WITHDRAWN

LONGMAN
BIBLIOGRAPHY
OF COMPOSITION
AND RHETORIC
1984–1985

LONGMAN SERIES IN
COLLEGE COMPOSITION AND COMMUNICATION

Advisory Editor: Harvey Wiener
LaGuardia Community College
The City University of New York

LONGMAN BIBLIOGRAPHY OF COMPOSITION AND RHETORIC 1984–1985

Erika Lindemann

The University of North Carolina at Chapel Hill

Longman

New York & London

Executive Editor: Gordon T. R. Anderson
Senior Production Editor: Ronni Strell
Text Design: Laura Ierardi
Cover Design: Joseph DePinho
Production Director: Eduardo Castillo
Compositor: UNC Printing Department
Printer and Binder: Malloy Lithographing, Inc.

Associate Editor: J. Randal Woodland

Longman Bibliography of Composition and Rhetoric: 1984–1985

Copyright © 1987 by Erika Lindemann

Longman Inc., 95 Church Street, White Plains, N.Y. 10601

Associated companies: Longman Group Ltd., London;
Longman Cheshire Pty., Melbourne; Longman Paul Pty., Auckland;
Copp Clark Pitman, Toronto; Pitman Publishing Inc., New York

Library of Congress Cataloging-in-Publication Data
Lindemann, Erika.
   Longman bibliography of composition and rhetoric,
1984-1985.

   (Longman series in college composition and communication)
   1. English language—Rhetoric—Study and teaching—
Bibliography. 2. English language—Composition and
exercises—Study and teaching—Bibliography. I. Title.
II. Series.
Z5818.E5L55   1987   016.808′042′07   87-2653
[PE1404]
ISBN 0-582-28376-0

87 88 89 90 9 8 7 6 5 4 3 2 1

PE
1404
L55
1984/85

CONTENTS

PREFACE   vii

CONTRIBUTING BIBLIOGRAPHERS   xi

JOURNAL ABBREVIATIONS   xiii

1   BIBLIOGRAPHIES AND CHECKLISTS   1

2   THEORY AND RESEARCH—Entries that discuss concepts or hypotheses, that explain how people learn, that describe fields or general methodologies, that examine historical developments, that review previous explanations of a subject, or that advance conclusions drawn from empirical evidence.   6

    Rhetorical Theory, Discourse Theory, and Composing   6
    Literature   46
    Reading   53
    Linguistics and Grammatical Theory   62
    Psychology   77
    Education   90
    Cross-Disciplinary Studies   94
    Other   98

3   TEACHER EDUCATION, ADMINISTRATION, AND SOCIAL ROLES—Entries that discuss the education of teachers, that examine administrative or personnel policies and procedures, that describe services supporting classroom instruction, or that treat relations between educational institutions and society.   112

    Teacher Education   112
    Administration   118
    Support Services   121
    Role in Society   128
    Other   130

4   CURRICULUM—Entries that explain teaching methods, that describe courses or units of instruction, or that combine theory with practice in a specific subject area or skill.   132

    General Discussions   132
    Preschool Education   141
    Elementary Education (K–8)   141
    Secondary Education (9–12)   154

Higher Education   169
  Developmental Writing   169
  Freshman Composition   175
  Advanced Composition   190
  Business Communication   191
  Scientific and Technical Communication   196
  Communication in Other Disciplines   202
Adult Education   208
English as a Second Language   209
Research and Study Skills   215
Other   218

5   TEXTBOOKS AND INSTRUCTIONAL MATERIALS—Entries that describe text-   221
books and other print and nonprint media used to support classroom instruction.

General Discussions   221
Elementary Materials (K–8)   222
Secondary Materials (9–12)   224
Higher Education Materials   225
  Developmental Writing   225
    Handbooks   225
    Rhetorics   225
    Readers   227
    Workbooks   228
    Special Texts   230
  Freshman Composition   231
    Handbooks   231
    Rhetorics   232
    Readers   235
    Workbooks   238
    Special Texts   239
  Advanced Writing   240
    Rhetorics   240
    Readers   241
    Composition and Literature Texts   241
    Business and Technical Writing   241
    Special Texts   243
Videotapes, Films, and Filmstrips   244
Recordings   247
Computer Programs and Other Materials   247

6   TESTING, MEASUREMENT, AND EVALUATION—Entries that examine ways   262
to assess students' work, that describe statistical or analytical techniques to
measure or evaluate teaching and learning, or that discuss appropriate criteria
for and uses of tests, scales, or other instruments.

Evaluation of Students   262
Evaluation of Teachers   273
Evaluation of Programs   274
Other   274

AUTHOR INDEX   276

PREFACE

The *Longman Bibliography of Composition and Rhetoric* offers teachers and researchers an annual classified listing of scholarship on written English and its teaching. This volume cites over 3800 titles that, with few exceptions, were published during the 1984 and 1985 calendar years. The bibliography lists each work once, annotates all citations, cross references them when appropriate, and indexes all authors and editors. A group of 151 contributing bibliographers, whose names appear on pp. xi–xii, prepared the citations and annotations.

SCOPE OF THE BIBLIOGRAPHY

The *Longman Bibliography* includes works that treat written communication, the processes whereby human beings compose and understand written messages, and methods of teaching people to communicate effectively in writing. The bibliography lists entries in six major categories (see the Contents for a fuller description of these categories):

Bibliographies and Checklists
Theory and Research
Teacher Education, Administration, and Social Roles
Curriculum
Textbooks and Instructional Materials
Testing, Measurement, and Evaluation

The bibliography makes few restrictions on the format, medium, or purpose of the works it includes, so long as the subject of the work falls into one of the six categories. It lists only published works: books, articles, monographs, published collections (of essays, conference presentations, or working papers), textbooks, bibliographies and other reference works, computer software, films, microforms, videotapes, and sound recordings. Although it excludes masters theses, book reviews, and works written in languages other than English, it includes citations for unpublished doctoral dissertations appearing in *Dissertation Abstracts International*. It also includes review articles that discuss several works, define movements or trends, or survey an individual's contribution to the discipline.

SOURCES

The *Longman Bibliography* cites works from four major sources.

PERIODICALS

Journals publishing articles on composition and its teaching are one source. Each journal is identified by an abbreviation (an alphabetical list of journal abbreviations appears on pp. xiii–xv). This volume includes approximately 2500 citations for journal articles. Editors of journals excluded from the list of journal abbreviations may request inclusion by writing to me and submitting a copy of the journal's editorial policy and a sample issue for review.

PUBLISHERS

A second source of materials is commercial publishers and university presses. These publishers, whose participation in the project is voluntary, provided contributing bibliographers with the written information necessary to prepare entries for approximately 450 scholarly books and instructional materials and for nearly 130 computer programs, videotapes, and cassette recordings. By and large, contributing bibliographers were unable to examine these materials.

This volume incorporates all textbooks appearing in the 1984 and 1985 "Bibliography of Writing Textbooks," published in the *Journal of the Council of Writing Program Administrators*. It also includes essay collections, books that bring together essays, articles, or papers by several authors. The bibliography annotates these collections but does not annotate each essay. However, the index lists all authors contributing to the collection, unless the annotation says otherwise.

DISSERTATION ABSTRACTS INTERNATIONAL (DAI)

DAI represents a third source of citations. Not all degree-granting institutions list their unpublished doctoral dissertations in *DAI*. However, this volume includes approximately 450 entries drawn from *DAI*. Since the contributing bibliographers have not examined these dissertations, the citations serve only to direct readers to the appropriate abstracts in *DAI*. Users of this volume will want to consult the *DAI* abstracts for additional information, including who supervised the degree candidate's work and which institution granted the degree.

RESOURCES IN EDUCATION (RIE)

A fourth source of materials in the *Longman Bibliography* is the Educational Resources Information Center (ERIC), a federally funded document-retrieval system coordinated by 16 clearinghouses. ERIC indexes its materials in two reference works. Journal articles appear in *Cumulative Index to Journals in Education (CIJE);* the list of journal abbreviations includes 95 journals indexed in *CIJE*.

Resources in Education (RIE), on the other hand, indexes documents in the ERIC microfiche collection, which is available in 2600 regional libraries or directly from ERIC. These documents, frequently published elsewhere, include government documents, research and project reports, bibliographies, and conference papers. Documents indexed in *RIE* receive a six-digit "ED" number (e.g., ERIC ED 199 701) and are cross referenced under various subject headings or "descriptors." This volume of the *Longman Bibliography* includes over 350 selected documents indexed in *RIE*.

Some documents may be listed in *RIE* and may be available in ERIC for several years after they were written. For convenience and to ensure comprehensiveness, the *Longman Bibliography* reports ERIC documents cited in *RIE* during the years covered in the current volume; that is, this volume cites ERIC documents listed in *RIE* in 1984 and 1985, even though the works may have an earlier date of publication. Also as a convenience, each ERIC entry includes the six-digit "ED" number.

Contributing bibliographers working with ERIC materials have developed criteria for determining what documents to include in this volume.

Substantiveness

Substantive documents of general value to composition teachers and researchers are included. Representatives of such publications are curriculum guides, federal government final reports, and technical reports from various publication series, such as those published by the University of Illinois Center for the Study of Reading and the newly established Centers for the Study of Writing.

Relevance

Documents that seem to represent concerns of high interest to researchers are included. The topics of functional literacy, computers, and revision, for example, represent concerns of greater relevance than the teaching of handwriting.

Inclusiveness

All papers on composition and rhetoric available in ERIC and delivered at the annual meetings of the Conference on College Composition and Communication (CCCC) and the National Council of Teachers of English (NCTE—Fall and Spring conventions) are included. Papers delivered at other regional and national meetings, such as those of the American Educational Research Association (AERA), the International Reading Association (IRA), and the Modern Language Association (MLA), are selected for inclusion on the basis of their substantiveness and relevance.

Reference value

Items for which the ERIC microfiche system might provide unique access are included. Representative of entries meeting this criterion would be books or collections of articles no longer available from their original publishers.

Alternate access

Many professional organizations regularly make copies of book and monograph publications available as ERIC microfiche. And many papers presented as reports or conference talks and available in ERIC are later published as monographs or as articles in journals. When such information is available, the entry in this volume will include ERIC ED numbers to indicate an alternate source of access to the document. However, users of this volume should keep in mind that although a book in ERIC reflects the exact contents of the published work, an article in ERIC is a manuscript that may see substantial revision before it is published.

Criteria for excluding from this volume items cited in *RIE* are as follows:

Communication theory. ERIC documents broadly concerned with human communication or with language study in general, rather than with composition and rhetoric, are routinely excluded.

Local interest. ERIC documents concerned with composition and rhetoric but judged to be primarily of local interest are excluded. For example, this volume omits annual evaluation reports of writing programs in local schools.

Availability. Publications of commercial publishers and other organizations that are listed in *RIE* and assigned an ERIC ED number but that are not available through the ERIC microfiche system are omitted.

Users of the *Longman Bibliography* may wish to supplement this resource by consulting *RIE* or various computer-assisted retrieval systems that access ERIC documents. Copies of most documents indexed in *RIE* can be purchased in paper or microform from the ERIC system (order forms appear in the back of monthly issues of *RIE*). ERIC clearinghouses also make available free or inexpensive guides to special topics of interest to rhetoric and composition teachers and researchers. Current addresses for these clearinghouses, especially the ERIC Clearinghouse on Foreign Languages and Linguistics (ERIC/FLL) and the ERIC Clearinghouse on Reading and Communication Skills (ERIC/RCS), appear on the inside back cover of each monthly issue of *RIE*.

Authors, publishers, and editors may send offprints of articles, copies of books, or microforms to me for possible inclusion in the *Longman Bibliography;* however, I will be unable to return these materials.

The items listed in the annual bibliography are not housed in any single location or owned by any single individual. The *Longman Bibliography* lists and describes these materials but does not provide users of the bibliography any additional means of retrieving them. However, users of the volume will find librarians extremely helpful in finding copies of particular works. Some materials may be available through interlibrary loan, OCLC and on-line catalogues, ERIC and other information-retrieval systems, or in state and university libraries. To locate materials cited in this volume, ask your librarian to help you.

CONTRIBUTING BIBLIOGRAPHERS

The reliability and usefulness of the *Longman Bibliography's* annual volumes depend primarily on a large group of contributing bibliographers. Contributing bibliographers accept responsibility for compiling accurate entries in their areas of expertise, for preparing brief, descriptive annotations for each entry, for determining where each entry will appear within the six sections of the bibliography, for cross referencing entries when appropriate, and for submitting completed entries to me by a specified deadline.

To ensure consistency, contributing bibliographers receive a *Handbook for Contributing Bibliographers* to guide them in their work, and they fill out a printed form for each entry. Contributing bibliographers agree to serve a three-year term and, thereafter, may request reappointment for another two-year term. In return for their valuable service to the profession, they receive a copy of each annual volume they have helped to prepare. Graduate students, teachers, researchers, or other individuals who wish to become contributing bibliographers may write to me.

ANNOTATIONS

Annotations accompany almost all entries in this volume. They describe the document's contents and are intended to help users determine the document's usefulness. Annotations are brief—50 words or fewer for books and 25 words or fewer for all other documents. Annotations are also meant to be descriptive, not evaluative. They explain what a work is about but leave readers to judge for themselves the work's merits. Most annotations fall into one of three categories: they present the document's thesis, main argument, or major research finding; they describe the work's major organizational divisions; or they indicate the purpose or scope of the work.

CROSS REFERENCES

This volume lists the citation and annotation for each document only once, in one of the six major sections of the bibliography. Every entry, however, is numbered so that cross references to other sections are possible. Cross references are necessary because much scholarship in composition and rhetoric is interdisciplinary. Cross references appear as a listing of entry numbers preceded by *See also,* which is at the end of each major division of the bibliography.

A publication of this scope depends on many people, especially those who offered advice, encouragement, and criticism during its planning and preparation. Robert Bain, Walter Glanze, Mary Hinkle, Kimball King, Joel Myerson, Marilyn Norstedt, and Patrick Scott provided helpful suggestions for organizing the project and for developing the *Handbook for Contributing Bibliographers.* The contributing bibliographers also deserve thanks for their significant contribution to this volume, work often made troublesome because procedures were new and some materials difficult to locate. Their energy and professional commitment to the project kept it moving forward; their questions and suggestions improved this volume.

The project has also enjoyed the financial support of the Council of Writing Program Administrators, Dean Samuel R. Williamson of the College of Arts and Sciences at the University of North Carolina–Chapel Hill, the University of North Carolina's Research Council, and Joseph M. Flora, chair of the University of North Carolina's Department of English. Lois Lineberger, Tramble Turner, Sandra Monroe, Betsy Denton, and especially J. Randal Woodland provided invaluable editorial assistance. Michael Padrick, Dan Wingate, Larry Mason, and Roger Deese offered important technical support in computer programming and computer typesetting.

Gordon T. R. Anderson of Longman Inc. believed in the importance of this work from its inception and patiently nurtured it through three years of planning and preparation. Ronni Strell at Longman gave wise, professional editorial advice at several stages in the preparation of the manuscript.

The profession profits from having among its ranks scholars whose bibliographical work, in part, has shaped this volume. Gary Tate, Richard L. Larson, Winifred Horner, Michael Moran, and Ronald Lunsford, and the members of the CCCC Committee on a Bibliography in Composition have all helped to set high standards for bibliographical resources in the field. Such resources have become increasingly important since the 1960s, when the profession began to witness an explosion of scholarship on writing and its teaching. Our profession now boasts a growing collection of historical, theoretical, empirical, and pedagogical studies to support teachers and researchers in their work. But without adequate bibliographical resources, our professional library remains inaccessible. This volume benefits from the work of those who, in the past 10 years, have given us access to that library. Those who have helped prepare the *Longman Bibliography of Composition and Rhetoric* hope that it will assist teachers and researchers to answer the thoughtful questions they raise in working with student writers.

Erika Lindemann

CONTRIBUTING BIBLIOGRAPHERS

Peter Adams
Jim Addison
Clara Alexander
Ken Autrey
David Bartholomae
Walter Beale
Larry Beason
Cynthia Bechtel
Richard Behm
Joye Pettigrew Berman
Gay Bernat
Lynn Z. Bloom
Virginia A. Book
Marianne Brokaw
Lady Falls Brown
Dawn L. Bruton
Mary Louise Buley-Meissner
Barbara Cambridge
Gregory Clark
John Clifford
Alice Cole
Benjamin W. Conarroe
Susan Currier
Donald A. Daiker
Thomas E. Dasher
Kenneth W. Davis
Bonnie Devet
Collett B. Dilworth
Judith Dobler
William A. Dodd
Angela G. Dorenkamp
Russel K. Durst
Carlota C. Dwyer
Robert M. Esch
Paul Eschholz
Timothy J. Evans

Helen V. Fairbanks
Linda Ferriera-Buckley
Yitua Firdyiwek
Gretchen Flesher
Sandra Squire Fluck
Bill Forssburg
Sarah D'Eloia Fortune
Stephen Freniere
Janice W. Frost
Richard Fulkerson
Patricia Goubil Gambrell
Ellen F. Gardiner
Sara S. Garnes
Jonathan A. Gates
Dennis Gendron
Anne Ruggles Gere
Joan I. Glazer
Gwendolyn Gong
Kay Gore
Mary Lou V. Greenfield
C. W. Griffin
Nedra Grogan
Evonne Kay Halasek
Jeanne W. Halpern
Kathy Haney
Jim Hanlon
Tori Haring-Smith
Jeanette Harris
Sarah E. Harrold
Patrick Hartwell
Christopher G. Hayes
Janice N. Hays
Laura Helms
Dixie Elise Hickman
Betsy Hilbert
Deborah H. Holdstein

Sylvia A. Holladay
Janie Hydrick
Jack Jobst
Dianna Johansen
Kenneth Kantor
Patricia P. Kelly
Joyce Kinkead
James Kinney
Alexandra R. Krapels
Elizabeth Larson
Janice M. Lauer
Barbara Lombardo
William Lutz
Steven Lynn
James D. Marshall
Cheryl L. Martin
Stefan E. Martin
Beryl C. Martinson
Rhoda Maxwell
Donald A. McAndrew
Ben W. McClelland
Lisa J. McClure
Ellen McDaniel
Ilona McGuiness
Vincent P. Mikkelsen
Walter S. Minot
Susan Miller
Joseph O. Milner
Max Morenberg
Stephanie Morris
Neil Nakadate
William F. Naufftus
Virginia Nees-Hatlen
Marie Wilson Nelson
Elizabeth F. Penfield
Virginia G. Polanski

James Postema
John W. Presley
Paul W. Ranieri
Duane Roen
Lois M. Rosen
Audrey J. Roth
Ruthann Ruehr
Sara L. Sanders
Dolores J. Sarafinski
Mary Sasse
Pearl Saunders
Judith Scheffler
Christopher S. Schreiner
Cynthia L. Selfe
Jeanne H. Simpson

Barbara M. Sitko
Robert C. Small, Jr.
Louise Z. Smith
Mark E. Smith
Marian Sousa
Freda F. Stohrer
James Strickland
Patricia Sullivan
Dan J. Tannacito
Josephine K. Tarvers
Nathaniel Teich
John Trimbur
Myron Tuman
Christine A. Vonder Haar
Billie J. Wahlstrom

Preston L. Waller
Barbara Weaver
Robert H. Weiss
Christopher G. Wenger
Robert C. Wess
Katherine L. Wheatley
Robert D. Whipple
Barbara Whitehead
James D. Williams
Michael M. Williamson
Jeanne K. Wilson
W. Ross Winterowd
Art Young

JOURNAL ABBREVIATIONS

ABCAB	The American Business Communication Association Bulletin	CLEd	Children's Literature in Education
		CollM	Collegiate Microcomputer
		CollT	College Teaching
AdEd	Adult Education	ComEd	Communication Education
AdLBEd	Adult Literacy and Basic Education	ComM	Communication Monographs
AERJ	American Educational Research Journal	CompEd	Computers and Education
		ComQ	Communication Quarterly
ALAN	The Alan Review	ComR	Communication Research
AmA	American Anthropologist	CPsy	Cognitive Psychology
AmEd	American Education	CritI	Critical Inquiry
AmP	American Psychologist	CSc	Cognitive Science
ArEB	Arizona English Bulletin	CSSJ	Central States Speech Journal
AS	American Speech	Curr I	Curriculum Inquiry
ASBJ	American School Board Journal	CurrR	Curriculum Review
ASch	The American Scholar		
		Daedalus	Daedalus: Journal of the American Academy of Arts and Sciences
BADE	Bulletin of the Association of Departments of English		
		DAI	Dissertation Abstracts International
BL	Brain and Language	DP	Developmental Psychology
BRMMLA	Rocky Mountain Review of Language and Literature		
		EdPsy	Educational Psychologist
		EdRev	Educational Review
CalE	California English	EdRQ	Educational Research Quarterly
CC	Computers and Composition	EEd	English Education
CCC	College Composition and Communication	EJ	The English Journal
		ELAB	English Language Arts Bulletin
CCR	Community College Review	ELTJ	English Language Teaching Journal
CD	Child Development	EN	English News
CE	College English	EnEd	Engineering Education
CEAF	CEA Forum	EngR	English Record
CEd	Childhood Education	EQ	English Quarterly
CEJ	Connecticut English Journal	ES	English Studies
CET	Carolina English Teacher	ESC	English Studies in Canada
CHE	Chronicle of Higher Education	ET	English in Texas
CHum	Computers and the Humanities	ETC	ETC: A Review of General Semantics
CI	Cognition and Instruction	ExC	Exceptional Children
CJCJ	Community and Junior College Journal	ExEx	Exercise Exchange

FEN	Freshman English News	L&S	Language and Speech
FLA	Foreign Language Annals	LaEJ	Louisiana English Journal
FlaEJ	Florida English Journal	Lang&S	Language and Style
FS	Feminist Studies	LangS	Language Sciences
GCQ	Gifted Child Quarterly	Language	Language: Journal of the Linguistic Society of America
HCR	Human Communication Research	LArts	Language Arts
HD	Human Development	Leaflet	The Leaflet
HER	Harvard Educational Review	LEd	Liberal Education
HT	History Teacher	Ling	Linguistics
IaEB	Iowa English Bulletin	LL	Language Learning
ICUT	Improving College and University Teaching	LPLP	Language Problems and Language Planning
IdahoEJ	Idaho English Journal	M&C	Memory and Cognition
IE	Indiana English	MarylandJ	Maryland Journal
IlEB	Illinois English Bulletin	MedEd	Medical Education
Intell	Intelligence	MichET	Michigan English Teacher
IPM	Information Processing and Management	MLJ	The Modern Language Journal
		MLQ	Modern Language Quarterly
IRAL	International Review of Applied Linguistics in Language Teaching	MLS	Modern Language Studies
		MM	Media and Methods
		MSE	Massachusetts Studies in English
JAF	Journal of American Folklore		
JBS	Journal of Black Studies	NCET	North Carolina English Teacher
JBW	Journal of Basic Writing	NebEC	Nebraska English Counselor
JC	Journal of Communication		
JDEd	Journal of Developmental Education	OrE	Oregon English
JEd	Journal of Education	P&L	Philosophy and Literature
JEdG	Journal for the Education of the Gifted	P&R	Philosophy and Rhetoric
JEdM	Journal of Educational Measurement	PADS	Publication of the American Dialect Society
JEdP	Journal of Educational Psychology		
JEdR	Journal of Educational Research	PCTEB	PCTE Bulletin
JEngL	Journal of English Linguistics	PhiDK	Phi Delta Kappan
JFR	Journal of Folklore Research	PhS	Philosophical Studies
JLD	Journal of Learning Disabilities	PMS	Perceptual and Motor Skills
JMCTE	Journal of the Mississippi Council of Teachers of English	Poetics	Poetics
		PPR	Philosophy and Phenomenological Research
JMEd	Journal of Medical Education		
JNT	Journal of Narrative Technique	PR	Partisan Review
JourEd	Journalism Educator	Pre-Text	Pre-Text
JPC	Journal of Popular Culture	Psychology	Psychology
JPsy	Journal of Psychology	PsyR	Psychological Review
JPsyR	Journal of Psycholinguistic Research	PsyT	Psychology Today
JQ	Journalism Quarterly	PT	Poetics Today
JR	Journal of Reading	QJS	Quarterly Journal of Speech
JSEd	Journal of Special Education		
JSHD	Journal of Speech and Hearing Disorders	Raritan	Raritan
		Reader	Reader
JT	Journal of Thought	RER	Review of Educational Research
JTEd	Journal of Teacher Education	Rhetorica	Rhetorica
JTW	Journal of Teaching Writing	RIE	Resources in Education
JTWC	Journal of Technical Writing and Communication	RR	Rhetoric Review
		RRQ	Reading Research Quarterly

RSQ	Rhetoric Society Quarterly	TETYC	Teaching English in the Two-Year College
RT	Reading Teacher	Thought	Thought
RTE	Research in the Teaching of English	TWM	Teachers and Writers Magazine
SAm	Scientific American	TWT	Technical Writing Teacher
SAR	South Atlantic Review	UEJ	Utah English Journal
SCETCN	SCETC Newsletter	VEB	Virginia English Bulletin
SCL	Studies in Canadian Literature	VLang	Visible Language
SECOL	The SECOL Bulletin		
SFS	Science Fiction Studies	WAC	Writing across the Curriculum
SLATE	SLATE Newsletter	WaEJ	Washington English Journal
SNNTS	Studies in the Novel	WC	Written Communication
SSCJ	Southern Speech Communication Journal	WCJ	Writing Center Journal
ST	Science Teacher	WD	Writers Digest
Statement	Statement	WJSC	Western Journal of Speech Communication
Style	Style		
SubStance	SubStance	WLN	Writing Lab Newsletter
		WLWE	World Literature Written in English
TCL	Twentieth Century Literature	WPA	Journal of the Council of Writing Program Administrators
TEd	Today's Education	Writer	The Writer
TESOLQ	Teachers of English to Speakers of Other Languages Quarterly	WWays	Word Ways

LONGMAN
BIBLIOGRAPHY
OF COMPOSITION
AND RHETORIC
1984–1985

1

BIBLIOGRAPHIES AND CHECKLISTS

1. Agee, Hugh, ed. *High Interest-Easy Reading: For Junior and Senior High School Students.* 4th ed. Urbana, Ill.: NCTE, 1984. 96 pages

   Annotates 378 books published between 1979 and 1982 and grouped into 18 categories. Prepared primarily for teenagers' use in recreational reading.

2. Autrey, Ken. *Word Processing and Writing Instruction.* Selected Reference Sources in Rhetoric and Composition. Columbia, S.C.: Department of English, University of South Carolina, 1985. 20 pages

   Contains 56 annotated entries grouped in five sections: introductions and surveys, research and case study reports, teaching suggestions, reports on software, and books. Also includes names and addresses for 13 journals and an author index.

3. Beard, John. "Annotated Bibliography: Selective Dictionaries on Usage and Style." *CEJ* 16 (Spring 1985): 119–121.

   Describes 10 dictionaries.

4. Beard, John. "Annotated Bibliography: Selective Dictionaries on Usage and Style." *ET* 17 (Fall 1985): 36–37.

   Annotates 10 books on usage and style.

5. Benoit, William L., and Bill D. Wallace. "Bibliographies of Several Approaches to Rhetorical Criticism." *RSQ* 15 (Summer–Fall 1985): 179–194.

   Groups works according to eight critical approaches and subdivides each group into theoretical statements and applications.

6. *Bilingual, Bicultural, and Bidialectal Reading and Communications: Abstracts of Doctoral Dissertations.* Urbana, Ill.: ERIC/RCS, 1984. ERIC ED 250 710 [10 pages]

   Reprints 13 abstracts from *Dissertation Abstracts International* 45 (July–December 1984).

7. Bohn, Willard. "Roman Jakobson's Theory of Metaphor and Metonymy: An Annotated Bibliography." *Style* 18 (Fall 1984): 534–550.

   A select, annotated bibliography of studies that apply, develop, or challenge Jakobson's binary model of metaphor.

8. Copeland, Evelyn, ed. *Recommended English Language Arts Curriculum Guides, K–12.* Urbana, Ill.: ERIC/RCS and NCTE, 1984.

   Lists and annotates model curricula. Includes curriculum guides recommended from 1982–1984.

9. Dieterich, Daniel J., and Richard H. Behm. "Annotated Bibliography of Research in the Teaching of Literature and the Teaching of Writing." *RTE* 18 (May 1984): 201–218.

   Lists citations in three areas: literature and media study, writing, and teacher education. Divides each area into preschool and elementary, secondary, and college and adult.

10. Durst, Russel K., and James D. Marshall. "Annotated Bibliography of Research in the Teaching of English." *RTE* 18 (December 1984): 417–438.

    Lists and annotates works published in 1983 and 1984 in the four areas of writing, language, literature, and teacher education.

11. Durst, Russel K., and James D. Marshall. "Annotated Bibliography of Research in the Teaching of English." *RTE* 19 (December 1985): 405–425.

    Entries in writing, language, literature, and teacher education. Prepared with the cooperation of ERIC.

12. Dyson, Anne Haas. "Research Currents: Writing and the Social Lives of Children." *LArts* 62 (October 1985): 632–639.

    Surveys studies on young children's unofficial writing, the permeable boundary of freewriting, and the relationship between children's social lives and writing.

13. Ede, Lisa S. "Audience: An Introduction to Research." *CCC* 35 (May 1984): 140–153.

    A bibliographic essay on audience. Discusses analysis, empirical research, and theoretical studies.

14. *English Language Arts Skills and Instruction: Abstracts of Doctoral Dissertations.* Urbana, Ill.: ERIC/RCS, 1984. ERIC ED 251 856 [9 pages]

    Reprints 12 abstracts from *Dissertation Abstracts International* 45 (July–December 1984).

15. Evans, Eileen B., and Pamela S. Rooney. "Reports that Meet Audience Needs: A Selective, Annotated Bibliography of Articles, 1950–1982." *TETYC* 11 (December 1984): 40–52.

    An annotated bibliography of articles by professional writers on approaches to audience in annual reports, auditor's reports, and general business reports.

16. Giannasi, Jenefer, and Robert F. Denton. "Stylistics Annual Bibliography: 1982–1983." *Style* 18 (Fall 1984): 391–533.

    A comprehensive, annotated bibliography of articles on style and stylistics. Book-length sources are annotated elsewhere.

17. Holbrook, Hilary Taylor. "ERIC/RCS Report: Writing Teachers Learning about Writing." *LArts* 61 (October 1984): 647–651.

    A bibliography of articles on types of in-service programs and their influences on teaching methods and attitudes.

18. Holbrook, Hilary Taylor. "Qualities of Effective Writing Programs." *ArEB* 28 (Fall 1985): 104–109.

    Reviews ERIC documents that focus on the foundations of a successful writing program. Discusses the roles of teachers and administrators.

19. Jacoby, Jay. "Checklist of Recent Writing Center Scholarship: April 1983 through March 1985." *WCJ* 5 and 6 (Winter–Spring 1985): 46–57.

    Lists articles, books, and ERIC documents that "have an explicit and direct connection with writing center theory, methodology, and operation."

20. Kazemek, Francis E., and Pat Rigg. *Adult Literacy: An Annotated Bibliography.* Newark, Del.: IRA, 1984. ERIC ED 248 484 [49 pages]

    Presents the recent work on adult literacy, divided into five sections: present state, current views, critiques of views, research, and teaching methods.

21. Lansing, Margaret L. *Computers in Composition: A Bibliography of Research and Practice.* Urbana, Ill.: ERIC/RCS, 1984. ERIC ED 249 499 [22 pages]

    Summarizes 50 studies divided into 16 topics. Designed to help classroom teachers use computers effectively in teaching writing.

22. Lehr, Fran. "Evaluating Language Development." *OrE* 6 (Fall 1984): 20–21, 30.

    Examines materials in ERIC data base for evaluating the language ability of children entering school and for planning appropriate instruction.

23. Lehr, Fran. "Teaching Thinking Skills in English/Language Arts." *ArEB* 28 (Fall 1985): 23–25.

    Surveys and annotates ERIC documents focusing on thinking skills.

24. Lehr, Fran. "Teaching Thinking Skills in English/Language Arts." *OrE* 7 (Fall 1985): 13–14.

    Examines ERIC data base for materials on teaching critical reasoning to students in upper elementary through college years.

25. Liggett, Sarah. "The Relationship between Speaking and Writing: An Annotated Bibliography." *CCC* 35 (October 1984): 334–344.

A 70-item annotated bibliography of cross-disciplinary theories and research on the relationship between speaking and writing.

26. Linn, Michael D., and Maarit-Hannele Zuber. *The Sound of English: A Bibliography of Language Recordings.* Urbana, Ill.: NCTE, 1984. 84 pages

    Annotates 190 English-language recordings, chosen because they illustrate a variety of social, regional, or historical speech patterns. Includes an extensive index and a list of producers and distributors.

27. McCarthy, Bernice. "Learning Styles and Right/Left Modes of Learning: A Selected Bibliography." *SCETCN* 18 (Fall 1985): 18–20.

    A 44-item bibliography. Some items are annotated.

28. McIlvaine, Robert M., and Joan C. Condravy. *Writing across the Curriculum: An Annotated Bibliography.* Urbana, Ill.: ERIC/RCS, June 1983. ERIC ED 234 421 [32 pages]

    A 200-item bibliography for all levels of instruction.

29. Meir, Margaret. "Teacher Commentary on Student Writing in the Process-Oriented Class." *ArEB* 28 (Fall 1985): 77–81.

    Reviews ERIC articles about teachers' comments on student writing.

30. Mikelonis, Victoria M., and Vicki Gervickas. "Using Computers in the Technical Writing Classroom: A Selected Bibliography, 1978–1984." *TWT* 12 (Fall 1985): 161–176.

    A survey of articles about the choice, content, and uses of computers in technical writing classrooms.

31. Mochamer, Randi Ward. *Teaching Writing as Thinking across the Secondary Curriculum: An Annotated Bibliography.* Urbana, Ill.: ERIC/RCS, 1985. ERIC ED 259 401 [46 pages]

    Reviews and annotates studies intended to help content area teachers develop a rationale and instructional models for cross-curricular writing. Presents four recommendations for implementing such a program.

32. Monson, Dianne L., ed. *Adventuring with Books: A Booklist for Pre-Kindergarten through Grade Six.* Urbana, Ill.: NCTE, 1985. 395 pages

    Annotates nearly 1700 books published between 1981 and 1984 and selected on the basis of literary and artistic quality; organized by genre. Includes a directory of publishers and a listing of professional books on children's literature.

33. Moran, Michael G., and Ronald F. Lunsford, eds. *Research in Composition: A Bibliographic Sourcebook.* Westport, Conn.: Greenwood Press, 1984. 506 pages

    Sixteen bibliographic essays summarize current research on reading and writing; survey major issues in research methods, evaluation, and assignment making; and review scholarship on the basics of punctuation, usage, vocabulary development, spelling, sentences, and paragraphs. Two appendixes discuss textbooks and usage manuals.

34. Murdock, Phil, and H. William Birns. *A Beginner's Guide to Teaching Technical Writing: An Annotated Bibliography.* Urbana, Ill.: ERIC/RCS, 1984. ERIC ED 245 243 [12 pages]

    Intended for secondary and college teachers beginning a course in technical writing. Sources are grouped in five sections: bibliographic sources, theory and philosophy, guide to teaching technical writing, texts, and journals and useful addresses.

35. Nancarrow, Paula R., Donald Ross, and Lillian S. Bridwell, comps. *Word Processors and the Writing Process: An Annotated Bibliography.* Westport, Conn.: Greenwood Press, 1984. 146 pages

    An alphabetically arranged, annotated listing of materials, most published since 1980, that "might help those who are interested in the ways computers can help writers, especially university students, with the art and craft of writing."

36. Newby, James E. "Language, Literature, and Communication: An Annotated Bibliography of Books by Black Authors." *JBS* 15 (December 1984): 155–176.

    Lists 62 items, ranging in focus from rhetoric and communication theory to literature, linguistics, stylistics, dialect and idiom, and cultural analysis.

37. Potter, Cheryl L. "Teaching Writing through Computers: An Annotated Bibliography." *EngR* 36 (1985): 17–20.

    A bibliography of 32 books on computer-based instruction for college and high school students.

38. Puma, Vincent, John Harwick, and Jim Mealy. *Cognitive Approaches to Writing: An Introductory Annotated Bibliography.* Urbana, Ill.: ERIC/RCS, 1983. ERIC ED 233 375 [7 pages]

Lists sources applying cognitive psychology to the writing process.

39. Quet, Danielle. "A Checklist of Mauritian Creative Writing in English (1920–1982): Addenda and Update (to 1982)." *WLWE* 23 (Spring 1984): 312–315.

Bibliography of poetry, drama, and short and long fiction.

40. Rabinowitz, Isaac. "Pre-Modern Jewish Study of Rhetoric: An Introductory Bibliography." *Rhetorica* 3 (Spring 1985): 137–144.

A bibliography of premodern Jewish studies of rhetoric. Cites original theoretical works and modern studies of them.

41. *Reading and Writing: Abstracts of Doctoral Dissertations.* Urbana, Ill.: ERIC/RCS, 1984. ERIC ED 245 206 [7 pages]

Reprints five abstracts from *Dissertation Abstracts International* 44 (January–June 1984).

42. *Reading and Writing: Abstracts of Doctoral Dissertations.* Urbana, Ill.: ERIC/RCS, 1984. ERIC ED 251 822 [10 pages]

Reprints 12 abstracts from *Dissertation Abstracts International* 45 (July–December 1984).

43. *Reading and Writing: Abstracts of Doctoral Dissertations.* Urbana, Ill.: ERIC/RCS, 1985. ERIC ED 259 313 [7 pages]

Reprints six abstracts from *Dissertation Abstracts International* 45 (January–June 1985).

44. Reese, Paul. "An Annotated Bibliography of *The Journal of Technical Writing and Communication:* 1981–1984." *JTWC* 15 (1985): 373–380.

Covers such subjects as the state of the profession, pedagogy, and theory, discussed in 75 articles.

45. Schwartz, Helen J. "A Selected Bibliography on Computers in Composition." *CCC* 35 (February 1984): 71–77.

An annotated bibliography of 47 entries in composition instruction.

46. Suhor, Charles, and Deborah Fox. "Update: The Phonics Wars." *OrE* 7 (Fall 1985): 20–21.

Examines ERIC data base for current views of the role of phonics in reading instruction.

47. Tanner, William E. "101 Sources for Teachers of Basic Writing." *ET* 16 (Fall 1984): 29–33.

A bibliography of sources, arranged in six categories, for teachers of underprepared students. Most items were published after *Errors and Expectations* (1977).

48. *Teacher Characteristics and Teacher Education in Reading and English Language Arts Instruction: Abstracts of Doctoral Dissertations.* Urbana, Ill.: ERIC/RCS, 1985. ERIC ED 259 315 [11 pages]

Reprints 16 abstracts from *Dissertation Abstracts International* 45 (January–June 1985).

49. *Teaching of Writing: Abstracts of Doctoral Dissertations.* Urbana, Ill.: ERIC/RCS, 1984. ERIC ED 246 451 [28 pages]

Reprints 38 abstracts from *Dissertation Abstracts International* 44 (January–June 1984).

50. *Teaching of Writing: Abstracts of Doctoral Dissertations.* Urbana, Ill.: ERIC/RCS, 1984. ERIC ED 250 712 [16 pages]

Reprints 33 abstracts from *Dissertation Abstracts International* 45 (July–December 1984).

51. *Teaching of Writing: Abstracts of Doctoral Dissertations.* Urbana, Ill.: ERIC/RCS, 1985. ERIC ED 259 379 [20 pages]

Reprints 39 abstracts from *Dissertation Abstracts International* 45 (January–June 1985).

52. Weaver, Barbara. "Bibliography of Writing Textbooks (Spring 1984)." *WPA* 7 (Spring 1984): 43–55.

An extensive annotated bibliography of developmental, freshman, advanced, and professional writing textbooks published during the 1983–1984 academic year.

53. Weaver, Barbara. "Bibliography of Writing Textbooks (Spring 1985)." *WPA* 8 (Spring 1985): 39–56.

An extensive, annotated bibliography of developmental, freshman, advanced, and professional textbooks published during the 1984–1985 academic year.

54. Winkler, Victoria M., and Jean L. Mizuno. "Advanced Courses in Technical Writing: Review of the Literature, 1977–1984." *TWT* 12 (Winter 1985): 33–49.

Reviews the literature to "find out what kinds of subject matter and pedagogical approaches are used in advanced technical writing courses."

55. *Written Language and Writing Abilities: Abstracts of Doctoral Dissertations.* Urbana, Ill.: ERIC/RCS, 1984. ERIC ED 246 452 [16 pages]

Reprints 33 abstracts from *Dissertation Abstracts International* 44 (January–June 1984).

56. *Written Language and Writing Abilities: Abstracts of Doctoral Dissertations.* Urbana, Ill.: ERIC/RCS, 1985. ERIC ED 259 378 [12 pages]

Reprints 16 abstracts from *Dissertation Abstracts International* 45 (January–June 1985).

See also 167, 1643, 1745, 2938, 3019, 3426, 3671, 3733

2
THEORY AND RESEARCH

RHETORICAL THEORY, DISCOURSE THEORY, AND COMPOSING

57. Adams, Katherine H. "Forms of Discourse: What Their Originators Intended." *TETYC* 11 (December 1984): 17–22.

Argues that early nineteenth-century rhetoric textbooks stressed creativity and flexibility in forms of discourse. Subsequent textbooks established more rigid classifications.

58. Altimore, Michael. "The Rhetoric of Scientific Controversy: Recombinant-DNA." *DAI* 44 (February 1984): 2586A.

Analyzes the rhetoric, specifically the type of argument, used by participants in the controversy over recombinant-DNA.

59. Anderson, Floyd D. "*De Doctrina Christiana* 2.18.28: The Convergence of Athens and Jerusalem." *RSQ* 15 (Summer–Fall 1985): 102–104.

Argues that the passage is significant because it epitomizes Augustine's uniquely successful effort to synthesize Hebraism and Hellenism.

60. Anderson, Norman A. "'Goodwrite': Orwell's Use of Language in *1984*." *IIEB* 72 (Fall 1984): 14–21.

Examines Orwell's attitudes about the "misuse of language" and his warnings about "bad writing practice" in *1984*.

61. Annas, Pamela J. "Style as Politics: A Feminist Approach to the Teaching of Writing." *CE* 47 (April 1985): 360–371.

Discusses the situation of women students as writers and describes the assumptions behind the course Writing as Women.

62. Anson, Christopher M. "Composition and Communicative Intention: Exploring the Dimensions of Purpose in College Writing." *DAI* 46 (July 1985): 90A.

Examines rhetorical, educational, and psychological purposes for writing and relates them to case studies of four freshmen writers.

63. Applebee, Arthur N. "Writing and Reasoning." *RER* 54 (Winter 1984): 577–596.

Reviews research on the contributions of written language to intellectual development and the role of writing in school and culture. Identifies areas of needed research.

64. Armstrong, Cherryl. "A Process Perspective on Poetic Discourse." Paper given at the CCCC Convention, New York, March 1984. ERIC ED 243 108 [11 pages]

Presents a case study of the process of composing a poem.

65. Arrington, Phillip K. "Tropes, Invention, and the Composing Process." *DAI* 45 (December 1984): 1740A.

Argues for a more dynamic, process-oriented view of Kenneth Burke's four "master" tropes.

66. Atwater, Deborah F. "A Dilemma of Black Communication Scholars: The Challenge of Finding New Rhetorical Tools." *JBS* 15 (September 1984): 5–16.

Argues for a "culturally valid [Afrocentric] rhetorical criticism," based on black rhetoric as a product of oral language, tradition, and situation.

67. Austin, Doris E. "Reading to Write: The Effect of the Analysis of Essays on Writing Skills in College Composition Classes." *DAI* 45 (September 1984): 771A.

Finds that providing a full rhetorical context for reading and analysis helps students develop mature essays.

68. Aycock, Coleen K. "New Critical Rhetoric and Composition." *DAI* 46 (August 1985): 427A.

Argues that new critical theory gains substantial weight in the context of modern rhetorical theory and practice.

69. Baghban, Marcia. "A Month in the Life of a Writing Six-Year-Old." Paper presented at the NCTE Spring Conference, Columbus, April 1984. ERIC ED 244 265 [23 pages]

Reports on a one-month study of a child's writing.

70. Baker, Deborah Carol. "A Rhetorical Analysis of Communication Style in Initial Meetings of Small Groups." *DAI* 44 (May 1984): 3204A.

Indicates that contextual constraints affect style and communication functions. *Ethos* is a result of individual stylistic choices and strategies.

71. Balkema, Sandra J. "The Composing Activities of Computer Literate Writers." *DAI* 45 (June 1985): 3569A.

Writers' activities illustrate the need for straightforward text entry and for facility in planning, directing form and content, and revising and composing simultaneously.

72. Bank, Stanley. "Student Writers Perceive Process and Product." *EdRQ* 9 (1984–1985): 28–39.

Studies writing samples and perceptions about writing of 134 high school students identified as basic. Results suggest the importance of developing ideas and being able to revise and edit.

73. Barabas, Christine P. "The Nature of Information in Technical Progress Reports: An Analysis of Writer Intentions, Texts and Reader Expectations." *DAI* 45 (May 1985): 3342A.

Indicates that good and poor report writers differ in composing strategies and in their assumptions about purpose and audience.

74. Barnes, Linda L. "Communicative Competence in the Composition Classroom: A Discourse Analysis." *DAI* 45 (March 1985): 2856A.

Examines the effects on students of teachers' written comments on papers.

75. Bartelo, Dennise. *Getting the Picture of Reading and Writing: A Look at the Drawings, Composing, and Oral Language of Limited English Proficiency Children.* Urbana, Ill.: ERIC/RCS and NCTE, 1984. ERIC ED 245 533 [50 pages]

A descriptive study of first graders.

76. Bartlett, Elsa J., and Jay C. Wilson. *A Study of Narrative Rhetoric.* Washington, D.C.: NIE, 1982. ERIC ED 234 414 [197 pages]

Stories written by New York City students in grades three through eight show age-related differences in structure and rhetorical complexity.

77. Barzun, Jacques. "Behind the Blue Pencil: Censorship or Creeping Creativity." *ASch* 54 (Spring 1985): 385–388.

Critiques modern copyediting practices, which flatten out and standardize written language.

78. Bates, Patricia T. "Writing Performance and Its Relationship to the Writing Attitudes, Topic Knowledge, and Writing Goals of College Freshmen." *DAI* 46 (August 1985): 366A.

Results indicate that students write better when there is less anxiety, blocking, and attributing success or failure to chance and when they have specified writing goals.

79. Baudin, Fernand. "The Visual Editing of Texts." *VLang* 18 (Winter 1984): 81–86.

Claims that writing is an image as well as a message and recommends teaching children to be conscious of how their texts look on the page.

80. Baumlin, James S. "Decorum, Kairos, and the 'New' Rhetoric." *Pre-Text* 5 (Fall–Winter 1984): 171–183.

Defends classical rhetoric, especially the concept of decorum, against criticisms of Brannon and Knoblauch's *Rhetorical Traditions and Modern Writing.*

81. Bayer, John George, Jr. "The Shifting Function of Rhetoric in Early Nineteenth-Century American Education and *Belles Lettres*." *DAI* 44 (January 1984): 2180A.

Investigates the relationship between the rhetorical tradition in education and the development of *belles lettres* in nineteenth-century America.

82. Bazerman, Charles. "The Writing of Scientific Nonfiction." *Pre-Text* 5 (Spring 1984): 39–66.

A study of the writing and revision of one scientific paper suggests that scientific texts are influenced by both scientific evidence and rhetorical context.

83. Beach, Richard, and Lillian S. Bridwell, eds. *New Directions in Composition Research*. Perspectives in Writing Research. New York: Guilford Press, 1984. 418 pages

Twenty studies examine research methods in composition, the composing process, the contexts in which writers work, and instructional contexts.

84. Beach, Richard, and JoAnne D. Liebman-Kleine. "The Writing/Reading Relationship: Implications of Research in Cognition for Reading and Writing." *Reader* 11 (Spring 1984): 23–35.

Uses schema theory to develop a theoretical model of how writers can become their own best reader.

85. Becker, Joseph D. "Multilingual Word Processing." *SAm* 251 (July 1984): 96–107.

Explores the potential for text editing in complex languages, such as Japanese, and for computer-generated translations.

86. Benoit, William L. "Isocrates on Rhetorical Education." *ComEd* 33 (April 1984): 109–119.

Reviews Isocrates' life and views on rhetorical education. Suggests that Isocrates and his work have been long overlooked.

87. Benton, Stephen L., John A. Glover, and Barbara S. Plake. "Employing Adjunct Aids to Facilitate Elaboration in Writing." *RTE* 18 (May 1984): 189–200.

Investigates the relative effectiveness of posing higher-order questions prior to and during writing and posing lower-order questions after writing to increase writers' elaboration.

88. Bereiter, Carl, and Marlene Scardamalia. "Learning about Writing from Reading." *WC* 1 (April 1984): 163–188.

Finds that students from age three to graduate school picked up rhetorical knowledge when exposed to single examples of literary types.

89. Berkenkotter, Carol. "Student Writers and Their Audiences: Case Studies of the Revising Decisions of Three College Freshmen." Paper presented at the Canadian Council of Teachers of English, Montreal, May 1983. ERIC ED 236 618 [14 pages].

Protocol analyses of essays revised by five writers responding to different audiences suggest that peer evaluations are not always beneficial.

90. Berkenkotter, Carol. "Student Writers and Their Sense of Authority over Texts." *CCC* 35 (October 1984): 312–319.

Studies three revisers and their relationship to peer groups: the resisting reviser, the inner-directed reviser, and the reviser who loses authority over the text.

91. Berlin, James A. "Rhetoric and Poetics in the English Department: Our Nineteenth-Century Inheritance." *CE* 47 (September 1985): 521–532.

A historical analysis of the literature/composition split in English departments. Emphasizes the damage done to rhetoric by its separation from a current and progressive poetics.

92. Berlin, James A. *Writing Instruction in Nineteenth-Century American Colleges*. Studies in Writing and Rhetoric. Carbondale, Ill.: Southern Illinois University Press, 1984. 114 pages

Describes the major rhetorical theories influencing nineteenth-century education, including classical, psychological-epistemological, and romantic. Discusses today's rhetorical traditions in light of the recent past.

93. Bernhardt, Stephen A. "The Politics of Teaching Orwell's 'Politics and the English Language.'" *IIEB* 72 (Fall 1984): 2–6.

Argues that Orwell's six stylistic principles for practicing writers, if accepted without examination, lead to "bad teaching."

94. Bernhardt, Stephen A. "The Writer, the Reader, and the Scientific Text." *JTWC* 15 (1985): 163–174.

Argues, using examples from journal articles in the natural sciences, that scientific writers do intrude personally into the text at particular junctures.

95. Bernhardt, Stephen A., and Bruce C. Appleby. "Collaboration in Professional Writing with the Computer: Results of a Survey." *CC* 3 (November 1985): 29–42.

Reports on an investigation of how writers collaborate via microcomputer and how such collaboration is viewed within departments.

96. Berthoff, Ann E. "'The Hand of the Mind': A Model for Teaching the Composing Process." *IaEB* 33 (1984): 1–3.

Argues that the hand in action can model the mind in the process of composing.

97. Berthoff, Ann E. "Is Teaching Still Possible? Writing, Meaning, and Higher Order Reasoning." *CE* 46 (December 1984): 743–755.

Argues against misusing theories of cognitive development to explain why college students cannot reason. Offers alternatives.

98. Berthoff, Ann E., ed. *Reclaiming the Imagination: Philosophical Perspectives for Writers and Teachers of Writing.* Upper Montclair, N.J.: Boynton/Cook, 1984. 286 pages

A collection of 51 readings by artists, philosophers, and scientists who consider how human beings make sense of the world, how they learn and know. Sections cover perception and the apprehension of form, language and the making of meaning, interpretation and the act of knowing, and artists at work. Authors are not indexed in this volume.

99. Besner, Neil. "Process against Product: A Real Opposition?" *EQ* 18 (Fall 1985): 9–16.

Shows where the process and product models meet in theory and practice. Argues that a less polarized view of process and product can enrich classroom practice.

100. Bevilacqua, Vincent M. "Campbell, Vico, and the Rhetorical Science of Human Nature." *P&R* 18 (1985): 23–30.

Offers a reading of Campbell's rhetorical analysis of mind in light of Vico's "science of the imagination."

101. Bevilacqua, Vincent M. "The Rhetorical Theory of John Constable's Reflections upon Accuracy of Style." *Rhetorica* 2 (Spring 1984): 63–73.

Shows Constable's stylistic rhetoric to be the result of his age, his neoclassical frame of reference, and his immediate rhetorical inheritance.

102. Bieke, Kathleen A. "The Audience Awareness of Competent Writers during Expository Writing." *DAI* 46 (November 1985): 1263A.

Investigates two possible definitions of audience awareness: a consciousness of readers and the construction of audience characteristics and attitudes.

103. Bjork, Robert E. "Language and the Healing Arts: Some Recent Texts on Medical Writing." *JTWC* 15 (1985): 49–53.

Three recent textbooks suggest how literature and composition studies as well as scientific studies can be combined to help produce a theory of medical writing.

104. Blair, Carole. "An Archaeological Critique of the History of Rhetorical Theory: Beyond Historical-Critical Dualism in the Analysis of Theoretical Discourse." *DAI* 45 (July 1984): 16A.

Uses Foucault's work to argue that flawed historiographic assumptions and methods have produced an inaccurate history of rhetoric. Advocates using Foucault's "research attitude."

105. Blazer, Bonita. "The Development of Writing in Kindergarten: Speaking and Writing Relationships." *DAI* 45 (November 1984): 1294A.

An ethnographic study reveals a developmental process characterized by interactions within and between social and symbolic systems and enhanced by oral language competencies.

106. Boice, Robert. "The Neglected Third Factor in Writing: Productivity." *CCC* 36 (December 1985): 472–480.

Reports on an experiment in which academicians in a contingency condition became more productive writers than those in a controlled or spontaneous condition.

107. Bolotta, Rene L. "Composing as Becoming: From Process to Holomovement." *DAI* 46 (July 1985): 91A.

Explores writing as an activity that "becomes the dialectical dialoguing of the writer's nonlocal language planes throughout the implicate order ground in the holomovement."

108. Books, Larry Wayne. "An Instructional Application of Schema Theory." *DAI* 44 (April 1984): 3221B.

Finds that instruction in schema theory and text organization significantly facilitated both comprehension and recall of scientific texts.

109. Booley, Heather A. "Discovery and Change: How Children Redraft Their Narrative Writing." *EdRev* 36 (1984): 263–275.

Investigates ways in which 14-year-olds make structural and stylistic changes in redrafting narratives.

110. Bormann, Dennis R. "Some 'Common Sense' about Campbell, Hume, and Reid: The Extrinsic Evidence." *QJS* 71 (November 1985): 395–421.

Argues that Campbell's *Philosophy of Rhetoric* was influenced by Reid's Scottish Common Sense Realism and constituted an attack on Hume's skepticism.

111. Branco, David J. "Dramaturgical Rhetoric: Erving Goffman's Interactional Theory of Communication-Conduct." *DAI* 44 (February 1984): 2290A.

Formulates a rhetorical theory based upon Goffman's work that sees rhetoric deriving from "social processes of power and victimage."

112. Brand, Alice G. "Hot Cognition: Emotions and Writing Behavior." Paper presented at the CCCC Convention, Detroit, March 1983. ERIC ED 236 677 [28 pages]

Calls for further investigation of the role of emotion in writing.

113. Brandes, Paul D. "Printings of Aristotle's *Rhetoric* during the Fifteenth and Sixteenth Centuries." *ComM* 52 (December 1985): 368–376.

Demonstrates the widespread availability of the work to Renaissance scholars. Traces the development of the *Rhetoric* from manuscript to book form.

114. Brandt, Deborah. "Social Foundations of Reading and Writing." *Reader* 11 (Spring 1984): 14–21.

Discusses writers' interrupting their writing to read what they have written. Argues that all composing strategies are socially based.

115. Brandt, Deborah. "Versions of Literacy." *CE* 47 (February 1985): 128–138.

A review essay describing four recent books and discussing trends in contemporary research on literacy.

116. Brandt, Deborah. "Writer, Context, and Text." *DAI* 44 (April 1984): 3045A.

Explores how social and semantic contexts bear on writing processes and on the character of finished texts.

117. Branham, Robert J., and W. Barnett Pearce. "Between Text and Context: Toward a Rhetoric of Contextual Reconstruction." *QJS* 71 (February 1985): 19–36.

Surveys possible relations that texts may have to their contexts and examines speeches by Lincoln and Edward Kennedy in terms of these relationships.

118. Bredin, Hugh. "Metonymy." *PT* 5 (1984): 45–58.

Examines classical and modern theories and typologies of metonymy.

119. Brennan, Mark, and Roslin E. Brennan. *Literacy and Learning: The Human Factor.* New South Wales, Australia: Australian Institute of Criminology, 1984. ERIC ED 242 891 [354 pages]

Studies Australian prison inmates' attitudes toward literacy, including writing.

120. Brereton, John, ed. *Traditions of Inquiry.* New York: Oxford University Press, 1985. 191 pages

Eight essays examine the contributions of Wendell, Scott, Richards, Leonard, Burke, Baird, Braddock, and Shaughnessy to the teaching of writing.

121. Britton, B. K., and J. B. Black, eds. *Understanding Expository Text: A Theoretical and Practical Handbook for Analyzing Explanatory Texts.* Hillside, N.J.: Erlbaum, 1984. 424 pages

Fifteen papers by discourse theorists on such topics as prose analysis and structure, scientific discourse, implicit knowledge and schema theory, cognitive demands of reading, the role of memory, propositional analysis, and knowledge-based models of comprehension.

122. Britton, James. "Viewpoints: The Distinction between Participant and Spectator Role Language in Research and Practice." *RTE* 18 (October 1984): 320–331.

Reviews the categories for classifying discourse function and then examines both the theoretical underpinnings of "spectator role" and the implications of the spectator/participant distinction.

123. Brock, Bernard L. "Epistemology and Ontology in Kenneth Burke's Dramatism." *ComQ* 33 (Spring 1985): 94–104.

Discusses the evolution of Burke's rhetorical systems by examining his refinements of dramatism. Topics include social uses of language, reality, metaphor, and paradox.

124. Brock, Bernard L., Kenneth Burke, Parke G. Burgess, and Herbert W. Simons. "Dramatism as Ontology or Epistemology: A Symposium." *ComQ* 33 (Winter 1985): 17–33.

Reconstructs the debate between the authors concerning the role of dramatism as a literal, ontological system or as a metaphorical, epistemological system.

125. Brockriede, Wayne. "Constructs, Experience, and Argument." *QJS* 71 (May 1985): 151–163.

Offers a theoretical model for analyzing rhetorical communication. Constructs (theories), human experience, and arguments are points of a triangle giving the critic multiple interdependent perspectives.

126. Brodkey, Linda. "The Context of Cooperation in Academic Discourse." Paper presented at the CCCC Convention, New York, March 1984. ERIC ED 245 230 [10 pages]

Explores the effects of teacher-centered writing classrooms on students' initiation of writing.

127. Broughton, Bradford B. "'No Man Is Allowed to Spell Ill': Modern Communication Advice from an Eighteenth-Century Expert." *JTWC* 15 (1985): 157–161.

Describes Lord Chesterfield's advice on writing well and speaking effectively in letters to his son.

128. Brown, Jean E. "Helping Students Discover a Process for Writing: A 'Blooming' Art." *EQ* 16 (Winter 1984): 47–53.

Advocates using Bloom's taxonomy to discover the writing process and overcome errors.

129. Brummett, Barry. "Consensus Criticism." *SSCJ* 49 (Winter 1984): 111–124.

Develops a theory of rhetorical criticism consistent with the consensus theory perspective that rhetoric is epistemic. Presents illustrative examples.

130. Brummett, Barry. "The Representative Anecdote as a Burkean Method, Applied to Evangelical Rhetoric." *SSCJ* 50 (Fall 1984): 1–23.

Explains a method of discovering the representative anecdote of a discourse.

131. Brummett, Barry. "Rhetorical Theory as Heuristic and Moral: A Pedagogical Justification." *ComEd* 33 (April 1984): 97–107.

Argues that rhetorical theory cannot be explained by social science models. Proposes instead a pedagogical perspective.

132. Bryant, Deborah G. "The Composing Processes of Blind Writers." *DAI* 45 (May 1985): 3296A.

Examines differences in composing processes between blind and sighted writers and between individuals blind from birth and those blinded later in life.

133. Buddemeier, Richard E. *Discovering Writing Ownership in the Process of Learning to Write.* Urbana, Ill.: ERIC/RCS and NCTE, 1981. ERIC ED 234 377 [36 pages]

A case study examining a freshman who claims ownership of and meaning in writing in a 14-month collaborative effort with the researcher.

134. Buddemeier, Richard E. "Origins of the Freshman Writer: A View from the Middle School." Paper presented at the CCCC Convention, New York, March 1984. ERIC ED 245 227 [18 pages]

Compares the context of writing in middle schools with the context of freshman English.

135. Buehler, Mary F. "Rhetorical Foundations of Technical Communication." *DAI* 44 (June 1984): 3671A.

Traces the rhetorical foundations of technical communication through historical developments of technical elements.

136. Bunge, Nancy. *Finding the Words: Interviews with Writers Who Teach.* Athens, Ohio: University of Ohio/Swallow Press, 1984..

Includes interviews with 16 successful writers who teach. Contains individual accounts of their principles and methods and offers a variety of perspectives on the process of writing and on the writer's materials and responsibilities.

137. Burgess, Parke G. "The Dialectic of Substance: Rhetoric *Vs.* Poetry." *ComQ* 33 (Spring 1985): 105–112.

Examines poetic and rhetorical symbolic power. One arises from acts of identification/division within the text; the other, from acts that extend beyond the text.

138. Burke, Kenneth. *Attitudes toward History.* 3d ed. Berkeley and Los Angeles: University of California Press, 1984. 312 pages

Originally published in 1937, this edition includes "Afterword: Attitudes toward History: In Retrospective Prospect."

139. Burke, Kenneth. "Dramatism and Logology." *ComQ* 33 (Spring 1985): 89–93.

Discusses the distinction between dramatism and logology as analogous to the distinction between ontology and epistemology.

140. Burkhardt, Ross M. "Becky: A Case Study in Composition." *LArts* 61 (November 1984): 717–721.

Observing a 13-year-old examine an experience, compose a statement, and then write a poem expressing its significance helped a teacher understand the writing process.

141. Burleson, Brant R., and Kathleen E. Rowan. "Are Social-Cognitive Ability and Narrative Writing Skill Related?" *WC* 2 (January 1985): 25–43.

Finds no relationship between social cognitive ability and the rated quality of narrative essays.

142. Burtoff, Michele J. "The Logical Organization of Written Expository Discourse in English: A Comparative Study of Japanese, Arabic, and Native Speaker Strategies." *DAI* 45 (March 1985): 2857A.

Concludes that language groups have culturally "preferred" strategies, not culture-specific ones.

143. Butler, Maureen. "Levels of Engagement, Rhetorical Choices, and Patterns of Differentiation in the Writing of Four Eleventh Graders." *DAI* 45 (August 1984): 440A.

Studies two average and two advanced eleventh-graders' school-assigned writing and finds a "relationship between patterns of engagement and [audience] differentiation."

144. Callaghan, Patricia. "A Pedagogy of Process: A Rhetoric of Assent." *TETYC* 11 (December 1984): 6–16.

Describes paradigm shifts in composition textbooks and proposes a new pedagogy based on Booth's rhetoric of assent.

145. Campbell, James. "Politics and Conceptual Reconstruction." *P&R* 17 (1984): 156–170.

Examines the work of Dewey and Mead on the relationship of "conceptual reconstruction" to political activity.

146. Campbell, John Angus. "Insight and Understanding: The 'Common Sense' Rhetoric of Bernard Lonergan." *QJS* 71 (November 1985): 476–488.

Places the work of the late Catholic philosopher in the context of modern rhetoric's efforts to bridge the gap between objectivism and relativism.

147. Capps, Ronald Robert. "The Critical Connection: A Computer-Assisted Rhetorical Criticism of the Message of Harry F. Chapin." *DAI* 46 (November 1985): 1126A.

Uses the perspective of the "new rhetoric" to analyze Chapin's lyrics.

148. Carleton, Walter M. "On Rhetorical Knowing." *QJS* 71 (May 1985): 227–237.

Review essay placing Gregg's *Symbolic Inducement and Knowing* in the context of the debate on the extent to which all knowledge is essentially rhetorical.

149. Carrell, Patricia. "The Forum: The Author Responds [to Rankin, *TESOLQ* 18 (March 1984)]." *TESOLQ* 18 (March 1984): 161–168.

Defends her stand on cohesion's not leading to coherence by citing the work of Witte, Faigley, and Connor, among others.

150. Carroll, John Joseph. "Underlying Determinants of Complex Interpretations in Discourse." *DAI* 44 (March 1984): 2919B.

Demonstrates that the relevance of an utterance to its context can be specified in terms of the operation of linguistic rule systems.

151. Castellano, Rose Lynn. "An Anecdotal Inquiry into the Nature and Function of Mental Imagery in the Artistic Process of Creative and Interpretive Artists." *DAI* 44 (January 1984): 1956A.

Argues that imagery strategies of the creative process resemble those used in daily life. Imagery ability is an "attainable skill."

152. Cherwitz, Richard A., and James W. Hikins. *Communication and Knowledge.* Rhetoric/Communication Series. Columbia, S.C.: University of South Carolina Press, 1985. 200 pages

Develops a theory of rhetorical knowledge, one that documents the central role of communication in all efforts to obtain knowledge.

153. Cheshire, Barbara W. "The Effects of Writing Apprehension on Writing Quality." Paper presented at the CCCC Convention, Minneapolis, March 1985. ERIC ED 258 264 [16 pages]

Finds that freewriting does not reduce apprehension.

154. Chew, Charles R. *Reading and Writing: Connections and Instructional Practices.* Urbana, Ill.: ERIC/RCS and NCTE, 1984. ERIC ED 244 287 [7 pages]

Discusses links between reading and writing.

155. Chiseri-Strater, Elizabeth. "Composing in Context: Revision Strategies of Freshman Writers." *Leaflet* 84 (Winter 1985): 35–44.

Describes and analyzes the revising processes of six students over a period of one semester.

156. Chiseri-Strater, Elizabeth. "Connections, Contexts, and Curriculum in Composition." Paper presented at the CCCC Convention, New York, March 1984. ERIC ED 245 247 [12 pages]

Based on literacy studies of young children, suggests that college writing teachers need context-based studies of learning.

157. Church, Elizabeth, and Carl Bereiter. "An Investigation of the Awareness and Use of Style in Adolescent's Reading and Writing." Paper presented at the AERA Convention, New Orleans, April 1984. ERIC ED 245 204 [9 pages]

A study of eleventh graders' ability to recognize stylistic features in reading and to use them in writing.

158. Clark, Beverly L. "Revising by Computer." *EngR* 35 (Fourth Quarter 1984): 6–9.

Word processing yields two benefits to students in revising drafts: the "mechanical" benefit of easy correction and the "philosophical" benefit of freedom to rearrange segments.

159. Clark, Irene Lurkis. "Listening and the Teaching of Writing." *TETYC* 10 (Winter 1984): 121–128.

Describes experiments leading to the conclusion that reading aloud and listening is useful for self-evaluation during the revision of compositions.

160. Clifford, John. "Cognitive Psychology and Writing: A Critique." *FEN* 13 (Spring 1984): 16–18.

Argues that cognitive psychology, while useful, plays only a "minor" part in the humanists' task of exploring how writing makes meaning.

161. Cohen, Jodi Rise. "Implicit Theories of Meaning in Rhetorical Criticism." *DAI* 46 (September 1985): 553A.

Uncovers and compares meaning in 17 rhetorical critiques. Finds an emphasis on mental processes, not on substance or practical choices.

162. Collins, James L. "A Contextualized Perspective on Developmental Writing." Paper presented at the CCCC Convention, Detroit, March 1983. ERIC ED 236 620 [12 pages]

Argues that basic writers need meaningful writing practice that is sufficiently contextual.

163. Collins, Mary Evelyn. "An Approach to the Study of Kenneth Burke: Meaning and Readability." *DAI* 45 (February 1985): 2302A.

An Aristotelian examination of Burke's writing indicates that problems in comprehension stem from Burke's organization, his changing definition of terms, and his dialectic style.

164. Comprone, Joseph J. "An Ongian Perspective on the History of Literacy: Psychological Context and Today's College Student Writer." Paper presented at the CCCC Convention, New York, March 1984. ERIC ED 245 221 [20 pages]

Explores Ong's view of the history of literacy and the historical tradition of rhetoric.

165. Conley, Thomas M. "The Enthymeme in Perspective." *QJS* 70 (May 1984): 168–187.

Argues that modern rhetoricians have both oversimplified the Greek rhetoricians' notion of enthymeme and given it undue centrality, leading to an underestimation of Burke and Perelman.

166. Connors, Robert J. "Mechanical Correctness as a Focus in Composition Instruction." *CCC* 36 (February 1985): 61–72.

Examines cultural and pedagogical forces that shaped nineteeth-century rhetorical history with its emphasis upon mechanical correctness.

167. Connors, Robert J. "Review: Journals in Composition Studies." *CE* 46 (April 1984): 348–365.

Discusses the reasons why journals are founded and their function for the disciplinary community. Reviews 15 current journals in composition studies.

168. Connors, Robert J. "The Rhetoric of Explanation." Paper presented at the CCCC Convention, Detroit, March 1983. ERIC ED 236 623 [60 pages]

Examines the concept of explanatory discourse in the Western rhetorical tradition.

169. Connors, Robert J. "The Rhetoric of Explanation: Explanatory Rhetoric from Aristotle to 1850." *WC* 1 (April 1984): 189–210.

Traces the history of the rhetoric of explanation, whose purpose is essentially to inform, from Aristotle through the American nineteenth century.

170. Connors, Robert J. "The Rhetoric of Explanation: Explanatory Rhetoric from 1850 to the Present." *WC* 2 (January 1985): 49–73.

Traces the history of the rhetoric of explanation, whose pupose is essentially to inform, from Henry Day's *Art of Rhetoric* to the work of Kinneavy and D'Angelo.

171. Connors, Robert J., Lisa S. Ede, and Andrea A. Lunsford, eds. *Essays on Classical Rhetoric and Modern Discourse.* Carbondale, Ill.: Southern Illinois University Press, 1984. 291 pages

A collection of 17 essays in honor of Edward P.J. Corbett. Discussions compare classical and contemporary rhetorical theories; examine the rhetoric of Plato, Aristotle, and Isocrates; trace the role of rhetoric in American education; identify rhetorical principles in scientific and technical communication; and explore issues in rhetorical invention, *ethos,* and style.

172. Connors, Robert J., and Tim D. P. Lally. "A Comment on 'Journals in Composition Studies' [*CE* 46 (April 1984)] and a Response." *CE* 47 (January 1985): 77–80.

A comment by Lally on Connors's article and his response.

173. Cooper, Martha D. "The Implications of Foucault's Archeological Theory of Discourse for Contemporary Rhetorical Theory and Criticism." *DAI* 45 (January 1985): 1915A.

Argues that Foucault's theory and method allow less dependence on the rhetorical theories of previous ages, capture the quality of rhetoric as event, and generate implications for current rhetorical practice.

174. Corbett, Edward P. J. "The Cornell School of Rhetoric." *RR* 4 (September 1985): 4–14.

Traces the growth and development of Cornell's Department of Speech and Drama. Discusses its influence in restoring classical rhetoric and humanistic learning.

175. Corder, Jim W. "Argument as Emergence, Rhetoric as Love." *RR* 4 (September 1985): 16–32.

Analyzes the limitations of Rogerian argument with reference to threats, identity, and understanding. Proposes abandoning authoritative positions by learning to speak and hear "a commodious language."

176. Corder, Jim W. "Corder's Dialogues." *RSQ* 15 (Summer–Fall 1985): 119–130.

Presents two dialogues on the nature of rhetorical argument. Benjamin seeks to enlighten Billy Joe and Boone Bilberry.

177. Corder, Jim W. "From Rhetoric to Grace: Propositions 55–81 about Rhetoric, Propositions 1–54 and 82 *et seq.* Being as Yet Unstated; or, Getting from the Classroom to the World." *RSQ* 14 (Winter–Spring 1984): 15–28.

Seeks to formulate the central concerns of rhetoric in short, general propositions accessible to those outside the discipline.

178. Corder, Jim W. "A New Introduction to Psychoanalysis, Taken as a Version of Modern Rhetoric." *Pre-Text* 5 (Fall–Winter 1984): 137–169.

Examines ways in which psychological problems can be defined in rhetorical terms and explores the rhetor's role as therapist.

179. Corder, Jim W. "On the Way, Perhaps, to a New Rhetoric, but Not There Yet, and If We Do Get There, There Won't Be There Anymore." *CE* 47 (February 1985): 162–170.

Argues that there is no new rhetoric. Discusses the conditions necessary to generating a new rhetoric.

180. Cormier, Robert. "The Pleasures and Pains of Writing a Sequel." *Alan* 12 (Winter 1985): 1–3.

Cormier chronicles his thinking and writing processes in producing *Beyond the Chocolate War.*

181. Cox, Beverly, and Elizabeth Sulzby. "Children's Use of Reference in Told, Dictated, and Handwritten Stories." *RTE* 18 (December 1984): 345–365.

Examines the use of reference as a means of producing cohesive text in stories composed by nine kindergartners and nine second graders.

182. Crowhurst, Marion. *Revision Strategies of Students at Three Grade Levels.* Vancouver, Canada: Educational Research Institute of British Columbia, 1983. ERIC ED 238 009 [34 pages]

Finds little evidence for age- or ability-related differences in expressive and persuasive compositions of good and average writers in grades 5, 7, and 11.

183. Crowley, Sharon. "The Evolution of Invention in Current-Traditional Rhetoric: 1850–1970." *RR* 3 (January 1985): 146–162.

Concludes that, although classical invention is not completely absent in nineteenth-century texts, it is transformed and diminished.

184. Crowley, Sharon. "Neo-Romanticism and the History of Rhetoric." *Pre-Text* 5 (Spring 1984): 19–37.

Argues that modern literary critics misunderstand the nature of rhetoric because they continue nineteenth-century Romanticism's privileging of poetic over rhetorical discourse.

185. Crowley, Sharon. "On Poststructuralism and Compositionists." *Pre-Text* 5 (Fall–Winter 1984): 185–195.

Replies to an earlier article by Winterowd by arguing that poststructuralists, by undermining literary discourse, will help revive rhetoric.

186. Crusius, Timothy W. "Thinking (and Rethinking) Kinneavy." *RR* 3 (January 1985): 120–130.

Offers suggestions for merging aim and purpose to improve the "overall design of an essay." Also considers the relationships among *topoi,* aim, and purpose.

187. Culp, Mary Beth, and Sylvia Spann. "The Influence of Writing on Reading." *JTW* 4 (Fall 1985): 284–289.

Results of a study indicate that writing had a positive influence on reading. Calls for research on the precise effects.

188. Däumer, Elisabeth. "Gender Bias in the Concept of Audience." *Reader* 13 (Spring 1985): 32–41.

Case study of a student writer that focuses on how he subsumed his predominantly female audience into a generalized male reader.

189. D'Angelo, Frank. "Nineteenth-Century Forms/Modes of Discourse: A Critical Inquiry." *CCC* 35 (February 1984): 31–42.

Examines assumptions underlying nineteenth-century forms/modes of discourse and argues for their abolition "as the basis of serious composition teaching."

190. Dahl, Karin L. "Reading and Writing as Transacting Processes." *DAI* 46 (July 1985): 111A.

An ethnographic study of transactions between reading and writing as seen from the perspective of college-aged learners.

191. Daiker, Donald, Andrew Kerek, and Max Morenberg, eds. *Sentence Combining: A Rhetorical Perspective.* Carbondale, Ill.: Southern Illinois University Press, 1985. 408 pages

Twenty-three selected papers from the Second Miami University Conference on Sentence Combining. Focuses on sentence combining as a method of teaching ways of thinking about, perceiving, and organizing reality.

192. Daniel, Stephen H. "The Philosophy of Ingenuity: Vico on Proto-Philosophy." *P&R* 18 (1985): 236–243.

Reviews Vico's ideas on common sense as both free (ingenious) and constrained by guidelines or "topics."

193. Daniels, Tom D., and Kenneth D. Frandsen. "Conventional Social Science Inquiry in Human Communication: Theory and Practice." *QJS* 70 (August 1984): 223–240.

Defends the methodology of the social sciences as a useful, if limited, analytical tool for human communication.

194. de Beaugrande, Robert. "Writer, Reader, Critic: Comparing Critical Theories as Discourse." *CE* 46 (October 1984): 533–559.

Argues for "discourse processing" as a major critical tool by comparing it to theories of Hirsch, Fish, and Miller.

195. Dent, Cathy H. "Development of Discourse Rules: Children's Use of Indexical Reference and Cohesion." *DP* 20 (March 1984): 229–234.

In this study of children and adults, situational reference was constant in all ages, but textual reference clearly increased with age.

196. Desmond, William. "Hegel, Dialectic, and Deconstruction." *P&R* 18 (1985): 244–263.

Dialectic celebrates wholeness; deconstruction dissolves it. Reviews the literature on deconstruction and argues that we must "step beyond negativity."

197. Diffley, Kathleen Elizabeth. *"Harper's New Monthly Magazine,* 1866–1876: The Popular Rhetoric of Reconstruction." *DAI* 46 (July 1985): 185A.

Traces changes in the domestic rhetoric of *Harper's New Monthly Magazine* through the undermining influences of the Civil War and into the 1870s.

198. DiMare, Lesley Ann. "The Paranoid Style in Rhetoric: A Genre Study." *DAI* 45 (May 1985): 3238A.

Classifies the rhetorical strategies of Cleaver, Gutierrez, and Hargis as genera of the paranoid style. Examines their common contexts.

199. Dobrin, David N. "What's the Purpose of Teaching Technical Communication." *TWT* 12 (Fall 1985): 146–160.

Argues that we should reconceive our purposes and practices in teaching technical writing, teaching students as apprentices and encouraging teaching writing on the job.

200. Dobson, L. N. *The Progress of Early Writers as They Discover Writing for Themselves.* Vancouver, Canada: Educational Research Institute of British Columbia, 1983. ERIC ED 235 505 [47 pages]

Describes first graders learning to write simply by writing.

201. Doheny-Farina, Stephen. "Writing in an Emergent Business Organization: An Ethnographic Study." *DAI* 45 (May 1985): 3337A.

Examines the social processes and functions of a computer software company, focusing on the collaborative writing of an important document.

202. Doheny-Farina, Stephen. *Writing in an Emerging Organization: An Ethnographic Study.* Urbana, Ill.: ERIC/RCS and NCTE, 1984. ERIC ED 258 184 [39 pages]

Studies writing in a computer software organization, noting the importance of corporate "voice."

203. Dolby-Stahl, Sandra K. "A Literary Folkloristic Methodology for the Study of Meaning in Personal Narrative." *JFR* 22 (April 1985): 45–69.

Theoretically examines interrelations of interpreter, storyteller, and documented folk text, applying approaches of reader-response and subjective criticism to literary and folk narratives.

204. Dowdey, Diane. "The Trying out of the Essay: How Scientific Essayists Compose." Paper presented at the CCCC Convention, New York, March 1984. ERIC ED 243 150 [18 pages]

Studies professional and student writers.

205. Downey, Bill. *Right Brain/Write On: Overcoming Writer's Block and Achieving Your Creative Potential.* Englewood Cliffs, N.J.: Prentice Hall, 1984.

Shows writers how to increase creativity through right-brain thinking, with advice from famous writers.

206. Downey, Sharon Dee. "Toward a Theory of Rhetorical Genre." *DAI* 44 (March 1984): 2621A.

Posits a theory of rhetorical genre that provides continuity and precision and illuminates the relationship of social values to developmental rhetorical history.

207. Downing, Carol Ann. "An Examination of Rhetorical Strategies Utilized by Mary Harris (Mother) Jones within the Context of the Agitative Rhetorical Model Developed by John Waite Bowers and Donovan J. Ochs." *DAI* 46 (September 1985): 553A.

Uses Bowers and Ochs's model to analyze the rhetoric of "Mother Jones." Discusses limitations of the model used.

208. Dowst, Kenneth. "Bruner, Dewey, and the Teaching of Writing." *IaEB* 33 (1984): 4–8.

Discusses the application of Bruner's theory of language to the teaching of composition.

209. Dyson, Anne Haas. "Learning to Write/Learning to Do School: Emergent Writers' Interpretations of School Literacy Tasks." *RTE* 18 (October 1984): 233–264.

Examines the relationship between learning to write and learning to perform school writing tasks during a 14-week period in a kindergarten.

210. Dyson, Anne Haas. "Second Graders Sharing Writing: The Multiple Social Realities of a Literary Event." *WC* 2 (April 1985): 189–215.

Argues that a child's social life within the classroom and his or her interpretations of school writing tasks have implications for researchers.

211. Eastern Washington University Research Laboratory. "Drafting: The (W)hole in the Composing Process." *Statement* 20 (May 1985): 39–47.

Analyzes three approaches to teaching drafting: the discovery, journalistic, and problem-solving approaches. Includes bibliography.

212. Ede, Lisa S., and Andrea A. Lunsford. "Audience Addressed/Audience Invoked: The Role of Audience in Composition Theory and Pedagogy." *CCC* 35 (May 1984): 155–171.

Recommends an integrated approach to audience, reflecting the combined concepts of audience addressed and audience invoked.

213. Edelsky, Carole, and Karen Smith. "Is That Writing — Or Are Those Marks Just a Figment of Your Curriculum?" *LArts* 61 (January 1984): 24–32.

Examines pieces of "authentic" and "inauthentic" writing to show different relationships among the graphophonic, syntactic, semantic, and pragmatic systems used to produce a meaningful text.

214. Edwards, Bruce L., Jr. "The Politics of Nonliteracy: Logocentrism in the Classroom." Paper presented at the NCTE Convention, Detroit, November 1984. ERIC ED 252 863 [9 pages]

Argues that literacy is erroneously equated with human worth, leading to logocentrism, the valuing of writing over speech.

215. Ehrlich, Diane B. "A Study of the Word Processor and Composing: Changes in Attitude and Revision Practices of Inexperienced Student Writers in a College Composition Class." *DAI* 45 (January 1985): 2081A.

Indicates that word processing teaches writing as a recursive process — as revision rather than as recopying.

216. Elbow, Peter. "The Shifting Relationships between Speech and Writing." *CCC* 36 (October 1985): 283–301.

Discusses the differences and similarities between writing and speech, describes the flexibility of writing as a medium, and advocates shifting between apparently contradictory cognitive processes and mentalities.

217. Enos, Richard Leo. "Ciceronian *Dispositio* as an Architecture for Creativity in Composition: A Note for the Affirmative." *RR* 4 (September 1985): 108–110.

Argues that Cicero's ideas on arrangement mistakenly have been seen as rigid instead of as responsive to invention.

218. Enos, Richard Leo. "Heuristic Structures of *Dispositio* in Oral and Written Rhetorical Composition: An Addendum to Och's Analysis of the Verrine Orations." *CSSJ* 35 (Summer 1984): 77–83.

Reveals that the arrangement of arguments shifted markedly from compositions structured for oral arguments to those intended for public reading.

219. Enos, Theresa. "Rhetorical Revival." Paper presented at the CCCC Convention, New York, March 1984. ERIC ED 246 481 [8 pages]

Explores current trends in rhetoric and compares them to trends in literary study. Argues that rhetoric is becoming fragmented and moribund.

220. Erickson, Keith V. "The Significance of 'Doctrina' in Augustine's *De Doctrina Christiana*." *RSQ* 15 (Summer–Fall 1985): 105–107.

By using the concept of "doctrina," Augustine was able to legitimize the Christian use of hitherto pagan rhetorical arts.

221. Fagan, Bob. "Executive Writing and Internal Revision." *EQ* 18 (Summer 1985): 69–74.

Describes the process an executive named Peter uses to write a report.

222. Fagley, N. S., and Paul M. Miller. "The Context of the Contents Pyramid Model of Classroom Writing Competence." *RER* 55 (Spring 1985): 1–4.

Critiques Mosenthal's (1983) Contexts Pyramid Model in relation to models proposed by Bransford (1979) and Jenkins (1979). Argues that Mosenthal's model does not fully account for writing processes.

223. Farr, Marcia, ed. *Advances in Writing Research, Vol. l: Children's Early Writing Development.* Writing Research: Multidisciplinary Inquiries into the Nature of Writing. Norwood, N.J.: Ablex, 1985. 354 pages

A collection of five essays employing various research methods. Examines children's writing in conference/workshop classrooms, in different home settings, among bilingual and monolingual students participating in a school-based postal system, and among kindergartners whose interest, dominant intentions, and styles of functioning differ.

224. Farr, Marcia, and Mary Ann Janda. "Basic Writing Students: Investigating Oral and Written Language." *RTE* 19 (February 1985): 62–83.

Investigates the relation of oral to written language in one basic-writing college student who speaks vernacular black English. Challenges previous accounts of such writers' problems.

225. Fingrutd, Meryl Anne. "The Three Mile Island Commission and the Language of Legitimacy." *DAI* 46 (December 1985): 1742A.

A discourse analysis of transcripts from the President's Commission, analyzing four essential disputes about the accident at Three Mile Island.

226. Finkel, Candida A. "Reason and Rhetoric: The Influence upon Rhetoric of Major Philosophic Changes in the Concept of Reason." *DAI* 45 (June 1985): 3480A.

Studies the relationship between rhetoric and concepts of reason. Examines the critical importance of three Renaissance philosophers and of Aristotle's definition of rhetoric.

227. Fisher, Walter K. "Narration as a Human Communication Paradigm: The Case of Public Moral Argument." *ComM* 51 (March 1984): 1–22.

Compares and contrasts a proposed narrative paradigm with the traditional rational perspective on symbolic interaction. Synthesizes the argumentative, persuasive theme and the literary, aesthetic theme.

228. Fisher, Walter R. "The Narrative Paradigm: An Elaboration." *ComM* 52 (December 1985): 347–367.

Relates the paradigm to major social, scientific, and humanistic theories and applies it to an interpretation and assessment of the conversation between Socrates and Callicles.

229. Fisher, Walter R., and Wayne Brockriede. "Kenneth Burke's Realism." *CSSJ* 35 (Spring 1984): 35–42.

Compares and contrasts Burke with Plato, Aristotle, Campbell, and Perelman.

230. Flower, Linda S., and John R. Hayes. "Images, Plans, and Prose: The Representation of Meaning in Writing." *WC* 1 (January 1984): 120–160.

Proposes a multiple-representation thesis to show how writers move between the "languages" of thought and of formal prose.

231. Flower, Linda S., and John R. Hayes. "Response to Marilyn Cooper and Michael Holzman, 'Talking about Protocols' [*CCC* 34 (October 1983)]." *CCC* 36 (February 1985): 94–97.

Rebuts the criticism of protocol analysis by explaining the difference between protocol methodology and Wundt's method of introspection and by discussing the differing influences of protocols on mental processes.

232. Fontaine, Sheryl I. *Evidence of Audience Awareness in the Writing and Writing Processes of Nine- and Eighteen-Year-Olds.* Urbana, Ill.: ERIC/RCS and NCTE, 1984. ERIC ED 258 183 [27 pages]

Observes four students at each age, finding little audience awareness in younger writers.

233. Fontaine, Sheryl I. "Writing for an Audience: How Writers at Three Age Levels Demonstrate an Awareness of the Audience and Respond to Two Contrasting Audiences." *DAI* 45 (December 1984): 1668A.

Findings indicate that older writers adapted their writing processes to the more distant reader by analyzing the audience, setting goals, and reviewing their texts.

234. Fox, Sharon E., and Nancy G. Platt. "Using Videotapes for Illustrations of Writing Research Findings." Paper presented at NCTE Convention, Columbus, April 1984. ERIC ED 252 876 [23 pages]

Argues for the usefulness of videotaping children's writing experiences in order to capture the contextual integrity of the classroom writing situation.

235. Fox, Tom. "Analyzing Language in Terms of the Intersubjectivity of Communities and Authority." *Reader* 11 (Spring 1984): 38–48.

Case study of a student writer that focuses on how her language adapts to her perception of communities and the authority within them.

236. Fredin, Eric S. "Assessing Sources: Interviewing, Self-Monitoring, and Attribution Theory." *JQ* 61 (Winter 1984): 866–873.

Argues that the process of newsgathering affects the conclusions journalists and their editors draw. Journalists work in a highly manipulative environment.

237. Freedman, Sarah Warshauer, ed. *The Acquisition of Written Language: Response and Revision.* Writing Research: Multidisciplinary Inquiries into the Nature of Writing. Norwood, N.J.: Ablex, 1985. 312 pages

A collection of 13 studies that examine written language acquisition and ways of responding to students' oral and written performances to encourage revision. Investigates the use of computers, conferences, and small groups, among other strategies.

238. Fregoe, David Harry. "A Schematization of Poetical, Rhetorical, and Poetical-Rhetorical Discourse." *DAI* 44 (May 1984): 3205A.

Finds that intrinsic and extrinsic categories have characterized the relationship of rhetoric and poetry. Proposes a model of poetical discourse, rhetorical discourse, and "poetical-rhetorical discourse."

239. Frentz, Thomas S. "Rhetorical Conversation, Time, and Moral Action." *QJS* 71 (February 1985): 1–18.

Attempts to use MacIntyre's ethical theories as the basis for a socially effective moral system by giving them rhetorical dimensions.

240. Fulkerson, Gerald. "Augustine's Attitude toward Rhetoric in *De Doctrina Christiana:* The Significance of 2.37.55." *RSQ* 15 (Summer–Fall 1985): 108–111.

Argues that Augustine rejected the study of rhetorical precepts because he thought imitation a more useful path to real eloquence.

241. Gaines, Robert. "Philodemus on the Three Activities of Rhetorical Invention." *Rhetorica* 3 (Summer 1985): 155–163.

Argues that the Epicurean rhetorician posits intellection, an activity prior to discovery and judgment, as the only act proper to rhetorical invention.

242. Gaonkar, Dilip Parameshwar. "Aspects of Sophistic Pedagogy." *DAI* 46 (September 1985): 554A.

Indicates the importance of *politike techne* to sophistic teaching and theory. Discusses humanism, rationalism, and utilitarianism as distinguishing pedagogical features.

243. Garner, Ruth, Vivian Belcher, Evelyn Winfield, and Terrie Smith. "Multiple Measures of Text Summarization Proficiency: What Can Fifth-Grade Students Do?" *RTE* 19 (May 1985): 140–153.

Finds summarizing a text a multiple-component operation. Most fifth graders studied recognized good summaries but were not so adept at producing or reflecting upon them.

244. Garrett, Mary Margaret. "The *Mo-Tzu* and the *Lu-Shih Ch'un-Ch'iu:* A Case Study of Classical Chinese Theory and Practice of Argument." *DAI* 45 (September 1984): 681A.

Applying Piaget's model to argumentation indicates the value of epistemological theory in analyzing culture-bound assumptions.

245. Garver, Eugene. "Richard McKeon's Chapter in the History of Rhetoric; or, Why Does McKeon Write So Funny?" *RSQ* 14 (Winter–Spring 1984): 3–14.

Argues that McKeon's difficult prose style is a logical consequence of his philosophical beliefs and of his notion of the role of rhetoric.

246. Gay, Pamela. *How Attitude Interferes with the Performance of Unskilled College Freshman Writers.* Washington, D.C.: NIE, 1983. ERIC ED 234 417 [164 pages]

Finds that the cumulative development of negative attitudes, attributable to misconceptions about writing and to teacher attitudes, hinder development of writing abilities.

247. Gee, T. W. "Of Ships and Sealing Wax." *EQ* 18 (Summer 1985): 82–88.

Students employing both an outline and a rough draft scored significantly better and produced essays of significantly higher quality than those who did not.

248. Geisler, Cheryl, David S. Kaufer, and Erwin R. Steinberg. "The Unattended Anaphoric 'This': When Should Writers Use It?" *WC* 2 (April 1985): 129–155.

Finds that demarcational, syntactic, and semantic reference did not predict readers' judgments. Suggests a classification based on the functional notions of topic and form.

249. Gere, Anne Ruggles, and Robert D. Abbott. "Talking about Writing: The Language of Writing Groups." *RTE* 19 (December 1985): 362–381.

Analyzes the "idea units" of fifth, eighth, and twelfth graders critiquing peers. Finds that all groups focused on content, but responses varied with mode of discourse.

250. Ghadessy, Moshen. "Going beyond the Sentence: Implications of Discourse Analysis for the Teaching of the Writing Skill." *IRAL* 22 (August 1984): 213–218.

Reinterprets Winter's (1976) discourse categories according to the degree of the writer's involvement.

251. Gillam-Scott, Alice. "'Treading Softly': Dealing with the Apprehension of Older Freshman Writers." Paper presented at the CCCC Convention, New York, March 1984. ERIC ED 244 260 [15 pages]

Reports on a study of older, apprehensive writers in college.

252. Glauner, Jeffrey. "Written Discourse: A Model for Pragmatic Analysis." *DAI* 46 (October 1985): 964A.

Argues for the effectiveness of the developed model as a mechanism for the pragmatic analysis of written discourse.

253. Goebel, George H. "Early Greek Rhetorical Theory and Practice: Proof and Arrangement in the Speeches of Antiphon and Euripides." *DAI* 44 (May 1984): 3376A.

Concludes that rhetorical theory shows continuity from its beginnings to the fourth century.

254. Goodman, Yetta. *A Two-Year Case Study Observing the Development of Third- and Fourth-Grade Children's Writing Processes.* Tucson: University of Arizona, College of Education, 1984. ERIC ED 241 240 [432 pages]

Reports a study of 10 Papago Indian third- and fourth-grade writers.

255. Goodwin, Pearl. "An Interview with Gloria Miklowitz." *Alan* 11 (Winter 1984): 40–42, 44.

A writer of young adult novels discusses why and how she writes and what she hopes to accomplish through writing.

256. Gorrell, Robert M. "Bottom as Rhetorician: Voice and Tone." *RR* 2 (January 1984): 157–162.

Offers suggestions for establishing a balance among voice, argument, and tone.

257. Grabe, William P. "Towards Defining Expository Prose within a Theory of Text Construction." *DAI* 45 (February 1985): 2501A.

Concludes that the term "expository prose" may be valid as a general genre type.

258. Graesser, Arthur C., Eric W. Lewis, Patricia L. Hopkinson, and Hank A. Bruflodt. "The Impact of Different Information Sources on Idea Generation: Writing off the Top of Our Heads." *WC* 1 (July 1984): 341–364.

Analyzes the extent to which the number and quality of ideas generated could be predicted by formal education, mass media, social interaction, and direct experience.

259. Grassi, Ernesto. "Humanistic Rhetorical Philosophizing: Giovanni Pontano's Theory of the Unity of Poetry, Rhetoric, and History." *P&R* 17 (1984): 135–155.

Discusses the work of a Renaissance humanist who rejects rational argument and locates understanding in metaphor and "rhetorical speech."

260. Graves, Richard L., ed. *Rhetoric and Composition: A Sourcebook for Teachers and Writers.* Upper Montclair, N.J.: Boynton/Cook, 1984. 376 pages

A collection of 38 readings, many reprinted from journals, in six sections: introduction; motivating student writing; the sentence: a reluctant medium; beyond the sentence; the pedagogy of composition: from classical rhetoric to current practice; and new perspectives, new horizons.

261. Greenberg, Valerie D. "Literature and the Discourse of Science: The Paradigm of Thomas Mann's *The Magic Mountain*." *SAR* 50 (January 1985): 59–73.

Suggests that modern writers have attempted to reunite literary and scientific discourse artificially separated by romantic writers.

262. Greene, John O. "A Cognitive Approach to Human Communication: An Action Assembly Theory." *ComM* 51 (December 1984): 289–306.

Presents an initial model of cognitive structures and processes underlying the production of verbal and nonverbal behaviors in ongoing interaction.

263. Greene, John O. "Evaluating Cognitive Explanations of Communication Phenomena." *QJS* 70 (August 1984): 241–254.

Suggests that cognitive approaches to the study of human communication should meet three kinds of standards: necessary, sufficient, and aesthetic requirements.

264. Gregg, Richard B. *Symbolic Inducement and Knowing.* Rhetoric/Communication Series. Columbia, S.C.: University of South Carolina Press, 1984. 160 pages

Synthesizes the claims that we know because we perceive symbolically. Examines the physiological, linguistic, and social implications of symbolic inducement. Links symbolic inducement to a critique of rhetoric.

265. Gregory, Marshall W. "Writing, Literacy, and Liberal Arts." *BADE* 82 (Winter 1985): 27–32.

Argues that using practicality to justify the teaching of writing trivializes it but that teaching writing as a literal and literary art enriches it.

266. Grieb, Kenneth J. "The Writing on the Walls." *JPC* 18 (Summer 1984): 78–91.

Rather than expressing the views of the opposition, graffiti in Mexico reflects the values of the government and ruling party.

267. Groppe, John D. "Reality as Enchantment: A Theory of Repetition." *RR* 2 (January 1984): 165–174.

Applies to different modes of discourse Berger's view that reality is sustained by repetition.

268. Gross, Alan G. "The Form of the Experimental Paper: A Realization of the Myth of Induction." *JTWC* 15 (1985): 15–26.

The conventional organization of the experimental paper realizes the myth that inductive science "can lead directly from sensory experience to reliable knowledge."

269. Gross, Alan G. "Style and Arrangement in Scientific Prose: The Rules behind the Rulers." *JTWC* 14 (1984): 241–253.

Describes the goals that editors of a scientific journal try to achieve in their revisions of style and arrangement.

270. Grunig, James E., Shirley Ramsey, and Larissa A. Schneider. "An Axiomatic Theory of Cognition and Writing." *JTWC* 15 (1985): 95–130.

Constructs a theory of writing and cognition, drawing on behaviorial sciences and humanities, and presents research to support portions of the theory.

271. Guthrie, John T. "Cognition for Composition." *JR* 27 (May 1984): 747–749.

Protocol analysis shows that successful writers recognize their readers' needs, indicating this awareness in the quantity, quality, relevance, and structure of the information they provide.

272. Guthrie, John T. "Expression of Narrative and Opinion." *RT* 37 (May 1985): 906–908.

Reviews the research of Hidi and Hildyard describing the distinctions between learning to write stories and opinion essays.

273. Guthrie, John T. "Learning to Write Coherently." *RT* 37 (January 1984): 430–432.

Presents results of King's research on cohesion in the writing of first- and second-grade children.

274. Guthrie, John T. "Writing Connections." *RT* 37 (February 1984): 540–542.

Describes constituents in stories of first and second graders as researched by King and Rentel.

275. Halloran, S. Michael. "The Birth of Molecular Biology: An Essay in the Rhetorical Criticism of Scientific Discourse." *RR* 3 (September 1984): 70–83.

Analyzes *ethos* in Watson and Crick's paper on DNA. Finds a "self-consciously genteel style" that contributes to a particular scientific paradigm.

276. Halpern, Jeanne W. "Differences between Speaking and Writing and Their Implications for Teaching." *CCC* 35 (October 1984): 345–357.

Uses edited transcripts from a two-year study on oral biography to discuss differences between spoken and written discourse. Analyzes voice, text, and audience adaptation.

277. Hample, Dale. "A Third Perspective on Argument." *P&R* 18 (1985): 1–23.

Argues that there is a private, cognitive form of argument underlying the public forms traditionally studied by rhetoricians.

278. Harbert, Kathy Lynn. "A Neuropsychological Framework for the Assessment of Competing Theories of Rhetoric as Epistemic." *DAI* 45 (April 1985): 3025A.

Presents a metatheoretical framework compatible with current cognitive theory for understanding symbols of thought and language.

279. Harned, Jon. "The Intellectual Background of Alexander Bain's 'Modes of Discourse.'" *CCC* 36 (February 1985): 42–50.

Argues that inadequate attention to Bain's intellectual milieu and his motivation for developing the modes have obscured the true historical importance of his taxonomy.

280. Harned, Jon. "Stanley Fish's Theory of the Interpretive Community: A Rhetoric for Our Time?" *FEN* 14 (Fall 1985): 9–13.

Discusses interpretive community and its relationship to composition/rhetorical theory.

281. Harpine, William D. "Can Rhetoric and Dialectic Serve the Purposes of Logic?" *P&R* 18 (1985): 96–112.

Asks Toulmin's question and argues that the limits of logic are beyond proof, that theorists need an "adequate" logical theory for evaluating rhetorical acts.

282. Harris, Jeanette. "Rewriting: A Note on Definitions." *RR* 2 (January 1984): 102–104.

Defines rewriting as a process involving revising, editing, and proofreading, arguing that such a model "enables us to view rewriting as a process within a process."

283. Harris, Jeanette. "Student Writers and Word Processing: A Preliminary Evaluation." *CCC* 36 (October 1985): 323–330.

A case study of six students indicates that, although they felt word processors made writing easier, faster, and neater, it did not encourage extensive macrostructure revisions.

284. Harris, Joseph. "The Plural Text/The Plural Self: Roland Barthes and William Coles." Paper presented at the CCCC Convention, Minneapolis, March 1985. ERIC ED 257 084 [15 pages]

Argues that Barthes and Coles offer significant theories for approaching style, stressing complexity and the dialectic of writing and the self.

285. Harris, Muriel. "Visualization and Spelling Competence." *JDEd* 9 (1985): 2–5.

Reports on a study that confirms the importance of visualization in spelling. Describes appropriate teaching strategies.

286. Harste, Jerome, Carolyn L. Burke, and Virginia A. Woodward. *The Young Child as Writer-Reader and Informant.* Washington, D.C.: NIE, 1983. ERIC ED 234 413 [479 pages]

Reports on the processes involved in learning literacy among children three to six years old.

287. Harvey, Irene E. "Contemporary French Thought and the Art of Rhetoric." *P&R* 18 (1985): 199–215.

Examines Sartre, Barthes, Ricoeur, Foucault, Derrida, and Lacan in reference to the "art of rhetoric."

288. Haselkorn, Mark P. "A Pragmatic Approach to Technical Writing." *TWT* 11 (Winter 1984): 122–124.

Argues that technical writing should be limited to the study and teaching of pragmatic conventions relevant to actual technical writing situations.

289. Hashimoto, Irvin Y. "Persuasion as Ethical Argument." *RR* 4 (September 1985): 46–53.

Argues that students need practical help in understanding complex terms such as "be good" and "be decent" in argument.

290. Hashimoto, Irvin Y. "Structured Heuristic Procedures: Their Limitations." *CCC* 36 (February 1985): 73–81.

Posits limitations for structured heuristics: cognitive style and experience motivation, hobby horses, metaphor, formats, and conventions.

291. Haskell, Dale E. "The Rhetoric of the Familiar Essay: E.B. White and Personal Discourse." *DAI* 44 (June 1984): 3671A.

Examines eight White essays to show how essays can evince compelling arguments by using a modern generative and lyrical *ethos*.

292. Hauser, Gerard A. "Aristotle's Example Revisited." *P&R* 18 (1985): 171–180.

Argues that Aristotle means "literally" that an example moves from part to part, that it is an argument based on unmediated influence.

293. Hawthorne, Joan. "The Importance of Prewriting: A Case Study." *Statement* 20 (October 1984): 32–41.

An apprehensive college student was able to write successfully with specific guidance in pre-writing activities.

294. Heald-Taylor, B. Gail. "Scribble in First Grade Writing." *RT* 38 (October 1984): 4–8.

First-grade children use scribble in their writing for specific and varied purposes.

295. Heath, Robert L. "Kenneth Burke's Break with Formalism." *QJS* 70 (May 1984): 132–143.

Traces Burke's movement from formalism to dramatism in a series of letters written to Frank in 1922.

296. Heidegger, Martin. *Early Greek Thinking.* David Farrell Krell and Frank A. Capuzzi, trans. New York: Harper & Row, 1984. 129 pages

Four essays written between 1943 and 1954 explicate key words used by the early Greeks to describe the premetaphysical interplay of language and thought; originally published in 1975.

297. Henrick, John. "An Elaborate Medieval Mnemonic." *WWays* 17 (May 1984): 97–99.

Describes a mnemonic device for remembering parts of Theophrastus's and Ariston's syllogisms. Challenges readers to find a better, more contemporary mnemonic device.

298. Herrington, Anne J. "Where Are We Now? Reflections on the Penn State Rhetoric Conference and Composition." *PCTEB* 50 (November 1984): 16–20.

Reviews presentations by featured speakers Halloran, Booth, Elbow, and Faigley as reflecting current concerns in writing pedagogy.

299. Herrington, Anne J. "Writing in Academic Settings: A Study of the Contexts for Writing in Two College Engineering Courses." *RTE* 19 (December 1985): 331–361.

A study of the same students and professors in different courses reveals "distinct forums": different issues, lines of reasoning, and social purposes.

300. Herrstrom, David Sten. "Technical Writing as Mapping Description onto Diagram: The Graphic Paradigms of Explanation." *JTWC* 14 (1984): 223–240.

Argues that technical writing functions to explain, allowing a reader to visualize relationships, while imaginative writing functions to present, leaving relationships and structure implicit.

301. Higgs, Rosalee O. "The Impact of Discourse Mode, Syntactic Complexity, and Story Grammar on the Writing of Sixth Graders." *DAI* 45 (August 1984): 80A.

Expository writing "elicited more complex syntax" than narrative writing, and students used their knowledge of story grammar elements better in expository writing than in narrative writing.

302. Hoagland, Nancy L. "The Role of Audience in the Revision Strategies of Basic Writers." *DAI* 46 (October 1985): 915A.

Findings suggest four modes of response expected from an audience: response to formal elements, to meaning, to personal appeals to the reader, and to the persona created in the writing.

303. Hoffman, Stevie, and Belinda McCully. "Oral Language Functions in Transaction with Children's Writing." *LArts* 61 (January 1984): 41–50.

Uses the notion of tenor to examine the role of oral language in influencing the writing of young children. Includes sample scripts.

304. Hogan, Homer. "A Phenomenological Approach to Paragraph Analysis." *RSQ* 14 (Summer–Fall 1984): 105–118.

A theoretical discussion of the relations between effective paragraphing and "fundamental movements" of consciousness.

305. Hogan, J. Michael. "Historiography and Ethics in Adam Smith's Lectures on Rhetoric, 1762–1763." *Rhetorica* 2 (Spring 1984): 75–91.

Delineates Smith's treatment of historiography, explaining its differentiation from other genres, its arrangement, and especially its emphasis on emotions and morality.

306. Hollinger, Robert. "Practical Reason and Hermeneutics." *P&R* 18 (1985): 113–122.

Argues that Gadamer, Habermas, MacIntyre, Taylor, Kuhn, and Rorty appropriate Aristotle's notions of *phronesis, praxis,* and rhetoric.

307. Hood, Michael Dennis. "Aristotle's Enthymeme: Its Theory and Application to Discourse." *DAI* 45 (September 1984): 682A.

Analyzes Aristotle's enthymeme in the context of his epistemology, concluding that it works as a generative principle of discourse. Lists applications for teaching composition.

308. Howell, Sharon L. "Metaphorical Analysis of the Evolution of the Female Identity, 1961–1982." *DAI* 44 (June 1984): 3540A.

Using content analysis and Burkean perspectives on metaphor, traces the development of the rhetorical creation of female identity.

309. Hrushovski, Benjamin. "Poetic Metaphor and Frames of Reference: With Examples from Eliot, Rilke, Mayakovsky, Mandelshtam, Pound, Creeley, Amichai, and the *New York Times*." *PT* 5 (1984): 5–43.

Analyzes examples of extended metaphors in poetic and nonpoetic texts.

310. Hudson, Sally A. "Contextual Factors and Children's Writing." *DAI* 45 (December 1984): 1669A.

Results indicate that, although the contextual factors of assigned writing varied little across grades, the audiences, purposes, and genres for self-sponsored writing expanded with age.

311. Hull, Glynda A. *The Editing Process in Writing: A Performance Study of Experts and Novices*. Pittsburgh: University of Pittsburgh Learning Research and Development Center, 1984. ERIC ED 245 254 [26 pages]

Studies the editing performance of college undergraduates.

312. Hull, Glynda A. "The Editing Process in Writing: A Performance Study of Experts and Novices." *DAI* 45 (September 1984): 829A.

Finds that, although expert college writers correct more errors than novice college writers, neither group makes many corrections.

313. Hult, Christine A. *Frames, Content Organization, and Themes in Student Expository Essays: An Analysis of Discourse Structure*. Urbana, Ill.: ERIC/RCS and NCTE, 1982. ERIC ED 235 482 [30 pages]

Finds that better high school writers more effectively organize, unify, and control essays than average or below average writers who can benefit from direct instruction.

314. Humes, Ann. *Designing Text for Information Processing*. Technical Report, no. 86. Los Alamitos, Calif.: Southwest Regional Laboratory for Educational Research, 1984. ERIC ED 249 940 [23 pages]

Reports on studies by linguists and psychologists that develop principles for constructing readable prose for both print and computer media.

315. Jacobi, Martin J. "Literature as Equipment for Writing: Applications of Kenneth Burke's Dramatism to the Teaching of Composition." *DAI* 45 (January 1985): 2081A.

Concludes that students using Burke's dramatic analyses expanded their perspective of literature when they read and their awareness of audience when they wrote.

316. Jacobs, Suzanne E. "Composing the In-Class Essay: A Case Study of Rudy." *CE* 46 (January 1984): 34–42.

Describes a student writer's difficulties in avoiding writer-based compositions.

317. Jamieson, Barbara C. *Features of Thematic and Information Structure in Oral and Written Narratives of Good and Poor Writers*. Urbana, Ill.: ERIC/RCS and NCTE, 1983. ERIC ED 258 177 [28 pages]

Compares the oral and written responses to films of 24 community college students.

318. Jensen, Julie M., ed. *Composing and Comprehending*. Urbana, Ill.: National Conference on Research in English and ERIC/RCS (distributed by NCTE), 1984. ERIC ED 243 139 [200 pages]

A collection of 19 essays examining the relationships among reading, writing, and other language skills. Summarizes research on children's uses of language and describes instructional strategies.

319. Johansson, Stig. "Word Frequency and Text Type: Some Observations Based on the LOB Corpus of British English Texts." *CHum* 19 (January–March 1985): 23–36.

Presents an analysis of 500 British English texts in 15 categories of writing, listing works of different grammatical types characteristic of those categories.

320. Johnson, Nan. "Rhetoric and Literature: Politics, Theory, and the Future of English Studies." *BADE* 77 (Spring 1984): 22–25.

Identifies sources of philosophical and theoretical estrangement and argues for a pluralistic definition of English studies.

321. Johnstone, Henry W. "Aristotle, Hegel, and *Argumentum ad Hominem*." *RSQ* 15 (Summer–Fall 1985): 131–144.

Maintains that an *argumentum ad hominem* may be formally valid and that both Aristotle and Hegel share this view.

322. Jones, Merrill Anway. "A Rhetorical Study of Winthrop Rockefeller's Political Speeches, 1964–1971." *DAI* 45 (February 1985): 2302A.

Uses the theories of Bitzer, Borman, and Burke to analyze Rockefeller's speeches.

323. Jordan, Mark D. "Authority and Persuasion in Philosophy." *P&R* 18 (1985): 67–85.

In the *Theaetetus,* Protagoras and Parmenides are for Socrates figures of sophistical and philosophical authority.

324. Journet, Debra. "Rhetoric and Sociology." *JTWC* 14 (Winter 1985): 339–350.

Describes one example of a scientific debate that relies on traditional rhetorical techniques of persuasion.

325. Kai-Kee, Elliot. "Social Order and Rhetoric in the Rome of Julius II (1503–1513)." *DAI* 44 (March 1984): 2851A.

Describes how the rhetoric of learned Romans in the reign of Julius II reflected the era's closely integrated social structure and political exigencies.

326. Kantrowitz, Bruce Michael. "Editorial Economics: Consequences of Policy Alternatives—A Reader-Based Quantitative Analysis." *DAI* 46 (September 1985): 542A.

Compares the "effects of editorial treatment and nontreatment on different audiences." Responses indicate the value of technical editing and the importance of audience in writing.

327. Karpen, James. "Can Classical Rhetoric Meet Today's Needs?" *ELAB* 26 (Spring 1985): 7–8.

Argues that because classical rhetoric was devised for an oral culture, modern approaches are more effective in today's pluralistic culture.

328. Karpen, James. "The Digitized Word: Orality, Literacy, and the Computerization of Language." *DAI* 45 (March 1985): 2855A.

Surveys the movement from the memorized to the printed to the "digitized" word in the processes of literary expression, information management, education, and thought.

329. Katriel, Tamar, and Marcelo Dascal. "What Do Indicating Devices Indicate?" *P&R* 17 (1984): 1–16.

Examines devices to "foreground" speakers' attitudes toward layers of meaning.

330. Kean, Donald K. "Persuasive Writing: Role of Writers' Verbal Ability and Writing Anxiety When Working under Time Constraints." *DAI* 45 (March 1985): 2787A.

Findings indicate that "verbal ability facilitates persuasive writing performance, while writing anxiety inhibits it." The availability of additional writing time did not necessarily result in improved writing.

331. Keech, Catharine L. "Apparent Regression in Student Writing Performance as a Function of Unrecognized Changes in Task Complexity." *DAI* 45 (March 1985): 2787A.

Presents a discourse typology that describes what students do differently from one writing occasion to the next. Suggests application for theories of cognitive development to writing.

332. Kegley, Pamela H. "The Effect of Mode of Discourse on Student Writing Performance." *DAI* 45 (November 1984): 1373A.

Analysis of variance "revealed significant differences between the mean score for narrative writing and those for descriptive, expository, and persuasive writing." Proposes implications for writing assessment.

333. Kehl, D. G., and Donald Heidt. "The Rhetoric of Cow and the Rhetoric of Bull." *RSQ* 14 (Summer–Fall 1984): 129–138.

Drawing examples largely from propaganda and advertising, the authors recommend a rhetorical taxonomy based on Perry's concepts of bull (generalizations) and cow (undigested facts).

334. Keller, Joseph. "The Rediscovery of Linguistic Creativity." *Thought* 60 (March 1985): 18–30.

Uses concepts of discourse analysis to examine the relationships between linguistic creativity and the "foundational sentences" of theology.

335. Kennedy, Mary Lynch. "The Composing Process of College Students Writing from Sources." *WC* 2 (October 1985): 434–456.

Reveals strong associations between reading level and the use of study-skill reading strategies and between postreading-prewriting strategies and composing strategies.

336. Kevelson, Roberta. "C. S. Peirce's Speculative Rhetoric." *P&R* 17 (1984): 16–29.

Reviews Peirce's work on semiotic methodology and speculative rhetoric.

337. Killingsworth, M. Jimmie. "The Essay and the Report: Expository Poles in Technical Writing." *JTWC* 15 (1985): 227–233.

Suggests a theory of expository writing: "In the *essay,* data are subordinated to ideas; in the *report,* data are dominant."

338. King, Andrew A. "St. Augustine's Doctrine of Participation as a Metaphysic of Persuasion." *RSQ* 15 (Summer–Fall 1985): 112–115.

Discusses Augustine's belief that fallen man could persuade himself of God's truth only through the study of opaque signs. Compares this "participation" with Burke's "identification."

339. Klauk, E. Russell. "Staging and Text Comprehensibility: It's What's 'Up Front' That Counts." Paper presented at the NCTE Convention, Columbus, April 1984. ERIC ED 249 473 [27 pages]

Argues that staging, a method for writers to mark the prominence of ideas, can be used to produce a well-structured and coherent text.

340. Kneupper, Charles W., ed. *Oldspeak/Newspeak: Rhetorical Transformations.* Arlington, Tex.: Rhetoric Society of America, 1985. 267 pages

A collection of 21 essays on a variety of topics, including political and religious rhetoric, *statis* theory, rhetorical systems in America, the rise and fall of rhetoric in classical education, the influence of audiences on writers, psychological strategies used in building and understanding paragraphs, Cicero, Orwell's *1984,* and Campbell's and Wertheimer's approaches to rhetoric.

341. Kneupper, Charles W. "Rhetoric as Epistemic: A Conversation with Richard A. Cherwitz." *Pre-Text* 5 (Fall–Winter 1984): 197–235.

Discusses the ways in which rhetoric creates and undermines various images of reality.

342. Kneupper, Charles W. "The Tyranny of Logic and the Freedom of Argumentation." *Pre-Text* 5 (Summer 1984): 113–121.

Claims that formal logic is an inappropriate method of instruction for argumentative writing.

343. Knoblauch, C. H., and Lil Brannon. *Rhetorical Traditions and the Teaching of Writing.* Upper Montclair, N.J.: Boynton/Cook, 1984. 182 pages

Argues that modern rhetorical theory and the pedagogy knowledgeably based on it offer a richer basis for writing instruction than classical rhetorical theory and its view of mind, language, and the world.

344. Koch, Barbara J. "The Forum: Comments on Karyn Thompson-Panos and Maria Thomas-Ruzic's 'The Least You Should Know about Arabic: Implications for the ESL Writing Instructor' [*TESOLQ* 17 (December 1983)]." *TESOLQ* 18 (September 1984): 542–545.

Points out sources for parallelism and coordination in Arabic by referring to features of Arabic rhetoric. Cautions contrastive rhetoricians to be objective.

345. Kotler, Janet. "On I. A. Richards — and Some Other Things." *ABCAB* 48 (March 1985): 2–4.

Argues that recent research on writing as a process is not persuasive and that discussions of how teachers actually handle their classes and students should receive more attention.

346. Kozicki, Henry. "Trouble in Composition: A Review Essay." *JTW* 3 (Spring 1984): 117–129.

Reviews Horner's *Composition and Literature.* Questions composition as a subject and the role of composition faculty.

347. Kraftchick, Steven John. "*Ethos* and *Pathos* Appeals in Galatians Five and Six: A Rhetorical Analysis." *DAI* 46 (December 1985): 1659A.

Examines Paul's use of *ethos* and *pathos* to further his argument in Galatians and looks at rhetorical proof structures.

348. Kremers, Marshall N. "The Practical Rhetoric of Samuel P. Newman." *DAI* 45 (July 1984): 167A.

Studies the first college rhetoric textbook written by an American, Newman's *Practical System of Rhetoric* (1827).

349. Krippendorff, Klaus. "An Epistemological Foundation for Communication." *JC* 34 (Summer 1984): 21–36.

Argues that the epistemological view taken from cybernetics provides a more powerful base for studies of human communication theory than does the ontological view of scientific inquiry.

350. Kroll, Barry M. "Rewriting a Complex Story for a Young Reader: The Development of Audience-Adapted Writing Skills." *RTE* 19 (May 1985): 120–139.

Analyzes developing audience-adapted writing skills in students from fifth grade to college. Finds a shift from the lower grades' "word-oriented" strategies to the higher grades' "meaning-oriented" approach.

351. Kroll, Barry M. "Social-Cognitive Ability and Writing Performance: How Are They Related?" *WC* 2 (July 1985): 293–305.

Concludes that social-cognitive ability relates most strongly to an oral task and very weakly to writing tasks.

352. Kroll, Barry M. "Writing for Readers: Three Perspectives on Audience." *CCC* 35 (May 1984): 172–185.

Assesses three views on audience – "rhetorical," "informational," "social" – from theoretical and pedagogical perspectives.

353. Kucer, Stephen. "The Making of Meaning: Reading and Writing as Parallel Processes." *WC* 2 (July 1985): 317–336.

Discusses a general theory of text processing that delineates the parallel operations in reading and writing.

354. La Roche, Mary G., and Sheryl S. Pearson. "Rhetoric and Rational Enterprises: Reassessing Discourse in Organizations." *WC* 2 (July 1985): 246–268.

Claims that rhetoric reveals underlying paradigms in organizations. The paradigms are determined by the nature of communal behavior and by the nature of thinking human beings.

355. Laib, Nevin K. "Territoriality in Rhetoric." *CE* 47 (October 1985): 579–593.

Discusses principles of social and territorial rhetoric and argues that viewing rhetoric as a territorial art has significant consequences.

356. Lake, Randall A. "Order and Disorder in Anti-Abortion Rhetoric: A Logological View." *QJS* 70 (November 1984): 425–443.

Applies Burke's cycle of terms for order to an analysis of antiabortion rhetoric.

357. LaMar, Helen J. "Naming Oneself Writer: Three Writing Lives." *DAI* 45 (November 1984): 1320A.

Interviews with three writers reveal three stages of "naming": early intuitive knowledge, engagement in writing, and a commitment to a writing career.

358. Land, Robert E., Jr. "Effect of Varied Teacher Cues on Higher and Lower Ability Seventh- and Eleventh-Grade Students' Revision of Their Descriptive Essays." *DAI* 45 (November 1984): 1320A.

Finds that addition and deletion revisions were increased by the content revision cue and that, as writers mature, they employ acquired revision strategies in better ways.

359. Lang, Helen S. "Philosophy as Text and Context." *P&R* 18 (1985): 158–170.

Uses the reception of Aristotle's *Physics* to demonstrate how meaning is determined by the historical relation between the text and the various contexts of argument.

360. Langer, Judith A. "Children's Sense of Genre: A Study of Performance on Parallel Reading and Writing." *WC* 2 (April 1985): 157–187.

Compares ways children used to organize their knowledge across genres (story and report) and domains (reading and writing).

361. Langer, Judith A. "The Effects of Available Information on Responses to School Writing Tasks." *RTE* 18 (February 1984): 27–44.

Explores relationships between topic knowledge and writing quality, concluding that organized information aids in addressing theses, but that "unintegrated information" suffices for elaborative writing tasks.

362. Langer, Judith A. *Effects of Topic Knowledge on the Quality and Coherence of Informational Writing.* Urbana, Ill.: ERIC/RCS and NCTE, 1983. ERIC ED 234 418 [38 pages]

Finds a strong and consistent relation between topic-specific background knowledge and the quality of writing among 97 tenth graders.

363. Langer, Judith A. *Reading and Writing in School-Age Children: A Developmental View.* Urbana, Ill.: NCTE Research Foundation, 1984. ERIC ED 258 135 [331 pages]

Tests children at grades three, six, and nine, finding that reading and writing tasks tap similar processes and cognitive strategies.

364. Larsen, Elizabeth K. "A History of the Composing Process." *DAI* 45 (November 1984): 1381A.

Studies how the composing process has changed through history and concludes that no single composing process can be mandated.

365. Lauer, Janice M. "Composition Studies: Dappled Discipline." *RR* 3 (September 1984): 20–29.

Discusses the "multimodel" nature of composition studies, uses Habermas to map its professional development, and analyzes the advantages and risks of its range and modes of inquiry.

366. Lederman, Marie Jean, Michael Ribaudo, and Susan R. Ryzewic. "A National Survey on the Assessment and Improvement of the Academic Skills of Entering Freshmen: Some Implications for Writing Program Administrators." *WPA* 7 (Spring 1984): 11–16.

Results of a survey reveal a need for writing programs to strengthen the skills of a high proportion of academically ill-prepared incoming freshmen.

367. Lefevre, Karen B. "Infinite Conversation: A Social Perspective on Rhetorical Invention." *DAI* 45 (February 1985): 2507A.

Concludes that composition theory and pedagogy should take into account the social relationships that underlie invention.

368. Leff, Michael C. "Recovering Aristotle: Rhetoric, Politics, and the Limits of Rationality." *QJS* 71 (August 1985): 362–373.

Review essay dealing with Arnhart's *Aristotle on Political Reasoning: A Commentary on the "Rhetoric"* and Beiner's *Political Judgment.*

369. Lentz, Tony M. "From Recitation to Reading: Memory, Writing, and Composition in Greek Philosphical Prose." *SSCJ* 51 (Fall 1985): 49–70.

Posits three stages in the developing relationship between memory and writing.

370. Lewis, Clayton W. "Burke's Act in *A Rhetoric of Motives.*" *CE* 46 (April 1984): 368–376.

Attempts to redress a problem with Burke's writings: they emphasize act and slight writing pedagogy.

371. Lewis, Clayton W., and Charles W. Kneupper. "The Relation of Agency to Act in Dramatism: A Comment on 'Burke's Act' [*CE* 46 (January 1984)] and a Response." *CE* 47 (March 1985): 305–312.

A comment by Kneupper on Lewis's article and Lewis's response.

372. Lewis, Dorothy P. "The Role of Interest in Students' Writing Fluency and the Quality of the Product." *DAI* 45 (December 1984): 737A.

A study of twelfth graders raises questions about traditional language arts pedagogy.

373. Lipson, Carol S. "Francis Bacon and *Plain* Scientific Prose: A Reexamination." *JTWC* 15 (1985): 143–155.

Francis Bacon, supposedly the father of modern scientific prose, espoused rhetorical principles that conflict with those of writers who support a plain style in scientific writing.

374. List, Kathleen L. "Coherence and Cohesion: Contextualization of Oswald Ducrot's General Theory of Language." *DAI* 46 (October 1985): 966A.

Translates and analyzes Ducrot's work and concludes that unsaid meaning relations improve nonnative interpretation of discourse.

375. Littlefield, Robert Stephen. "An Analysis of the Persuasion and Coercion Used by the Carter Administration to Promote Human Rights in Argentina, Brazil, and Chile." *DAI* 44 (March 1984): 2623A.

Characterizes two means of persuasion and their interaction. Indicates why coercion was unsuccessful. Suggests new grounds for the analysis of diplomatic persuasive strategies.

376. Long, Roberta, and Laurie Bulgarella. "Social Interaction and the Writing Process." *LArts* 62 (February 1985): 166–172.

A tape of three first graders writing a story together revealed a high level of thinking on story content, structure, and grammar.

377. Lotto, Edward. "The Technology of Writing: Lessons from Laramie." *PCTEB* 50 (November 1984): 21–24.

Reviews presentations by featured speakers Ong, Ohmann, Laskowski, Kinney, and Green to point out the role of writing in a technological age.

378. Lotto, Edward. "The Writer's Subject Is Sometimes a Fiction." *WCJ* 5 and 6 (Spring–Winter 1985): 15–20.

Using modern theories of literary criticism and examples from his tutoring, shows that student writers often view their subjects only in terms of familiar conventions or their own experiences.

379. Lunsford, Andrea A. "Rhetoric: A Key to Survival." *EQ* 17 (Winter 1984): 3–15.

Describes tensions in defining "rhetoric" and recommends rehabilitating the rhetorical tradition. Affirms rhetoric as a means for living in and improving the world.

380. Lunsford, Andrea A., and Lisa S. Ede. "Classical Rhetoric, Modern Rhetoric, and Contemporary Discourse Studies." *WC* 1 (January 1984): 78–100.

Demonstrates that characteristic assumptions giving classical rhetoric its power can be found in an unsystematic and fragmented way in contemporary rhetoric.

381. Lutz, Jean A. "A Study of Professional and Experienced Writers Revising and Editing at the Computer and with Pen and Paper." *DAI* 44 (March 1984): 2755A.

Concludes that writers revise and edit differently at the word processor than with pen and paper.

382. Lyne, John. "Rhetorics of Inquiry." *QJS* 71 (February 1985): 65–73.

Sees rhetoric as an increasingly popular form of intellectual inquiry for an academic community that is moving beyond both objectivism and relativism.

383. Maden, Thomas F. "A Problem with Johnstone's." *P&R* 18 (1985): 86–95.

Argues that Johnstone's *The Problem of the Self* fails to establish its argument that the "self is the locus of a contradiction."

384. Maloney, Henry B. "You Write What You Read." *EJ* 74 (September 1985): 28–32.

Humorous description of the author's dilemma in selecting a dissertation topic.

385. Manabe, Takashi. "A Speech-Act-Theory-Based Interpretation Model for Written Texts." *DAI* 46 (November 1985): 1265A.

Suggests that speech-act theory, with variations, may be applied to written texts.

386. Marder, Daniel. "Envisioning and Revisioning." *RR* 3 (September 1984): 13–19.

Speculates on the need to adjust self and expression to audience and communication.

387. Markels, Robin Bell. *A New Perspective on Cohesion in Expository Paragraphs.* Studies in Writing and Rhetoric. Carbondale, Ill.: Southern Illinois University Press, 1984. 110 pages

Asserts that cohesion is of greatest importance in its relationship to unity and emphasis and must be considered a part of the surface structure of written language as well as the deep structure.

388. Marks, Dorothy. "When Children Write Science Fiction." *LArts* 62 (April 1985): 355–361.

Using one fourth grader's science fiction, a teacher attempts to understand the genre and the student's handling of voice, of history, and of time.

389. Marshall, Bruce A. *A Historical Commentary on Asconius.* Columbia, Mo.: University of Missouri Press, 1985. 384 pages

Studies Asconius's commentaries on Cicero's speeches.

390. Matalene, Carolyn. "Contrastive Rhetoric: An American Writing Teacher in China." *CE* 47 (December 1985): 789–808.

Identifies some of the differences between Chinese and Western rhetoric that confront an American writing teacher in China.

391. Matsuhashi, Ann, and Karen B. Quinn. "Cognitive Questions from Discourse Analysis: A Review and a Study." *WC* 1 (July 1984): 307–339.

Demonstrates the potential of discourse analysis for exploring cognitive processes that occur during writing.

392. Mayher, John S., and Rita S. Brause. "Learning through Teaching: Lessons from a First Grader." *LArts* 61 (March 1984): 285–290.

By analyzing drafts of her students' writing, a first-grade teacher charts the students' writing growth and clarifies her own concept of good writing.

393. McAndrew, Donald A. *The Effect of an Assigned Rhetorical Context on the Holistic Quality and Syntax of the Writing of High and Low Ability College Writers.* Urbana, Ill.: ERIC/RCS and NCTE, 1981. ERIC ED 235 481 [35 pages]

Reports on an experiment involving two samples from 60 students. Finds that the task and the assigned rhetorical context produced no significant effect.

394. McAndrew, Donald A. "Qualitative Research and Questions about Teaching Writing." *EngR* 36 (1985): 2–4.

Emphasizes the value of qualitative research in exploring questions about the process of learning to write.

395. McAndrew, Donald A. "Scribal Fluency and Syntactic Fluency." Paper presented at the CCCC Convention, New York, March 1984. ERIC ED 243 146 [14 pages]

Studies the relationship between handwriting speed and syntactic structures produced by college writers.

396. McCarron, William. "Changing the Technical Writing Paradigm." *JTWC* 15 (1985): 27–33.

Argues that technical writing is persuasive as well as referential, somewhere between science writing and advertising, and involves discovery as well as recording.

397. McCarthy, Patricia, Scott Meier, and Regina Rinderer. "Self-Efficacy and Writing: A Different View of Self-Evaluation." *CCC* 36 (December 1985): 465–471.

A prediction study of 137 freshmen showed that self-efficacy significantly related to essay quality as successfully demonstrated in 19 self-assessment skills.

398. McCartney, Robert. "Constructing the Self through Writing." *RSQ* 14 (Summer–Fall 1984): 119–128.

Argues, using the theories of Mead and modern rhetoricians and essays by his own students, that we construct our identities through writing.

399. McCleary, William J. "The Movement from Personal to Group Identity in Expressive Discourse." Paper presented at the CCCC Convention, Minneapolis, March 1985. ERIC ED 255 925 [25 pages]

Explores Kinneavy's theory of expressive discourse, viewing it as a process as well as an aim.

400. McClelland, Ben W., and Timothy R. Donovan, eds. *Perspectives on Research and Scholarship in Composition.* New York: MLA, 1985. 266 pages

A collection of 13 essays assessing the major scholarship in areas shaping the theory and practice of composition studies. Examines theoretical issues in rhetoric, composition, literature, and linguistics. Discusses research on collaborative learning, cognition, the competence of young writers, error, technical communication, and artificial intelligence. Includes bibliography.

401. McCord, Phyllis Frus. "Reading Nonfiction in Composition Courses: From Theory to Practice." *CE* 47 (November 1985): 747–762.

An approach to using nonfiction in composition courses. Suggests reflexive reading as a strategy for composition pedagogy.

402. McCulley, George A. "Writing Quality, Coherence, and Cohesion." *RTE* 19 (October 1985): 269–282.

Concludes that coherence in the persuasive writing of 17-year-olds includes but exceeds Halliday and Hasan cohesion indexes. Validates Bain's primary criterion for writing quality.

403. McCutchen, Deborah. "Writing as a Linguistic Problem." *Ed Psy* 4 (1984): 226–238. ERIC ED 258 204.

Argues that researchers overemphasize planning-level processes, neglecting the importance of text-level processes.

404. McKeough, Anne. "Developmental Stages in Children's Narrative Composition." Paper presented at the AERA Convention, New Orleans, April 1984. ERIC ED 249 461 [18 pages]

Studies 60 children ages 4, 6, 8, and 10. Finds that narratives proceed through increasingly complex substages and are related to working memory.

405. McMillen, Liz. "Writing Skills Taught in College Said to Muddy Clear Expression." *CHE* 31 (4 December 1985): 29.

Speakers at the 1985 National Council of Teachers of English meeting argue that college students are mistakenly taught how to write in a tradition of *belles lettres* rather than learning models of on-the-job writing.

406. McPhillips, Shirley P. "The Spirit of Revision: Listening for the Writer's Conscience." *LArts* 62 (October 1985): 614–618.

Taping the revision conferences of seven fifth graders shows the students moving inside their stories to consider issues of transition, focus, balance, tone, and cohesion.

407. McQuade, Donald, ed. *The Territory of Language: Linguistics, Stylistics, and the Teaching of Composition.* Rev. ed. Carbondale, Ill.: Southern Illinois University Press, 1985. 288 pages

A revised and expanded version of a 1979 collection. Contains 26 articles, several new to this edition.

408. Meisenhelder, Susan. "Redefining 'Powerful' Writing: Toward a Feminist Theory of Composition." *JT* 20 (Fall 1985): 184–195.

Argues that, in persuasion, the reader-writer relationship should not be characterized by "I" foisting meaning on "You," but by one working interactively toward "shared" meaning.

409. Melia, Trevor. "And Lo the Footprint... Selected Literature in Rhetoric and Science." *QJS* 70 (August 1984): 303–312.

A review essay on Kind's *Mathematics: The Loss of Certainty,* Munevar's *Radical Knowledge,* and Weiner's *Notes on the Methodology of Scientific Research.*

410. Menasche, Lionel. "Discourse Mode, Enabling Metaphors, and Styles of Closure in the Composing Process: Two Case Studies Based on Interruption Interviews." *DAI* 46 (November 1985): 1217A.

Examines the effects of mode on composing processes and ways writers represent composing to themselves. Suggests that writers use individual "enabling metaphors" and "styles of closure."

411. Mendiola, Sandra E. "Written English of Mexican American Students: A Study of Grammar, Structure, and Organization." *DAI* 45 (December 1984): 1760A.

Finds that college bilinguals educated in America write better English than those educated partly in Mexico.

412. Meyer, Bonnie, and Roy O. Freedle. "Effects of Discourse Type on Recall." *AERJ* 21 (Spring 1984): 121–143.

Finds that comparison/contrast, causation, and problem/solution discourse organizations facilitated learning more than did description.

413. Meyrowitz, Joshua. "The Adultlike Child and the Childlike Adult: Socialization in an Electronic Age." *Daedalus* 113 (Summer 1984): 19–48.

Describes recent reunification of social-psychological constructions of "child" and "adult" and how separate information systems — literacy, print, and media — are determiners.

414. Miller, Gerald R., and Michael J. Sunnafrank. "Theoretical Dimensions of Applied Communication Research." *QJS* 70 (August 1984): 255–263.

Argues that applied research in communication should be carried out in a theoretical context and that theoretical and applied work can be mutually supportive.

415. Miller, Keith D. "The Influence of a Liberal Homiletic Tradition on *Strength to Love* by Martin Luther King, Jr." *DAI* 45 (April 1985): 3026A.

King's imaginative and literal borrowing from the work of Social Gospel preachers to create his *ethos* illustrates a collision of oral homiletic and literary traditions.

416. Miller, Thomas P. "Eighteenth-Century Scottish Rhetoric in Its Socio-Cultural Context." *DAI* 46 (November 1985): 1287A.

Relates the development of eighteenth-century Scottish rhetoric to the Act of Union in 1707.

417. Minor, Dennis E. "Albert Einstein on Writing." *JTWC* 14 (1984): 13–18.

Finds the scientific thinking and writing process of Einstein to be based on the earlier theories of Mach, an Austrian physicist.

418. Minor, Dennis E. "Newspeak, *1984,* and Technical Writing." *JTWC* 15 (1985): 365–372.

Concludes that, while technical writers must operate under some linguistic constraints, they must keep them from limiting the range of thought itself.

419. Moffett, James. "Liberating Inner Speech." *CCC* 36 (October 1985): 304–308.

Views the sustained development of a line of thought, audience, mode of discourse, and re-reading as a means of rejuvenating inner speech to surprise habitual thought patterns.

420. Mohan, Bernard A., and Winnie Au-Yeung La. "Academic Writing and Chinese Students." *TESOLQ* 19 (September 1985): 515–534.

A comparison of students from Hong Kong and British Columbia indicates that developmental factors, rather than first language interference, affect discourse organization.

421. Monahan, Brian D. "Revision Strategies of Basic and Competent Writers as They Write for Different Audiences." *RTE* 18 (October 1984): 288–304.

Contrasts the revision strategies of four basic and four competent twelfth graders in writing compositions for two different audiences, teachers, and peers.

422. Moore, Mary Candace. "The Theory, Practice, and Rhetoric of Loyalty." *DAI* 44 (February 1984): 2602A.

Examines the rhetoric of arguments made concerning the dissolution or preservation of relations.

423. Moore, Michael T. "The Relationship between the Originality of Essays and Variables in the Problem-Discovery Process: A Study of Creative and Noncreative Middle School Students." *RTE* 19 (February 1985): 84–95.

Results indicate a relationship between problem-discovery and originality in essays produced by middle school writers. Examines whether student writers' problem-finding behavior is observable.

424. Moran, Charles. "The Word Processor and the Writer: A Systems Analysis." *CC* 2 (November 1984): 1–5.

Examines the effect of word processing on his own and his friends' writing. Finds different effects for different writers.

425. Moran, Michael G. "Joseph Priestley, William Duncan, and Analytic Arrangement in Eighteenth-Century Scientific Discourse." *JTWC* 14 (1984): 207–215.

Describes a five-stage heuristic introduced by Joseph Priestley, the eighteenth-century rhetorician and scientist.

426. Morrison, Toni. "Memory, Creation, and Writing." *Thought* 59 (December 1984): 385–290.

Addresses connections between memory and invention and describes the writer's compact with a reader, to whom she wants to respond on the "same plane as a preliterate or illiterate reader would."

427. Moxley, Joseph M. "Five Writers' Perceptions: An Ethnographic Study of Composing Processes and Writing Functions." *DAI* 45 (December 1984): 1670A.

Analyzes the perceptions of one experienced and four inexperienced writers regarding writing development and related variables.

428. Mulderig, Gerald P. "Gertrude Buck's Rhetorical Theory and Modern Composition Teaching." *RSQ* 14 (Summer–Fall 1984): 95–104.

Buck, a Vassar professor who died in 1922, was "an important, though unacknowledged, precursor of today's New Rhetoricians," particularly in her interest in psychology.

429. Munch, James Michael. "The Effects of Rhetorical Questions on Cognitive Elaboration and Persuasion in Dyadic Exchange Processes." *DAI* 44 (February 1984): 2566A.

Investigates the persuasive impact of rhetorical questions in buyer/seller exchanges.

430. Mura, Susan Zachary Swan. "Gricean Pragmatics as Rhetoric: Prospectus and Proof for a Metatheory." *DAI* 45 (July 1984): 18A.

Proposes a metatheory for a rhetorically based pragmatics. Suggests using Grice's theory with additions from Burke, Perelman, Toulmin, and Wallace.

431. Murphy, James J. "Rhetoric in the Earliest Years of Printing, 1465–1500." *QJS* 70 (February 1984): 1–11.

Examines the choices made by early printers publishing rhetorics. Finds that Italy led in printing classical treatises; France and Germany printed the largest number of contemporary works.

432. Murray, Donald. "On the Cutting Edge: Writing." *TEd* (1984–1985): 54–55.

Describes writing as a process of making meaning through a cycle of texts: the texts of intent, of reality, and of response.

433. Myers, Greg. "The Social Construction of Two Biologists' Proposals." *WC* 2 (July 1985): 219–245.

Shows that two biologists engaged in communal writing respond to and develop a disciplinary consensus as they write and rewrite.

434. Myers, Miles. *The Teacher-Researcher: How to Study Writing in the Classroom.* Urbana, Ill.: ERIC/RCS and NCTE, 1985. 177 pages

Includes an overview of general guidelines for research design; chapters on analyzing syntax, text, cognition in information processing, and context. Discusses studies of error, student attitudes toward writing, and teachers' approaches to writing instruction.

435. Naylor, Kathleen J. "Concepts Eighth-Grade Remedial Students Hold about Reading and Writing." *DAI* 45 (October 1984): 1083A.

An examination of student writing samples, dramatic play, and cloze activity reveals that remedial eighth graders did not have clear concepts of their reading and writing processes.

436. Neuner, Jerome L. "Text Studies and Teaching Lessons from Cohesion Analysis." *EngR* 36 (1985): 8–12.

Discusses the relationship between the presupposing and presupposed world in a text and cohesive chains. Suggests five major types of cohesion.

437. Newell, Sara E. "A Socio-Pragmatic Perspective of Argument Fields." *WJSC* 48 (Summer 1984): 247–261.

A case study of the Utah legislature illustrates Toulmin's "fields of argument"; notes that maintaining "the web of justification" limits strategies for disagreement.

438. Newkirk, Thomas. "Archimedes' Dream." *LArts* 61 (April 1984): 341–350.

Shows, using writings by his young daughter, that early writing has a variety of functions and is not always based on oral speech.

439. Newkirk, Thomas. "The Hedgehog or the Fox: The Dilemma of Writing Development." *LArts* 62 (October 1985): 593–603.

An examination of early writing shows a need for a "more adequate model [that] will show the ways in which development occurs in a variety of discourse forms."

440. Newkirk, Thomas. "The Lowly List." *IaEB* 33 (1984): 11–17.

Studies a young child's use of lists and suggests that lists have special classificatory power, freeing words from sentences.

441. Ng, En Tzu Mary. "The Pronoun and Topic of Discourse: A Functional Perspective in Text." *DAI* 46 (August 1985): 413A.

Shows how formal surface chains of pronouns reveal the topic of the discourse.

442. Nickerson, Sheila. "The Tao of Writing." *DAI* 46 (December 1985): 1613A.

Suggests that creative writing, "viewed as psychotechnology and not as a skill," can facilitate "self-transcendence."

443. Nilsen, Alleen Pace. "Winning the Great He/She Battle." *CE* 46 (February 1984): 151–157.

Argues that contemporary writers are usually aware of sexist problems in selecting pronouns but often are unaware of solutions. Offers suggestions.

444. Norman, Barbara Ann. "The Black Muslims: A Rhetorical Analysis." *DAI* 45 (October 1985): 841A.

Uses the Coleman model of social change as a framework for analyzing the rhetoric of Black Muslims and the process of altering perceptions about blacks.

445. North, Steve. "Journal Writing across the Curriculum: A Reconsideration." *FEN* 14 (Fall 1985): 2–4, 8–9.

Journals are context-dependent, serving epistemic purposes in composition classes; in other courses, journals may be more formalist.

446. Nothstine, William Lee. "Philosophical Hermeneutics as a Basis for Rhetorical Practice, Theory, and Criticism." *DAI* 45 (July 1984): 18A.

Uses Gadamar's philosophical hermeneutics to argue that rhetoric has positive ethical value and offers "fundamental knowledge beyond technical or theoretical knowledge."

447. Nunn, Grace G. "Peer Interaction during Collaborative Writing at the Fourth- and Fifth-Grade Level." *DAI* 45 (July 1984): 105A.

Finds that oral language played an important role in maintaining interpersonal relationships, in problem solving, and in critical awareness of language and ideas.

448. O'Brien, Edward Joseph. "The Nature of the Search for Referents in Discourse Processing." *DAI* 45 (April 1985): 3360B.

Studies how texts are processed using referents and finds support for the work of Kintsch and van Dijk.

449. O'Donnell, Angela M., Donald F. Dansereau, Thomas Rocklin, Judith Lambiotte, Velma I. Hythecker, and Celia O. Larson. "Cooperative Writing: Direct Effects and Transfer." *WC* 2 (July 1985): 307–315.

Students who cooperated on written tasks outperformed those who worked individually.

450. O'Donnell, Holly. "ERIC/RCS Report: The Effect of Topic on Writing Performance." *EEd* 16 (December 1984): 243–249.

Reviews recent research on writing topics.

451. Ohmann, Richard. "Literacy, Technology, and Monopoly Capital." *CE* 47 (November 1985): 675–689.

Discusses computer literacy as a political issue involving dominance and equality in a democracy.

452. Olenn, Valjeane M. "The Dual Function of Narrative in a Child's Writing." *LArts* 61 (April 1984): 376–382.

A case study of a fourth grader who used a narrative heuristic to organize a piece of research writing. Based on Calkins' Atkinson Academy scripts.

453. Oliver, Lawrence J. "The Case against Computerized Analysis of Student Writings." *JTWC* 15 (1985): 309–322.

Concludes that computerized text-analysis systems like Writer's Workbench are deficient, limited, and without solid empirical foundation.

454. Oliver, Lawrence J. "Pitfalls in Electronic Writing Land." *EEd* 16 (May 1984): 94–100.

Reviews research suggesting that computerized text analysis may not lead to better writing.

455. Olson, Gary M. *Composition and Comprehension of Simple Texts.* Washington, D.C.: NIE, 1983. ERIC ED 236 575 [236 pages]

Prints studies related to thinking-out-loud experiments.

456. Oring, Elliott. "Dyadic Traditions." *JFR* 21 (April 1984): 19–28.

Defines *dyad* as the smallest unit of social interaction, characterized by informality, and discusses rhetorical implications for audience relationships.

457. Overbeck, Lois More. "Developing Self-Awareness about Writing Processes: The Perry Model and the Remedial Writer." Paper presented at the CCCC Convention, New York, March 1984. ERIC ED 246 476 [13 pages]

Suggests parallels between Perry's learning model and the discoveries of composition theory and research.

458. Packer, Martin J. "Concealment and Uncovering in Moral Philosophy and Moral Practice." *HD* 28 (March–April 1985): 108–112.

Describes research that supports McIntyre's account of moral reasoning and discourse. Discusses discrepancies between the content and the underlying concerns and interests of such discourse.

459. Page, Gina, and Peter O. Evans. "Whom Do Children Write for: A Study of Audience for School Compositions." *EQ* 17 (Fall 1984): 45–53.

Investigates the nature of the audience children perceived and the feelings of importance they attached to these audiences.

460. Paramour, Sally, and Andrew Wilkinson. "The Disruption of the Probable: Narrative Writing in Children Seven to Thirteen." *LArts* 62 (April 1985): 391–403.

A study of three groups of students, ages 7, 10, and 13, who write a progression of narratives: simple chronicles, simple stories based on disruptions of probabilities, and highly developed stories.

461. Parris, Peggy. "Setting Free the Birds: Heuristic Approaches to the Teaching of Creative Writing at the College Level." *DAI* 44 (February 1984): 2463A.

Concludes that heuristics such as the tagmemic invention matrix and Burke's pentad are useful for beginning creative writers.

462. Pellegrini, A. D., Lee Galda, and Donald L. Rubin. "Context in Text: The Development of Oral and Written Language in Two Genres." *CD* 55 (August 1984): 1549–1555.

Tests Halliday's model of context/text relations in oral and written, narrative and persuasive language of children in grades one, three, and five.

463. Pellegrini, A. D., Lee Galda, and Donald L. Rubin. "Persuasion as a Social-Cognitive Ability." Paper presented at the AERA Convention, New Orleans, April 1984. ERIC ED 243 164 [21 pages]

Studies first, third, and fifth graders' oral and written persuasion and cognitive role taking.

464. Perdue, Virginia A. "Writing as an Act of Power: Basic Writing Pedagogy as Social Practice." *DAI* 45 (August 1984): 441A.

Argues the positivist shortcomings of both process- and product-centered pedagogy and suggests an "alternative, critical pedagogy" based on the principles of Freire and Foucault.

465. Perelman, Chaim. "The New Rhetoric and the Rhetoricians: Remembrances and Comments." *QJS* 70 (May 1984): 188–196.

Surveys and criticizes studies of his work that have appeared in America, concluding with the recommendation that Americans read books in foreign languages.

466. Perelman, Chaim. "Rhetoric and Politics." *P&R* 17 (1984): 129–134.

Argues the importance of philosophical discourse for the preservation of a "universal community."

467. Perkins, Terry M. "Isocrates and Plato: Relativism *Vs.* Idealism." *SSCJ* 50 (Fall 1984): 49–66.

A comparative analysis of the merits of Isocrates' relativism and Plato's idealism.

468. Perl, Sondra. *Coding the Composing Process: A Guide for Teachers and Researchers.* Washington, D.C.: NIE, 1984. ERIC ED 240 609 [103 pages]

Describes a method for analyzing the composing process.

469. Petersen, Bruce T. "Ideology and Pseudo-Politics in the Teaching of Literature and Composition." *Reader* 11 (Spring 1984): 1–13.

Discusses the political implications of the process/product debate in composition pedagogy and the reader-response/formalist debate in literary criticism.

470. Petersen, Bruce T. "Technical Writing, Revision, and Language Communities." Paper presented at the CCCC Convention, New York, March 1984. ERIC ED 245 246 [11 pages]

Studies writers on the job and notes that students are often taught the least important aspects of writing on the job.

471. Peterson, Linda. "Repetition and Metaphor in the Early Stages of Composing." *CCC* 36 (December 1985): 429–443.

Discusses Richard Wright's uses of repetition and metaphor during planning and editing/revising *Black Boy*.

472. Petrosko, Joseph M., Marjorie M. Kaiser, and Julia C. Dietrich. "Relationships among Writing Ability, Grade, Apprehension, and Knowledge of the Composing Process." Paper presented at the AERA Convention, New Orleans, April 1984. ERIC ED 249 523 [28 pages]

Studies 496 students in grades 6 through 12. Finds that knowledge of appropriate composing behavior was a significant predictor of ability, as was low apprehension.

473. Phelps, Louise Wetherbee. "Dialectics of Coherence: Toward an Integrative Theory." *CE* 47 (January 1985): 12–29.

Seeks to transform the process/product polarity in composition studies into an integrative theory of discourse.

474. Philips, Leon C. "A Comparative Study of Two Approaches for Analyzing Black Discourse." *DAI* 45 (October 1985): 841A.

Proposes a "culture-sensitive African based approach" to the rhetorical criticism of black public discourse.

475. Piazza, Carolyn L., and Carl M. Tomlinson. "A Concert of Writers." *LArts* 62 (February 1985): 150–158.

A year-long study shows that kindergarten students who engaged in social interactions during drafting learned about functions, audiences, and speaking/writing relationships.

476. Pickering, Samuel, Jr. "Composing a Life." *CE* 47 (May 1985): 289–294.

An autobiographical account by a writing teacher about composing sentences, composing essays, and composing his life.

477. Pickrel, Paul. "Identifying Clichés." *CE* 47 (May 1985): 252–261.

Discusses problems in defining and identifying clichés.

478. Pierstorff, Don K. "Why We Need an English Teachers' Meeting." *TETYC* 11 (October 1984): 12–15.

Argues that theoretical models of the composing process are ineffective at translating theory into teaching practice.

479. Pollard, Rita. "Fourth Graders' Personal Narrative Writing: A Study of Perceptions of Personal Narrative Discourse and of Narrative Composing Decisions and Strategies." *DAI* 45 (August 1984): 441A.

Studies 13 fourth graders to find that they had already internalized narrative schema similar to that described by text linguistics. Gives recommendations for instruction.

480. Pollard, Rita. *Fourth Graders' Understanding of Personal Narrative Discourse.* Urbana, Ill.: ERIC/RCS and NCTE, 1984. ERIC ED 247 571 [30 pages]

Studies 13 fourth graders, finding that they could articulate a narrative schema similar to that of text linguists and could use it in their writings.

481. Pollard-Gott, Lucy, and Lawrence T. Frase. "Flexibility in Writing Style: A New Discourse-Level Cloze Test." *WC* 2 (April 1985): 107–117.

Finds that the ability to change features of style is characteristic of the experienced writer and can be measured by the cloze test.

482. Poole, Marshall Scott, David R. Seibold, and Robert D. McPhee. "Group Decision Making as a Structurational Process." *QJS* 71 (February 1985): 74–102.

Explains structurational theory, as developed by Giddens and others, and recommends it as a basis for analyzing group decision-making processes.

483. Popken, Randall L. "A Study of the Paragraph in Academic Writing." *DAI* 46 (October 1985): 966A.

Analyzes paragraphs from 13 major academic journals for relative and informal variations.

484. Powell, Mava Jo. "Conceptions of Literal Meaning in Speech Act Theory." *P&R* 18 (1985): 133–158.

Charts the "terminological incoherence" of Austin, Searle, and the "nondescriptivists."

485. Prelli, Lawrence John. "A Rhetorical Perspective for the Study of Scientific Discourse." *DAI* 45 (April 1985): 3027A.

Establishes a rhetorical perspective for scientific discourse and presents procedures for using it critically.

486. Pufahl, John P. "Lou LaBrant." *EJ* 73 (May 1984): 71–72.

Places LaBrant among important "ancestors" of writing research because her monographs anticipate current composition theory.

487. Quick, Doris M. "Audience Awareness and Adaptation Skills of Writers at Four Different Grade Levels." *DAI* 44 (January 1984): 2133A.

Writers in grades 4, 8, and 12 showed some awareness of audience, but only college writers exhibited consistent adaption skills.

488. Quinn, Dennis P. "Rhetorical Analysis of Intellectual Processes in Student Writing: Linguistics Cues in the Quality-Rated Writing of College Prefreshmen." *DAI* 45 (March 1985): 2855A.

Concludes, contrary to Odell, that no correlation exists between the frequency of linguistic cues and a text's relative "quality."

489. Quinn, Mary P. "Critical Thinking and Writing: An Approach to the Teaching of Composition." *DAI* 44 (April 1984): 3045A.

Synthesizes devlopmental learning theory with writing pedagogy by making critical thinking a primary concern.

490. Rafoth, Bennett A. "Audience Adaptation in the Essays of Proficient and Nonproficient Freshman Writers." *RTE* 19 (October 1985): 237–253.

Good writers use more information from a videotaped interview of their audience than poor writers. Both groups adapted more explicit statements than subtle ones.

491. Rafoth, Bennett A. "Audience Awareness and Adaptation in the Persuasive Writing of Proficient College Freshmen." *DAI* 45 (March 1985): 2788A.

Findings indicate that audience awareness is a strong predictor of high inference adaptations. Proficient writers took greater advantage of information when more was provided.

492. Raimes, Ann. "What Unskilled Writers Do as They Write: A Classroom Study of Composing." *TESOLQ* 19 (June 1985): 229–258.

Uses thinking-aloud protocols to describe writing processes of eight students. Concludes that each writer of a second language is unique and differs from writers of a first language.

493. Rankin, Dorothy S. "The Forum: Comments on Patricia Carrell's 'Cohesion Is Not Coherence' [*TESOLQ* 16 (December 1982)]." *TESOLQ* 18 (March 1984): 158–162.

Disagrees with Carrell's criticism of Halliday and Hasan's cohesion theory and argues that cohesion theory complemented by Kaplan's contrastive rhetoric can aid ESL acquisition.

494. Rankin, Elizabeth D. "Revitalizing Style: Toward a New Theory and Pedagogy." *FEN* 14 (Spring 1985): 8–13.

Argues that privileging invention has caused style to fall "on bad times." Provides background and outlines criteria for a theory of style.

495. Ratteray, Oswald M. T. "Expanding Roles for Summarized Information." *WC* 2 (October 1985): 457–472.

Identifies seven types of summaries, defines them, briefly traces the history of their use, and discusses the potential role for each.

496. Reed, W. Michael, John K. Burton, and Patricia P. Kelly. "The Effects of Writing Ability and Mode of Discourse on Cognitive Capacity Engagement." *RTE* 19 (October 1985): 283–297.

Uses primary task/secondary task paradigm to measure the engagement of basic, average, and honors freshmen in descriptive, narrative, and persuasive writing.

497. Reid, Joy. "The Forum: Comments on Vivian Zamel's 'The Composing Processes of Advanced ESL Students: Six Case Studies' [*TESOLQ* 17 (June 1983)]." *TESOLQ* 18 (March 1984): 149–153.

Questions Zamel's conclusions because intensive ESL writers differ from freshmen ESL writers and points out that contrastive rhetorics are well established rather than questionable.

498. Reid, Joy. "The Forum: The Author Responds [to Spack, *TESOLQ* 19 (June 1985)]." *TESOLQ* 19 (June 1985): 398–400.

Defends the teaching of outlining "as part of the invention process" for preuniversity ESL students.

499. Reid, Joy. "The Forum: The Radical Outliner and the Radical Brainstormer: A Perspective on Composing Processes." *TESOLQ* 18 (September 1984): 529–533.

Discusses two polar approaches to composing and suggests that much research may have reflected the researcher's own bias in composing.

500. Reinhardt, Alan J. "Breaking Ground: A Study in Interdisciplinary Writing at a Rural Community College." *DAI* 44 (January 1984): 2133A.

Results suggest that an interdisciplinary approach may affect both the attitudes and progress of freshman writers.

501. Reither, James A. "Writing and Knowing: Toward Redefining the Writing Process." *CE* 47 (October 1985): 620–628.

Argues for redefining the writing process to include substantive social knowing.

502. Reynolds, Mark. "Free Writing's Origin." *EJ* 73 (May 1984): 81–82.

Discusses Brande as an originator of freewriting.

503. Rice, Eileen M. "Tutor and Child: Partners in Learning." *LArts* 61 (January 1984): 18–23.

A case study of a seven-year-old writer shows how a teacher-tutor was able to increase his writing fluency and confidence.

504. Richardson, Leonard E. "Does the New Rhetoric Work? A Comparison of Freshman Writing Performance under Instructors Trained in the New Rhetoric with Instructors Not Trained in the New Rhetoric." *DAI* 44 (April 1984): 3052A.

A study of six freshman composition classes shows that students taught structured heuristics made some gains.

505. Ricoeur, Paul. "Toward a 'Postcritical Rhetoric.'" *Pre-Text* 5 (Spring 1984): 9–16.

Responds to articles in the *Ricoeur and Rhetoric* issue of *Pre-Text* [4 (Fall–Winter 1983)].

506. Roberts, Elizabeth Ann. "A Rhetorical Analysis of the Security Clearance Hearing of J. Robert Oppenheimer Utilizing Selected Concepts of Kenneth Burke." *DAI* 45 (April 1985): 3027A.

Burke's concepts allow a "focused analysis" of the Oppenheimer verdict.

507. Robinson, Jay L. "Literacy in the Department of English." *CE* 47 (September 1985): 482–498.

Expresses doubt that contemporary English departments will change enough to teach literacy effectively.

508. Rodrigues, Raymond J. "Moving away from Writing-Process Worship." *EJ* 74 (September 1985): 24–27.

Reevaluates the process method. Advocates pluralizing the writing curriculum to balance structure and individual guidance.

509. Roen, Duane H. "Coherence in Writing." *EJ* 73 (September 1984): 35–36.

Suggests that coherence in writing demands clear thinking and that the value of using transitions to accomplish coherence is overstated.

510. Roginski, Jim. "An Interview with Jane Yolen: Author of Fantasy and Fairy Tale." *Alan* 12 (Spring 1985): 37–38, 40, 42.

A storyteller and writer discusses her life, traces her roots to an oral tradition, and notes the restrictiveness of the fairy-tale mode.

511. Root, Robert L., Jr. "Assiduous String-Savers: The Idea Generating Strategies of Professional Expository Writers." Paper presented at the CCCC Convention, Minneapolis, March 1985. ERIC ED 258 205 [15 pages]

Examines the invention strategies of six professional writers.

512. Root, Robert L., Jr. "Style and Self: The Emergence of Voice." *JTW* 4 (Spring 1985): 77–85.

Research on professional expository writers confirms Flower and Hayes and Bereiter. Finds that achieving automaticity comes through "immersion in context and experience in expression."

513. Rose, Mike, ed. *When a Writer Can't Write: Studies in Writer's Block and Other Composing Process Problems.* Perspectives in Writing Research. New York: Guilford Press, 1985. 272 pages

Eleven studies employing different research methods examine the emotional, cognitive, and situational factors that impede composing in young writers, college and graduate students, nonnative speakers of English, and experienced writers.

514. Rose, Mike. *Writer's Block: The Cognitive Dimension.* Studies in Writing and Rhetoric. Carbondale, Ill.: Southern Illinois University Press, 1984. 132 pages

Suggests six basic causes of writer's block, surveys recent work on the composing process, presents case studies, and makes recommendations for instruction.

515. Rose, Mike, and Barbara Apstein. "A Comment on 'The Language of Exclusion' [*CE* 47 (April 1985)] and a Response." *CE* 47 (December 1985): 871–873.

A comment by Apstein on Rose's article and Rose's response.

516. Rosen, Jay. "Structuralism in Reverse." *ETC* 41 (Spring 1984): 38–45.

Warns that current mass-marketing practices use language that fails to make important distinctions. The market also controls what is published.

517. Rottweiler, Gail P. "Systematic Cohesion in Published General Academic English: Analysis and Register Description." *DAI* 45 (February 1985): 2512A.

Analyzes cohesion devices in academic texts and discusses implications for text linguistics and writing pedagogy.

518. Rowland, Robert C. "The Rhetoric of Menachem Begin: The Myth of Redemption through Return." *DAI* 44 (May 1984): 3206A.

Draws on work by Campbell and Eliade to analyze Begin's use of myth to respond to the Holocaust.

519. Rowland, Robert C., and Deanna F. Womack. "Aristotle's View of Ethical Rhetoric." *RSQ* 15 (Winter–Spring 1985): 13–32.

Argues that Aristotle's theories on rhetoric, ethics, and politics are consistent with each other and are valuable to any democratic society.

520. Rubens, Brenda. "Phenomenology, Metaphor, and Computer Documentation: A Move toward a More Self-Conscious Approach in Technical Writing." *JTWC* 14 (1984): 19–28.

Concludes that not even science can escape using metaphorical language. Describes a trend toward a more personalized, "friendly" style in computer textbooks and manuals.

521. Rubin, Donald L. "Response to Burleson and Rowan [*WC* 1 (January 1984)]." *WC* 2 (January 1985): 45–48.

Notes differences in sample size, observation, and statistics for the Burleson and Rowan studies.

522. Rubin, Donald L. "Social Cognition and Written Communication." *WC* 1 (April 1984): 211–245.

Discusses the interaction of five distinctly identifiable dimensions of social cognition: subskills, coordination of perspective, content domain, content stability, and audience.

523. Rygiel, Dennis. "On the Neglect of Twentieth-Century Nonfiction: A Writing Teacher's View." *CE* 46 (April 1984): 392–400.

Discusses the paucity of rhetorical criticism of twentieth-century English nonfiction and the implications for teachers of writing.

524. Rygiel, Dennis, and Douglas Brent. "A Comment on 'On the Neglect of Twentieth-Century Nonfiction' [*CE* 46 (April 1984)]." *CE* 47 (January 1985): 80–85.

A comment by Brent on Rygiel's article and Rygiel's response.

525. Sacksteder, William. "Hobbes: Philosophical and Rhetorical Artifice." *P&R* 17 (1984): 30–46.

Examines interrelationships between Hobbes's rhetorical expertise and his philosophic strictures.

526. Samuels, Marilyn Schauer. "Technical Writing and the Recreation of Reality." *JTWC* 15 (1985): 3–13.

Argues that technical writing is one kind of creative writing because the technical writer recreates reality using a knowledge of facts, audience, and situation.

527. Sanchez-Escobar, Angel. "A Contrastive Study of the Rhetorical Patterns of English and Spanish Writing." *DAI* 45 (November 1984): 1321A.

Reveals significant differences between the organization and style of English and Spanish paragraphs and essays.

528. Sanders, Robert E. "Style, Meaning, and Message Effects." *ComM* 51 (June 1984): 154–167.

Examines stylistic options as a resource for strategic communication when conventions and protocols for structuring discourse do not apply or are rejected.

529. Santmire, Toni E. "Cognitive Development in Writing." Paper presented at the NCTE Convention, Columbus, Spring 1984. ERIC ED 249 505 [15 pages]

Uses Piaget's categories of cognitive development as a way to describe the writing of 100 junior high school students.

530. Scardamalia, Marlene, and Pamela Paris. "The Function of Explicit Discourse Knowlege in the Development of Text Representations and Composing Strategies." *CI* 2 (1985): 1–39.

The structural representations of adult writers are mediated by gist, intention, and language. Younger writers' representations are generally unmediated.

531. Schneider, Annette E. "Shaping Thought and Utterance: The Function of Rereading in the Writing Process." *DAI* 46 (November 1985): 1218A.

Examines how rereading functioned in the composing process of skilled and unskilled college writers. Finds rereading to be significant only for the skilled writers.

532. Scholes, Robert. "Is There a Fish in This Text?" *CE* 46 (November 1984): 653–664.

Not a spoof of reader-response theory but rather a parable comparing the views of Agassiz with other major thinkers and writers.

533. Schollmeier, Paul. "A Classical Rhetoric of Modern Science." *P&R* 17 (1984): 209–220.

Argues that Mill's logic of science is a rhetoric of science and that Mill's concept of induction is the same as Aristotle's concept of example.

534. Schrag, Calvin O. "Rhetoric Resituated at the End of Philosophy." *QJS* 71 (May 1985): 164–174.

Calls for a dialogue between rhetoric and philosophy, with philosophy accepting persuasion rather than absolute proof and rhetoric looking beyond practical persuasion to the pursuit of truth.

535. Schreiner, Margaret Rizza. "Created to Praise: The Christian Rhetoric of Gerard Manley Hopkins." *DAI* 44 (February 1984): 2547A.

Examines the controlling influence of baroque esthetics, scholasticism, religious rule, and orthodox sacramental theology on Hopkins' poetic language.

536. Schultz, Anne. "Swords or Ploughshares? A Rhetorical Choice." *JTW* 3 (Fall 1984): 145–155.

Contrasts two ends of rhetoric—shared inquiry *vs.* winning—and regards choice as crucial to approaching all of life.

537. Schumacher, Gary M., George R. Klare, Frank Cronin, and John D. Moses. "Cognitive Activities of Beginning and Advanced College Writers: A Pausal Analysis." *RTE* 18 (May 1984): 169–187.

Reports the results of studying pauses in the writing process and suggests that cognitive activities during writing may become more highly automated with experience.

538. Schuster, Charles I. "Mikhail Bakhtin as Rhetorical Theorist." *CE* 47 (October 1985): 594–607.

Discusses the significance of Bakhtin's contribution to rhetorical theory.

539. Schwartz, Mimi. "Response to Writing: A College-Wide Perspective." *CE* 46 (January 1985): 55–62.

Presents results of a survey on the prose styles preferred by academics from various disciplines.

540. Schwartz, Mimi, Susan H. Kaye, and Beverly Sauer Levy. "Two Comments on 'Response to Writing: A College-wide Perspective' [*CE* 46 (January 1984)] and a Response." *CE* 47 (February 1985): 181–184.

Comments by Kaye and Levy to Schwartz's article and Schwartz's response.

541. Scott, Kathleen F. "Children's Revision Abilities: Reading and Rewriting as Component Processes." *DAI* 46 (November 1985): 1237A.

Reveals that the revision process placed unique reading demands upon writers, which were managed differently by good and poor readers.

542. Scott, Patrick. "The Textual Basis of Rhetorical Research: Some Bibliographical Questions." *RSQ* 14 (Winter–Spring 1984): 43–52.

Argues that students of rhetoric must understand the textual variations in rhetorical classics, whereas bibliographers can learn from composition research on revision strategies.

543. Scott, Robert L. "Chaim Perelman: Persona and Accommodation in the New Rhetoric." *Pre-Text* 5 (Summer 1984): 89–95.

Concludes that *The New Rhetoric* and Perelman's article in *The Quarterly Journal of Speech,* 70 (May 1984), show him to be a practicing rhetor as well as a rhetorical theorist.

544. Selfe, Cynthia L. "The Predrafting Processes of Four High- and Four Low-Apprehensive Writers." *RTE* 18 (February 1984): 45–64.

Suggests that high-apprehensive writers grasp rhetorical situations more slowly, perceive their papers less holistically, and spend less time organizing ideas than low-apprehensive writers.

545. Selfe, Cynthia L. "Reading as a Writing and Revising Strategy." Paper presented at the CCCC Convention, New York, March 1984. ERIC ED 244 295 [24 pages]

Discusses case studies of college freshmen composing aloud to examine their use of reading while writing.

546. Shanahan, Joseph B. "Reader Response Literature: A Source for Effective Descriptors of the Revision Stage in the Process of Writing." *DAI* 45 (February 1985): 2426A.

Examines similarities between responding to a piece of literature and revising a piece of writing. Describes one poet's revison strategies according to Miller's reader-response terms.

547. Shapiro, Nancy S. "Rhetorical Maturity and Perry's Model of Intellectual Development: Competence, Context, and Cognitive Complexity in College Student Writing." *DAI* 46 (August 1985): 368A.

Investigates the relationship between intellectual maturity, as defined by Perry's model, and rhetorical maturity, as measured by Diederich's writing scale and the Levels of Context (audience awareness) Scale.

548. Shelly, Lynn B. "The Writer and the Text: Deconstruction and the Teaching of Composition." *DAI* 45 (December 1984): 1671A.

Compares definitions of writers and texts appearing in composition textbooks with those found in modern criticism.

549. Shugar, Debora. "Croll, Flacius Illyricus, and the Origin of Anti-Ciceronianism." *Rhetorica* 3 (Summer 1985): 269–284.

Argues that Illyricus's *Clovis* reveals that Renaissance anti-Ciceronianism emerges out of a resurgent Biblicism and the rediscovery of Hellenistic rhetoric.

550. Shuman, R. Baird. "Computer Revolution, Phase Two." *IlEB* 73 (Fall 1985): 2–11.

Describes four communication revolutions and discusses the educational uses of computers.

551. Shumway, David R. "A Unified Field Theory for English." *Reader* 14 (Fall 1985): 45–67.

Opposes constituting the writing process as the object of a discipline because process models fail to provide a social context for writing.

552. Siemers, Curtis Bernard. "Memory, Essences, and Ethics: Richard M. Weaver's Theory of Ethical Public Speaking." *DAI* 44 (April 1984): 2926A.

Develops a "rhetorical-ethical theory of speech criticism" to apply to public speeches.

553. Simons, Herbert W. "Chronicle and Critique of a Conference." *QJS* 71 (February 1985): 52–64.

Summarizes and analyzes the major themes of the University of Iowa's 1984 conference on "The Rhetoric of the Human Sciences."

554. Simons, Herbert W., and Aram A. Aghazarian. *Politically Speaking: Form and Genre in Political Discourse*. Rhetoric/Communication Series. Columbia, S.C.: University of South Carolina Press, 1985. 200 pages

Explores the problems and possibilities of a generic approach to the study of rhetoric, with particular emphasis on political rhetoric. A series of essays on form and genre combining insights from literary studies, rhetorical theory, sociolinguistics, and philosophy.

555. Skulicz, Matthew. "Some Analogies between Computer Programming and the Composing Process." Paper presented at the New York State English Council, Amherst, October 1984. ERIC ED 250 720 [28 pages]

Argues that, if students know that writing is a system, then they can use the procedures of programming to better understand the writing process.

556. Slevin, James F. "Review: Acclaiming the Imagination." *CE* 47 (September 1985): 514–520.

Reviews Berthoff's contribution to composition theory and practice.

557. Sloan, Gary. "The Frequency of Transitional Markers in Discursive Prose." *CE* 46 (February 1984): 158–179.

Composition textbooks promote the use of transitional markers, but do professional writers use them? An analysis of 25 college essays suggests "sometimes."

558. Sloss, Gail Sam. "The Methods of Science: The Social Side." *DAI* 44 (February 1984): 2602A.

A study testing the influence of three strategies for presenting research results on the likelihood of positive evaluation by an audience.

559. Smith, Edward E., and Lorraine Goodman. "Understanding Written Instructions: The Role of an Explanatory Schema." *CI* 1 (1984): 359–396.

An experimental study finds that written instuctions with steps are easier to understand if a rationale is given for each step.

560. Smith, Hugh T. "The Process Approach Comes to Big-Time Football." *EJ* 73 (September 1984): 38–39.

A fictional interview illustrates that the student gains self-discovery when process is stressed more than product.

561. Smith, John H. "Rhetorical Polemics and the Dialectics of *Kritik* in Hegel's Jena Essays." *P&R* 18 (1985): 31–57.

Reviews Hegel's first years in Jena to trace the genesis of his mode of dialectical logic as a reaction against Kant, Jacobi, and Fichte.

562. Smith, Rochelle. "Paragraphing for Coherence: Writing as Implied Dialogue." *CE* 46 (January 1984): 8–21.

Uses reader-response theory to explain that paragraphs cohere through an implied dialogue between writer and reader.

563. Smith, William L., Glynda A. Hull, Robert E. Land, Jr., Michael T. Moore, Carolyn Ball, Donald E. Dunham, Linda S. Hickey, and Constance W. Ruzich. "Some Effects of Varying the Structure of a Topic on College Students' Writing." *WC* 2 (January 1985): 73–89.

Finds that the structure of a topic made a difference in the quality, fluency, and number of errors in student writing, but not in the error ratio.

564. Solomon, Martha. "The Rhetoric of Dehumanization: An Analysis of Medical Reports of the Tuskegee Syphilis Project." *WJSC* 49 (Fall 1985): 233–247.

A case study of scientific reports suggests that rhetorical conventions can obscure and deemphasize the ethical, nonscientific perspective.

565. Spack, Ruth. "The Forum: Comments on Joy Reid's 'The Radical Outliner and the Radical Brainstormer: A Perspective on Composing Processes' [*TESOLQ* 18 (September 1984]." *TESOLQ* 19 (June 1985): 396–398.

Reminds Reid of what "outlining" means traditionally and underscores Reid's definition of outlining as organization occurring after the generation of ideas rather than before.

566. Sparshatt, Francis. "Text and Process in Poetry and Philosophy." *P&L* 9 (April 1985): 1–20.

Discusses the nature of philosophical writing and thinking and their relationships to rhetoric and literature.

567. Stanwood, P. G., and Heather Asals. *John Donne and the Theology of Language.* Columbia, Mo.: University of Missouri Press, 1985. 384 pages

Discusses and annotates passages from Donne's sermons to reveal the assumptions of Donne and his contemporaries regarding language. Designed for students "of theology and rhetoric." Glossary included.

568. Steinbach, Rosanne, Marlene Scardamalia, and Carl Bereiter. "Teaching Independent Reflective Processes in Writing: A Follow-Up Study." Paper presented at the AERA Convention, New Orleans, April 1984. ERIC ED 249 522 [11 pages]

Studies 29 sixth graders who had been taught reflective planning skills in writing one year earlier. Results showed that cognitive changes persisted.

569. Sternglass, Marilyn. "Applying Text-Processing Principles to College Writing." Paper presented at the Pennsylvania State Conference on Rhetoric and Composition, State College, Pa., July 1982. ERIC ED 235 492 [13 pages]

Examines some ways macrostructures are used in text processing and production.

570. Sternglass, Marilyn. "How Commitment to a Task Stimulates Critical Thinking Processes." Paper presented at the CCCC Convention, New York, March 1984. ERIC ED 248 506 [12 pages]

Studies basic and traditional college writers, finding that personal commitment to a task helps students exercise more complex cognitive strategies.

571. Stevenson, John W. "Writing as a Liberal Art." *LEd* 70 (Spring 1984): 57–62.

Argues against Hirsch's contention that "a minimum level of competency" is the aim of writing courses.

572. Stewart, Donald C. "Some History Lessons for Composition Teachers." *RR* 3 (January 1985): 134–144.

Argues that knowing the history of the profession gives teachers flexibility and the theoretical breadth to be liberated from current-traditional rhetoric.

573. Stewart, Donald C. "The Status of Composition and Rhetoric in American Colleges, 1880–1902: An MLA Perspective." *CE* 47 (November 1985): 734–746.

A discussion of rhetoric and composition studies in the Modern Language Association at the end of the nineteenth century.

574. Stoddard, Eve Walsh. "The Role of *Ethos* in the Theory of Technical Writing." *TWT* 11 (Spring 1984): 229–241.

Argues that *ethos* can be an effective form of appeal in technical discourse, particularly in attracting the attention of the audience to instructions.

575. Stoddard, Sara E. "Texture, Pattern, and Cohesion in Written Texts: A Study with Graphic Perspective." *DAI* 45 (March 1985): 2862A.

Analyzes three cohesion types to discover the relative cohesiveness, ambiguity, and complexity of texts.

576. Strickland, James. "The Computer as a Tool for the Invention Stage of Writing." Paper given at the New York State English Council Meeting, Uniondale, N.Y., October 1983. ERIC ED 236 693 [23 pages]

Reports on a study in progress on whether or not computer-assisted systematic heuristics help improve the quality of ideas in writing.

577. Stutman, Randall K., and Sara E. Newell. "Beliefs *Vs.* Values: Salient Beliefs in Designing a Persuasive Message." *WJSC* 48 (Fall 1984): 362–372.

Suggests that using "values" to analyze audiences and formulate persuasive messages is inappropriate. Proposes four alternative belief strategies and a five-step process.

578. Sullivan, Patricia Ann. "A Rhetorical Approach to the Criticism of Autobiography." *DAI* 44 (June 1984): 3542A.

Uses the work of Mead and Iser to argue that autobiographical discourse be classified as poetical, rhetorical, and rhetorical-poetical.

579. Sutton, Jane Susan. "A Phenomenological Prestructure in Interpreting Aristotle's *Rhetoric.*" *DAI* 46 (August 1985): 300A.

Analyzes the "inconsistency" of the proofs and establishes a "contextual Sophistic prestructure" in which to reexamine the proofs and the *Rhetoric.*

580. Svaldi, David Paul. "Symbols of Sand Creek: A Case Study in the Rhetoric of Extermination." *DAI* 44 (May 1984): 3206A.

Uses Berkhofer's "rhetorical functionalism" to analyze rhetoric about Sand Creek. Lists characteristics of the rhetoric of extermination that can be applied to other situations.

581. Swope, John W. "Making Writing Mean Rather Than Making It Right." *VEB* 35 (Spring 1985): 26–36.

Discusses research on cognitive dissonance as the basis for revision.

582. Taufen, Phyllis. "Connecting." *WaEJ* 8 (Fall 1985): 7–8.

Talking before writing makes the process easier.

583. Taylor, Karl K. "The Different Summary Skills of Inexperienced and Professional Writers." *JR* 27 (May 1984): 691–699.

Uses protocol analysis to reveal that professionals who summarize are more adept than inexperienced writers at reading, notetaking, abstracting, monitoring, analyzing, and writing.

584. Telotte, J. P. "Narration, Desire, and a Lady from Shanghai." *SAR* 49 (January 1984): 56–71.

Discusses the rhetorical principles of narration illustrated by the structure of the film, *Lady from Shanghai.*

585. Thomas-Ruzic, Maria, and Karyn Thompson-Panos. "The Forum: The Authors Respond [to Koch, *TESOLQ* 18 (September 1984)]." *TESOLQ* 18 (September 1984): 545–547.

Generally agree with Koch's comments, but point out that the scope of their article did not permit such elaboration as Koch provided.

586. Tinkler, John F. "Humanism as Discourse: Studies in the Rhetorical Culture of Renaissance Humanism, Petrarch to Bacon." *DAI* 44 (March 1984): 2755A.

Uses Kuhn, Kristeller, and others to define the rhetorical paradigm linking Renaissance and classical humanism.

587. Tomlinson, Barbara. "Talking about the Composing Process: The Limitations of Retrospective Accounts." *WC* 1 (October 1984): 429–445.

Identifies three limitations of writers' comments about their own writing processes and discusses ways to improve the validity of this research method.

588. Tompkins, Phillip K. "On Hegemony— 'He Gave It No Name'— and Critical Structuralism in the Work of Kenneth Burke." *QJS* 71 (February 1985): 119–131.

A review essay focusing on *Representing Kenneth Burke,* but also considering books by Lentricchia, Donoghue, Eagleton, and Culler.

589. Trimbur, John. "Literature and Composition: Separatism or Convergence?" *JTW* 3 (Spring 1984): 109–115.

Believes that Horner's *Composition and Literature* indicates a trend. Analyzes the reasons for viewing reading as the "convergence of literacy and literature under the rubric of writing."

590. Tripp, Ellen. "A Muddle in the Modes: or, Pinpointing Process." *TETYC* 11 (December 1984): 26–28.

Defines three process modes: explanation, instruction, and the narrative report. Defines process analysis as explanation.

591. Turner, Alberta. "Inviting Poems by Free Association: A Method of Discovering What We Mean." *JEd* 166 (1984): 136–143.

Suggests that free association induces from the preconscious mind raw material for poetry, but it also helps initiate fresh hypotheses and provoke discussion in any field.

592. Vande Kopple, William J. "Sentence Topics, Syntactic Subjects, and Domains in Texts." *WC* 2 (October 1985): 339–357.

Finds evidence that syntactic subjects not corresponding to sentence topics are scarcely recalled and interfere with subjects' recall of topical material.

593. Vande Kopple, William J. "Some Exploratory Discourse on Metadiscourse." *CCC* 36 (February 1985): 82–93.

Defines metadiscourse as "discourse about discourse," discusses its types, and explores its uses and abuses.

594. VanOosting, James. "The Use of Imaginative Literature for Communication Theory Construction: Some Precautions." *QJS* 71 (May 1985): 218–226.

Argues that imaginative literature can provide a reliable data base for communication theories only if certain precautions are observed.

595. Vause, Corinne Jordan. "The Sermons of Innocent III: A Rhetorical Analysis." *DAI* 45 (June 1985): 3482A.

Analyzes sermons in their historical and rhetorical contexts, using Burkean theories.

596. Veit, Walter. "The Potency of Imagery — the Impotence of Rational Language: Ernesto Grassi's Contribution to Modern Epistemology." *P&R* 17 (1984): 221–239.

Reviews Grassi's work with Italian humanists and a suppressed classical literature that questioned the concept of logical truth.

597. Viglionese, Paschal C. "The Inner Functioning of Words: Iconicity in Poetic Language." *VLang* 19 (Summer 1985): 373–386.

Analyzes several examples of Italian poetry to show the union of visual expression and content. The significance of this expression is iconic.

598. Vulgamore, Melvin L. "The Rhetoric of Being and Becoming." *LEd* 71 (Summer 1985): 167–172.

Notes the importance of rhetoric in a liberal education.

599. Waldo, Mark L. "Romantic Rhetoric for the Modern Student: The Psychorhetorical Approach of Wordsworth and Coleridge." *RR* 4 (September 1985): 64–79.

Finds that these poets are not responsible for the current-traditional paradigm. Instead they anticipate current theories of language and cognition.

600. Walker, Sue. "How Typewriters Change Correspondence: An Analysis of Prescription and Practice." *VLang* 18 (Spring 1984): 102–117.

Discusses the prescriptions developed for business correspondence to meet the relative inflexibility of the typewriter. Expresses interest in the effect the word processor will have.

601. Wason-Ellam, Linda. "The Relationship of Sentence Expansion with Pictorialization on Grade Six Writing." *DAI* 45 (August 1984): 409A.

Investigates the interaction of gender, prior achievement, and pictorialization on sentence expansion in narrative and expository modes.

602. Weaver, Richard M. *Language Is Sermonic: Richard M. Weaver on the Nature of Rhetoric.* Edited by Richard L. Johannesen, Rennard Strickland, and Ralph T. Eubanks. Baton Rouge, La.: Louisiana State University Press, 1985. 230 pages

Collects eight of Weaver's essays on the nature of traditional rhetoric and its role in shaping society. Argues against society's reverence for relativism and the consequent disregard for values. Uses his Southern background and classical education as a backdrop for his scrutiny of our misuse of language.

603. Weissberg, Robert C. "Given and New: Paragraph Development Models from Scientific English." *TESOLQ* 18 (September 1984): 485–500.

Offers given/new information paradigm as an alternative to modes approach. Provides classroom application.

604. Welch, Cyril. "An Introduction to Writing." *P&R* 17 (1984): 73–98.

A philosopher examines the question, "What is writing?"

605. Welch, Cyril. "Talking." *P&R* 18 (1985): 216–235.

A meditation on talking, with reference to the relation between speech and writing.

606. Whalen, Tim. "A History of Specifications: Technical Writing in Perspective." *JTWC* 15 (1985): 235–245.

Traces a history of specification over several thousand years to help us understand some of the conventions and constraints of this form of technical writing.

607. White, Lana J. "A Concept to Inform the Teaching of Writing." *DAI* 44 (February 1984): 2459A.

Suggests that writing is best described as a discovery process for the writer-reader rather than being divided into categories such as description, argument, exposition, and narration.

608. Wicking, Jeffrey Bruce. "A Study of Source Evaluation and the Relationship between Changes in Source Evaluation and Dissonance Reduction." *DAI* 45 (December 1984): 1814A.

Investigates the notion that satisfaction with communication sources is influenced by source valence and the reduction of cognitive dissonance, not attraction, homophily power, and credibility.

609. Wiethoff, William E. "The Merits of *De Doctrina Christiana* 4.11.26." *RSQ* 15 (Summer–Fall 1985): 116–118.

Argues that the passage is significant because it shows the consistency of Augustine's rhetoric and suggests the impact of his experience on his rhetorical theory.

610. Wiethoff, William E. "Pietro Bembo and Standards for Oral and Written Discourse." Paper presented at the Central States Speech Association, Indianapolis. April 1985. ERIC ED 254 894 [29 pages].

Uses the writings of Renaissance humanist Bembo to question traditional assumptions about oral and written discourse.

611. Williams, James D. "Coherence and Cognitive Style." *DAI* 45 (April 1985): 3125A.

A study of 44 college freshmen concludes that coherence in discourse is related more to developmental than to pedagogical factors.

612. Williams, James D. "Coherence and Cognitive Style." *WC* 2 (October 1985): 473–491.

Finds that cognitive style correlated significantly with discourse coherence.

613. Wilson, Robert L. "Paragraph Logic." *Statement* 21 (October 1985): 30–31.

Discusses the functions of transitions and topic sentences in paragraphs.

614. Winterowd, W. Ross. "Kenneth Burke: An Annotated Glossary of His Terministic Screen and a 'Statistical' Survey of His Major Concepts." *RSQ* 15 (Summer–Fall 1985): 145–177.

An alphabetically arranged series of definitions and commentaries on the major concepts developed in eight books by Burke.

615. Winterowd, W. Ross. "The Politics of Meaning: Scientism, Literarism, and the New Humanism." *WC* 2 (July 1985): 269–292.

Argues for a realignment of literary studies under the aegis of rhetoric to account for both the scientismic and literalist view of meaning.

616. Witte, Stephen P. "Topical Structure and Writing Quality: A Study of the Argumentative Texts of College Writers." Paper presented at the AERA Convention, Montreal, September 1982. ERIC ED 233 345 [34 pages]

Finds that freshman writers discover content for topics introduced and distinguish between crucial and noncrucial topics.

617. Wolf, Dennie. "Ways of Telling: Text Repertoires in Elementary School Children." *JEd* 167 (1985): 71–88.

Concludes that educators need to recognize children's ability to adapt language across different tasks, and to help them use that skill in the classroom.

618. Wong, Samuel G. "True Sentences: Studies in the Art of Investigative Prose in the Seventeenth Century." *DAI* 45 (December 1984): 1764A.

Argues that Browne and Burton shape the validity of information in their investigative prose through interpretive perspectives.

619. Woods, William F. "Nineteenth-Century Psychology and the Teaching of Writing." *CCC* 36 (February 1985): 20–41.

Discusses the influence of faculty psychology, principles of association, and organicist theory on composition pedagogy.

620. Woodson, Nancy P. "Oral and Textual Composing Patterns of Beginning Writers." *DAI* 46 (December 1985): 1547A.

Findings indicate that most beginning writers link situational speaking and writing strategies and that they respond better to "dialogic" essay prompts.

621. Worncik, Barbara. "Charles Rollin's *Traite* and the Rhetorical Theories of Smith, Campbell, and Blair." *Rhetorica* 3 (Winter 1985): 45–65.

Examines the reciprocal relations between Rollin's *Traite* and the rhetorical theories of Smith, Campbell, and Blair.

622. Yancey, Kathleen B. "Scripts, Schemas, and Scribes: Needed Dimensions of the Composing Process." *DAI* 44 (March 1984): 2749A.

Indicates that models of composing processes generally ignore affect and creativity, an omission that could be resolved on the macrolevel with script/schemata concepts.

623. Yeshayahu, Shen. "On Importance Hierarchy and Evaluation Devices in Narrative Texts." *PT* 6 (1985): 681–698.

Examines semantic and structural features contributing to the hierarchical organization of narrative texts.

624. Yoos, George E. "The Rhetoric of Cynicism." *RR* 4 (September 1985): 54–62.

Defines cynicism, gives examples of its use by famous writers, and analyzes its "moral points of view."

625. Young, George M. "The Development of Logic and Focus in Children's Writing." *L&S* 28 (April–June 1985): 115–127.

Describes an experiment measuring the development of logic and focus in children's writing.

626. Zamel, Vivian. "The Forum: The Author Responds [to Reid, *TESOLQ* 18 (March 1984)]." *TESOLQ* 18 (March 1984): 154–158.

Maintains that Reid misinterprets process approach, cognitive development, and schema theory.

627. Zeiger, William. "The Exploratory Essay: Enfranchising the Spirit of Inquiry in College Composition." *CE* 47 (September 1985): 454–466.

Characterizes the familiar, inquiry essay and the persuasive expository essay, arguing that college composition programs include both.

See also 5, 33, 628, 629, 636, 672, 680, 682, 687, 691, 695, 700, 719, 751, 773, 777, 814, 829, 830, 834, 915, 949, 974, 977, 978, 1013, 1031, 1039, 1055, 1067, 1086, 1092, 1097, 1107, 1115, 1127, 1160, 1169, 1192, 1195, 1207, 1214, 1217, 1225, 1249, 1313, 1338, 1345, 1927, 1957, 2077, 2110, 2138, 2479, 2520, 2558, 2605, 2643, 2664, 2676, 2677, 2703, 2716, 2743, 2823, 2918, 3068, 3615, 3714, 3799, 3807

LITERATURE

628. Anderson, Wayne C. "'Perpetual Affirmations, Unexplained': The Rhetoric of Reiteration in Coleridge, Carlyle, and Emerson." *QJS* 71 (February 1985): 37–51.

Examines the way three nineteenth-century writers used mere repetition as a persuasive technique for propositions that are both unexplained and unprovable.

629. Anderson, Wayne C. "The Rhetoric of Silence in the Discourse of Coleridge and Carlyle." *SAR* 49 (January 1984): 72–90.

Discusses Coleridge's and Carlyle's rhetorical technique of avoiding the examination of areas they thought "by definition incommunicable," in order to force reader participation.

630. Angenot, Marc. "The Emergence of the Anti-Utopian Genre in France: Souvestre, Girandeaux, Robida, *et al.*" *SFS* 12 (July 1985): 129–133.

Traces the origin of Orwell and Huxley's twentieth-century anti-utopias to nineteenth-century French writers hostile to socialism, industrialization, and rational "progress."

631. Arnold, Richard. "'Thoughts Grow Keen and Clear': A Look at Lampman's Revisions." *SCL* 10 (1985): 170–176.

Traces changes in the poet's "visionary outlook" by examining revisions of "Vision" and "Power."

632. Arrow, Ralph. "Consciousness as Doubt." *TCL* 30 (Winter 1984): 465–474.

Explores the use of doubles in texts as a means of oscillating between experience and consciousness without being overwhelmed by unorganized experience or trapped in predetermined linguistic structures.

633. Bal, Mieke. "The Rhetoric of Subjectivity." *PT* 5 (1984): 337–376.

Uses the story of Samson and Delilah to illustrate that the structure of reality in fiction and in history are similarly subjective.

634. Barker, Wendy. "Playing Time, Working Play: Poetry Writing as Part of the Field." *ET* 16 (Spring 1985): 9–13.

Concludes that writing poetry improves student writing since it requires imaginative as well as intellectual effort and teaches the value of time spent alone.

635. Beiderwell, Bruce. "The Coherence of *Our Mutual Friend*." *JNT* 15 (Fall 1985): 234–243.

Demonstrates the narrative techniques of "opposition and repetition."

636. Bellamy, Joe David. *American Poetry Observed: Poets on Their Work.* Urbana, Ill.: University of Illinois Press, 1984. 328 pages

Presents interviews with 18 writers, comparing their theories with their practices in writing.

637. Berg, Temma F. "From Pamela to Jane Gray; Or, How Not to Become the Heroine of Your Own Text." *SNNTS* 17 (Summer 1985): 115–137.

Proposes that women need not wait for new plots but can learn to "rewrite the texts that have written us."

638. Boswell, Bill. "Recreating the Text: Reflections on the Teaching of Literature." *EQ* 17 (Summer 1984): 2–15.

Makes suggestions for encouraging students to deal with texts in several genres.

639. Bowerstock, G. W. "The Art of the Footnote." *ASch* 53 (Winter 1983–1984): 54–62.

Historical review and appreciation of the footnote as a "work of art and an instrument of power."

640. Brownstein, Marilyn L. "Postmodern Language and the Perpetuation of Desire." *TCL* 31 (Spring 1985): 73–88.

Examines postmodernists' reaction against the "tyranny" of symbolic forms in modernist literature by paralleling Freudian and object relations theories of desire with neurophysiological accounts of bimodal consciousness.

641. Burns, Robert Alan. "Isabelle Valancy Crawford's Poetic Technique." *SCL* 10 (1985): 53–80.

Examines Crawford's development as a writer, including her use of metaphor and dialect in a variety of poetic forms.

642. Cain, William E. *The Crisis in Criticism: Theory, Literature, and Reform in English Studies.* Baltimore City, Md.: The Johns Hopkins University Press, 1984. 336 pages

Examines the academic, professional, and institutional contexts of literary studies. Focuses on the relationships among theory, text, and teaching.

643. Cain, William E. "Review — Deconstruction: An Assessment." *CE* 46 (December 1984): 811–820.

Reviews four books published in 1982 and 1983 on deconstruction. Speculates on how this critical field gained respectability.

644. Cairns, P. "Style, Structure, and the Status of Language in Chinua Achebe's *Things Fall Apart* and *Arrow of God.*" *WLWE* 25 (Spring 1985): 1–9.

Examines Achebe's use of public, rather than private, language to reconstruct Ibo history and public experience.

645. Campbell, Jane. "Reaching Outwards: Versions of Reality in *The Middle Ground.*" *JNT* 14 (Winter 1984): 17–32.

Explores the effect of a narrative technique, "inconclusiveness," on the audience.

646. Carey, Robert F. "The Reader, the Text, the Response: Literary Theory and Reading Research." *EQ* 18 (Fall 1985): 17–23.

Synthesizes some of the voices criticizing literary theory and analyzes theories of value to those interested in reading theory, research, and praxis.

647. Carrier, David. "Of Narratology." *P&L* 8 (April 1984): 32–42.

Debates the tenets of recent theories of narratology through an examination of how texts function.

648. Cascardi, A. J. "Skepticism and Deconstruction." *P&L* 8 (April 1984): 1–14.

Reviews the distinctions between "skepticism" and "deconstruction" and argues that this recent alignment "seriously mistakes the nature and intent of deconstruction."

649. Chambers, Aidan. *Booktalk: Occasional Writing on Literature and Children.* New York: Harper & Row, 1985. 224 pages

Presents essays on ways to help children read and talk about their reading. Includes two previously unpublished essays, "Tell Me: Are Children Critics?" and "Ways of Telling," about the narrative structure of his own books.

650. Chittick, Kathryn. "Interview with Malcolm Ross." *SCL* 9 (1984): 241–266.

Explores Ross's development as a writer, editor, scholar, teacher, and educational leader.

651. Clark-Beattie, Rosemary. "*Middlemarch*'s Dialogic Style." *JNT* 15 (Fall 1985): 199–218.

Examines "dialogical" prose, which manipulates the distance between spoken and written forms.

652. Comprone, Joseph J. "Literary Theory and Composition: Creating Communities of Readers and Writers." Paper presented at the CCCC Convention, Minneapolis, March 1985. ERIC ED 254 855 [15 pages]

Reviews interpretive theories in literary criticism, arguing that they can help reconceptualize writing across the curriculum.

653. Craig, Randall. "Plato's *Symposium* and the Tragicomic Novel." *SNNTS* 17 (Summer 1985): 158–173.

Explores connections between the Socratic dialogue and the novel. Examines the juxtaposition of the serious and comic in *Symposium* and modern tragicomic fiction.

654. Davis, Robert Murray. "The Frontiers of Genre: Science-Fiction Westerns." *SFS* 12 (March 1985): 33–41.

Compares and contrasts the conventions of the western and of science fiction, especially as combined in the works of Jakes and Boyd.

655. DeGraaff, Robert M. "Self-Articulating Characters in *David Copperfield.*" *JNT* 14 (Fall 1984): 214–222.

Posits Dickens's characters as products of the "rhetorical force" of his style.

656. Dingwaney, Anuradha, and Lawrence Needham. "'A Sort of Previous Lubrication': De-Quincy's Preface to *Confessions of an English Opium-Eater.*" *QJS* 71 (November 1985): 457–469.

Uses the Preface to argue that DeQuincy's prose style was often consciously rhetorical rather than merely expressive.

657. Dowling, David. "*A Passage to India* through 'The Spaces between the Words.'" *JNT* 15 (Fall 1985): 256–266.

Finds a correspondence between the limits of language and the limits of perception in the narrative.

658. Ebersole, Peter, and Karen DeVogler-Ebersole. "Depth of Meaning in Life and Literary Preference." *Psychology* 21 (1984): 28–30.

Discusses the link between subjects' preferences for literary selections and subjects' concepts of the depths of their own meanings of life.

659. Eizykman, Boris. "Temporality in Science-Fiction Narrative." *SFS* 12 (March 1985): 66–87.

Argues that early science fiction misses potential openness by using future tense mostly to recount events in the narrator's past. Examines recent experiments in more complex temporal schemes.

660. Feasley, Florence G. "Copywriting and the Prose of Hemingway." *JQ* 62 (Spring 1985): 121–126.

Argues that Hemingway's prose illustrates how intensely language can be used for the effective ad writer and copywriter.

661. Filloy, Richard A. "Deciding the Authorship of a Doubtful Text: The Case of John Selden's *Table-Talk.*" *QJS* 70 (February 1984): 41–52.

Examines the rhetorical process by which a reader is persuaded of the authenticity of a text.

662. Fitting, Peter. "'So We All Became Mothers': New Roles for Men in Recent Utopian Fiction." *SFS* 12 (July 1985): 156–183.

Examines seven 1970s novels for the impact on feminism on utopian visions.

663. Fox, Ronda. "A Study of Metaphor in the Writing of Nine- and Thirteen-Year-Olds, College Freshmen, and Graduate Students in the Humanities and in the Sciences." *DAI* 45 (December 1985): 1668A.

Findings indicate that metaphor production and processing increased with age and that they became discipline-specific in graduate studies.

664. Fuller, Steven. "Is There a Language Game That Even the Deconstructionist Can Play?" *P&L* 9 (April 1985): 104–109.

Responds to Cascardi's "Skepticism and Deconstruction," "reasserting deconstruction's skeptical credentials and then...showing how those credentials enable the deconstructionist to play a...language-game."

665. Gadomski, Kenneth E. "Narrative Style in *King Horn* and *Havelock the Dane.*" *JNT* 15 (Spring 1985): 133–145.

Considers how the narrator in the oral tradition guides the audience's response and creates a role for the audience.

666. Gerlack, John. "Closure in Henry James's Short Fiction." *JNT* 14 (Winter 1984): 60–67.

Explores James's failure to construct open endings in short stories as successfully as in novels.

667. Graham, Robert J. "David Bleich's Subjective Criticism: Reading, Response, and Values in the Teaching of Literature." *EQ* 17 (Spring 1984): 54–59.

Suggests that Bleich's subjective approach to literature can encourage student discussions of value questions raised by the selection.

668. Graham, Robert J. "Decoding the Rise: Critique, Competence, and Textuality in the Teaching of Poetry." *EQ* 18 (Summer 1985): 2–15.

Reccommends using the students' own texts as the starting point for exploring the power of textuality and the constriction and release of meaning.

669. Green, Lawrence D. "'We'll Dress Him Up in Voices': The Rhetoric of Disjunction in *Troilus and Cressida.*" *QJS* 70 (February 1984): 23–40.

Sees the inconsistencies of characters in Shakespeare's play as a systematic series of disjunctions arguing that "magnificent language... actually encourages despicable actions."

670. Hansen, Tom. "Letting Language Do: Some Speculations on Finding Found Poems." *ET* 15 (Winter 1984): 51–65.

Discusses the found poem of lyrical intensity, the subversive found poem, and the found fragment.

671. Harker, W. John. "The New Imperative in Literary Criticism." *VLang* 19 (Summer 1985): 256–372.

Attributes the rise of reader-response criticism to developments in notions about private verse and asks for a new literary criticism that recognizes the interaction between text and reader.

672. Harshaw (Hrushovski), Benjamin. "Fictionality and Fields of Reference: Remarks on a Theoretical Framework." *PT* 5 (1984): 227–251.

Examines ways that language interacts with experience and fictional worlds to influence readers' interpretations of literature.

673. Hellweg, Paul. "Writers' Link-O-Grams." *WWays* 18 (August 1985): 190.

Presents a puzzle based on the names of 25 famous authors, with a link word between halves of each name.

674. Henrick, John. "There Once Was a Digital Limerick." *WWays* 17 (February 1984): 53–54.

Illustrates digital verse, defines criteria, and uses a mathematical formula to produce a digital stanza.

675. Hillocks, George, and Larry Ludlow. "A Taxonomy of Skills in Reading and Interpreting Fiction." *AERJ* 21 (Spring 1984): 7–24.

Empirically determines the hierarchical and taxonomic nature of four sets of questions for interpreting fiction.

676. Hirsch, E. D., Jr. "Meaning and Significance Reinterpreted." *CritI* 11 (December 1984): 202–225.

Revises Hirsch's earlier distinction between meaning and significance based upon the realization "that meaning is not simply an affair of consciousness and unconsciousness."

677. Homan, Margaret. "'Syllables of Velvet': Dickinson, Rossetti, and the Rhetorics of Sexuality." *FS* 11 (Fall 1985): 569–593.

Examines the rhetoric of poetry as it contributes to the cultural constitution of gender.

678. Johnston, Kenneth G. "Hemingway and Freud: The Tip of the Iceberg." *JNT* 14 (Winter 1984): 68–73.

Explores the relationship between the discourse of "omission" and personal experience.

679. Jones, James Lyle. "Close, Naked, and Natural: Rhetoric and John Dryden's *Essay of Dramatic Poesy*." *DAI* 45 (July 1984): 17A.

Analyzes the persuasive possibilities of Dryden's *Essay* in terms of its 1668 audience and its intellectual and social milieus.

680. Kirkwood, William G. "Parables as Metaphors and Examples." *QJS* 71 (November 1985): 422–440.

Argues that parables (and by implication all narratives) function both on metaphoric and exemplary levels and are rhetorical because they seek to influence the audience.

681. Kuiper, Koenraad. "The Nature of Satire." *Poetics* 13 (December 1984): 459–473.

Satire depends on readers in particular contexts perceiving an intent to change their understanding of a situation, similar form in the satire and its object, and humor.

682. LeClair, Tom, and Larry McCaffery, eds. *Anything Can Happen: Interviews with Contemporary American Novelists*. Urbana, Ill.: University of Illinois Press, 1983. 320 pages

Twenty-six previously published interviews of major contemporary American novelists. Includes remarks on craft.

683. Lemieux, Jacques. "Utopias and Social Relations in American Science Fiction, 1950–1980." *SFS* 12 (July 1985): 148–155.

Argues that science fiction is the imaginative expression of a scientific/technical petty bourgeoisie.

684. Levin, Harry. "The Implication of Explication." *PT* 5 (1984): 97–109.

Examines roles of literary interpreters and critics, who read and sometimes "rewrite" literature for scholars and for students.

685. Lide, Barbara, and Francis Lide. "Literature in the Composition Class: The Case Against." *RR* 2 (January 1984): 109–122.

Presents reasons why literature is an "inefficient and roundabout" way to improve academic writing.

686. Lieber, Justin. "The Future Present Tense." *P&L* 9 (October 1985): 203–211.

Examines science fiction within the context of classical philosophy, noting "the best and most representative science fiction speaks of the future...casting into relief...the present."

687. Losse, Deborah N. "The Representation of Discourse in the Renaissance Nouvelle." *PT* 5 (1984): 585–595.

Contrasts the frequent intervention of a first-person narrator with other discursive forms, such as interior monologue, to provide insights into characters in fiction.

688. LoVerso, Marco. "Language Private and Public: A Study of Wiseman's *Crackpot*." *SCL* 9 (1984): 78–94.

Analyzes Wiseman's treatment of language as a mediating device between the person and society.

689. Lyne, John. "Semiotics Self-Signifying: The Ongoing Constitution of Sign Studies." *QJS* 70 (February 1984): 80–90.

A review essay on five books about semiotics by Culler, Deely, Hervey, Merrill, and Scholes.

690. Maclean, Marie. "Metamorphoses of the Signifier in 'Unnatural Languages.'" *SFS* 11 (July 1984): 166–173.

Analyzes "unnatural languages" in science fiction as attempts to explore connections between language and choice. Classifies alterations of signifier-signified relationships.

691. Mailloux, Steven. "Rhetorical Hermeneutics." *CritI* 11 (June 1985): 620–641.

Rhetorical hermeneutics "gives up the goals of Theory and continues theorizing about interpretation only therapeutically." It must "also provide histories of how particular theoretical and critical discourses have evolved."

692. Maine, Barry. "*U.S.A.*: Dos Passos and the Rhetoric of History." *SAR* 50 (January 1985): 75–86.

Argues that the literary and cinematic techniques Dos Passos used have obscured the importance of *U.S.A.* as historical narration.

693. Marsland, Elizabeth. "Literature as Interaction: Readers and 'Non-readers' in First World War Propagandist Poetry." *Poetics* 13 (December 1984): 489–500.

Argues that patriotic poetry united a large, popular "us" against a [literal] enemy. Protest poetry aligned elite readers against lies or establishment beliefs about "them."

694. Mason, Kenneth M., Jr. "George Eliot's *Mill on the Floss*: Tragic Harvest and Pastoral Deceit." *JNT* 15 (Spring 1985): 169–182.

Explores the "implications of narrative detail and method" in shaping the audience's response.

695. Matalene, H. W. "The Interactionism of the *Ancien Régime*: or, Why Does Anybody Ever Bother to Listen to Anybody Else?" *CE* 46 (January 1984): 22–31.

Surveys literary and rhetorical history to prove that the *Ancien Régime* never ended.

696. Mathieson, Kenneth. "The Influence of Science Fiction in the Contemporary American Novel." *SFS* 12 (March 1985): 22–32.

Posits six structural and linguistic characteristics as criteria for identifying science fiction and evaluating its influence on mainstream fiction.

697. McDonald, Christie V. *The Dialogue of Writing: Essays in Eighteenth-Century French Literature*. Atlantic Highlands, N.J.: Humanities Press, 1984. 109 pages

Analyzes dialogue as a genre and critical principle informing the discussion of the works of Rousseau and Diderot. Examines relationships between texts and writers, texts and readers, and between texts and other texts to gain insights into the complex acts of writing and reading.

698. McGann, Jerome J. "Some Forms of Critical Discourse." *CritI* 11 (March 1985): 339–417.

Distinguishes five elementary forms of critical discourse. Focuses specifically upon two nonnarrative forms and their relation to the form of critical narrative.

699. Miall, David S. "The Structure of Response: A Repertory Grid Study of a Poem." *RTE* 19 (October 1985): 254–268.

Undergraduates chart responses to eight aspects of internal structure in Coleridge's "Frost at Midnight." Resulting grids "map boundary" between common and individual responses.

700. Miller, Carolyn R. "Genre as Social Action." *QJS* 70 (May 1984): 151–167.

Argues that genre is distinct from form and should be seen as rhetorical action, which acquires meaning from situation and social context.

701. Mir, Maqsood Hamid. "The Phenomenological Response Theory: A Model for Synthesizing Reader Response and Literary Texts in Teaching College English." *DAI* 44 (May 1984): 3390A.

Suggests that pedagogical questions developed in reader-response theory may provide heuristics for writing assignments.

702. Mizener, Heather. "Microcomputers in the English Classroom: What Are the Effects of Computer Graphics and Interactive Computer-Assisted Learning on Student Comprehension of a Poem?" *EQ* 18 (Summer 1985): 89–96.

Finds that students using the microcomputer spent more time on the lesson and were more involved in it but did not comprehend the lesson significantly better.

703. Mulderig, Gerald P. "The Rhetorical Design of Carlyle's *Life of John Sterling.*" *JNT* 14 (Spring 1984): 142–150.

Examines a variety of rhetorical strategies used to establish biography.

704. Murray, Heather. "Metaphor and Metonymy, Language and Land in Ethel Wilson's *Swamp Angel.*" *WLWE* 25 (Autumn 1985): 241–252.

Examines the figurative, semantic, syntactic, and formal features of the fictional world and the narrative process.

705. Natalle, Elizabeth Jo. "The Function of Feminist Theatre as a Rhetorical Medium within the Women's Movement." *DAI* 44 (January 1984): 1971A.

A rhetorical analysis of 20 feminist plays.

706. Niesz, Anthony J., and Norman N. Holland. "Interactive Fiction." *CritI* 11 (September 1984): 110–129.

Using computers to write fiction leads to a new genre, "interactive fiction," in which the reader becomes part of the fiction and "writing and reading as processes replace writing and reading as products."

707. Norris, Christopher. "Reason, Rhetoric, Theory: Empson and deMan." *Raritan* 5 (Summer 1985): 89–106.

Examines each theorist's argument on the relationship between grammar and rhetoric.

708. Orlov, Paul A. "Technique as Theme in *An American Tragedy.*" *JNT* 14 (Spring 1984): 75–93.

Explores the relationship between the narrative techniques and the theme of "selfhood."

709. Orr, Leonard. "The Canon of Criticism and the Hierarchy of Genres." *MSE* 9 (1984): 13–24.

Argues "that the traditional critical canon itself militates against the traditional public view of the low place of critical writing compared to literary works."

710. Panja, Shormishtha. "A Self-Reflexive Parable of Narration: *The Faerie Queene VI.*" *JNT* 15 (Fall 1985): 277–288.

Examines the importance of closure in light of structuralist and poststructuralist narratology.

711. Plandott, Dinnah. "William Faulkner: The Tragic Enigma." *JNT* 15 (Spring 1985): 97–119.

Reverses the usual reading process, from specific to abstract, by first constructing a paradigm to encompass the work's complexity.

712. Quet, Danielle. "Mauritian Voices: A Panorama of Contemporary Creative Writing in English, Part Two." *WLWE* 23 (Spring 1984): 303–312.

Examines the literary effects of the English language and British education on Hindu and Muslim elites in Mauritius.

713. Quinn, Arthur. "'Meditating Tacitus': Gibbon's Adaptation to an Eighteenth-Century Audience." *QJS* 70 (February 1984): 53–68.

Sees Gibbon's rhetorical task as adapting Tacitus's gloomy analysis of the Roman Empire to the needs of an optimistic British Empire.

714. Rabinowitz, Nancy Sarkin. "'Faithful Narrator' or 'Partial Eulogist': First-Person Narrator in Brontë's *Villette.*" *JNT* 15 (Fall 1985): 244–255.

Explores the "sense of female power," a mode of discourse developed in the heroine's narration.

715. Reddy, Maureen T. "Gaskell's 'The Grey Woman': A Feminine Palimpset." *JNT* 15 (Spring 1985): 183–193.

Examines the feminine perspective of the narrative.

716. Renan, Yael. "Disautomatization and Comic Deviations from Models of Organizing Experience." *Style* 18 (Spring 1984): 160–176.

Argues that satirists create perceptual shifts by deviating from common organizations of reality, omitting conventional frames and adding or substituting unconventional ones.

717. Richardson, Janette. "Affective Artistry on the Medieval Stage." *QJS* 70 (February 1984): 12–22.

Sees the rhetoric of the Brome *Abraham and Isaac* as a dramatic version of the four levels of medieval preaching: literal, tropological, allegorical, and anagogical.

718. Ryan, Marie Laure. "Fiction as a Logical, Ontological, and Illocutionary Issue." *Style* 18 (Spring 1984): 121–139.

Redefines fiction as the linguistic representation of a representation, which has never been produced as a genuine reflection of reality by someone real.

719. Ryan, Marie Laure. "The Modal Structure of Narrative Universes." *PT* 6 (1985): 717–755.

Examines the representation of temporal arrangements in narrative texts.

720. Scanlon, Patrick M. "Emblematic Narrative and the Argument of Love in Sidney's *New Arcadia*." *JNT* 15 (Fall 1985): 219–233.

Explores the emblem as a narrative technique.

721. Scholes, Robert. *Textual Power: Literary Theory and the Teaching of English.* New Haven: Yale University Press, 1985. 192 pages

Analyzes the values and institutional tendencies in poststructuralist literary theory. Argues that we should stop studying literature and study texts instead. Includes chapters on teaching reading, interpretation, and criticism.

722. Schulte, Ranier. "Transferral of Poetic Frontiers: Renovation and Innovation." *WLT* 59 (Autumn 1985): 525–530.

Concludes that Americans do not translate international works into their language to the extent that the Germans and French do, consequently missing opportunities to appreciate Hispanic poetry.

723. Schuster, Charles I. "Confessions of a Writer: The Art of Richard Selzer." *RR* 3 (September 1984): 84–93.

An interview with a nonfiction writer who discusses his working habits and literary influences.

724. Scott, Robert L. "Narrative Theory and Communication Research." *QJS* 70 (May 1984): 197–204.

A review essay on five recent books by Genette, Jameson, Mitchell, and Chatham.

725. Secor, Marie. "Perelman's Loci in Literary Argument." *Pre-Text* 5 (Summer 1984): 97–110.

Defines Perelman's concept of loci in the context of classical rhetoric and illustrates it by literary arguments published in a single issue of *PMLA*.

726. Sipple, William L. "A Coherent Pedagogy for Teaching Literature and Writing." Paper presented at the CCCC Convention, Minneapolis, March 1985 ERIC ED 257 107 [15 pages]

Offers a tagmemic problem-solving approach to reading literature, analyzing it, and writing about it.

727. Somay, Bülent. "Towards an Open-Ended Utopia." *SFS* 11 (March 1984): 25–38.

Traces the progress of utopian visions from dogmatic utopian texts to open-ended utopian texts, in that utopia functions as an "absent paradigm" that the reader helps to reconstruct.

728. Speck, Bruce W. "The 'Spiritual' Problem in the Literature Classroom." *NebEC* 29 (Summer 1984): 5–8.

Discusses students' attitudes about literature and its relationship to social, personal, and spiritual dilemmas.

729. Stiebel, Arlene. "But Is It Life? Some Thoughts on Modern Critical Theory." *MLS* 14 (Summer 1984): 3–12.

Criticizes modern critical theory as relying too heavily on the reader to complete a text. Refers to Fish and Iser.

730. Talal, Marilynn. "Tasting Poetry." *ET* 16 (Spring 1985): 37–44.

Advocates exploring the sense of taste to help writers discover new details and sharpen other senses by evoking memories and association.

731. Tittler, Jonathan. "Approximately Irony." *MLS* 15 (Spring 1985): 32–46.

Gives an extended definition of irony, both subjective and objective (intended and accidental), demonstrating that neither is strictly objective or subjective.

732. Wagner, Linda W. "Sylvia Plath's Specialness in Her Short Stories." *JNT* 15 (Winter 1985): 1–14.

Distinguishes between factual "autobiographical" writing and thematic writing.

733. Weinberg, Henry H. "Centers of Consciousness Reconsidered." *PT* 5 (1984): 767–773.

Considers the simultaneous existence of both nonreflective and reflective thought in single sentences or expressions, especially in Flaubert's writing.

734. Weinsheimer, Joel C. *Gadamer's Hermeneutics: A Reading of Truth and Method.* New Haven: Yale University Press, 1985. 296 pages

A comprehensive exposition of *Truth and Method* for nonspecialist readers.

735. Wexler, Joyce. "Modernist Writers and Publishers." *SNNTS* 17 (Fall 1985): 286–295.

Argues that the alleged indifference of modernist writers to the reading public oversimplifies their relations with publishers and audiences and encourages postmodernists in refusing "to serve the reader."

736. Wirth-Nesher, Hana. "The Ethics of Narration in D. M. Thomas's *The White Hotel.*" *JNT* 15 (Winter 1985): 15–28.

Weighs techniques for "shaping truth" in individual and collective narrations of experience.

737. Wolpow, Edward R. "Shakespearean Word (514) Ways (82)." *WWays* 18 (May 1985): 85–86.

Focuses on Shakespeare's use of number words. Includes a transaddition puzzle.

738. Woodmansee, Martha. "The Interests in Disinterestedness: Karl Philipp Moritz and the Emergence of the Theory of Aesthetic Autonomy in Eighteenth-Century Germany." *MLQ* 45 (March 1984): 22–47.

Argues that art shifted in Germany from being an instrument of human purpose to becoming a self-sufficient totality in a "theology of art" fashioned to rescue literature from a market economy.

739. Zoran, Gabriel. "Towards a Theory of Space in Narrative." *PT* 5 (1984): 309–335.

Examines four-dimensional relationships between time and space in real-world and fictional-world settings.

See also 68, 91, 117, 118, 136, 180, 184, 185, 194, 196, 261, 275, 300, 309, 315, 320, 378, 469, 471, 505, 510, 535, 548, 588, 589, 594, 597, 599, 804, 819, 848, 850, 867, 923, 989, 1274, 1322, 1325, 1443, 2040, 2518, 3820

READING

740. Anderson, Richard C., and Commission on Reading. *Becoming a Nation of Readers: The Report of the Commission on Reading.* Urbana, Ill.: National Academy of Education, National Institute of Education, and the Center of the Study of Reading, [1985]. 147 pages

Presents commissioners' interpretations of current knowledge about reading and its teaching. Suggests solutions for serious problems in reading instruction such as lack of parental involvement, poor teacher education curricula, and insufficient time devoted in classes to reading and writing.

741. Baddeley, Alan. "Reading and Working Memory." *VLang* 18 (Autumn 1984): 311–322.

Finds evidence that the articulatory loop is not essential for most fluent reading but important for accurately processing complex texts.

742. Baker, Linda. "Differences in the Standards Used by College Students to Evaluate Their Comprehension of Expository Prose." *RRQ* 20 (Spring 1985): 297–311.

Given only general instructions, students usually used lexical standards for comprehension, but rarely external and internal consistency. Students of lower ability used primarily lexical standards for comprehension.

743. Barnes, James A. "An Analysis and Comparison of Reading and Writing Levels of Third-, Fifth-, and Seventh-Grade Students as Measured by Readability Formulae." *DAI* 45 (July 1984): 78A.

Finds significant relationships between measures of writeability and reading. Students wrote progressively below reading-grade level as grade level increased.

744. Baumann, James F. "The Effectiveness of a Direct Instruction Paradigm for Teaching Main Idea Comprehension." *RRQ* 20 (Fall 1984): 93–115.

Concludes that 66 sixth graders taught by a direct instruction paradigm were better able to comprehend main ideas than those taught by a basal reader or by vocabulary development exercises.

745. Bebout, Linda. "Asymmetries in Male-Female Word Pairs." *AS* 59 (Spring 1984): 13–30.

Data from 116 Ontario subjects indicate that "lady" is a sexless synonym for "woman" but that "gentleman" and "man" work somewhat differently.

746. Beck, Isabel L., Margaret McKeown, Richard C. Omanson, and Martha T. Pople. "Improving the Comprehensibility of Stories: The Effects of Revisions That Improve Coherence." *RRQ* 19 (Spring 1984): 263–277.

Altering surface and knowledge problems in two stories enhanced the comprehension of 48 skilled and less skilled third-grade students.

747. Bereiter, Carl, and Marlene Bird. "Use of Thinking Aloud in Identification and Teaching of Reading Comprehension Strategies." *CI* 2 (1985): 131–156.

An analysis of protocols from adults thinking aloud while reading suggests four teaching strategies that are tested and discussed.

748. Birkmire, Deborah P. "Text Processing: The Influence of Text Structure, Background Knowledge, and Purpose." *RRQ* 20 (Spring 1985): 314–326.

Recognizing textual elements was affected by text structure, while reading rate was influenced by both text structure and background knowledge.

749. Black, J. L., D. W. K. Collins, J. N. DeRoach, and S. R. Zubrick. "A Detailed Study of Sequential Saccadic Eye Movements for Normal and Poor-Reading Children." *PMS* 59 (October 1984): 423–434.

Finds that sequential saccadic eye movements are not diagnostically useful for the early detection of dyslexia.

750. Black, J. L., D. W. K. Collins, J. N. DeRoach, and S. R. Zubrick. "Smooth Pursuit Eye Movements in Normal and Dyslexic Children." *PMS* 59 (August 1984): 91–100.

Finds that abnormally high saccadic eye movements in low-velocity smooth-movement tracking was highly diagnostic for early detection of reading problems and dyslexia.

751. Bond, Sandra J., and John R. Hayes. "Cues People Use to Paragraph Text." *RTE* 18 (May 1984): 147–167.

The authors use three studies on the paragraph to construct a successful process model of paragraphing using only formal cues as opposed to semantic cues.

752. Book, Cassandra L., Gerald G. Duffy, Laura R. Roehler, Michael S. Meloth, and Linda G. Vavrus. "A Study of the Relationship between Teacher Explanation and Student Metacognitive Awareness during Reading Instruction." *ComEd* 34 (January 1985): 29–36.

Results indicate that low group student readers of teachers trained to give explicit explanation are more aware of reading processes than students of teachers not similarly trained.

753. Browne, Beverly Ann. "Processing Expository Text: The Effects of Propositional Number and Vocabulary Difficulty in Mature Readers." *DAI* 46 (November 1985): 1675B.

Examines the effects of variations in vocabulary difficulty in expository prose on word inference, word recall, and memory of factual content of passages.

754. Bruskin, Carol, and Marion Blank. "The Effects of Word Class on Children's Reading and Spelling." *BL* 21 (March 1984): 219–232.

"In spelling and reading, third and fifth graders [showed] more accurate responses to nouns and verbs than to noncontent words of matched length and frequency."

755. Burani, Cristina, Dario Salmaso, and Alfonso Caramazza. "Morphological Structure and Lexical Access." *VLang* 18 (Autumn 1984): 348–358.

Finds that root-morphemic and word surface frequency contribute to variation in lexical decision times. Supports a model of lexical organization that represents words in morphologically decomposed form.

756. Calhoun, Mary Lynne, and Christine L. Allegretti. "Processing of Short Vowels, Long Vowels, and Vowel Digraphs by Nondisabled Readers." *PMS* 59 (December 1984): 951–956.

Using pseudo-words, no effects on recognition time were found for short vowels, long vowels, or vowel digraphs. Calls for an empirically supported complexity scale taking rule conditionality and rule consistency into account.

757. Carell, Patricia L. "The Effects of Rhetorical Organization on ESL Readers." *TESOLQ* 18 (September 1984): 441–469.

Indicates that certain discourse types facilitate greater recall than others for intermediate ESL readers, and that Spanish, Arabic, and Oriental students display different recall patterns.

758. Cavedon, Adel, Cesare Cornoldi, and Rossana DeBeni. "Structural *Vs*. Semantic Coding in the Reading of Isolated Words by Deaf Children." *VLang* 18 (Autumn 1984): 378–387.

Suggests that the main reading problem for deaf children concerns coding words less deeply during reading than other readers do.

759. Chall, Jeanne S., and Catherine Snow. *Families and Literacy: The Contribution of Out-of-School Experiences to Children's Acquisition of Literacy*. Washington, D.C.: NIE, 1982. ERIC ED 234 345 [681 pages]

Reports on an 18-month study of the home environment of second, fourth, and sixth graders. Finds correlations between reading ability and an emotionally positive home climate.

760. Clark, Curtis L. "Reader, Writer, and Text Context Variables as Influences on the Comprehensibility of Text." *DAI* 45 (September 1984): 795A.

Examining comprehensibility from a symbolic-interactionist perspective shows that "both reader variables and qualities of the writer's text affected comprehension performance."

761. Clark, Frances L., Donald D. Deshler, Jean B. Schumaker, Gordon R. Alley, and Michael M. Warner. "Visual Imagery and Self-Questioning: Strategies to Improve Comprehension of Written Material." *JLD* 17 (March 1984): 145–149.

Finds that six adolescents improved comprehension scores following three to four hours of instruction in each of two strategies.

762. Colligan, Robert C., and Lee E. Bajuniemi. "Multiple Definitions of Reading Disability: Implications for Preschool Screening." *PMS* 59 (October 1984): 467–475.

Finds that preschool students at highest risk for later reading disability were immature males, weak in number concepts and in symbol recognition.

763. Collins, Carmen. "The Power of Expressive Writing in Reading Comprehension." *LArts* 62 (January 1985). 48–54

College students in a developmental reading course who wrote expressively for 10 minutes a day improved their self-concepts and their comprehension skills.

764. Connor, Ulla. "The Forum: Recall of Text: Differences between First and Second Language Readers." *TESOLQ* 18 (June 1984): 239–256.

Advanced ESL learners (Japanese and Spanish) and native English speakers show differences in total recall but no significant difference in recall of superordinate ideas.

765. Copeland, Kathleen. "The Effect of Writing upon Good and Poor Writers' Learning from Prose." *DAI* 46 (August 1985): 367A.

Students in a writing activity group performed significantly better than students subject to multiple-choice questions, directed rereading, or unrelated activity.

766. Culp, Mary Beth, and Sylvia Spann. "The Influence of Writing on Reading." Paper presented at the AERA Convention, New Orleans, April 1984 ERIC ED 243 083 [14 pages]

Studies the effects of writing on the reading achievement of first-year college students.

767. DiCecco, Joseph Vincent. "Elaboration during Text Comprehension." *DAI* 44 (April 1984): 3222B.

Studies a specific type of elaboration, the inference, and concludes that readers' intentions and motivations are the keys to inferencing.

768. Drake, Dorothy A., and Linnea C. Ehri. "Spelling Acquisition: Effects of Pronouncing Words in Memory for Their Spellings." *CI* 1 (1984): 297–329.

Suggests that the process of pronouncing letters establishes the letters as "sound symbols" in lexical memory.

769. Duran, Elva. "Teaching Functional Reading in Context to Severely Handicapped and Severely Handicapped Autistic Adolescents of Limited English Proficiency." *Psychology* 22 (1985): 57–62.

Discusses language difficulties faced by the handicapped and explains several methods of integrating functional reading exercises with students' daily activites.

770. End, Laurel J. "Unearthing Grounds: Some Studies of Metaphor Comprehension." *DAI* 45 (April 1985): 3358B.

Examines the grounds of metaphors and concludes that, although pairs of metaphors can share a common ground, such grounds are fragile and subject to interference.

771. Fairbrother, Helen Anne. "The Roles of Author Structure, Subjective Structure, and Reader Variables in the Recall of Written Materials." *DAI* 46 (October 1985): 1363B.

Assesses the stability of a technique to analyze readers' perceptions of text structure and explores the relationship between reader variables and text recall.

772. Finn, Seth. "Information-Theoretic Measure of Reader Enjoyment." *WC* 2 (October 1985): 358–376.

Investigates the role of syntactic and semantic unpredictability in determining readers' evaluation of journalistic prose.

773. Fleming, Margaret, ed. "Reading and Writing Connections." *ArEB* 27 (Special Issue, Winter 1985). ERIC ED 253 885 [177 pages].

Special issue, made available in ERIC. Articles listed separately in this volume.

774. Flores d'Arcais, Giovanni. "Lexical Knowledge and Word Recognition: Children's Reading of Function Words." *VLang* 18 (Autumn 1984): 359–377.

Reports a lower availability of function words such as connectives and prepositions as compared to contrast words.

775. Fogliani-Messina, Teresa M., and Anne M. Fogliani. "Perceptual Experience in Learning to Read." *PMS* 59 (October 1984): 479–482.

Field-independent 10-year-olds scored significantly higher for accuracy, but not for speed or comprehension.

776. Gernsbacher, Morton Ann. "Memory for Surface Information in Nonverbal Stories: Parallels and Insights to Language Processes." *DAI* 45 (September 1984): 1046B.

Examines the language phenomenon that, shortly after comprehension, surface information becomes less available to subjects presented with "wordless" narratives.

777. Gerrig, Richard Jay. "Lexical Innovations and Theories of Comprehension." *DAI* 45 (December 1984): 1939B.

Exploits the properties of lexical innovations to contrast modular and interactive theories of language comprehension.

778. Gibbs, Vanita M., and Robert L. Pabst, eds. *Reading: The Core of Learning.* David C. Waterman, comp. Terre Haute, Ind.: Indiana State University Curriculum Research and Development Center, 1984. ERIC ED 241 903 [60 pages]

Seven papers presented at the Thirteenth Annual Reading Conference, June 1983.

779. Gildea, Patricia Mae. "On Resolving Ambiguity: Can Context Constrain Lexical Access?" *DAI* 45 (July 1984): 382B.

Contrasts exhaustive and selective access theories of interpreting ambiguous words in context. Concludes that the dominant meaning is available while the subordinate meaning is context-dependent.

780. Grant-Davie, Keith A. "Between Fact and Opinion: Readers' Representations of Writers' Aims in Expository, Persuasive, and Ironic Discourse." *DAI* 46 (December 1985): 1613A.

Compares more and less skilled readers' interpretations of texts.

781. Guthrie, John T. "Rhetorical Awareness." *JR* 28 (October 1984): 92–93.

Summarizes Odell and Goswami's work and suggests that students must learn to analyze rhetorical constraints of a document.

782. Haddad, Heskel M., Nancy S. Isaacs, Karin Onghena, and Ayala Mazor. "The Use of Orthoptics in Dyslexia." *JLD* 17 (March 1984): 142–144.

Finds that of 73 children with reading difficulty, "orthoptic exercises" improved the "reading mechanism" of those with "poor fusional amplitudes" but not those with dyslexia alone.

783. Hare, Victoria Chou, and Kathleen M. Borchardt. "Summarization Skills." *RRQ* 20 (Fall 1984): 62–78.

Concludes that 22 low-income, minority high school students over three two-hour sessions improved their summarization skills but failed to improve their ability to recognize topic sentences.

784. Hartman, Diane M. "An Investigation into the Predictive Relationship of Ten Writing Assessment Variables to Reading Comprehension." *DAI* 45 (November 1984): 1353A.

Examines the "predictive relationship of five qualitative and five quantitative measures of writing to reading comprehension of ninth grade students." Finds 7 of the 10 variables significant.

785. Hausfeld, Steven Russel. "Acoustic Recoding in Silent Prose Reading." *DAI* 45 (September 1984): 1047B.

Examines contending hypotheses about the role of recoding in reading. Finds that, although acoustic recoding plays a crucial role, subjects are unaware of it.

786. Haussler, Myna M. *Transitions into Literacy.* Urbana, Ill.: ERIC/RCS and NCTE, 1982. ERIC ED 235 479 [30 pages]

A longitudinal study of eight nonreaders developing print awareness in kindergarten and grade one.

787. Heisel, Marsel, and Gordon Larsen. "Literacy and Social Milieu: Reading Behavior of the Black Elderly." *AdEd* 34 (Winter 1984): 63–70.

Assesses the literacy of 132 elderly blacks in a large city to determine how the lack of traditional education affected them.

788. Heydorn, Bernard W. "Treatment *Vs.* Non-treatment in Reduction of Symbol Reversals by First-Grade Children." *PMS* 59 (August 1984): 36–38.

Finds that practice in correcting reversed symbols did not enhance reduction of errors among first graders.

789. Hynds, Susan D. "Interpersonal Cognitive Complexity and the Literacy Response Processes of Adolescent Readers." *RTE* 19 (December 1985): 386–402.

Compares eleventh graders' written impressions of peers with their impressions of fictional characters.

790. Johnson, Barbara E. "Elementary Students' Comprehension of Anaphora in Well-Formed Stories." *JEdR* 78 (March–April 1985): 221–223.

Sixth graders achieved significantly higher levels of comprehension in anaphora than did third graders.

791. Johnson-Cohen, Lois R. "Syntax and Reading Comprehension: A Sector Analysis of Syntactic Changes Made by College Students." *DAI* 45 (July 1984): 170A.

Compares original academic texts with students' rewritten versions and suggests that rewriting exercises did not significantly alter students' reading comprehension.

792. Johnston, Peter H. "Understanding Reading Disability: A Case Study Approach." *HER* 55 (May 1985): 153–177.

Using verbal reports by three "adult disabled readers," examines social and psychological factors behind reading failure.

793. Keenan, Stacey A. "Effects of Chunking and Line Length on Reading Efficiency." *VLang* 18 (Winter 1984): 61–80.

Finds that placing one phrase of text on a line hindered rather than facilitated reading.

794. Kerns, Kimberley, and Sadie N. Decker. "Multifactorial Assessment of Reading Disability: Identifying the Best Predictors." *PMS* 60 (June 1985): 747–753.

Identifies variables that help assess reading disability: WISC-R Information and Digit Span, family history, the Colorado Perceptual Speed Test, and the letters subtest of the Colorado Expressive Fluency Test.

795. Kieras, David E. *The Role of Prior Knowledge in Operating Equipment from Written Instructions.* Arlington, Va.: Office of Naval Research, 1985. ERIC ED 253 858 [36 pages]

Describes several experiments, noting the strong role of prior knowledge and supporting a "consensus model" of cognition.

796. Kintgen, Eugene R., and Norman N. Holland. "Carlos Reads a Poem." *CE* 46 (September 1984): 478–491.

Uses protocol analysis and other research techniques to study how people read and comprehend poems.

797. Kramsch, Claire. "Literary Texts in the Classroom: A Discourse." *MLJ* 69 (Winter 1985): 356–366.

Urges restoring the teaching of literature to language classes. Uses discourse and reading theory to advocate reading literature as a social activity.

798. Langer, Janet. "Examining Background Knowledge and Text Comprehension." *RRQ* 19 (Summer 1984): 468–481.

Concludes that, for 161 sixth-grade students, measures of background knowledge could predict passage-specific comprehension.

799. Ledford, Suzanne Y. "The Relationships among Selected Sixth-Grade Students' Reading Schemata, Reading Achievement, and Writing Sophistication." *DAI* 45 (September 1984): 797A.

Finds significant relationships among reading schemata, reading achievement, writing sophistication, gender, socioeconomic level, and ethnic background.

800. Lee, James F. "The Acquisition of Orthographic Structures by Monolingual Spanish-Speaking Children and Its Relationship to Reading Achievement." *DAI* 46 (October 1985): 965A.

Concludes that monolingual Spanish-speaking children acquire orthographic structures in an identifiable progression, which is not correlated with reading achievement.

801. Lemons, Robert, and R. N. Malatesha. "Improving Reading through Training to Listen." *PMS* 60 (June 1985): 788–790.

Both structured and passive listening instruction enhanced reading achievement in the experimental but not the control group of remedial students in the third grade.

802. Levy, Betty Ann, and John Begin. "Proofreading Familiar Text: Allocating Resources to Perceptual and Conceptual Processes." *M&C* 12 (November 1984): 621–632.

Indicates that more spelling errors were detected when familiar rather than unfamiliar passages were proofread, indicating a resource allocation explanation.

803. Lewis, Janice. "Support for Reading and Writing as Shared Developmental Processes." Paper presented at the Western College Reading and Learning Association, Denver. March 1985. ERIC ED 254 826 [15 pages]

Reviews studies of reading/writing relationships, criticizing the tendency to teach reading and writing separately.

804. Liebman-Kleine, JoAnne D. "Reading, Writing, and Thinking: Toward a Problem-Solving Theory of Reading Literary Narrative." *DAI* 45 (September 1984): 829A.

Employs principles from composition theory to make literary reading a problem-solving process that promotes learning.

805. Lucas, Margery Marie. "Lexical Access during Sentence Comprehension: Context Effects, Frequency Effects, and Decision Processes." *DAI* 46 (July 1984): 384B.

Investigates the processing of ambiguous words in sentences. Finds that lexical access is automatic and that resolution is attentional.

806. Lucey, Wayne. "First Reader: An Individualized Reading." *EQ* 16 (Winter 1984): 10–13.

Describes First Reader, an individualized reading program. Claims that it provides a nonthreatening context for discussion and allows a student to use individual preferences.

807. Massaro, Dominic A. "Reading Ability and Knowledge of Orthographic Structure." *VLang* 18 (Autumn 1984): 323–334.

Explores the relationship between reading ability and the use of orthographic structure in fourth graders.

808. Masterson, Jacqueline. "Surface Dyslexia and Its Relationship to Developmental Disorders of Reading." *VLang* 18 (Autumn 1984): 388–396.

Finds the same symptoms in adults with surface dyslexia and children with reading disorders.

809. McKeown, Margaret. "The Acquisition of Word Meaning from Context by Children of High and Low Ability." *RRQ* 20 (Summer 1985): 482–496.

The low-ability group of 30 fifth-grade students misunderstood the relationship between word and context. Semantic interference affected high and low groups. Argues that meaning acquisition is a complex task.

810. Mosenthal, James H., and Robert J. Tierney. "Cohesion: Problems with Talking about Text." *RRQ* 19 (Winter 1984): 240–244.

Discounts Halliday and Hasan by asserting that cohesive ties are the result, not the cause, of the text's coherence.

811. Muncer, Steven J., and Steven Jandreau. "Morphemes, Syllables, Words, and Reading." *PMS* 59 (August 1984): 14.

Finds that morphemic presentation of reading materials (*vs.* whole word or syllabic presentation) might facilitate learning to read.

812. Nagy, William E., Patricia A. Herman, and Richard C. Anderson. "Learning Words from Context." *RRQ* 20 (Winter 1985): 233–253.

Concludes that 58 eighth-grade students learned vocabulary from context. Suggests that such learning accounts for much vocabulary growth in the school years.

813. Neville, Donald D., and Evelyn F. Searls. "The Effect of Sentence-Combining and Kernel-Identification Training on the Syntactic Component of Reading Comprehension." *RTE* 19 (February 1985): 37–61.

Infers that sentence-combining and kernel-identification training enabled sixth-graders in an experimental reading group to comprehend and retain the ability to comprehend longer, more complex sentences.

814. Newkirk, Thomas, and Nancy B. Lester. "A Comment on 'Looking for Trouble: A Way to Unmask Our Reading' [*CE* 46 (December 1984)] and a Response." *CE* 47 (November 1985): 765-769.

A comment by Lester on Newkirk's article and Newkirk's response.

815. Oka, Evelyn Reiko. "Metacognitive and Motivational Aspects of Children's Reading Comprehension." *DAI* 46 (August 1985): 677B.

Demonstrates different perspectives on how metacognitive and motivational factors jointly influence children's learning and achievement.

816. Oluwu, Terry Adekunle. "Recalculation of Four Traditional and Two Cloze-Derived Readability Formulas." *DAI* 45 (March 1985). 2685A

A study proposing and testing new readability formulas using new criterion passages.

817. Orasanu, Judith, ed. *Reading Comprehension: From Research to Practice.* Hillside, N.J.: Erlbaum, 1986. 432 pages

Twenty papers on such topics as cognitive processes in reading, the role of prior knowledge, linguistic perspectives on literacy, the relation of reading and writing, language development, personal computers, and literacy training programs for adults.

818. Parker, Frank. "Dyslexia: An Overview." *JBW* 4 (Fall 1985): 58–67.

Presents "an operational definition of dyslexia, some attendant characteristics, four competing accounts of the nature of the disorder, and some brief suggestions for remediation."

819. Perkins, Leroy. "Reading and the Unwritten Test." *ArEB* 27 (Winter 1985): 6–9.

Describes the relationship between reading and writing "as mirrors we look into to see ourselves."

820. Pickering, D. M., and Judith A. Bower. "Psycholinguistic Performance of Children Varying in Socioeconomic Status and Home-Language Background." *PMS* 61 (December 1985): 1143–1146.

Verbal deficits in English were associated with delayed reading achievement only when English was the native language.

821. Pinelli, Thomas E., Virginia M. Cordle, and Raymond F. Vondran. "The Function of Report Components in the Screening and Reading of Technical Reports." *JTWC* 14 (1984): 87–94.

Surveys engineers and scientists to determine which components of a report are initially reviewed and in what order they are then read.

822. Pitts, Murray M., and Bruce Thompson. "Cognitive Styles as Mediating Variables in Inferential Comprehension." *RRQ* 19 (Summer 1984): 426–435.

Three cognitive styles (field-independence/field-dependence, conceptual tempo, and attentional style) mediated comprehension for 128 fourth, fifth, and sixth graders.

823. Pontius, Anneliese A. "Dyslexia Subtype with Simultaneous Processing of Intraobject Spatial Relations in an 'Ecological Syndrome.' " *PMS* 61 (December 1985): 1107-1120.

Finds that Australian aboriginal schoolchildren who distorted spatial relations in drawing the human face were also prone to dyslexia and low literacy skills.

824. Prola, Max. "Irrational Beliefs and Reading Comprehension." *PMS* 59 (December 1984): 777–778.

Finds that, among college students, endorsement of irrational beliefs correlated negatively with reading comprehension. Irrational beliefs seemed to disrupt cognitive processes, affecting intellectual functioning and academic performance.

825. Radway, Janice. "Interpretive Communities and Variable Literacies: The Functions of Romance Reading." *Daedalus* 113 (Summer 1984): 49–73.

An ethnographic study of the implications of romance readers' self-perceptions for a theory of variable literacies.

826. Reinking, David, and Robert Schreiner. "The Effects of Computer-Mediated Text on Measures of Reading Comprehension and Reading Behavior." *RRQ* 20 (Fall 1985): 536–552.

Using computers to present definitions, paraphrases, additional information, and main ideas to 104 fifth and sixth graders increased the students' comprehension of selected passages.

827. Roach, Donald A. "Effects of Cognitive Style, Intelligence, and Sex on Reading Achievement." *PMS* 61 (December 1985): 1139–1142.

Reading achievement correlated positively with field independence, analytic conceptual style, intelligence, and sex. Suggests that measures of cognitive style and intelligence may be one and the same.

828. Roberts, Donald F., Christine M. Bachen, Melinda C. Hornby, and Pedro Hernandez-Ramos. "Reading and Television: Predictors of Reading Achievement at Different Age Levels." *ComR* 11 (January 1984): 9–49.

Examines the relationship between television viewing behavior and reading achievement within a framework that includes socioeconomic status, home environment, and involvement with print and television.

829. Roen, Duane H., and Gene L. Piché. "The Effects of Selected Text-Forming Structures on College Freshmen's Comprehension of Expository Prose." *RTE* 18 (February 1984): 8–25.

Results of a reading-recall experiment challenge rhetorician's claims that "cohesive ties," such as conjunctions, ellipses, and statements of rhetorical intention, facilitate reader comprehension.

830. Rogers, Robert. "Three Times True: Redundancy in Ambiguous Texts." *PT* 6 (1985): 591–605.

Examines the role and form of linguistic and propositional redundancy that readers use to verify meaning in ambiguous texts.

831. Roller, Cathy M. "The Effects of Reader- and Text-Based Factors on Writers' and Readers' Perceptions of the Importance of Information in Expository Prose." *RRQ* 20 (Summer 1985): 437–457.

Concludes that category membership and goal relatedness affected perceptions of information's importance. Reader- and text-based factors varied according to types of writing.

832. Rosenblatt, Louise M. "Viewpoints: Transaction *Vs.* Interaction — A Terminological Rescue Operation." *RTE* 19 (February 1985): 96–107.

Examines the implications for research in distinguishing "transaction" and "interaction." Differences in the current use of these terms reflect differences in paradigms.

833. Salzer, Richard T. "Early Reading and Giftedness: Some Observations and Questions." *GCQ* 28 (Spring 1984): 95–96.

Preschoolers who had taught themselves to read also had traits identified as typical of verbally gifted children.

834. Scholes, Robert, and Reed Way Dasenbrock. "A Comment on 'Is There a Fish in this Text?' [*CE* 46 (November 1984)] and a Response." *CE* 47 (October 1985): 650–653.

A comment by Dasenbrock on Scholes's article and Scholes's response.

835. Scruggs, Thomas E., and Debra Tolfa. "Improving the Test-Taking Skills of Learning-Disabled Students." *PMS* 60 (June 1985): 847–850.

Learning-disabled second and third graders trained in test taking improved their performance on the Word Study Skills subtest of the SAT but not on the Reading Comprehension subtest.

836. Sheen, Sy-Yng, and Charles E. Heerman. "Intercorrelations of Measures of Reading and Writing: Implications for College Research on Reading and Writing." *PMS* 60 (April 1985): 677–678.

Argues that tests of the effects of sentence combining on reading comprehension should include a cloze test as well as a standardized reading test.

837. Simion, Francesca, Beatrice Benelli, and Franca Farantini. "Is Activation of Different Codes Related to Age and Stimulus Material?" *VLang* 18 (Autumn 1984): 335–341.

Finds that, where higher-order operations are required to compare stimuli, the nature of the stimuli affects the types of codes activated. For both types of stimuli the level of accuracy also changes as a function of age.

838. Singer, Hindy, and R. B. Ruddell, eds. *Theoretical Models and Processes of Reading*. 3d ed. Hillside, N.J.: Erlbaum, 1985. 960 pages

A collection of 47 papers on such topics as the reading process, the development of reading skills, speech and writing, and reading and cognition functioning.

839. Slater, Wayne H., Michael F. Graves, and Gene L. Piché. "Effects of Structural Organizers on Ninth-Grade Students' Comprehension and Recall of Four Patterns of Expository Text." *RRQ* 20 (Winter 1985): 189–202.

Both providing an outline of a passage before students read and having students take notes facilitated comprehension recall.

840. Stanovich, Keith E., Anne E. Cunningham, and Dorothy J. Feeman. "Intelligence, Cognitive Skills, and Early Reading Progress." *RRQ* 19 (Spring 1984): 278–303.

A study of first, second, and third graders shows that reading comprehension and general intelligence increased with age.

841. Swaffar, Janet K. "Reading Authentic Texts in a Foreign Language: A Cognitive Model." *MLJ* 69 (Spring 1985): 15–34.

Describes the communicative and cognitive benefits of reading full texts in a cultural context. Suggests instructional models for this kind of reading in foreign language classes.

842. Taylor, Barbara M., and Richard Beach. "The Effects of Text Structure on Middle-Grade Students' Comprehension and Production of Expository Text." *RRQ* 19 (Winter 1984): 134–146.

For 114 seventh-grade students, instruction and practice in a hierarchical summary procedure "enhanced" the students' recall of social studies material, while awareness of textual structure seemed to improve expository writing.

843. Taylor, Carol A. "The Relative Effects of Reading or Writing a Prose or Diagrammatic Summary upon the Comprehension of Expository Prose." *DAI* 45 (October 1984): 1085A.

Concludes that "summaries appear to facilitate the comprehension of expository prose, but the effect depends on the kind of material read."

844. Taylor, Maravene Elizabeth. "The Effects on Text Recall of Local and Global Organization Variations." *DAI* 45 (April 1985): 3324B.

Examines whether sentence subject consistency and the organization of subtopics could affect recall. Finds that both played significant roles in enhancing recall.

845. Tierney, Robert J., and Margie Leys. *What Is the Value of Connecting Reading and Writing?* Reading Education Report, no. 55. Urbana, Ill.: University of Illinois Center for the Study of Reading, 1984. ERIC ED 251 810 [42 pages]

Argues that reading and writing work together — as tools for information storage and retrieval, for discovery and logical thought, and for communication and self-indulgence.

846. Tierney, Robert J., and P. David Pearson. *Toward a Composing Model of Reading.* Reading Education Report, no. 43. Urbana, Ill.: University of Illinois Center for the Study of Reading, 1983. ERIC ED 233 329 [29 pages]

Views the way readers create meaning as similar to the way writers create meaning.

847. Vasos, Helen. "Semantic Processing in Bilinguals." *DAI* 46 (July 1984): 388B.

Finds that a taxonomic category label in a subject's second language can evoke a more restricted meaning than the native language equivalent.

848. Vipond, Douglas, and Russell A. Hunt. "Point-Driven Understanding: Pragmatic and Cognitive Dimensions of Literacy Reading." *Poetics* 13 (June 1984): 261–277.

Distinguishes literary reading as "point-driven" rather than story- or information-driven.

849. Walker, Pat Neff, Jr. "Cognitive Processes in Reading Comprehension." *DAI* 44 (February 1984): 2586B.

Reports on experiments designed to investigate two separate areas of cognitive processes in reading comprehension.

850. Weaver, Constance. "Parallels between New Paradigms in Science and in Reading and Literary Theory: An Essay Review." *RTE* 19 (October 1985): 298–316.

Argues that quantum physics and transactional reading/literary theories share basic tenets.

851. Winograd, Peter N. "Strategic Difficulties in Summarizing Texts." *RRQ* 19 (Summer 1984): 404–425.

Finds that poor readers were unable to pick out what the author thought was important, to find main ideas throughout the passage, and to "transform" the original text.

852. Wood, Shaila Penelope. "The Limits of Readability." *TETYC* 10 (Winter 1984): 129–133.

Reviews research to show that reading instruction should help students develop skills, expectations, and the judgment to process whatever materials they encounter.

853. Zakariya, Sally Banks. "To Boost Kids' Reading Skills, Pack away the Workbooks and Bring on the Books." *ASBJ* 172 (August 1985): 17–21.

Summarizes *Becoming a Nation of Readers*. Suggests ways for teachers, administrators, and parents to improve students' reading and writing skills.

See also 41, 42, 43, 67, 75, 84, 114, 154, 157, 187, 190, 318, 335, 353, 360, 363, 426, 435, 448, 675, 681, 701, 937, 951, 956, 974, 976, 988, 994, 1067, 1086, 1159, 1178, 1218, 1224, 1253, 1344, 1363, 1515, 1957, 2004, 2051, 2096, 2344, 2418, 2562, 2848, 2862, 2990, 3118, 3143, 3825, 3840

LINGUISTICS AND GRAMMATICAL THEORY

854. Aarts, Jan, and Willem Meijs, editors. *Corpus Linguistics: Recent Developments in the Use of Computer Corpora in English Language Research.* Costerus New Series, vol. 45. Amsterdam: Rodopi (distributed in the U.S. by Humanities Press), 1984. 230 pages

A collection of 14 papers read at the 1983 Conference on the Use of Computer Corpora in English Language Research, University of Nijmegen. Papers fall into two groups: the compilation and analysis of large computer corpora and the exploitation of corpora that have been available for some time.

855. Addison, James C., Jr. *The Lexical Cohesion of Combined and Decombined Sentences.* Urbana, Ill.: ERIC/RCS and NCTE, 1984. ERIC ED 247 526 [18 pages]

Studies how combined and decombined sentences work. Finds text analysis inconclusive, but interviews showed that small words (*it, and*) linked meaning and wording systems.

856. Afghari, Akbar. "Grammatical Errors and Syntactic Complexity in Three Discourse Categories: An Analysis of English Compositions Written by Persian Speakers." *DAI* 45 (March 1984): 771A.

Investigating the effect of task on grammatical errors and syntactic complexity revealed significant differences related to mode of discourse.

857. Akiyama, M. Michael. "Are Language-Acquisition Strategies Universal?" *DP* 20 (March 1984): 219–228.

This study finds cultural differences in language acquisition between American and Japanese children and suggests that language acquisition has both universal and specific aspects.

858. Algeo, John. "Usage." *PADS* 71 (1984): 31–53.

Surveys research in usage most needed and reports findings in three groups: aims, sources or techniques, and dissemination of results.

859. Almeida, Jose C. "The Interplay of Cohesion and Coherence in Native and Nonnative Written Academic Discourse." *DAI* 46 (November 1985): 1263A.

Concludes that native and nonnative writing contain coherence and cohesive features that interrelate.

860. Ames, Jay. "Czech These Homographs— Please!" *WWays* 17 (February 1984): 61–62.

Includes, with editors' changes, words in a Czech-French dictionary that illustrate direct borrowings from English.

861. Andersen, Elaine S. "The Acquisition of Sociolinguistic Knowledge: Some Evidence from Children's Verbal Role Play." *WJSC* 48 (Spring 1984): 125–144.

Examines young children's ability to select topics, sentence structures, lexical items, and phonological features to "fit" different roles in their nonlinguistic repertoire.

862. Aoun, Joseph. *A Grammar of Anaphora.* Linguistic Inquiry Monographs, no. 11. Cambridge, Mass.: MIT Press, 1985. 192 pages
Annotation not available.

863. Arakelian, Paul G. "Prescriptive Nonsense: The Nonrestrictive Relative Clause." *FEN* 14 (Spring 1985): 18–20.

Argues that "pause or intonation have very little to do with the restrictiveness of a modifier" and that English speakers assume "all relative clauses are restrictive."

864. Ashley, Leonard R. N. "Fragging the Froggies." *WWays* 18 (May 1985): 125.

Invites readers to provide acceptable substitutions for French words that have been assimilated into English.

865. Ashley, Leonard R. N. "Horsing Around." *WWays* 17 (November 1984): 254.

Word game illustrating the impact of equine words on human vocabulary. Requires players to write proverbs (i.e., "boisterous fun"—"horsing around").

866. Ashley, Leonard R. N. "Onomastics-Cha-Cha-Cha." *WWays* 18 (August 1985): 164.

Discovers linguistic surprises in dance names. Presents a quiz.

867. Bachtin, Nicholas. "English Poetry in Greek: Notes on a Comparative Study of Poetic Idioms." *PT* 6 (1985): 333–356.

Discusses diachronic and synchronic linguistic interference that complicates the idiomatic translation of poetry.

868. Backman, Sven, and Goran Kjellmer, eds. *Papers on Language and Literature.* Gothenburg Studies in English, no. 60. Goteborg, Sweden: Acta Universitatis Gothoburgensis, 1985. 399 pages

A collection of 32 articles, of which 3 (by Charles Barber, Goran Kjellmer, and Per Linell) note changes in educated British English, analyze the loss of prepositions in English, and discuss important functions of language for emotive communication.

869. Bailey, Charles-James N. "The Concept of Balance and Linguistic Naturalness." *LangS* 6 (October 1985): 229–238.

Argues that linguistic studies should analyze language in more natural contexts. In particular, function should not be totally separated from structure.

870. Basham, Charlotte, and Pat Rounds. "Brief Reports and Summaries: A Discourse Analysis Approach to Summary Writing." *TESOLQ* 18 (September 1984): 527.

Explores factors contributing to ESL learners' difficulties in writing summaries by analyzing original texts and students' summaries and by interviewing students.

871. Beauzee[?]. "'Grammar' from Diderot's *Encyclopédie.*" *Substance* 13 (1894): 66–79.

A statement of eighteenth-century French grammatical theory, known alternately as General, Universal, or Philosophical Grammar. Published for the first time in English.

872. Bennett, Jo Ann. "An Exploration of Some Linguistic Differences between Speaking and Writing." *DAI* 46 (August 1985): 681B.

Discusses some developmental and sociolinguistic approaches to differences between spoken and written languages and considers such differences within situational contexts.

873. Bergerson, Howard W. "The Great Haiku." *WWays* 18 (November 1985): 225–231.

Creative story about finding a Talking Manuscript on the Funk and Wagnalls porch. Presents word play and 17-letter haiku. Satirizes Ronald Reagan.

874. Berwick, Robert. *The Acquisition of Syntactic Knowledge.* Series in Artificial Intelligence. Cambridge, Mass.: MIT Press, 1985. 350 pages

Annotation not available.

875. Biber, Douglas E. "A Model of Textual Relations within the Written and Spoken Modes." *DAI* 45 (November 1984): 1382A.

Proposes a model to account for linguistic relationships between written and spoken English and describes the place of several genres in speech and writing.

876. Billman, Dorrit Owen. "Procedures for Learning Syntactic Categories: A Model and Text with Artificial Grammars." *DAI* 44 (April 1984): 3221B.

Investigates one method of using new knowledge in learning syntactic categories and tests the prediction for a rule in context and in isolation.

877. Boomer, Garth. "The Ideal Classroom for Language Development." *EQ* 17 (Fall 1984): 54–64.

Elaborates on characteristics of the classroom ideal for language development.

878. Borgmann, Dmitri A. "An Alien Lexicon." *WWays* 18 (February 1985): 27–35.

Describes the vocabulary in English related to alien or extraterrestrial life.

879. Borgmann, Dmitri A. "Bowdlerized Alphabet Soup." *WWays* 18 (August 1985): 179–180.

Provides a humorous recipe for bowdlerizing alphabet soup, using such techniques as the Sanskrit alphabet, magnetizing letters, and "clothing" letters.

880. Borgmann, Dmitri A. "The *G* Spot." *WWays* 18 (February 1985): 62–64.

Describes rules and exceptions governing words with the letter *g*.

881. Borgmann, Dmitri A. "Horse Proverbs." *WWays* 18 (February 1985): 38–39.

Presents 25 "authentic" proverbs about horses.

882. Borgmann, Dmitri A. "Majestic Palindrome." *WWays* 18 (February 1985): 6–15.

Describes word, name and sentence, and verse palindromes. Presents "all known quality word and name palindromes," including foreign-language palindromes.

883. Borgmann, Dmitri A. "Occult Occupations." *WWays* 18 (February 1985): 58–61.

Lists occupational titles in the film industry, pointing out their alphabetical imbalance, their interchangeable parts, and the unavailability of definitions for these occupations.

884. Borgmann, Dmitri A. "Our Feathered Friends." *WWays* 18 (February 1985): 36–37.

Provides a test of "linguistic structures embedded within greater linguistic structures," using words exclusively related to birds.

885. Borgmann, Dmitri A. "Some Odd Title Malarkey." *WWays* 18 (February 1985): 19–26.

Presents, through recreational logology, a "surefire, simple formula for creating titles" for papers, based on numerical values and related to the magic number 227.

886. Borgmann, Dmitri A. "Speaking of Fingers." *WWays* 18 (February 1985): 16–18.

Describes various names for individual fingers of the human hand. Records words for size, shape, and places on fingers and fingernails.

887. Borgmann, Dmitri A. "To Act or Not to Act." *WWays* 18 (February 1985): 53–54.

Provides 33 proverbs urging one to immediate action. Lists 33 proverbs that contradict the advice in the earlier list.

888. Borgmann, Dmitri A. "Webster's Fourth: Another Review." *WWays* 18 (November 1985): 214–216.

Reviews the 1985 multivolumed "Webster's Fourth." Includes satiric anecdotes about various entries. Expresses delight at recreational linguistics entries.

889. Brasch, Walter M. *Black English and the Mass Media.* Lanham, Md.: University Press of America, 1984. 376 pages

Analyzes mass media and the evolution of American black English.

890. Bredin, Hugh. "Roman Jakobson on Metaphor and Metonymy." *P&L* 8 (April 1984): 89–103.

Critiques Jakobson's "Two Aspects of Language and Two Types of Aphasic Disturbances," argu-

ing that language and speech demand more than "two fundamental operations."

891. Bridges, Jean Bolen. "Dialect Interference: A 'Standard' Barrier." *WLN* 8 (June 1984): 9–12.

Argues that, by recognizing dialect differences, teachers can teach Standard Edited English more effectively. Cites 24 features of black English that may cause interference.

892. Briggs, Charles L. "The Pragmatics of Proverb Performances in New Mexican Spanish." *AmA* 87 (December 1985): 793–810.

Shows how performances of proverbs by Mexicans connect basic cultural and linguistic patterns with current social interaction.

893. Brodner, Frederick. *The Loom of Language.* New York: Norton, 1985. 720 pages

Describes the origins, growth through history, and present use of language for communication, with an emphasis on groupings of foreign languages for acquiring new languages.

894. Brooke, Maxey. "Diphthongs." *WWays* 18 (May 1985): 111.

Suggests the possibility of creating 98 diphthongs and identifies 38 from dialects in the Deep South and East Texas.

895. Brooke, Maxey. "Peripatetic Words." *WWays* 17 (August 1984): 153–154.

Comments on complex borrowings in English.

896. Brooke, Maxey. "Uh-Huh." *WWays* 18 (November 1985): 250.

Provides numerous definitions of the term "uh-huh."

897. Brooke, Robert E. "Writing and Commitment: Some Psychosocial Functions of College Writing." *DAI* 45 (February 1985): 2507A.

Combines elements of composition theory and poststructuralism in order to understand writing in relationship to culture and individuality.

898. Butters, Ronald S. "When Is English 'Black English Vernacular'?" *JEngL* 17 (1984): 29–36.

Concludes that a white female adolescent whose voice was mistakenly identified by blacks as black probably had mastered prosodic features.

899. Carlson, Greg N. "Thematic Roles and Their Role in Semantic Interpretation." *Ling* 22 (1984): 259–279.

Proposes an analysis of semantic interpretation that includes thematic roles. Argues that thematic roles are neither semantic nor syntactic, but have an "intermediate" status instead.

900. Carmona, Ralph Chris. "Language and Ethnic Politics: Bilingualism in Los Angeles City Schools, 1975–1980." *DAI* 45 (June 1985): 3733A.

Examines the historical basis of bilingual education, including a case study of its development in the Los Angeles Unified School District from 1975 to 1980.

901. Carpenter, Ronald H., and Richard E. Hersh. "A Stylistic Index of Deteriorating Military Morale: Using Form in Correspondence for Intelligence Purposes." *Lang&S* 18 (Spring 1985): 185–191.

Using letters written by British soldiers during the American Revolution, tests the hypothesis that stylistic analysis of personal correspondence may yield useful military intelligence.

902. Carrell, Patricia. "Inferencing in ESL: Presuppositives and Implications of Factive and Implicative Predicates." *LL* 34 (March 1984): 1–21.

Investigates how ESL learners draw presuppositive and implicative inferences from English sentences.

903. Cassidy, Frederic G. "Regional Speech and Localisms." *PADS* 71 (1984): 32–35.

Reports progress on the *Dictionary of American Regional English* (five proposed volumes) and the archiving of data collected.

904. Castaneda, Hecto-Neri. "The Semantics and the Causal Roles of Proper Names." *PPR* 46 (September 1985): 91–113.

Proposes the theory of Restricted-Variable/Retrieval View to explain the use of proper names in daily life.

905. Ching, Marvin K. L. "Discourse Theory and Its Relevance to the Teaching of Composition." *SECOL* 8 (Summer 1984): 84–99.

Explains how discourse analysis of lexical choice, topicalization, and the structure of a sentence in relation to another sentence can be helpful to composition teachers.

906. Choueka, Yaacov, and Serge Lusignan. "Disambiguation by Short Contexts." *CHum* 19 (July–September 1985): 147–157.

Describes an experiment in computerized text processing. Finds that four surrounding words in a text is sufficient context to determine a word's meaning unambiguously.

907. Clark, Ann K. "Style and the Sign: Conditions for a Theory of Style." *Lang&S* 17 (Winter 1984): 48–56.

Studies the relationships between the sign and what it signifies while analyzing the positions of four earlier theorists.

908. Cook, John Granger. "A Text Linguistic Approach to the Gospel of Mark." *DAI* 46 (December 1985): 1660A.

Demonstrates how linguistics can aid Biblical exegesis. Analyzes the macrostructure, syntax, semantics, and pragmatics of the Gospel of Mark.

909. Corbin, Kyle. "Subtransposals From A to Z." *WWays* 18 (November 1985): 220–224.

Describes strategies various contestants used in word contest involving "substitute-letter transposals." Reveals that computer users did not outscore winners.

910. Cresswell, M. J. *Structured Meanings: The Semantics of Propositional Attitudes.* Cambridge, Mass.: MIT Press, 1985. 202 pages

A study of propositional attitudes. Fifteen chapters divided into three parts treat sense and reference, what meanings are, and formal semantics.

911. Cronell, Bruce. "Black English Influences in the Writing of Third- and Sixth-Grade Students." *JEdR* 77 (March–April 1984): 233–236.

Finds that a significant portion of writing errors were linked to black English dialect influences.

912. Cronell, Bruce. "Language Influences in the English Writing of Third- and Sixth-Grade Mexican-American Students." *JEdR* 78 (January–February 1985): 168–173.

Several types of error in these children's writing were influenced by Spanish and Chicano language usage.

913. Cullen, Roxanne M. "Toward a Pedagogy of Rewriting." *DAI* 46 (August 1985): 411A.

Claims that text linguistics can expand our understanding of revision.

914. Curtis, Jan K. *The Teacher's Role in Natural Literacy Acquistion.* San Jose: California Association of Teachers of English, April 1984. ERIC ED 245 559 [24 pages]

Argues for redesigning literacy curricula based on research in language acquisition.

915. Dahbi, Mohammed. "The Development of English Writing Skills by Moroccan University Students." *DAI* 46 (November 1985): 1264A.

Reveals significant differences in writing skills between first-year and third- and fourth-year Moroccan students.

916. Daiker, Donald, Andrew Kerek, and Max Morenberg. *Sentence Combining and the Teaching of Writing.* Akron, Ohio: L&S Press, 1979. ERIC ED 259 393 [246 pages]

Twenty-two papers from the Miami University Conference on Sentence Combining, October 1978, now available in ERIC. Essays treat the theory of sentence combining, research in sentence combining, and sentence combining in the classroom.

917. Dansei, Marcel. "A Glossary of Lectal Terms for the Description of Language Variation." *LPLP* 9 (Summer 1985): 115–124.

Defines 24 terms used in empirical linguistics.

918. Deese, Rebecca. "The Development of Hierarchical Structures of Adjective Usage." *DAI* 44 (April 1984): 3215B.

Finds that moving from concrete to abstract meanings led to a description of positive, but not negative, adjectival hierarchies.

919. Devereux, Robert. "Shortenings, Blends, and Acronyms." *WWays* 17 (November 1984): 210–215.

Describes how new words are created by adding on letters to familiar words. Defines and illustrates "blends." Distinguishes "acronyms" from "abbreviations." Illustrates phonemic acronyms.

920. Dicker, Susan, and Ken Sheppard. "Brief Reports and Summaries: The Effect of Multiple Drafts on Structural Accuracy in Writing." *TESOLQ* 19 (May 1985): 168–170.

Indicates that multiple drafting does not improve surface-level correctness. Suggests that the process approach may not influence "structural accuracy and sophistication of ESL student writing."

921. Dolinsky, Claudia. "Cultural and Linguistic Barriers to Consumer Information Processing: Information Overload in a Hispanic Population in the United States." *DAI* 46 (August 1985): 473A.

Concludes that information overload occurs in a nonnative but proficient language speaker sooner than it does in native language speakers.

922. Dougherty, Eleanor Donnelly. "Cognitive Models of Face-to-Face Interaction: A Semiotic Approach." *DAI* 45 (December 1984): 1805A.

A study of cognitive representations, in both schema models and sign models, of an occasion of a face-to-face meeting with verbal interaction.

923. Eckler, A. Ross. "Are Acrostic Messages Real?" *WWays* 18 (August 1985): 187–189.

Tries to determine whether odd patterns of letters (specifically in Shakespeare's verse) are intentional or coincidental.

924. Eckler, A. Ross. "Clothes Encounters." *WWays* 18 (May 1985): 76–81.

Discusses word play in names of women's and men's clothing stores.

925. Eckler, A. Ross. "Name Play." *WWays* 18 (August 1985): 137–139.

Suggests word play appropriate for a logologist's inscriptions in yearbooks, wedding books, or retirement books.

926. Eckler, A. Ross. "A New Type of Reference Work." *WWays* 17 (November 1984): 243–246.

Discusses how a transitive verb can be expressed as the sum of two other transitive verbs. Reviews privately published book by Henry Burger.

927. Eckler, A. Ross. "Renaming the Months." *WWays* 18 (August 1985): 167–168.

Attempts to apply logological rules to the names of the months.

928. Eckler, A. Ross. "A Sound-Alike Dictionary." *WWays* 17 (May 1984): 80–81.

Suggests the usefulness of a sound-alike dictionary based on a study of 150 words containing consonants *nrst* and vowels arranged in 24 groups.

929. Eiss, Harry. "Detective Acrostics." *WWays* 18 (November 1985): 253–254.

Presents word games using acrostics and double acrostics using detective fiction.

930. Elkhatib, Ahmad S. "Case Studies of Four Egyptian College Freshman Writers Majoring in English." *DAI* 46 (October 1985): 969A.

Classifies and explains underprepared foreign students' lexical problems.

931. Elliot, Brian A. "A Classification and Analysis of Errors in the Written French of Francophone Welland, Ontario, Secondary School Students." *DAI* 46 (November 1985): 1264A.

Classifies errors and possible causes into 35 groups, each with one general error type.

932. Epes, Mary. *Tracing Errors to Their Sources: A Study of the Encoding Processes of Adult Basic Writers.* Washington, D.C.: NEH, 1983. ERIC ED 238 024 [66 pages]

Finds an overriding influence of nonstandard dialect on the encoding behavior of adult basic writers, especially in two highly stigmatized error categories.

933. Fauconnier, Gilles. *Mental Spaces: Aspects of Meaning Construction in Natural Language.* Cambridge, Mass.: MIT Press, 1985. 185 pages

Investigates how language builds up "mental spaces" and constructs relations within and between them.

934. Fleming, Margaret. "Beyond Grammar and Usage." *CEJ* 16 (Spring 1985): 9–12.

Argues that "grammar is how language actually IS used, devoid of value judgments; usage is how it SHOULD BE used in a particular context."

935. Foster, Dan. "Coherence, Cohesion, and Deixis." Paper presented at the CCCC Convention, New York, March 1984. ERIC ED 245 223 [9 pages]

Studies the relationship between text coherence and the universe of discourse.

936. Foster, Deborah Dene. "Structure and Performance of Swahili Oral Narrative." *DAI* 45 (November 1984): 1488A.

Describes how oral language, as a medium of expression, communicates. Posits a theory for narrative analysis.

937. Fountoukidis, Dona Lee. "The Effect of Sentence Contexts on the Use of Orthographic Structure in Word Recognition by College Students." *DAI* 44 (January 1984): 2272B.

Investigates the effect of semantic and syntactic context on the use of orthographic structure in word recognition.

938. Frank, Alan. "Consonant-Characterized Words." *WWays* 17 (May 1984): 76–79.

Reports on the most prolific consonant groups in words, lists least productive consonant groups, and provides a puzzle with 22 problems.

939. Frank, Alan. "Infinite-Tile Scrabble." *WWays* 17 (November 1984): 216–217.

Presents graph of Scrabble game, using an infinite pool of tiles. Grand score for two players is 7096. Lists possible moves.

940. Frow, John. "Language, Discourse, Ideology." *Lang&S* 17 (Fall 1984): 302–315.

Analyzes *Language as Ideology.* Book's argument that the "grammar of a language is its theory of reality" supports a theory of language based on relationships of meaning and power.

941. Funt, Robert. "Opusopuscule." *WWays* 17 (May 1984): 120–124.

Presents excerpts from a book of palindromes in a logological commonplace book.

942. Giora, Rachel. "Notes towards a Theory of Text Coherence." *PT* 6 (1985): 699–715.

Argues that intersentential cohesion "has little to offer for the investigation of text coherence."

943. Grant, Jeff. "Ars Magna: The Ten Square." *WWays* 18 (November 1985): 195–207.

Presents tautonymic 10 × 10 grid for word puzzles.

944. Grant, Jeff. "Q Palindromes." *WWays* 17 (November 1984): 223.

Presents problematic letter *q* and word game problems. Lists obscure palindromic words beginning with the letter. Lists words with *q* not followed by *u*.

945. Green, Karen. "Is a Logic for Brief Sentences Possible?" *PhS* 47 (January 1985): 29–55.

Argues that a logic for brief sentences is not possible.

946. Green, Michael. "Talk and Doubletalk: The Development of Metacommunication Knowledge about Oral Language." *RTE* 19 (February 1985): 9–24.

Pilot interviews with children identify significant age differences in three levels of metacommunication knowledge and five factors that influence the understanding of speaker meaning in oral language.

947. Hakuta, Kenji. *Mirror of Language: The Debate on Bilingualism.* New York: Harper & Row, 1984. 240 pages

Challenges current theories of child and adult language learning and discusses the intellectual and social implications of bilingualism and bilingual education.

948. Halliday, M. A. K. *An Introduction to Functional Grammar.* Baltimore: Edward Arnold, 1985. 432 pages

A systemic grammar examining the clause as message and as interaction, constituency, word groups and phrases, the clause complex, intonation and rhythm, cohesion and discourse, metaphorical modes of expression, and the analysis of a text.

949. Harman, Lesley Diana. "The Modern Stranger: On Language and Membership." *DAI* 44 (May 1984): 3499A.

Constructs a theoretical framework for a "language of membership" that implicates the modern stranger in the mode of discourse of urban society.

950. Harris, John S. "The Naming of Parts: An Examination of the Origins of Technical Scientific Vocabulary." *JTWC* 14 (1984): 183–191.

Examines the sources of technical and scientific vocabulary, including foreign language root words, names of inventors and discoverers, and names of common shapes and functions.

951. Harris, Roy. "The Semiology of Textualization." *LangS* 6 (October 1984): 271–286.

To understand a text, the reader must be aware of its nonlinguistic signs.

952. Harste, Jerome, Virginia A. Woodward, and Carolyn L. Burke. "Examining Our Assumptions: A Transactional View of Literacy and Learning." *RTE* 18 (February 1984): 84–108.

Argues that literacy is governed by sociopsycholinguistic processes, discusses the need for a unifying theory of language learning, and advocates reading-writing tasks for preschoolers.

953. Hartwell, Patrick. "Grammar, Grammars, and the Teaching of English." *CE* 47 (February 1985): 105–127.

Argues that teaching grammar to improve writing ability is ineffective and that composition theorists and researchers should move on to more interesting areas of inquiry.

954. Hartwell, Patrick, and Martha Kolln. "Comment on 'Grammar, Grammars, and the Teaching of Grammar' [*CE* 47 (February 1985)] and a Response." *CE* 47 (December 1985): 874–879.

A comment by Kolln on Hartwell's article and Hartwell's response.

955. Hartwell, Patrick, Joseph Williams, Richard D. Cureton, Carole Moses, and Edward A. Vavra. "Four Comments on 'Grammar, Grammars, and the Teaching of Grammar' [*CE* 47 (February 1985)] and a Response." *CE* 47 (October 1985): 641–650.

Comments by Williams, Cureton, Moses, and Vavra on Hartwell's article and Hartwell's response.

956. Hatta, Takeshi. "Reading Processes in Japanese: Do the Japanese Have Script-Specific Mechanisms?" *LangS* 7 (October 1985): 355–363.

Reports on an experiment suggesting that different types of scripts require different processing mechanisms.

957. Hayes, Ira. "An Experimental Study of Sentence Combining as a Means of Improving Syntactic Maturity, Writing Quality, and Grammatical Fluency in the Compositions of Remedial High School Students." *DAI* 45 (February 1985): 2424A.

Suggests that teacher personality rather than a particular method accounts for effectiveness in teaching writing skills. The sentence-combining group experienced growth in several factors of syntactic maturity.

958. Hellweg, Paul. "Phobia and Counterphobia." *WWays* 18 (May 1985): 82.

Presents a list of 10 phobia words and their opposites.

959. Henrick, John. "Formal Analogy Is Best." *WWays* 18 (May 1985): 97.

Presents a game with a series of mottos that the reader should match to specific occupations.

960. Henrick, John. *"That's* in a Name." *WWays* 18 (August 1985): 162–163.

Presents anagrams from personal names that also describe the person associated with the name.

961. Henzell-Thomas, Jeremy. "Teaching the Use of Connectives Expressing Concession." *ELTJ* 39 (October 1985): 279–281.

Distinguishes concession from contrast and distinguishes among types of concession. Suggests eight criteria for writing material to practice concession.

962. Hoffman, Paul. "Kripke on Private Language." *PhS* 47 (January 1985): 23–28.

Investigates how Kripke has not distinguished between private and public language.

963. Hopper, Robert, and Robert A. Bell. "Broadening the Deception Concept." *QJS* 70 (August 1984): 288–302.

A study based on responses by 221 undergraduates concludes that words signaling deception can usefully be grouped in one of six categories.

964. Hudelson, Sarah. "The Forum: Kan Yu Ret an Rayt in Ingles: Children Become Literate in English as a Second Language." *TESOLQ* 18 (June 1984): 221–238.

Reviews recent research in the development of second-language reading and writing skills. Offers suggestions for applying findings in the classroom.

965. Hutchinson, Jean E. "Constraints on Children's Implicit Hypotheses about Word Meanings." *DAI* 45 (April 1985): 3352B.

An experiment with children's language learning reveals that preschoolers spontaneously constrained meanings of new nouns, thus greatly simplifying language learning.

966. Hyde, Janet Shibly. "Children's Understanding of Sexist Language." *DP* 20 (July 1984): 697–706.

Children are overwhelmingly likely to respond to the "gender-neutral *he*" as male. Gender-related pronouns affect children's occupational stereotypes.

967. Innis, Robert E., ed. *Semiotics: An Introductory Anthology.* Bloomington, Ind.: Indiana University Press, 1985. 352 pages

A collection of 15 essays by major figures in the development of semiotics. Questions addressed include what is a sign? Why are there signs? How many kinds of signs are there? What are their respective powers and uses. Authors include Pierce, de Saussure, Langer, Levi Strauss, Jakobson, Barthes, and Eco.

968. Isaak, Mark. "More Sound-Spelling Correspondences." *WWays* 18 (August 1985): 184–186.

Provides spellings for particular pronunciations.

969. Isaak, Mark. "Sound-Spelling Correspondences." *WWays* 19 (May 1985): 101–106.

Extends the list of words from the *American Heritage Dictionary* that presents various spellings for particular sounds.

970. Jamieson, Barbara C. "Features of the Thematic and Information Structures of the Oral and Written Language of Good and Poor Writers." *DAI* 45 (December 1985): 2425A.

Finds that better writers made more adjustments from speaking to writing. Suggests that aspects of the functional sentence perspective can provide a conceptual framework for analysis and instruction.

971. Jeffries, Sophie. "English Grammar Terminology as an Obstacle to Second Language Learning." *MLJ* 69 (Winter 1985): 385–390.

Reports on a study showing that the more familiar college students are with English grammar terminology, the better they will perform in beginning language courses.

972. Joseph, John. "The Elaboration of an Emerging Standard." *LangS* 6 (April 1984): 39–52.

A dialect that attains a standard status undergoes elaboration, a process beginning with transference of structural and lexical elements from a "high" culture.

973. Kahane, Henry, and Renee Kahane. "Linguistic Aspects of Sociopolitical Keywords." *LPLP* 8 (Summer 1984): 143–160.

Analyzes four characteristics of terms "which in their totality and interdependence reflect and reveal the essence" of social and political movements.

974. Kane, Roberta. "A Longitudinal Analysis of Primary Children's Written Language in Relation to Reading Comprehension." *DAI* 45 (September 1984): 797A.

A syntactic analysis of narrative and expository writing reveal differences due to purposes. Finds that complexity in writing seemed related to reading comprehension.

975. Kay, Paul, and Willett Kempton. "What Is the Sapir-Whorf Hypothesis?" *AmA* 86 (March 1984): 65–79.

Reviews and tests empirically the hypothesis; then reevaluates it in light of research findings.

976. Kent, Carolyn E. "A Linguist Compares Narrative and Expository Prose." *JR* 28 (December 1984): 232–236.

Argues that narratives are agent-oriented, time-bound, chronologically linked. Expository texts are subject-oriented, not time-bound, and logically linked using parallelism and repeated subjects.

977. King, Jeffrey C. "A Formal Semantics for Some Discourse Anaphora." *DAI* 46 (December 1985): 1646A.

Attempts a formal semantics for singular anaphoric pronoun occurrences and definite descriptions whose quantifier antecedents occur in other sentences.

978. King, Stephen W., and Kenneth K. Sereno. "Conversational Appropriateness as a Conversational Imperative." *QJS* 70 (August 1984): 264–273.

Applies Grice's concept of "implicature" to the study of interpersonal communication.

979. Kobayashi, Hiroe. "Brief Reports and Summaries: Rhetorical Patterns in English and Japanese." *TESOLQ* 18 (December 1984): 737–738.

An analysis of 676 writing samples reveals that Japanese ESL students display a preference for first-language rhetorical patterns.

980. Kucer, Stephen. "Text Coherence as an 'In-Head' Phenomenon." Paper presented at the CCCC Convention, Detroit March 1983. ERIC ED 233 301 [15 pages]

Finds that globally incoherent texts written by 13 basic writing students require readers to make major inferences.

981. Lance, Mark Norris. "Reference without Causation." *PhS* 45 (May 1984): 335–351.

Argues that causal theory of reference is not helpful in accounting for primitive reference.

982. Lauton, David. "Arrant Solecisms." *AS* 59 (Summer 1984): 131–148.

Oral usage data collected from 41 subjects on the past tense forms of *run* and *dive* show the inadequacies of common dictionary usage notes.

983. Laycock, Don. "Dictionaries and Podism." *WWays* 18 (November 1985): 241–242.

Presents a neologism, "podism,"—"a state of mental bias, like sexism and racism," the attitude that all civilization, science, and culture originated in the Northern Hemisphere.

984. Laycock, Don. "A Rude Word in the Alphabet Soup." *WWays* 18 (May 1985): 91–94.

Presents an exchange of letters between Horace Greerly and the Paragon Soup Company, resulting from Greerly's finding a rude word spelled out in his alphabet soup.

985. Lederer, Richard. "Jack and the Twoderful Beans." *WWays* 18 (August 1985): 169–170.

Uses inflationary language to retell the story of "Jack and the Beanstalk."

986. Lederer, Richard. "What Do You Call a Naked Grizzly?" *WWays* 18 (November 1985): 235–236.

Provides puzzle using homophones; answers included.

987. Lehmann, W. P., and Winfield S. Bennett. "Human Language and Computers." *CHum* 19 (April–June 1985): 77–83.

Discusses why computer processing of natural language is difficult and how it is being attempted.

988. Lima, Susan Diane. "Morphological Encoding in the Reading of Sentences." *DAI* 46 (September 1985): 986B.

Finds that pseudo-prefixed words required more fixation time than prefixed words and that lexical access to a prefixed word is achieved by "stripping."

989. Lovelace, Martin John. "The Presentation of Folklife in the Biographies and Autobiographies of English Rural Workers." *DAI* 44 (May 1984): 3455A.

Attempts to describe the conventions of personal experience narration (spoken and written) among rural English working men.

990. Lumsden, David. "Does Speaker's Reference Have Semantic Relevance?" *PhS* 47 (January 1985): 15–21.

Explains the nature of semantic reference.

991. Lycan, William B. *Logical Form in Natural Language.* Cambridge, Mass.: MIT Press, 1984. 348 pages

A discussion of truth-theoretic semantics and its relationship to pragmatics and psychology. Details the anatomy of the notion of linguistic meaning, explores the interface between formal languages and natural language, and defends the autonomy of linguistic semantics as a branch of scientific psychology.

992. Mark, Vera. "Ways of Telling: Social Dimensions of Written Gascon in Lectoure, France." *DAI* 46 (August 1985): 459A.

Examines how writers construct images of personal, community, and ethnic identity as well as represent, challenge, and influence social relations.

993. Martin, Marilyn. "Advanced Vocabulary Teaching: The Problem of Synonyms." *MLJ* 68 (Summer 1984): 130–137.

Describes the way in which stylistic register, grammatical privileges, idiomatic collocation, and semantic features are essential for nonnative speakers learning new vocabulary.

994. Martinet, Jeanne. "The Child's Access to Writing and Reading." *LangS* 6 (April 1984): 73–80.

Argues that a writing system that does not evolve with spoken language causes problems in learning to read and write.

995. Mayher, John S. "Grammar and Consciousness." *CEJ* 15 (Spring 1984): 29–30.

Cites research to argue against the continued teaching of grammar as an aid for writing improvement.

996. McCartney, Kathleen. "Effect of Quality of Day-Care Environment on Children's Language Development." *DP* 20 (March 1984): 244–260.

The quality of day-care environment predicted four measures of intellectual and language development, with the level of the caretaker's speech more important than that of peers.

997. McClure, Erica F., and Margaret S. Steffensen. "A Study of the Use of Conjunctions across Grades and Ethnic Groups." *RTE* 19 (October 1985): 217–236.

Identifies a common order to mastering four conjunctions by third, sixth, and ninth graders of three ethnicities. Finds slower acquisition for lower socioeconomic minorities.

998. McConochie, Jean Alice. "Simplicity and Complexity in Scientific Writing: A Computer Study of Engineering Textbooks." Paper given at the International Congress of Applied Linguistics, 1975. ERIC ED 233 570 [23 pages]

Finds that writing in engineering employs a smaller subset of English grammatical structures than literary writing.

999. McCreedy, Lynn A. "Aspects of Reference, Coherence, and Style in Three Genres of Navajo Texts." *DAI* 44 (April 1984): 3050A.

Studies Coyote stories, prayers, and personal narratives and finds that discourse structure and cohesion "interrelate in a principled way across a stylistic continuum."

1000. McDonald, Janet L. "The Meaning of Semantic and Syntactic Processing Cues by First and Second Language Learners of English, Dutch, and German." *DAI* 45 (February 1985): 2717B.

Concludes that second-language learners shift from cue mapping appropriate to the first language to that appropriate to the second.

1001. Meziani, Ahmed. "Moroccan Learners' English Errors: A Pilot Study." *IRAL* 22 (November 1984): 297–310.

Classifies grammatical errors in 50 essays written by high school students in Rabat after two years of English classes.

1002. Miller, S. R. "Performatives." *PhS* 45 (March 1984): 247–259.

Explains the nature of *ifids*—"illocutionary force indicating devices"—in relation to Austin's speech-act theories.

1003. Morice, Dave. "Palindromania." *WWays* 18 (November 1985): 247–249.

Lists palindromes and poems composed from them. Plays games with Stein's "rose is a rose." Makes poems out of the names Gogol and Isis.

1004. Morrow, Daniel Hibbs. "Dialect Interference in Writing: Another Critical View." *RTE* 19 (May 1985): 154–180.

Criticizes recent treatments of "dialect interference" in writing, especially Hartwell's 1980 *RTE* article. Offers suggestions for more sophisticated study.

1005. Mosenthal, James H., and Robert J. Tierney. *Cohesion: Problems with Talking about Text—A Brief Commentary.* Technical report, no. 298. Urbana, Ill.: University of Illinois Center for the Study of Reading, 1983. ERIC ED 236 566 [15 pages]

Reports on studies indicating that the concept of cohesion does not describe a text's unity. Cohesion appears to be an effect rather than a cause of coherence.

1006. Moser, Paul K. "Types, Tokens, and Propositions: Quine's Alternative to Propositions." *PPR* 44 (March 1984): 361–375.

Argues that Quine's assault on propositions is "in part defective " and "undermines" Quine's ideas on "truth bearers."

1007. Muncer, Steven J., and George Ettlinger. "In and behind a Lenneberg Paradigm." *JPsyR* 13 (1984): 57–68.

A study suggests that chimps may be able to learn some rules of syntax but that they are not able to be creative with that syntax.

1008. Nahir, Moshe. "Language Planning Goals: A Classification." *LPLP* 8 (Fall 1984): 294–327.

Proposes a classification of 11 language planning goals reflecting "deliberate, institutionally organized attempts at affecting the linguistic or sociolinguistic status or development of language."

1009. Nash, Walter. *The Language of Humor: Style and Technique in Comic Discourse.* White Plains, N.Y.: Longman, 1985. 181 pages

Analyzes the linguistic patterns, stylistic functions, and social and cultural contexts of humor. Examines a wide range of comic material, including jokes, graffiti, aphorisms, advertisements, anecdotes, puns, parodies, and passages of comic fiction.

1010. Nattinger, James R. "The Forum: Communicative Language Teaching: A New Viewpoint." *TESOLQ* 18 (September 1984): 391–407.

Offers a computational metaphor for communicative language teaching (CLT). Shows how CLT influences classroom practices, including writing.

1011. Nava, John M. "A Study of Prepositions in Written Language: Grades Three through Eight." *DAI* 46 (December 1985): 1546A.

Observes a decrease in the variety of prepositions used and meanings for them among students in grades seven and eight. Calls for further examination of this "plateau."

1012. Netsu, Machiko. "The Role of Error Analysis in Clarifying Linguistic Distinctions between English 'When' and Its Japanese Equivalents." *IRAL* 22 (August 1984): 191–202.

Explores the nature of errors learners make in producing Japanese temporal constructions. Interlingual transfer and incomplete explanations are factors.

1013. Nida, Eugene A. "Rhetoric and Styles: A Taxonomy of Structures and Functions." *LangS* 6 (October 1984): 287–305.

Clarifies the structures and functions of discourse in terms of the processes they represent and in terms of intentionality, coherence, and effectiveness.

1014. Nilsen, Don L. F. "The Humor of Idiomatic English." *EngR* 36 (1985): 12–13.

Discusses idiomatic phrases and the humor created by their use and misuse. Includes a bibliography.

1015. Norment, Nathaniel, Jr. "Contrastive Analyses of Organizational Structures and Cohesive Elements in Native and ESL Chinese, English, and Spanish Writing." *DAI* 45 (July 1984): 172A.

Finds that English, Chinese, and Spanish writers in college employ distinctive organizationl structures across modes when writing both in their native languages and in English.

1016. Oi, Kyoko M. "Cross-Cultural Differences in Rhetorical Patterning: A Study of Japanese and English." *DAI* 45 (February 1985): 2511A.

Finds that Americans writing English use fewer connectives and more synonyms than the Japanese do when writing either English or Japanese.

1017. Ortony, Andrew, Terence J. Turner, and Nancy Larson-Shapiro. "Cultural and Instructional Influences on Figurative Language Comprehension by Inner City Children." *RTE* 19 (February 1985): 25–36.

Examines the influence of special instruction on Harlem school children's comprehension of figurative language. Supports "language experience" over "cognitive constraints" view of figurative language comprehension.

1018. Owen, William Foster. "Interpretive Themes in Relational Communication." *QJS* 70 (August 1984): 274–287.

A study based on 118 people of conversational themes that married couples, dating couples, relatives, live-in friends, and non-live-in friends use to interpret their relationships.

1019. Partridge, Harry B. "Good-Bye, Dr. Wombat!" *WWays* 17 (February 1984): 13–18.

Creative piece, relying on etymology, epigrams, and limericks to advance plot.

1020. Peng, Fred C. C. "Mental Processing of Information: A Neurolinguistic Approach." *LangS* 6 (October 1984): 340–374.

Describes what information is and how it is mentally processed. Proposes a theory called "force enhancement," which explains the tasks of mental processing.

1021. Phillips, Louis. "The Apple-Sauce Chronicles." *WWays* 17 (November 1984): 229–232.

Lists jokes based on homonyms, reversals of first and last name parts, and spoonergrams. Presents puns with movie titles and names of real/fictional notables.

1022. Phillips, Louis. "The Fall of the Dictionary of Webster." *WWays* 18 (August 1985): 148.

A humorous account of the "fall" of the dictionary that alludes to Poe's "Fall of the House of Usher."

1023. Polarin, A. B. "'Pseudo-Grammatical' and 'Pseudo-Lexical' Errors in Written EL2 Texts." *IRAL* 22 (February 1984): 59–63.

These errors appear to be caused by "phonographic" errors resulting from the interaction between English phonology and graphology.

1024. Pollack, Philip L. "Two-Letter Interjections." *WWays* 18 (May 1985): 98–100.

Lists and groups two-letter interjections according to feelings, commands, and statements.

1025. Posner, Jeanne. "General Semantics in the Classroom: The Relationship between the Degree of Intensionality of Elementary School Teachers' Language Behavior and Students' Attitudes towards Teachers and School." *DAI* 45 (January 1985): 1917A.

Finds that students' attitudes improved as teachers used more intensional language.

1026. Powell, Marcy S. "Word Division." *ES* 65 (October 1984): 452–458.

Notes variation in syllabification among dictionaries and between British and American usage. To provide consistency, offers six principles for phonetic and four for morphemic divisions.

1027. Preston, Dennis R. "Linguistics: Science's Best-Kept Secret." *IE* 7 (Spring 1984): 16–22.

Defines a linguist's work and argues that all language teachers pursue linguistic interests.

1028. Preston, Dennis R. "My Little Deuce Coo?" *IE* 8 (Spring 1985): 34.

Analyzes *coup* words as doublets, words long in the language but lately given "foreign" pronunciations as a sign of erudition.

1029. Price, Glanville. *The Languages of Britain.* Baltimore: Edward Arnold, 1985. 248 pages

Examines the languages spoken in Britain since the earliest records and studies their roles in the development of the English language.

1030. Quirk, Randolph, Sidney Greenbaum, Geoffrey Leech, and Jan Svartik. *A Comprehensive Grammar of the English Language.* White Plains, N.Y.: Longman, 1985. 1779 pages

A description of current American and British English, incorporating research in semantics, pragmatics, and text linguistics. Nineteen chapters on parts of speech, phrases, sentences, clauses, and information processing; three appendixes on word formation, punctuation, and stress, rhythm, and intonation; includes bibliography.

1031. Raskin, Victor. "Jokes." *PsyT* 19 (October 1985): 24–39.

Provides a semantic theory of humor to match human intuition. Addresses the question, "How does the text convey humor?"

1032. Ridgeway, Doreen, Everett Waters, and Stan A. Kuczaj II. "Acquisition of Emotion–Descriptive Language: Receptive and Productive Vocabulary Norms for Ages Eighteen Months to Six Years." *DP* 21 (September 1985): 715–724.

Produces normative data for children's understanding of emotion – describing adjectives from ages 18 to 71 months.

1033. Robinson, James Adolph. "The Relationship between Person Characteristics and Attitudes toward Black and White Speakers of Informal Nonstandard English." *DAI* 45 (September 1984): 683A.

Examines how the cognitive complexity and racial bias of speakers affect their listening attitudes.

1034. Rogers, Margaret. "On Major Types of Written Errors in Advanced Students of German." *IRAL* 22 (February 1984): 1–39.

A study of syntactic, morphological, lexical, orthographic, and translation errors in 26 essays written in a freewriting exercise.

1035. Rosner, Mary. "Putting 'This and That To- gether' to Question Sentence-Combining Re- search." *TWT* 11 (Spring 1984): 221–228.

Argues that we need to know more about how syntactic structures, such as subordinate clauses, function in various technical documents and disciplines.

1036. Roth, Froma P., and Nancy J. Spekman. "Assessing the Pragmatic Abilities of Children: Part 1 Organizational Framework and Assess- ment Parameters." *JSHD* 49 (February 1984): 2–11.

Presents clinicians with an approach to assessing the abilities of children to employ the rules gov- erning language use in social situations.

1037. Roth, Froma P., and Nancy J. Spekman. "Assessing the Pragmatic Abilities of Children: Part 2 Guidelines, Considerations, and Specific Evaluation Procedures." *JSHD* 49 (February 1984): 12–17.

Presents guidelines, procedures, and activities for the clinical evaluation of children's abilities to employ the rules governing language use in social contexts.

1038. Rousseau, Jean-Jacques. *Discourses and the Essay on the Origin of Languages.* Edited by Vic- tor Gourevitch. Perennial Library. New York: Harper & Row, 1985. 320 pages

Essays on language, culture, and social and lit- erary theory.

1039. Rubin, Andee, and Jane Hansen. *Reading and Writing: How Are the First Two 'R's' Re- lated?* Reading Education Report, no. 51. Ur- bana, Ill.: University of Illinois Center for the Study of Reading, 1984. ERIC ED 248 464 [26 pages]

Argues that reading and writing are similar pro- cesses and therefore should be taught together for real communicative purposes.

1040. Russell, Willis. "New Words." *PADS* 71 (1984): 54–59.

Summarizes the lexical research needed in Amer- ican English in the following areas: etymology, slang, new words and meanings, and a data base of neologisms for researchers.

1041. Saksena, Anuradha. "Linguistic Models, Pedagogical Grammars, and ESL Composition." *IRAL* 22 (May 1984): 137–143.

ESL grammar texts based on theoretical descrip- tive linguistics have students practice passive constructions, unreduced relative clauses, and nominalization—all undesirable structures for composition.

1042. Scarcella, Robin C. "Cohesion in the Writing Development of Native and Nonnative English Speakers." *DAI* 45 (November 1984): 1386A.

Indicates that more proficient writers vary im- plicit with explicit lexical ties to produce coherent prose. Less proficient writers seldom use implicit ties.

1043. Scarcella, Robin C. "How Writers Orient Their Readers in Expository Essays: A Compara- tive Study of Native and Nonnative English Writers." *TESOLQ* 18 (December 1984): 671–688.

Indicates that native and nonnative English writers orient readers differently, the latter using longer orientations and fewer attention-getting types.

1044. Schaefer, James Frank. "The Interpretation of Action in Dramatic Language." *DAI* 45 (No- vember 1984): 1241A.

Proposes a unified dramatic-linguistic approach to interpreting dramatic texts. Reviews dramatic theory, studies of dramatic language, and cog- nitive psychology.

1045. Schneider, Thomas. "Terminology: Teaming Up *Homo Faber* and *Homo Linguisticus.*" *CHum* 19 (April–June 1985): 103–108.

Describes problems associated with proliferating terminology in technical fields and suggests a computer data base as one means of managing the problem.

1046. Schnur, Elizabeth Sue. "Lexical Develop- ment." *DAI* 44 (April 1984): 3218B.

Examines how children master impressive quan- tities of words and how their linguistic sophisti- cation helps them take advantage of linguistic contexts.

1047. Schuster, Edgar H. "Let's Get Off the Myth- mobile." *EJ* 74 (October 1985): 40–43.

Discusses five commonly taught rules of writing and grammar, refuting them by giving examples of well-known authors who broke these rules.

1048. Scott, Bill. "Communication, Creativity, and Form/Content Relationships in Linguistic Texts." *Lang&S* 17 (Summer 1984): 217–233.

Postulates a "systematic range of form-content relationships" that has at one extreme the theoretical dominance of content over form; at the other, form over content.

1049. Shanahan, Timothy. *The Nature of the Reading-Writing Relationship: A Multivariate Approach.* Urbana, Ill.: ERIC/RCS and NCTE, 1982. ERIC ED 233 337 [38 pages]

Examines the relationships among multiple measures of reading and writing in the second and fifth grade.

1050. Shipley, Joseph T. *The Origins of English Words: A Discursive Dictionary of Indo-European Roots.* Baltimore City, Md.: The Johns Hopkins University Press, 1984. 672 pages

An anecdotal, eclectic tracing of the origins of words in linguistics, literature, history, folklore, anthropology, philosophy, and science. Organized alphabetically and written in prose, rather than in the abbreviated style of a conventional dictionary.

1051. Shore, Cecilia, Barbara O'Connell, and Elizabeth Bates. "First Sentences in Language and Symbolic Play." *DP* 20 (September 1984): 872–880.

In this longitudinal study, direct symbolic play variables contributed unique explained variance to different language variables.

1052. Small, Robert C., Jr. "Three Reasons Why We Shouldn't Teach Grammar and One Why We Should (Sort of)." *CEJ* 18 (Spring 1985): 1–4.

Argues against the traditional teaching of grammar because it is ineffective, too abstract, and time consuming. Thinks grammar can best be studied in linguistics, not writing, courses.

1053. Smith, Herb. "The Fallacy of 'Correct' Usage: An Empirical Study." *EQ* 17 (Spring 1984): 102–108.

Finds variation in the expectations university faculty have about usage.

1054. Smith, Michael. "On the Birth (and Death?) of a Word." *WWays* 18 (November 1985): 232–234.

Describes birth of new words in English, "specker" for example.

1055. Spack, Ruth. "Invention Strategies and the ESL College Composition Student." *TESOLQ* 18 (December 1984): 649–670.

Reviews first-language theory on invention. Offers evidence that, once taught, ESL students benefit from first-language invention strategies, some requiring adaptation for ESL learners.

1056. Spangler, G. A. "Reference and Identification." *PPR* 46 (December 1985): 333–336.

Argues that reference and identification are not the same.

1057. Stanback, Marsha Houston. "Code-Switching in Black Women's Speech." *DAI* 44 (April 1984): 2927A.

Studies the speech of two black and two white women friends.

1058. Sternglass, Marilyn. *Writing Based on Reading: Reading Based on Writing.* Paper presented at the CCCC Convention, Detroit, March 1983 ERIC ED 234 389 [10 pages]

Finds that students need to balance their use of causal chains of inferences in writing based on outside sources with a reader's needs.

1059. Strage, Amy Alexandra. "Children's Mastery of Co-Reference Restrictions on Pronominal and Null Anaphora." *DAI* 45 (March 1985): 3096B.

After testing 40 subjects to see how they handled anaphora, finds that their interpretations were co-determined by structural and functional hypotheses formed during childhood.

1060. Sumners, William. "Artificial Adreverbums." *WWays* 18 (August 1985): 158.

Creates several "questionable forward-and-backward" palindromes, each beginning with "demi."

1061. Sumners, William. "A Tale of Two Crossword Dictionaries." *WWays* 17 (August 1984): 171–174.

Presents results of a "brief investigation of two crossword dictionaries" to determine sources authors used to compile dictionaries.

1062. Tabbert, Russell. "Parsing the Question 'Why Teach Grammar?'" *EJ* 73 (December 1984): 38–42.

Argues that few significant benefits result from teaching grammar and that reading and writing remain the center of language arts curriculum.

1063. Tarlinskaja, Marina. "Rhythm-Morphology-Syntax-Rhythm." *Style* 18 (Winter 1984): 1–26.

Argues that relations between rhythmical and grammatical qualities of English verse are reciprocal. Poets use different rhythms characteristic of different parts of speech to connect ideas.

1064. Templeton, Shane, and Patricia Thomas. "Performance and Reflection: Young Children's Concept of Word." *JEdR* 77 (January–February 1984): 139–146.

A study of tasks involving structural and significative features of words supports an interactive model of development, with language performance and metalinguistic knowledge working together.

1065. Tesdell, Lee S. "Brief Reports and Summaries: ESL Spelling Errors." *TESOLQ* 18 (June 1984): 333–334.

A study of advanced ESL learners speaking Arabic, Chinese, Malay, or Spanish indicates no need to adapt spelling instruction to language group.

1066. Tex, William Winkelman. "The Language of the News: A Comparative Semantic Analysis of the Language of Network Television and New York City Newspaper News Reports." *DAI* 45 (July 1984): 8A.

Uses the intensional characteristics defined by Korzybski to analyze the language of news reports on television and in newspapers on the same topics.

1067. Thomas, Gordon P. "Reading, Writing, and Mutual Knowledge." *DAI* 46 (October 1985): 961A.

Examines the views of Flower and Hayes and of Hirsch on writing and reading in relation to philosophical notions of shared knowledge of linguistic conventions.

1068. Tibbetts, Arn M. "Beware of Black Holes in the English Language." *ABCAB* 48 (March 1985): 1, 26–28.

Argues that "black holes," or troublesome abstractions, are a serious and pervasive problem in writing.

1069. Tichy, Paul. "Subjunctive Conditionals: Two Parameters *Vs.* Three." *PhS* 45 (March 1984): 147–179.

Explains how subjunctive conditionals are best interpreted by using a three-parameter theory proposed by Mill, Ramsey, and Chisholm.

1070. Ulrich, Eugene. "Double Entendre Headlines." *WWays* 17 (August 1984): 136–137.

Finds ambiguity in numerous headlines.

1071. Ulrich, Eugene. "Rhyme-Forced Proverbs." *WWays* 18 (August 1985): 165–166.

Attempts to make nonrhyming proverbs rhyme, at times changing their messages.

1072. Van Ostade, Ingrid Tieken-Boon. "'I will be drowned and no man shall save me': The Conventional Rules for *Shall* and *Will* in Eighteenth-Century English Grammars." *ES* 66 (April 1985): 123–142.

A study of 38 grammars from 1700 to 1798 finds that rules are consistent before Johnson but that his dictionary's rules are more complex. No developing pattern was found.

1073. Vanden Bergh, Bruce, Janay Collins, Myrna Schultz, and Keith Adler. "Sound Advice on Brand Names." *JQ* 61 (Winter 1984): 835–840.

Concludes that phonetic symbolism, especially words beginning with plosives, is significant in recalling and recognizing brands.

1074. Weinstein, Gail. "Literacy and Second Language Acquisition: Issues and Perspectives." *TESOLQ* 18 (September 1984): 471–484.

Reviews a study conducted at a Thai refugee camp, compares research in literacy and second-language acquisition, and suggests ethnography as a means to improve ESL teaching.

1075. Weixelbaum, Elia S. "Formal Language with Oracles." *DAI* 44 (June 1984): 3861B.

Studies the relativization of formal language and concludes that relativized regular languages derive from abstract families of language theory.

1076. Whaley, Charles Philip. "Determinants of Lexical and Semantic Decision Time." *DAI* 45 (November 1984): 1609B.

Explores the relative contribution of a large number of factors on the lexical access stage and the semantics association stage.

1077. Williams, Stephen Meredith. "Memory for Unilateral Speech." *Psychology* 22 (1985): 47–70.

Includes "four experiments [that] investigated the possibility of monoaural ear differences due to left hemisphere speech specialization beyond the phonological/perceptual stage."

1078. Wilson, George M. "Pronouns and Pronominal Description: A New Semantic Category." *PhS* 45 (January 1984): 1–30.

Argues that descriptions can exhibit "chief semantic" characteristics of pronouns.

1079. Wolpow, Edward R. "Jejuniana." *WWays* 17 (February 1984): 31–33.

Builds words from *jejune*. Lists obscure medical terms and notes that dictionaries leave out many words used often.

1080. Wolpow, Edward R. "Names on the Border." *WWays* 17 (May 1984): 86–87.

Examines cities' names that reflect their location on state or national borders. Suggests generic, specific, and international border categories.

1081. Wolpow, Edward R. "Webster's Fourth: A Review." *WWays* 18 (November 1985): 212–213.

Provides a hypothetical review of a 1990 edition of the dictionary, predicting some of the anticipated changes.

1082. Woods, William F. "The Cultural Tradition of Nineteenth-Century 'Traditional' Grammar Teaching." *RSQ* 15 (Winter–Spring 1985): 3–12.

Traces the teaching of grammar from Roman times to the nineteenth century and defines three standard "myths" about the beneficial effects of grammar instruction.

1083. Woolard, Kathryn Ann. "The Politics of Language and Ethnicity in Barcelona, Spain." *DAI* 44 (February 1984): 2513A.

A matched guise experiment examining the sociolinguistic basis for ethnic classification of speakers of Catalan and Castilian.

1084. Wright, Sandra. "A Description of the Variance between the Oral and Written Language Patterns of a Group of Black Community College Students." *DAI* 46 (November 1985): 1267A.

Concludes that nonstandard patterns of written language among black community college students "may not result from oral language interference."

1085. Wyckham, Robert C. "Students' Linguistic Skills and the Language of Television Advertising." *EQ* 17 (Spring 1984): 22–30.

A survey of 264 Canadian elementary school teachers reports that the language of television advertising influences students' ability to learn standard English usage.

1086. Yaden, David B., Jr. "Reading Research in Metalinguistic Awareness: Findings, Problems, and Classroom Applications." *VLang* 18 (Winter 1984): 5–47.

Concludes that, although children are largely unaware of the structure of both speech and print, experience with written language is the most efficient way to enhance metalinguistic growth.

1087. Yau, Margaret S. S., and Joe Belanger. "Syntactic Development in the Writing of EFL Students." *EQ* 18 (Summer 1985): 107–118.

Shows that Chinese students learning English broaden their use of syntactic options in much the same ways as native speakers do.

See also 150, 195, 237, 276, 303, 309, 374, 403, 407, 420, 429, 443, 517, 575, 622, 625, 690, 712, 745, 770, 776, 847, 1088, 1105, 1113, 1120, 1135, 1150, 1157, 1170, 1175, 1176, 1198, 1199, 1209, 1218, 1238, 1254, 1444, 1456, 1468, 1471, 1480, 1491, 1544, 1858, 1866, 1879, 2365, 2411, 2474, 2690, 2708, 2839, 2983, 3008, 3036, 3050, 3053, 3054, 3536, 3847

PSYCHOLOGY

1088. Acredolo, Linda P., and Susan W. Goodwyn. "Symbolic Gesturing in Language Development: A Case Study." *HD* 28 (January–February 1985): 40–49.

A case study of Kate between 12.5 and 17.5 months. Describes the development of gestures and its relationship to the early advent of language.

1089. Alfieri-Fenston, Gloria. "Writing: A Thumbprint of Self." *EngR* 35 (Fourth Quarter 1984): 10–13.

Anxiety research shows that students' attitudes toward writing are often assignment-related.

1090. Arca, Maria. "Strategies for Categorizing Change in Scientific Research and in Children's Thought." *HD* 27 (September–December 1984): 335–341.

Argues that interplay between discrete and continuous change is critical in our understanding scientific progress and in the child's understanding of states and changes.

1091. Balamore, Usha, and Robert H. Woznick. "Speech Action Coordination in Young Children." *DP* 20 (September 1984): 697–706.

Study supports Vygotsky's claim that meaningful concomitant vocalization facilitates the reorganization of unsuccessful action.

1092. Beatty, Michael J., and Steven K. Payne. "Is Construct Differentiation Loquacity? A Motivational Perspective." *HCR* 11 (Summer 1985): 605–612.

Two studies of undergraduate texts suggest that motivaton influences both loquacity and cognitive complexity as measured by the Role Category Questionnaire.

1093. Beatty, Michael J., and Steven K. Payne. "Listening Comprehension as a Function of Cognitive Complexity: A Research Note." *ComM* 51 (March 1984): 85–89.

Two studies test the assumption that comprehension is partly dependent upon an individual's level of cognitive complexity.

1094. Berk, Laura E., and Ruth A. Garvin. "Development of Private Speech among Low-Income Appalachian Children." *DP* 20 (March 1984): 271–286.

Supports Vygotsky: most private speech is cognitively self-guiding. Finds cultural and sex differences in rate but not in form of development.

1095. Bickhard, Mark H., Robert G. Cooper, and Patricia E. Mace. "Vestiges of Logical Positivism: Critiques of Stage Explanations." *HD* 28 (September–October 1985): 240–258.

Argues that attacks on the "stage" concept in Piagetian development derive from faulty assumptions grounded in logical positivism.

1096. Bizzell, Patricia. "William Perry and Liberal Education." *CE* 46 (September 1984): 447–454.

Discusses some of psychologist Perry's levels of development pertaining to college students, especially focusing on cultural influences.

1097. Boice, Robert. "Cognitive Components of Blocking." *WC* 2 (January 1985): 91–104.

Identifies seven cognitive components of blocking (listed in descending order of importance): work apprehension, procrastination, dysphoria, impatience, perfectionism, evaluation anxiety, and rules.

1098. Bonitatibus, Gary J., and John H. Flavell. "Effect of Presenting a Message in Written Form on Young Children's Ability to Evaluate Its Communication Adequacy." *DP* 21 (March 1985): 455–461.

First graders could evaluate the referential-communicative adequacy of two-word messages better if they saw them written out.

1099. Brainerd, C. J., and J. Kingma. "On the Independence of Short-Term Memory and Working Memory in Cognitive Development." *CPsy* 17 (April 1985): 210–247.

Nine experiments support the hypothesis that "short-term" memory and information processing do not overlap but develop independently of each other.

1100. Brown, Margery. "Do Confusing Information and Egocentric Instructions Influence Perception?" *PMS* 59 (August 1984): 15–20.

Although differences in instructions did not affect the performance of field-dependent or field-independent males, clear feedback enhanced performance. Deliberately confusing feedback was more disorienting to field-dependent students.

1101. Bullock, Mary. "Causal Reasoning and Developmental Change over the Preschool Years." *HD* 28 (July–August 1985): 169–191.

Preschoolers share some principles of causal reasoning with adults, but there are developmental changes in the conception and use of these principles.

1102. Carpenter, Carol. "Relationships between Two Distinct Personality Types and Their Composing Processes." *DAI* 45 (September 1984): 771A.

Results indicate that intuitive-perceptive types used an exploratory process, while sensing-judging types used a more structured, planned approach.

1103. Carrier, Carol, Verns Higson, Victor Klimoski, and Eric Peterson. "The Effects of Facilitative and Debilitative Achievement Anxiety on Notetaking." *JEdR* 77 (January–February 1984): 133–138.

In this study, debilitating anxiety was associated with poor performance. "Helpful" levels of anxiety, however, contributed to good performance.

1104. Carroll, John B., Lawrence Kohlberg, and Rheta DeVries. "Psychometric and Piagetian Intelligences: Toward Resolution of Controversy." *Intell* 8 (January–March 1984): 67–91.

Reexamines the problem of whether or not psychometric and Piagetian measurements gauge a similar course of development.

1105. Cavenaugh, John C., Deirdre A. Kramer, Jan D. Sinnott, J. Camp Cameron, and Robert P. Markley. "On Missing Links and Such: Interfaces between Cognitive Research and Everyday Problem Solving." *HD* 28 (May–June 1985): 146–168.

Discusses claims that relativistic and dialectical reasoning represent a post-formal-operational structure.

1106. Chapman, Michael, Jochen Brandtstädter, John A. Meacham, Harriet Nerlove Mischel, Ellen A. Skinner, James Youniss, and Paul B. Baltes. "Intentional Action as a Paradigm for Developmental Psychology: A Symposium." *HD* 27 (May–August 1984): 113–144.

A symposium of seven essays questioning "whether and to what extent action [theory] may constitute a useful paradigm for developmental psychology."

1107. Cheng, Patricia W., and Keith J. Holyoak. "Pragmatic Reasoning Schemas." *CPsy* 17 (October 1985): 391–416.

Everyday reasoning is guided by schematic structures that are "primarily the products of induction from recurring experience with classes of goal-related situations."

1108. Chi, Michelene T. H. "Changing Conception of Sources of Memory Development." *HD* 28 (January–February 1985): 50–56.

Critiques the two general trends in memory research: on strategies and on metamemory. Offers a third, knowledge, that rectifies some inconsistencies in the other two.

1109. Chinen, Allen B. "Modal Logic: A New Paradigm of Development and Late-Life Potential." *HD* 27 (January–February 1984): 42–56.

Argues that four "logical modalities" — necessity, possibility, universality, existential — govern successive stages in life. Optimal adult development includes awareness of these modes.

1110. Chipman, S. F., J. W. Segal, and R. Glaser, eds. *Thinking and Learning Skills.* Vol. 2: *Research and Open Questions.* Hillside, N.J.: Erlbaum, 1985. 640 pages

Thirty-two theoretical papers on knowledge acquisition, relations between language and problem-solving skills, whether or not logical thinking can be taught, child and adult thinking patterns, and socialization.

1111. Cravens, Hamilton. "The Wandering IQ: American Culture and Mental Testing." *HD* 28 (May–June 1985): 113–130.

Shows how one research movement on mental functioning was a product of cultural assumptions.

1112. Crosson, Bruce. "Subcortical Functions in Language: A Working Model." *BL* 25 (July 1985): 257–292.

Proposes a model of language production that involves cortical and subcortical structures. Argues that this theory is specific enough to generate testable hypotheses.

1113. Eagney, Peggy. "Language and Cognition: The Relation of Linguistic Ability to Performance of a Cognitive Task in Deaf Children." *DAI* 44 (January 1984): 2271B.

Attempts to use the range of skill among deaf children to show the relation of language to cognitive development.

1114. Eckensberger, Lutz H., John A. Meacham, Ernst E. Boesch, Hans Furth, Irving E. Sigel, James V. Wertsch, Benjamin Lee, and Adrienne E. Harris. "Action Theory, Control, and Motivation: A Symposium." *HD* 27 (May–August 1984): 163–210.

A symposium of six essays discussing action theory and its affective, social, communicative aspects. Includes a discussion by participants.

1115. Ede, Lisa S. "Is Rogerian Rhetoric Really Rogerian?" *RR* 3 (September 1984): 40–48.

Analyzes assumptions underlying Rogers's humanistic psychology. Concludes that the Rogerian rhetoric found in textbooks contradicts and distorts his principles.

1116. Einhorn, Hillel J., and Robin M. Hogarth. "Ambiguity and Uncertainty in Probabilistic Inference." *PsyR* 92 (October 1985): 433–461.

Proposes and begins to test a model for making decisions in ambiguous situations.

1117. Elifson, Joan M., and Katherine R. Stone. "Integrating Social, Moral, and Cognitive Developmental Theory: Implications of James Fowler's Epistemological Paradigm for Basic Writers." *JBW* 4 (Fall 1985): 24–37.

Examines Fowler's paradigm and explains its usefulness for integrating stage theory with composition research.

1118. Englert, Carol S., and Elfrieda H. Hiebert. "Children's Developing Awareness of Text Structures in Expository Materials." *JEdP* 76 (1984): 65–74.

Reports on the effects of four major expository text types on comprehension. Data support the notion that knowledge of discourse types underlies effective expository comprehension.

1119. Enright, Robert D., Christina C. Franklin, Daniel K. Lapsley, and Kurt Steuck. "Longitudinal and Cross-Cultural Validation of the Belief-Discrepancy Reasoning Construct." *DP* 20 (January 1984): 143–149.

A study of children and adolescents suggests that tolerance for "disagreeing others" develops in reasoning stages that are longitudinally and cross-culturally robust.

1120. Evans, Mary Ann. "Self-Initiated Speech Repairs: A Reflection on Communicative Monitoring in Young Children." *DP* 21 (March 1985): 365–371.

Older children more consistently repaired their speech, but even young children practiced considerable communicative monitoring.

1121. Fisher, Bernice. "Guilt and Shame in the Women's Movement: The Radical Ideal of Action and Its Meaning for Feminist Intellectuals." *FS* 10 (Summer 1984): 185–222.

Analyzes the discourse of the feminist movement as a negotiation of feelings toward criticism of the movement through which its members construct collective values.

1122. Fisk, William R. "Responses to 'Neutral' Pronoun Presentations and the Development of Sex-Biased Responding." *DP* 21 (March 1985): 481–485.

Children in this study did not respond to "he" as if it were gender neutral, whereas "they" and "s/he" elicited non-male-biased responses.

1123. Franenglass, Marni H., and Rafael M. Diaz. "Self-Regulating Functions of Children's Private Speech: A Critical Analysis of Vygotsky's Theory." *DP* 21 (March 1985): 357–364.

Suggests that experimental failures to observe private speech may be methodological. Supports Vygotsky's theories, finding children's private speech increasing with task failure.

1124. Frederiksen, Norman, Sybil Carlson, and William C. Ward. "The Place of Social Intelligence in a Taxonomy of Cognitive Abilities." *Intell* 8 (October–December 1984): 315–337.

Reports few significant relationships between cognitive and social variables. Initial question posed should be how the elements of two large taxonomic systems relate.

1125. Freedman-Stern, Renee, Hanna K. Ulatowska, Temple Baker, and Christine DeLacoste. "Disruption of Written Language in Aphasia: A Case Study." *BL* 22 (July 1984): 181–205.

Describes the discourse structure of an aphasic using narrative texts, letters, and expository texts. Results focus on coherence and cohesion.

1126. Freeman, Mark. "History, Narrative, and Life-Span Developmental Knowledge." *HD* 27 (January–February 1984): 1–19.

A comprehensive study of development must utilize narrative, dialectics, and hemeneutics to achieve a more complete sense of the "parameters of possiblity that cultures allow."

1127. Freeman, Mark. "Paul Ricoeur on Interpretation: The Model of the Text and the Idea of Development." *HD* 28 (November–December 1985): 295–312.

Examines the works of Ricoeur, arguing connections between the interpretation of text via metaphor and the development of individuals through self-understanding.

1128. Frese, Michael, and Judith Stewart. "Skill Learning as a Concept in Life-Span Developmental Psychology: An Action Theoretic Analysis." *HD* 27 (May–August 1984): 145–162.

Uses skill learning to understand life-span development, especially interrelations between task analysis and structures of action, opting for an interactive paradigm of development.

1129. Garnsey, Susan M., and Gary S. Dell. "Some Neurolinguistic Implications of Prearticulatory Editing in Production." *BL* 23 (September 1984): 64–73.

Posits that a prearticulatory editor "monitors planned output [both semantic and syntactic] for deviations from the speaker's intentions and repairs such deviations if found."

1130. Garvey, William D., Stephen D. Gottfredson, and James G. Simmons. "A Comparison of Two Major Scientific Information Exchange Processes in Psychology: 1962 and 1975." *AmP* 39 (January 1984): 11–21.

Using surveys taken in 1962 and 1975, discusses changes in communicating psychological research results, both orally and in journals.

1131. Gassaniga, Michael S. "The Social Brain." *PsyT* 19 (November 1985): 29–30, 32–34, 36, 38.

Theorizes that our brains are divided into independent units that often work apart from our conscious and verbal selves and lead to the creation of beliefs.

1132. Gati, Stamar, and Amos Tversky. "Weighting Common and Distinctive Features in Perceptual and Conceptual Judgments." *CPsy* 16 (July 1984): 341–370.

Results show that in verbal descriptions, common features are more salient than distinctive features, while with pictorial stimuli, distinctive features are more salient.

1133. Gernsbacher, Morton Ann. "Surface Information Loss in Comprehension." *CPsy* 17 (July 1985): 324–363.

Studies the loss of surface form during the comprehension of nonverbal stimuli and draws general conclusions about the differences between skilled and less-skilled comprehenders.

1134. Globerson, Tamar, Eliya Weinstein, and Ruth Sharabany. "Teasing out Cognitive Development from Cognitive Style: A Training Study." *DP* 21 (July 1985): 682–691.

Cognitive development and cognitive style are distinctively different dimensions. With training, field-dependent subjects performed as well as developmentally comparable field-independent subjects.

1135. Gordon, Alice M. "Adequacy of Responses Given by Low-Income and Middle-Income Kindergarten Children in Structured Adult-Child Conversations." *DP* 20 (September 1984): 880–892.

When day-care teachers modeled complex language, disadvantaged children were capable of high-quality language interactions.

1136. Gray, William M., and Lynne Hudson. "Formal Operations and the Imaginary Audience." *DP* 20 (July 1984): 584–594.

Measurement problems produced mixed results in this study of adolescent egocentrism, suggesting that the phenomenon is complex and differential.

1137. Greene, John O. "Speech Preparation Processes and Verbal Fluency." *HCR* 11 (Fall 1984): 61–84.

Three experiments suggest that speech fluency is facilitated by the preparation of a content-free, organized sequence in advance of actual production.

1138. Greenspan, Steven L., and Erwin M. Segal. "Reference and Comprehension: A Topic-Comment Analysis of Sentence-Picture Verification." *CPsy* 16 (October 1984): 556–606.

Concludes that the interpretation of a sentence depends on both anaphoric and exophoric factors. Studies the interrelationship of topic, subject, object, and prepositions.

1139. Gustafsson, Jan-Eric. "A Unifying Model for the Structure of Intellectual Abilities." *Intell* 8 (July–September 1984): 179–203.

Proposes a three-level model of the structure of cognitive abilities: the *g* factor at the top followed by two broad factors dealing with verbal and figural information.

1140. Haan, Norma. "Processes of Moral Development: Cognitive or Social Disequilibrium?" *DP* 21 (September 1985): 996–1006.

Social disequilibrium together with individual strategies of handling conflict predicted development; points toward an interactive experience of moral-social conflict as explaining moral development.

1141. Hardy-Brown, Karen, and Robert Plomin. "Infant Communicative Development: Evidence from Adoptive and Biological Families for Genetic and Environmental Influences on Rate Differences." *DP* 21 (March 1985): 378–385.

Parental general intelligence was moderately predictive of infant communicative development. Argues for genetic factors.

1142. Harris, Adrienne. "Desire in History: A Review of *The Structure of Freudian Thought*." *HD* 27 (January–February 1984): 20–30.

Uses Feffers' *The Structure of Freudian Thought* to analyze the issues of continuity and change as they relate to developmental theory.

1143. Haskins, Ethelbert W. "Black: Defiance, Sensationalism, and Disaster." *ETC* 41 (Winter 1984): 398–401.

Examines psychological dangers of using "black" to unify a racial group: the term neglects important differences, holds negative connotations, and perpetuates stereotypes.

1144. Hastak, Manoj. "Assessing the Role of Brand- and Advertisement-Related Cognitive Responses as Mediators of Communication Effects on Cognitive Structure." *DAI* 45 (December 1984): 1811A.

Consumer reactions to print advertisements substantiated the idea that different cognitive response types mediate advertising's effects on audience.

1145. Hattenhauer, Darryl. "Erikson on Freud on Irma: The Rhetoric of the Patriarchy." *RSQ* 14 (Winter–Spring 1984): 29–42.

Argues that Freud and Erikson, in their analysis of Freud's Irma dream, used a rhetoric of scientific progress to disguise their sexism.

1146. Haugh, Jane A. M. "Investigation of the Relationship between Children's Metacognitive Awareness about the Purpose of Reading and Writing." *DAI* 45 (August 1984): 476A.

Studies the effects of age, educational experience, and gender on metacognitive awareness among 50 second and fifth graders.

1147. Hawkins, J., R. D. Pea, J. Glick, and S. Scribner. "'Merds that Laugh Don't Like Mushrooms': Evidence for Deductive Reasoning by Preschoolers." *DP* 20 (July 1984): 584–594.

Under highly limited conditions, preschoolers could reason deductively and showed sensitivity to the task context. They could not fully use deductive reasoning where appropriate.

1148. Herman, Lewis M., Douglas G. Richards, and James P. Wolz. "Can Dolphins Understand Sentences? Notes from the Field: Tursiops Truncatus Teaches Us about Language Acquisition." *ST* 52 (October 1985): 20–25.

Concludes that dolphins are able to understand sentences expressed in the grammar of the artificial acoustic or gestural language taught to them.

1149. Hess, Thomas M. "Aging and Context Influences on Recognition Memory for Typical and Atypical Script Actions." *DP* 21 (September 1985): 1139–1151.

Age differences in prose memory appeared related to the extent that distinctive context information was encoded.

1150. Hill, Jane C., and Michael A. Arib. "Schemas, Computation, and Language Acquisition." *HD* 27 (September–December 1984): 282–296.

Studies, through a computer model of language development in the two-year-old, the relationship between Piaget's schema theory and language acquisition.

1151. Hirst, William, Joseph LeDoux, and Susanna Stein. "Constraints on the Processing of Indirect Speech Acts: Evidence from Aphasiology." *BL* 23 (September 1984): 26–33.

Relates the understanding of indirect speech acts to the general roles given to the two hemispheres of the brain.

1152. Hooper, Frank H., Judith O. Hooper, and Karen K. Colbert. "Personality and Memory Correlates of Intellectual Functioning in Adulthood: Piagetian and Psychometric Assessments." *HD* 28 (March–April 1985): 101–107.

A research report. Adults in three age groups functioned at the formal-operational level but showed structural modifications on the basis of age and individual factors.

1153. Hopkins, Richard L. "Education and the Right Hemisphere of the Brain: Thinking in Patterns for a Computer World." *JT* 19 (Summer 1984): 104–114.

Analyzes hemispheric research, stressing its tendency to overgeneralize. Emphasizes the increasing role of the right hemisphere in understanding current society.

1154. Kagan, Jerome. *The Nature of the Child.* New York: Basic Books, 1984. 309 pages

A developmental psychologist argues that early childhood experiences do not inexorably shape our lives, that moral development is based less on abstract reasoning than on feelings, and that the influence of parents is both less deterministic and more subtle than is commonly thought.

1155. Keller, Monika, and Siegfried Reuss. "An Action-Theoretical Reconstruction of the Development of Social-Cognitive Competence." *HD* 27 (May–August 1984): 211–220.

Social knowledge is increasingly constructed through negotiation, via discourse among equals, among mutually shared standards of moral acceptability and legitimacy.

1156. Kellerman, Kathy. "Memory Processes in Media Effects." *ComR* 12 (January 1985): 83–131.

Examines the nature of memory, issues of retention and recall of messages, and methods of promoting retention and recall.

1157. Kim, Kyung J. "Development of the Concept of Truth-Functional Negation." *DP* 21 (March 1985): 462–472.

Most children under five have trouble with negative sentences. They lack an explicit understanding of truth-functional negation as defined in logic.

1158. Kimura, Doreen. "Male Brain, Female Brain: The Hidden Differences." *PsyT* 19 (November 1985): 50–52, 54, 56–58.

Compares brain organization of men and women. Concludes that very little can be predicted about an individual's mental abilities based on sex.

1159. Kintsch, Walter, and James G. Greeno. "Understanding and Solving Word Arithmetic Problems." *PsyR* 92 (January 1985): 109–129.

Proposes a processing model that relates text comprehension to problem solving that children use for word problems. The model accounts for problem difficulty.

1160. Kipnis, David, and Stuart Schmidt. "The Language of Persuasion." *PsyT* 19 (April 1984): 40–42, 44–46.

Explores connections between choices of influence strategy (assertiveness, flattery, compromise) and objectives, power positions, and expectations or biases.

1161. Kitchener, Robert F. "Holistic Structuralism, Elementarism, and Piaget's Theory of 'Relationalism'." *HD* 28 (November–December 1985): 281–294.

Suggests that Piaget's structuralism is committed both to transactionalism and to additive composition laws.

1162. Kotovsky, K., John R. Hayes, and H. A. Simon. "Why Are Some Problems Hard? Evidence from Tower of Hanoi." *CPsy* 17 (April 1985): 248–294.

Analyzes the cognitive overload common in solving complex problems. Discusses the relevance of planning, training, practice, and drill.

1163. Kurfiss, Joanne. "Developmental Perspectives on Writing and Intellectual Growth in College." Paper presented at the CCCC Convention, New York, May 1984. ERIC ED 248 516 [20 pages]

Using the theories of Piaget, Kohlberg, and Perry, argues for a better match between the learner's level of development and instructional design.

1164. Labouvie-Vief, Gisela, and Renee Lawrence. "Object Knowledge, Personal Knowledge, and Processes of Equilibration in Adult Cognition." *HD* 28 (January–February 1985): 25–39.

Critiques Piaget's model of subject-object equilibrium and suggests extending his model to stress a more interpersonal dialogic basis for personal knowledge.

1165. Lanky, Edward, Cheryl R. Kaus, and Paul A. Roodin. "Life Experience and Mode of Coping: Relation to Moral Judgment in Adulthood." *DP* 20 (September 1984): 1159–1167.

Finds higher levels of moral reasoning in affirmative copers and discusses relationships between life experience and cognitive variables.

1166. Lesser, Ronnie, and Marilyn Paisner. "Magical Thinking in Formal Operational Adults." *HD* 28 (March–April 1985): 57–70.

Describes research showing that formal-operational logic and beliefs in "magical" causation can co-exist in adults. Suggests that affect is intertwined with cognition.

1167. Levi, Laurie S., and Anthony Grasha. "Motivational Processes and Personal Attributes of Writers: An Exploratory Study." Paper presented at the APA Convention, Anaheim, January 1983. ERIC ED 239 304 [10 pages]

Finds some characteristics of productive writers among faculty across the curriculum.

1168. Levine, Charles, Lawrence Kohlberg, and Alexandra Hewer. "The Current Formulation of Kohlberg's Theory and a Response to Critics." *HD* 28 (March–April 1985): 94–100.

Summarizes a monograph that clarifies meta-ethical assumptions behind Kohlberg's model of justice reasoning, modifies the model, and denies charges of sexual, cross-cultural, and ideological bias.

1169. Levy, Jerre. "Right Brain, Left Brain: Fact or Fiction." *PsyT* 19 (May 1985): 38–39, 42–44.

Surveys major theories and research, concluding that "normal people have. . .one gloriously differentiated brain, with each hemisphere contributing its specialized abilities."

1170. Longhorn, Ian. "The Semantics of Self-Removal." *ETC* 41 (Fall 1984): 299–301.

Explores psychological differences between using third- and first-person plural pronouns. Argues that third person creates ghost writers and apparent but nonexistent dichotomies.

1171. Lucariello, Joan, and Katharine Nelson. "Slot-Filler Categories as Memory Organizers for Young Children." *DP* 21 (March 1985): 272–282.

Supports the hypothesis that "scripts" provide a basis for categorical structures in semantic memory.

1172. MacLennon, Richard N., and Douglas N. Jackson. "Accuracy and Consistency in the Development of Social Perception." *DP* 21 (January 1985): 30–36.

Finds that inferential accuracy about the behavior of other persons, studied independent from language development, increased as a function of age.

1173. Mandl, Heinz, Nancy L. Stein, and Tom Trasbasso, eds. *Learning and Comprehension of Text.* Hillside, N.J.: Erlbaum, 1984. 480 pages

Fifteen papers by discourse theorists and educational psychologists on the cognitive processing of texts, the role of knowledge, schema theory, texts and the learning process, and the outcomes and implications of intervention research.

1174. Mandler, Jean. "Stories: The Function of Stories." Paper presented at the APA Convention, Anaheim, August 1983. ERIC ED 238 247 [36 pages]

Outlines the differences between story schema and story grammar. Based on research on how children and adults understand stories.

1175. Markman, Ellen M., and Jean E. Hutchinson. "Children's Sensitivity to Constraints on Word Meaning: Taxonomic *Vs.* Thematic Relations." *CPsy* 16 (January 1984): 1–27.

Discusses four studies to argue that "linguistic impact may [help] to shape the conceptual structure of a child in the direction of greater taxonomic organization."

1176. Mather, Patricia L., and Kathryn N. Black. "Hereditary and Environmental Influences on Preschool Twins' Language Skills." *DP* 20 (March 1984): 303–308.

Vocabulary comprehension was significantly influenced by heredity, whereas performance skills were influenced by family environment.

1177. McBride, Mary, and Thomas P. Mullen. "Looking for Our Little Brother." *ETC* 41 (Summer 1984): 148–151.

Emphasizes the need to monitor our internal censor, the metaphors we use to describe actions and our selves.

1178. McCleary, Carol Anne. "Semantic Organization and Classification in Aphasia." *DAI* 44 (April 1984): 3225B.

After testing anterior and posterior aphasics, finds that the disrupted semantic organization of posterior aphasics caused problems for them in classification.

1179. McCutchen, Deborah, and Charles A. Perfetti. *Coherence and Connectedness in the Development of Discourse Production.* Washington, D.C.: NIE, 1982. ERIC ED 233 336 [44 pages]

Describes developmental differences observed in children's writing. Proposes a model of computer simulation designed to account for aspects of coherence and connectedness.

1180. McGuiness, Diane. *Skool Daze: What Happens When Children Fail to Learn.* New York: Harper & Row, 1985. 288

Argues that teachers and psychologists are too quick to apply the "learning-disabled" label to children and often fail to recognize normal differences in brain function and development, especially gender-related differences. Describes and advocates remediation programs that focus on individual strengths and weaknesses.

1181. Motley, Michael T. "Slips of the Tongue." *SAm* 253 (September 1985): 116–127.

Explores why people make slips of the tongue and discusses techniques for inducing slips for the purposes of the study.

1182. Mounoud, Pierre. "A Point of View on Ontogeny." *HD* 27 (September–December 1984): 329–334.

Notes a contradicton between Piaget's use of "environment" in phylogeny and in ontogeny. Poses a more balanced view, one he calls systemic.

1183. Muehling, Darrel D. "The Moderating Effect of Message-Response Involvement on the Processing of Comparative and Noncomparative Advertising." *DAI* 46 (December 1985): 1690A.

Studies whether comparative advertisements are processed differently from noncomparative ads.

1184. Mumford, Michael, and William A. Owens. "Individuality in a Developmental Context: Some Empirical and Theoretical Considerations." *HD* 27 (March–April 1984): 84–108.

Because current developmental theory tends to support "interactionist" positions, human development must be studied from a dialectical perspective. "Type Models" may assist this approach.

1185. Murphy, Gregory L., and Douglas L. Medlin. "The Role of Theories in Conceptual Coherence." *PsyR* 92 (July 1985): 289–316.

Argues that theories and world knowledge inform a person's meaning for concepts. Seeks to add "conceptual coherence" to the growing interest in mental models.

1186. Nelson, Lin. "Promise Her Everything: The Nuclear Power Industry's Agenda for Women." *FS* 10 (Summer 1984): 291–314.

Analyzes attempts to promote nuclear power through public communications as a source of new equality and self-determination for women.

1187. Nelson-Le Gall, Sharon A. "Motive-Outcome Matching and Outcome Foreseeability: Effects of Attribution and Intentionality on Moral Judgments." *DP* 21 (March 1985): 332–337.

Young children's judgments were influenced by more than the consequences of an action. They could analyze others' goals and motives in certain situations.

1188. Nickerson, Jeff. "The Mind's Eye and the CRT Terminal: Towards a Diagrammatic Interface." *VLang* 19 (Summer 1985): 387–399.

Contrasts human beings and computers, focusing especially on the difference between the parallel processing of human beings and the sequential processing of current machines.

1189. Olson, Sheryl L., John E. Bates, and Kathryn Bayles. "Mother-Infant Interaction and the Development of Individual Differences in Children's Cognitive Competence." *DP* 20 (January 1984): 166–179.

Finds a significant link between parent-infant verbal interaction and children's developing cognitive competence. Socioeconomic status was a second predictor of later competence.

1190. Overton, Willis, James P. Byrne, and David P. O'Brien. "Developmental and Individual Differences in Conditional Reasoning: The Role of Contradiction Training and Cognitive Style." *DP* 21 (July 1985): 692–701.

Suggests that the prerequisite logical competence required for formal conditional reasoning appears at around the twelfth grade. Reflective style further enhanced performance.

1191. Parsons, John W. *A Study of Writing Behavior with Pre/Post Monitoring Using the Omnibus Personality Inventory, Derived from Erik Erickson's Theory of Personality.* Urbana, Ill.: ERIC/RCS and NCTE, 1982. ERIC ED 235 478 [45 pages]

Finds that freewriting improves the attitudes of high school students toward themselves and toward writing.

1192. Pellegrino, James W. "Anatomy of Analogy." *PsyT* 19 (October 1985): 48–54.

Explains the three general types of thought processes people use to solve analogy problems and their relation to research on information-processing theory.

1193. Petersen, Bruce T. "Conceptual Patterns in Industrial and Academic Discourse." *JTWC* 14 (1984): 95–107.

A study of writing samples from industry and the academic world concludes that technical writing operates at levels of abstraction beyond the reporting of information.

1194. Phelps, Louise Wetherbee. "Foundations for a Modern Psychology of Composition." *RR* 3 (September 1984): 30–37.

Focuses on "written language as a function of the human mind." Key concepts include the constructive power of the mind and the primacy of context.

1195. Pitta, Dennis Anthony. "An Experimental Investigation of the Relationships of Some Message and Receiver Characteristics on Communication Success." *DAI* 45 (January 1985): 2174A.

Studies the effect of message (implication or assertion), repetition, cognitive style, and audience involvement upon aided and unaided recall and verbatim, conceptual, and inferential belief.

1196. Powers, Stephen, and Richard L. Lopez, Jr. "Perceptual, Motor, and Verbal Skills of Monolingual and Bilingual Hispanic Children: A Discriminant Analysis." *PMS* 60 (June 1985): 999–1007.

Whereas monolingual preschoolers knew names of body parts better, bilingual children were superior in following complex directions and in perceptual-motor coordination.

1197. Pratt, Michael W., and Sandra MacKenzie-Keating. "Organizing Stories: Effects of Development and Task Difficulty on Referential Cohesion in Narrative." *DP* 21 (March 1985): 332–337.

Referential problems in children's and adults' narratives were influenced by task difficulty and cognitive style. Developmental factors, presentational mode, and familiarity/practice also influenced results.

1198. Pratt, Michael W., Jennifer McLaren, and Garth Wickens. "Rules as Tools: Generalization of Verbal Self-Regulative Communication by First-Grade Speakers." *DP* 20 (September 1984): 893–902.

Suggests that verbal self-regulation training can improve children's referential communication skills and can generalize this training.

1199. Premack, David. "Possible General Effects on Language Training on the Chimpanzee." *HD* 27 (September–December 1984): 268–281.

Language training allows a chimpanzee to solve problems—specifically conceptual ones—that were unsolvable previously. Such a change "resembles" that of a normal child.

1200. Pritchard, Ruie. "The Fear of the Blank Page." *NCET* 41 (Summer 1984): 16–18.

Reviews research on writing apprehension and presents the Daly and Shamo instrument for assessment.

1201. Pruchno, R. A., F. C. Blow, and M. A. Smyer. "Life Events and Interdependent Lives: Implications for Research and Intervention." *HD* 27 (January–February 1984): 31–41.

"Positing multiple effects of life events will lead ...to a more thorough understanding of events themselves [and] will ultimately help to explain developmental differences."

1202. Reed, Michael W. "Cognition and Writing Research: How Applicable Is It to Instruction." *VEB* 35 (Spring 1985): 94–99.

Reviews research on cognitive processes, especially human memory, to see how applicable it might be to writing instruction.

1203. Reid, Barbara V. "An Anthropological Reinterpretation of Kohlberg's Stages of Moral Development." *HD* 27 (March–April 1984): 57–64.

Uses a "grid/group" theory of environmental constraints and group allegiances to explain movement through Kohlberg's moral stages.

1204. Reigstad, Thomas J. "Perspectives on Anxiety and the Basic Writer: Research, Evaluation, and Instruction." *JBW* 4 (Spring 1985): 68–77.

Summarizes current literature on writing apprehension. Describes a SUNY-Buffalo program for dealing with highly apprehensive writers.

1205. Reinke, Barbara J., Abbie M. Ellicott, Rochelle L. Harris, and Emily Hancock. "Timing of Psychosocial Changes in Women's Life." *HD* 28 (September–October 1985): 259–280.

A symposium of four papers "to investigate regularities in timing of psychosocial experiences among [adult middle-class] women."

1206. Reiser, Brian J., John B. Black, and Robert P. Abelson. "Knowledge Structures in the Organization and Retrieval of Autobiographical Memories." *CPsy* 17 (January 1985): 89–137.

Supports the superiority of activities over general actions as effective cues for retrieving autobiographical memories. Argues against cues that are either too general or too specific.

1207. Rentel, Victor M., and Martha L. King. *A Longitudinal Study of Coherence in Children's Written Narratives, 31 March 1981–31 March 1982.* Washington, D.C.: NIE, 1983. ERIC ED 237 989 [70 pages]

Describes a developmental learning progression of cohesive choices made by 36 grade school children sampled every four months over a period of four years.

1208. Rest, James R., and Stephen J. Thoma. "Relation of Moral Judgment Development to Formal Education." *DP* 21 (July 1985): 709–714.

On measures of moral judgment and thinking, the high-education group showed increasing gains over the low-education group, years in college adding significantly to the predictability of moral judgment in young adulthood. Complements other studies relating formal education to moral judgment.

1209. Rice, Mabel. "A Cognition Account of Differences between Children's Comprehension and Production of Language." *WJSC* 48 (Spring 1984): 145–154.

Addresses psychological differences between children's linguistic performances and their retrieval mechanisms and underlying cognitions.

1210. Robinson, Ann, and John F. Feldhusen. "Don't Leave Them Alone: Effects of Probing on Gifted Children's Imaginative Explanations." *JEdG* 7 (Spring 1984): 156–163.

"Probing" questions about a puzzling reading passage produced higher-level thinking in both gifted and nongifted sixth-grade students.

1211. Robinson, E. J., and S. J. Whittaker. "Children's Responses to Ambiguous Messages and Their Understanding of Ambiguity." *DP* 21 (March 1985): 446–454.

When young children were not free to point at potential referents, they were less inclined to make a single interpretation of an ambiguous message.

1212. Roe, Kiki V., Antonia Divas, Antigone Karagellis, and Arnold Roe. "Sex Differences in Vocal Interaction with Mother and Stranger in Greek Infants: Some Cognitive Implications." *DP* 21 (March 1985): 372–377.

Suggests that early differences in vocal-interactional patterns and cognitive processing may be attributable to differences in parental behavior toward male/female children.

1213. Rowe, H. A. H. *Problem Solving and Intelligence*. Hillside, N.J.: Lawrence Erlbaum, 1984. 314 pages

Investigates the structural components of the problem-solving process, develops a classification of problem-solving strategies, and discusses individual and group differences.

1214. Rubin, David C. "The Subtle Deceiver: Recalling Our Past." *PsyT* 19 (September 1985): 38–39, 42–46.

Discusses autobiographical memory, the sources of vivid memories, and retrieval strategies people use to access memory.

1215. Runco, Mark A. "Reliability and Convergent Validity of Ideational Flexibility as a Function of Academic Achievement." *PMS* 61 (December 1985): 1075–1081.

Ideational flexibility and fluency and measured IQ correlated significantly with academic achievement, especially among students in the gifted quartile.

1216. Runco, Mark A. "Teachers' Judgments of Creativity and Social Validation of Divergent Thinking Tests." *PMS* 59 (December 1984): 711–717.

Teachers' evaluations of "creative" students correlated with measured IQ and scores on Wallach and Kogan divergent thinking tests.

1217. Russell, James. "Should I Believe You, or What You Say? Children's Belief of Children's Statements." *DP* 20 (March 1984): 261–270.

Older children made complex inferences about messages in light of their speakers, while younger children did not assess statements in terms of speakers' intentions.

1218. Schadler, Margaret, and Daniel O'Connell. "Temporal Analyses of Children's Comprehension during Oral Reading." *JPsyR* 13 (1984): 259–273.

Concludes that temporal measures are highly sensitive to comprehension processes and that children comprehend stories as they read and compare story content with what they know about the world.

1219. Schooler, Carmi. "Psychological Effects of Complex Environments during the Life Span: A Review and Theory." *Intell* 8 (October–December 1984): 259–281.

"Provides evidence [in both sexes] that environmental complexity is related to more effective cognitive functioning across all stages of the life span."

1220. Schumacher, Gary M., George R. Klare, and Frank Cronin. "Cognitive Processes during Pauses in Writing." Paper presented at the National Reading Conference, Clearwater Beach, Fla., December 1982. ERIC ED 236 624 [18 pages]

Finds that longer pauses by freshmen and a greater number of cognitive activities by upperclassmen reflect differences in degrees of skill and the quality of writing.

1221. Segal, J. W., S. F. Chipman, and R. Glaser, eds. *Thinking and Learning Skills*. Vol. 1: *Relating Instruction to Research*. Hillside, N.J.: Erlbaum, 1985. 568 pages

Twenty-two papers on teaching thinking skills, intervention research, cognitive strategies and text structures, developing reading and thinking skills in content areas, and problem-solving skills.

1222. Sevcik, Ann. "Thinking about Names." *ETC* 41 (Winter 1984): 387–388.

Argues that changing the names we use changes our perceptions and behavior. Uses change from "student" to "learner" to illustrate.

1223. Shanahan, T. "Nature of the Reading-Writing Relationship: An Exploratory Multivariate Analysis." *JEdP* 76 (1984): 466–477.

When multiple reading and writing measures were administered to 256 second graders and 251 fifth graders, canonical correlational analysis demonstrated that reading and writing were significantly related.

1224. Shankweiler, Donald, Suzanne T. Smith, and Virginia A. Mann. "Repetition and Comprehension of Spoken Sentences by Reading-Disabled Children." *BL* 23 (November 1984): 241–257.

Finds that limits on working memory kept poor readers from recalling certain sentences and that some indications of a deficiency in comprehension ability also existed.

1225. Shapiro, Nancy S. "Rhetorical Maturity and Perry's Scheme of Cognitive Complexity." Paper presented at the CCCC Convention, Minneapolis, March 1985. ERIC ED 255 935 [29 pages]

Tests 70 college students on three measures, finding that the cognitive complexity scale has a significant relationship to both writing competence and audience awareness.

1226. Shattuck, Roger. "Words and Images: Thinking and Translation." *Daedalus* 114 (Fall 1985): 201–214.

Reviews literature on conceptualization preceding language to affirm that thinking is possible without arbitrary signs. Each medium requires "translation" to language.

1227. Shock, Diane H. "The Writing Process: Effects of Life-Span Development on Imaging." *DAI* 45 (December 1984): 1672A.

Finds that, although life-span development seemed to influence the subject matter of images, it appeared to have little effect on writing approaches and styles.

1228. Shultz, Thomas R., and Diane Wells. "Judging the Intentionality of Action-Outcomes." *DP* 21 (January 1985): 83–89.

Young children could assess intentionality by matching information on the action's state against information regarding outcome. Only older children used objective rules consistently.

1229. Siegel, Alexander W. "Martha Muchow: Anticipations of Current Issues in Developmental Psychology." *HD* 28 (July–August 1985): 217–224.

Sees Muchow's work as anticipating the current interest in contextualism in both developmental psychology and environmental cognition.

1230. Sigman, Marion, and Judy A. Ungerer. "Cognitive and Language Skills in Autistic, Mentally Retarded, and Normal Children." *DP* 20 (March 1984): 293–302.

Deficits in symbolic/imitative abilities, not in sensorimotor skills, are linked to impaired language development in autistic children. Impaired social development is also considered.

1231. Smetana, Judith G. "Children's Impressions of Moral and Conventional Transgressors." *DP* 21 (July 1985): 715–724.

Pre-adolescent children inferred personality characteristics from information regarding behavior. They constructed qualitatively different psychological impressions of moral and conventional transgressors.

1232. Smith, Lydia A. H. "The Function of Language for the Young Child: A Report on Research and Experiences in England, 1972–1982." *JEd* 166 (1984): 273–290.

Discusses the work of Susan and Nathan Isaacs, concluding that interaction with adults helps children mature.

1233. Snarey, John R., Joseph Reimer, and Lawrence Kohlberg. "Develoment of Social Moral Reasoning among Kibbutz Adolescents: A Longitudinal Cross-Culture Study." *DP* 21 (January 1985): 3–17.

Supports the validity of Kohlberg's structural-developmental understanding of moral judgment, finding no sex differences and fewer cultural differences than expected.

1234. Sonderegger, Theo B., ed. *Nebraska Symposium on Motivation, 1984: Psychology and Gender.* Nebraska Symposium on Motivation. Lincoln, Neb.: University of Nebraska Press, 1985. 326 pages

A collection of eight essays, two of which discuss gender differences in cognitive and effective development. One essay discusses the different ways males and females value math and English. Another suggests that social roles based on gender may change as strength becomes less important and language skills more important.

1235. Sonnenschein, Susan. "Feedback from a Listener Affects Children's Referential Communication Skills." *DP* 20 (March 1984): 287–292.

Young children learn to assess message adequacy by watching listeners flounder with inadequate messages, but they do not improve their own skills without specific feedback.

1236. Stafford, Juliene Lanette. "Skilled Problem-Solving Ability and the Effects of Practice in Young and Elderly Adults." *DAI* 44 (March 1984): 2917B.

Studies how age differences relate to problem-solving abilities and concludes that both young and old people approach novel problems similarly.

1237. Standiford, Sally N. "Metacomprehension." *ArEB* 27 (Winter 1985): 25–28.

Explains how teachers can help students reflect on their own activities.

1238. Terrace, H. S. "In the Beginning Was the 'Name.'" *AmP* 40 (September 1985): 1011–1028.

Discusses the importance of referential naming ability on the language acquisition, vocabulary, and syntax of apes and children. Includes extensive bibliography.

1239. Tietjen, Anne Marie, and Lawrence Walker, Jr. "Moral Reasoning and Leadership among Men in a Papua New Guinea Society." *DP* 21 (November 1985): 982–992.

Suggests that, in this non-Western society, morality is differently defined than in Western societies. Necessitates expansion of Kohlbergian scoring materials.

1240. Ulvund, Stein Erik. "Predictive Validity of Assessments of Early Cognitive Competence in Light of Some Current Issues in Developmental Psychology." *HD* 27 (March–April 1984): 76–83.

Suggests that predictions of infants' later intellectual development should take into account individual and environmental variables.

1241. Van der Veer, R., and M. H. van Ijzendoorn. "Vygotsky's Theory of the Higher Psychological Processes: Some Criticisms." *HD* 28 (January–February 1985): 1–9.

Criticizes Vygotsky's dichotomizing lower and higher psychological processes. Culture influences these processes. Thus, they are not as "natural" or "hereditary" as previously argued.

1242. Vernon, Philip A., Sue Nador, and Lida Kantor. "Group Differences in Intelligence and Speed of Information Processing." *Intell* 9 (April–June 1985): 137–148.

"Generally, the results support the hypothesis that speed of processing is an important factor underlying intelligence," though "number of puzzling findings" remain.

1243. Vernon, Philip A., Sue Nador, and Lida Kantor. "Reaction Times and Speed of Processing: Their Relationship to Timed and Untimed Measures of Intelligence." *Intell* 9 (October–December 1985): 357–374.

After affirming the hypothesis, argues that more intelligent subjects use increased speeds of processing to retrieve information faster, answer questions more quickly, and prevent overburdening of short-term memory's capacity.

1244. Walker, Lawrence J., Brian de Vries, and Sandra L. Bichard. "The Hierarchical Nature of Stages of Moral Development." *DP* 20 (September 1984): 960–966.

Supports the notion of invariant hierarchical stages of moral development, showing that they are not dependent on linguistic variables.

1245. Wallesch, Claus-W., Leif Henriksen, Hans-H. Kornhuber, and Olaf B. Paulson. "Observations on Regional Blood Flow in Cortical and Subcortical Structures during Language Production in Normal Man." *BL* 25 (July 1985): 224–233.

Finds increased brain activity during language production in both left hemispheric and selected bilateral regions of the brain.

1246. Walter, Katya M. "Writing in Three Disciplines Correlated with Jungian Styles." *DAI* 46 (August 1985): 414A.

Concludes that upper-division students in English, journalism, and business communications use different cognitive styles.

1247. Waltz, Alfred Jacob. "The Influence of the Interaction of Cognitive Style, Information Presentation Style, and Problem Type on Problem Comprehension and Decision Effectiveness." *DAI* 46 (August 1985): 464A.

Provides a model of cognitive style based on psychological theory and relevant to a managerial environment.

1248. Wapner, Seymour. "Martha Muchow and Organismic and Developmental Theory." *HD* 28 (July–August 1985): 209–213.

Considers a German psychologist's observations of urban children. Integrates developmental and psychological approaches to the studying of children's knowledge of their environment.

1249. Warren, David J. "Zen in the Art of Dissertation Writing: A Phenomenological Study of Self-Discovery through the Dissertation Process." *DAI* 46 (July 1985): 292B.

Revealed that, although few students seek self-discovery through the writing of a dissertation, most find it.

1250. Weiner, Bernard, and Stephen Handel. "A Cognition-Emotion-Action Sequence: Anticipated Emotional Consequences of Causal Attributions and Reported Communication Strategy." *DP* 21 (January 1985): 102–107.

Finds developmental changes in communication strategies used in socially delicate situations but age constancy in understanding that situation.

1251. Wiggers, Michiel, and Cornelis F. M. van Fiesout. "Development of Recognition of Emotions: Children's Reliance on Situational and Facial Cues." *DP* 21 (March 1985): 332–337.

Finds evidence for a clear developmental trend from centration to de-centration in recognizing emotions according to types of cues.

1252. Yap, Johnny N. K., and R. De V. Peters. "An Evaluation of Two Hypotheses Concerning the Dynamics of Cognitive Impulsivity: Anxiety-over-Errors or Anxiety-over-Competence?" *DP* 21 (September 1985): 1055–1064.

Reflective children were more motivated to avoid errors in their performance than were impulsive children, who were anxious about competence.

1253. Yore, Larry D., and Lloyd O. Ollila. "Cognitive Development, Sex, and Abstractness in Grade-One Word Recognition." *JEdR* 78 (March–April 1985): 242–247.

Students with high cognitive development recognized more words than those with lower development; females, more than males.

1254. Zecker, Steven, M. Tanenhaus, Alan Glaros, and R. Whitman. "Subvocal Motor Activity and Contextual Processing." *JPsyR* 13 (1984): 177–193.

Minimization of subvocal motor activity negatively affected the subjects' contextual processing ability during listening tasks; researchers conclude that subvocal activity is important in establishing context.

1255. Zelinski, Elizabeth M., Michael J. Gilewski, and Leah L. Light. "Adult Age Differences in Memory for Prose: The Question of Sensitivity to Passage Structure." *DP* 20 (November 1984): 1181–1192.

Suggests that the old are as sensitive to passage structure as the young, although they remember less of what they read.

See also 38, 63, 98, 121, 160, 175, 178, 195, 205, 262, 279, 330, 331, 398, 428, 429, 442, 544, 547, 577, 608, 619, 640, 754, 789, 795, 822, 824, 838, 922, 966, 996, 1007, 1032, 1051, 1064, 1256, 1282, 1293, 1297, 1299, 1356, 1380, 1413, 1426, 1444, 1451, 1815, 1869, 1872, 2416, 2489, 2631, 2653, 3687, 3728

EDUCATION

1256. Alesandri, Kathryn Lutz, Janice J. Langstaff, and C. Merlin. "Visual-Verbal and Analytic-Holistic Strategies, Abilities, and Styles." *JEdR* 77 (January–February 1984): 139–146.

Finds that analytic processing habits may facilitate learning but that study strategies are most effective when they complement the individual's style.

1257. Alpert, Bracha R. "The Use of Writing in Instruction: Context and Consequences." *DAI* 46 (October 1985): 914A.

Investigates different uses of writing for subject matter learning, students' attitudes toward writing, composing processes, and teacher-student interactions.

1258. Andrews, John D. W. "Discovery and Expository Learning Compared: Their Effects on Independent and Dependent Students." *JEdR* 78 (November–December 1984): 80–89.

Both dependent and independent learners benefitted most from a discovery-learning approach.

1259. Bennett, Robert A. "Academic Learning Time, Mastery Learning, and All That..." *SLATE* 9 (May 1984).

Discusses academic learning time and mastery learning, evaluating their influence on test scores, classroom time, growth in English, and writing.

1260. Boomer, Garth. "English Teaching: Art and Science." Paper presented at the NCTE Convention, Detroit, November 1984. ERIC ED 257 058 [28 pages]

Describes the various roles enacted by English teachers.

1261. Boyer, Ernest L., and Carnegie Foundation for the Advancement of Learning. *College: A Carnegie Foundation Report on the Undergraduate Experience in America.* New York: Harper & Row, 1985. 368 pages

Examines the undergraduate experience, including the transition from secondary school to college, instructional resources and change, the preparation college offers for work and citizenship, and ways to evaluate colleges.

1262. Bryant, Coralie. "Teaching Students to Read Poetry Independently: An Experiment in Bringing Together Research and the Teacher." *EQ* 17 (Winter 1984): 48–57.

Demonstrates that, when teacher and students become involved in classroom research, student-centered learning results.

1263. Burns, Gerald Thomas. "From the 'English School' towards 'English': Secondary Vernacular Study and the Origins of Modern American Education." *DAI* 46 (September 1985): 733A.

Traces the evolution of English as a secondary school subject.

1264. Cervero, Ronald M. "Is a Common Definition of Literacy Possible?" *AdEd* 36 (Fall 1985): 50–54.

Reviews current understandings of adult literacy, argues that a common definition is not feasible, but nonetheless examines the need for a common definition.

1265. Clarke, Robert, T. Gerrity, R. Laverdiere, and B. Johns. "Age as a Factor in Teacher Job Satisfaction." *Psychology* 22 (1985): 19–23.

Concludes that a positive linear relationship exists between teacher age and overall satisfaction with work and co-workers.

1266. Corbett, Stephen S., and William Flint Smith. "Identifying Student Learning Styles: Proceed with Caution!" *MLJ* 68 (Autumn 1984): 212–221.

Finds that the Edmonds Learning Style Identification Exercise failed to predict learning styles for groups of students, although it did predict accurately individual preferences.

1267. Curtis, W. Scott, and Edward T. Donlon. "Ten-Year Follow-Up Study of Deaf-Blind Children." *ExC* 50 (February 1984): 449–455.

Examines the communication, adjustment, and learning abilities of deaf-blind students who had begun special programs 10 years earlier (1970).

1268. Deshler, Donald D., Jean B. Schumaker, and B. Keith Lenz. "Academic and Cognitive Interventions for LD Adolescents: Part I." *JLD* 17 (February 1984): 108–117.

Describes a study that taught seven learning-disabled adolescents a number of written-language learning strategies.

1269. Deshler, Donald D., Jean B. Schumaker, and B. Keith Lenz. "Academic and Cognitive Interventions for LD Adolescents: Part II." *JLD* 17 (March 1984): 170–179.

Describes a study that used "cooperative planning efforts between [learning disabled] and regular class teachers to facilitate" students' transferring writing strategies to regular class settings.

1270. DiStefano, Philip, and Jo Ellen Killion. "Assessing Writing Skills through a Process Approach." *EEd* 16 (December 1984): 203–208.

Finds that, when teachers attended an in-service session describing process-model approaches to writing instruction, their students' writing improved.

1271. Doty, Ralph. "Chrysippus' Theory of Education." *JT* 20 (Summer 1985): 70–75.

Analyzes the stoic Chrysippus' theory of education, especially his emphasis on proper usage as a means of identifying good instruction and good teachers.

1272. Facione, Peter A. "Toward a Theory of Critical Thinking." *LEd* 70 (Fall 1984): 253–261.

Recommends that research be undertaken to structure a systematic and comprehensive method of teaching critical thinking at all levels.

1273. Fitzgerald, Jill, Dixie Lee Spiegel, and Tamsen Banks Webb. "Development of Children's Knowledge of Story Structure and Content." *JEdR* 79 (November–December 1985): 101–108.

Over grades four through six, children acquired greater knowledge about structural complexity in stories but evidenced little growth in knowledge of content.

1274. Gaines, Bette C. "An Analysis of the Relationship between Teaching Behaviors and Student Achievement in Learning to Write Essays about Poetry." *DAI* 45 (September 1984): 772A.

Studies interactions among institutional and environmental factors and their effects on student learning.

1275. Gee, James Paul. "Narrativization of Experience in the Oral Style." *JEd* 167 (1985): 9–35.

A stylistic analysis of a narrative produced in the oral mode by a black second grader.

1276. Graves, Donald H. *A Researcher Learns to Write*. Portsmouth, N.H.: Heinemann, 1984. 208 pages

A collection of Graves's work since the mid-1970s. Introductions to each article discuss the author's own development as a writer. Includes many pieces that were previously unpublished, inaccessible, or written specifically for this volume.

1277. Harste, Jerome, Virginia A. Woodward, and Carolyn L. Burke. *Language Stories and Literacy Lessons*. Portsmouth, N.H.: Heinemann, 1984. 252 pages

A study of preschool literacy learning, revealing children's considerable mastery of oral and written language prior to formal instruction. Argues for a new language arts curriculum based upon the child's natural facility to deal with the complexities of language.

1278. Hoetker, James, and Tom Albritton. "Teacher Perceptions of the Effects of the Writing Skills Enhancement Program: A Report of a Survey." *FlaEJ* 21 (Fall 1985): 2–5.

Summarizes 47 responses to a questionnaire about teachers' attitudes toward a statewide rule that limits writing class size but prescribes weekly writing assignments.

1279. Hogan, Michael Phinney. "Writing as Punishment." *EJ* 74 (September 1985): 40–42.

Survey results indicate that most teachers disapprove of punitive writing assignments.

1280. Jackson, Brian. "The Teaching of Defined Concepts: A Test of Gagne and Brigg's Model of Instructional Design." *JEdR* 78 (March–April 1985): 224–227.

Suggests that results about the superiority of discovery-learning methods are inconclusive.

1281. Kearney, Patricia, Timothy G. Plax, and Nancy J. Wendt-Wasco. "Teacher Immediacy for Affective Learning in Divergent College Classes." *ComQ* 33 (Winter 1985): 61–74.

Studies teacher communication behaviors as potential indicators of student affective learning. Focuses on product- or task-oriented *versus* people-oriented content.

1282. Kiewra, Kenneth A. "Investigating Notetaking and Review: A Depth of Processing Alternative." *EDPsy* 20 (Winter 1985): 23–32.

Concludes that studies of notetaking should manipulate levels of notetaking and/or review and should examine data for levels of learning outcomes.

1283. Knight, John H. "The Question of Quality: A Little Help from Our Friends." *IIEB* 71 (Spring 1984): 49–52.

Examines the results of a seven-year experiment with a planned program of television viewing. Provides suggestions for teachers and parents.

1284. Lane, Harlan. *When the Mind Hears: A History of the Deaf*. New York: Random House, 1984. 608 pages

Told from the point of view of the deaf. Traces the history of attempts to educate the deaf with sign language and the reactions against such attempts by users of oral language.

1285. Lazerson, Marvin, Judith Black McLaughlin, and Bruce McPhearson. "Learning and Citizenship: Aspirations for American Education." *Daedalus* 113 (Fall 1984): 59–74.

Relates complex critical thinking to contemporary definitions of literacy for citizenship.

1286. Maher, Frances. "Pedagogies for the Gender-Balanced Classroom." *JT* 20 (Fall 1985): 48–64.

Discusses gender-balanced, interactive pedagogy and regards writing assignments as an "important way" to build on personal experiences.

1287. McFarland, James L. "The Role of Speech in Self-Development, Self-Concept, and Decentration." *ComEd* 33 (July 1984): 231–236.

Reviews research that argues that speech is primary and enables individuals to move from egocentrism to selflessness, which leads to self-actualization.

1288. North, Stephen M. "Designing a Case Study Method for Tutorials: A Prelude to Research." *RR* 4 (September 1985): 88–99.

Analyzes the theoretical and practical assumptions underlying case studies and favors "the participant-observer version."

1289. Oglesby, Kent. "What Is the Meaning of 'Liberal' in a Liberal Education?" *Statement* 20 (February 1985): 45–50.

Argues that a liberal education stimulates students to learn by reasoning their way to discovery. Includes a bibliography on liberal education.

1290. Plante, Patricia R. "Of Course, Johnny Can't Read." *LEd* 71 (Summer 1985): 159–162.

Two assumptions about education account for students' inability to read, write, or speak effectively: that one can learn without self-discipline and that formal structures or books are unnecessary.

1291. Platt, Nancy G. *The Context for Writing: A Descriptive Study of One Family-Grouped Informal First- and Second-Grade Classroom.* Urbana, Ill.: ERIC/RCS and NCTE, 1982. ERIC ED 235 480 [34 pages]

A study based on participant observation shows children creating their own culture with their teacher.

1292. Ravitch, Diane. *The Schools We Deserve: Reflections on the Educational Crisis of Our Time.* New York: Basic Books, 1984. 300 pages

A collection of essays on a variety of educational issues, including the use and misuse of tests, the place of the humanities in the curriculum, desegregation, bilingual education, the debate about educational quality, and the relationship of the schools and society.

1293. Ricketts, Jeffrey Neil. "The Influence of Cognitive Learning Style on Achievement in Linguistics." *DAI* 44 (May 1984): 3505A.

Analyzes the concept, "cognitive learning style," and its role when included in a general model of educational achievement.

1294. Robinson, Susan F. "Coherence in Student Writing." *DAI* 45 (December 1984): 1671A.

Finds developmental differences in the skill with which students at different age and ability levels connected ideas across sentence boundaries.

1295. Saldiver, Rhoda Gail Hill. "The Influence of the National Council of Teachers of English on the Treatment of Blacks and Black Educational Issues as Reflected in NCTE Publications." *DAI* 46 (September 1985): 805A.

Analyzes the treatment of blacks as they are presented in the major publications of the National Council of Teachers of English from 1911 to 1983.

1296. Savitz, Fred R., and Gwendolyn Anthony. "Creativity: A Missing Stimulus to Learning among the Gifted/Talented." *Psychology* 21 (1984): 15–18.

Discusses the need to develop curricula and environments that will increase creativity among gifted and talented students.

1297. Scardamalia, Marlene, Carl Bereiter, and Rosanne Steinbach. "Teachability of Reflective Processes in Written Composition." *CSc* 8 (April–June 1984): 173–190.

Finds that sixth graders improved at reflecting on individual ideas after instruction in thinking aloud, self-questioning, and synthesizing conflicting ideas.

1298. Schlatter, Franklin D. *SLATE* 10 (Summer 1985).

Reprints Dusel's report on teaching load, published originally in the *Illinois English Bulletin* 43 (October 1955).

1299. Speigle, Joan E., and Lyn Schaefer. "Longitudinal Evaluation of the Effects of Two Compensatory Preschool Programs on Fourth-through Sixth-Grade Students." *DP* 21 (July 1985): 702–708.

The Learning to Learn program, a cognitive developmental approach, including the teaching of problem-solving strategies, was more effective than Head Start.

1300. Spurlin, Joni E., Donald F. Dansereau, Celia O. Larson, and Larry W. Brooks. "Cooperative Learning Strategies in Processing Descriptive Text: Effect of Role and Activity Level on Learner." *CI* 1 (1984): 451–463.

Analyzes the impact of specific roles and activities for each member of a dyad in cooperative learning.

1301. Stevenson, Harold W., Shin-ying Lee, James Stigler, G. William Lucker, Chen-chin Hsu, and Seiro Kitamura. "Family Variables and Reading: A Study of Mothers of Poor and Average Readers in Japan, Taiwan, and the United States." *JLD* 17 (March 1984): 150–156.

Finds that the mothers of poor readers may hinder children's progress by overestimating their children's abilities, underestimating their own possible influence, and failing to help their children.

1302. Warnock, John, and Sue Holt. "Gifted and Talented Education." *SLATE* 10 (May 1985).

Surveys issues involved in identifying gifted students and designing curriculum. Lists strategies for action and 20 references.

1303. Watson, Ken. "Recent Australian Research in the Teaching of English." *EQ* 18 (Fall 1985): 44–55.

Reviews recent Australian research on spelling, reading, assessment, and the use of computers to teach English.

1304. Wiener, Harvey S. "Multicultural Literacy for Faculty: Accommodating Nonnative Speakers of English in Content Courses." *RR* 4 (September 1985): 100–107.

Extends Hirsch's "cultural literacy" to faculty, suggesting a need for greater awareness of the varied heritages students bring to class.

1305. Wolfe, Denny. "Opting for 'Newthink': Interdisciplinary English in the Decades Ahead." *EJ* 73 (October 1984): 28–31.

Argues for a holistic and humanistic restructuring of education to achieve interdisciplinary balance. Presents language as the unifying principle.

1306. Wolfthal, Maurice. "The Way We Were: Students in the Golden Age." *Daedalus* 113 (Fall 1984): 161–167.

Recounts examples and statistics showing that large numbers of students have been deficient in reading and writing at "level" throughout the twentieth century.

1307. Woods, William F. "The Reform Tradition in Nineteenth-Century Composition Teaching." *WC* 2 (October 1985): 377–390.

Presents the history and characteristics of the "reform tradition" that provided the basis for the early progressive teaching of the 1890s.

1308. Zbrodoff, Nadia J. "Writing Stories under Time and Length Constraints." *DAI* 46 (November 1985): 1219A.

Finds that time and length constraints influence measures of the writing process. Recommends controlling these constraints in future research.

See also 63, 413, 462, 489, 503, 793, 900, 952, 966, 1064, 1103, 1134, 1180, 1431, 1538, 1557, 1612, 1668, 1669, 1746, 1793, 1804, 2021, 2090, 2095, 2098, 3740, 3750

CROSS-DISCIPLINARY STUDIES

1309. Anderson, Kristine F. "An Interview with James Kinneavy on Writing across the Curriculum Programs." *WAC* 2 (December 1984): 4–5.

Discusses the nature, value, current use, and future direction of writing across the curriculum programs on college campuses.

1310. Barnum, Carol M. "Industrial Engineering Technology and English: Team Work on the Senate Project." *WAC* 3 (December 1985): 5.

Summarizes a successful team-teaching project using writing and speaking in an industrial engineering course.

1311. Beach, Richard. "The Effect of Reading Ability on Seventh Graders' Narrative Writing." Paper presented at the AERA Convention, New Orleans, April 1984. ERIC ED 246 401 [22 pages]

Examines the relationship of reading ability and writing quality.

1312. Carbaugh, Donal A. "On Persons, Speech, and Culture: American Codes of 'Self,' 'Society,' and 'Communication' on 'Donahue.'" *DAI* 45 (August 1984): 342A.

Uses the work of Burke to propose a three-featured theory for describing cultural communication codes. Analyzes "Donahue talk" and other speech events as sociocultural performances.

1313. Cassell, Richard M. "Esthetic Transformations: Visual, Stylistic, Syntactic, and Rhetorical Features in the Writing Process of S. J. Perelman." *DAI* 44 (January 1984): 2146A.

Studies Perelman's *Westward Ha!* to develop a writing process model showing how cognition, style, and rhetoric interact at each stage of composition.

1314. Covert, Laurie Anne Schmid. "A Fantasy-Theme Analysis of the Rhetoric of the Symbionese Liberation Army: Implications for Bargaining with Terrorists." *DAI* 45 (April 1985): 3024A.

Analysis adds information to bargaining models and supplies "communication strategies."

1315. Diefenbeck, James A. *A Celebration of Subjective Thought.* Philosophical Explorations Series. Carbondale, Ill.: Southern Illinois University Press, 1984. 280 pages

Distinguishes between "objective" thinking as guided and controlled by accepted philosophies and data and "subjective" thinking as "appropriate to the subject as active agent or first cause." Argues that the former is epistemologically inadequate for dealing with questions of value.

1316. Dionisopoulos, George N. "Corporate Rhetoric of the Atomic Power Industry after Three Mile Island." *DAI* 45 (April 1985): 3024A.

Identifies rhetorical strategies of purification and transcendence in analyzing the rhetoric of atomic power industry.

1317. Evans, Vella Neil. "Woman's Image in Authoritative Mormon Discourse: A Rhetorical Analysis." *DAI* 46 (December 1985): 1439A.

Uses diverse rhetorical techniques to analyze Mormon discourse concerning women from 1830 to 1984.

1318. Fagan, William T., Julie M. Jensen, and Charles R. Cooper, eds. *Measures for Research and Evaluation in the English Language Arts, Vol. 2.* Urbana, Ill.: ERIC/RCS and NCTE, 1985. 245 pages

Supplements the 1975 edition. Offers descriptions of over 80 research instruments, giving their date of construction, stated purpose, and information about their validity.

1319. Finn, Seth, and Donald F. Roberts. "Source, Destination, and Entropy: Reassessing the Role of Information Theory in Communication Research." *ComR* 11 (October 1984): 453–476.

Applies information theory to such issues as readability, the cloze procedure, redundancy, and other aspects of human communication. Bibliography included.

1320. Fulmer, Hal W. "The Defiant Legacy: Southern Clergy and a Rhetoric of Redemption for the Reconstruction South." *DAI* 46 (December 1985): 1440A.

Analyzes the rhetoric of Southern protestant clergy from 1865 to 1867, tracing the effect of major issues and attitudes they developed upon the contemporary South.

1321. Giroux, Henry A. "Critical Pedagogy, Cultural Politics, and the Discourse of Experience." *JEd* 167 (1985): 22–41.

Argues that a "critical pedagogy" must be developed, creating a "critically affirmative language" to establish a new educational discourse.

1322. Gopen, George D. "Rhyme and Reason: Why the Study of Poetry is the Best Preparation for the Study of Law." *CE* 46 (April 1984): 333–347.

Argues that skills developed in the study of poetry are the same as those needed in a successful law career.

1323. Greeley, Andrew W. "The Making of a Storyteller." *Thought* 59 (December 1984): 391–401.

A sociologist-novelist connects narrative form with sociology and with "narrative theology" or story as a basis of religion.

1324. Grunig, James E., Shirley Ramsey, and Larissa A. Schneider. "An Axiomatic Theory of Cognition and Writing." Paper presented at the Association for Education in Journalism and Mass Communications, Corvallis, Oreg., August 1983. ERIC ED 233 353 [57 pages]

Constructs a "deep theory" of the relationships among language, cognition, and writing.

1325. Harris, Wendell V. "Signs of the Times: Language as Sign in These Times." *ComQ* 32 (Winter 1984): 20–77.

Surveys 12 recent books dealing with interdisciplinary issues involving the role of language in human "understanding, relationships, and action." Topics include culture, literature, and semiotics.

1326. Hayes, David A., and Kathleen Copeland. "Effects of Selected Writing Tasks upon the Transfer of Prose Learning." Paper presented at the National Reading Conference, Clearwater Beach, Fla., December 1982. ERIC ED 233 364 [14 pages]

Finds that writing in conjunction with reading affects the inferences of ninth graders in different ways depending on the writing task.

1327. Hines, Roger B. "Writing across the Curriculum in the Cobb County Schools." *WAC* 2 (December 1984): 2–3.

Lists three goals of the writing across the curriculum program in the Cobb County School System and reports on progress after one year.

1328. Hornbeck, David E. "Some Requirements of Technical Report Writing in Civil Engineering Technology." *WAC* 1 (May 1984): 7.

Explains three levels of report writing for civil engineering technology.

1329. Huberman, Elizabeth. "Writing across the Curriculum: An Unfinished Story." *CEAF* 14 (1984): 2–4.

Argues that delays in implementing a writing across the curriculum program are caused by inertia, faculty unwillingness to increase their workload, and lack of funding or administrative support.

1330. Hyde, Michael J. "Emotion and Human Communication: A Rhetorical, Scientific, and Philosophical Picture." *ComQ* 32 (Spring 1984): 120–132.

Explores the relationship between emotion and rhetoric in human communication. Discusses the contributions of Plato, Aristotle, Burke, and communication theorists.

1331. Jolliffe, David A. "Audience, Subject, Form, and Ways of Speaking: Writers' Knowledge in the Disciplines." *DAI* 46 (August 1985): 367A.

Case studies reveal that biology, literature, and social work have rhetorics and composing operations specific to each discipline.

1332. Kurfiss, Joanne. "Do Students Really Learn from Writing?" *WAC* 3 (December 1985): 3–4.

Offers a rationale for and ways of implementing writing across the curriculum.

1333. Kurland, Daniel J. "Increasing the Theoretical Base of Developmental Education: Case Studies — Grammar, Reading, Science." Paper presented at the National Association for Developmental Education, Philadelphia, March 1984. ERIC ED 248 460 [26 pages]

Argues for greater concern about theoretical frameworks that support instruction in grammar, critical reading, and introductory science courses.

1334. Lönroth, Lars. "The Intellectual Civil Servant: The Role of the Writer and the Scholar in Nordic Culture." *Daedalus* 113 (Spring 1984): 107–136.

Surveys the history of literacy and cultural developments in each Nordic country, describing socialist policies that create state-supported writing and oral continuity.

1335. Lieber, Michael D. "Analogic Ambiguity: A Paradox of Proverb Usage." *JAF* 97 (October–December 1984): 423–441.

Examines the application of analogies to critical thinking. Using ethnographic and literary examples, reveals the ambiguous structures of proverbs in rhetorical and social terms.

1336. Lopez, John Michael. "Rhetoric of National Development Policy Making: The 'Ideology of National Development' and Administration of President Juscelino Kubitschek of Brazil during 1956–1958." *DAI* 46 (September 1985): 546A.

Analyzes "language-mediated shifts of attention" that affected policy development. Proposes a "rhetoric of development policy making" that could be useful in comparative studies.

1337. Mashat, Soraya Hassam. "A Rhetorical Analysis of the Image of Saudi Women in Two Specific Cross-Cultural Media Messages." *DAI* 46 (December 1985): 1431A.

An analysis of two films indicates the importance of recognizing cultural differences in presenting one culture to another accurately.

1338. McClosky, Donald N. "The Literary Character of Economics." *Daedalus* 113 (Summer 1984): 97–119.

Describes the literary nature of economic "science," seeing the field as constituted by writing and rhetoric.

1339. McLaughlin, Daniel. "Literacy in Navajoland: Functions and Effects of Power." Paper presented at the Ethnography in Education Research Forum, Philadelphia, March 1985. ERIC ED 257 324 [33 pages]

Observes literacy among the Navajo, finding diglossia (Navahos communicate orally in Navajo, but write in English) and layers of context and power.

1340. Meyers, Miles. *The Speech Events Structuring Written Composition.* Urbana, Ill.: ERIC/RCS and NCTE, 1980. ERIC ED 239 248 [32 pages]

Examines data to find a correlation between levels of writing competency and four types of speech events: encoding, conversation, presentation, and ritual.

1341. Morris, Barry Alan. "The Unconscious Conspiracy: Reaganomics and the Rhetorical Emergence of the Corporate Citizen." *DAI* 45 (February 1985): 2303A.

Describes the rhetorical campaign of the "corporate citizen" for legitimacy as an "individual" social voice.

1342. Morrow, Susan R. "An Overview of Writing across the Curriculum." *WAC* 1 (May 1984): 2–3.

Describes the development of the writing across the curriculum movement and links it to research in cognitive psychology.

1343. Morrow, Susan R., and James McKay. "An Interview with Dr. Harris T. Travis." *WAC* 2 (May 1985): 6–7.

Describes the need for and value of writing across the curriculum programs, especially at technical colleges.

1344. Newell, George E. "Learning from Writing in Two Content Areas: A Case Study/Protocol Analysis." *RTE* 18 (October 1984): 265–287.

Suggests that essay writing is more effective than notetaking or answering study questions in enabling eleventh-grade students to integrate what they read with what they know.

1345. Niles, Lyndrey A. "Rhetorical Characteristics of Traditional Black Preaching." *JBS* 15 (September 1984): 41–52.

Examines problems facing the rhetorical critic of black sermons and identifies sermon types and their qualities (e.g., "call-response").

1346. Pradl, Gordon M. "On Coming to Terms with the Real Literacy Crisis." *ETC* 41 (Fall 1984): 248–266.

Discusses whether literacy is defined as mere communication or as a process of social transformation. Recommends four ways to implement a responsible literacy program.

1347. Saloom, B. George. "Communication in a Technological Environment." *WAC* 3 (December 1985): 6–9.

Emphasizes the importance of good speaking and writing skills for students seeking successful business careers.

1348. Sharplin, Wanda S., and Theda P. Birdsong. "Student Attitudes toward Writing: A New Assessment." *LaEJ* 24 (Winter 1985): 25–33.

Finds that valuing writing correlates positively with students' grade point averages and progress toward degree, although teachers do not provide sufficient opportunities for writing.

1349. Smith, Earl. "Career and Communication Skills." *WAC* 2 (May 1985): 4–5.

Uses personal examples to argue for the importance and practice of writing in school and in the marketplace.

1350. Sola, Michele, and Adrian T. Bennett. "The Struggle for Voice: Narrative, Literacy, and Consciousness in an East Harlem School." *JEd* 167 (1985): 88–110.

An anthropological and ethnographic study of writing in an East Harlem school reveals the struggle for voice among students.

1351. Stamps, Dory. "The Library as Classroom: An Opportunity for Writing across the Curriculum." *WAC* 2 (December 1984): 3–4.

Offers advice to non-English faculty on how to use the library as laboratory for student writing and learning experiences.

1352. Street, R. I., and J. N. Cappella, eds. *Sequence and Pattern in Communicative Behavior.* The Social Psychology of Language, no. 3. Baltimore: Edward Arnold, 1985. 304 pages

A collection of essays drawing on work in social psychology, speech communication, and linguistics. Examines how social relationships develop, are maintained, and fail.

1353. Stricklen, Simon A., Jr. "A Note of Caution." *WAC* 2 (May 1985): 3.

Questions the validity of writing across the curriculum programs and argues against their special role on college campuses.

1354. Taylor, Barbara M. "Improving Middle-Grade Students' Reading and Writing of Expository Text." *JEdR* 79 (November–December 1985): 119–125.

Sixth-grade students benefited from learning how to analyze social science texts. They did not benefit from instruction in writing essays on social science topics.

1355. Thaiss, Christopher J. *Language across the Curriculum: ERIC Digest.* Urbana, Ill.: ERIC/RCS and NCTE, 1984. ERIC ED 250 699 [12 pages]

Describes language across the curriculum for administrators, policy makers, and teachers. Discusses faculty training, classroom techniques, and curricular change.

1356. Thompson, Richard A. "Language, the Brain, and the Question of Dichotomies." *AmA* 8 (March 1984): 98–105.

Presents evidence from four fields showing that the dichotomous model of hemisphericity sheds little light on *cultural* differences in systems of thought, belief, and custom.

1357. Tulkoff, Joseph. "Communication in Industry." *WAC* 2 (December 1984): 6–7.

Describes the importance of writing skills for engineers working for industry.

1358. Veit, Richard. "1984 Visited: English Debased? Students Illiterate?" *ETC* 41 (Winter 1984): 409–415.

Attacks the view that language and literacy are declining, points to similar criticisms throughout history, and traces changes in historical interpretation.

1359. Wertheimer, Molly. "Some Philosophical and Psychological Presuppositions in Four Theories of Listening in Rhetoric." *DAI* 45 (January 1985): 1918A.

Investigates the nature of listening—a "unitary process or a complex of activities"—by examining the rhetorical theories of Aristotle, Augustine, Campbell, and Woolbert.

1360. Wess, Robert C. "An Interview with Toby Fulwiler." *WAC* 3 (December 1985): 9–11.

Explains several types of writing across the curriculum programs and discusses how to implement them.

1361. Whitenton, James B. "Expertise and Overlap on the College Campus." *WAC* 2 (May 1985): 2–3.

Argues for reinforcing concepts that overlap in college courses to deepen student knowledge. Encourages collection of course information for broadening teacher awareness.

1362. Williamson, Michael M. "The Function of Writing in Three College Undergraduate Curricula." *DAI* 45 (September 1984): 775A.

A study of the function of writing in biology, sociology, and English reveals that different registers are associated with different disciplines.

1363. Zinkhan, George, and Edward Blair. "An Assessment of the Cloze Procedure as an Advertising Copy Test." *JQ* 61 (Summer 1984): 404–408.

Concludes that the cloze procedure can differentiate advertisements, predicting which will be most successful for a particular target group.

1364. Zins, Daniel L. "Teaching English in a Nuclear Age." *CE* 47 (April 1985): 387–406.

Discusses the obligation of English teachers to confront the nuclear predicament in teaching rhetoric and literature. Includes a list of resources.

See also 28, 31, 36, 66, 152, 203, 264, 266, 267, 296, 308, 375, 456, 458, 532, 539, 554, 558, 566, 623, 633, 644, 647, 648, 652, 663, 664, 733, 739, 850, 890, 942, 975, 1041, 1096, 1109, 1111, 1126, 1152, 1168, 1226, 1257, 1305, 1396, 1437, 1836, 2226, 2765, 2822, 2938, 3707, 3814

OTHER

1365. Algren, Edith. "A Rhetorical Analysis of the Role of the Movement against Teaching in English in the Public Schools of Puerto Rico within the Puerto Rican Movement toward Political Autonomy, 1898–1949." *DAI* 45 (May 1985): 3237A.

Examines the shifting stance of the movement's spokespersons in four historical periods and the relationship of language to educational and political concerns.

1366. Andersen, Kenneth E. "Communication Ethics: The Non-Participant's Role." *SSCJ* 49 (Spring 1984): 219–228.

Explores the role of receivers in communication transactions.

1367. Andersen, Peter A., Janis F. Andersen, and Shirley M. Mayton. "The Development of Nonverbal Communicaton in the Classroom: Teachers' Perceptions of Students in Grades K–12." *WJSC* 49 (Summer 1985): 188–203.

Examines perceptions of students' nonverbal regulations in conversation and their expression of emotions.

1368. Anderson, Janice Walker. "A Quantitative and Qualitative Analysis of Mobil's Advocacy Advertising in *The New York Times*." *DAI* 46 (August 1985): 297A.

Examines advertising by Mobil from 1970 to 1983, including long-term positive and short-term negative advertising.

1369. Arnett, Nancy Carol. "John F. Kennedy's 1960 Presidential Campaign: Rhetorical Strategies and Image Projection." *DAI* 44 (April 1984): 2924A.

Uses Burke's work to analyze and evaluate the effectiveness of campaign strategies. Focuses on religious issues.

1370. Aschauer, Mary Ann, and Fred D. White. "Towards a Marriage of Two Minds: The Word Processor and Natural Habits of Thought in the 'Discovery' Stage of Composing." Paper presented at the Spring Conference of the Delaware Valley Writing Council, Villanova, Pa., February 1984. ERIC ED 243 129 [18 pages]

Discusses the relationship between lateralization of brain organization and word processing as a heuristic for writing.

1371. Atari, Omar F. "A Contrastive Analysis of Arab and American University Students' Strategies in Accomplishing Written English Discourse Functions: Implications for EFL." *DAI* 44 (April 1984): 3047A.

Concludes that Arab students use counterproductive rhetorical strategies when writing English.

1372. Babcock, John Gilbert Chittenden. "The Role of Public Discourse in the Soil Conservation Movement, 1865–1935." *DAI* 46 (October 1985): 838A.

Studies 11 key figures—their issues, themes, and appeals—and resulting legislation.

1373. Banker, Stephen Robert. "He Who Gaffes Last: A Rhetorical Analysis of the Gaffes of Reagan and Carter in the 1980 General Election Campaign." *DAI* 46 (July 1985): 18A.

A rhetorical analysis of campaign gaffes helps to explain Reagan's election.

1374. Barker, Larry L., Kittie W. Watson, and Robert Kibler, Jr. "An Investigation of the Effect of Presentations by Effective and Ineffective Speakers on Listening Test Scores." *SSCJ* 49 (Spring 1984): 309–318.

Examines differences in listening comprehension test scores when "effective" and "ineffective" speakers present Brown Carlsen and STEP listening tests.

1375. Barnes, Judith A. "Gender Portrayal in Magazine Advertising." *DAI* 45 (February 1985): 2291A.

Finds that from 1953 to 1983 gender portrayal became less stereotyped overall, but that from 1979 to 1983 it began to become more traditional.

1376. Baron, Naomi S. "Computer-Mediated Communication as a Force in Language Change." *VLang* 18 (Spring 1984): 118–141.

Examines the effects of using computers as a replacement for writing and speech.

1377. Bartley, Shirley. "The Man in the Arena: A Rhetorical Analysis of Theodore Roosevelt's Inventional Stance, 1910–1912." *DAI* 45 (September 1984): 681A.

Focuses on Roosevelt's discourse, his definition and creation of issues, his construction of arguments, his choice of language, and the justification for his policies.

1378. Bennett, W. Lance. "Communication and Social Responsibility." *QJS* 71 (August 1985): 259–288.

Uses two Reagan administration statements on El Salvador to criticize "negative communication," which denies failures of preconceptions to fit facts.

1379. Benson, Thomas W. "The Rhetorical Structure of Frederick Wiseman's *Primate*." *QJS* 71 (May 1985): 204–217.

Rhetorically analyzes Wiseman's 1974 documentary film about the treatment of animals in a scientific research center.

1380. Biggers, Thompson, and John T. Masterson. "Communication Apprehension as a Personality Trait: An Emotional Defense of a Concept." *ComM* 51 (December 1984): 381–390.

Applies an emotion-based theory of human response to resolving methodological and conceptual problems associated with the trait-state nature of communication apprehension.

1381. Black, Edwin. "Ideological Justifications." *QJS* 70 (May 1984): 144–150.

Analyzes a *New York Times* editorial on mob activity during the 1977 power blackout to reveal liberal political assumptions and values.

1382. Boiarsky, Carolyn. "What the Authorities Tell Us about Teaching Writing: Results of a Survey of Authorities on Teaching Composition." Paper presented at the NCTE Spring Conference, Columbus, Ohio, April 1984. ERIC ED 243 145 [48 pages]

Reports on a survey of writers published by the National Council of Teachers of English.

1383. Bowman, Joel P. "From Chaos to K-Mart: Beyond the You-Attitude." *ABCAB* 47 (December 1984): 16–20.

Discusses how the "you-attitude" theory of business communications applies to the business environment itself.

1384. Bradac, James, Jr., and Anthony Mulac. "A Molecular View of Powerful and Powerless Speech Styles: Attributional Consequences of Specific Language Features and Communicator Intentions." *ComM* 51 (December 1984): 307–319.

Two studies examine the interaction of style's power and the communicator's intentions in a hypothetical job interview.

1385. Brenner, Douglas Francis. "The Rhetoric of the Moral Majority: Transforming Perceptions of Opposition." *DAI* 45 (June 1985): 3478A.

Examines the stance and strategies the Moral Majority used against its opposition in its first four years.

1386. Brezezinski, Evelyn J. "Review of The Assessment of Educational Progress Information Retrieval System Ver.115 (NAEPIRS), by L. M. Rudner et al." *JEdM* 22 (Spring 1985): 41–52.

Reviews a data-base program designed to provide information on findings of the National Institute of Education's National Assessment of Educational Progress.

1387. Brodsky, Allen. "The Simple-Language Bill Isn't Quite So Simple." *ABCAB* 47 (June 1984): 9–10.

Outlines objections to Pennslyvania's proposed Plain Language Contract Act.

1388. Brown, Mary Helen. "That Reminds Me of a Story: Speech Action in Organizational Socialization." *WJSC* 49 (Winter 1985): 27–42.

Examines role-related learning based on structural, technological, and personality information revealed through stories told by employees.

1389. Brown, Peter D. "English and the Computer." *EQ* 16 (Winter 1984): 55–62.

Describes the shaping of thoughts by computer learning and language learning. Comments on the teacher's responsibility.

1390. Buckelew, Roy Edward. "The Political Preaching of Jerry Falwell: A Rhetorical Analysis of the Political Preaching of Rev. Jerry Falwell in Behalf of the Moral Majority during the 1980 Political Campaign." *DAI* 44 (January 1984): 1970A.

From five perspectives, asks five questions about Falwell's preaching. Concludes that he was effective only among fundamentalist Christian voters.

1391. Bulsys, Joseph Algirdas. "An Analysis of Dwight D. Eisenhower's Public Imagery of the Soviet Union and Communist China as Presented in Selected Speeches and News Conferences: 1953–1961." *DAI* 46 (October 1985): 839A.

Examines Eisenhower's rhetorical role during the Cold War and finds his imagery "coherent, consistent," and "idealistic."

1392. Burgchardt, Carl R. "Discovering Rhetorical Imprints: LaFollette, 'Iago,' and the Melodramatic Scenario." *QJS* 71 (November 1985): 441–456.

Argues, using LaFollette's speeches as examples, that a speaker's life work often exhibits an imprint, a recurring rhetorical pattern.

1393. Burleson, Brant R. "Role-Taking and Communication Skills in Childhood: Why They Aren't Related and What Can Be Done about It." *WJSC* 48 (Spring 1984): 155–170.

Reviews the literature on role taking and adaptive communication. Recommends several modifications in existing theory and research practices.

1394. Burns, Thomas. "Format Preferences in Editorial Cartooning." *JQ* 61 (Spring 1984): 182–184.

Argues that an editorial refuting an editorial cartoon can reverse reader opinion more easily than the converse.

1395. Buttny, Richard. "Accounts as a Reconstruction of an Event's Context." *ComM* 52 (March 1985): 57–77.

A student-teacher conference illustrates how the construction of an event's context is crucial to understanding how accounts function to change meanings in problematic situations.

1396. Casmir, Fred L. "The Theoretical Integration of Levels of Human Communication." *ComQ* 32 (Winter 1984): 62–70.

Provides a "thought model" for studying the fundamental differences between communication processes and their products.

1397. Caulfield, Peter J. "Rhetoric and the Equal Rights Amendment: Contemporary Means of Persuasion." *DAI* 45 (February 1985): 2507A.

Examines the persuasive rhetorical formats used in discourse about the Equal Rights Amendment. Finds that anti-ERA discourse relied on emotional appeals, while pro-ERA discourse focused on rational economic appeals.

1398. Charland, Maurice Rene. "Discourse and Power: The Construction in Public Communication of a *Peuple Quebecois*." *DAI* 44 (June 1984): 3539A.

Indicates that motives for political action are created in public discourse and describes forms used to elicit action.

1399. Ching, Liu Mei. "Women and the Media in China: An Historical Perspective." *JQ* 62 (Spring 1985): 45–52.

From 1900 to 1910, Chinese women began their fight for media careers with help from male reformists and China's first women journalists.

1400. Cianciolo, Patricia J. "Reading, Literature, and Writing from Writers' Perspectives." *EJ* 74 (December 1985): 65–69.

Explains six attitudes that good writers share, according to writers of young people's literature.

1401. Collins, James. "Some Problems and Purposes of Narrative Analysis in Educational Research." *JEd* 167 (1985). 57–70

Suggests that examining class and ethnic differences in narrative style can improve the study of the communicative bases of learning activities.

1402. Cooper, Rose Marie. "A Critical Analysis of the Rhetoric of Myrtle Fillmore, Co-Founder of Unity." *DAI* 45 (June 1985): 3479A.

Uses historical, biographical, and critical approaches to analyze Fillmore's writings, which stress the central importance of thought in life.

1403. Corley, Joseph Russell. "A Communication Study of Arthur F. Holmes as a World View Advocate." *DAI* 44 (May 1984): 3204A.

Using Brown's model of rhetorical processes concerning worldview meaning and application, finds that Holmes's rhetoric is architectonic and productive.

1404. Daniell, Beth. "Toward a Definition of Literacy." Paper presented at the NCTE Convention, Detroit, November 1984. ERIC ED 257 114 [14 pages]

Discusses numerous problems in defining literacy, including separating literacy from the mastery of a standard dialect, and notes the connection between literacy and culture.

1405. Dates, Jannette Lake, and Oscar Gandy, Jr. "How Ideological Constraints Affected Coverage of the Jesse Jackson Campaign." *JQ* 62 (Autumn 1985): 595–600.

Examines conflict resolution in mainstream media that concentrated on Jackson's style, rarely addressing his stand on important issues for fear of appearing racist.

1406. Delgado, Joseph Figueroa. "The Metaphorical Construction of Political Reality: Luis Muñoz." *DAI* 46 (October 1985): 840A.

Uses the work of Lakoff, Johnson, and Bormann in metaphorical-transfer criticism and fantasy theme analysis to examine Muñoz's public speeches from 1948 to 1952.

1407. Donelson, Ken. "Sublime Laws That Change Our Messy World." *Statement* 20 (February 1985): 51–60.

A compilation of humorous laws covering all eventualities, including writing and literature. Example: Never turn your back on a unicorn that dislikes you.

1408. Douglas, George, ed. *The History of Business Writing*. Urbana, Ill.: Association for Business Communication, 1985.

Annotation not available.

1409. Dowling, Ralph Edward. "Rhetorical Vision and Print Journalism: Reporting the Iran Hostage Crisis to America." *DAI* 45 (December 1984): 1571A.

Uses Bormann's fantasy theme analysis to discuss the shared rhetorical vision of the press and U.S. readers during the Iranian hostage crisis.

1410. Drew, Dan G., and Stephen D. Reese. "Children's Learning from a Television Newscast." *JQ* 61 (Spring 1984): 83–89.

Finds that children in higher grades remembered more news stories than children in lower grades. Film clips increased unaided recall consistently through grade levels.

1411. Dunbar, Nancy Reeve. "A Critical Examination of the Concept of Argument Fields: The Laetrile Case." *DAI* 45 (December 1984): 1572A.

Analyzes argumentation across a variety of fields and discusses the reasons for and the nature of variation in argumentation.

1412. Dupree, James Vincent. "A Burkean Analysis of the Messages of Three Television Preachers: Jerry Falwell, Robert Schuller, and Jimmy Swaggert." *DAI* 45 (July 1984): 16A.

Analyzes three preachers' perspectives, reasons for action, and audience identification strategies, revealing their differences, similarities, and potential for success.

1413. Edie, William F., and Jon W. Paulson. "Communicator Attitudes, Communicator Style, and Communication Competence." *WJSC* 48 (1984): 390–407.

Examines relationships among style variables, attitudes, perceived competence, and variations in competence dependent on attitude types.

1414. Ekman, Paul, Wallace V. Friesen, and John Bear. "The International Language of Gestures." *PsyT* 18 (May 1984): 64–69.

Discusses how every little movement has a meaning all its own, depending on the culture in which a person makes it.

1415. Elam, Ohakwe Temple. "Argument and National Security Decision: A Systematic Examination of the 1975 United States Angola Decision." *DAI* 45 (December 1984): 1572A.

Uses approaches to decision making advanced by Berkowitz, Bock, and Fusillo to analyze American intervention in Angola. Finds a dominant rhetoric of maintaining a balance of power.

1416. Elliot, Norman. "Communicative Development from Birth." *WJSC* 48 (Spring 1984): 184–196.

Locates communicative development in three kinds of interactive change.

1417. Elliott, Appele Gan Marietta. "A Dramatistic Analysis of Rev. Albert Cleage's Role in the Black Protest Movement from 1960 to 1969." *DAI* 45 (June 1985): 3479A.

Examines strategies, fantasy themes, and the redemptive process in Cleage's work for insights into his rhetoric and his relationship to the movement.

1418. Ellis, A. W. *Reading, Writing, and Dyslexia: A Cognitive Analysis.* Hillside, N.J.: Erlbaum, 1984. 160 pages

Covers the following topics: written language, reading by ear and eye, word recognition, acquired dyslexia, syntax, spelling, learning to read and write, developmental dyslexia, and dysgraphia.

1419. Ellsworth, Elizabeth Ann. "The Power of Interpretive Communities: Feminist Appropriation of *Personal Best*." *DAI* 45 (November 1984): 1225A.

Analyzes feminist public discourse and film reviews in feminist publications for strategies of interpretation in opposition to actions of film industry.

1420. Erwin, Dan Roland. "A Study in the Preaching of John Claypool: The Rhetorical Function of Narrative." *DAI* 45 (February 1985): 2302A.

Argues that narrative functions rhetorically to inculcate personal and social values and to create new perceptions of reality.

1421. Ewing, Charles Burgess. "An Analysis of Frank Capra's War Rhetoric in the 'Why We Fight' Films." *DAI* 44 (May 1984): 3205A.

Uses Ivie's model to reveal the pattern of "victimage rhetoric" in four films. Three *topoi* depict the "image of savagery."

1422. Feezel, Jerry D. "Toward a Confluent Taxonomy of Cognitive, Affective, and Psychomotor Abilities in Communication." *ComEd* 34 (January 1985): 1–11.

Presents Feezel's Confluent Taxonomy, which organizes learner activity hierarchically in three dimensions: mental, social, and physical involvement.

1423. Fishman, Andrea R. "Reading, Writing, and Meaning: A Literacy Study among the Amish." *DAI* 46 (July 1985): 91A.

An ethnographic study of the functions, uses, perceptions, and transmission of reading and writing among members of an Amish family.

1424. Fokerts, Jean, and Stephen Lacy. "Journalism History Writing, 1975–1983." *JQ* 62 (Autumn 1985): 585–588.

Four recent works on the history of journalism challenge Carey's indictments of journalism history as "excessively trivial" and "dull and unimaginative."

1425. Friday, Robert Andrew. "Rhetorical Analysis of Daniel Berrigan's Defense at the Trial of the Catonsville Nine." *DAI* 45 (August 1984): 342A.

Uses Weaver's Scope's Trial analysis as a basis for examining Berrigan's defense from the perspectives of dialectic, rhetoric, and poetic.

1426. Gaidis, William C. "A Test of Deductive Reasoning in an Advertising Context." *DAI* 44 (February 1984): 2516A.

Studies consumer acceptance of rational advertising messages as the result of building and testing mental representations of the messages.

1427. Gardner, Holly Frances. "Membership and Language Use: An Investigation into the Internal Sequential Organization of Naturally Occurring Stories from a Social Interaction Perspective." *DAI* 45 (August 1984): 649A.

Investigates the internal ordering of narratives in conversation, focusing on the sequential placement of elements in relation to the story's closing in two kinds of organization.

1428. Gay, John Franklin. "The Rhetorical Strategies and Tactics of Malcolm X." *DAI* 46 (December 1985): 1440A.

Uses movement theory to analyze Malcolm X's rhetorical strategy. Uses a traditional approach to analyze his rhetorical tactics.

1429. Gaziano, Cecilie. "Neighborhood Newspapers and Neighborhood Leaders: Influences on Agenda Setting and Definition of Issues." *ComR* 12 (October 1985): 568–594.

The agendas and issues defined by neighborhood leaders are more attuned to residents' concerns than agendas and definitions of issues in neighborhood papers.

1430. Gibson, Dirk Cameron. "Neither God Nor Devil: A Rhetorical Perspective on the Political Myths of J. Edgar Hoover." *DAI* 44 (June 1984): 3539A.

Uses traditional techniques of rhetorical criticism to analyze Hoover's handwritten comments on internal FBI memos.

1431. Goelman, Hillel, Antoinette Oberg, and Frank Smith, eds. *Awakening to Literacy.* Portsmouth, N.H.: Heinemann, 1984. 256 pages

A collection of 15 studies examining literacy from several perspectives, in several countries, and through different research methods. Discusses the role of parents, peers, school teachers, and cultural influences in enabling children to read and write.

1432. Griffin, Charles James Grant. "Charles Finney's Prayer: A Dramatistic Interpretation of Charles Grandison Finney's Lectures on Revivals of Religion, 1834–1835." *DAI* 44 (June 1984): 3540A.

Uses Burke's dramatistic vocabulary to analyze Finney's revival lectures and discuss the presence of prayerlike qualities.

1433. Griffin, Leland. "When Dreams Collide: Rhetorical Trajectories in the Assassination of President Kennedy." *QJS* 70 (May 1984): 111–131.

Using Burke's dramatistic method, the author sees the assassination in terms of the opposing rhetorics of Kennedy and Oswald.

1434. Grim, Patricia Ann. "From Strict Neutrality to the Fourteen Points: Woodrow Wilson's Communication Strategies in World War One." *DAI* 45 (August 1984): 343A.

Analyzes the rhetorical strategies that Wilson, his supporters, and his opponents used before and during U.S. involvement in World War I.

1435. Gross, Alan M. "Public Debates as Failed Social Dramas: The Recombinant-DNA Controversy." *QJS* 70 (November 1984): 397–409.

Applies Turner's concept of social drama to the public debate over DNA research and other public debates concerning science and technology.

1436. Gross, Gerald, ed. *Editors on Editing.* 2d ed. New York: Harper & Row, 1984. 352 pages

A collection of essays on the art, craft, and business of being an editor. Includes samples of editor-author correspondence.

1437. Hamid, Abdel Rahim Nur Eldin. "African Political Rhetoric: An Analysis of Persuasive Strategies in the Discourse of President Gaafar M. Nimeiri of the Sudan, 1970–1980." *DAI* 44 (March 1984): 2622A.

Works from the theoretical position of "situational communication" to conduct a content analysis and qualitative assessment of speeches. Finds eight strategies and four rhetorical characteristics.

1438. Hanisko, SandraLee Mary. "Foreign Affairs Perspectives toward Revolution in El Salvador: The Unfolding of U.S. Officials' Rhetorical Experiences." *DAI* 46 (September 1985): 554A.

Examines the *Congressional Record* and finds two rhetorical perspectives on the controversy: the cold war perspective and the human rights theme.

1439. Haskins, Jack B., and Mark Miller. "The Effects of Bad News and Good News on a Newspaper's Image." *JQ* 61 (Spring 1984): 3–13.

Agrees with the general perception that there is too much bad news, but finds a declining readership when a paper is "too good to be true."

1440. Haskins, Jack B., Mark Miller, and Jan Quarles. "Reliability of the News Direction Scale for Analysis of the Good-Bad News Direction." *JQ* 63 (Autumn 1984): 524–528.

Scale measures negative-positive dimensions of news stories. Includes 21 definitions for bad news and 20 definitions for good news.

1441. Hogan, J. Michael. "Public Opinion and American Foreign Policy: The Case of Illusory Support for the Panama Canal Treaties." *QJS* 71 (August 1985): 302–317.

Argues that, with help from the media, supporters of the treaties successfully popularized the myth that voter opposition to the treaties had diminished.

1442. Homenick, Michael P. "Spelling: A Complex, Task-Dependent Ability." *DAI* 45 (September 1984): 773A.

Finds no relationships between spelling ability and complexity in writing, although other measures of complexity were significant.

1443. Hoover, Judith D. "Irvin S. Cobb: A Rhetorical Biography." *DAI* 44 (June 1984): 3540A.

Analyzes persuasive strategies in Cobb's humor, fiction, and propagandistic pieces.

1444. Housel, Thomas J. "Understanding and Recall of Television News." *JQ* 61 (Autumn 1984): 505–508.

Reports that linguistic complexity and advances in cognitive psychology have been incorporated as variables in recalling television news.

1445. Hunter, Carman St. John, and David Harman. *Adult Illiteracy in the United States: A Report to the Ford Foundation.* New York: McGraw-Hill, 1985. 240 pages

Defines adult illiteracy in America and evaluates the programs and services currently available.

1446. Hynds, Ernest C. "Editorials, Opinion Pages Still Have Vital Roles at Most Newspapers." *JQ* 61 (Autumn 1984): 634–639.

Reports no change in amounts of space allotted editorials or in editors' attitudes toward the impact of the opinion page on its readers.

1447. Japp, Phyllis M. "Esther or Isaiah?: The Abolitionist-Feminist Rhetoric of Angelina Grimke." *QJS* 71 (August 1985): 335–348.

Suggests that two 1838 speeches by Grimke foreshadowed basic feminist rhetorical personae: the supplicatory mode of Esther and the prophetic mode of Isaiah.

1448. Jefferson, Bonnie Sharp. "The Rhetorical Restrictions of a Devil Theory: The Anti-Communist Press's View of Communism, 1945-1947." *DAI* 46 (August 1985): 299A.

Examines the anti-Communist press's work and attitudes that restricted options open to the Truman administration and that had other negative consequences.

1449. Jefferson, Patricia Ann. "Spokesmen for a Holy Cause: A Rhetorical Examination of Selected Leaders of the New Religious-Political Right." *DAI* 45 (November 1984): 1238A.

Examines the public discourse of Falwell, Robison, and Dixon as leaders of the new religious political right.

1450. Johnson, John R. "The Role of Inner Speech in Human Communication." *ComEd* 33 (July 1984): 211–222.

Examines Vygotsky's and Sokolov's concept of inner speech as central to understanding intrapersonal and extrapersonal spoken language.

1451. Kahan, Lisa D., and D. Dean Richards. "Effects of Two Types of Familiarity on Children's Referential Communication Abilities." *ComM* 52 (September 1985): 280–287.

While controlling for the complexities of the stimulus, examines the effects of immediate experience and recognizability on kindergartners' and third graders' referential communication.

1452. Kiewe, Amos. "An Analysis by Rhetorical Models of the Sadat-Begin Peace Negotiation from Inception to Completion." *DAI* 45 (October 1984): 985A.

Uses a Burkean dramatistic approach to analyze the speeches and styles of Sadat and Begin.

1453. King, Robert L. "Transforming Scandal into Tragedy: A Rhetoric of Political Apology." *QJS* 71 (August 1985): 289–301.

Criticizes Edward Kennedy and Nixon for describing Chappaquiddick and Watergate as "tragedies" and notes that the press uncritically adopted these descriptions.

1454. Kurzbard, Gary. "Ethos and Industry: A Critical Study of Oil Industry Advertising from 1974 to 1984." *DAI* 46 (August 1985): 299A.

Uses a Burkean framework to analyze the discourse of the oil industry, particularly the advertising of the Mobil and Exxon corporations.

1455. Laba, Martin. "Narrative and Talk: A Study in the Folkloric Communication of Everyday Conversational Exchange." *DAI* 45 (July 1984): 267A.

Examines how narrative is fashioned in a folkloric performance occasioned by conversation, focusing on the continuity between the performance and the conversation.

1456. Lebrun, Yvan. "Sign Aphasia." *LangS* 7 (April 1985): 143–154.

The semiology of sign aphasia found in the deaf parallels that of oral and written language aphasia.

1457. Lemert, James B. "News Context and the Elimination of Mobilizing Information: An Experiment." *JQ* 61 (Summer 1984): 243–249.

Finds that journalists eliminated information allowing people to act on their attitudes in political stories more than in business or gardening news.

1458. Lent, John A. "Cuban Mass Media after Twenty-Five Years of Revolution." *JQ* 62 (Autumn 1985): 609–615.

Traces the development of media in Castro's Cuba, which supports three national dailies, 54 radio stations, three television stations, and numerous periodicals.

1459. Lentz, Richard Glenn. "Resurrecting the Prophet: Dr. Martin Luther King, Jr., and the News Magazines." *DAI* 44 (February 1984): 2279A.

Analyzes three magazines' coverage of King.

1460. Lessl, Thomas M. "Science and the Sacred Cosmos: The Ideological Rhetoric of Carl Sagan." *QJS* 71 (May 1985): 175–187.

A Burkean analysis of Sagan's *Cosmos,* arguing that it attempts to create a quasireligious attitude toward science.

1461. Lopez, Consuelo. "C.L.R. James: The Rhetoric of a Defiant Warrior." *DAI* 44 (June 1984): 3541A.

Analyzes the sources and use of James's rhetorical strategies to foster and further Marxist movements and to create a persuasive *ethos.*

1462. Lumsden, D. Barry, and Frank Fuller. "Publishing Opportunities for Community College Educators." *CCR* 12 (Summer 1984): 48–60.

Identifies 15 periodicals specifically of interest to community college personnel and describes what authors need to know before submitting manuscripts.

1463. Lyons, Mary Ethel. "A Rhetoric for American Catholicism: The Transcendental Voice of Isaac T. Hecker." *DAI* 45 (September 1984): 683A.

Analyzes Hecker's sermons to reveal their expression of transcendental ideas in language appropriate to his age.

1464. MacKenzie, Scott Bradley. "The Role of Attention in Mediating the Effect of Advertising on Attribute Importance." *DAI* 44 (February 1984): 2562A.

Two experiments tested the hypothesis that the amount of attention drawn to an attribute by an advertisement mediates advertising's effect on attribute importance.

1465. Makau, Josina M. "The Supreme Court and Reasonableness." *QJS* 70 (November 1984): 379–396.

Reviews Supreme Court opinions on economic regulation and racial discrimination cases to discover how the court defines the concept of reasonableness.

1466. Marshall, Melvin Jay. "An Analysis of Values Expressed in the Presidential Speeches of John F. Kennedy." *DAI* 46 (November 1985): 1126A.

Uses Rokeach's value hierarchies and cluster analysis to examine the values of the culture expressed in Kennedy's speeches.

1467. Marvin, Carolyn. "Constructed and Reconstructed Discourse: Inscription and Talk in the History of Literacy." *ComR* 11 (October 1984): 563–594.

Explores four models of literacy. Argues that the definition of literacy consists in "written and oral practices organized around texts in a particular culture."

1468. McClure, Malcolm McKenzie. "Accounting as Language: A Linguistic Approach to Accounting." *DAI* 45 (July 1984): 219A.

Establishes an analogy between sentences and accounting entries to argue for the similarity of accounting and natural language. Analyzes the nature of accounting change.

1469. McComb, Karen B., and Fredric M. Jablin. "Verbal Correlates of Interviewer Empathic Listening and Employment Interview Outcomes." *ComM* 51 (December 1984): 353–371.

Analyzes audio/videotapes of screening interviews to determine relationships among interviewees' verbal behaviors, the perceptions of interviewers as empathic listeners, and interview outcomes.

1470. McKenzie, Taylor A. "Booker T. Washington in Atlanta Revisited." *DAI* 46 (November 1985): 1127A.

Analyzes the political and social environment in which Washington delivered his Cotton States Exposition Speech. Focuses on Washington's education and background.

1471. McManus, Walter Stewart. "Effects of Language Characteristics on Earnings: Hispanic Men in the United States." *DAI* 44 (February 1984): 2538A.

Describes research on the role of language in the assimilation of Hispanic men into the labor market and the effect of language skills on their wages.

1472. Monroe, Mark Paul. "Individuals Unite: Paradox as a Rhetorical Strategy in the Political Discourse of Barry Goldwater and the Resurgence of Conservatism in American Politics, 1950–1964." *DAI* 44 (June 1984): 3541A.

Defines "paradoxical rhetoric" and identifies paradox as a rhetorical strategy in three areas of Goldwater's discourse.

1473. Motley, Michael T., and Carl Camden. "Nonlinguistic Influences on Lexical Selection: Evidence from Double Entendres." *ComM* 52 (June 1985): 124–135.

Examines the assumption that lexical activation operates within only one semantic network at a time and is instigated only by the linguistic parameters of the encoded message.

1474. Murphy, Bren Adair Ortega. "Rhetorical Strategies of Chicago Regional Theaters in the 1970's: A Case Study of Audience Development." *DAI* 45 (June 1985): 3481A.

Using the neo-Aristotelian concept of *ethos* and Burke's concept of identification, analyzes audience development strategies.

1475. Murrel, Sharon Lynne. "The Impact of Communicating through Computers." *DAI* 44 (June 1984): 3533A.

Evaluates the impact of two approaches on idea generation and group decision making.

1476. Nelson, Kate. "Tilting at Windbags: My Losing Battle with Business Jargon." *EJ* 73 (September 1984): 61–62.

An editor/writer argues that professional, often unreadable, jargon in the business world intentionally separates the professional from the masses.

1477. "The New Deal Publicity Operation: Fountain for the Modern Presidency." *JQ* 61 (Spring 1984): 35–48.

Analyzes how President Franklin D. Roosevelt depended on an established publicity bureau for "accurate information" while denying that he had formed it.

1478. Nogle, Victoria Louise. "A Rhetorical Criticism of Women's Music and the Lesbianfeminist Movement." *DAI* 46 (September 1985): 554A.

Argues that the rhetorical message of lesbianfeminist music is a principal way in which the movement accomplishes its rhetorical tasks.

1479. O'Hair, Dan, Michael J. Cody, and Ralph R. Behnke. "Communication Apprehension and Vocal Stress as Indices of Deception." *WJSC* 49 (Fall 1985): 286–300.

Examines variables in simulated job interviews to test theories of anticipatory responses to communication interaction.

1480. Oishi, Noriko, Teiko Sumino, and Masamichi Nagahata. "A Case of Developmental Dyslexia and Dysgraphia." *LangS* 7 (April 1985): 85–108.

Case report of a boy with developmental dyslexia. Analyzes the processes and problems he went through to acquire reading and writing skills.

1481. Olson, Lester Clarence. "Emblems of American Community: A Study in Rhetorical Iconology." *DAI* 45 (April 1985): 3027A.

Explores the evolution of historical meaning and the "suasory function" of icons representing the American colonies.

1482. Oravec, Christine. "Conservationism *Vs.* Preservationism: The 'Public Interest' in the Hetch Hetchy Controversy." *QJS* 70 (November 1984): 444–458.

An analysis of the first national dispute between conservationists and preservationists, the debate between 1901 and 1913 over building a dam in Yosemite Park.

1483. Ormrod, Jeanne Ellis. "Visual Memory in a Spelling Matching Task: Comparison of Good and Poor Spellers." *PMS* 61 (August 1985): 183–188.

Good spellers are equally able to identify matched and mismatched pairs. Poor spellers have more trouble with mismatches than matches. Supports Frith's "partial cues" explanation of poor spelling performance.

1484. Ozick, Cynthia. "The Question of Our Speech: The Return to Aural Culture." *PR* 51 (1984): 755–773.

Argues from James and nineteenth-century English textbooks that modern culture is aural and lacks the "serious" attention to written language of an earlier age.

1485. Palmerton, Patricia Ruby. "Terrorism and the Media: A Rhetorical Critical Analysis of the 'Crisis in Iran.'" *DAI* 45 (June 1985): 3481A.

Analyzes the news coverage of CBS and ABC during the crisis and the terrorists' rhetorical strategies.

1486. Parker, Robert P., and Frances A. Davis, eds. *Developing Literacy: Young Children's Use of Language.* Newark, Del.: IRA, 1983. ERIC ED 253 843 [192 pages]

Eleven essays investigating the relationships among all aspects of language from the researcher's, teacher's, psychologist's, and anthropologist's points of view. Suggests ways in which older people may help young children become literate.

1487. Patterson, John Willard. "Holy Humor: The Religious Rhetoric of Grady Nutt." *DAI* 44 (April 1984): 2925A.

Examines the relationship of religious piety and humor, concentrating on five genres in Nutt's work.

1488. Penley, Mary Constance. "The Rhetoric of the Photograph in Film Theory." *DAI* 45 (November 1984): 1225A.

Uses Barthes's work to analyze concepts of filmic images in the films of Kracauer, Bazin, and Metz.

1489. Pollay, Richard W. "Twentieth-Century Magazine Advertising." *WC* 1 (January 1984): 56–77.

Finds that the level of information richness varied significantly with decade, page size, product class, format, and rhetorical style at the discretion of the copywriter.

1490. Post, Louis A. "Operational Guidelines for Authors, Communicators, and Managers." *JTWC* 14 (1984): 227–287.

Concludes that effective technical writers can save a company money by efficiently bridging the gap between scientists and managers.

1491. Prigatano, George P., James R. Roueche, and David J. Fordyce. "Nonaphasic Language Disturbances after Closed Head Injury." *LangS* 7 (April 1985): 217–229.

Examines three nonaphasic language disturbances —talkativeness, tangential verbalizations, and peculiar phraseology—and how they compromise communication.

1492. Pritchard, David. "Race, Homicide, and Newspapers." *JQ* 62 (Autumn 1985): 500–507.

Finds that newspapers are less likely to publish stories about homicides with minority suspects and victims than about homicides with white suspects and victims.

1493. Rabine, Leslie W. "Romance in the Age of Electronics: Harlequin Enterprises." *FS* 11 (Spring 1985): 39–60.

Describes the rhetoric of Harlequin romances as dictated by corporate agenda. Discusses increasing demands by authors for autonomy, weakening the corporate rhetoric.

1494. Railsback, Celeste Condit. "The Contemporary American Abortion Controversy: Stages in the Argument." *QJS* 70 (November 1984): 410–424.

Traces seven stages in the American controversy over abortion, beginning with a professional debate in 1960 and concluding with a public stalemate in 1980.

1495. Ramaprasad, Jyotika. "Foreign Policy and Press Coverage: A Study of *The New York Times* Coverage of India from 1973 to 1980." *DAI* 46 (September 1985): 542A.

Examines newspaper coverage of changes in Indian and American foreign policy.

1496. Rampolla, Mary Lynn. "A Vision of the Past: Crisis and Historical Consciousness in Worcester, 1095–c.1140." *DAI* 46 (November 1985): 1376A.

Examines the relationship between the writing of history and periods of crisis, focusing on the Worcester cathedral priory in the period after the Norman Conquest.

1497. Rank, Hugh. "Outside Limits." *RR* 4 (September 1985): 80–86.

Describes natural and artificial constraints affecting the overall structure of writing.

1498. Reid-Nash, Naomi Kathleen. "Rhetorical Analysis of the Painting of Hieronymous Bosch." *DAI* 45 (December 1984): 1573A.

Finds Burke's cluster analysis a useful approach for examining the visual arts. Counters the notion that Burke's work is idiosyncratic.

1499. Resnick, Daniel P., ed. *Literacy in Historical Perspective*. Washington: Library of Congress, 1983. ERIC ED 237 942 [170 pages]

Eight papers presented at the Literacy in Historical Perspective Conference, Washington, July, 1980. Topics include the spread of literacy; the impact of the printing press on attitudes toward literacy; discriminatory assessments of black literacy; and historical discussions focusing on England, America, China, and Russia.

1500. Richardson, Jacques G. "The Changing Role of Periodicals in Scientific-Technical Communication." *JTWC* 14 (1984): 1–12.

Surveys tendencies in publishing scientific and technical journals. Projects worldwide trends expected to develop during the 1980s and the 1990s.

1501. Robertson, Jean Ellis. "Language in Oral Histories: The Shape of Disclosure about the Past." *DAI* 45 (July 1984): 224A.

Identifies three genres of oral historical discourse, examining the relationship between duration of events, negatives, modals, finite verbs, and chronological presentation.

1502. Roddy, Vanessa K. "I'm Sick of Reading about Writing." *EJ* 74 (September 1985): 43.

Complains about "endless advice" on teaching writing.

1503. Rushing, Janice Hocker. "*E.T.* as Rhetorical Transcendence." *QJS* 71 (May 1985): 188–203.

Sees the film *E.T.* as embodying a "mythic rhetoric," in which the title character represents collaboration rather than combat and transcendence rather than dialectic.

1504. Ryan, Michael, and David Martinson. "Ethical Values: The Flow of Journalistic Information and Public Relations Persons." *JQ* 61 (Spring 1984): 27–34.

Reports that ethical values among public relations persons varied when asked to comment on hypothetical situations involving firing a coach or disposing of nuclear waste from a research lab.

1505. Ryman, David H., Paul Naitoh, and Carl E. Englund. "Decrements in Logical Reasoning Performance under Conditions of Sleep Loss and Physical Exercise: The Factor of Sentence Complexity." *PMS* 61 (December 1986): 1179–1188.

Using the active voice resulted in better performance on logical reasoning tasks at all fatigue levels. Whereas sleep loss affected response to active voice instructions, response to passive voice instructions was stable.

1506. Salwen, Michael B. "The Reporting of Public Opinion Polls during Presidential Years, 1968–1984." *JQ* 62 (Summer 1985): 272–277.

Newspaper polls are misleading when subtle differences in question wording, type of population sampled, and timing of the sample are not consistent.

1507. Samra, Rise Jane. "The Changing Image of the Chrysler Corporation (1979–1980): A Dramatistic Analysis." *DAI* 46 (November 1985): 1127A.

Uses Burkean techniques to analyze the Chrysler-financed media campaign as well as uncontrolled media coverage of the corporation.

1508. Sauter, Kevin O'Brien. "The Speaking of Hubert H. Humphrey in the 1968 Presidential Campaign: A Study Using Certain Concepts of Milton Rokeach." *DAI* 45 (April 1985): 3028A.

A study indicating the usefulness and limitations of Rokeach's concepts in "qualitative rhetorical analysis of public discourse."

1509. Schanche, Carol. "An Editor's Evaluation." *EJ* 73 (February 1984): 31.

A National Council of Teachers of English editor describes a change in attitude from being "competitive" to seeking cooperation between writer and editor.

1510. Schooley, Bill Jaye. "George Vanderhoff: Nineteenth-Century Elocutionist in America." *DAI* 45 (October 1985): 841A.

Studies Vanderhoff's contributions as an educator, entertainer, and practitioner of oral interpretation of literature.

1511. Schreiner, Eleanor Lynn. "In Quest of the Mexican Ethos: Patterns of Communication." *DAI* 45 (December 1984): 1573A.

Analyzes the communicative behavior of urban Mexicans and develops a model of "macrostrategies for intercultural communication."

1512. Schwartz, Marc J., and John F. Dovidio. "Reading between the Lines: Personality Correlates of Graffiti Writing." *PMS* 59 (October 1984): 395–398.

College undergraduates who write "private" graffiti score higher on creativity measures, are more externally oriented, and view graffiti more positively than non-graffiti-ists.

1513. Scott, Robert L., and James F. Klumpp. "'A Dear Searcher into Comparison': The Rhetoric of Ellen Goodman." *QJS* 70 (February 1984): 69–79.

Argues that syndicated columnist Goodman relies primarily on analogy as a rhetorical strategy.

1514. Segers, May C. "The Catholic Bishops' Pastoral Letter on War and Peace from a Feminist Perspective." *FS* 11 (Fall 1985): 619–647.

Analyzes the role of women in preparing the statement and assesses ideological affinities between feminist pacifism and the letter.

1515. "Seven Headliners Tell What It Took to Turn Them into Readers." *ASBJ* 172 (August 1985): 22–23.

Anecdotes by Isaac Asimov, Susan Stamberg, Bill Bradley, Daniel Boorstin, Fred Rogers, Katharine Graham, and Darryl Strawberry, who discuss their personal involvement with reading, writing, and communicating.

1516. Shepherd, Gregory J., and Barbara J. O'Keefe. "The Relationship between the Developmental Level of Persuasive Strategies and Their Effectiveness." *CSSJ* 35 (Fall 1984): 137–152.

Two experiments assess the role four persuasion strategies play in gaining compliance.

1517. Shoemaker, Pamela J. "Media Treatment of Deviant Political Groups." *JQ* 61 (Spring 1984): 66–75.

Finds that the mass media tend to ridicule more heavily political groups perceived as deviant (KKK) than groups representing the status quo (League of Women Voters).

1518. Siefert, Marsha. "The Dynamics of Evaluation: A Case Study of Performance Reviews." *PT* 5 (1984): 111–127.

Uses Pavarotti's career to illustrate how published reviews, especially in America, mirror and shape a performer's success.

1519. Smith, Bonnie G. "Seeing Mary Beard." *FS* 10 (Fall 1984): 399–416.

Examines Beard's *On Understanding Women* (1931) as a revisionist history presenting a multiplicity of voices in a new rhetoric of history.

1520. Smith, Craig R. "Daniel Webster's July 17 Address: A Mediating Influence in the 1850 Compromise." *QJS* 71 (August 1985): 349–361.

Argues that this speech was particularly directed toward Southerners, as Webster's earlier March speech on the 1850 Compromise had primarily appealed to Northerners.

1521. Smith, Ron F., and Linda Decker-Amos. "Of Lasting Interest? A Study of Change in the Content of the *Reader's Digest*." *JQ* 62 (Spring 1985): 127–131.

Reports that, since its inception in 1922, *Reader's Digest* has published fewer factual articles and more pieces examining how to live a better, healthier life.

1522. Smith, Stephen Austin. "The South of the Mind: Rhetorical Methodology of the Contemporary South." *DAI* 45 (August 1984): 344A.

An analysis of the cultural mythology of the contemporary South indicates new mythic themes of racial equality, regional distinctiveness, and place and community.

1523. Spencer, Gregory Horton. "The Relationship between Christian Conversion and the Rhetoric of Malcolm Muggeridge." *DAI* 46 (November 1985): 1127A.

Analyzes Muggeridge's discourse according to five stages of religious conversion.

1524. St. Dizier, Byron. "The Effect of Newspaper Endorsements and Party Identification on Voting Choice." *JQ* 62 (Autumn 1985): 589–594.

Finds that, since 1965, newspaper endorsements have had stronger effects than political party affiliation on voting returns.

1525. Steinfield, Charles William. "Communicating via Electronic Mail: Patterns and Predictors of Use in Organizations." *DAI* 45 (July 1984): 5A.

Examines the purpose of using electronic mail and factors leading to different use patterns.

1526. Strine, Mary S., and Michael E. Pacanowsky. "How to Read Interpretive Accounts of Organizational Life: Narrative Bases of Textual Authority." *SSCJ* 50 (Spring 1985): 283–297.

Proposes a schema for categorizing interpretive research. Examines authorial stance and status and author-audience contact in four contemporary accounts of organizational life.

1527. Swarts, Valerie Renee. "The Function of Natural Law Warrants in the Rhetorical Discourse of Women's Suffrage, 1848–1920." *DAI* 46 (August 1985): 300A.

The analysis indicates that natural law was a primary argument in women's demands for enfranchisement.

1528. Tarpley, J. Douglas. "American Newsmagazine Coverage of the Supreme Court, 1978–1981." *JQ* 61 (Winter 1984): 801–804.

Examines how and why the media report on the Supreme Court, focusing primarily on First Amendment decisions.

1529. Timmis, John H., III. "Textual and Information-Theoretic Indexes of Style as Discriminators between Message Sources." *ComM* 52 (June 1985): 136–155.

Twelve indexes applied to three message sources provide an operationalized basis for the rhetorical criticism of communication style.

1530. Trachsel, Mary. "Formal and Functional Notions of Literacy in the History of American Education." Paper presented at the NCTE Convention, Detroit, November 1984. ERIC ED 257 115 [13 pages]

Notes the pedagogical shift from "formal" to "functional" definitions of literacy.

1531. Turner, Judith Axler. "An Enterprising 'Scruffy' Teaches Computers to Think…in English." *CHE* 30 (17 April 1985): 5–6.

Article evaluates the work of Schank, a Yale artificial intelligence researcher who writes computer programs that converse with humans using a "semantic design."

1532. Walden, Ruth. "Editorial Rights, Constitutional Restraints of Editors of State-Supported Newspapers." *JQ* 62 (Autumn 1985): 616–625.

Proposes an analytical framework for defining protected editorial discretion among government editors of official campus newspapers at state-supported high schools and universities.

1533. Walters, Keith. "Ethnographic Studies of Literacy and the Classroom Teacher." Paper presented at the NCTE Convention, Detroit, November 1984. ERIC ED 257 116 [20 pages]

Reviews ethnographic studies, noting the home-school discontinuity and drawing conclusions for teachers.

1534. Waltman, John L., and Steven P. Golen. "Publishing Opportunities in Business Communication." *ABCAB* 47 (September 1984): 1–10.

Presents results, in tabular form, of a questionnaire concerning opportunities for publishing articles on business communication topics in a variety of journals.

1535. Wander, Philip. "The Rhetoric of American Foreign Policy." *QJS* 70 (November 1984): 339–361.

Finds two prevailing argumentative forms in American foreign policy rhetoric: prophetic dualism and technocratic realism.

1536. Warburton, Terrence L. "Toward a Theory of Humor: An Analysis of the Verbal and Nonverbal Codes in 'Pogo.'" *DAI* 45 (December 1984): 1573A.

Using Berger's method of content analysis, discusses Pogo's "comedic style" and proposes a theory of humor.

1537. Warnock, John. "Cultural Literacy: A Worm in the Bud?" *BADE* 82 (Winter 1985): 1–7.

Analyzes the meaning and impact of Hirsch's concept of cultural literacy and argues for incorporating Barthes's idea of "the writerly."

1538. Watson, Arden K., and Carley H. Dodd. "Alleviating Communication Apprehension through Rational Emotive Therapy: A Comparative Evaluation." *ComEd* 33 (July 1984): 257–266.

Reports results of a five-year study of the effects of rational emotive therapy *vs.* a skills approach in reducing communication apprehension.

1539. Weatherson, Michael Allen. "'A Political Revivalist': The Public Speaking of Hiram W. Johnson, 1866–1945." *DAI* 46 (December 1985): 1443A.

Analyzes Johnson's discourse and its role in the progressive movement and foreign policy affairs.

1540. Weiler, Michael. "The Rhetoric of Neo-Liberalism." *QJS* 70 (November 1984): 362–378.

Finds that neo-liberal rhetoric continues certain liberal traditions but departs from them by promoting pragmatism, innovation, and entrepreneurial values.

1541. Weiner, Jack. "The Destalinization of Dmitrii Shostakovich's *Song of the Forests* op. 81 (1949)." *BRMMLA* 38 (1984): 214–222.

Analyzes this oratorio, written during the Stalin years and edited later, to demonstrate its gradual elimination of praise for Stalin.

1542. Welch, Barbara. "Being-in-the-Body: A Reflection upon American Self-Medication Drug Advertising." *DAI* 45 (February 1985): 2293A.

Uses Illich's approach to analyze the development of self-medication drug advertising since 1776.

1543. Welch, Richard Francis. "A Methodology for the Rhetorical Analysis of Aesthetic Communication: A Burkean Approach." *DAI* 45 (August 1984): 345A.

Uses a Burkean approach to analyze four films. Concludes that uncovering motives worked well in autobiographical films but not so well in other genres.

1544. Wells, Gordon. *The Meaning Makers: Children Learning Language and Using Language to Learn*. Portsmouth, N.H.: Heinemann, 1985. 256 pages

Based on the Bristol study. Follows the language development of a sample of children from their first words to the end of their elementary education. Many spoken and written examples (also available on cassette) indicate the active role children play in their own learning.

1545. Wilson, Clint C., II, and Felix Gutierrez. *Minorities and Media*. Beverly Hills, Calif.: Sage, 1985. 248 pages

Analyzes the relationship between American mass media and four non-European minorities: Asian, blacks, Latinos, and Native Americans. Argues that historically the media molded public perceptions of minorities around stereotypes, but that media are being altered by ethnically targeted advertising, greater visibility of minorities, and increases in minority-controlled media.

1546. Worthington, Everett L., Jr., Robert M. Tipton, Janet S. Cromley, Thomas Richards, and Robert H. Janke. "Speech and Coping Skills Training and Paradox as Treatment for College Students Anxious about Public Speaking." *PMS* 59 (October 1984): 394.

Training in relaxation techniques and self-instruction to reduce anxiety was as or more effective than training in speaking skills in alleviating anxiety about public speaking.

1547. Zeider, Martin A. "Creative Technical Writing: The Key to Successful Grantspersonship." *JTWC* 15 (1985): 69–73.

A wry look at the art of getting successful scientific grants.

See also 20, 85, 164, 174, 197, 236, 279, 584, 660, 722, 817, 893, 908, 1066, 1073, 1144, 1183, 1210, 1247, 1557, 1802, 1835, 1837, 1895, 2718, 3753, 3849

3

TEACHER EDUCATION, ADMINISTRATION, AND SOCIAL ROLES

TEACHER EDUCATION

1548. Armour, Maureen. "Energy Rx for Writing Teachers: Plug into a Network." *LArts* 62 (November 1985): 759–764.

A grant allowed four writing teachers to form a support network. Teachers meet regularly to write and to share observations about learning in their classrooms.

1549. Beach, Richard. "Components of Composition Inservice: Theory, Categories, Attitudes, and Behaviors." *EEd* 16 (May 1984): 83–93.

Describes an in-service program to improve teachers' assessment of student writing and their use of conferences.

1550. Bell, Elizabeth. "The Peer Tutor as Principal Benefactor in the Writing Center; or, It's Not Just for English Teaching Anymore." *WLN* 9 (May 1985): 10–13.

Argues that tutoring trains students to be effective, knowledgeable teachers and to develop leadership skills valuable in business and the professions.

1551. Bergeson, Mary Alice. "Communication Training for Adolescents and Their Teachers." *DAI* 44 (February 1984): 2290A.

Finds that training of middle school students and teachers improved their "communication cognitions and behavior."

1552. Black, Janet K., Margaret Griffin, Rose Spicola, and Peggy Lazarus. "Teachers Teach Their Teachers: Implications for Facilitating Professional Growth." Paper presented at the NCTE Spring Conference, Columbus, April 1984. ERIC ED 255 916 [26 pages]

Describes a two-week summer institute at North Texas State University designed to make teachers aware of recent writing research.

1553. Brannon, Lil, and Gordon M. Pradl. "The Socialization of Writing Teachers." *JBW* 3 (Spring/Summer 1984): 28–37.

Describes the training of graduate students teaching expository writing at New York University.

1554. Brown, Betsy E., and John T. Harwood. "Training and Evaluating Traditional and Nontraditional Instructors of Composition." *JBW* 3 (Spring/Summer 1984): 63–73.

Concludes that "with adequate training and supervision, faculty or lecturers from disciplines besides English can provide effective instruction in composition."

1555. Burnham, Christopher. "Recruiting, Training, and Supporting Volunteer Basic Writing Instructors: A Working Program." *JBW* 3 (Spring/Summer 1984): 14–27.

Describes a program involving cross-disciplinary faculty.

1556. Burris, Leslie, Andrea Cassidy, Ava Lamaster, Nell Meriwether, and Sarah Liggett. "Student Teaching the Second Time: High School Teachers in the College Classroom." *LaEJ* 24 (Fall 1985): 18–23.

Describes an internship program at Louisiana State University—Baton Rouge, arguing that it benefits interns, school districts, secondary and university students, and the university's English department.

1557. Campbell, Anne. "The Effects of Inservice Training Using a Transactional Approach to Early Language Training upon Teachers of Multiply Handicapped Children in a Public School Setting." *DAI* 44 (January 1984): 2261A.

Examined the effects of using *A Transactional Approach to Early Language Training* for inservice training of teachers of the severe or profound multiply handicapped.

1558. Check, Joseph W., Denise Burden, and Peter Golden. "Reading, Writing, Teaching: Classroom Teachers Discuss Literature on the Teaching of Writing." *HER* 55 (November 1985): 464–477.

Panel discussion and brief reviews of literature on the teaching of writing.

1559. Clark, Thomas. "*Writer's Digest's* 1985 Guide to Writers Conferences, Seminars, and Workshops." *WD* (May 1985): 39–50.

For teachers interested in honing their own writing, a comprehensive, geographical guide.

1560. Copeland, Celia A. "The Writing Conference: In Search of Something to Say." *ET* 15 (Winter 1984): 31–36.

Explores why a personal conference is helpful to both the writing teacher and the gifted student. Emphasizes the teacher's role as a guide and questioner.

1561. Cotton, Helen D. S. "The Teaching of Creative Writing in Selected Colleges and Universities, 1970–1980: Issues, Activities, and Trends." *DAI* 45 (June 1985): 3569A.

A survey of teachers, articles, and course outlines reveals that creative writing teachers were usually qualified specialists who used varied methods and emphasized imagination and writing skills.

1562. Daniels, Harvey, and Steven Zemelman. *A Writing Project: Training Teachers of Composition from Kindergarten to College.* Portsmouth, N.H.: Heinemann, 1985. 256 pages

A study of the Writing Project movement in America. Presents a philosophical rationale, a guide to workshop activities, and a review of research confirming the effectiveness of such projects. Based on the Illinois Writing Project.

1563. DeBrosse, James. "Diary of a Mad English Teacher." *SCETCN* 18 (Fall 1985): 1, 22–28.

An anectodal essay chronicling the disappointments a part-time college English teacher experiences in his first year of teaching.

1564. Eblen, Charlene. "Peter Elbow's 'Believing Game': A Focus for a Writing Conference." Paper presented at the CCCC Convention, New York, March 1984. ERIC ED 249 510 [13 pages]

Encourages teachers to practice Elbow's "believing game" with small groups of other teachers, in hopes that the teachers will then use it with students.

1565. Erickson, Lori. "The Graduate Student, Forty-Five Years Later." *CE* 47 (December 1985): 852–855.

Discusses a 1940 article by Hade Saunders about the lack of creativity in graduate education in English. Recognizes similarities in contemporary graduate education.

1566. Evans, Peter J. A. "Challenges to the Teaching of English in Canada." *EQ* 16 (Winter 1984): 18–22.

Discusses three issues facing the profession in Canada: teacher qualifications, the return to basics, and the assignment of unqualified teachers from other disciplines to teach English.

1567. Gage, Thomas, and John C. Schafer. "Humboldt State University's Master's Program in the Teaching of Writing." *WPA* 7 (Spring 1984): 27–34.

Outlines and evaluates Humboldt's program, showing both the sequence and content of required courses.

1568. Gardner, Susan S. "The Teaching of Writing from the Perspective of Secondary English Teachers." *DAI* 46 (October 1985): 915A.

Study reveals a complex interaction among three themes: freedom and control, uncertainty, and the teacher's view of a student's mind.

1569. Garnes, Sara. "Preparing the Ideal Teacher of Basic Writing." *JBW* 3 (Spring/Summer 1984): 4–13.

Defines three essential qualities of the teacher—commitment, curiosity, and confidence—and describes the training program at The Ohio State University.

1570. Giannelli, Gary. "Why Abraham Lincoln Flunked Freshman Comp or 'Abe! This Essay Is Written on an Envelope!'" *EJ* 73 (September 1984): 85–86.

Regrets that composition teachers emphasize neatness and format over content.

1571. Gibson, Claude L. "Not Just to Teach but to Profess." Paper presented at the CCCC Convention, Minneapolis, March 1985. ERIC ED 255 929 [7 pages]

Discusses the need for composition teachers to be informed about recent theory and applications.

1572. Gould, June. "The Morning After." *TWM* 15 (March–April 1984): 10–12.

Describes an in-service writing course for teachers to help them identify with the writing process of their students.

1573. Gremore, Robert. "Community Faculty: Part-Time Teachers Who Connect the Composition Classroom to the World of Work." *WPA* 8 (Fall–Winter 1984): 57–64.

Discusses the implementation of a "community faculty" program at Metropolitan State University in Minnesota. Outlines training procedures.

1574. Groff, Patrick. "The National Commission on Teacher Education." *NebEC* 30 (Fall 1984): 7–11.

Reviews and evaluates the purposes for establishing the commission.

1575. Grogg, Patricia Marcum. "On Teaching." *ABCAB* 47 (December 1984): 9–10.

Discusses three qualities of a good teacher.

1576. Hairston, Maxine. "Breaking Our Bonds and Reaffirming Our Connections." *BADE* 81 (Fall 1985): 1–5.

Calls for rhetoricians and writing teachers to stand on their own as professionals who no longer need the approval of those who teach literature.

1577. Hairston, Maxine. "Breaking Our Bonds and Reaffirming Our Connections." *CCC* 36 (October 1985): 272–282.

Address to the Conference on College Composition and Communication. Advocates that rhetoricians and writing teachers make a psychological break from literary critics.

1578. Handlen, Tom. "English Teachers Will Write—with the Right Incentive." *EJ* 73 (September 1984): 41.

Asserts the value of composition teachers' doing their own writing. Describes an in-house faculty newsletter as a way to publish teachers' works.

1579. Hanning, R. W. "The Classroom as Theater of Self: Some Observations for Beginning Teachers." *BADE* 77 (Spring 1984): 33–43.

Explores an analogy between acting and teaching. Emphasizes the paradox implicit in authority combined with vulnerability.

1580. Hansen, Jane. "Teachers Share Their Writing." *RT* 38 (May 1985): 836–840.

Describes a research project in which teachers developed their own writing community, then replicated it in their classrooms.

1581. Haring-Smith, Tori. "The Importance of Theory in the Training of Teaching Assistants." *BADE* 82 (Winter 1985): 33–39.

Outlines five models, providing examples and citations, and argues for one that combines theory with practice as illustrated by a sample syllabus.

1582. Hartwell, Patrick. "Choosing Your Doctoral Program." *JBW* 3 (Spring/Summer 1984): 74.

Presents a brief list of questions to consider when examining composition and rhetoric programs.

1583. Hashimoto, Irvin Y. "Sensitizing Beginning Teachers of Writing." *JBW* 3 (Spring/Summer 1984): 55–62.

Analyzes comma splice errors to demonstrate an approach to dealing with sentence problems.

1584. Helstrom, Ward. "Economics, Elitism, and Teacher Apprentice Programs." *BADE* 77 (Spring 1984): 26–32.

Argues that economics and attitude prevent the improvement of apprentice programs. Calls for reform.

1585. Hunt, Maurice. "Essay Evaluation as a Framework for Teaching Assistant Training." *FEN* 14 (Fall 1985): 19–21.

Describes a plan that begins with extensive study of departmental essay standards and proceeds to other pedagogical concerns.

1586. Jacoby, Adrienne. "An Investigation of the Historical Backgrounds of Elementary School Classroom Teachers Concerning Written Composition and Its Effects on Curricular Decisions and Teaching Concerning Writing: A Case Study." *DAI* 45 (December 1984): 1703A.

Finds that teachers lacked knowledge about instructional methods, expectations, evaluation, classroom management, curriculum, and processes related to writing.

1587. Julian, Kathy. "Learning to Write in a 'Teaching of Composition' Class." *NCET* 42 (Summer 1985): 16–18.

Explains how the course taught teachers to write, to emphasize individuality, to delay editing, and to value review.

1588. Kearns, Edward A. "Practicing What We Teach in Writing." *EJ* 64 (October 1985): 28–33.

Examines the process of teaching writing and its implications for teacher education programs. Advocates extensive practice in both critical and creative writing.

1589. Kelly, Lou. "Writing as Learning for Basic Writing Teachers and Their Students." *JBW* 3 (Spring/Summer 1984): 38–54.

Describes a seminar-practicum that treats basic writing "like writing at all levels of development . . . as the humanistic discipline that is basic to all humanistic study."

1590. Lackie, Joyce C., Phyllis Endicott, and Patricia Mulesky. "Successful Peer Tutoring for Prospective Composition Teachers." *Statement* 20 (October 1984): 23–31.

Describes a program in which future teachers assist with basic writing classes and tutor in a writing lab as part of their training.

1591. Lindemann, Erika. "Teaching as a Rhetorical Art." Paper presented at the CCCC Convention, Detroit, March 1983. ERIC ED 234 406 [11 pages]

Suggests ways teachers can discover and maintain communicative interactions in teaching writing.

1592. Lindemann, Erika. "Teaching as a Rhetorical Art." *CEAF* 15 (1985): 9–12.

Argues that writing teachers are effective rhetoricians if they know what goes on in a writing class, what makes a good writing assignment, and what their comments say to students about writing.

1593. Lockward, Diane. "An Open Letter to Writing Conference Speakers." *EJ* 74 (September 1985): 33–34.

Offers suggestions for improving the content of writing conferences.

1594. Logan, Kenneth J. "Writing Instruction: From Preaching to Practice." *LArts* 62 (November 1985): 754–758.

Explores his own writing behavior and its implications for teaching. Advocates reading, creating writing environment, learning to focus, writing from experience, and listening for the language of learners.

1595. Lumley, Dale. "Learning to Write: A History of Boxes, Plain and Neat." *EJ* 73 (September 1984): 82–84.

Urges composition teachers to teach the craft of writing but also to teach writing as a way to discover and grow.

1596. Macrorie, Ken, ed. *Twenty Teachers.* New York: Oxford University Press, 1984. 250 pages

A collection of first-person profiles of successful educators who discuss teaching and their attitudes toward students. Concludes with Macrorie's "open letter about schools," which summarizes the qualities that enable teachers to help students do "good works."

1597. Magistrale, Tony. "Generating Nonfiction: Writing across the Curriculum." *CEJ* 16 (Fall 1984): 51–56.

Describes a writing across the curriculum workshop for college faculty that emphasizes writing as a tool for learning. Specific suggestions include multiple drafts, journals, collaboration, and audience awareness.

1598. Malamud, Randy. "Teaching Freshmen: A Rite of Passage in Academe." *CHE* 31 (6 November 1985): 104.

Reminisces about beginning college teaching as a teaching assistant responsible for three sections of introductory composition.

1599. Marshall, Kristine E. "A Passion and an Aptitude: Turn-of-the-Century Recommendations for English Teacher Preparation." *EJ* 73 (March 1984): 63–70.

Looks at evolving pedagogical training for English teachers, especially the need for subject matter "specialization."

1600. Middleton, Francine K. "Beginning to Write." *LaEJ* 24 (Fall 1985): 41–46.

Reflects on writing a paper in the fourth grade and suggests that teachers can learn about the writing process from their own experience.

1601. Mikkelsen, Nina. "Teacher as Partner in the Writing Process." *LArts* 61 (November 1984): 704–711.

Describes how she discovered her own story in a writing institute and how the experience helped her become a writing partner with her students.

1602. Mikkelsen, Nina. "Teaching Teachers: What I Learn." *LArts* 62 (November 1985): 742–753.

A teacher describes how she writes to learn: writing about students, talking with students, publishing students' work, helping students assess themselves, and, finally, answering her own questions.

1603. Mitchell, G. A. "The Development of Oral Skills for the Presentation of Technical Information." *JTWC* 14 (1984): 109–112.

Describes the use of public speaking exercises to develop oral skills of technical teachers in Great Britain.

1604. Nugent, Harold E., and Susan Monroe Nugent. "Providing Connections: English and Education." *Leaflet* 83 (Fall 1984): 11–15.

Describes a course and practicum for English teachers on the teaching of critical thinking, reading, and writing.

1605. Nye, Naomi Shihab. "The Integrity of the Odd: Responses to Writing by Students." *ET* 16 (Spring 1985): 52–56.

Regrets that teachers usually show little tolerance for writing they consider odd. Argues that, although the meaning may sometimes be mystifying, teachers should accept the unusual.

1606. Oftendahl, Joan L. "Secondary English Methods Courses in the Midwest." *EEd* 17 (October 1985): 152–161.

Finds that both practicing teachers and methods professors ranked strategies for teaching composition as the most important topic to be covered in English methods courses.

1607. Parker, Robert P. "Writing Courses for Teachers: Outcomes and Contexts." *LArts* 61 (November 1984): 693–703.

Describes a writing course for teachers in which the social and intellectual context enables teachers to become writers able to create a similar context for their students.

1608. Perl, Sondra, James Carter, and Nancy Wilson. *How Teachers Teach the Writing Process.* Washington, D.C.: NIE, 1985. ERIC ED 255 920 [895 pages]

Describes a three-year project studying 10 elementary teachers trained in a process approach. Includes articles and papers resulting from the project.

1609. Perrin, Robert. "The Anticipated Problems of Future Teachers of English." Paper presented at the NCTE Spring Conference, Houston, March 1985. ERIC ED 254 857 [12 pages]

Argues that many new teachers face disillusionment. Discusses a questionnaire used in advanced composition.

1610. Pittman, David A. "Observations of a Student Teacher *in Medias Res;* or, a 'Sub' Article." *IE* 9 (Winter 1985): 41–42.

Anecdotally presents the experiences of a high school student teacher.

1611. Pouncey, Peter R. "On a Background for Teachers." *AmEd* 20 (1984): 2–12.

Argues that all teachers should have a strong background in the humanities.

1612. Powers, Stephen, and Mark Rossman. "Student Satisfaction with Graduate Education: Dimensionality and Assessment in a College Education." *Psychology* 22 (1985): 46–49.

Identifies factors leading to student satisfaction: intellectual stimulation of instruction and peers, freedom to influence school policy, professor/student interactions, and university facilities.

1613. Pytlik, Betty P. "Making Connections between Colleges and High Schools through Inservice Teacher Training." Paper presented at the CCCC Convention, Minneapolis, March 1985. ERIC ED 255 939 [12 pages]

Describes an Ohio in-service program, noting that it improves teacher performance and high school–college relationships.

1614. Ranieri, Paul. "The Teacher as Student — and Engineer." *JTW* 3 (Spring 1984): 17–22.

Stresses the importance of teachers being lifetime learners. Defines teaching as a creative, problem-solving activity.

1615. Reed, Patricia Ann. "I Have Been to the Mountain: Summer Study at Bread Loaf." *PCTEB* 50 (November 1984): 3–6.

Describes opportunities available to teachers accepted to the Bread Loaf Program and some probable effects on their teaching and research.

1616. Richards-Beale, Kaye C. "A Study of Inservice Education in the Teaching of Writing in North Carolina Public School Systems 1981–1982." *DAI* 45 (July 1984): 72A.

Finds that in-service education is based on "needs perceived by administrators," lacks "coordination and articulation," and is evaluated more on "changes in teachers' attitudes" than on changes in learning.

1617. Roberts, David D. "New Teachers and Staff Grading Sessions: Three Problems." *FEN* 13 (Fall 1984): 20–21.

Discusses ways to make grading sessions more productive.

1618. Roberts, David H. "Mississippi's Living Room War on Literacy." *JMCTE* 8 (Fall 1985): 15–18.

Promotes Mississippi's new summer writing projects for teachers.

1619. Robinson, Sam. "Planning Processes of a Student Teacher: Understanding the Purpose for Teaching English." *EQ* 17 (Spring 1984): 90–96.

Investigates the dependence of curriculum planning on the teacher's knowledge of the content and the purpose for teaching it.

1620. Roderick, Jessie A., and Louise M. Berman. "Dialoguing about Dialogue Journals." *LArts* 61 (November 1984): 686–692.

Teachers exchange dialogue journals to learn what their students experience and how to use the technique better for communication and self-discovery.

1621. Romano, Tom. "It Takes One to Know One." *ELAB* 26 (Spring 1985): 10–11.

Demonstrates that smugness in a writing teacher can be deadly both to the student and to the profession. Speaks favorably of the Ohio Writing Project.

1622. Schwartz, Helen J. "The Confessions of Professor Strangelove; or, An Apology for Literacy." *CC* 2 (August 1985): 6–16.

Describes the author's experiences learning about and teaching with computers. Includes advice for other humanists.

1623. Shuman, R. Baird. "Within a Budding Grove: America's Schools and the Nation at Risk Report." *IlEB* 71 (Spring 1984): 3–9.

Notes the problems that led to the report, reviews the recommendations, and indicates the kind of teacher education needed if change is to take place.

1624. Smith, Ronald E. "Literacy and the English Teacher: Observations and Suggestions." *EJ* 74 (December 1985): 22–27.

Discusses the problem of illiteracy and proposes possible responses, including changing teacher education programs.

1625. Smith, William L. "Using a College Writing Workshop in Training Future English Teachers." *EEd* 16 (May 1984): 76–82.

Describes a program in which prospective teachers tutor students in writing as part of their professional preparation.

1626. Soven, Margot. "Changes in Teaching Practices: What Happens after the Writing across the Curriculum Workshop?" Paper presented at the CCCC Convention, New York, March 1984. ERIC ED 248 520 [11 pages]

Argues for continued interaction after the workshop, describing major changes in content area writing instruction.

1627. Sullivan, Patrick. "Writing Lab Tutors Design a Tutor Training Program." *WLN* 9 (September 1984): 11–12.

Tutors suggest 18 problems that a training program should address.

1628. Susi, Geraldine Lee. "The Teacher/Writer: Model, Learner, Human Being." *LArts* 61 (November 1984): 712–716.

Studies students' reactions to teacher/writers and teacher/writers' own reactions. Finds that the various roles of teachers had positive effects on students.

1629. Talmage, Harriet, Ernest Poscarella, and Sue Ford. "The Influence of Cooperative Learning Strategies on Teacher Practices, Student Perceptions of the Learning Environment, and Academic Achievement." *AERJ* 21 (Spring 1984): 163–179.

Shows that teachers can learn cooperative goal structuring strategies, which have a significant influence on students' reading but not on language arts.

1630. Taylor, Sharon J. "Beyond the Experts: A Teacher's Perception of Grammar Instruction." *DAI* 45 (December 1984): 1672A.

Concludes that teachers had been using an ineffective approach to grammar instruction but lacked methods and materials to implement a more effective model.

1631. Thompson, C. Lamar. "Is Effective Teaching of the Language Arts an Art?" *NebEC* 30 (Winter–Spring 1985): 26–27.

Lists 10 metaphorical characteristics for effective teaching of the language arts.

1632. Thompson, Edgar H. "The Effect of a Feedback System on Teacher Performance in Writing Conferences." *DAI* 45 (January 1985): 1982A.

Discussing taped writing conferences enabled an instructor to conduct more student-centered, content-specific conferences. A second instructor's attitudes changed because of the feedback.

1633. Tierney, Robert J., David L. Tucker, Margaret Gallagher, P. David Pearson, and Avon Crismore. *The Metcalf Project: Teacher-Researcher Collaboration in Reading and Writing Instruction.* Reading Education Report, no. 56. Urbana, Ill.: University of Illinois Center for the Study of Reading, 1985. ERIC ED 252 818 [39 pages]

Describes a three-year collaboration between teachers and researchers that results in participating teacher-researchers training their colleagues.

1634. Tirrell, Mary Kay. "Teaching Assistants as Teachers and Writers: Developmental Issues in TA Training." Paper presented at the CCCC Convention, Minneapolis, March 1985. ERIC ED 257 061 [12 pages]

Describes a training program for teaching assistants based on cognitive theory and the concept of teacher as writer.

1635. Trimmer, Joseph F. "Faculty Development and the Teaching of Writing." *WPA* 9 (Fall–Winter 1985): 11–18.

Identifies three faculty attitudes toward writing instruction and draws implications for faculty development.

1636. Vacca, JoAnne, and Anthony Manna. "Professional Growth of Secondary English Teachers." *EEd* 17 (October 1985): 162–169.

Finds that secondary English teachers ranked written composition as their first choice for in-service programs.

1637. Vallecorsa, Ada L., Naomi Zigmond, and Lola M. Henderson. "Spelling Instruction in Special Education Classrooms: A Survey of Practices." *ExC* 52 (September 1985): 19–24.

Examines current practices in special education programs for teaching spelling. Suggests approaches for "improving training and practice" of special education instructors.

1638. Vardell, Sylvia M. "Teaching Teachers to Teach Writing: Raising Your Composition Consciousness." Paper presented at the NCTE Spring Conference, Houston, April 1985. ERIC ED 258 220 [11 pages]

Describes an in-service program using a videotape presentation.

1639. Wagner, Mary Jo. "What Secondary Teachers Should Know about Children's Writing." *VEB* 35 (Spring 1985): 100–106.

Explains what secondary teachers can learn from examining the writing of elementary students and from research about children's writing.

1640. Young, Art. "Rebuilding Community in the English Department." *BADE* 77 (Spring 1984): 13–21.

Analyzes what is involved in becoming a community of scholars who teach and study writing, reading, and literature as one subject.

See also 1265, 1270, 1360, 1688, 1691, 1698, 1757, 1782, 1900, 1926, 2039, 2101, 2222, 2627, 2715, 2926, 2968, 3115, 3141, 3142, 3452, 3601, 3662

ADMINISTRATION

1641. Briscoe, Mary Louise. "Reflections on Academic Burnout." *BADE* 79 (Winter 1984): 1–7.

Analyzes the causes and effects of burnout and suggests ways to identify, prevent, and cope with it.

1642. Brown, Peggy Ann, ed. "Writing Programs." *Forum for Liberal Education* 7 (Special Issue, October 1984): ERIC ED 249 850 [21 pages].

Describes ways to maintain and strengthen college writing programs and outlines programs at 15 colleges and universities.

1643. Bruffee, Kenneth A. "The WPA as (Journal) Writer: What the Record Reveals." *WPA* 9 (Fall–Winter 1985): 5–10.

A former editor gives an overview of articles published in *WPA* 1979–1985 and notes examples of programmatic self-criticism.

1644. Ceci, Stephen J., and Douglas Peters. "Letters of Reference: A Naturalistic Study of the Effects of Confidentiality." *AmP* 39 (January 1984): 29–31.

Discusses the "confidential" designation for faculty letters evaluating graduate school applicants in terms of ratings given and details provided.

1645. Conference for Secondary School English Department Chairpersons. *Position Statement on the Role of Secondary School English Department Chairs.* Urbana, Ill.: NCTE, 1985. 3 pages

Offers 15 recommendations for defining the role of a chairperson. Recommendations comment on compensation for department administration, curriculum decisions, and effective cooperation with support services and within the department.

1646. Corbett, Marlene. "Two Specific Suggestions." *IIEB* 71 (Spring 1984): 52–56.

Outlines the effects of class size on writing instruction and offers solutions. Urges disconnecting the public address system.

1647. Couture, Barbara. "Why an English Department Should Join with Industry in Planning a Professional Writing Program." *TWT* 11 (Spring 1984): 167–174.

Concludes that English departments and representatives from private and government organizations should collaborate in planning professional writing programs.

1648. Gere, Anne Ruggles. "Review: *Evaluating College Writing Programs.*" *WPA* 7 (Spring 1984): 35–42.

Reviews Witte's and Faigley's work, compares their model for qualitative evaluation of writing programs with the program evaluation outline of the Council of Writing Program Administrators.

1649. Gopen, George D. "Every Spring a New Haystack: A Method for the Annual Evaluation of New Composition Texts." *WPA* 7 (Spring 1984): 17–25.

Describes the method Loyola University of Chicago uses to evaluate new composition textbooks.

1650. Graham, Jean Bettis. "Serious about Keeping Good Teachers? Help Them Reclaim Lost Teaching Time." *ASBJ* 172 (January 1985): 35–36.

An English teacher describes her work schedule, arguing that teachers need more release time and smaller classes to teach thinking and writing more effectively.

1651. Hartzog, Carol P. "Freshman English 1984: Politics and Administrative Process." *WPA* 8 (Fall–Winter 1984): 7–16.

Offers suggestions for ways writing program adminstrators can become better politicians to improve the state of freshman English and the status of composition.

1652. Holbrook, Hilary Taylor. *Qualities of Effective Writing Programs: ERIC Digest.* Urbana, Ill.: ERIC/RCSand NCTE, 1984. ERIC ED 250 694 [12 pages]

Describes successful classroom practices, inservice training programs, schoolwide writing programs, and administrative strategies.

1653. *Incentives for Excellence.* Urbana, Ill.: NCTE, 1984. 1 page

Suggestions for school board members who want to improve morale, professionalism, and the quality of education in their districts.

1654. Lupack, Barbara T. "Writing across the Curriculum: Designing an Effective Model." Paper presented at the Midwest Writing Center, Iowa City, October 1983. ERIC ED 238 025 [11 pages]

Offers an approach to involving departments in the development of student literacy.

1655. Mier, Margaret. *Class Size and Writing Instruction: ERIC Digest.* Urbana, Ill.: ERIC/RCS and NCTE, 1984. ERIC ED 250 689 [12 pages]

Reports on the relationship between class size and writing achievement, stressing contradictory results of studies.

1656. Müller, Kurt E., and R. Douglas LeMaster. "Criteria Used in Selecting English Faculty in American Colleges and Universities." *BADE* 77 (Spring 1984): 51–57.

Finds continued interest in hiring PhDs and reports on full-time faculty hired from 1980–1982 by two-year, BA/MA, and doctoral departments.

1657. Myres, John. "Help Teachers Let Kids Know What Your Schools Expect." *ASBJ* 172 (February 1985): 29.

Using written "classroom orientation policies" helps students, parents, teachers, and administrators understand what is expected in the classroom and for homework.

1658. Polin, Linda G. "Identifying the Program Variables in College Composition Programs." Paper presented at the AERA Convention, Montreal, April 1983. ERIC ED 234 395 [39 pages]

A study of the California State system shows a need for stating program goals in terms of student gains and for faculty development in teaching writing.

1659. Potts, Maureen A. "The Administration of a Basic Writing Program." *ET* 16 (Fall 1984): 24–28.

Students, faculty, and personnel outside the English department represent three areas of concern that the basic writing administrator must address.

1660. Rose, Mike. *The Freshman Writing Program: A Descriptive Report.* Urbana, Ill.: ERIC/RCS and NCTE, 1984. ERIC ED 247 567 [61 pages]

Describes the writing program at UCLA, presenting placement testing procedures, curricular principles, course descriptions, and staffing concerns.

1661. Rose, Mike. "The Language of Exclusion: Writing Instruction at the University." *CE* 47 (April 1985): 341–359.

Examines five popular notions and some false assumptions about writing that often inform policy discussions at the university.

1662. Schlatter, Franklin D. "The Implications of Large English Classes." *IIEB* 71 (Spring 1984): 34–36.

Draws attention to 16 implications of overloaded

English classrooms, especially as they relate to the teacher's ability to provide instruction in composition.

1663. Schlatter, Franklin D. "When English Teachers Face Large Classes." *SLATE* 10 (April 1985).

Reviews issues concerning class size and argues for smaller classes. Includes bibliography.

1664. Skinner, B. F. "The Shame of American Education." *AmP* 39 (September 1984): 947–954.

Critiques many calls for educational reform and suggests improvements in education that "give students and teachers better reasons for learning and teaching."

1665. Staples, Katherine. "Money, Status, and Composition: Assumptions Underlying the Crisis of Part-Time Instruction." Paper presented at the CCCC Convention, New York, March 1984. ERIC ED 243 118

Discusses the problems of using part-time instructors.

1666. Sternglass, Marilyn. "High School Teachers Teaching College Composition: Implementing a Collaborative High School–University Project." *JTW* 3 (Fall 1984): 249–261.

Discusses how to plan and implement a collaborative project in which high school teachers teach college composition.

1667. Stratton, R. E. "The Profession, 1984 (Part One)." *RR* 3 (January 1985): 164–178.

Criticizes professional bureaucracies and argues against assumptions favored by journals published by the National Council of Teachers of English. Disputes the notion that "departments of literature and composition should remain unified."

1668. Taylor, Raymond G. "The Potential Impact of Humanistic Psychology on Modern Administrative Style, Part I: Humanistic Psychology— An Overview." *Psychology* 21 (1984): 20–24.

Reviews the development of humanistic psychology, describes current forms of humanistic psychology, and discusses its potential impact on administrators.

1669. Taylor, Raymond G. "The Potential Impact of Humanistic Psychology on Modern Administrative Style, Part II: Administrative Models and Psychological Variants." *Psychology* 21 (1984): 1–9.

Explains six administrative models with respect to humanistic psychology and suggests a "modified person-oriented administrative system" in education.

1670. Trimbur, John. "'Writing and Undergraduate Education': A Report on the First Annual NEWPA Fall Meeting." *WPA* 9 (Fall–Winter 1985): 59–61.

Notes current issues in writing across the curriculum and freshman composition that arose in discussions at a regional conference of writing program administrators.

1671. Wallace, M. Elizabeth. "The Richness of Language and the Poverty of Part Timers: Impact and Invisibility." *CE* 46 (October 1984): 580–586.

Assesses the impact of teaching part-time on the teachers, on students, and on the profession.

1672. Wallace, M. Elizabeth, William K. Buckley, David Healy, and Nina D. Zin. "Three Comments on 'The Richness of Language and the Poverty of Part-Timers' [*CE* 46 (October 1984)] and a Response." *CE* 47 (September 1985): 537–544.

Comments by Buckley, Healy, and Zin on Wallace's article, and Wallace's response.

1673. Yager, Joel, Gordon D. Strauss, and Kenneth Tardiff. "The Quality of Deans' Letters from Medical Schools." *JMEd* 59 (June 1984): 471–478.

Discusses the language and details found in excellent and poor letters written about students applying to residency programs. Offers recommendations for writers, readers, and students.

1674. Young, Art, Mike Gorman, and Margaret Gorman. "The 1983–1984 Writing and Literature Survey: Courses and Programs." *BADE* 79 (Winter 1984): 48.

Reports on courses, enrollment, section sizes, and percentage of instructional effort devoted to writing and to literature. Notes an interest in writing across the curriculum.

See also 18, 1278, 1309, 1355, 1566, 1584, 1640, 1678, 1728, 1784, 1787, 1926, 2125, 2559, 2826, 3718, 3760, 3834, 3836

SUPPORT SERVICES

1675. Barbour, James, Barney Gaines, and Michael J. Hogan. "1983–1984 Salaries for Teaching As-

sistants in English Departments." *BADE* 78 (Summer 1984): 45–50.

Reports on the teaching load, salary, tuition, salary minus tuition, and salary per course minus tuition in 68 PhD-granting departments.

1676. Barker, Thomas T. "The English Microlab Registry: A Tool for Researchers in Computers and Composition." *CC* 1 (August 1984): 8–9.

Describes the registry, what information is available from it, and how to participate in it.

1677. Bosco, Jay J. "The Experience of a Peer Tutor." *WLN* 9 (January 1985): 13–14.

Argues that peer tutors can be effective teachers because they understand students' problems with classes and assignments.

1678. Brown, Alan. "The High School Writing Center: Surviving Our Mistakes." *WLN* 9 (June 1985): 4–6.

Argues that, when establishing a new center, a director needs to cultivate faculty as well as administrative support.

1679. Brown, Alan. "Writing Centers: How They Succeed and Fail." *DAI* 46 (July 1985): 91A.

Identifies characteristics of successful and unsuccessful writing centers and offers recommendations for directors.

1680. Carmusin, Amy. "Let the Students Help." *WLN* 9 (1984): 10–11.

Tutors enroll in year-long writing and editing course and serve on committees related to the writing center program.

1681. Catroppa, Barbara. "Writing for Publication: Advice from Classroom Teachers." *LArts* 61 (December 1984): 836–841.

A survey of teachers who published during a five-year period showed that they wanted to share their experience and had the support of colleagues, family, or professors.

1682. Chase, Geoffrey W. "Integrating the Writing Center into the Curriculum." *WLN* 9 (February 1985): 1–4.

Describes the writing center at the School of Interdisciplinary Studies at Miami University as an integral part of the curriculum.

1683. Chase, Geoffrey W. "Small Is Beautiful: A Plan for the Decentralized Writing Center." *WLN* 9 (April 1985): 1–4.

Recommends locating small centers in dormitories. Advocates creating "decentralized writing centers designed to serve various academic divisions and programs."

1684. Chiteman, Michael D. "From Writing Lab to Interdisciplinary Academic Support Center: Cost-Effective Guidelines." *WLN* 8 (March 1984): 1–4.

Suggests expanding tutorial services by using interdisciplinary volunteer faculty and student interns. Recommends soliciting additional funds from university organizations and alumni. [Reprinted in *WLN* 9 (November 1984): 1–4.]

1685. Clark, Irene Lurkis. "Leading the Horse: The Writing Center and Required Visits." *WCJ* 5 and 6 (Spring–Winter 1985): 31–34.

Describes a survey of students attending the University of Southern California's Writing Center. A policy of required attendance increased the number of student visits.

1686. Covington, David H., Ann E. Brown, and Gary B. Blank. "An Alternative Approach to Writing across the Curriculum." *WPA* 8 (Spring 1985): 15–23.

Describes "decentralized writing programs" in the Department of Forestry and the School of Engineering at North Carolina State University.

1687. Curtis, Deborah. "Writing Center Promotion: 'The Hard Sell.'" *WLN* 9 (February 1985): 6.

Suggests that writing center staff can increase student patronage through personal contacts with professors and classes.

1688. D'Arcy, Pat. "Inservice: Learning How to Share." *IaEB* 33 (1984): 9–10.

Shows the similarities between successful language teaching and successful in-service programs.

1689. Davis, Irma. "The Rewards and Tribulations of Meeting the Writing Needs of Untraditional Students in Advanced Composition." Paper given at the CCCC Convention, New York, March 1984. ERIC ED 245 461 [9 pages]

Discusses the role of a writing center in encouraging publication by sponsoring a writer's conference.

1690. Davis, Kevin. "The Davis and Elkins Academic Resource Center." *WLN* 9 (January 1985): 7.

Discusses techniques for dispelling the negative image writing centers frequently have.

1691. Davis, Kevin. "Shopping: Peer Tutors as Cantaloupes." *WLN* 10 (October 1985): 12–13.

Cites compassion, conscientiousness, good writing and reading skills, and openness to other ideas as desirable characteristics of good tutors.

1692. Ewing, Noreen J. "Small Really *Is* Beautiful: The Success of a Writing Center." *WLN* 10 (September 1985): 1–3.

Suggests seven ways to use a limited budget and eight ways to promote a writing center's services.

1693. Gale, Steven H. "1983–1984 Average Salaries in Nationally Rated Graduate English Departments." *BADE* 78 (Summer 1984): 43–44.

Presents high, low, average, and median salaries by rank for public and private universities.

1694. Gills, Paula. "A Reader Responds." *WLN* 9 (April 1985): 6–8.

Suggests ways to recognize different types of learning disabilities and to deal with them.

1695. Glassman, Susan. "Recruiting and Selecting Peer Tutors." *WLN* 8 (February 1984): 1–4.

Suggests seven ways to recruit nonsalaried peer tutors. Explains the selection process, focusing on an applicant's potential for developing an individual, effective tutoring style.

1696. Glassman, Susan. "Training Peer Tutors Using Video." *WCJ* 5 and 6 (Spring–Winter 1985): 40–45.

Describes the procedures and benefits of having writing center tutors produce videotapes of tutoring sessions as part of their training.

1697. Glauner, Jeffrey. "Peer Tutors as a Part of the Collaborative Close Community Network: A Response to Betty Neumann's Questions." *WLN* 10 (November 1985): 4–5.

Discusses how and why peers should be tutors.

1698. Goldberg, Mark F. "Inservice Guidelines: Some Implications from Exemplary Composition Programs." *EEd* 17 (February 1985): 35–38.

Outlines five steps necessary for successful in-service instruction.

1699. Goldsmith, James. "Reinventing the Wheel: Very Quickly." *WLN* 9 (June 1985): 1–3.

A novice director recounts his experiences in developing a center attended by hostile basic writers.

1700. Grattan, Mary. "The Writing Center as a Consulting Service for Content Area Faculty." *WLN* 9 (March 1985): 1–3.

Suggests that writing centers develop content area laboratories, assigment guides, worksheets, and booklets for other disciplines that require but do not teach writing.

1701. Gregor, Margaret Ann Norville. "The Provision of Learning Resources Center Services to Off-Campus Community College Students." *DAI* 45 (March 1985): 2682A.

Studies the relationships among decision-making processes that determine the availability of off-campus services offered by learning resource centers.

1702. Harris, Jeanette. "The Role of the Writing Center in Basic Writing." *ET* 16 (Fall 1984): 20–23.

Argues that basic writers need instruction in the creation of writing rather than in the elimination of surface errors. Tutors can help.

1703. Harris, Muriel. "Theory and Reality: The Ideal Writing Center(s)." *WCJ* 5 and 6 (Spring–Winter 1985): 4–9.

Describes the ideal writing center as a "friendly support place for students," not a "materials-centered facility."

1704. Hart, Dabney. "Peer Group Tutoring." *WLN* 9 (November 1984): 11–12.

Argues that supplementing center staff by regular faculty members of all ranks benefits students as well as faculty.

1705. Hartstein, Marc. "Objectivity in Tutoring." *WLN* 9 (October 1984): 9–10.

Argues that tutors presented with papers straining their objectivity can decline to read them, can act as an unsympathetic audience, or can side with the student by encouraging the strongest arguments.

1706. Haviland, Carol P. "Writing Centers and Writing across the Curriculum: An Important Connection." *WCJ* 5 and 6 (Spring–Winter 1985): 25–30.

Describes three types of writing across the curriculum programs, including a tutorial series for students applying to professional schools, sponsored by the Writing Center at Montana State University.

1707. Held, Nadine. "Hire Junior College Students as Tutors? Why Not? (Ideas for Hiring and Funding Tutors at the Junior College)." *WLN* 10 (September 1985): 6–7.

Cites five sources of tutors and six ways to pay them.

1708. Hemmeter, Thomas. "Spreading the Good Word: The Peer Tutoring Report and the Public Image of the Writing Center." *WPA* 9 (Fall–Winter 1985): 41–50.

Describes training intended to teach peer tutors to write clear, descriptive, nonevaluative tutoring reports for faculty.

1709. Henry, George H. "The Council: How Shall It Survive?" *CE* 46 (November 1984): 668–678.

Traces the changing purpose of the National Council of Teachers of English.

1710. Holmes, Elizabeth. "Individual Instruction." *WLN* 9 (April 1985): 9–10.

Urges peer tutors to be peers, not teachers, to let students be themselves, and to evolve a flexible style.

1711. Holmes, Leigh Howard. "Expanding Turf: Rationales for Computers in Writing Labs." *WLN* 9 (June 1985): 13–14.

Cites eight reasons why computers can be useful in the writing center.

1712. Hurlow, Marcia. "Alleviating Writing Anxiety in Individual and Small Group Settings." Paper given at the Writing Centers Association, West Lafayette, Ind., May 1983. ERIC ED 238 008 [9 pages]

Advocates peer tutoring in a writing lab and discusses problems and techniques.

1713. Johnson, Joann B. "Reevaluation of the Question as a Teaching Tool." *WLN* 10 (December 1985): 1–4.

Shows the inhibiting effect of questions in tutorials and concludes that statements or paraphrases are more effective.

1714. Kail, Harvey. "The Best of Both Worlds." *WLN* 9 (December 1984): 1–5.

Argues that writing laboratories can provide walk-in service as well as credit-bearing courses for remedial and advanced students.

1715. Kinkead, Joyce. "Outreach: The Writing Center, the Campus, and the Community." *WLN* 10 (November 1985): 5–8.

Describes how centers can expand their services to students, to other departments, to local teachers, and to others interested in writing.

1716. Knight, Susan J. "The Peer Tutor as Counselor." *WLN* 9 (June 1985): 7–9.

Suggests that the tutor can "help students cope with their anxieties about writing — frustrations which range from adjusting to college life to dealing with professors' differing expectations."

1717. Kotker, Joan Garcia. "Computers and Tutors." *CC* 1 (August 1984): 6–7.

Argues that computers in the writing lab have helped tutors by saving time and by providing a new teaching method.

1718. Kotker, Joan Garcia. "Expanding the Non-credit Writing Lab." *WLN* 8 (May 1984): 10–11.

Restructuring five-day classes into one lecture, two grammar labs, and two composition classes produced the same number of compositions but enabled more grammar instruction.

1719. Lassner, Phyllis. "Conferencing: The Psychodynamics of Teaching Contraries." *WCJ* 4 (Spring–Summer 1984): 22–30.

Using Elbow's concepts of "paternal" and "maternal" teaching, as well as theories from Britton, Vygotsky, and Winnicott, describes the tutor's role as moving from "nurture and support " to "standards and firmness."

1720. Lauby, Jacqueline. "Note: This writing center will *not* correct your dangling modifiers, teach you comma rules, or have you underline nouns once, verbs twice." *WLN* 9 (September 1984): 8.

Discusses how writing center tutors can function as informed readers for skilled writers.

1721. Lauby, Jacqueline. "Wanted: Someone Conversant with the Turabian Style Sheet to Help Edit My Thesis." *WLN* 8 (May 1984): 11–12.

Suggests that writing centers could train tutors to act as "tutors-as-editors for graduate students and faculty."

1722. Leahy, Richard. "Competency Testing and the Writing Lab." *WLN* 9 (March 1985): 12–14.

Describes how to prepare students for competency examinations that test editing and mechanical skills.

1723. Lederman, Marie Jean. "Evolution of an Instructional Resource Center: The CUNY Experience." *BADE* 82 (Winter 1985): 43–47.

Traces the history of the Instructional Resource Center, which collects and disseminates information on basic skills instruction and research, listing major research projects, conferences, and publications.

1724. Lee, Joyce W. "Daily Writing: A Manageable and Successful Reality." *EngR* 36 (1985): 20–24.

Discusses the symbiotic relationship between writing and comprehension as the basis for a writing laboratory methodology.

1725. Loris, Michelle Carbone. "The Workshop Skills Center: A Cross-Disciplinary Full Language Development Center." *WLN* 9 (December 1984): 6–8.

The center provides "a place to try out, develop, expand, and strengthen...language abilities" for "students at all levels and from every discipline."

1726. Luckett, Clinton. "Adapting a Conventional Writing Lab to the Berthoff Approach." *WCJ* 5 and 6 (Spring–Winter 1985): 21–24.

Describes difficulties in changing student and faculty perceptions of a writing laboratory from that of a "fix-it shop" to a place where students work on the making of meaning, as Berthoff advocates.

1727. Lupack, Barbara T. "Early Alert: Reaching Students in Time." *WLN* 8 (May 1984): 3–5.

Describes an intrusive method for identifying students needing assistance, for evaluating their weaknesses, and for providing appropriate help.

1728. Malankowsi, James R., and Peter H. Wood. "Burnout and Self-Actualization in Public School Teachers." *JPsy* 117 (May 1984): 23–26.

Studies show that teachers with high "self-actualization" are less prone to burnout. Teachers who deal with larger numbers of students are more prone to burnout.

1729. Malbec, Toby W. "Using Interviewing Techniques." *WLN* 8 (June 1984): 5–6.

Like an interviewer, a tutor should use open-ended questions so that students will diagnose their own writing problems and provide their own corrections.

1730. Marcus, Harriet. "The Writing Center: Peer Tutoring in a Supportive Setting." *EJ* 73 (September 1984): 66–67.

Peer tutoring provides supportive, nonjudgmental feedback for students of all ability levels.

1731. Markline, Judy. "Peer Tutors in the Community College." *WLN* 10 (December 1985): 11–12.

Argues that community colleges should employ peer tutors. Describes a way to select, train, and compensate tutors.

1732. Martin, Kathy. "Perry Meridian High School's Writing Lab." *WLN* 8 (May 1984): 5–6.

Describes the development and use of a high school writing center.

1733. Martin, Kathy. "The Writing Lab's Image." *WLN* 8 (March 1984): 8.

Reports on successful methods for encouraging students and faculty to use the writing lab.

1734. McAndrew, Donald A. "From Writing Center to Center for Writing: A Heuristic for Development." *WLN* 9 (January 1985): 1–5.

Suggests ways to expand a center's services to reach a diversity of clients in varied locations on and off campus.

1735. McCully, Michael. "The Writing Lab and Freshman Composition: A Mutual Redefinition." *WLN* 9 (May 1985): 1–5.

Describes restructuring a composition program to include the writing center to achieve greater coherence.

1736. McGrath, Susan. "Drawing the Line." *WLN* 9 (December 1984): 9–10.

Suggests how to deal with students who only want help with proofreading, who come at the last minute, or who ask for local, but need global, revision.

1737. McPherson, Elisabeth. "Then, Now, and Maybe Then..." *CE* 46 (November 1984): 697–701.

Describes the successes of leadership in the National Council of Teachers of English in areas such as minority involvement and intellectual freedom for teachers.

1738. Melnick, Jane R. "The Politics of Writing Conferences: Describing Authority through Speech Act Theory." *WCJ* 4 (Spring–Summer 1984): 9–21.

Uses three case studies and speech act theory to analyze authority in tutor-student conferences. Argues that tutors should assert their authority "decisively" but also clarify its limits.

1739. Morehead, David R., Annelise M. Pejtersen, and William Rouse. "The Value of Information and Computer-Aided Information Seeking: Problem Formulation and Application to Fiction Retrieval." *IPM* 20 (1984): 583–601.

Describes the formulation of a value function modeled on human response to a data base of novels. Attempts to take on-line search beyond the limits of keywords.

1740. Moseley, Ann. "From Factory to Workshop: Revising the Writing Center." *WCJ* 4 (Spring–Summer 1984): 31–38.

Advocates a revised concept of the writing center. It should no longer be a "factory" that merely distributes learning materials but should use a workshop approach that relies on a process approach to writing.

1741. Murray, Patricia Y., and Linda Bannister. "The Status and Responsibilities of Writing Lab Directors: A Survey." *WLN* 9 (February 1985): 10–11.

Reports on directors' academic status, salaries, responsibilities, and work loads. Describes how labs are perceived and suggests improvements.

1742. Nash, Thomas. "New Directions for Writing Labs." *WLN* 9 (September 1984): 2–7.

A survey of the types and functions of writing centers.

1743. Neuleib, Janice. "Research in the Writing Center: What to Do and Where to Go to Become Research-Oriented." *WLN* 9 (December 1984): 10–13.

Shows how case studies, protocol analyses, surveys, rhetorical studies, computer-assisted instruction, and progress analyses can be conducted in the center.

1744. Noppen, Mick. "Speaking of Writing." *WLN* 10 (September 1985): 9–10.

Advocates talking through ideas prior to writing them down to increase a student's creativity and confidence.

1745. Olson, Gary A., ed. *Writing Centers: Theory and Administration.* Urbana, Ill.: NCTE, 1984. 247 pages

A collection of 20 essays examining the functions, administration, and funding of writing centers. Discusses the implications of research and theories for collaborative learning and tutorial instruction. Describes the selection, training, and evaluation of tutors. Suggests strategies for tutoring ESL, business and technical, and reluctant students. Includes extensive bibliography.

1746. Perrin, Robert. "The Archives of *English Journal.*" Paper given at the NCTE Spring Conference, Houston, March 1985. ERIC ED 254 858 [13 pages]

Reviews issues of the journal since 1912, noting continuing and new concerns.

1747. Purves, Alan C. "NCTE: The House of Intellect or Spencer Gifts." *CE* 46 (November 1984): 693–696.

Argues that the National Council of Teachers of English changed from an organization allied with higher education and theoretical concerns to a bureaucracy focusing on skills acquisition.

1748. Reigstad, Thomas J., and Donald A. McAndrew. *Training Tutors for Writing Conferences.* Theory and Research into Practice. Urbana, Ill.: ERIC/RCS and NCTE, 1984. 43 pages

Discusses the importance of training tutors to recognize the proper hierarchy of concerns in a student's composition so that teachers can use classroom time more effectively.

1749. Rouse, William, and Sandra H. Rouse. "Human Information Seeking and Design of Information Systems." *IPM* 20 (1984): 129–138.

Argues that current designs lack a theoretical basis for assessing the value of information in a human problem-solving context. Concludes that the most important practical consideration is flexibility.

1750. Russel, Mark. "Assessment and Intervention Issues with the Nonspeaking Child." *ExC* 51 (September 1984): 64–71.

Examines the development and uses of mechanical aids for communicatively impaired individuals.

1751. Samuels, Shelly. "Emphasizing Oral Proofreading in the Writing Lab: A Multifunction Technique for Both Tutors and Students." *WLN* 9 (October 1984): 1–4.

Discusses using oral proofreading to reveal errors unnoticed and uncorrected, errors noticed and corrected, and errors corrected orally but unacknowledged by writers.

1752. Scanlon, Leone. "Learning Disabled Students at the Writing Center." *WLN* 9 (January 1985): 9–11.

Discusses methods tutors can use to assist learning-disabled students.

1753. *SCETCN* 17 (Spring 1984).

Abstracts of presentations given at the February 1984 convention in Washington, D.C. Includes text of luncheon address by Anthony Hecht on "English and Technology."

1754. *SCETCN* 18 (Spring 1985).

Abstracts of presentations given at the February 1985 convention in Greenville, S.C.

1755. Shoval, Peretz. "Principles, Procedures, and Rules in an Expert System for Information Retrieval." *IPM* 21 (1985): 475–487.

Describes a system that assists users in choosing appropriate keywords for a data-base search.

1756. Simmons, Nancy, and Jane Brill. "Resources for Writing Centers." *EJ* 74 (October 1985): 78–79.

Reviews several writing textbooks for teachers or tutors to use in writing centers.

1757. Simpson, Jeanne H. "Defining the Status of Writing Center Tutors." *WLN* 9 (February 1985): 4–6.

Describes a training program for graduate student tutors that includes weekly discussions, required readings in writing pedagogy, and instruction in professional ethics and demands.

1758. Simpson, Jeanne H. "So Demanding a Job." *WLN* 9 (January 1985): 5–6.

Discusses some economic and professional problems writing center directors face.

1759. Simpson, Jeanne H. "What Lies Ahead for Writing Centers: Position Statement on Professional Concerns." *WCJ* 5 and 6 (Spring–Winter 1985): 35–39.

The National Writing Center Association's statement on the rights, responsibilities, and qualifications of writing center directors and guidelines for the operation of a center.

1760. Smith, Sandy. "Ego States and the Writing Staff." *WLN* 9 (October 1984): 4–7.

Transactional analysis describes three ego states in communication: child, parent, adult. Argues that tutors are more effective using a child/adult role in tutoring passive students.

1761. Sollisch, James. "The Eternal Rough Draft: A Metaphor for Training Peer Tutors." *WLN* 10 (December 1985): 12–14.

Explains how a "tutor training program [can] be a model of training program [can] be a model of writing as writing as learning." By writing, tutors know and understand the problems of student writers.

1762. Sollisch, James. "From Fellow Writer to Reading Coach: The Peer Tutor's Role in Collaboration." *WCJ* 5 and 6 (Spring–Winter 1985): 10–14.

Emphasizes the tutor's role as a reader rather than a fellow writer. Explains "prediction exercises" in which responders attempt to guess what will come next in a student paper.

1763. Stebbins, Peter J. "The Journal as a Sounding Board." *WLN* 9 (March 1985): 11.

Journals can help tutors identify and solve tutoring problems.

1764. Stewart, Jon. "Why I'm a Writing Tutor." *WLN* 10 (December 1985): 10.

"Getting others to see that writing has a rational structure is [the] most important job at the Writing Center."

1765. Stoddart, Pat. "Computers as Tools for Writing at Logan High School." *WLN* 9 (May 1985): 5–6.

Describes using computers in the writing center to facilitate interdisciplinary writing projects.

1766. Sullivan, Patrick. "Do You Object to Tutors Assisting Your Students with Their Writing?" *WLN* 10 (December 1985): 6–8.

Suggests the need for policy statements to inform faculty about centers. Lists 10 ways to advertise.

1767. Sullivan, Patrick. "The Politics of the Drop-In Writing Center." *WLN* 8 (May 1984): 1–3.

Suggests policies for discussing grades, proofreading, and informing teachers of the help a student receives.

1768. Tackach, James. "Theory Z Management and the College Writing Center." *WCJ* 4 (Spring–Summer 1984): 1–8.

Suggests that writing center directors use a method of management that emphasizes stable employment, nonspecialization, implicit control, collective responsibility, and a holistic concern for people.

1769. Thomas, Dene K. "A Transition from Speaking to Writing: Small Group Writing Conferences." *DAI* 45 (March 1985): 2856A.

Analyzes freshman tutorial conferences in order to suggest ways to improve student writing processes.

1770. Truscott, Robert Blake. "Tutoring the Advanced Writer in a Writing Center." *WLN* 9 (June 1985): 14–16.

Describes minicourses in research writing, career writing, stylistics, creative writing, and other types of professional writing.

1771. Vick, Richard D. "The Western Illinois University Writing Center." *WLN* 9 (November 1984): 7–9.

Explains the center's objectives, the makeup and training of the staff, the materials used, and future plans.

1772. Weglarz, Mike. "Better Tutoring through Peer Tutor Interaction." *WLN* 9 (February 1985): 9.

Peer tutors enroll in a two-semester course emphasizing tutoring techniques and writing as process and taught by the center's director.

1773. Wills, Linda Bannister. "Competency Exam Performance and the Writing Lab." *WLN* 8 (June 1984): 1–4.

Stresses "the importance of one-to-one contextual instruction on students' improvement of their scores on an error-recognition type competency exam."

1774. Willson, Robert F., Jr. "Using a Small Endowment to Improve Writing." *BADE* 82 (Winter 1985): 48–49.

Describes how funds were used to improve morale, encourage professional development, supplement the writing lab, and sponsor writing workshops for teachers and students.

1775. Wolfe, Johnny S., Thomas L. Updike, and Jerry R. Wilder. "The Need for Organizational Change among Programs of Student Personnel Services throughout Higher Education." *Psychology* 22 (1985): 40–48.

Concludes that the "student personnel services area has become an illogical, sometimes conflicting, mixture of functions and responsibilities" and that planning and reorganization are needed.

1776. Woodward, Pauline. "The Writing Center Community: Getting It Together." *WLN* 8 (April 1984): 5–8.

Describes a weekly training forum attended by selected faculty and professional and peer tutors who discuss course assignments and tutoring techniques.

1777. Wright, Richard R. "The English Examiner: A Helpful Solution." *WPA* 8 (Spring 1985): 35–38.

Describes the writing proficiency requirement in the Graduate School at Iowa State University and the role of the English Examiner.

1778. Zander, Sherri. "The H.O.T. T.U.B. Method: How Other Tutors Teach Us Better." *WLN* 9 (January 1985): 11–12.

As part of their training, tutors tutor each other. Questionnaires and taped sessions reveal strengths and weaknesses of tutoring techniques.

See also 19, 30, 1295, 1351, 1550, 1627, 1672, 1915, 1939, 2070, 2238, 2302, 2404, 2408, 2414, 2426, 2433, 2456, 2913, 2933, 3019, 3106, 3114, 3122, 3380, 3789, 3846

ROLE IN SOCIETY

1779. Allen, Diane. "New Coalition Criticizes Reports on Education Reform." *NebEC* 30 (Fall 1984): 17–20.

Presents a five-point statement to provide a foundation for the successful reform of English programs.

1780. Allen, Diane. "To Improve Literacy, First Educate the Public and Its Decision Makers, NCTE Commissioners Say." *Statement* 20 (October 1984): 54–60.

Reports recommendations of National Council of Teachers of English commissioners about teaching reading, literature, language, and media and about professional concerns.

1781. Appleby, Bruce C. "The Last Great Humanitarians." *IlEB* 71 (Spring 1984): 21–24.

Argues that English teachers, the last great humanitarians, have the chance to help people realize the centrality of language in all human behavior.

1782. Barnes, Sylvia. "An Analysis of the Value of Writing as Perceived by English Teachers and by a Sample Population in Huntsville, Alabama." *DAI* 46 (December 1985): 1544A.

English teachers agreed with the general population on the function of writing but placed greater importance on writing at every level of schooling.

1783. Barton, Ben F., and Marthalee S. Baron. "Communication Models for Computer-Mediated Information Systems." *JTWC* 14 (1984): 289–306.

Concludes that technical communication specialists should be centrally involved in the research and design of computer-mediated information systems.

1784. Beidler, Peter G. "What Can You Do with an English Major?" *CE* 47 (January 1985): 39–42.

Describes the careers of 150 graduates of Lehigh University's English program.

1785. Bell, T. H. "Suggested Priorities and Goals for American Education." *AmEd* 20 (1984): 30–32.

Outlines seven major goals for American education, beginning with a commitment to general literacy.

1786. Bell, T. H. "Toward a Learning Society." *AmEd* 20 (1984): 2–3, 11.

Discusses the federal government's efforts to combat adult functional illiteracy.

1787. Chopra, Raj K. "A Crisp, Clear Annual Report Is an Asset for Your Schools." *ASBJ* 172 (November 1985): 44–45.

Describes the effectiveness of a plain-English, corporate-style annual report to communicate a school system's successes and goals to students, parents, and the community.

1788. Douglas, George. "English Education and the New Technocracy." *IlEB* 71 (Spring 1984): 25–31.

Illustrating with the American "modern technological argument" that spelling "reasonably well" is good enough, states that "problems of the spirit" undermine excellence in education.

1789. Duke, Charles R., and Ruth Ann Futrell. "Myth or Reality: The Value of English in the Working World." *IE* 7 (Winter 1984): 25-35.

Excerpts from 14 interviews with people in farming, manufacturing, and automobile clean-up examine how material taught in English classes carries over to everyday life.

1790. Farnsworth, Briant J., and Ione M. Garcia. "Do Our Elementary Schools Teach What Society Wants?" *Psychology* 21 (1984): 59-64.

Concludes that major differences exist among adminstrators, teachers, parents, and students concerning education's responsibility in supporting societal needs.

1791. Hackworth, Robert. "Legislative Reform: An Interview with Florida Senator Jack Gordon." *JDEd* 8 (1985): 22-23.

Discusses the possible origins and impact of legislative reforms, focusing on the Gordon Rule and the College-Level Academic Skills Program in Florida.

1792. Hennelly, John. "Business Writing Where It Counts." *EJ* 73 (February 1984): 85-88.

An English teacher describes an eight-session business writing workshop.

1793. Hirsch, E. D., Jr. "'English' and the Perils of Formalism." *AmSch* 53 (Summer 1984): 369-379.

Ties the separation of reading, writing, and literature to New Criticism. Argues against reading and writing as general skills and for education as broad-scale acculturation.

1794. Hogan, Robert F. "The Hatch Amendment." *SLATE Starter Sheet* 10 (October 1985).

Reprints the amendment and regulations, discusses misinterpretations, warns of efforts to pass a Pupil Rights Amendment at the state level, and outlines courses of action.

1795. *Incentives for Excellence: What School Board Members Can Do to Encourage Excellence.* Urbana, Ill.: NCTE,1984. ERIC ED 241 960 [6 pages]

Describes how school board members can work to improve language arts instruction.

1796. Irmscher, William F. "Toward Excellence." *IlEB* 71 (Spring 1984): 10-17.

Examines major threats to excellence in English and defines efforts by the National Council of Teachers of English to combat censorship, loss of status, and unbalanced curriculum. Reviews "Essentials of English."

1797. Keck, Judith W. "Fighting Censorship Incidents with Rationale Writing." *ELAB* 26 (Spring 1985): 23.

Advocates preparing a professional defense against censorship before incidents occur by writing an analysis of the purposes and goals for all materials taught.

1798. Klitgaard, Robert. *Choosing Files.* New York: Basic Books, 1984. 288 pages

Examines how society allocates scarce positions at elite universities and in business and government positions that give a few young people a substantial lifetime advantage. By focusing on Harvard admissions, discusses the measurement of potential, the uses and misuses of standardized tests, affirmative action, and the costs and benefits of compensatory programs.

1799. Meek, Margaret, and Jane Miller, eds. *Changing English: Essays for Harold Rosen.* Portsmouth, N.H.: Heinemann, 1984. 268 pages

A collection of 22 essays tracing changes in educational research, curricula, teaching methods, and public assessments of education. Focuses on Great Britain but discusses concerns applicable to English instruction in America as well.

1800. Morgan, Lyle W., Jr. "Censorship in the Public School and the College Classroom: A (non) Classical Approach." *NebEC* 29 (Spring 1984): 34-38.

Cites examples of attempted censorship and ways to prepare to deal with such attempts.

1801. Orris, JanEdward. "General Education in the Community College: A Megatrendian View." *CCR* 13 (Summer 1985): 3-11.

Discusses the relevance of Naisbitt's five key points from *Megatrends* to education in community colleges today.

1802. Papagan, Harry G. "Are Writing Teachers at Risk? A Review of Higher Education Court Cases." *CCR* 13 (Summer 1985): 35-45.

Reviews the courts' positions on academic matters, finds support for academic autonomy, and concludes that composition teachers probably will not be challenged by the courts.

1803. Pitts, Beverly, and Jim Guffin. "The Write Right Image." *JTW* 3 (Spring 1984): 7–16.

Describes the views of students, the public, and teachers concerning teachers of writing. Emphasizes the common goals of teachers in elementary, secondary, and university levels.

1804. Seldon, Ramsey W. "Towards Excellence in the Language Arts." *Statement* 19 (May 1984): 15–21.

Advocates teaching language as a set of cognitively integrated skills and recognizing these skills as integrated with learning in every subject.

1805. SLATE Steering Committee. *SLATE* 10 (February 1985).

Summarizes 1984 activities, presents notes from the National Council of Teachers of English's Committee against Censorship, and reports briefly on issues in education.

1806. SLATE Steering Committee. *SLATE* 10 (March–April 1985).

Reports on activities mandating a certain number of compositions, on available Starter Sheets, on sessions at the National Council of Teachers of English meeting, and on the Statement of Teaching Composition.

1807. SLATE Steering Committee. *SLATE* 10 (September 1985).

Summarizes SLATE committee meeting and reports from representatives. Presents updates on censorship and mandated writing programs.

1808. Snyder, Fritz. "Copyright Law and the Community College." *CCR* 13 (Fall 1985): 23–31.

Discusses the key provisions of the 1976 Copyright Act and their implications for community college humanities curricula.

1809. Tucker, Robert L. "Antidote to Rejection." *EJ* 74 (April 1985): 58–59.

Describes how teachers "can become a powerful force for better education" by writing regularly for local media.

1810. West, Edwin G. "Are American Schools Working? Disturbing Cost and Quality Trends." *AmEd* 20 (1984): 11–21.

Reviews major findings of national studies of education.

1811. Whitburn, Merrill D. "Freedom in the Research and Teaching of Rhetoric: University Industry Cooperation." *BADE* 79 (Winter 1984): 37–39.

Examines the advantages and constraints of specialists' becoming involved with industry. Argues for close cooperation to preserve academic freedom.

1812. Worthington, Pepper. "Expectations *Vs.* Reality: A Conflict for Teachers." *NebEC* 30 (Fall 1984): 23–27.

Examines conflicts that arise for teachers when expectations developed for students are not fulfilled after graduation.

See also 390, 405, 451, 507, 1008, 1074, 1292, 1301, 1321, 1334, 1339, 1346, 1347, 1349, 1404, 1423, 1431, 1484, 1544, 1573, 1623, 1661, 1734, 1836, 1864, 1940, 2014, 2171, 2472, 2876, 2964, 2972, 2974, 3808

OTHER

1813. Brostoff, Anita. "Using the Document Design Approach in Consulting." Paper given at the CCCC Convention, Minneapolis, March 1985. ERIC ED 254 867 [24 pages]

Uses the project's text, "Writing in the Professions," to outline steps in consulting.

1814. Cetron, Marvin J., Barbara Soriano, and Margaret Gayle. *Schools of the Future: How American Business and Education Can Cooperate to Save Our Schools.* New York: McGraw-Hill, 1985. 176 pages

An extended discussion of what schools will be like in the twenty-first century. Sponsored by the American Association of School Administrators.

1815. Eichorn, Dorothy H., and Gary R. VandenBos. "Dissemination of Scientific and Professional Knowledge: Journal Publication within the APA." *AmP* 40 (December 1985): 1309–1316.

An overview of publication and editorial practices in the APA. Lists characteristics leading to manuscript acceptance or rejection, focusing on content, organization, and language used.

1816. Fish, Marjorie Jane. "A Study of Mass Communication Research and Scholarship." *DAI* 46 (July 1985): 290A.

Reviews the history of the field from the 1930s on and discusses the impact "of institutional structures on research activity."

1817. Jung, M. A. "So Proudly We Hail: The Faculty Lounge." *LaEJ* 23 (Winter 1984): 23–27.

Compares M*A*S*H and the faculty lounge, noting its contribution as a sounding board for teachers.

1818. Miller, James E., Jr. "ADE and the English Coalition." *BADE* 79 (Fall 1985): 16–19.

Describes the Association of Departments of English's role in the formation of the Coalition of English Association.

1819. Oram, Virginia White. "Writing Teachers Can't Write Either." *JTW* 4 (Spring 1985): 127–130.

Laments jargon and poor writing in writing journals and texts. Suggests that teachers of writing should write better.

1820. Ort, Daniel. "In a Subjunctive Mood Indigo." *CHE* 31 (16 October 1985): 88.

Argues that English professors bear the heaviest burden among college teachers because they have more homework from writing classes and seldom can supplement income with consulting.

1821. Rivers, William E. "The Current Status of Business and Technical Writing." *BADE* 82 (Winter 1985): 50–54.

Surveys 915 departments about enrollment, staffing, and hiring patterns. Predicts expanding enrollments, continued need for faculty trained in composition and literature, and new jobs.

1822. Roueche, John E., George A. Baker, III, and Suanne D. Roueche. "College Responses to Low-Achieving Students: A National Study." *AmEd* 20 (1984): 31–34.

Reports survey results on universities' responses to underprepared students.

1823. Shields, Ronald Eugene. "Marjorie Gullan: Speech Teacher, Lecturer, Public Reader, and Pioneer in Choral Speaking." *DAI* 44 (March 1984): 2624A.

Discusses the interdependence of Gullan's professional activities.

See also 3103

4
CURRICULUM

1824. Adams, Alice B. "Dyslexia: Hidden Handicap in the Classroom." *TETYC* 12 (December 1985): 259–264.

Describes methods of diagnosing and helping dyslexic students.

1825. Arons, Arnold B. "'Critical Thinking' and the Baccalaureate Curriculum." *LEd* 71 (Summer 1985): 141–157.

Discusses a list of thinking-reasoning processes basic to analysis and critical thinking. Argues that abstract logical reasoning can be developed in the undergraduate curriculum.

1826. Beck, James. "Removing Four Roadblocks to Bias-Free Reading and Writing." *EJ* 74 (October 1985): 56–58.

Discusses four common misconceptions about critical reading and suggests ways to increase students' awareness of logical arguments.

1827. Bennett, William J. "To Reclaim a Legacy." *AmEd* 21 (1985): 4–15.

Argues for a return to a strong core curriculum in the humanities.

1828. Bereiter, Carl. "Review of *Writing and the Writer* by Frank Smith (1982)." *CurrI* 14 (1984): 211–216.

Critiques the interpretive treatment of curricular topics, as represented in Smith's book, specifically the failure to adapt to principles of empirical science.

1829. Berger, Allen. *What Do Governors and Educators Recommend to Improve Reading and Writing?* Pittsburgh: University of Pittsburgh School of Education, 1984. ERIC ED 245 244 [161 pages]

Presents statements from approximately 150 political and educational leaders.

1830. Block, Richard A. "Education and Thinking Skills Reconsidered." *AmP* 40 (May 1985): 574–575.

Argues that college students should be taught metacognitive organizing and thinking skills using real-world problems and emphasizing writing skills. Includes brief bibliography.

1831. Blue, Kay. "Future Read, Future Write, Future Ready." *CurrR* 24 (November–December 1984): 47–49.

Discusses ways in which language arts teachers can use a futures perspective to enhance skills in reading, writing, research, and discussion. Emphasizes writing future scenarios and problem solving.

1832. Boiarsky, Carolyn. "An Inquiry into the Relative Frequency of Various Practices for Teaching Writing in the Classroom as Perceived by Authorities in the Field." *DAI* 45 (August 1984): 440A.

A survey of teaching practices at the primary, middle, secondary, and postsecondary levels reveals a "tentative set of norms for teaching writing" and frequent recommendations for a process approach.

1833. Boiarsky, Carolyn. "What the Authorities Tell Us about Teaching Writing: A Survey." *JTW* 3 (Fall 1984): 213–223.

Analyzes data from 101 authorities to establish tentative norms for the frequency of various kinds of writing tasks at the primary, middle, secondary, and postsecondary levels.

1834. Brent, Harry. "Prolegomenon to Our Recognition of the Teaching of Grammar as Part of the Teaching of Writing." *CEJ* 16 (Spring 1985): 71–73.

Questions the proposition that "learning grammar does not help students to write better."

1835. Britton, James, Margaret Gill, William Washburn, Stuart Middleton, Mike Torbe, and Arthur N. Applebee, eds. *English Teaching: An International Exchange*. Portsmouth, N.H.: Heinemann, 1984. 208 pages

A collection of 22 essays previously published that examine issues and practices in the teaching of literacy, both in America and in other countries.

1836. Brooks, Charlotte K., ed. *Tapping Potential: English and Language Arts for the Black Learner*. Urbana, Ill.: NCTE, 1985. 330 pages

A collection of 43 essays focusing on ways to improve instruction for black students in the areas of language, reading, writing, and literature. Offers suggestions for working with dialect-speaking students, improving students' self-concepts, introducing students to African and Afro-American literature and culture, and teaching writing and vocabulary. Examines issues raised by the *King* case, testing programs, and attempts to define "the canon."

1837. Bruffee, Kenneth A. "Collaborative Learning and the 'Conversation of Mankind.'" *CE* 46 (November 1984): 635–652.

Places collaborative learning in a theoretical context as a major pedagogical force involving much more than "merely throwing students together with their peers."

1838. Cavallari, Susan D. "Hot-Spots: the Journal as Nonfiction." *CEJ* 16 (Fall 1984): 32–36.

Suggests strategies to make journal writing productive: listing, portraits, clustering, daydreaming, freewriting, composing letters and dialogues.

1839. Chall, Jeanne S. "Literacy: Trends and Explorations." *AmEd* 20 (1984): 16–22.

Attributes recent gains in literacy in the early grades to challenging instructional programs.

1840. Christenson, Eric H. "Taking Risks in Composition." *EJ* 74 (September 1985): 63–64.

Suggests that the best way to teach writing is by personal demonstration.

1841. Clark, Christopher M., and Susan Florio-Ruane. *The Written Literary Forum: Combining Research and Practice*. Research Series, no. 138. East Lansing, Mich.: Michigan State University Institute for Research on Teaching, 1984. ERIC ED 243 132 [33 pages]

Suggests a model for bringing research and practice together.

1842. Clark, John R., and Anna Lydia Motto. "We're Entitled to a Title." *ArEB* 28 (Fall 1985): 61–64.

Argues for teaching students how to write titles for essays.

1843. Clark, Thomas L. "The Dictionary Is NOT the Secular Bible." *CEJ* 15 (Spring 1984): 31–39.

Suggests several ways to introduce students to lexicography and thereby enhance their editing and rewriting skills.

1844. Clark, Wilma. "Writing to Learn in All Subjects." *SLATE* 9 (April 1984).

Reviews the theory, practice, and goals of writing across the curriculum programs, listing strategies for building a districtwide program and for writing in various disciplines.

1845. Corbett, Edward P. J. "A Collegiate Writing Program for the 1980's." *BADE* 78 (Summer 1984): 20–23.

Predicts trends for freshman and upper-level courses, pointing out staffing and computer needs.

1846. Cronin, Frank. "Beginning Writing: Pleasure and Progress." *WaEJ* 7 (Winter 1985): 19–21.

Difficulties in learning to write should lead teachers to devise manageable subroutines and create enjoyable assignments.

1847. Davis, Frederica. "In Defense of Grammar." *EEd* 16 (October 1984): 151–161.

Discusses the justifications for including formal grammar in the curriculum.

1848. de Beaugrande, Robert. "Forward to the Basics: Getting Down to Grammar." *CCC* 35 (October 1984): 358–367.

Argues against a basic grammar characterized by vague or technical terms and recommends one that is accurate, workable, economical, compact, operational, and immediate.

1849. Dohaney, M. T. "Reading and Writing Development: Must It End with High School Graduation?" *EQ* 17 (Winter 1984): 48–57.

Argues that institutions of higher learning must teach the reading and writing skills necessary to process knowledge.

1850. Dudley, Pat. "Mother, May I Implement the Writing Process?" *ET* 15 (Summer 1984): 9–11.

Compares instituting writing programs to a recursive children's game. Lists 101 steps for implementing a writing curriculum.

1851. Duin, Ann. "Implementing Cooperative Learning Groups in the Writing Curriculum: What Research Shows." Paper presented at the Minnesota Council of Teachers of English Meeting, Mankato, Minn., May 1984. ERIC ED 251 849 [17 pages]

Reviews 800 studies on cooperative learning, showing its effectiveness and outlining methods for using it in writing classes.

1852. Duke, Charles R., ed. *Writing Exercises from Exercise Exchange, Vol. 2*. Urbana, Ill.: NCTE, 1984. 335 pages

Includes more than 75 classroom-tested suggestions that have appeared in *Exercise Exchange* over the last seven years.

1853. Eagleson, Robert D., ed. *English in the Eighties*. Adelaide, Australia: Australian Association for the Teaching of English, 1982. ERIC ED 233 390 [164 pages]

Fourteen papers presented at the Third International Conference for the Teaching of English, Sydney, Australia, 1980.

1854. Eastern Washington University Research Laboratory. "Peer Groups Free Teachers." *LaEJ* 23 (Fall 1984): 49–53.

Summarizes the work of five proponents of peer editing. [Excerpted from *IdahoEJ* 6 (Fall 1983).]

1855. Engel, Bernard F. "Reading Verse Aloud in Composition Classes." *CEJ* 16 (Spring 1985): 110.

Reading verse aloud helps students test reading ability, practice rhythms, understand metaphor and symbolism, and practice reading for sense.

1856. Fagan, Edward R. "Reading in the Writing Classroom." *EngR* 35 (Fourth Quarter 1985): 2–5.

Examines the relationship between the reading and writing skills with the intent of enhancing both skills.

1857. Fagan, Edward R. "Writing: Description." *CEJ* 15 (Spring 1984): 91–92.

Suggests one way to use prewriting techniques to teach descriptive writing.

1858. Fearn, Leif. "Writing and Grammar." *CEJ* 16 (Spring 1985): 13–15.

Argues that workbook exercises by themselves are useless. Students must be able to use what they have learned in sentences of their own.

1859. Flinn, Jane Zeni. "An Accountability Model for School Writing Programs." *EEd* 16 (May 1984): 101–110.

Shows how writing programs based on the National Writing Project model can meet accountability criteria.

1860. Flood, James, and Diane Capp. "The Reading/Language Arts Curriculum of Secondary Schools: What Has Been and What Might Be." *EEd* 17 (May 1985): 79–90.

Argues that oral language is primary in the development of reading and writing skills.

1861. Fowler, Lois. "The Structuralists: Word Order and Teaching Writing." *CEJ* 16 (Spring 1985): 44–47.

Suggests activities that stress the importance of word order in speaking and writing the English language.

1862. Fox, Robert R. "Writers in the Schools and a Revolution in Literary Publishing: Two Aspects of the Literary Revival in Texas." *ET* 16 (Fall 1985): 21–27.

Argues that inviting poets to visit schools for a term affects how reading and writing are taught.

1863. Franklin, Phyllis. "From the Editor." *BADE* 81 (Fall 1985): i–ii.

Analyzes *Integrity in the College Curriculum*, criticizing its assessment of the curriculum and calling for further study of the tensions between teaching and specialization.

1864. Freedman, Morris. "Those Futile Attempts to Legislate Literacy." *CHE* 27 (1 February 1984): 80.

Argues that current attempts to legislate good writing are doomed because thay omit reading skills and vocabulary borrowed from the student's milieu.

1865. Freedman, Sarah Warshauer, and Robert C. Calfee. "Understanding and Comprehending." *WC* 1 (October 1984): 459.

Suggests changing the reading and writing curriculum on the basis of students' performance in almost solving a problem but needing some guidance.

1866. Gann, Marjorie. "Teaching Grammar: Is Structural Linguistics Really Better?" *EQ* 17 (Spring 1984): 31–53.

Finds strengths and weaknesses in traditional, structural, and transformational approaches, with no approach emerging as more effective than the others.

1867. Gaspar, Dennis. "Writing Teachers as Researchers: Looking Closely at What We Do." *EN* 6 (1984): 48–52.

Argues that successful writing teachers must conduct research about their students.

1868. Gere, Anne Ruggles. "From Practice to Theory: Talk-Write." *WaEJ* 8 (Fall 1985): 27–28.

Compares strategies that unite speaking and writing.

1869. Glaser, Robert. "Education and Thinking: The Role of Writing." *AmP* 39 (February 1984): 93–104.

Reviews major theories of cognition and suggests teaching strategies to improve cognitive skills.

1870. Glassman, Steve. "Modelling and Showing: An Approach for the Junior Fiction Workshop." *ELAB* 26 (Spring 1985): 4–6.

Argues that the genres of fiction have internal rules. Young writers can best learn the rules by enlarging on models. Demonstrates with samples.

1871. Goldberg, Mark F. "An Update on the National Writing Project." *PhiDK* 65 (January 1984): 356–357.

Discusses the growth of the National Writing Project, begun in 1974 as the Bay Area Writing Project. Examines the project's potential for improving student writing.

1872. Greenfield, Adele. "Writing by Intuition." *Writer* 98 (February 1985): 14–16, 45.

Provides exercises designed to help the writer "focus on right-brained intuition."

1873. Grimm, Nancy. "Classroom Management: Using Small Groups Effectively." *ArEB* 28 (Fall 1985): 52–60.

Demonstrates how to develop and model response groups. Offers a checklist for teachers on improving the quality of group work.

1874. Grossman, Florence. "Turning Them on to Poetry." *IaEB* 33 (1984): 34–35.

Describes how to help students generate poetry by asking them to remember imaginative childhood games.

1875. Halpern, Jeanne W., and Sarah Liggett. *Computers and Composing: How the New Technologies Are Changing Writing.* Studies in Writing and Rhetoric. Carbondale, Ill.: Southern Illinois University Press, 1984. 144 pages

Discusses how new electronic hardware is changing writers' composing habits and how these changes can and should be incorporated into the classroom. Includes bibliography.

1876. Hanna, Stanley. "Writing to Learn: Whose Responsibility?" *EN* 6 (1984): 53–58.

Discusses the relationship between writing and learning.

1877. Harris, Muriel. "Encouraging Mature, Not Premature, Editing." *CEJ* 15 (Spring 1985): 67–69.

Discusses strategies that encourage students to edit their writing at the appropriate time in the writing process.

1878. Hart, Mary. "Oral History in the Classroom." *Statement* 21 (October 1985): 39–42.

Discusses how work with oral histories can enhance students' writing, editing, literary, and research skills.

1879. Hattenhauer, Darryl. "A New Approach to the Teaching of Developmental Grammar." *ELAB* 26 (Spring 1985): 14–15.

Advocates learning grammar while learning to write by beginning with whole discourse and focusing on grammatical problems in texts, instead of by moving from grammar to discourse.

1880. Hawley, Christopher S. "The Thieves of Academe: Plagiarism in the University System." *ICUT* 32 (Winter 1984): 35–39.

Analyzes questionnaire data to examine plagiarism. Proposes strategies for responding and questions for further research.

1881. Hocks, Elaine. "A Method of Interpreting and Writing about Literature." *WLN* 8 (May 1984): 6–9.

Describes a technique enabling students to interpret literature, establish a thesis, and develop necessary support for the analytic essay.

1882. Hodges, V. Pauline, and William Johnson. "Basic Language Skills?" *Statement* 20 (October 1984): 17–22.

Argues that schools more than ever need to teach "basic" English skills, especially those that foster critical thinking.

1883. Hoffman, Eleanor M. "Raising the Dead; or, from Syllabus to Lesson Plan." *ArEB* 28 (Fall 1985): 26–34.

Shows how to develop a lesson plan in terms of goal, audience, content, form, and context. Gives two examples.

1884. Hogan, Homer. "Teaching Rhetorical Classification." *EQ* 16 (Winter 1984): 65–74.

Recommends teaching the formal outline to use in composition and computer programming.

1885. Holbrook, Hilary Taylor. "ERIC/RCS Report: Visual Literacy Comes of Age." *ET* 15 (Winter 1984): 66–71.

Examines criteria for literacy other than reading and writing, asking questions of television, film, and advertising media. Points to a need for a visual curriculum.

1886. Hollingsworth, Craig R. "Poetry and Drama: Alternatives in the Composition Course." *EJ* 74 (September 1985): 60–62.

Literature review indicates that composing poetry and drama improves students' language skills and essay writing.

1887. Huber, Carole A. "Metaphor in Twentieth-Century Theory of Teaching Composition: As a Trope, an Aid to Expression, a Problem-Solving Strategy, and a Way of Knowing." *DAI* 44 (February 1984): 2459A.

Recommends teaching metaphorical thinking in a pedagogy that recognizes how reality is constructed through rhetoric.

1888. Hunt, Peter, and Sarah Wilkinson. "Technical Communication: The Academic Dilemma." *JTWC* 15 (1985): 35–42.

Two British writers conclude, after a sabbatical tour, that the teaching of technical writing in the United Kingdom and the United States is mediocre.

1889. Illinois Community College Board. *Results of the Survey of Community Colleges on the Teaching of Writing.* Springfield, Ill.: Illinois State Board of Education, 1984. ERIC ED 250 051 [12 pages]

Reports that community colleges frequently have placement tests, see writing skills as constant over the past 10 years, and support in-service training in teaching writing.

1890. James, Janis. "Freewriting, Feedback, and Self-Confidence." *ELAB* 26 (Spring 1985): 12–13.

Cycles of student writing and communication with the teacher establish the trust necessary for real growth in writing. Argues for ideas before form.

1891. Kelly, Patricia P., and Robert C. Small, Jr., eds. "What We Know about the Teaching of Writing." *VEB* 35 (Special Issue, Spring 1985). ERIC ED 257 118 [129 pages].

Special issue of a journal, made available in ERIC. Articles listed separately in this volume.

1892. Knapp, John V. "Strategies for Individual Progress in Reading Literature and Writing Compositions." *EngR* 35 (Second Quarter 1984): 2–7.

Negotiating contracts between students and teachers teaches students how to learn and how to judge their learning.

1893. Kraft, Robert G. "Group-Inquiry Turns Passive Students Active." *CollT* 33 (Fall 1985): 149–154.

Describes group-inquiry techniques that increase students' involvement in oral and written discussions.

1894. Kroitor, Harry P., and Elizabeth Tebeaux. "Bringing Literature Teachers and Writing Teachers Closer Together." *BADE* 78 (Summer 1984): 28–32.

Argues that teaching fundamental principles in all English courses will unify English studies and therefore have positive effects on students and faculty.

1895. Laine, Chet. "Is Research Being Used in the English Classroom?" *ELAB* 25 (Spring 1984): 19–22.

Examines studies of the ways in which classroom teachers use and fail to use current research in language arts, linguistics, and the learning process.

1896. Land, Darren F. "Meaning through Language: Personal Journals." *EQ* 17 (Fall 1984): 11–19.

Explores the use of personal journal writing as a means of self-expression, self-discovery, and synthesizing school and life.

1897. Larsen, Richard B. "Arguing for Computer-Based Composition Instruction." Paper presented at the CCCC Convention, New York, March 1984. ERIC ED 246 480 [11 pages]

Argues that English teachers must accept microcomputers in the composition classroom. Suggests that their most powerful application is word processing.

1898. Leahy, Richard. "The Power of the Student Journal." *CollT* 33 (Summer 1985): 108–112.

Discusses using journals for all graded work in linguistics and literature classes.

1899. Lee, Helen C. "More Words, Better Writing Processes." *CEJ* 16 (Spring 1985): 105–107.

Discusses the benefits of using computers and the Bank Street Writer in composition classes.

1900. Liggett, Sarah. "Collaborative Writing from Start to Finish." *LaEJ* 24 (Fall 1985): 24–29.

Discusses the experiences of teachers who write collaboratively.

1901. Litvack, Mark. "Writing: The Living Organism." *Statement* 21 (October 1985): 25–29.

Argues for a holistic approach to teaching composition.

1902. Loeb, Helen M. "Writing Courses in the Engineering College Curriculum." *JTWC* 15 (1985): 43–48.

A survey of 150 engineering colleges finds that freshman and upper-division writing courses are required or recommended and are considered successful and important.

1903. Lotto, Edward. "Assignment Making: The Teachers and the Critics." *PCTEB* 5 (April 1984): 15–22.

Argues that theorists overemphasize the non-academic audience and neglect the academic audience.

1904. Lucking, Robert, and Pamela Benner. "Orwell, Computers, and the Teaching of English." *IE* 8 (Fall 1984): 16–18.

Despite some negative effects, computers can be "helpful teaching tools."

1905. Madigan, Chris. "The Tools That Shape Us: Composing by Hand *Vs.* Composing by Machine." *EEd* 16 (October 1984): 143–150.

Suggests that microcomputers may help reshape students' writing processes.

1906. Marechal, Linda S. "Writing as Problem Solving across the Curriculum." *ET* 15 (Spring 1984): 33–41.

Advocates creating more positive assignments that are based on process, discovery, arrangement, and style.

1907. Maxwell, John C. "How to Kill a Writer." *IE* 9 (Winter 1985): 39–40.

Discourages the use of writing as punishment. [Reprinted from *Education Week* 28 (August 1985).]

1908. McDermond, Dawn. "Teachers Should Write, Writers Should Teach." *UEJ* (1985): 23–25.

A teacher models writing for her class by drafting a short story, sharing it, and asking the students for critiques.

1909. NCTE Commission on Composition. "Teaching Composition: A Position Statement." *CE* 46 (October 1984): 612–614.

A "statement [for] teachers, parents, and administrators [to be used] in understanding the power of writing and...teaching."

1910. NCTE Commission on Composition. "Teaching Composition: A Position Statement." *LArts* 61 (October 1984): 652–653.

States essential principles of writing to guide teachers, parents, and administrators in understanding the power of writing and how to teach it effectively.

1911. NCTE Commission on Composition. *Teaching Composition: A Position Statement.* Urbana, Ill.: NCTE, 1985. 5 pages

Defines principles in the teaching of writing.

1912. NCTE Commission on Composition. "Teaching Composition: A Position Statement." *Statement* 20 (February 1985): 77–78.

Discusses the act of writing, the purposes and scenes for writing, teachers of writing, and the means of writing instruction.

1913. Newkirk, Thomas. "In Defense of the Teacher-as-Audience." *Leaflet* 84 (Winter 1985): 50–56.

Argues that teachers are a valid audience for student writing because they are representatives of the interpretive community the student gradually enters.

1914. Nordberg, Beverly. "Let's Not 'Write a Report.'" Paper presented at the NCTE Spring Conference, Columbus, Ohio, April 1984. ERIC ED 244 279 [20 pages]

Discusses writing across the curriculum as a way of improving the quality of student papers.

1915. North, Stephen M. "The Idea of a Writing Center." *CE* 46 (September 1984): 433–446.

Writing centers help students with basics, but their primary purpose is to lead beginning and advanced writers to a better understanding of the writing process.

1916. Phelps, Terry O. "Beyond Teacher-Based Instruction in Language Arts." *ArEB* 28 (Fall 1985): 4–11.

Argues that the key to student-based instruction is good questioning "on the students' level to facilitate higher order mental processes."

1917. Pilarcik, Marlene A. "Composite Compositions: A Group Effort." *PCTEB* 51 (April 1985): 15–17.

Argues for group-centered writing activities as a way to improve students' awareness of the writing process.

1918. Polanski, Virginia G. "Producing Metaphors and Similes That Work." *EQ* 16 (Winter 1984): 29–36.

Describes methods used by researchers at three grade levels to elicit original metaphors and similes: structural tasks, definitions and models, and theses to be supported.

1919. Raffetto, William G. "The Cheat." *CJCJ* 56 (October–November 1985): 26–27.

Lists 14 forms of academic dishonesty, 5 directly pertinent to writing. Suggests 7 preventive measures for faculty.

1920. Resch, Paula C. *Suzuki and the Teaching of Writing: A Surprising Connection.* Urbana, Ill.: ERIC/RCS and NCTE, 1984. ERIC ED 251 181 [11 pages]

Argues that Suzuki music and writing process instruction are similar, especially in their assumptions that performance precedes subskills and that all children can learn.

1921. Rich, Sharon J. "Whole Language: The Inner Dimension." *EQ* 18 (Summer 1985): 15–22.

Describes how one teacher used the "whole language" approach to motivate children to make sense of their worlds.

1922. Roderick, John M., and Lois Ann Ryan. "On Keeping a Journal." *CEJ* 15 (Spring 1984): 81–86.

Surveys the literature on using personal journals in the classroom. Aims to help teachers decide whether or not they will use journals.

1923. Rodrigues, Dawn. "Peer Review Possibilities." *CEJ* 15 (Spring 1984): 80.

Discusses three functions of peer writing groups. They provide an audience for student writers, a reason for revision, and help for the teacher.

1924. Rouse, John. "Scenes from the Writing Workshop." *CE* 47 (May 1985): 217–236.

A narrative of students and teachers talking, reading, writing, and learning in a writing workshop.

1925. Rushing, Joe B. "The Humanities: Endangered Species?" *CJCJ* 56 (December 1985–January 1986): 16–18.

Asserts that, for the survival of the humanities, faculty need a pervading conviction about the centrality of the humanities in all disciplines.

1926. Scovic, Stephen P. "Some of Those Ideas We Mistook for Panaceas Deserve Another Chance." *ASBJ* 172 (July 1985): 28–29.

Describes traditional and alternative methods for curriculum, testing, and measurement. Discusses strategies for successfully combining them.

1927. Selzer, Jack. "Exploring Options in Composing." *CCC* 35 (October 1984): 276–284.

Argues for flexible composing styles to accommodate different aims, situations, and writers.

1928. Simard, Rodney. "Reducing Fear and Resistance by Attacking the Myths." *CollT* 33 (Summer 1985): 101–107.

Identifies eight misconceptions that interfere with writing and proposes ways to dispel them.

1929. Slanger, George. "Dualism in the Teaching of English: What I Learned from Education Courses." *EEd* 17 (December 1985): 220–231.

Describes the difficulty of evaluating what is not directly taught in writing instruction.

1930. Sommers, Jeffrey. "Teaching as Rhetorical Situation." *FEN* 13 (Spring 1984): 11–13.

Suggests that teachers consider their audiences by recalling their own experiences as students.

1931. Squire, James R. "The Modes of Discourse." *CEJ* 15 (Spring 1985): 52–53.

Suggests that teachers use the modes of discourse to structure a curriculum that provides a variety of experiences in reading and writing prose.

1932. Stafford, Kim R. "Thirteen Questions: Finding Voices for Writing Fiction." *OrE* 6 (Fall 1984): 26–27.

Uses job interview questions for beginning writers to answer as a strategy for developing authentic voices for fictional characters.

1933. Staley, George, and Joe Kincheloe. "Not *All* Writing Is Good Writing: The Killing of the Spirit." *EN* 6 (1984): 45–47.

Discusses problems in evaluating writing.

1934. Stiff, Rebecca. "Debunking the Rules of the Game." *EJ* 74 (October 1985): 61–62.

Discusses 10 misconceptions students have about writing.

1935. Strickland, James. *Deactivating the Writing Program.* Urbana, Ill.: ERIC/RCS and NCTE, 1983. ERIC ED 236 627 [13 pages]

Advises teachers on how rigid rules, magical thinking, misdirection, and immaturity undermine the development of writing.

1936. Suhor, Charles. "Curriculum Models: You Get What You Ask For." *ET* 15 (Spring 1984): 8–23.

Examines the traditional curriculum model and weaknesses in its approach to teaching writing. Compares it to the process model, which is less formulaic.

1937. Suhor, Charles. "Thinking Skills in English —and across the Curriculum." *ArEB* 27 (Winter 1985): 1–5.

Argues that language as a way of thinking and learning "is an essential element in every classroom."

1938. Suhor, Charles. "1984 Report on Trends and Issues in English: A Summary of Reports from the NCTE Commissions." *ET* 15 (Summer 1984): 30–33.

Summarizes reports in the areas of language, curriculum, literature, reading, composition, and media.

1939. Suhor, Charles, and Michael Spooner. *Second Annual Trends and Issues Statements.* Urbana, Ill.: ERIC/RCS and NCTE, 1985. ERIC ED 252 881 [14 pages]

Summarizes discussions among commissions and standing committees of the National Council of Teachers of English. Defines 15 trends and isssues in teaching English language arts.

1940. Suhor, Charles, and Michael Spooner. "Second Annual Trends and Issues Statements: NCTE Commissions and Standing Committees." *Statement* 20 (May 1985): 52–60.

Reports on trends and issues in language, literature, composition, reading, media, curriculum, research, and censorship discussed at the 1983 National Council of Teachers of English meeting in Denver.

1941. Sulkes, Stan. "Hopeless, but Not Serious: Comparing Results from Writing Classes with Those of Other Disciplines." *FEN* 14 (Spring 1985): 20–22.

Concludes that students in other disciplines also have difficulty showing knowledge in new contexts.

1942. Swope, John W. "Journals: Capturing Students' Individual Responses to Literature." *VEB* 35 (Winter 1985): 35–41.

Explains using response journals that focus on emotions and difficulties as a means of gathering students' immediate responses to longer pieces of fiction.

1943. Taylor, Karl K. "Teaching Summarization Skills." *JR* 27 (February 1984): 389–393.

Argues that summarization skills include careful reading, looking for structures, analyzing material, checking for accuracy, and thinking before writing. Pedagogy emphasizes peer response and induction.

1944. Thomas, Timothy A. "A Student Looks at Writing to Learn." *Statement* 21 (October 1985): 18–24.

Discusses a composition curriculum based upon a process approach to teaching writing. Draws on National Writing Project curricula.

1945. Thomas, Trudelle. "Using a Personal Journal." *ELAB* 25 (Spring 1984): 8–9.

Discusses the value of organizing a writing class around the keeping of a personal journal. Gives examples of journal-writing activities.

1946. Thompson, Loren C., and Alan M. Frager. "Teaching Critical Thinking: Guidelines for Teacher-Designed Content Area Lessons." *JR* 28 (November 1984): 122–127.

Presents five guidelines for developing lessons to teach critical thinking. Guidelines advocate transferring thinking skills from speaking to writing situations. Analyzes sample plan.

1947. Travers, D. Molly Murison. "The Poetry Teacher: Behavior and Attitudes." *RTE* 18 (December 1984): 367–384.

Reviews research on poetry in the classroom. Suggests the importance of the teacher over the method in developing student attitudes and reading competence.

1948. Tritt, Michael. "Collaboration in Writing: From Start to Finish and Beyond." *EQ* 17 (Spring 1984): 82–86.

Suggests that, by writing collaboratively, students learn and gain confidence, sharing strengths to work out difficulties.

1949. Vivion, Michael, and George A. McCulley. "Primary Traits: Combining Instruction and Evaluation." *ArEB* 28 (Fall 1985): 89–100.

Offers a method to reduce teachers' "red line fever" by using primary traits for prewriting, rewriting, and evaluating.

1950. Waller, Gary F. "Working within the Paradigm Shift: Poststructuralism and the College Curriculum." *BADE* 8 (Fall 1985): 6–12.

Defends the infusion of poststructuralism into curriculum and describes Carnegie-Mellon's revised program, one based on discourse and built on language, history, and culture.

1951. Walvoord, Barbara Fassler. "Freshmen, 'Focus,' and Writing across the Curriculum." *FEN* 14 (Fall 1985): 13–17.

Offers strategies for teaching students that all discourse needs focus and for showing how to make sections of a paper fit the purpose of the whole.

1952. Weber, Paul, and Judy Freund. "The Wisconsin Program for the Gifted Is a Lab for Innovation." *PhiDK* 65 (January 1984): 366.

Argues that a Wisconsin elementary school's gifted and talented program has benefited the entire school, providing a receptive atmosphere for curriculum innovation.

1953. White, Edward M., and Linda G. Polin. *Research in Effective Teaching of Writing, Phase I.* Washington: NIH, 1983. ERIC ED 239 292 [248 pages]

Describes and evaluates current practices in composition programs at 19 California State University campuses.

1954. White, Edward M., and Linda G. Polin. "Research on Composition Programs: Faculty Attitudes and Beliefs about the Teaching of Writing." *WPA* 8 (Fall–Winter 1984): 37–45.

Summarizes results of a California State University system survey revealing differences in faculty attitudes about the teaching of writing.

1955. Wilson, Robert L. "Writing for Survival." *NebEC* 29 (Spring 1984): 23–24.

Advocates providing opportunities to build students' confidence in using language to increase the likelihood of success in life.

1956. Woolings, Marty. "Meaning through Language: Writing Folders." *EQ* 17 (Fall 1984): 20–25.

Reports that writing folders encouraged regular writing, increased motivation to write, and individualized the approach to writing in London, Ontario, schools.

1957. Youngblood, Ed. "Reading, Thinking, and Writing: Using the Reading Journal." *EJ* 74 (September 1985): 46–48.

Argues that reading journals improves students' reading, writing, and thinking skills.

1958. Ziegler, Alan. *The Writing Workshop,* Vol. 2. New York: Teachers and Writers Collaborative, 1984. 244 pages

"Deals with what you might say to students to inspire them to write." Emphasizes product and divides suggestions into "openers" and "orientations." Includes a "catalogue of assignments."

See also 21, 49, 50, 51, 96, 211, 445, 498, 499, 508, 565, 803, 817, 853, 891, 995, 1062, 1263, 1285, 1286, 1293, 1304, 1327, 1346, 1664, 1713, 1744, 1779, 1780, 2090, 2098, 2628, 3443, 3453, 3844

PRESCHOOL EDUCATION

1959. Bertrand, Nancy, and Steven H. Fairchild. "Reading Readiness through Writing." Paper given at the NCTE Spring Conference, Columbus, Ohio, April 1984. ERIC ED 244 234 [9 pages]

Discusses possible uses of writing to prepare children for reading instruction.

1960. Borus, Dixie N. "The Development of Knowledge about Word Reading and Word Writing in Three-, Four-, and Five-Year-Old Children." *DAI* 45 (October 1984): 1081A.

Investigates relationships among word reading and word writing behaviors of preschool children.

1961. Ehri, Linnea C. "Learning to Read and Spell." Paper given at the AERA Convention, New Orleans, April 1985. ERIC ED 259 302 [43 pages]

Reviews studies of children's acquisition of reading and spelling skills.

1962. Farr, Marcia. "State of the Art: Children's Early Writing Development." Paper given at the AERA Convention, New Orleans, April 1984. ERIC ED 247 587 [19 pages]

Considers studies of early writing development in the context of emergent literacy.

1963. Glenn, Sheila M., and Cliff C. Cunningham. "Nursery Rhymes and Early Language Acquisition by Mentally Handicapped Children." *ExC* 51 (September 1984): 72–74.

Examines the effect of nursery rhymes, particularly when combined with a parent's voice, on language development in preschool handicapped children.

1964. Hall, Susan E. M. "OAD MAHR GOS and Writing with Young Children." *LArts* 62 (March 1985): 262–265.

Kindergartners using invented spelling write Mother Goose rhymes, which teachers use to discuss written language.

1965. Himley, Margaret. "First Encounters of a Written Kind: Points of Entry and Paths of Development for Three Beginning Writers." *DAI* 44 (May 1984): 3373A.

Addresses how and why children begin to use the resources of written language to make meaningful texts. Offers suggestions for conducting more effective writing research.

1966. Hipple, Marjorie L. "Journal Writing in Kindergarten." *LArts* 62 (March 1985): 255–261.

Using daily journals to communicate, 23 kindergartners who could not read enhanced their self-concept and their development in oral language skills, listening, and reading.

1967. Seittelman, Estelle M. "Write about Our Roots." *EngR* 35 (First Quarter 1984): 15–17.

A continuing curriculum for teaching creative writing from kindergarten through elementary school.

1968. Springate, Kay W. "Developmental Trends and Interrelationships among Preprimary Children's Knowledge of Writing and Reading Readiness Skills." *DAI* 45 (March 1985): 2755A.

Findings indicate that knowledge of the communicative purposes of listing, labeling, and letter writing increased across groups of three-, four-, and five-year-olds.

1969. Warash, Barbara Gibson. "Computer Language Experience Approach." Paper given at the NCTE Spring Conference, Columbus, Ohio, April 1984. ERIC ED 244 264 [14 pages]

Describes the use of microcomputers in early childhood language activities.

1970. Zenai, Ruth. "The Language Arts and Music: Recent Research." *ArEB* 27 (Fall 1984): 61–64.

Discusses how music can help children read and write.

See also 952, 1277, 1431, 1533, 2044, 3008, 3754

ELEMENTARY EDUCATION (K–8)

1971. Afflerbach, Peter. "Overcoming Children's Reluctance to Revise Informational Writing." *JTW* 4 (Fall 1985): 170–176.

Proposes two approaches to encourage revision: persuasive writing and "common ground" writing in content area reports.

1972. Amberg, Margaret, Ray La Point, Mary Rose Redlich, and Beth Torrison. *A Guide to Easing Writing's Rigors: Having Fun with Language.* Edited by Linda Christensen, Lori Hamann, and John M. Kean. Madison, Wis.: University of Wisconsin, Department of Curriculum and Instruction, 1983. ERIC ED 249 517 [118 pages]

Noting that fun with language engenders love and understanding, calls for teachers to model writing and suggests 12 class activities.

1973. Anderson, Margaret A., Nona A. Tollefson, and Edwyna C. Gilbert. "Giftedness and Reading: A Cross-Sectional View of Differences in Reading Attitudes and Behaviors." *GCQ* 29 (Fall 1985): 186–189.

Describes sex- and age-related differences affecting the enjoyment of and participation in reading activities by gifted students.

1974. Armington, David. "Invented Spelling." *TWM* 15 (May–June 1984): 1–6, 8.

Describes using "invented spelling" to help young children write words from their own speech before they know the correct spelling.

1975. Ashby-Davis, Claire. "Teaching Reading and Writing through the Study of Grammar: A Metacognitive Approach." *CEJ* 16 (Spring 1985): 25–38.

Discusses abstractions needed to apply grammar to acts of reading and writing. Describes pilot studies.

1976. Atwell, Nancie. "Writing and Reading Literature from the Inside Out." *LArts* 61 (March 1984): 240–252.

Describes a literate environment in which eighth graders read writing and write readings. Samples of two students' work show how they got "inside" reading and writing.

1977. Avery, Carol S. "Growth in Process: Three Stories." *PCTEB* 5 (November 1985): 3–12.

Case studies of three first graders whose first writing experiences were in the classroom using the process approach.

1978. Bartelo, Dennise. "A Writing Center Approach to Children's Literature for Kindergarten Children." *Leaflet* 84 (Spring 1985): 11–14.

Describes two learning centers with readiness and writing activities keyed to specific children's books.

1979. Baru, Ellen. "Finding the Writer's Magic." *LArts* 62 (November 1985): 730–739.

A professional writer's regular visits brought a fifth-grade writing class and their teacher confidence and self-discipline.

1980. Bauman, Gail A. "A Case Study Examination of the Development of the Writing Process Behaviors of Kindergarten Children as Demonstrated in an Informal Classroom Writing Center." *DAI* 46 (October 1985): 889A.

In a qualitative, descriptive case study, the writing of kindergarten children was shown to be influenced by their drawing, home environments, previous experiences, and interactional uses of language.

1981. Beachem, Michael T. "An Investigation of Two Writing Process Interventions on the Rhetorical Effectiveness of Sixth-Grade Writers." *DAI* 45 (February 1985): 2386A.

Examines the effects of the New Jersey Writing Project and Sustained Student Summary Writing on sixth graders' expressive and persuasive writing. Students in the New Jersey Writing Project improved in expressive writing.

1982. Beckman, Judy, and Joan Diamond. "Picture Books in the Classroom: The Secret Weapon for the Creative Teacher." *EJ* 73 (February 1984): 102–104.

Examines several "sophisticated picture books" that can enhance creative thinking/writing skills.

1983. Blackburn, Ellen. "Common Ground: Developing Relationships between Reading and Writing." *LArts* 61 (April 1984): 367–375.

Describes a first-grade program based on complementary principles of the writing and the reading processes. Considers invention, choice, discussion, revision, and publication.

1984. Bloome, David. *Getting Access to and Control of Reading and Writing Resources: K–8.* Urbana, Ill.: NCTE Research Foundation, 1984. ERIC ED 251 830 [235 pages]

Studies students' use of reading and writing resources in the school and the community.

1985. Boutin, Frances, and Chelle King. "Composition/Grammar: The Partner Joins the Language Arts Team." *ET* 15 (Spring 1984): 24–32.

Examines the development, implementation, validation, and revision of a total language arts program for kindergarten through eighth grade. Includes objectives that should be adapted to a teacher's style.

1986. Braig, Deborah E. "Six Authors in Search of an Audience: Dialogue Journal Writing of Second Graders." *DAI* 45 (November 1984): 1295A.

Finds that dialogue journals helped children develop audience awareness and written language abilities.

1987. Brause, Rita S., and John S. Mayher. "Learning through Teaching: Adele Fiderer Reflects with Her Fifth Graders." *LArts* 62 (September 1985): 539–543.

A collaborative partnership in which fifth graders wrote books for first graders.

1988. Brazee, Phyllis. "Helping Students Read and Write in Expository Materials." *Statement* 19 (May 1984): 9–14.

Suggests that sentence expansion/reduction and follow-up paragraph writing help students learn to read and write exposition.

1989. Brewster, Marty. "Stepping Down to Creativity." *ELAB* 25 (Spring 1984): 10–11.

Discusses methods for stimulating creativity in junior high school students. Suggests writing assignments and grading strategies.

1990. Bromley, Karen D. "Précis Writing and Outlining Enhance Content Learning." *RT* 38 (January 1985): 406–411.

Both précis writing and outlining resulted in improved learning and in positive attitudes for two groups of fifth graders.

1991. Bromley, Karen D. "SSW: Sustained Spontaneous Writing." *CEd* 62 (September–October 1985): 23–29.

Defines "sustained spontaneous writing" and describes ways of implementing it in the classroom.

1992. Burrows, Alvina Truet, Doris C. Jackson, and Dorothy O. Saunders. *They All Want to Write: Written English in the Elementary School.* 4th ed. Hamden, Conn.: The Shoe String Press, 1984. 238 pages

First published in 1939, offers elementary teachers, curriculum planners, and teacher educators practical suggestions for daily writing exercises. Distinguishes between personal and practical writing, includes samples of children's writings,

reviews recent research, and suggests how to integrate reading, writing, and literature. Includes bibliography.

1993. Butler, Andrea, and Jan Turbill. *Towards a Reading-Writing Classroom.* Portsmouth, N.H.: Heinemann, 1984. 90 pages

A guide showing how the process approach to the teaching of writing can be used in the elementary classroom to teach reading more effectively.

1994. Butler, Andrea, and Jan Turbill, eds. *Towards a Reading-Writing Classroom.* Rozelle, Australia: Primary English Teaching Association, 1984. ERIC ED 250 650 [96 pages]

Describes theoretical approaches and instructional strategies for integrating reading and writing.

1995. Cacha, Frances B. "The Writing Process in the Elementary Social Studies Program." *ArEB* 27 (Fall 1984): 65–68.

Describes how teachers can use the stages of process writing to integrate social studies and language arts.

1996. Cacha, Frances B. "Writing Theory and Word Processing with Elementary Students." *ArEB* 28 (Fall 1985): 35–39.

Describes a five-month study of six fourth graders who learned to use word processing.

1997. Chapman, Diane L. "Poet to Poet: An Author Responds to Child-Writers." *LArts* 62 (March 1985): 235–242.

A visit from a poet helped fifth and sixth graders see that writing is hard work and involves researching and experimenting with meaning, shapes, and word choice.

1998. Chou, Frank H., and Susan A. Vaught. *Student Selection of Topic and the Length of Sample Writing.* Urbana, Ill.: ERIC/RCS, 1982. ERIC ED 236 683 [31 pages]

Finds that sixth-grade students write more when they choose their own topics.

1999. Chudy, Gladys L. "Grammar, an Imposition." *CEJ* 16 (Spring 1985): 97–98.

Suggests that grammar is best taught in conjunction with other language arts materials such as word games, individualized writing conferences, and passages from literature.

2000. Church, Susan M. "Blossoming in the Writing Community." *LArts* 62 (February 1985): 175–179.

A teacher who has experienced the rewards of a writing community is able to create such a community with three seventh-grade resource students.

2001. Clark, Christopher M., and Susan Florio. *Understanding Writing in School: A Descriptive Study of Writing and Its Instruction in Two Classrooms.* Research Series, no. 104. East Lansing, Mich.: Michigan State University Institute for Research on Teaching, 1982. ERIC ED 239 257 [239 pages]

Describes a naturalistic study of writing-related activities and teacher attitudes in two elementary classrooms.

2002. Clark, John R. "Writing in the Shortest Forms." *ExEx* 31 (Fall 1985): 36–37.

Discusses the usefulness of poetry's "short-short forms" in teaching writing. Stresses the importance of continuous writing and frequent revision.

2003. Clark, Ruth Anne, Shirley C. Willihnganz, and Lisa L. O'Dell. "Training Fourth Graders in Compromising and Persuasive Strategies." *ComEd* 34 (October 1985): 331–342.

Explores the effects of training children to construct persuasive arguments and to compromise in situations where their interests conflict with their audience's interests.

2004. Collins, James P. "Linguistic Perspective on Minority Education: Discourse Analysis and Early Literacy." *DAI* 45 (September 1984): 830A.

Explores the nature of communication in formal learning environments and identifies some discourse skills children must learn to become literate.

2005. Coombs, Marjorie. "Writing across the Curriculum: An Experiment That Worked." *UEJ* (1984): 2–5.

Describes a year-long, accelerated, two-period, Science/Language Arts class for eighth graders, taught by an English teacher and a science teacher.

2006. Cranley, Sharon J. "A Comparison between Scavenger Hunts and the Presentation of Vocabulary." *ET* 15 (Summer 1984): 25–27.

Reviews research on using visual images in direct teaching and advocates having students find or create pictorial representations of vocabulary.

2007. Crews, Ruthellen. "Teaching Writing as an Extension of the Directed Reading Activity." Paper given at the Florida Reading Association, Hollywood, Fla., October 1983. ERIC ED 239 241 [12 pages]

Describes how to integrate writing activities with content reading.

2008. Curran, Doris. "Teaching Standard English as a Second Language to American Third Graders." *IE* 7 (Spring 1984): 3–4.

After composing and revising, pupils are accountable for complete sentences, subject-verb agreement, and proper pronoun forms.

2009. Curran, Doris. "When Children Ask 'Why?': Teaching Research Skills in the Primary Grades." *IE* 9 (Winter 1985): 26–29.

Presents a sequence of simple to more sophisticated research techniques. Suggests reference books.

2010. Day, Margaret M. "Characteristics of the Concept of Audience in Fifth-Grade Writing." *DAI* 45 (July 1984): 103A.

Describes characteristics of audience considered by fifth-grade writers. Findings show that assigning an audience affected the organization and length of essays.

2011. Dismuke, Diane. "Toward Tomorrow: Writing." *TEd* (1985–1986): 54–55.

Describes a writing program in which kindergartners write phonetically with computers, first graders use editing symbols, and second graders make up complex questions about their stories.

2012. Dixon, Diane J. "The Effect of Poetry on Figurative Language Usage in Children's Descriptive Prose Writing." *DAI* 45 (February 1985): 2387A.

Results show that the use of poetry does not necessarily increase figurative language in students' writing.

2013. Donohue, Christine. "A Study of the Impact of a Special Writing Program on the Reading and Writing Achievement of Gates Students in a New York City Junior High School Remediation Program." *DAI* 46 (September 1985): 659A.

Reports significant increases in writing achievement and reading comprehension for the experimental group.

2014. Donsky, Barbara V. "Trends in Elementary Writing Instruction, 1900–1959." *LArts* 61 (December 1984): 795–803.

Examines language textbooks over a 60-year period and traces the cyclic nature of instruction as textbooks responded to educational and societal needs.

2015. Drescher, Carolyn S. "Throw the Horse over the Fence Some Grass." *CEJ* 16 (Spring 1985): 86–88.

Argues for drills in grammar, correct punctuation, usage, and sentence combining for student writers in junior high school.

2016. Dudley-Marling, Curtis C. "Microcomputers, Reading, and Writing: Alternatives to Drill and Practice." *RT* 38 (January 1985): 388–391.

Advocates using microcomputers to encourage meaningful written language.

2017. Duggan, Tamia. "They Can Write on the First Day." *WaEJ* 6 (Spring 1984): 21–22.

First graders begin keeping journals on the first day of class and publish their work throughout the year.

2018. Duncan, Patricia H. "What Do Children Understand about Their Own Compositions?" Paper given at the NCTE Spring Conference, Houston, March 1985. ERIC ED 255 936 [10 pages]

Observes five children in grade one, finding early development of metacognitive knowledge of story structure.

2019. Duvall, Betty J. "Kindergarten Performance for Reading and Matching Four Styles of Handwriting." *DAI* 45 (February 1985): 2388A.

Explores kindergartners' ability to match typeset letters to handwritten manuscript, cursive, italic, and D'Nealia letters. Cursive was more difficult to read, write, and match. Italic was the easiest.

2020. Dyson, Anne Haas. "Copying: Composing with Training Wheels?" *CEJ* 15 (Spring 1984): 50–51.

Argues that writing experiences for young children should focus on communicating intended meaning and not simply on forming letters.

2021. Dyson, Anne Haas. "Emerging Alphabetic Literacy in School Contexts: Toward Defining the Gap between School Curriculum and Child Mind." *WC* 1 (January 1984): 5–55.

Observes that teachers approach literacy from the perspective of curriculum, students from the perspective of cultural and personal experiences.

2022. Dyson, Anne Haas. "Research Currents: Who Controls Classroom Writing Contexts?" *LArts* 61 (October 1984): 618–626.

Compares the writing activities, or events, of preschoolers and second graders to show that school activities should be structured to increase children's control over written language.

2023. Dyson, Anne Haas. *Understanding the How's and Why's of Writing: Children's Concepts of Writing in Grade Two.* Athens, Ga.: University of Georgia and the NCTE Research Foundation, 1984. ERIC ED 249 535 [135 pages]

Describes three case studies of second-grade writers, focusing on their concepts of writing and their writing behaviors in school.

2024. Ediger, Marlow. "Issues in Designing the Language Arts Curriculum." *ArEB* 27 (Winter 1985): 158–164.

Provides guidelines for determining the objectives, scope and sequence, methodology, aids, and organization of the elementary school language arts curriculum.

2025. Evans, Christine Sobray. "Writing to Learn in Math." *LArts* 61 (December 1984): 828–835.

Using writing as a way to learn multiplication and geometry, a test class of fifth graders scored higher on a posttest than did the students in the control group.

2026. Farr, Marcia. *Writing Growth in Young Children: What We Are Learning from Research.* The Talking and Writing Series, K–12. Washington: Dingle Associates, 1983. ERIC ED 233 389 [22 pages]

Synthesizes classroom-based studies of children's writing development.

2027. Ferguson, Anne M., and Jo Fairburn. "Language Experience for Problem Solving in Mathematics." *RT* 38 (February 1985): 504–507.

Concludes that a language experience approach is a useful strategy for assisting remedial second graders in solving word problems.

2028. Ferguson, John. "English for the Remote Learner." *EQ* 17 (Fall 1984): 65–66.

Describes a nontraditional English program provided by the private sector and designed for the remote learner.

2029. Fountas, Irene C. "An Investigation of the Effect of a Story Mapping Program on the Development of Story Schema in Selected Second-Grade Students." *DAI* 45 (December 1984): 1637A.

Finds that change in children's ability to select and describe the elements of a story were significantly greater than the change in their ability to use the story element in speaking and writing.

2030. Freemer, Phillip T. "Grammar and Writing: A Positive Connection through Revision." *CEJ* 16 (Spring 1985): 42–43.

Describes a writing activity in which writers must make grammar-based choices while engaged in revision.

2031. Friedman, Sheila. "'If You Don't Know How to Write, You Try': Techniques That Work in First Grade." *RT* 38 (February 1985): 516–521.

Describes strategies for teaching first graders to write.

2032. Fulwiler, Toby. "Writing and Learning, Grade Three." *LArts* 62 (January 1985): 55–59.

Uses four journal entries written by third graders over a year to show that journals can be used to develop "more autonomous thinking."

2033. Gambrell, Linda B. "Dialogue Journals: Reading/Writing Interaction." *RT* 38 (February 1985): 512–515.

Suggests a procedure for using journals in which students and teachers converse in writing.

2034. Ganz, Alice. "Writing to Shape Experience." *EngR* 36 (1985): 16–19.

Finds that, in second graders, movement from egocentrism to sociocentrism is fostered by emphasizing the making of meaning rather than by correcting mechanical details.

2035. Garrity, Patricia J. "Learning to Listen." *CEJ* 15 (Spring 1984): 75–79.

Describes experiences in learning to use conferences in a writing program.

2036. Geller, Linda Gibson. *Wordplay and Language Learning for Children.* Urbana, Ill.: NCTE, 1985. 104 pages

Demonstrates how wordplay—rhythmic verse, nonsense, humor, and parody—can be used to aid students' cognitive development and language learning.

2037. Giordano, Gerard. "Analyzing and Remediating Writing Disabilities." *JLD* 17 (February 1984): 65–128.

Advocates writing exercises (as opposed to copying) and illustrates some that emphasize communicative goals and build on the communicative competencies of children with writing disabilities.

2038. Giza, Marie. "What in the World Is There in a Comic Book?" *MarylandJ* 19 (1984): 28–30.

Advocates having elementary students create their own comic books as a way to teach reading, writing, vocabulary, grammar, spelling, and punctuation.

2039. Goldberg, Mark F. "Sharing a Successful Writing Program." *ArEB* 27 (Fall 1984): 7–10.

Praises the Bay Area Writing Project as the model that increased writing in English classes and the content areas.

2040. Golden, Joanne M. "Children's Concept of Story in Reading and Writing." *RT* 37 (March 1984): 578–584.

Illustrates children's concept of story with examples of writings and retellings. Suggests ways teachers can help children extend and refine these concepts.

2041. Goodman, Jesse, and Kate Melcher. "Culture at a Distance: An Anthroliterary Approach to Cross-Cultural Education." *JR* 28 (December 1984): 200–207.

Developed by Margaret Mead, this approach to a culture through its folklore uses webbing to guide reading, reading folktales to generate writing.

2042. Gordon, Naomi M., ed. *Classroom Experiences: The Writing Process in Action.* Portsmouth, N.H.: Heinemann, 1984. 128 pages

A collection of seven essays discussing how to implement a process-based writing curriculum in kindergarten through the eighth grade. Also offers advice on staff development and communicating with parents.

2043. Grabe, Mark, and Cindy Grabe. "The Microcomputer and the Language Experience Approach." *RT* 38 (February 1985): 508–511.

Finds the word processor an effective tool in helping children read and write.

2044. Hall, Susan E. M. "Seven and One-Half Ways to Kill a Young Writer." *JTW* 4 (Fall 1985): 178–182.

A kindergarten teacher advocates accepting individual approaches to and the experimentation of young writers. Lists eight "blunt instruments" that can kill the desire to write.

2045. Hannan, Elspeth, and Gord Hamilton. "Writing: What to Look for, What to Do." *LArts* 61 (April 1984): 364–366.

A chart to help teachers identify the writing behavior of young children, interpret the behavior, and select suitable program strategies.

2046. Hansen, Jane, Thomas Newkirk, and Donald H. Graves, eds. *Breaking Ground: Teachers Relate Reading and Writing in the Elementary School.* Portsmouth, N.H.: Heinemann, 1985. 212 pages

A collection of 20 articles by classroom teachers and teacher educators that examine how process approaches in writing can be used successfully in teaching reading. Advocates combining reading and writing to help students understand the world.

2047. Hardt, Ulrich H. "Teaching Children to Write Poetry." *OrE* 7 (Fall 1985): 16–19.

Games and exercises for students composing poems.

2048. Harrison, Sam. "Writing by Ear: An Approach to Creativity in the Classroom." *FlaEJ* 21 (Spring 1985): 7–9.

A county writer-in-residence tells how he encounters children in creative writing by letting them decide what "sounds right."

2049. Healy, Mary K. "Writing in a Science Class: A Case Study of the Connections between Writing and Learning." *DAI* 45 (January 1985): 2017A.

Analyzes a seventh-grade biology teacher's writing assignments. Although students wrote almost every day, they rarely made personal, meaningful, or speculative connections to the subject. Concludes that teachers could benefit from inservice programs connecting writing and learning in the subject areas.

2050. Hewitt, Geof. "Hooking the Mind to the Hand." *TWM* 15 (March–April 1984): 1–4.

Describes a method of eliciting poetry from sixth-grade students.

2051. Hill, Margaret H. "The Case: Writing as a Remediation Device for Disabled Readers." *ArEB* 27 (Winter 1985): 153–157.

Argues that writing helps disabled readers "establish a structure for reading."

2052. Hink, Kaye E. "Let's Stop Worrying about Revision." *LArts* 62 (March 1985): 249–254.

Using an observational journal, a first-grade teacher found that more revision of students' writing occurred than she had suspected.

2053. Hodges, Richard E. "Spelling." *ArEB* 27 (Winter 1985): 47–50A.

Discusses the development of spelling ability and its implications for instruction.

2054. Holdaway, Don. *Stability and Change in Literacy Learning.* Portsmouth, N.H.: Heinemann, 1984. 72 pages

Assesses the new role of writing instruction in a language arts curriculum that has traditionally been concerned almost exclusively with reading instruction.

2055. Hubbard, Ruth. "Second Graders Answer the Question 'Why Publish?'" *RT* 38 (March 1985): 658–662.

Concludes that publishing children's work helps them gain a sense of authorship, of audience, and of extended time.

2056. Hubbard, Ruth. "Write-and-Tell." *LArts* 62 (October 1985): 624–630.

First graders' sharing sessions confirm the students' writing, bring out additional narrative details, develop students' oral language skills, and provide a supportive class community.

2057. Hudgins, Nancy L. "Imagery: Its Relationship to Children's Written Compositions." *DAI* 45 (November 1984): 1285A.

Finds that involving children in manipulations and rotation techniques before writing helps them generate topics and handle the writing task.

2058. Hudson, Sally A. *Context and Children's Writing.* Urbana, Ill.: ERIC/RCS, 1985. ERIC ED 258 176 [28 pages]

Studies school- and self-sponsored writing of 20 children, grades one to five, concluding that real assignments foster growth.

2059. Jackson, Rex. *The Effects of the Mason Thinking and Writing Program on the Skills of Second Grade Children.* Princeton, N.J.: Applied Educational Research, 1985. ERIC ED 258 191 [81 pages]

Finds significant effects on most measures, including writing quality and sentence maturity.

2060. Jacobs, Suzanne E. "The Development of Children's Writing: Language Acquisition and Divided Attention." *WC* 2 (October 1985): 414–433.

Suggests that teachers use a list of the kinds of language learning underway in the elementary school to influence children's writing processes.

2061. Jacobs, Suzanne E. "Investigative Writing: Practice and Principles." *LArts* 61 (April 1984): 356–363.

Describes a method of teaching fourth and fifth graders to process information by posing questions on a central topic. Response groups maintain interest and a better understanding of information.

2062. Jacoby, Adrienne. "Word Processing with the Elementary School Student: A Teaching and Learning Experience for Both Teachers and Students." Paper given at the Spring Conference of the Delaware Valley Writing Council, Villanova, Pa., February 1984. ERIC ED 246 449 [8 pages]

Discusses word processing in composition instruction.

2063. Jaggar, Angela, and M. Trika Smith-Burke, eds. *Observing the Language Learner.* Newark, Del., and Urbana, Ill.: International Reading Association and NCTE, 1985. 250 pages

A collection of 17 essays that present research on child language development and advocate creating environments to allow language learning to occur naturally. Based on "kid watching," most of the essays describe aspects of language learning, explain their importance, and show teachers what to look for and how to interpret what they see and hear.

2064. Johnson, Sue. "Generating Enthusiasm for Writing at the Elementary School Level." *WaEJ* 6 (Winter 1984): 24–26.

Approach includes journal writing, writing in response to reading, writing groups, writing a school newspaper, and a writing bulletin board.

2065. Jones, Margaret B., and Denise D. Nessel. "Enhancing the Curriculum with Experience Stories." *RT* 39 (October 1985): 18–22.

Illustrates ways to integrate the language experience approach with basal readers and the content areas.

2066. *Junior High Language Arts Course of Study.* Oak Park, Ill.: Oak Park Public School District Ninety-Seven, February 1984. ERIC ED 241 921 [5 pages]

Presents a curriculum outline.

2067. Karlin, Robert, and Andrea R. Karlin. "Writing Activities for Developing Reading Comprehension." Paper given at the IRA Convention, Anaheim, May 1983. ERIC ED 234 370 [22 pages]

Suggests how reading teachers can use writing activities to develop and reinforce reading lessons.

2068. Kasten, Wendy C. "The Behaviors Accompanying the Writing Process in Selected Third- and Fourth-Grade Native American Children." *DAI* 45 (February 1985): 2389A.

Examines the use and types of resources, revisions, oral language, and behaviors related to composing among third- and fourth-grade Native American children.

2069. Kelley, Kathleen R. "The Effect of Writing Instruction on Reading Comprehension and Story Writing Ability." *DAI* 45 (December 1984): 1703A.

Instruction in both a sentence/paragraph structure approach and a six-step writing approach contributed to development in reading comprehension and writing achievement.

2070. Keville, Richard. "Kids Find Publishing a Moving Experience." *ASBJ* 171 (November 1984): 39.

Using a mobile publishing lab in a rural school district improved students' reading, grammar skills, and enthusiasm for writing.

2071. Kinney, Martha A. "A Language Experience Approach to Teaching Expository Text Structure." *RT* 38 (May 1985): 854–856.

A study of 15 first graders concludes that the language experience method is an effective way to teach text structure.

2072. Knighten, Katherine Wells. "The Computer and Seventh Graders: An Anecdotal Report." *IIEB* 73 (Fall 1985): 49–53.

Describes experiences during computer sessions of drill and practice and short, directed writing using a cluster of four VAX 11780s.

2073. Koening, Jeffrey L. "Enhancement of Middle School Students' Written Production through the Use of Word Processing." *DAI* 45 (March 1985): 2787A.

While control group subjects showed more positive attitudes toward the constructs "writing" and "computers," the treatment group subjects spent significantly more time on revising written work.

2074. Kreeft, Joy. "Dialogue Writing: Bridge from Talk to Essay Writing." *LArts* 61 (February 1984): 141–150.

Argues that a dialogue journal between student and teacher can help students move from oral conversation to independent writing. Includes a study of a sixth grader's journal.

2075. Kroll, Barry M. "Audience Adaptation in Children's Persuasive Letters." *WC* 1 (October 1984): 407–427.

Indicates that children are able to adapt letters and oral messages to their readers' needs by including context-creating statements, descriptive information, and persuasive appeals.

2076. Kurth, Ruth J., and Linda J. Stromberg. "Using Word Processing in Composition Instruction." Paper given at the American Reading Forum, Sarasota, Fla., December 1984. ERIC ED 251 850 [16 pages]

Studies 18 remedial elementary school writers who learned to use word processing. Finds that word processing did not replace good teaching of the writing process.

2077. Lampert, Judy E. "Class Discussion and One-to-One Interaction: Their Effects on the Decisions of Fourth Graders to Write." *JEdR* 78 (May–June 1985): 315–318.

The type of prewriting activity had no effect on the decision to write. Girls' choices appeared adversely affected by the discussion activity.

2078. Langer, Judith A. *Children's Sense of Genre: A Study of Performance on Parallel Reading and Writing Tasks.* Urbana, Ill.: ERIC/RCS, 1984. ERIC ED 249 474 [42 pages]

Studies children's notions of what stories and reports are, how they can be organized, and when to use them. Finds differentiated notions of stories and reports and their structure.

2079. Langer, Judith A. *Literacy Instruction in American Schools: Problems and Perspectives.* Urbana, Ill.: ERIC/RCS, 1984. ERIC ED 249 475 [54 pages]

Proposes an alternative to focusing on subskills in literacy instruction, namely, instructional scaffolding, a student-centered, collaborative model based on what the student knows.

2080. Levine, Denise Stavis. "The Biggest Thing I Learned but It really Doesn't Have to Do with Science." *LArts* 62 (January 1985): 43–47.

Classroom research with seventh graders showed that open-ended expressive writing with the class as audience improved concept learning in science.

2081. Lott, Carolyn J. "The Effects of the Microcomputer Word Processor on the Composition Skills of Seventh-Grade Students." *DAI* 46 (December 1985): 1545A.

Compares the effects on the writing of seventh graders of word processors and paper and pencil. Students using word processors scored higher on the development index.

2082. Manna, Anthony, and Ronald F. Kingsley. "Discovering Language Options through 'Scripting.'" *ELAB* 26 (Fall 1985): 13–16.

Through a guided dramatic process, students develop material for brief scenes, transforming cold print into expressive language.

2083. Matthews, Jacklyn, and Susan Douglas Turner. "Writing with Style." Paper given at the NCTE Spring Conference, Houston, March 1985. ERIC ED 257 103 [14 pages]

Describes a developmental writing program for grades three to six, stressing prewriting, peer editing, and publishing.

2084. May, Mary Jo. "Newtonian Expedition: Using Nature as a Basis for Discovery Writing." *ExEx* 31 (Fall 1985): 34–35.

Encourages relating English to science and problem solving. Describes a class walk.

2085. McCarthy, Lucille, and Ellen J. Braffman. "Creating Victorian Philadelphia: Children Reading and Writing the World." *CurrI* 15 (1985): 121–151.

Describes the "Phil-A-Kid" enrichment program for 9- to 13-year-olds in which students learned about Victorian Philadelphia through reading, writing, and fields trips.

2086. McDonald, Joyce. "Strategies for Improving Research Reporting in Grades Five through Eight." *IE* 9 (Winter 1985): 13–14.

Presents three strategies to lay the groundwork for research skills: narrowed topics, multisource requirements, and in-text citations.

2087. McGee, Lea M., and Donald J. Richgels. "Teaching Expository Text Structure to Elementary Students." *RT* 38 (April 1985): 739–748.

Presents a method for teaching five expository text structures to elementary students.

2088. McKensie, Lee, and Gail E. Tomkins. "Evaluating Students' Writing: A Process Approach." *JTW* 3 (Fall 1984): 201–212.

Demonstrates how evaluation works in each stage of the writing process. Includes an Integrated Evaluation Checklist of questions to ask at each stage.

2089. McKeown, Margaret, Isabel L. Beck, Richard C. Omanson, and Martha T. Pople. "Some Effects of the Nature and Frequency of Vocabulary Instruction on the Knowledge and Use of Words." *RRQ* 20 (Fall 1985): 525–535.

High frequency and extended, rich instruction helped fourth-grade students with vocabulary development.

2090. McVitty, Walter, ed. *Children and Learning: Some Aspects and Issues.* Portsmouth, N.H.: Heinemann, 1984. ERIC ED 258 169 [120 pages]

A collection of 13 essays arranged under three headings: changing views about learning, children and literacy learning, and children learning through media.

2091. Michener, Darlene M. "A Quasi-Experimental Study of the Effects of Reading Aloud to Third-Grade Students as Reflected in Their Written Composition Skills." *DAI* 46 (December 1985): 1545A.

Finds significant effects for the reading aloud treatment. Calls for developing more valid and reliable instruments.

2092. Modaff, John, and Robert Hopper. "Why Speech is 'Basic.'" *ComEd* 33 (January 1984): 37–42.

Discusses the functions and importance of speech instruction, especially at elementary levels. Emphasizes that speech is a necessary condition for literacy.

2093. Mosenthal, Peter. "The Effect of Classroom Ideology on Children's Production of Narrative Text." *AERJ* 21 (Fall 1984): 679–689.

Finds that academic or cognitive/developmental differences among teachers influenced children's narrative texts.

2094. Moss, Joy F. *Focus Units in Literature: A Handbook for Elementary School Teachers.* Urbana, Ill.: NCTE, 1984. 238 pages

Aims to develop critical and creative skills by reading sequences of stories aloud to students. Suggests discussion questions and other classroom activities. Includes bibliographies for 13 focus units.

2095. Moss, R. Kay. *Transactions among Teachers and Children.* Urbana, Ill.: ERIC/RCS, 1985. ERIC ED 258 188 [30 pages]

Examines two kindergarten classrooms, finding children more self-reliant in "natural" classrooms than in "standardized" classrooms.

2096. Moxley, Roy. "The Compositional Approach to Reading in Practice and Theory." *JR* 27 (April 1984): 636–643.

Argues that writing and reading rely on the ability to "compose." Advocates copying, cloze exercises, dictation, and writing texts to teach reading.

2097. Newman, Judith M. *The Craft of Children's Writing.* Portsmouth, N.H.: Heinemann, 1985. 72 pages

A case study examining writing samples of a first grader. Indicates how teachers and parents can help children become comfortable and successful writers.

2098. Newman, Judith M., ed. *Whole Language: Theory in Use.* Portsmouth, N.H.: Heinemann, 1985. 220 pages

A collection of 18 essays, some previously published, that advise teachers about putting whole language theory into practice. Views reading and writing as tools for finding out about the world and encourages students to become active participants in learning.

2099. Nugent, Susan Monroe, ed. *Developing Audience Awareness.* Lexington, Mass.: New England Association of Teachers of English (distributed by NCTE), 1985. 56 pages

A collection of seven articles focusing on how teachers have helped their students become better writers by having them concentrate on audience. Appeared as *The Leaflet,* 84 (Winter 1985). Authors are not indexed in this volume.

2100. Ogden, Barbara. "Pulling the Switch: Promoting Better Independent Reading." *ET* 16 (Summer 1985): 17–19.

Advocates reading-immersion periods so that students become excited about reading.

2101. Olson, Judy, and Jeanice Midgett. "Alternative Placements: Does a Difference Exist in the LD Populations?" *JLD* 17 (February 1984): 101–103.

Uses the Picture Story Language Test as one of several tests administered to learning disabled students. Recommends that all preservice teachers of learning-disabled students learn to teach writing.

2102. Olson, Mary W. "A Dash of Story Grammar and . . . Presto! A Book Report." *RT* 37 (February 1984): 458–461.

Suggests a specific story outline for book reports, based on story grammar research and tested at the second- and fifth-grade levels.

2103. Paulet, Robert O. "The Whole Language Approach: Will It Be Used in Quebec and Manitoba?" *EQ* 17 (Winter 1984): 30–35.

Describes ways in which Quebec and Manitoba are implementing the whole language approach, integrating listening, speaking, reading, and writing around experiential learning.

2104. Paulis, Chris. "The Adaptation of Short Stories into Screenplays: A Language Arts Program for the Gifted." *MarylandJ* 19 (1984): 7–13.

Describes a three-phase summer course for gifted middle school students who chose, adapted, and produced two short stories on videotape.

2105. Paulis, Chris. "A Few Blood Gurgling Screams: Accidental Humor from Student Detective Stories." *EJ* 73 (January 1985): 73–74.

Reports "charming blunders" middle school student make when assigned to write mysteries. Discusses advantages of students' taking chances with language.

2106. Perrin, Robert. "Writing in the Elementary Classroom." Paper given at the Indiana Teachers of Writing Conference, Indianapolis, September 1984. ERIC ED 251 854 [17 pages]

Reports on a survey of 26 elementary teachers about the activities, beliefs, and recommendations they had about teaching writing.

2107. Phenix, Jo, and Elspeth Hannan. "Word Processing in the Grade One Classroom." *LArts* 61 (December 1984): 804–812.

Using computers for six weeks, first graders learned about drafts, manipulating writing, taking risks, and revising. They retained these habits after computers were removed.

2108. Piggins, Carol Ann. "Act to Write." *ELAB* 26 (Fall 1985): 31–32.

Suggests methods of creative listening to help students notice and eventually generate accurate and vivid detail.

2109. Pinnell, Gay Su, and Martha L. King, eds. "Access to Meaning/Spoken and Written Language." *Theory into Practice* 23 (Special Issue, Summer 1984). ERIC ED 250 683 [99 pages].

Explores how language functions to give children access to meaning. Views speaking and writing as social, interactive processes.

2110. Pinnell, Gay Su, and Martha L. King, eds. *Access to Meaning: Spoken and Written Language.* Columbus, Ohio: Ohio State University College of Education, 1984. ERIC ED 250 683 [99 pages]

A collection of 12 essays that explore how language functions to allow children access to meaning. Details the interactive nature of speaking and writing.

2111. Pratee, Doris. "Using Extended Reading to Motivate Elementary Compositions." *ArEB* 27 (Winter 1985): 73–77.

Suggests activities to encourage writing in conjunction with reading.

2112. Pringle, Ian, and Aviva Freedman. *A Comparative Study of Writing Abilities in Two Modes at the Grade Five, Eight, and Twelve Levels.* Ontario, Canada: Ontario Department of Education, 1985. ERIC ED 258 202 [145 pages]

Examines transactional and narrative writing for quality, complexity, story structure, and error. See also the authors' *The Writing Abilities of a Selected Sample of Grade Seven and Eight Students* ERIC ED 217 412/413.

2113. Ramsey, Esther Leota K. "Motivating Junior High School Students to Write." *IE* 8 (Spring 1985): 12-13.

Describes producing class books, collections of student writing, to motivate students.

2114. Ramsey, Esther Leota K. "Two Viewpoints." *IE* 8 (Spring 1985): 13.

Argues the appropriateness of a one-word entry.

2115. Roberts, Jean M. "A Case Study of Thirty Events of 'Writing Lessons' in a Fourth-Grade Classroom." *DAI* 46 (November 1985): 1187A.

A naturalistic investigation of how participants construe and context influences writing events. Finds that the teacher-centered classroom limits student writers.

2116. Rodrigues, Dawn. "Using Computers in the Language Arts Curriculum." *CurrR* 24 (May–June 1985): 25-28.

Discusses word processing as a way to integrate computers into classroom instruction.

2117. Roper, Helen D. "Spelling, Word Recognition, and Phonemic Awareness among First-Grade Children." *DAI* 45 (January 1985): 2052A.

Finds that, for 100 first graders, phonemic awareness contributed to improving spelling, word recognition, and the ability to identify letter-sound correspondences. As skills developed, reliance on phonemic awareness varied.

2118. Rosenburg, Ruth. "Wordplay Magic." *ExEx* 29 (Spring 1984): 24-30.

Describes a method for teaching the "apt usage" of words by using lapel buttons, bumper stickers, and T-shirt slogans.

2119. Roubicek, Henry L. "An Investigation of Story Dramatization as a Prewriting Activity." *DAI* 45 (August 1984): 403A.

A counterbalanced design study involving 39 fifth graders shows that story dramatization is an effective prewriting technique.

2120. Rouse, John. "On Children Writing Prose." *LArts* 61 (October 1984): 592-599.

A writer visits P.S. 230, in Brooklyn, where children think about writing and discover their own intentions and where teachers allow risk taking.

2121. Ryder, Willet, and Eleanor Ryder. "The Arts in Language Arts: Activities Relating Visual Art to the Language Arts in the Elementary School Level." *ArEB* 27 (Fall 1984): 57-60.

Describes how oragami puppets, balloon pen-pals, and portaits of famous American women integrate art, reading, and writing.

2122. Saidel, Lois F. "The Effects of Calligraphic Tuition on Handwriting Skills Attainment in Grades Three, Five, and Seven." *DAI* 45 (February 1985): 2391A.

Examines the effects of calligraphic instruction on the handwriting quality and preferences of third, fifth, and seventh graders. Results do not support the use of universal calligraphic instruction.

2123. Schumm, Jeanne S., and Marguerite C. Radencich. "Readers'/Writers' Workshop: An Antidote for Term Paper Terror." *JR* 28 (October 1984): 13-19.

Argues that middle school students should be taught a systematic method for writing term papers using modeling, problem solving, and in-class writing.

2124. Smith, Nancy J. "The Word Processing Approach to Language Experience." *RT* 38 (February 1985): 556-559.

Reviews articles on and gives suggestions for using word processors with the language experience approach.

2125. Smith, Roland M. "Try These Fifteen Dandy Ideas for Saving Money—and Improving Instruction." *ASBJ* 172 (February 1985): 30-32.

Describes a "young author plan" and reading activities used in a school system's program to promote excellence while cutting costs.

2126. Smith, Vernon H. "Teaching Beginning Writing *Vs.* Nurturing Beginning Writers." Paper given at the Indiana Teachers of Writing Conference, Indianapolis, September 1984. ERIC ED 254 847 [39 pages]

Examines the effect of frequent writing without teacher correction at grades one and two, concluding that students benefit from "nurture," not "instruction."

2127. Staab, Claire F., and Karen Smith. "Classroom Perspectives on Teaching Writing." *RT* 38 (May 1985): 841-844.

Suggests two methods for organizing content so that student writing is functional.

2128. Stalker, Linda. "Research Can Be Contagious." *IE* 9 (Winter 1985): 22-23.

Describes activities in an eighth-grade career unit that involves research techniques.

2129. Staton, Jana. *Thinking Together: Language Interaction in Children's Reasoning.* The Talking and Writing Series, K–12. Washington: Dingle Associates, 1983. ERIC ED 233 379 [51 pages]

Shows how written or oral dialogues between teacher and student can be a way of thinking.

2130. Stockard, Connie H. "Things the Teachers Did Not Say." *CEd* 61 (September–October 1984): 18–21.

A narrative about a five-year-old whose teachers frustrate her attempts at writing.

2131. Stotsky, Sandra. "Helping Beginning Writers Develop Writing Plans: A Process for Teaching Informational Writing in the Middle School and Beyond." *Leaflet* 84 (Winter 1985): 2–17.

Describes a method that gives students experience with informational writing through whole-class lessons.

2132. Stotsky, Sandra. "Imagination, Writing, and the Integration of Knowledge in the Middle Grades." *JTW* 3 (Fall 1984): 157–190.

Classifies five types of "imaginative informational writing" and suggests way to generate such assignments.

2133. Strong, William. "Writing to Learn—Across the Curriculum." *UEJ* (1985): 3–16.

Argues for writing in content areas at all levels. Suggests possible lesson plans.

2134. Swicord, Barbara. "Debating with Gifted Fifth and Sixth Graders: Telling It Like It Was, Is, and Could Be." *GCQ* 28 (Summer 1984): 127–129.

Examines how the principles of debate can be introduced to and used by elementary school students, particularly gifted students.

2135. Teich, Nathaniel, Bev Chadburn, Greg Robins, and Stanley A. Wonderley. "Wordless Books for Teaching Writing." *OrE* 7 (Spring 1985): 4–9.

Describes narrative picture books without words and presents classroom activities. Includes 65-item bibliography.

2136. Testerman, Jean. "The Teaching behind the Test Scores." *MarylandJ* 19 (1984): 31–33.

Argues that junior high school students improve in all language arts when the arts are integrated. Includes sample weekly schedule and materials.

2137. Thaiss, Christopher J. *Learning Better, Learning More: In the Home and across the Curriculum.* The Talking and Writing Series, K–12. Washington: Dingle Associates, 1983. ERIC ED 233 383 [36 pages]

Describes five situations in which writing and speaking experiences are used as a way of learning subject matter.

2138. Thaiss, Christopher J., and Charles Suhor, eds. *Speaking and Writing, K–12: Classroom Strategies and the New Research.* Urbana, Ill.: NCTE, 1984. 262 pages

A collection of nine essays. Presents research on students' development of oral communication skills and their ability to write "elaborated texts," discusses the role of teacher-student dialogue and new technologies, suggests ways to integrate language arts and promote favorable environments for learning, and examines the assessment of students' language skills.

2139. Tompkins, Gail E., and Eileen Tway. "Adventuring with Words." *CEd* 61 (May–June 1985): 361–365.

Discusses the value of and identifies resources for wordplay and word games, riddles, jokes, rhymes and verse, and word histories.

2140. Turvey, Joel. "What's Your Creature?" *OrE* 7 (Fall 1985): 4.

Outlines assignments for writing about creatures in Greek mythology and for creating imaginary mythological creatures.

2141. Tutolo, Daniel. "Beginning Writing in Italy." Paper given at the IRA Convention, Atlanta, May 1984. ERIC ED 246 416 [18 pages]

Describes writing instruction and students in the first three grades in Italy.

2142. Tway, Eileen. *Time for Writing in the Elementary School.* Theory and Research into Practice. Urbana, Ill.: ERIC/RCS and NCTE, 1984. 32 pages

Argues that many students are not writing to their potential because of pressures for time. Offers activities designed to provide students with adequate writing time.

2143. Tway, Eileen. *Writing Is Reading: Twenty-Six Ways to Connect.* Theory and Research into Practice. Urbana, Ill.: ERIC/RCS and NCTE, 1985. 48 pages

Recommends using children's literature to combine reading and writing processes. A practice section includes ideas such as bookmaking, script writing, and storytelling. Includes two booklists.

2144. Wagner, Mary Jo. "A Comparison of Fifth Graders' Oral and Written Stories." *DAI* 45 (February 1985): 2392A.

Examines fifth graders' oral and written stories. Oral stories were longer than written ones, but students preferred their written stories, results differing from Sawkins' (1971) findings.

2145. Warsley, Dale. "Sourdough Writing: Teaching Computer Fiction Writing." *TWM* 16 (January–February 1985): 1–6.

Describes using an Atari computer to interest elementary students in writing fiction and to introduce them to computers.

2146. Wegner, Judy A. "Reading Is Fun? Or Reading Is Fun!" *NebEC* 29 (Spring 1984): 27–30.

Offers several techniques to interest adolescents in reading.

2147. Whitin, David J. "Children and Children's Authors." *LArts* 61 (December 1984): 813–821.

Because these third and fourth graders were writers, they could correspond confidently with well-known authors and understand the authors' advice about writing.

2148. Whitin, David J. "Lessons Learned by a Writing Teacher." *IE* 8 (Winter 1985): 3–5.

A third-grade teacher learns that students can discover their own topics, can give mutual support in several ways, and deserve respect as writers.

2149. Willinsky, John. "To Publish and Publish and Publish." *LArts* 62 (June 1985): 619–623.

A writer helps students publish their writings in a variety of ways, recreating the history of their publication from oral presentations to computer processing.

2150. Willinsky, John. "The Writer in the Teacher." *LArts* 61 (October 1984): 585–591.

Describes a first- and second-grade classroom fashioned around the teacher's personal concept of literacy. Children engage in script and print, in performance and publication.

2151. Willis, Meredith Sue. "Personal Fiction Writing: Writing Dialogue." *TWM* 16 (September–October 1984): 9–12.

Advocates dialogue writing to help elementary students to begin to write. Includes examples from fifth-grade students.

2152. Wiseman, Donna. "Helping Children Take Early Steps toward Reading and Writing." *RT* 37 (January 1984): 340–344.

Describes early reading and writing behaviors of children and suggests ways to encourage these efforts.

2153. Wood, Karen D. "Probable Passages: A Writing Strategy." *RT* 37 (February 1984): 496–499.

Presents a technique for using story frames in making predictions about basal reader selections.

2154. Woodley, John, Carol Woodley, and Yetta Goodman. "Invented Spelling." *ArEB* 27 (Winter 1985): 39–46.

Examines invented spellings as clues to a child's language development.

See also 8, 14, 22, 23, 24, 46, 105, 209, 234, 294, 318, 406, 459, 480, 617, 649, 744, 747, 765, 768, 835, 877, 964, 994, 1275, 1276, 1486, 1580, 1601, 1608, 1637, 1790, 1835, 1839, 1847, 1908, 1967, 1970, 2160, 2179, 2186, 2191, 2213, 2214, 2223, 2251, 2287, 2319, 2354, 2361, 2366, 3009, 3010, 3055, 3452, 3465, 3730, 3731, 3754

SECONDARY EDUCATION (9–12)

2155. Addison, James C., Jr. "A Cognitively Based Composition Course: The Need for Sequence." *NCET* 42 (Winter 1985): 28–33.

Explains assumptions for a writing curriculum based on cognitive development and describes 15 writing assignments.

2156. Alberghene, Janice M. "Writing in *Charlotte's Web*." *CLEd* 16 (Spring 1985): 32–44.

Argues that White's *Charlotte's Web* is a book about the style and craft of the fictive artist.

2157. Anderson, Judi. "From Poetry to Journal to Creative Response: An Introductory Strategy." *IlEB* 72 (Spring 1985): 56–62.

Describes student "word awareness journals" and provides "lexicons" as springboards to the "generation of original free verse poems."

2158. Arnold, Kathy. "Cutting Class: The Writer's Workshop." *ET* 15 (Summer 1984): 19–20.

Discusses how to organize a two-day writer's workshop during the last six weeks of school to encourage interest at the end of the year.

2159. Arnold, Kathy. "Writer's Workshop: A Debriefing." *ET* 17 (Fall 1985): 23–24.

Describes a writer's workshop held at the year's end. Includes activities for a two-day workshop.

2160. Arnold, Linda K., and Andrea L. Watson. "Teaching through Publication: An Unusual Approach to Motivating Students." *Statement* 21 (October 1985): 5–11.

Discusses teaching writing by having students submit work for writing contests.

2161. Askew, Lida. "You Talk Like a Thesaurus." *EJ* 73 (September 1984): 100–101.

Explains a group composition assignment that is also analyzed and critiqued by groups of students.

2162. Atwell, Nancie. "Everyone Sits at a Big Desk: Discovering Topics for Writing." *EJ* 74 (September 1985): 35–39.

Discusses how to use student-selected writing topics. Suggests resources and includes writing samples and student responses.

2163. Bailey, Adrienne Y. "Writing, Reform, and Optimism." *JTW* 4 (Spring 1985): 7–17.

Reviews the place of writing in the College Board's Educational Equality Project.

2164. Baldwin, Dean R. "What's Wrong with 'What I Did on My Summer Vacation'?" *EJ* 73 (February 1984): 61–62.

Argues that teachers can liven up "our most hackneyed theme topic" by focusing on subject, audience, and intent.

2165. Ballard, Leslie. "A Composition Program for High School Seniors." *IE* 8 (Winter 1985): 6–8.

Three composition courses among other language electives generate concentrated work and student enthusiasm.

2166. Barnes, Douglas, Dorothy Barnes, and Stephen Clarke. *Versions of English.* Portsmouth, N.H.: Heinemann, 1984. 442 pages

A description and critique of the varieties of English instruction currently offered to British 15- to 17-year-olds under the labels of "English," "English language," "English literature," or "communication studies." Based on empirical observa-

tions of school fifth and sixth forms and colleges of Further Education.

2167. Barry, Francis J. "Small Group Discussion as a Prewriting Activity: A Naturalistic Inquiry." *DAI* 45 (February 1985): 2423A.

Examines twelfth graders' discourse moves, social skills, and procedures for planning and developing compositions. Finds discussion a useful prewriting, anxiety-relieving activity.

2168. Bathke, Julia. "Writing the Covenant." *ET* 17 (Fall 1985): 25–29.

Examines how modern writing theory can be put to practice in a curriculum by combining grammar, poetry, and writing.

2169. Baumlin, James S. "Bringing the Writing Process into the Literature Class." *ET* 16 (Winter 1985): 13–15.

Examines how to incorporate process-centered writing into the literature class. Freewriting can precede discussion and analysis. [Reprinted in *ET* 16 (Summer 1985): 27–29.]

2170. Beem, Jane A. "Overcoming Roadblocks in the Composition Class." *IIEB* 71 (Spring 1984): 41–46.

Examines ways a successful writing teacher can establish an atmosphere of trust with students and project a positive attitude toward the writing process.

2171. Bennett, Bruce. "Writers in Their Places." Paper given at the International Writing Association Convention, Norwich, England, April 1985. ERIC ED 258 255 [19 pages]

Reviews 11 case studies of teenage writers, noting the social role of writing.

2172. Birdsong, Theda P., and Wanda S. Shaplin. "English Curriculum for College-Bound Students: A Report on the 1982 State Task Force Study." *LaEJ* 23 (Fall 1984): 89–95.

Presents a Louisiana Board of Regents task force's recommendations relating to course content, writing practice, and skills level.

2173. Bleeker, Gerrit. "Using Young Adult Fiction to Reintegrate the Language Arts." *Alan* 11 (Winter 1984): 33–34, 44.

Argues for reintegrating the teaching of language arts. Suggests activities for teaching Paterson's *Bridge to Terabithia*.

2174. Booth, Jim. "Why Johnny Writes Badly." *NCET* 42 (Summer 1985): 11–12.

Argues that teachers fail to make instruction clear, neglect the authentic student voice, and are too concerned too early in the writing process about correctness.

2175. Brostoff, Anita. "Using Problem Solving to Think and Write: Tagmemics for High School Students." Paper given at the CCCC Convention, Detroit, March 1983. ERIC ED 234 384 [15 pages]

Provides three tagmemic heuristics.

2176. Brown, Alan. "Hearing the Voice: A Study of Hemingway's Style." *IlEB* 72 (Spring 1985): 53–56.

Describes "altering" an author's style to teach students sentence expansion, formal and colloquial vocabulary, and their own voice.

2177. Brown, Lawrence W. "Teaching English with Andy Rooney." *EJ* 73 (September 1984): 65.

Using Rooney's writing as a model can produce simple, direct, and colorful student writing.

2178. Bruffee, Kenneth A. "Ideas: After the Fact Outlines." *WaEJ* 6 (Winter 1984): 29.

Writing outlines after a draft is completed can help students see where they need to revise.

2179. Bushman, John H. "A Writing Sequence for the Junior High/Middle and Secondary School English Curriculum." *VEB* 35 (Spring 1985): 3–9.

Calls for a better sense of sequence in writing curricula (because of shifts to developmental notions about learners) and to the process approach to writing.

2180. Calhoun, Anga Windsor. "Lesson Plan: Phase Autobiography." *FlaEJ* 20 (Fall 1984): 43–44.

An eight-day lesson plan for having students write an autobiography.

2181. Campbell, Gracemarie. "The Resource Paper, Again." *EJ* 73 (February 1984): 72–74.

Offers three aids for teaching students to compose research papers.

2182. Carter, John Marshall. "Practicing What We Teach: The Teacher as Writing Model." *NCET* 42 (Summer 1985): 15.

Advocates that teachers-as-writers move through the entire writing process alongside their students.

2183. Carter, John Marshall. "Thinking across the Curriculum: A Prewriting Scavenger Hunt." *NCET* 42 (Winter 1985): 8–11.

Discusses the use of broad questions to promote thinking across the curriculum as a prelude to interdisciplinary writing.

2184. Chapman, Marcia. "Building Writing Competence and Confidence with Small Group Revision." *EN* 6 (1984): 14–16.

Discusses means of using peer-response groups.

2185. Chew, Charles R., ed. *Computers in the English Program: Promises and Pitfalls.* New York State English Council Monographs. Albany, N.Y.: New York State English Council (distributed by NCTE), 1984. ERIC ED 257 083 [148 pages]

A collection of 14 essays that discuss the role of computers in writing instruction in the schools. Provides advice about developing guidelines and selection criteria for software and about using computers to help students revise paragraphs, essays, and other kinds of writing. Includes brief descriptions of software for writing, reading, and language instruction.

2186. Chew, Charles R. "Writing Instruction: Commitment to Improvement." Paper given at the Queensboro Reading Council Meeting, Bayside, N.Y., March 1984. ERIC ED 244 283 [8 pages]

Discusses key factors in effective writing instruction.

2187. Cisneros, Sandra. "A Translation Exercise." *ET* 16 (Spring 1985): 48–50.

Advocates presenting poems in a foreign language to allow students to listen to language. After listening, students attempt a translation.

2188. Clinton, DeWitt. "Communicating with Live Writers: SASE Enclosed." *ExEx* 31 (Fall 1985): 38–39.

Provides ways of putting students in advanced writing courses in touch with "live, published writers." Introduces students to audience-based writing.

2189. Colasurdo, Anthony P. "The Literary Magazine as Class Project." *EJ* 74 (February 1985): 82–84.

Discusses producing a literary magazine in a mass media class.

2190. Collins, Kathleen. "Teaching Fiction Writing through Anticipatory Affirmation." *TWM* 16 (May–June 1985): 4–5.

Describes using stream of consciousness and flashback methods to encourage students writing fiction.

2191. Craven, Jerry. "Allowing Students to Enjoy Writing." *ET* 17 (Fall 1985): 18–20.

Argues that writing and writing instruction have become too rule governed, that students like to express themselves and try new identities. Suggests activities for expression and playacting.

2192. Crowe, Chris. "*Laissez Faire* and the Writing Process." *ArEB* 28 (Fall 1985): 101–103.

A satiric essay on creativity and the writing process.

2193. Crowe, Michael R., Robert E. Abram, and Leslie A. Bart. *Alternative Environments for Basic Skills Development.* Columbus, Ohio: Ohio State University National Center for Research in Vocational Education, 1984. ERIC ED 246 179 [187 pages]

Studies the impact on reading and writing of work-study programs for secondary students.

2194. Culver, Steven. "Evaluation: The Compleat Conference Rolebook." *VEB* 34 (Spring 1984): 12–13.

Offers a set of negative rules for conferences.

2195. Curran, Jane M., ed. *Ideas Plus: A Collection of Practical Teaching Ideas, Book 2.* Urbana, Ill.: NCTE, 1985. 58 pages

Classroom-tested ideas in the areas of language exploration, literature, and prewriting and writing.

2196. Curran, Jane M., ed. *Ideas Plus: A Collection of Practical Teaching Ideas, Book 3.* Urbana, Ill.: NCTE, 1985. 64 pages

Classroom-tested ideas covering language exploration, literature, and prewriting and writing.

2197. Curtice, Carolyn Ann. "What Can a Computer Do for Me That I Am Not Already Doing?" *EJ* 73 (January 1984): 32–33.

Practical suggestions for teachers apprehensive about computer-assisted writing instruction.

2198. Cypert, Rick. "Experiencing the Topic." *ET* 16 (Summer 1985): 30–33.

Suggests staging confrontations and visits outside the classroom to aid invention and shock students into awareness of their topic.

2199. Danheiser, Thomas L. "Writing a Sonnet." *IE* 8 (Fall 1984): 9–10.

Writing a sonnet helps students read sonnets.

2200. Davis, Chuck. "Shakespeare: The Car Salesman." *WWays* 18 (August 1985): 149–150.

Finds advertising slogans in Shakespeare's plays and poetry.

2201. Davis, Ken, ed. *Writing by Imitation.* Kentucky English Bulletin, Fall 1984. Lexington, Ky.: Kentucky Council of Teachers of English (distributed by NCTE), 1984. 72 pages

A collection of articles that describe theoretical and practical applications of classical imitation in writing courses at all levels. Presents ways of using models to help students improve their writing. Appeared as *Kentucky English Bulletin* (Fall 1984). Authors are not indexed in this volume.

2202. Davis, Millie. "Discover Your Lemon." *VEB* 35 (Spring 1985): 65–67.

Explains using a lemon as a prewriting prompt to stimulate both the intuitional/creative and intellectual/scientific approaches to writing.

2203. de Beaugrande, Robert. "Yes, Teaching Grammar Does Help." *EJ* 73 (February 1984): 66–69.

Presents several techniques for grammar instruction supporting a "learner's grammar" based on natural communication.

2204. Dodd, Anne Wescott. "The Big Mac Approach to Teaching Grammar." *CEJ* 16 (Spring 1985): 94–96.

Advocates a "short, well-planned unit on the structure of English sentences" for ninth graders.

2205. Duin, Ann. "Investigating Students' Awareness of Their Own Composing." *EngR* 36 (1985): 26–28.

Discusses the use of conference groups, discussion, manuals, and introspection to create writing for specific audiences.

2206. Dunn, Saundra, Susan Florio-Ruane, and Christopher M. Clark. *The Teacher as Respondent to the High School Writer.* Research Series, no. 152. East Lansing, Mich.: Michigan State University Institute for Research on Teaching, 1984. ERIC ED 251 858 [32 pages]

Studies one high school creative writing class to learn about the socially negotiated nature of school writing. Finds that the teacher created other audiences and evaluators.

2207. Edwards, Grace Toney. "Group Conferencing: An Answer for Large Composition Classes." *VEB* 35 (Spring 1985): 37–41.

Advocates moving from individual to group conferences because of increased class size and possible unexpected benefits.

2208. Elias, Kristina M., Craig Abruzzo, Sue Casentino, and Kim Herbert. "Mea Culpa, Mea Culpa, Mea Maxima Grammatica Culpa." *CEJ* 16 (Spring 1985): 89–93.

Responses from high school students support the conclusion that a knowledge of grammar is important for writing well and that self-teaching grammar workbooks are useful.

2209. Ewald, Helen R. "Using Error Analysis in the Writing Lab for Correctness and Effectiveness." *WLN* 8 (January 1984): 6–8.

Argues that error analysis can expose assumptions causing grammatical errors, rhetorical ineffectiveness, and composition problems.

2210. Farrell, Pamela B. "Word Processing and High School Writing." *CC* 2 (November 1984): 5–7.

A survey of the effect of word processing on 110 high school students gives highest rating to its effect on revision.

2211. Fearing, Bertie E., and Jo Allen. *Teaching Technical Writing in the Secondary School.* Theory and Research into Practice. Urbana, Ill.: ERIC/RCS and NCTE, 1984. 56 pages

A study of the kinds of errors technical writers make and the forms their writing takes. A practice section offers sample lessons and activities. Includes bibliography.

2212. Fearn, Leif. "How They Write: A Study of Writers' Self-Reports." *CEJ* 16 (Fall 1984): 29–31.

Recommends that writing students read professional writers' self-reports (accounts of their struggles with writing) so that they can see their own experiences in the context of others'.

2213. Feingold, Carolyn. "Writing beyond the Curriculum: Three Current Nebraska Models for the Student Writers' Workshop." *NebEC* 31 (Fall 1985): 16–18.

Describes workshops for students in grades 7 through 12.

2214. Felten, Paul. "No, Teddy, 'Mommy Pretty' Lacks a Verb." *IE* 8 (Winter 1985): 9–10.

Argues that writers do not need grammatical lingo.

2215. Fischer, Lucille. "Getting Started." *FlaEJ* 20 (Fall 1984): 41–42.

Describes an activity for writing about circumstantial evidence presented to students as a list of facts.

2216. Fisher, Anita. "Mr. Browning and the Student Writer." *FlaEJ* 21 (Spring 1985): 10–12.

Describes using Browning's poetry as the basis of composition work for honors students. Notes other Victorian works to use.

2217. Fitzgerald, Sallyanne H. "Why Peer Editing Works in the Basic Writing Class." *NCET* 42 (Summer 1985): 19–21.

Argues that peer editing in a basic class can be successful when the process and the expectations are well defined.

2218. Flachmann, Kim. "An Organic Approach to Writing." *CalE* 21 (March–April 1985): 87–91.

Proposes that writing instruction take an "organic" rather than a "linear" approach. Suggests that students can visualize the whole essay by first drawing cartoons depicting content.

2219. Flaherty, Gloria P. "The Speaking/Reading/ Writing Connection: Interaction in a Basic Reading Classroom." *DAI* 45 (February 1985): 2463A.

Results support the dual roles of practitioner/ researcher, the value of discussion in instruction, and the relation between speaking and reading/ writing growth.

2220. Frith, Greg H., and Aquilla A. Mims. "Teaching Gifted Students to Make Verbal Presentations." *GCQ* 28 (Winter 1984): 45–47.

Offers rhetorical strategies that gifted students can use in speeches and oral reports. Contains sample exercises.

2221. Fulwiler, Toby. "Understanding Bad Writing." *CEJ* 15 (Spring 1984): 54–59.

In the context of a writing across the curriculum program, provides solutions to problems of mechanics, audience, conceptual abilities, and motivation.

2222. Gambell, Trevor J. "What High School Teachers Have to Say about Student Writing and Language across the Curriculum." *EJ* 73 (September 1984): 42–44.

Argues that, since language problems exist across the curriculum, all teachers must teach language, collaborating in their efforts to combat common problems.

2223. Garner, Cynthia. "'The Need of Being Versed in Country Things': A Thematic Approach." *ExEx* 31 (Fall 1985): 20–23.

Suggests a rural theme appropriate for ninth graders. Details activities for decorating classroom, planting flowers, and writing journals and travel brochures.

2224. Geiser, Patricia. "The English Connection." *IIEB* 71 (Winter 1984): 3–6.

Explains how field trips to art museums can be used to trigger writing assignments based on showing, not telling.

2225. George, Diana. "Creating Contexts: Using the Research Paper to Teach Critical Thinking." *EJ* 73 (September 1984): 27–31.

Collaborative learning and teaching critical thinking skills help students combat problems writing research papers.

2226. Gere, Anne Ruggles, ed. *Roots in the Sawdust: Writing to Learn across the Disciplines.* Urbana, Ill.: NCTE, 1985. 238 pages

A collection of 16 articles presenting techniques for writing in history, philsophy, art, German, mathematics, science, social studies, and special education classes. Discusses the benefits of writing to learn, the use of peer evaluation, and the reactions of students and teachers. Includes bibliography.

2227. Gillespie, Tim. "Tuna Fish, Eddie R., and Writing for Real." *EJ* 74 (April 1985): 30–32.

Discusses using letter writing to generate audiences and situations for basic writers.

2228. Glasser, William. *Control Theory in the Classroom.* Perennial Library. New York: Harper & Row, 1985. 160 pages

Discusses applications of control theory as a new teaching approach in the secondary school classroom. Recommends small learning teams, consisting of two to four students.

2229. Gleeson, Kitty, and Ken Holmes. "The Syncretic Model: A Process Approach to the Teaching of Reading and Writing in Tandem." *ET* 15 (Spring 1984): 42–53.

Argues that merging reading and writing adds power to each. Presents an approach using writing as a strategy of discovery.

2230. Gregg, Lynn C. "Conferencing: A Better Way to Composition." *NCET* 42 (Summer 1985): 23–26.

Offers a conferencing approach that allows teachers time with students, improves the quality of student writing, and decreases grading time.

2231. Hall, Chris. "Writing on a User-Friendly Topic: Language." *ExEx* 29 (Spring 1984): 43–45.

Presents a method of collecting the vocabulary of various speech communities.

2232. Hannon, Jody. "Sneaking Fun into Composition: News Writing." *EJ* 73 (September 1984): 33–34.

A minicourse in radio broadcasting as an alternative composition unit. Describes assignments and skills learned.

2233. Hannula, Joyce Jarosz. "The Shakedown of an Assumption." *ArEB* 28 (Fall 1985): 12–14.

Follows Martin's advice to use expressive writing "for trying out and coming to terms with new ideas" and offers writing/reading assignments.

2234. Harris, Catherine Mary. "Prewriting: A Hook for Reading." *ET* 17 (Fall 1985): 21–22.

Describes using flashback and stream of consciousness as prewriting activities that enable students to appreciate these techniques in literature.

2235. Hathaway, James. "Supplementary Notes on Student Writing and a Brief Anthology of Poetry by Students and Teachers." *ET* 16 (Spring 1985): 57–76.

Includes examples of poems derived from models and forms and poems written as exercises in metaphor.

2236. Heckler, Edward. "Dracula and the Adjective Clause." *ET* 17 (Fall 1985): 33–35.

Advocates teaching grammar as a process by having students create original sentences. Includes seven exercises for teaching relative pronouns.

2237. Henson, Leigh. "Discovering Theme through Writing: A Response-Oriented Approach to 'The Lottery.'" *IlEB* 72 (Spring 1985): 30–38.

Describes a strategy for teaching writing that guides students toward the interpretation of theme and serves as a prewriting activity.

2238. Herrmann, Andrea W. "Collaboration in a High School Computers and Writing Class: An Ethnographic Study." Paper given at the CCCC Convention, Minneapolis, March 1985. ERIC ED 258 256 [19 pages]

Studies eight writers, noting the value of collaboration.

2239. Hershon, Robert. "Lawrence Stazer: The Use and Pleasure of the Hoax." *TWM* 15 (January–February 1984): 7–10.

Describes a method for teaching high school seniors to write poetry by writing an imaginary persona.

2240. Hickerson, Benny. "Critical and Creative Readings, Thinking, and Writing with Texas Literature." *ET* 16 (Winter 1985): 24–29.

Believes that Texas students can easily identify with Texas authors and literature. Setting and characterization are major elements to be studied.

2241. Hindel, Lee J. "What I Would Like to Tell Teachers about Teaching Their Students to Write; or, somethin' like that." *Alan* 12 (Fall 1984): 15–16.

An 18-year-old novel competition winner suggests strategies for motivating and freeing high school students to write.

2242. Hipple, Ted. "Writing and Literature." *EJ* 73 (February 1984): 50–53.

Examines three ways teachers can "blend" writing with the study of literature.

2243. Hipple, Ted, and Joan Kaywell. "Composition and Literature: Twelve Writing Activities Derived from Commonly Taught Works." *FlaEJ* 21 (Fall 1985): 27–29.

Lists writing assignments teachers can use to satisfy Florida's Writing Skills Enhancement rule of weekly themes while still teaching literary works.

2244. Hirsch, S. Carl. "Understanding Fiction through Writing It." *EJ* 73 (September 1984): 77–81.

Describes a minicourse in writing fiction.

2245. Hitt, Valeria. "Bring in the Authors." *EJ* 73 (February 1984): 70–71.

A librarian suggests a variety of ways to reach published writers to invite into the classroom.

2246. Hodgins, Audrey, ed. *Ideas Plus: A Collection of Practical Teaching Ideas, Book 1.* Urbana, Ill.: NCTE, 1984. 58 pages

Classroom-tested ideas divided into four categories: literature: they can take it with them, assignment assortment for writers, prewriting and polishing, and fun and functional: projects, strategies, and diversions.

2247. Hoke, Diana L. "Don't Look Now, but Isn't That an Albatross behind You? Keeping the Research Paper Assignment Airborne." *IE* 9 (Winter 1985): 5–9.

Discusses eight study skills taught in a research paper project and ways of sequencing steps in the project.

2248. Holden, Marjorie H., and Mimi Warshaw. "A Bird in the Hand and a Bird in the Bush: Using Proverbs to Teach Skills and Comprehension." *EJ* 74 (February 1985): 63–67.

Discusses using proverbs to teach grammar, vocabulary, literary devices, ethnographic fieldwork, poetry, comprehension skills, and abstract thinking.

2249. Huffman, Suanne. "How Do You Spell 'Nonfiction'?" *CEJ* 16 (Fall 1984): 37–39.

Outlines a six-week nonfiction unit for ninth grade.

2250. Hurt, Madeline. "Developing Student Writing through Creative Awareness." *VEB* 35 (Spring 1985): 81–83.

Argues that asking high school students to assume the perspective of various creatures engenders new power in their writing.

2251. Hyler, Linda. "Teaching Writing through Programming." *CC* 2 (February 1985): 2–3.

Reports that junior high school students' writing habits improved by storyboarding stories and writing them on the computer in BASIC.

2252. Jacob, Kay. "Three Writing Assignments for *A Farewell to Arms.*" *IlEB* 72 (Spring 1985): 7–10.

Describes assignments designed to move students through a " hierarchy of levels of thinking," from "knowledge and comprehension" to "analysis, synthesis, and evaluation."

2253. Jones, Michael P. "The Making of a Poetry Program." *EJ* 74 (October 1985): 63–65.

Describes how poetry writing classes evolved in the curriculum of a secondary school.

2254. Kahn, Elizabeth, Carolyn Calhoun Walter, and Larry R. Johannessen. *Writing about Literature. Theory and Research into Practice.* Urbana, Ill.: ERIC/RCS and NCTE, 1984. 54 pages

A set of sequences designed to teach students to support an interpretation, explicate an implied relationship, and analyze an author's generalizations. Provides accompanying handouts for students.

2255. Kelly, Patricia P., Mary Pat Hall, and Robert C. Small, Jr. "Composition through the Team Approach." *EJ* 73 (September 1984): 71–74.

A case study describing a project for teaching composition by using teams of students. Cites several projected benefits for students.

2256. Kendall, John. "Fireproof Your School with Writing." *EJ* 74 (January 1985): 59–60.

Urges that teachers challenge students to preserve "physical descriptions" and "strong emotional feeling" about their school experiences in their writing.

2257. King, Don. "Generating the Light Bulb Essay." *ExEx* 30 (Fall 1984): 17–19.

Presents a technique for encouraging students to write a discovery essay.

2258. Kollar, Mary. "Speaking Up for Voice." *WaEJ* 8 (Fall 1985): 9–12.

Honest, engaging papers can be nourished by teachers who treat assignments as explorations and who encourage reading aloud.

2259. Kollar, Mary, and Rick Monroe. "Our Audience Is Real." *EJ* 73 (February 1984): 75–79.

Describes a "paper exchange" between eighth and twelfth graders as a way of creating real audiences.

2260. Lampert, Kathleen W. "Using Dialogues to Teach the Interpretive Process." *JTW* 4 (Spring 1985): 19–30.

Uses dialogues as a step between personal response and formal interpretation for an audience. Finds dialogues a "powerful alternative to the critical essay."

2261. Langer, Judith A., and Arthur N. Applebee. *Learning to Manage the Writing Process: Tasks and Strategies.* Urbana, Ill.: ERIC/RCS, 1983. ERIC ED 234 420 [17 pages]

Suggests a variety of techniques for teaching writing as process.

2262. Lansing, Margaret L. *Student Writers and Word Processors: A Case Study.* Urbana, Ill.: ERIC/RCS, May 1984. ERIC ED 249 491 [35 pages]

Studies two eleventh graders for six weeks, identifying two types of students, the planner and the reviser, and finding that computers support revisers over planners.

2263. Latta, Susan. "MTV and Video Music: A New Tool for the English Teacher." *EJ* 73 (January 1984): 38–39.

Discusses the advantages and uses of video music in developing analytical thinking and writing skills.

2264. Lawrence, Robert. "The Where Exercise: Seeing in Writing." Paper given at the National Conference on Developmental Education, Chicago, 1981. ERIC ED 237 997 [7 pages]

Proposes a classroom activity, coaching students to "see" objects prior to a writing assignment.

2265. LeBar, Barbara. "An Articulation Assignment." *IE* 7 (Winter 1984): 12–13.

The topic, "My Private *vs.* My Public Pastimes," generates student interest.

2266. Libby, Judith S. "Opening the Door: Writing and the Slow Learner in High School." *JTW* 3 (Spring 1984): 45–52.

Examines techniques for increasing the confidence of basic writers while immersing them in the writing process. Includes specific classroom activities, including collaborative writing.

2267. Lichtman, Sharon R. "A Primary Source Method of Teaching Biography." *CEJ* 16 (Fall 1984): 9–15.

Describes a nonfiction unit on primary-source biography for high school students.

2268. Lithicum, Frances. "Fable Magic." *ET* 17 (Fall 1985): 15–17.

An 11-day writing unit using students' original fables.

2269. Little, Sherry Burgus. "Using Revision to Teach Grammar." *CEJ* 16 (Spring 1985): 49–54.

Describes a workshop program that "individualizes the study of grammar" within the context of writing.

2270. Mabry, Phyllis. "A High School Classroom and One Computer: Relief from Those Drill and Practice Tasks." *IlEB* 73 (Fall 1985): 63–66.

Describes goals and procedures for using grammar programs initially with students of different academic levels and subsequently using computers for spelling and word processing.

2271. Mackey, Gerald. "Reading and Writing: An Interdisciplinary Program that Involved Everyone." *ExEx* 31 (Fall 1985): 40–42.

Presents cross-curricular reading assignments in English, science, social studies, and mathematics for grades 9 through 12.

2272. Malachowski, Ann Marie. "Advertising: A Research Subject for Persuasive Writers." *ExEx* 29 (Spring 1984): 34–35.

Discusses parallels between the persuasiveness of advertising and persuasive research paper topics.

2273. Marcusen, Ann B. "Discovering Values through the Writing Process." *UEJ* (1984): 6–10.

Describes a writing unit on prejudice for ninth graders.

2274. Marshall, James D. "The Effects of Writing on Student's Understanding of Literary Texts." Paper given at the NCTE Convention, Detroit, November 1984. ERIC ED 252 842 [24 pages]

Studies writing about literature in the eleventh grade. Finds that extensive writing in a personal or formal mode was better than restricted, unelaborated writing.

2275. Mathie, Craig. "Making the Medicine Go Down: An Alternative to the Book Report." *UEJ* (1984): 11–13.

Offers alternatives to the book report, using Summerfield's spectator/participant writing model.

2276. Matthews, Dorothy, ed. "Writing Assignments Based on Literary Works." *IlEB* 72 (Special Issue, Spring 1985). ERIC ED 255 923 [76 pages].

Makes available in ERIC a special journal issue. Articles listed separately in this volume.

2277. McCarron, William, and Doris A. Miller. "Supermarket Writing." *Statement* 21 (October 1985): 12–17.

Suggests exercises and responses to generate expressive writing, which the author compares to shopping in a supermarket.

2278. McCartney, Robert. "Teaching Composition as a Dialogue." *NCET* 41 (Winter 1984): 6–10.

Presents a method for student conferences built on Buber's I-Thou perspective on students and their writing.

2279. McDonald, Agnes. "Making Coffee from Scratch." *NCET* 43 (Fall 1985): 9–11.

Explains a writing/thinking activity centered on making coffee that was conceived to demonstrate "three significant life Realities."

2280. McDonald, Joseph P. "Teaching the Documentary Arts: Combining Writing with Research and Photography." *EJ* 74 (November 1985): 56–63.

Describes an experimental high school workshop in which 10 students composed a documentary.

2281. McQuade, Thomas F. "Proposition Analysis: A Curriculum to Teach High School Students How to Organize Essays." *DAI* 45 (August 1984): 401A.

Describes a 10-lesson curriculum for teaching proposition analysis, proposes a method for teaching coherence and invention, and presents theoretical and pre- and posttest support for the method.

2282. Mehlville District Curriculum Office and Teaching Staff. *English Curriculum Guide: Senior High Program.* St. Louis: Mehlville School District, 1984. ERIC ED 246 421 [38 pages]

Describes a high school English curriculum.

2283. Melvin, Mary P. "The Implications of Sentence Combining for the Language Arts Curriculum." Paper given at the NCTE Convention, Seattle, April 1983. ERIC ED 238 021 [14 pages]

Advocates sentence combining across the language arts curriculum to encourage the production of appropriate and interesting sentences.

2284. Merrill, Yvonne. "Writing across the Curriculum: The Marana Experience." *ArEB* 27 (Fall 1984): 1–6.

Traces the development of a high school writing across the curriculum program.

2285. Michaud, Ruth. "Them As Can Should Do." *EJ* 73 (February 1984): 38–42.

Supports writing with and for students as a successful teaching method benefiting both teacher and student.

2286. Mikulecky, Larry. "Preparing Students for Workplace Literacy Demands." *JR* 28 (December 1984): 253–257.

Argues that narrowly focused school reading and writing do not transfer as literacy skills needed in the workplace. Describes 18 activities that foster these skills.

2287. Miller, Margery Staman. "In Search of Self and Others: Reading and Writing Autobiography." *CEJ* 16 (Fall 1984): 20–22.

Describes a reading-and-writing approach to autobiography that emphasizes data collection, analysis and synthesis of data, and writing for a public audience.

2288. Ministry of Education, Jerusalem. *English Teacher's Journal* (Israel) 30 (July 1984): ERIC ED 253 103 [89 pages].

Contains 16 articles. Topics include teaching ESL in Israel at the elementary and secondary level, approved textbooks, heterogeneous classes and individualized learning, and a statistical survey of secondary English teachers.

2289. Morris, Ann R. "Composing in a Circle: Reading and Writing Story Cycles." *FlaEJ* 21 (Spring 1985): 2–6.

Illustrates how two story cycles that are assigned reading can become the basis for student-generated story cycles.

2290. Moxley, Joseph M. "Trends in Writing Instruction: A New Look at the Composing Process." *FlaEJ* 21 (Fall 1985): 22–26.

Traces the emergence of the process approach to teaching writing and suggests some ways of applying theory to the classroom.

2291. Mullican, James S. "Found Poetry." *ExEx* 30 (Spring 1985): 35–37.

Describes an honors seminar in writing poetry that teaches vividness and avoiding sentimentality. Shows how to find poems in news articles, editorials, and other contexts.

2292. Myres, John. *Writing to Learn across the Curriculum: Fastback 209.* Bloomington, Ind.:

Phi Delta Kappa Educational Foundation, 1984. ERIC ED 248 532 [38 pages]

Contains research-based information designed to make writing a learning process. Discusses implementation in specific subject areas and presents activities.

2293. Naff, Beatrice. "Writing and the Creative Connection." *VEB* 35 (Spring 1985): 107–108.

Draws connections between Ghiselin's *Creative Process* and the writing process in contemporary English classrooms.

2294. Nance, Ellen Harrison. "The Question of Audience in the Teaching of Composition." *ET* 15 (Summer 1984): 12–16.

Examines the history of audience analysis, methods for teaching students about audience, and the effectiveness of these techniques.

2295. Nees-Hatlen, Virginia. "Collaborating on Writing Assignments: A Workshop with Theoretical Implications." *JTW* 4 (Fall 1985): 234–246.

Reports on a workshop on designing writing assignments collaboratively emphasizing its theoretical and practical benefits.

2296. Nevada Joint Council on College Preparation. *Making High School Count: Report of the Nevada Joint Council on College Preparation.* Reno: University of Nevada System, 1984. ERIC ED 246 721 [21 pages]

Recommends skills and competencies high school graduates need for success in a four-year college program.

2297. Newton, Frances S. "Vanity Fare: Signs of the Times for Creative Writing." *NCET* 42 (Fall 1984): 9–11.

Urges using the language on T-shirts and bumper stickers to produce good writing.

2298. Niles, Alice. "Journals Are Worth the Time." *VEB* 35 (Spring 1985): 60–64.

Offers a rationale from developmental and rhetorical theories for the advantages of journal writing.

2299. Nugent, Harold E., and Susan Monroe Nugent. "The Double-Entry Journal in Literature Class." Paper given at the New England Association of Teachers of English Meeting, Providence, R.I., October 1984. ERIC ED 252 862 [14 pages]

Advocates using a journal in a literature class, the first entry being an affective response, the second being a response after small group discussion.

2300. Ogren, Roy. "A Composition Grading Policy That Gets Results." *CEJ* 16 (Spring 1985): 81–85.

Describes a policy that "pressures students into editing final drafts carefully and seeking extra help with basics."

2301. Olson, Gary A. "The Advanced Placement Language and Composition Course." *JTW* 3 (Spring 1984): 37–44.

Describes the content and methodology of an advanced placement course.

2302. Olson, Gary A., and Jane Bowman Smith. "Establishing a Writing Center in the High School." *JTW* 3 (Spring 1984): 53–62.

Discusses selling the idea, funding, location, staff, tutor training, daily operation forms, data collection, and advertising.

2303. Orden, J. Hannah. "Vocabulary Review: Making Words Your Own." *ExEx* 30 (Spring 1985): 33–34.

Links freewriting and personal responses to literature to developing vocabulary and meaningful word definitions.

2304. Palmer, William S. "Freewriting: Some Hints for Classroom Use." *NCET* 42 (Winter 1985): 21–27.

Describes steps to take with different grades and levels of students to improve on Elbow's power writing.

2305. Panwitt, Barbara. *Using Microcomputers for Instruction in Humanities and Social Sciences, Part II*. Reston, Va.: National Association of Secondary School Principals, 1984. ERIC ED 240 663 [8 pages]

Describes uses of computers for writing in several school subjects.

2306. Patten, Mack. "Hot Tubs or Sentence Combining." *EJ* 73 (September 1984): 63–64.

Argues that enthusiastic teachers using methods of teaching writing across the curriculum do not always produce interested students.

2307. Pendergrass, Paula. "Preventing Twenty-First-Century Illiteracy: A Return to the Classics." *IE* 9 (Fall 1985): 7–9.

Lists 11 benefits of reading classics. Emphasizes the value of dreams and goals to combat modern cynicism.

2308. Peters, William H. "Developing Reasoning Skills through an Integrated Curriculum Approach." Paper given at the NCTE Spring Conference, Houston, March 1985. ERIC ED 257 102 [9 pages]

Argues for integrating language, literature, and composition, offering, as an example, one tenth-grade unit, "The Inquiring Mind."

2309. Pevey, Jo Lundy. "Activity-Based Writing." *ExEx* 30 (Fall 1984): 22–23.

Lists questions, assignment options, and local places students could visit to generate a paper on a newly discovered dining place.

2310. Pipman, Millie H. "The Amount and Nature of Composition Instruction in Two Secondary English Classrooms." *DAI* 45 (August 1984): 486A.

Observes literature and composition classes to determine the time allocated for literature and composition instruction in each course and for phases of composing process.

2311. Pitts, Beverly, comp. "Media Literacy and Television News." *JTW* 4 (Fall 1985): 156–161.

Four television journalists discuss television news, including its limitations and effects, and how to teach intelligent viewing of television news.

2312. Pollard, Rita. "Another Look: Audience Awareness and the Younger Writer." *EngR* 36 (1985): 13–15.

Stresses the need to study the young writer's evolving competencies (rather than "deficiencies"). Examines how fourth graders amplify their narratives.

2313. Potts, Richard. "Proofreading: Conscious Decisions." *NCET* 41 (Winter 1984): 1–4.

Argues for developing consciousness of usage problems in editing and proofreading by using discrimination, identification, and translation drills.

2314. Pritchard, Ruie. "Who Needs the Practice? Research on Peer Writing Groups." *NCET* 42 (Fall 1984): 22–23.

Cites studies supporting the effectiveness of peer review, especially on organization and critical thinking.

2315. Queenan, Margaret. "To Understand a Magazine, Produce a Magazine." *ExEx* 30 (Spring 1985): 18–21.

Describes student magazines and outlines a 25-day production schedule.

2316. Rank, Hugh. *The Pep Talk: How to Analyze Political Language.* Park Forest, Ill.: Counter-Propaganda Press, 1984. 215 pages

Presents exercises in studying political language. Designed to develop students' analytical skills in both reading and writing.

2317. Reed, Michael D. "Language, Perception, and Racism." *ET* 17 (Fall 1985): 12–14.

Argues that we see the world through language. *The Grapes of Wrath* and *Huckleberry Finn* illustrate how to "look beyond our words."

2318. Reissman, Rose. "Humor Your Students to Good Usage." *CEJ* 16 (Spring 1985): 115.

Discusses how Russell Baker's essays can "serve as powerful motivators and effective teaching tools" in teaching usage.

2319. Reissman, Rose. "Let the Transitive Vampire Motivate Students to Good Grammar and Proper Style." *CEJ* 16 (Spring 1985): 16–19.

Suggests using a term-long saga or story for teaching grammar and style.

2320. Resch, Kenneth E. "'What Dya Mean Revise It, Mr. Resch — It's Done!'" *ArEB* 28 (Fall 1985): 48–51.

Suggests ways to emphasize the importance of revision in high school writing classes.

2321. Rodrigues, Raymond J. "The Computer-Based Writing Program from Load to Print." *EJ* 73 (January 1984): 27–30.

Supports the development of computer-assisted composition curricula with sample programs for prewriting, revising, and evaluating.

2322. Rodrigues, Raymond J. "Introducing Students to Primary Traits." *CEJ* 15 (Spring 1984): 93.

Suggests using the fable to help students understand "primary traits" and their function in evaluating student writing.

2323. Rodriguez, William Robert. "Three Approaches to Writing the First Poem." *EJ* 74 (April 1985): 33–37.

Describes "breath-grouping, prose poetry, and the repeater" as creative approaches to poetry writing.

2324. Rosenbaum, Nina Joy. "Problems with Current Research in Writing Using the Microcomputer." Paper given at the Spring Conference of the Delaware Valley Writing Council, Villanova, Pa., February 1984. ERIC ED 234 116 [19 pages]

Describes the use of microcomputers in secondary writing instruction.

2325. Rubano, Gregory. "From Biographical Research to Presentation in Writing." *CEJ* 16 (Fall 1984): 16–19.

Describes a biography unit for high school students that emphasizes library research, oral rehearsal, writing, peer conferences and peer editing, and dramatization.

2326. Salinger, Wendy. "From Abbot School to Deep Space: Teaching Writing in a Special Education Setting." *TWM* 16 (March–April 1985): 1–12.

Describes a teacher's experiences teaching writing at a special education facility for troubled adolescents.

2327. Schmidt, Gary D. "*Beowulf* and the Literary Question." *IIEB* 72 (Spring 1985): 15–20.

Describes short and long essay assignments designed to make *Beowulf* "more accessible to students and increase their awareness of the role of the poet."

2328. Schmidt, Gary D. "Painting and the Art of Rhetoric." *IIEB* 71 (Winter 1984): 15–18.

Recommends and describes specific famous paintings as stimulants to writing and aids for teaching focus, effective detail, and stance.

2329. Schrader, Vincent E. "Teaching Journalism on the Micro." *EJ* 73 (April 1984): 93–94.

Praises using the microcomputer to produce a school newspaper.

2330. Schwartz, Jeffrey. "Renga: Teaching a Collaborative Poem." *TWM* 15 (January–February 1984): 1–3.

Describes a method of teaching students to write Renga poetry, a collaborative method of writing poetry.

2331. Sears, Peter. "What Do You Say about a Terrible Poem?" *TWM* 16 (May–June 1985): 1–3.

Describes how a teacher should constructively criticize a bad poem written by a high school student.

2332. Segedy, Michael. "An Approach to Teaching and Writing Poetry." *VEB* 34 (Winter 1984): 47–50.

Describes a method to help students analyze and compose poems by locating who, when, where, and what.

2333. Self, Warren. "A Broadened Perception: Writing and Learning." *VEB* 35 (Spring 1985): 19–25.

Calls for the greater use of writing to help students learn instead of writing that serves teachers' purposes for evaluation.

2334. Shea, George B., Jr. "A Knight to Remember; or, It Wasn't Easy Seeing Green." *IlEB* 72 (Spring 1985): 11–14.

Using *Sir Gawain and the Green Knight,* describes prewriting exercises and four choices of audience that "exercise some of the choices that real writers make."

2335. Sheffield, Terry. "A Teenager's Guide to a Small Part of the Galaxy." *UEJ* (1985): 20–22.

Offers an assignment for high school students for writing a guidebook to their area.

2336. Sheilah, Allen. "Students' Journals: Is This Time Well Spent?" *EQ* 16 (Winter 1984): 37–42.

Uses samples of student work to show journals worthwhile.

2337. Shores, Phyllis. "If Only." *UEJ* (1985): 34–36.

Bemoans the interruptions in the classroom that disrupt the teaching of writing.

2338. Shuman, R. Baird. "School-Wide Writing Instruction." *EJ* 73 (February 1984): 54–57.

Suggests that writing practice can be implemented across the high school curriculum through ungraded expressive writing, journal writing, and publishing.

2339. Simmons, John S. "Writing Enhancement: Beyond Class Size." *FlaEJ* 21 (Fall 1985): 18–21.

Suggests activities to make composition instruction more effective. Advocates using workshops and group work, made easier by recently reduced class size in Florida.

2340. Simons, Elizabeth Radin. "The Folklore of Naming: Using Oral Tradition to Teach Writing." *TWM* 16 (November–December 1984): 9–12.

Describes how a teacher focused on students' names to encourage them to write about themselves and their heritage.

2341. Simons, Elizabeth Radin. "Levitation, Jokes, and Spin the Bottle: Contemporary Folklore in the Classroom—A Folklorist's View." *EJ* 74 (February 1985): 32–36.

Discusses studying folklore in high school to promote critical thinking and to improve writing.

2342. Sinatra, Richard. "Use of Three Writing Tasks at an Adolescent Treatment Center." *PMS* 59 (October 1984): 355–358.

Student papers prompted by slide presentations were given slightly higher holistic ratings than papers prompted by oral stimulation of the imagination or by data presented on a fact sheet.

2343. Singer, Hindy. "'A Writing Assignment—Do I Have to?'" *EN* 6 (1984): 4–5.

Discusses ways to motivate writing students.

2344. Singer, Hindy, and D. Donlan. *Reading and Learning from Text.* Hillside, N.J.: Erlbaum, 1985. 560 pages

A guide to improving reading skills in high school. Discusses several subject disciplines and developing schoolwide programs.

2345. Smith, Eugene. "Enlivening Students' Writing about Literature." *CEJ* 15 (Spring 1984): 14–15.

Suggests expressive and transactional writing tasks as alternatives to traditional writing assignments about literature.

2346. Smith, Michael W. *Reducing Writing Apprehension.* Theory and Research into Practice. Urbana, Ill.: ERIC/RCS and NCTE, 1984. 40 pages

A series of sample lessons designed to introduce the writing process and to exercise students' skills while causing as little apprehension as possible. Includes suggestions on evaluating students' work.

2347. Smitherman, Geneva, and Sandra Wright. "Black Student Writers, Storks, and Familiar Places." Paper given at the NCTE Convention, Detroit, November 1984. ERIC ED 259 328 [33 pages]

Compares 1969 and 1979 samples by black 17-year-olds writing for the National Assessment of Educational Programs.

2348. Snackey, Jan. "Poems, Patterns, and . . . Promises of Better Writing." *ET* 16 (Spring 1985): 45–47.

Argues that students appreciate the security of formal poetic structures when they write. Using established patterns helps students progress to more independent writing.

2349. Snow, Susan. "Ease Comes with Training, or What Suzuki Has to Show Us about Teaching Basic Skills." *UEJ* (1984): 14.

Applies the Suzuki method of teaching music to reading and writing.

2350. Spencer, Arlene. "Teaching the Rules First." *IE* 8 (Winter 1985): 13–14.

Students should learn spelling, grammar, and sentence structure before being taught creative writing.

2351. Stegman, Michael O. "Beyond Correctness: The Computer and the Composing Process." Paper given at the Spring Writing Conference of the New York Department of Education, Albany, N.Y., May 1984. ERIC ED 252 852 [21 pages]

Describes exercises to help students use computers for revision. Describes ways in which the computer has been successfully incorporated into English curriculum.

2352. Stockard, Connie H. "Major Poets Model for Student Writing." *ET* 16 (Spring 1985): 29–36.

Argues that children do not have to understand the messages of poems to use them as models for their own writing. Students can learn poetic forms using poetic models.

2353. Stotsky, Sandra. "A Proposal for Improving High School Students' Ability to Read and Write Expository Prose." *JR* 28 (October 1984): 4–7.

Argues that upper elementary and secondary students should read and write expository prose much sooner.

2354. Streff, Craig R. "The Concept of Inner Speech and Its Implications for an Integrated Language Arts Curriculum." *ComEd* 33 (July 1984): 223–230.

Presents eight implications for teaching about inner speech as a central feature of human communication.

2355. Stull, William L. "Sentence Combining: Pros, Cons, and Possibilities." *CEJ* 16 (Spring 1985): 55–60.

Provides an overview of the strengths and shortcomings of sentence combining in writing courses.

2356. Stupple, Donna-Marie. "How to Stop Worrying and Learn to Love Word Processing." *IlEB* 73 (Fall 1985): 54–58.

Using Acewriter, outlines the procedure used with 90 high school freshmen in an initial four-day word processing experience.

2357. Sullivan, Jenny N., and Merle O. Thompson. "Two Methods of Using Reading in a Writing Class." *VEB* 35 (Spring 1985): 88–93.

Discusses two means of incorporating reading in a writing class.

2358. Swander, Mary. "About a Wolf: Maybe Two Wolves." *TWM* 16 (November–December 1984): 6–9.

Describes how a teacher incorporates the students' sense of sound into their writing.

2359. Swanson, Marti. "Writing in the American Novel Class: My Debt to Clarence." *IlEB* 72 (Spring 1985): 2–7.

Describes 14 writing topics on Hawthorne, Twain, Dreiser, Hemingway, and Steinbeck.

2360. Tanner, Deborah. "An Introduction to Poetry Analysis through Showing Language." *UEJ* (1984): 20–26.

Presents a unit for teaching poetry to advanced placement students.

2361. Terpstra, Richard L. "A Problem-Solving Approach to Writing." *IE* 7 (Winter 1984): 20–24.

Students write memos in response to assignments written in memo form about real-life problems. Includes two assignments and two student responses for each.

2362. Thompson, Edgar H. "Making Writing Conferences Work." *VEB* 35 (Spring 1985): 42–47.

Describes five essential elements of a writing conference and explains a five-day sequence of writing and conferencing.

2363. Towns, Sanna Nimtz. "Techniques for Integrating Reading and Writing Instruction in Secondary and Postsecondary Reading." Paper given at the Mississippi Reading Association, Biloxi, Miss., January 1984. ERIC ED 244 251 [15 pages]

Suggests techniques for combining reading and writing instruction.

2364. Towrey, Suzanne. "Integrating the Language Arts Curriculum through the Interview." *WaEJ* 8 (Fall 1985): 19–24.

A local history project enables students to integrate speaking and writing.

2365. Tremmel, Robert. "Back Alley Editing: An Effective Way to Teach Grammar and Usage." *CEJ* 16 (Spring 1985): 5–8.

Argues for a "shift in emphasis from teacher's teaching grammar to student's learning grammar" and for incorporating grammar and usage study into "the composing of whole pieces of discourse."

2366. Tremmel, Robert. "Hospitality in the Classroom: The Teaching Stance of the Writers in the Schools." *JTW* 3 (Fall 1984): 191–199.

Advocates two principles of hospitality: respecting students' language and offering flexible audiences throughout the writing process.

2367. Tsujimoto, Joseph I. "Re-Visioning the Whole." *EJ* 73 (September 1984): 52–55.

Presents several revision strategies for high school students such as varying the point of view, varying the audience, and memory revision.

2368. Ulrich, Clint. "New Directions for Saskatchewan's Curriculum Guide for Division IV English." *EQ* 17 (Spring 1984): 87–89.

Suggests revising the nine-year-old curriculum to make it consistent with new approaches to teaching recommended by the committee.

2369. Viera, Carroll. "Composing Skills and Peer Review." *NCET* 42 (Fall 1984): 20–21.

Suggests combining the Cooper and Odell evaluation model with Denn's notions about the effectiveness of peer review groups.

2370. Walker, Laurence. "Grammar Teaching in Alberta." *EQ* 18 (Fall 1985): 24–34.

Describes the teaching of grammar in Alberta as deduced from approved textbooks, Department of Education reports, curriculum guides, public examinations, and anecdotal records.

2371. Wallace, Joan T. "Grammar Time." *CEJ* 16 (Spring 1985): 74–80.

Traces the history of grammar instruction over the past 25 years and concludes that grammar is best taught in the context of reading and writing.

2372. Walrath, Norma D. "Grammar Requires Patience. We Must Teach It!" *CEJ* 16 (Spring 1985): 108.

Discusses the need to teach grammar and to apply grammar to both speaking and writing.

2373. Walrath, Norma D. "Peer Editing and No Grading: Two Techniques That Work Partly." *CEJ* 15 (Spring 1984): 102.

Discusses advantages and disadvantages of these techniques. Reports that the paper load increased.

2374. Walsh, Dennis M. "A Case for Teaching Technical Writing in the High School." *ArEB* 26 (Spring–Summer 1984): 8–13.

Advocates a technical writing elective course for high school seniors.

2375. Watson, Deryn M. "Computer-Assisted Learning for School Pupils of History, French, and English in the United Kingdom." *CHum* 18 (July–December 1984): 233–241.

Describes the programs for computer-assisted learning in English that allow users to develop stories that can be "played back" on the computer.

2376. Wetherell, Rick. "Writing." *TEd* (1985–1986): 104.

Describes using a Writing Skills Development Sheet that encourages the revision of sentences.

2377. Whale, Kathleen B., and Trevor J. Gambell, eds. *From Seed to Harvest: Looking at Literature.* CCTE Monographs and Special Publications. Canadian Council of Teachers of English (distributed by NCTE), 1985. 110 pages

A collection of 14 essays presented at the 1982 Conference of the Canadian Council of Teachers of English, Saskatoon, Canada. Addresses seven themes: student as writer and responder, integration of language and literature, developing literary criticism, literature as tradition and identity, drama as literature, the adult reader and the adult writer, and critical analysis: third world literature and the media.

2378. Wheeler, Patricia M. "Students Describe Their Four-Step Writing Project." *NCET* 41 (Summer 1984): 5–8.

Describes a regimen that moves writing students through four steps: informal journal entries, usage targeting, peer review, and revision.

2379. Wiest, Donald. "Owning Writing." *VEB* 34 (Spring 1984): 14–17.

Argues that students who claim ownership of their writing take responsibility for pushing themselves through all of the steps of composing.

2380. Willis, Meredith Sue. *Personal Fiction Writing: A Guide to Writing from Real Life for Teachers, Students, and Writers*. New York: Teachers and Writers Collaborative, 1984. 192 pages

Presents 356 classroom-tested writing assignments in six categories: describing places, people, and action; writing dialogue and monologue; and creating structure. Also contains a section on revision.

2381. Winterowd, W. Ross. "Writing about Writing." *ExEx* 30 (Spring 1985): 26–27.

Gives an assignment for a paper describing the writer's composing process. Includes questions about self, time and place, implements, purpose, and the act of writing.

2382. Wolf, Susan J. "Putting Research in Its Place." *IE* 9 (Winter 1985): 33–34.

Suggests approaching topics through comparison/contrast or cause/effect and recognizing documentation as a research tool.

2383. Wolfe, Denny, and Carol Pope. "Developing Thinking Processes: Ten Writing-for-Learning Tasks throughout the Curriculum." *VEB* 35 (Spring 1985): 11–17.

Offers 10 suggestions for helping students use writing as a vehicle for learning in the disciplines and across grade levels.

2384. Womble, Gail. "Process and Processor: Is There Room for a Machine in the English Classroom?" *EJ* 73 (January 1984): 34–37.

A tenth-grade teacher's experiences with a computer-assisted writing experiment.

2385. Worthington, Pepper. "Shifting Gears: An Effective Purpose for English Grammar." *NCET* 41 (Summer 1984): 13–15.

Describes the effort to convince students to shift from informal to formal constructions to produce language appropriate to the writing task.

2386. Zarnowski, Myra. "What Katy Knew: Clues from a Student Journal." *EngR* 35 (Third Quarter 1984): 2–4.

Advocates using journals as a teaching technique in secondary education.

2387. Zbikowski, John. "'I Tried Peer Conferencing, but It Doesn't Work.'" *CEJ* 16 (Spring 1985): 111.

Describes a teacher's experience with peer conferencing and analyzes why the conferences did not seem to work.

2388. Ziegler, Alan. "The Writing Workshop: Volume 2." *TWM* 16 (September–October 1984): 1–6.

Describes what teachers should say to students to inspire them to write.

See also 8, 14, 23, 24, 34, 358, 509, 649, 783, 957, 1263, 1350, 1568, 1652, 1765, 1971, 1973, 1976, 1988, 2002, 2006, 2039, 2048, 2066, 2082, 2084, 2088, 2112, 2118, 2128, 2129, 2132, 2133, 2135, 2137, 2140, 2420, 2447, 2452, 2467, 2484, 2488, 2492, 2504, 2511, 2513, 2535, 2536, 2555, 2575, 2596, 2611, 2614, 2641, 2642, 2652, 2671, 2687, 2822, 2900, 2950, 2982, 3017, 3071, 3098, 3112, 3445, 3457, 3540, 3553, 3596, 3621, 3737

HIGHER EDUCATION

DEVELOPMENTAL WRITING

2389. Akst, Geoffrey, Ruth Davis, and Virginia Slaughter. *Microcomputers and Basic Skills in College: Applications in Reading, Writing, ESL, and Mathematics*. New York: CUNY Office of Academic Affairs, 1984. ERIC ED 246 839 [102 pages].

A collection of 26 essays on computing in general and on specific applications of computers to language instruction, including reading, vocabulary development, writing, and the study of English as a second language.

2390. Anderson, Kristine F. "Guidelines for Using Group Activities with Basic Writers." *ArEB* 28 (Fall 1985): 45–47.

Offers advice for using groups effectively in a student-centered basic writing class.

2391. Arkin, Marian, and Brian Gallagher. "Word Processing and the Basic Writer." *CEJ* 15 (Spring 1984): 60–66.

Describes developmental writing courses in which word processors were used with promising results.

2392. Benton, Kay Hutchison. "Writing without Pain (or at Least Less of It)." *WLN* 8 (January 1984): 8–9.

Describes the use of freewriting, personal topics, and oral reading to alleviate writer's block in ESL students and basic writers.

2393. Berg, Anna, and Gerald Coleman. "A Cognitive Approach to Teaching the Developmental Student." *JBW* 4 (Fall 1985): 4–23.

Reports on a program designed to improve students' cognitive and basic skills through a curriculum emphasizing "cognitive competencies."

2394. Besser, Mary Pamela. "Sentence Combining: A Model for Correcting Fragmentary Absolutes in Basic Writing Students' Essays." *ExEx* 30 (Spring 1985): 30–32.

Discusses techniques for achieving surface-structure transformations that eliminate fragments. Advocates reading papers backward aloud.

2395. Bizzell, Patricia. "What Happens When Basic Writers Come to College." Paper given at the CCCC Convention, New York, March 1984. ERIC ED 245 232 [15 pages]

Describes the clash between the world views of basic writers and of the academic community.

2396. Boggs, George R. *The Effect of a Developmental Writing Course on Student Persistence and Achievement: A Research Report.* Oroville, Calif.: Butte College, 1984. ERIC ED 244 687 [27 pages]

Studies the effectiveness of a developmental writing course on a subsequent freshman writing course.

2397. Boley, Tommy J. "Guidelines for a Basic Writing Program." *ET* 16 (Fall 1984): 5–10.

Lists and discusses 10 curricular guidelines for designing a basic writing course emphasizing students' thinking.

2398. Bradford, Annette. "Applications of Self-Regulating Speech in the Basic Writing Program." *JBW* 4 (Fall 1985): 38–47.

Explains why and how students can benefit from talking out loud to themselves or to others while composing.

2399. Brown, Margaret C. "A Revision Technique for Problem Paragraphs: Decombining and Recombining." *ELAB* 26 (Spring 1985): 8–9.

Demonstrates a method for decombining elements in a weakly written paragraph and recombining them according to a set of standards for effective writing.

2400. Campbell, Joann. "Waving to the Distant Reader: An Approach to Basic Writing." *JTW* 3 (Spring 1984): 91–97.

Advocates designing writing tasks with "a progressively abstract subject and progressively distant audience." Suggests treating the topic in four stages: for the self, for someone involved, for a mutual acquaintance, and for a future reader.

2401. Carino, Peter A. "The Annotated Paragraph: An Exercise for Developing Revision Skills in Basic Writing Classes." *ExEx* 31 (Fall 1985): 28–30.

Guides basic writers by providing "evaluative annotations" of each sentence in their drafts of paragraphs.

2402. Carino, Peter A. "Developing Basic Writing Topics in Response to Reading: A Cognitive-Model Approach." *IE* 8 (Spring 1985): 3–8.

Explains assignments that lead writers through the four levels of cognitive development in the Andrew Wilkinson model: describing, interpreting, generalizing, and speculating.

2403. Carroll, Joyce Armstrong. "Practical Strategies for Teaching Basic Writing." *ET* 16 (Fall 1984): 16–19.

Believes that unskilled writers need practical strategies for prewriting, writing, and rewriting. Discusses listing, freewriting, cubing, shaping, and revising.

2404. Carter, Lu, and Tracy Nerem. "Writers Clinic: A Diagnostic Tool." *NebEC* 19 (Summer 1984): 18–21.

Describes policies and procedures of a service staffed by students for students.

2405. Condravy, Joan C., and Robert M. McIlvaine. "From Practice to Publish: A Process-Centered Approach to Basic Skills English 100." Paper given at the CCCC Convention, Minneapolis, March 1985. ERIC ED 255 932 [8 pages]

Describes a developmental course at Slippery Rock State University, noting how procedures reflect current research.

2406. Corona, Laurel, and Bruce Keitel. "'ACCESS': Retaining Underprepared College Freshmen." *WPA* 9 (Fall–Winter 1985): 51–58.

Describes a literacy program and identifies five key factors in successful implementation of programs for underprepared students.

2407. Dairs, Suzanne, and Marta Martino. "Variability in Reader-Response Journals." *EngR* 35 (Third Quarter 1984): 5–7.

Compares reader-response journals of ESL and freshmen composition students responding to literature.

2408. Dillingham, Don. "A Peer Tutor's Views on the Group Tutorial." *WLN* 10 (October 1985): 11–12.

Describes several ways to make group tutoring effective.

2409. Dunbar-Odom, Donna. "Directed Journals: Reading, Writing, and Reasoning for the Basic Writing Student." *IE* 8 (Spring 1985): 17–22.

Students write essay responses to four required readings per week, giving reasons for their personal responses.

2410. Eldred, Janet. "Arguing from Experience: A Generative Model." *IE* 8 (Spring 1985): 9–11.

Examines Rodriguez's *Hunger of Memory* to study an author's process of writing.

2411. Epes, Mary. "Tracing Errors to Their Sources: A Study of the Encoding Processes of Adult Basic Writers." *JBW* 4 (Spring 1985): 4–33.

A research report emphasizing the influence of nonstandard dialect on writing and the need for direct grammar instruction.

2412. Fabien, Miriam G. "Using a Learning Styles Approach to Teaching Composition." *DAI* 45 (January 1985): 2071A.

Explores how individual learning styles can be used in teaching composition. Students were trained to adopt writing strategies suited to their learning styles.

2413. Frazer, Cynthia Lynch. "Reading and Writing: An Integrated Approach for Teaching Remedial English." *IE* 8 (Spring 1985): 14–16.

Presents a classroom model of reading, responding, and writing from the response.

2414. Friedmann, Thomas. "A Blueprint for Writing Lab Exercises." *WLN* 8 (January 1984): 1–4.

Describes the development of usage exercises to be used in a sequence.

2415. Gaudet, Marcia. "Using Museums in Writing Classes." *LaEJ* 24 (Winter 1985): 34–38.

Describes assignments designed to improve observation, critical thinking, and cultural awareness.

2416. Goldberg, Marilyn K. "Overfamiliarity: A Cognitive Barrier in Teaching Composition." *JBW* 4 (Spring 1985): 34–43.

Examines the work of Piaget, Polanyi, and other cognitive theorists to explain how "overfamiliarity" operates and how it affects learning.

2417. Gomez, Debra. "Ideas in Practice: Why Come to Class? Productive Class Time in a Developmental Writing Course." *JDEd* 8 (1985): 20–21.

Recommends having developmental writers work in small groups, suggesting corrections and improvements to each other.

2418. Hall, Christine K. "Writing as a Prereading Role Playing Exercise to Increase the Reading Comprehension of Remedial College Students." *DAI* 45 (December 1984): 1737A.

Investigates "role-playing activity" used before reading to increase reading comprehension.

2419. Hall, Phil. "Giving Silliness a Chance." *WLN* 9 (May 1985): 7–8.

Encourages the use of "a slightly silly brand of fantasy that lets students' creativity run free while clearing up problems with adequate development."

2420. Harris, Jeanette. "The Cloze Procedure: Writing Applications." *JTW* 4 (Spring 1985): 105–111.

Discusses exercises that teach expectation from context in writing as well as in reading.

2421. Hartnett, Carolyn. "The Form of Thinking for Basic Writers." Paper given at the CCCC Convention, Detroit, March 1983. ERIC ED 239 251 [16 pages]

Offers advice to teachers on how to get students to use cohesion in forming their thoughts into extended rhetorical patterns.

2422. Hashimoto, Irvin Y. "Adult Learning and Composition Instruction." *JBW* 4 (Spring 1985): 55–67.

Characterizes adult learners and presents a rationale for designing materials and methods to meet their needs.

2423. Holdstein, Deborah H., Tim Redman, and Linda DeCelles. "Evaluating Computer-Assisted Instruction for Writing." *CollM* 2 (Summer 1984): 101–106.

Argues for the effectiveness of tutorial computer-assisted instruction in composition classes. Discusses research on Write Well grammar software.

2424. Houpt, Sheri. "Inspiring Creative Writing through Conversation." *FLA* 17 (May 1984): 185–189.

Describes nine assignments that include in-class oral activities in the prewriting phase.

2425. Hunter, Linda. "Student Responses to Using Computer Text Editing." *JDEd* 8 (1984): 13–14, 29.

Reports favorable results for basic writers using computer text editing.

2426. Hurlow, Marcia. "Writing Labs and Linguistic Insecurity." *WLN* 9 (April 1985): 4–6.

Describes how tutors can recognize and help students suffering from writing anxiety.

2427. Jacobson, Beatrice. "The Apple in the Center." *WLN* 9 (November 1984): 9–10.

Argues that computers make all stages of the writing process easier and faster, encourage students to write more, and add a sense of professionalism.

2428. Joseph, Nancy. *Integrated Language Skills: An Approach to Developmental Studies.* Lake City, Fla.: Lake City Community College, 1984. ERIC ED 241 095 [14 pages]

Describes a comprehensive remedial language curriculum, including writing, for college students.

2429. Kalinevitch, Karen. "Developmental Writing: A Systematic and Creative Approach." *IE* 8 (Spring 1985): 29–33.

Describes an approach in which students move from writing simple through compound through complex sentences to creating paragraphs and an essay.

2430. King, Mary. "Proofreading Is Not Reading." *TETYC* 12 (May 1985): 108–112.

Finds that patiently listening to students read individual sentences they've written helps them become better able to correct errors.

2431. Lambert, Judith R. "Summaries: A Focus for Basic Writers." *JDEd* 8 (1984): 10–12, 32.

Describes a procedure for teaching summary writing, discussing the instructional, affective, and cognitive advantages of this method.

2432. Larochelle, Therese. "The Sentence: What Is It?" *CEJ* 16 (Spring 1985): 61–68.

Describes an approach to "sentence sense" for basic writers that includes defining the English sentence, identifying basic sentence elements, and practicing sentence-combining.

2433. Lauby, Jacqueline. "Understanding the Dyslexic Writer." *WLN* 9 (January 1985): 7–9.

Discusses some characteristics of dyslexic writers and suggests six strategies to help them.

2434. Lederman, Marie Jean, Michael Ribaudo, and Susan R. Ryzewic. "Basic Skills of Entering College Freshmen: A National Survey of Policies and Perceptions." *JDEd* 9 (1985): 10–13.

Reports on a survey of 1297 representative colleges and universities to determine the skill levels of entering freshmen. Discusses implications for faculty and administrators.

2435. LeTourneau, Mark S. "Typical ESL Errors and Tutoring Strategies." *WLN* 9 (March 1985): 5–8.

Cites examples of "some of the more common inflectional and grammatical errors" and tells "how a tutor might deal with them."

2436. Lewis, Ruby M. "Teaching English Composition to Developmental Students at the College Level: A Free Writing/Language Study Approach *Vs.* a Structured Writing/Language Study Approach." *DAI* 45 (March 1985): 2788A.

Finds no significant difference in writing quality among students exposed to the freewriting or the structured writing approaches.

2437. Loheyde, Katherine Jones. "Teaching Composition to Writing Impaired Students." *CEJ* 15 (Spring 1984): 87–90.

Points out problems with organizational patterns and logical relationships that "language-delayed" students have and suggests how to deal with these problems.

2438. Lyons, Chopeta. "Spelling Inventory." *JBW* 4 (Fall 1985): 80–83.

Presents a method for helping developmental students identify, analyze, and correct spelling errors.

2439. Madden, Thomas R. "Finding the Beef: A Journalistic Summary Method for the Basic Writer." *ExEx* 31 (Fall 1985): 24–26.

Presents a way of sharpening abstracting skills by using the lead of a news article.

2440. McAllister, Carole. "The Word Processor: A Visual Tool for Writing Teachers." *JDEd* 8 (1985): 12–15.

Recommends using microcomputer word processing programs in composition classes to facilitate writing and rewriting.

2441. Meesin, Charoon. "A Comparison of the English and Reading Achievement of Remedial and Nonremedial College Freshmen." *DAI* 45 (July 1984): 72A.

Students enrolled in a university's remedial program improved significantly and improved more than transfer students, but improvement did not match the entry achievement levels of nonremedial students.

2442. Meiser, Mary J. "A Cognitive-Process Approach to College Composition: A Comparative Study of Unskilled Writers." *DAI* 45 (January 1985): 2018A.

Two basic writing classes received either process instruction, consisting of specific writing strategies, or traditional instruction, including concentration on grammar. The process class made significant and higher gains in grammar and on three of the four writing measures.

2443. Morante, Edward A., Shari Faskow, and Irene Nomejko. "The New Jersey Basic Skills Assessment Program: Part II." *JDEd* 7 (Spring 1984): 6–9.

Evaluates remedial programs in New Jersey colleges and the impact of the New Jersey Basic Skills Assessment Program. Suggests future directions.

2444. Moss, Andrew. "Taking a New Look at Remedial Writing." *CHE* 29 (14 November 1984): 40.

Remedial writing courses, once termed "bonehead English," now go far beyond basic grammar and punctuation and include literature discussions and critical thinking.

2445. Nichols, Randall G. "The Effects of Computer-Assisted Writing on the Composing Process of Basic Writers." *DAI* 45 (February 1985): 2507A.

While computers do not affect writers' goals and plans, they change such factors as the amount of editing, reading, and word production.

2446. Ostereicher, M. H. "Developing College Writers through Mentoring." *EngR* 36 (1985): 22–25.

Discusses using peer tutors or mentors to support classroom learning and to benefit students.

2447. Portnoy, Kenneth. "Video in Script Writing Projects." *MM* 22 (November–December 1985): 13–15.

Describes using videotape to present elements in good stories and to help high school and college students assess the construction of their stories.

2448. Powell, Joyce E. "The Effects of Sentence Combining on the Writing of Basic Writers in the Community College." *DAI* 45 (February 1985): 2508A.

Examines the effects of *The English Modules* sentence-combining curriculum on college basic writers' syntactic fluency, quality, and usage errors. Syntactic fluency improved but quality declined as a result of the treatment.

2449. Preussner, Alanna, and Arnold Preussner. "Personalized Instruction in Basic Writing at Yankton College." *EN* 6 (1984): 7–9.

Describes a basic writing program at Yankton College.

2450. Rabianski-Carriuolo, Nancy. "Language Arts Research Provides Encouragment for Anxious Writers." *CEJ* 15 (Spring 1984): 72–74.

Offers suggestions to teachers for helping reluctant writers select topics, take hour-long essay examinations, and gain confidence with language skills.

2451. Rabianski-Carriuolo, Nancy. "The Teaching and Evaluation of Composition: Developmental College Freshmen." Paper given at the NCTE Convention, Detroit, November 1984. ERIC ED 253 888 [19 pages]

Discusses four aspects of a developmental writing course: meeting affective needs, assessing, instructing, and evaluating.

2452. Radencich, Marguerite C., and Jeanne S. Schumm. "To Byte or Not to Byte: Traditional and High-Tech Approaches to Writing Term Papers." *MM* 21 (September 1984): 9–12.

Presents a strategy for writing term papers, both with and without a word processor.

2453. Rankin, David. "Reading, Listening, Writing: An Integrated Approach to Teaching Exposition." *JBW* 4 (Fall 1985): 48–57.

Explains a procedure "designed primarily as an introduction to the written dialect for students who require developmental instruction."

2454. Reagan, Sally Barr. "The Effect of Combined Reading-Writing Instruction on the Composing Processes of Basic Writers: A Descriptive Study." Paper given at the CCCC Convention, New York, March 1984. ERIC ED 243 134 [11 pages]

Studies the effects of a college writing instructor team teaching with a reading instructor.

2455. Reegan, Sally B. "Double Exposure: Combined Reading-Writing Instruction." *DAI* 45 (March 1985): 2863A.

A case study of a reading-writing course for basic writers.

2456. Reimer, Daniel. "Teaching Theresa." *WLN* 9 (September 1984): 1–2.

Describes the role of computers in labs to facilitate text editing. Encourages students to work with their own texts during the learning process.

2457. Reynoso, Wendy Demko. "Brief Reports and Summaries: A Pilot Study of the Effect of Contrastive Instruction on the Standard English Proofreading Skills of Dialect Different Students." *TESOLQ* 18 (December 1984): 740–742.

A study of black, Hispanic, and Asian students indicated that contrastive instruction improves Standard English proofreading skills.

2458. Roof, Midge. "Dialect Collision and Student Trauma." *JTW* 3 (Spring 1984): 63–77.

Endorses viewing language as a "context-specific transaction" so that Standard Written English serves as the appropriate dialect only in specific contexts.

2459. Roueche, John E., George A. Baker III, and Suanne D. Roueche. "Access with Excellence: Toward Academic Success in College." *CCR* 12 (Spring 1985): 4–9.

Reviews several studies of underprepared students, focuses on a 1984 status survey of basic skills instruction, and discusses 11 common elements in successful programs.

2460. Rounds, Jeanine C., and Dan Anderson. "Placement in Remedial College Classes: Required *Vs.* Recommended." *CCR* 13 (Summer 1985): 20–27.

Reviews the literature on required remediation in college and notes a trend toward mandatory statewide placement.

2461. Scheffler, Judith. *Microcomputer Use in a Developmental Writing Course.* Drexel University Microcomputing Working Papers, no. 7. Philadelphia: Drexel University, 1984. ERIC ED 259 327 [25 pages]

Describes the use of a computer in a developmental writing course.

2462. Schwalm, David E. "Degree of Difficulty in Basic Writing Courses: Insights from the Oral Proficiency Interview Testing Program." *CE* 47 (October 1985): 629–640.

Discusses how performance levels from the Oral Proficiency Interview, developed by the Foreign Service Institute, can be applied to basic writing pedagogy and programs.

2463. Schwartz, Mimi. "Defining Voice through Letter Writing." *EngR* 35 (First Quarter 1984): 10–14.

Discusses using various kinds of letter writing to create/expose voice.

2464. Skulicz, Matthew. "Ideas in Practice: Writing for Publication in Developmental English." *JDEd* 9 (1985): 20–23.

Describes an in-class publication that involves developmental students in writing, editing, reacting, and publishing.

2465. Skulicz, Matthew. "Writing for Publication in Developmental English." Paper given at the National Association of Developmental Educators Meeting, Philadelphia, March 1984. ERIC ED 246 450 [18 pages]

Describes a developmental writing course.

2466. Sollisch, James. "Making Writing Real: A Step in the Developmental Process." *JDEd* 9 (1985): 12–15, 32.

Describes a sequence of classroom assignments stressing writing as communication and providing a responsive audience for student writers.

2467. Stay, Byron L. "Talking about Writing: An Approach to Teaching Unskilled Writers." *JTW* 4 (Fall 1985): 248–252.

Finds two valuable uses of talk: alleviating the social and psychological pressure of "unskilled" writers and encouraging rewriting.

2468. Stoffel, Judy. "Editing for Style *à la* Joseph Williams." *WLN* 10 (September 1985): 12–14.

Identifies and illustrates five of Williams's prescriptions for improving sentence quality.

2469. Summerlin, Charles Timothy. "Toward Defining 'Basic' Over Again." *BADE* 81 (Fall 1985): 32–35.

Analyzes learning-to-write and writing-to-learn, opposing views of basic writing, and argues for competence tempered by humanistic goals.

2470. Tabor, Kenneth. "Gaining Successful Writing in the Foreign Language Classroom." *FLA* 17 (April 1984): 123–124.

Describes a writing assignment that included group work in the prewriting stage, peer revision, and individual conferences with the instructor during class.

2471. Tremmel, Robert. "What Writing Lab Instruction Can Teach Us about Classroom Teaching: One Student's Progress." *IE* 8 (Spring 1985): 22–28.

Describes the consequences in the classroom of a basic writer's work in a writing lab.

2472. Wade, Philip. "Back to Basics: Notes from Underground." *TETYC* 11 (December 1984): 23–25.

Satirizes curriculum change in response to social pressures and suggests that college is not the place to teach basic writing.

2473. Ware, Elaine. "Visual Perception through 'Window Proofreading.'" *WLN* 9 (May 1985): 8–9.

Suggests that writers proofread more effectively by using a three-by-five card containing a small rectangular window to isolate words and punctuation.

2474. Wilson, Allison. "Black Dialect and the Freshman Writer." *JBW* 4 (Spring 1985): 44–54.

Argues that the "standard/nonstandard conflict" is not the primary source of writing problems. Proposes a "discourse-based approach" to writing instruction.

2475. Zimmerman, Jesse. "The Tutor's Corner." *WLN* 10 (November 1985): 9.

Describes how tutors can help students to begin composing, to revise, and to improve their writing by adjusting their response to different situations.

See also 285, 293, 302, 366, 1117, 1204, 1583, 1659, 1680, 1694, 1699, 1702, 1735, 1791, 1924, 2266, 2295, 2311, 2492, 2495, 2508, 2535, 2573, 2574, 2575, 2576, 2592, 2611, 2618, 2650, 2656, 2657, 2671, 2678, 2680, 2688, 2690, 2973, 3048, 3069, 3124, 3134, 3738, 3791, 3816, 3841, 3842

FRESHMAN COMPOSITION

2476. Adams, Katherine H. "From James Britton: The Rhetoric of Spectating." *FEN* 13 (Winter 1984): 15–17.

Presents a classroom construct that includes expressive writing, observation, "gossip," and reading/publication in each writing assignment.

2477. Anandam, Kamala. "Camelot: Dream or Reality?" *CollM* 2 (Summer 1984): 121–128.

Describes a computer-based program at Miami-Dade Community College that helps to foster communication between teachers and students, with specific reference to writing applications.

2478. Anson, Chris M. "Audience, Dissonance, and Invention: A Method for Reducing Egocentrism in Student Writing." *ExEx* 30 (Spring 1985): 12–14.

Presents a prewriting activity that teaches writers to "consider opposing views and make concessions," to decenter arguments and to solve problems.

2479. Anson, Chris M. *Composition and Communicative Intention: Exploring the Dimension of Purpose in College Writing.* Urbana, Ill.: ERIC/RCS, 1984. ERIC ED 257 076 [28 pages]

Reports on case studies of four freshmen, finding students' models of writing and literacy more important than the demands of specific writing tasks.

2480. Anson, Chris M. "The Peer-Group Conference: Rediscovering a Forgotten Audience." *Leaflet* 84 (Winter 1985): 18–23.

Advocates peer conferencing to develop audience sensitivity in student writers.

2481. Bacon, Nora. "Writing Assignments in a Women's Studies Composition Course." *EJ* 74 (May 1984): 29–33.

Describes writing assignments designed both to sharpen writing skills and to encourage feminist critical reading.

2482. Barton, Marcia. "I Settled for English: What Students Say about Learning to Write." *WaEJ* 6 (Spring 1984): 12–21.

Students' comments on final exminations in a composition course reveal discoveries students have made about their own writing.

2483. Beck, James. "'It *Must* Be Good': The High Craft of the Lowly Magazine Article." *ArEB* 26 (Winter 1984): 57–63.

Advocates writing feature articles in freshman composition.

2484. Beck, James P. "Is 'Process' Composing Really Teachable?" *CEJ* 15 (Spring 1984): 95–101.

Recounts experiences with the process approach, highlighting advantages and pointing out difficulties.

2485. Beck, James P. "More Student Accountability, Earlier." *IE* 7 (Winter 1984): 14–19.

Lists and briefly discusses 12 methods for changing "passive pupils" into "active authors."

2486. Beck, James P. "Picky But Potent: The 'Précis' as Cure-All for Reading and Writing Ills." *ArEB* 27 (Winter 1985): 54–66.

Presents a unit intended to help students read texts more thoroughly and write summaries more cogently.

2487. Bedetti, Gabriella. "Interdisciplinary Concepts of Teaching Voice." *EngR* 36 (1985): 15–16.

Discusses semiotics and a method of teaching college students voice, tone, and style.

2488. Beem, Beverly. "Using a Historic Site in a Writing Class." *CEJ* 16 (Fall 1984): 63–67.

Describes a freshman English course in which a historic site was selected as a focus for student writing.

2489. Beers, Susan E. "An Analysis of the Interaction between Students' Epistemological Assumptions and the Composing Process." Paper given at the CCCC Convention, New York, March 1984. ERIC ED 249 503 [16 pages]

Using Perry's scheme of intellectual development, argues that teachers should be aware of student's level of development.

2490. Bell, Kathleen L. "The Writing Apprehension of Successful College Freshman Writers: Six Case Studies." *DAI* 46 (August 1985): 367A.

Findings raise questions pertaining to anxiety and motivation, course requirements, locus of control, and error analysis in writing.

2491. Benesch, Sarah. "Improving Peer Response: Collaboration between Teachers and Students." Paper given at the CCCC Convention, New York, March 1984. ERIC ED 243 113 [11 pages]

Describes a collaborative approach for deriving guidelines for peer response to essays in first-year college writing courses.

2492. Benner, Pamela, Deborah Epperson, and Joe Toole. "Students Write on Writing." *JTW* 3 (Spring 1984): 23–36.

Three students identify six sources of writing anxiety and possible solutions, examine the teacher-student axis of responsibility, and discuss how collaboration expands an awareness of rhetorical context, especially audience.

2493. Boiarsky, Carolyn. "Plunging into Word Processing: A Community College Teacher's Experience." *IlEB* 73 (Fall 1985): 59–63.

Reviews a six-hour introduction to computers geared to teaching students at Illinois Central the "linguistic functions of revision," addition, deletion, substitution, and reordering.

2494. Bowman, Barbara. "Writing about Film in Nonfilm Courses." *JTW* 4 (Fall 1985): 290–294.

Advocates teaching film analysis through identification, description, and interpretation. Includes 19 questions for analysis without using film jargon.

2495. Bridgeman, Brent, and Sybil B. Carlson. "Survey of Academic Writing Tasks." *WC* 1 (April 1984): 247–280.

Finds that, although students need a variety of writing skills, disciplines do not agree on the kinds of writing required or the type of assessment preferred.

2496. Bridgford, Kim. "A Matter of Style: Developing Awareness through Writing." *IlEB* 72 (Spring 1985): 46–53.

Describes a procedure designed to help students see a "richness of different styles in works" from Beckett to the Bible.

2497. Bristow, Margaret. "A Grammar Assignment That Worked." *CEJ* 16 (Spring 1985): 48.

Suggests that students write summaries and evaluations of articles on the teaching of grammar to improve critical thinking, reading, and writing.

2498. Brown, Jane L. "Emphasizing Revision with Word Processing in Freshman English Classes." Paper presented at the Southeastern Writing Centers Association Convention, Atlanta, April 1985. ERIC ED 258 279 [13 pages]

Describes a course in which students use the Milliken Word Processor to learn word processing and computer-assisted revision.

2499. Brown, Jane L. "The Final Step: Helping Students Become Self-Critical Writers." *ArEB* 28 (Fall 1985): 65–68.

Offers suggestions for moving students from being dependent writers to becoming independent writers.

2500. Bryant, John. "Argument and Word Play: The Uses of Simile." *FEN* 13 (Winter 1984): 22–24.

Describes classroom exercises in creating similes.

2501. Buckler, Patricia Prandini. "Reading, Writing, and Psycholinguistics: An Integrated Approach Using Joyce's 'Counterparts.'" *TETYC* 12 (February 1985): 22–31.

Describes a freshman composition course using linked reading/writing exercises, combining Rosenblatt's model for reading with Moffett's model of writing.

2502. Cawelti, Scott. "Interpretive Structural Modeling." *IaEB* 33 (1984): 24–25.

Discusses the applications of interpretive structural modeling to the process of invention in writing.

2503. Chase, Dennis. "From Grammar to Billy Bob's: The Education of an English Teacher— Texas Style." *CEJ* 16 (Spring 1985): 20–24.

Recounts classroom experiences to illustrate the "difficulties involved in the teaching of traditional grammar" and to show inconsistencies and omissions in college handbooks.

2504. Chase, Dennis. "Pass the Peek Freans, Please: Some Food for Thought in Composition Classes." *LaEJ* 24 (Winter 1985): 1–13.

Describes how food can be used to motivate students to generate ideas and focus their writing.

2505. Clines, Raymond H. "Chaim Perelman Reexamined: An Application to Classroom Methodology." Paper given at the CCCC Convention, Minneapolis, March 1985. ERIC ED 251 846 [17 pages]

Argues that the exclusive stress on logic in argumentation has produced a misapplication of logic to teaching writing, especially to teaching argument.

2506. Colavito, Joseph J. "Avoiding Minimalist Thinking: Research Orientation in Freshman Composition." *IE* 9 (Winter 1985): 35–38.

Gives directed activities for cultivating observation and research through continued practice.

2507. Collins, James L., and Elizabeth A. Sommers, eds. *Writing On-Line: Using Computers in the Teaching of Writing.* Upper Montclair, N.J.: Boynton/Cook, 1985. 136 pages

A collection of 14 essays that examine how computers can be used to enhance writing instruction, the uses of microcomputers at various stages of composing, and the implications computers have for future teaching and research.

2508. Comprone, Joseph J., and Katharine J. Ronald. "Expressive Writing: Exercises in a New *Progymnasmata*." *JTW* 4 (Spring 1985): 31–53.

From a historical base, develops two stages of integrating expression and communication with exercise sequences, six for stage one and four for stage two.

2509. Cooper, Jan, Rick Evans, and Elizabeth Robertson. *Teaching College Students to Read Analytically: An Individualized Approach.* Urbana, Ill.: NCTE, 1985. 58 pages

Discusses the benefits of exploratory reading journals in developing the reflective state of mind of a good critical reader and presents three case studies discussing an underprepared, urban black athlete, a freshman English course, and two sophomore courses.

2510. Crisler, Jesse A. "Organizational Models for Student Composition." *IE* 8 (Winter 1985): 15–19.

Presents three assignments to develop organizational skills: interviewing classmates, collaborative outlining, and generating detail for a character sketch.

2511. Criswell, Dana. "Teaching Revision." *LaEJ* 23 (Fall 1984): 54–62.

Argues that teaching rewriting is central to teaching writing. Describes ways to go about it.

2512. Cross, John A., and Bob J. Curey. "The Effect of Word Processing on Writing." Paper given at the American Society for Information Science Meeting, Bloomington, Ind., May 1984. ERIC ED 247 941 [10 pages]

Studies three sections of English 101, half using computers, finding that the effects of the computer vary with the student, teacher, and context of the class.

2513. Crowley, Sharon. "Great Expectations: Composition Theory and Practice." *CEJ* 16 (Spring 1985): 99–104.

Advocates a process-oriented pedagogy in the writing classroom instead of a pedagogy based on the five-paragraph theme.

2514. Davis, James E. "Rewriting Bambara's 'My Man Bovanne.'" *IIEB* 72 (Spring 1985): 38–46.

Using illustrations from student work, argues that "students can improve both their writing" and understanding of literature by rewriting a given text.

2515. Davis, Mary. "Becoming: A Course in Autobiography." *EJ* 74 (May 1985): 34–36.

A teacher of college freshmen describes readings and "self-exploration" as an approach to writing a "slice of life" autobiography.

2516. Deen, Rosemary. "The Teacher and the Satan." *IaEB* 33 (1984): 31–33.

Argues that writing strings of sentences in class helps generate and clarify ideas.

2517. Delmar, P. Jay. "The Composition-Literature Course: Making the Impossible Possible." *EngR* 35 (Second Quarter 1984): 8.

Suggests that, by drawing upon literature, it is possible to generate any type of essay.

2518. Devlin, Frank. "Literature and the Freshman Writing Class." *FEN* 13 (Fall 1984): 10–15.

Argues that literature/composition courses have a new critical/current traditional composing bias. Presents a reader response/process alternative.

2519. Dice, Laura. "Generating Generative Metaphors." *ArEB* 27 (Spring–Summer 1984): 37–43.

Describes a method for writing metaphors.

2520. Doe, Sandra. "The Helix Papers: Essays and Research on Teaching Writing." *DAI* 44 (March 1984): 2749A.

Explains the helical curriculum and examines the composing processes of three students in such a course.

2521. Doe, Sue Rowe. "William Perry and One Student Profile." *Leaflet* 84 (Winter 1985): 24–29.

Describes the intellectual change in one student that resulted from his participation in a writing class.

2522. Dollieslager, Rick. "Composition by Word Processing: A Community College Program." *IIEB* 73 (Fall 1985): 41–48.

Indicates the problems, solutions, and potential of using a limited number of computers as tools in the writing classroom.

2523. Dorazio, Patricia. "Teaching Composition: A Way to Improve It." *CCR* 12 (Fall 1984): 29–31.

Reports on an experiment with Garrison's quick-conference method of composition instruction at Hudson Valley Community College.

2524. DuBois, Barbara. "Hat Tricks for Teaching Writing." *ExEx* 29 (Spring 1984): 20–21.

Illustrates how to resist lecturing and use group activities to teach the development of a thesis, organization, and collaboration with peers.

2525. Emmanuel, Lenny. "The Third Stanza." *JTW* 3 (Fall 1984): 269–284.

Recommends teaching the process of revision "with a thorough knowledge of grammatical and rhetorical skills."

2526. Engel, Mary. "Mining the Motherlode: Tapping the Natural Resources of Students' Journals." *ArEB* 28 (Fall 1985): 15–22.

Reviews the literature on journal writing and offers suggestions for linking journals to writing in freshman composition.

2527. Engel, Mary, and Thomas M. Sawyer. "Contractual Revision." Paper given at the CCCC Convention, Detroit, March 1983. ERIC ED 234 415 [18 pages]

Outlines the benefits of requiring students to form contracts specifying revision with peer tutors.

2528. Ewald, Helen R., and Nancy Roundy. "Prescribing Writer Options: A Heuristic Procedure for Freshman Composition." *EN* 6 (1984): 17–27.

Describes procedures for enhancing students' inventiveness in writing.

2529. Fazio, Gene, Judy Pearce, and Gwen Rowley. "Buddy Writing, Paragraph Skeletons, and Overhead Transparencies: Strategies for Teaching Paragraph Writing." *ArEB* 26 (Spring 1984): 34–41.

Describes alternatives to lecturing and worksheets to "involve students in developing their own skills."

2530. Fenton, Mary C. "Teaching Persuasion: A Positive Approach." Paper given at the Wyoming Conference on Freshman and Sophomore English, Laramie, Wyo., June 1983. ERIC ED 233 396 [15 pages]

Synthesizes four instructional models for argumentative writing.

2531. Finkle, Sheryl L. "Teaching Shirley Jackson's 'The Lottery': A Sensitizing Approach." *IIEB* 72 (Spring 1985): 65–71.

Develops a series of inductive reading activities to "sensitize students to the function of background knowledge and formal schemes in texts" and to their own writing.

2532. Flynn, Elizabeth A. "Gender Differences and Student Writing." Paper given at the CCCC Convention, Detroit, March 1983. ERIC ED 233 399 [11 pages]

Essays by five pairs of freshmen show that men and women confront different problems in their writing and adopt different attitudes toward it.

2533. Forrester, Kent. "Why Nothing Works." *TETYC* 11 (October 1984): 16–22.

Argues that writing demands a developed fluency in complex language skills that are difficult to teach. Includes recommendations for teachers.

2534. Forrester, Kent. "Writing and the Real World." *ArEB* 27 (Fall 1984): 79–81.

Argues for more instruction in expository writing, which reflects the "writing world outside the classroom."

2535. Foster, David. "Reader-Awareness for Inexperienced Writers: Textbooks *Vs.* Teachers." *JTW* 3 (Spring 1984): 79–89.

Contends that "inexperienced writers ought not to be asked to compose for specific audiences outside themselves until they have learned to write for the reader in themselves."

2536. Fowler, Lois. "Consider Autobiography." *CEJ* 16 (Fall 1984): 23–28.

Describes a college-level course based on autobiography that aims to help students develop essays about their experiences.

2537. Fox, Barry. "Confidence, Illumination, and Purging: Three Effects of Exploratory Language." *EQ* 17 (Fall 1984): 3–10.

Three students use writing to explore thoughts, rather than to state ideas already thought of, in five paragraph essays.

2538. Frazer, Cynthia Lynch, and Stephen Heady. "An Exercise in Research: Becoming Familiar with MLA." *IE* 9 (Winter 1985): 24–25.

A 12-question, in-class exercise about documentation.

2539. Freedman, Sarah Warshauer. *Teaching and Learning in the Individual Writing Conference.* Urbana, Ill.: NCTE Research Foundation, 1984. ERIC ED 251 835 [65 pages]

Studies first-year college writing conferences, female/nonwhite students focusing on microlevels, males on macrolevels, and teachers individualizing instruction according to students' needs.

2540. French, Tita. "A Good Crot Is Hard to Find." *RR* 3 (January 1985): 190–200.

Reports on a successful attempt to encourage creativity by asking writers to use Weather's Grammer B.

2541. Fulkerson, Tahita. "Make Your Students See Red: A Lesson on the Topic Sentence." *ExEx* 30 (Fall 1984): 8–9.

Draws an analogy between listing or excluding colored items noted in the classroom to restriction in topic sentence construction.

2542. Fulkerson, Tahita, and Sue Milner. "*1984:* A Rhetorical Perspective." *IE* 8 (Fall 1984): 10–15.

Demonstrates how the protagonist carries out activities like those of students in freshman composition: invention, audience and purpose analysis, arrangement, language analysis, and values clarification.

2543. Gebhardt, Richard. "Changing and Editing: Moving Current Theory on Revision into the Classroom." *RR* 2 (January 1984): 78–88.

Finds a lag between revision theory and classroom practice, advocates teaching drafting as a process of growth, and encourages the use of computers.

2544. George, Diana. "Working with Peer Groups in the Composition Classroom." *CCC* 35 (October 1984): 320–326.

Discusses strategies for facilitating interactions among group members. Classifies groups as task-oriented, leaderless, and dysfunctional.

2545. Gere, Anne Ruggles. "From Practice to Theory: Writing Groups." *WaEJ* 7 (Winter 1985): 22–23.

Social definitions of writing underlie and explain benefits normally attributed to writing groups.

2546. Glass, Tom. "How to Learn What You've Been Teaching: An Assignment Proposal." *ExEx* 30 (Fall 1984): 41–43.

Allows students to develop an assignment and convince the teacher of its importance.

2547. Goerdt, Arthur L. "Integrating a College Freshman Writing Course with Instruction in the Use of the Library." *ET* 16 (Summer 1985): 34–37.

Urges that library instruction stress content. Lists seven assignments for first-semester college English courses and five second-semester assignments.

2548. Goldstein, Richard M., and Charles W. Nelson. "Stand Up and Write: Completing the Freshman Communications Course." Paper given at the Central States Speech Association Meeting, Chicago, April 1984. ERIC ED 246 497 [11 pages]

Offers a course guide for integrating oral communication into a writing course.

2549. Gowen, Brent. "Response to Private Journal Writing." *ExEx* 31 (Fall 1985): 32–33.

Discusses private journal writing and students' written responses to their journals, directed to the class and teacher.

2550. Graves, Richard L. "The Way of a Large House: Synthesis in Teaching Composition." *RR* 3 (September 1984): 4–12.

Describes a way of teaching writing using several approaches: reading models, identifying with a passage, using response groups, analyzing structures, reading professional essays, and revising.

2551. Hadley, David. "Utilizing Local Resources in Teaching the Importance of Writing Skills." *ExEx* 29 (Spring 1984). 22–23

Describes resume writing and writing letters of application for summer jobs, arguing for "the experience of achieving a real purpose through a piece of writing."

2552. Hample, Dale. "Teaching the Cognitive Context of Argument." *ComEd* 34 (July 1985): 196–204.

Explains how to teach argumentation by combining a discussion of logic and audience analysis. Offers as an example the invention of value arguments.

2553. Harris, Jeane, and Steven Wilson. "Incoherence and Hamster-Heads." *FEN* 13 (Fall 1984): 17–20.

Assignments that "violate the expectations of freshmen writers" can produce prose that has "creativity, honesty, and charm."

2554. Harris, Jeanette. "Wading into Research: Preliminary Reading/Writing Activities." *IE* 9 (Winter 1985): 30–32.

Advocates writing a summary, a synthesis, and a critique as preliminary research activities.

2555. Harrison, Ellen. "How *Do* You Teach Them to Think?" *ArEB* 28 (Fall 1985): 71–76.

Advocates using the Christensen coding system in evaluating student writing.

2556. Hashimoto, Irvin Y. "'You Write with a Purpose,' 'You Breathe,' and Other Needless Assertions." *FEN* 13 (Winter 1984): 19–22.

Discusses generalizations and "bland ideas" commonly espoused in writing courses.

2557. Hawisher, Gail E., and Gary D. Schmidt. "Collaborative Writing: A Successful Strategy for Computer-Assisted Instruction." *IlEB* 73 (Fall 1985): 28–35.

Describes student-to-student computer interaction in Rhetoric 108 at the University of Illinois as instructors modified "conventional" and "creative" writing tasks.

2558. Heavilin, Barbara A. "Synectics as an Aid to Invention in English Composition 104 at Ball State University." *DAI* 45 (November 1984): 1381A.

Concludes that synectics helps students think analogically and divergently and develop a more positive attitude toward writing.

2559. Heller, Scott. "Fifty Lecturers Lose Their Jobs in a Dispute over How—and If—Writing Can Be Taught." *CHE* 30 (17 April 1985): 23–24.

The University of Texas's English Department fires 50 untenured temporary faculty and reconsiders the growth of its writing programs and the use of temporary teachers.

2560. Herrscher, Walter. "The Joy of Titles: Christening Your Composition." *TETYC* 12 (December 1985): 287–292.

Discusses methods of creating interesting and functional titles.

2561. Hodgins, Frank. "Computer Rhetoric at the University of Illinois." *IIEB* 73 (Fall 1985): 21–26.

Describes Computer Rhetoric 108, related to Project EXCEL, which "gives much greater emphasis to revising and rewriting than is ordinarily possible in freshman composition courses."

2562. Horning, Alice S. "Semantic Analysis, Readability, and the Teaching of Writing." *TETYC* 10 (Winter 1984): 95–103.

Shows how the results of readability research can be applied to help students improve their writing.

2563. Hudson, Kathleen A. "Writers Talk about Writing: An Eclectic Approach to Teaching Composition." *DAI* 45 (November 1984): 1388A.

Uses quotations from writers to provide ideas, materials, and directions for use in composition class.

2564. Hunt, Maurice. "Christensen Revamped: The Rhetorical Sentence as a Model of the Writing Process." *EngR* 36 (1985): 20–23.

Students learn to generate complex rhetorical sentences when they understand the "addition," any grammatical unit that is not a main clause.

2565. Hunt, Russell A. "Language Development in Young Children and Composition Class: The Role of Pragmatics." Paper given at the CCCC Convention, New York, March 1984. ERIC ED 248 542 [21 pages]

Argues that, since pragmatics has shown language learning to be social rather than cognitive, teachers should develop activities in which language serves real purposes.

2566. Jaech, Sharon. "Going Public: A Case for Reading Aloud in the Classroom." *RR* 3 (September 1984): 58–64.

Offers suggestions for helping students see writing as a social, public act. Stresses techniques that encourage each student to read aloud.

2567. Jason, G. James. "Using Philosophical Dilemmas to Teach Composition." *TETYC* 12 (October 1985): 185–190.

Describes how philosophical "thought experimentation" that constructs imaginary "what if" situations can prompt students to write on interesting topics.

2568. Johnson, Sabina Thorne. "The Language Journal: Bridge to Expository and Argumentative Writing." Paper given at the California Association of Teachers of English Meeting, San Francisco, February 1984. ERIC ED 246 472 [16 pages]

Examines the journal as a multimodel composition that teaches students sensitivity to language.

2569. Karloff, Kenneth. "The Intermediate Impossible: A Prewriting Activity for Creative Problem Solving." *ExEx* 30 (Spring 1985): 16–17.

Illustrates how using "ideas that normally would be discarded as useless" can help students develop topics.

2570. Katz, Sandra. "Teaching the Tagmemic Discovery Procedure: A Case Study of a Writing Course." *DAI* 45 (November 1984): 1320A.

Students developed the ability to use the tagmemic matrix to generate ideas and identify gaps in understanding.

2571. Kaufer, David S. "A Plan for Teaching the Development of Original Policy Arguments." *CCC* 35 (February 1984): 57–70.

Develops a pedagogy for policy arguments, giving steps for identifying sources of disputes and for resolving them based on the level of conflict.

2572. Kearns, Michael S. "Lyric Poems in the Composition Class: A Cognitivist Approach to Course Design." *JTW* 4 (Spring 1985): 55–76.

Uses critical moments, generative propositions, and collaborative learning as touchstones for a cognitivist approach. Provides detailed sequences of assignments with evaluations.

2573. Keller, Rodney D. "The Rhetorical Cycle: Reading, Thinking, Speaking, Listening, Discussing, Writing." Paper given at the CCCC Convention, Minneapolis, March 1985. ERIC ED 257 099 [13 pages]

Describes a prewriting sequence.

2574. Kessel, Barbara, and Dolores Rosenhaum. "Do-It-Yourself Placement Tests." *ArEB* 27 (Winter 1985): 138–148.

Describes a way of writing placement tests that draws on teachers across campus.

2575. Klaus, Carl, and Nancy Jones, eds. *Courses for Change in Writing: A Selection from the NEH/Iowa Institute.* Upper Montclair, N.J.: Boynton/Cook, 1984. 296 pages

A collection of writing courses originally designed in 1979 and 1980 by participants in the University of Iowa's Institute on Writing. Each course includes an explanatory essay followed by a sequence of writing assignments and related activities. Includes a bibliography.

2576. Kleine, Michael. "What Freshmen Say—and Might Say—to Each Other about Their Own Writing." *JTW* 4 (Fall 1985): 216–233.

Develops a taxonomy of four group roles—evaluators, immediate readers, helpful listeners, and role-playing audience—and suggests three strategies for implementing them.

2577. Knodt, Ellen Andrews. "The Aims Approach: More Effective Writing for the Real World." Paper given at the CCCC Convention, New York, March 1984. ERIC ED 248 509 [12 pages]

Argues that composition instruction based on the aims of discourse rather than the modes can help students understand purpose and function in writing.

2578. Kolln, Martha. "Rhetorical Grammar for Students." Paper given at the CCCC Convention, New York, March 1984. ERIC ED 243 109 [11 pages]

Presents a rationale for teaching grammar in the composition class.

2579. Koring, Heidi. "Reader Reaction Modes and the Teaching of Literature." *FEN* 13 (Fall 1984): 15–17.

Since writing is both expressive and transactional, students can learn that response modes should be appropriate to the text studied.

2580. Koring, Heidi. "Teaching Down East Down South." *IE* 7 (Spring 1984): 13–14.

Advocates using recordings of dialects to foster students' interest in their native dialect.

2581. Lampert, Kathleen W. "Using Dialogues to Teach Argumentation." *ExEx* 30 (Spring 1985): 6–10.

Uses dialogues to help students understand the "dialectic movement of formal argument."

2582. Lederman, Marie Jean. "Literature and Composition in the Two-Year College: Love Affair or One-Night Stand?" *TETYC* 12 (February 1985): 9–13.

Discusses the desirability of integrating literary study into writing courses.

2583. Lewis, Clayton W. "Acts with Language: An Approach to Composition." *FEN* 13 (Spring 1984): 1–4.

Offers stylistic/rhetorical analysis as one approach to teaching composition. Sees the student's text as a language act that the student can analyze.

2584. Libby, Judith S. "George Orwell: Inside the English Class." *IE* 8 (Fall 1984): 7–9.

Includes examples of six writing habits deplored by Orwell. Discusses exercises to counter these habits.

2585. Linn, Bill. "Shamrocks and Semi-Colons: Notes on an Old-Fashioned Pedagogy." *ArEB* 27 (Winter 1985): 67–72.

Reports on research in writing comparing American and Irish student writers.

2586. Loar, David. "A Small Matter of Perspective." *LaEJ* 23 (Winter 1984): 17–22.

Satirically classifies freshman students according to how they turn in in-class essays.

2587. Long, Russell C. "Technology against Itself: Defining Literacy in the Classroom." *LaEJ* 24 (Winter 1985): 14–20.

Advocates a course analyzing mass media so that students realize the supremacy of print literacy.

2588. Lynn, Steven W. "Readability and Revision." *TETYC* 10 (Winter 1984): 135–140.

Imagining a readability formula is a strategy for helping students control and organize thinking and writing.

2589. Lyons, Peter A. "Back to the Text: Discussing and Writing about Literature." *JTW* 3 (Fall 1984): 237–247.

Uses a "cumulative inferential paradigm" to teach the movement from specific facts in a text to inferences based on those facts.

2590. MacAllister, Joyce B. "'Textual Conditioning,' Propriety, and Ethical Appeal in Traditional and Contemporary Rhetoric." *TETYC* 10 (Winter 1984): 113–120.

Finds that, in a sample of current textbooks, students are not offered alternatives to formulas for style. Concludes that teachers should build on a rhetorical tradition and psycholinguistic research.

2591. Maddox, Kathleen S. "Techniques to Teach Audience Awareness." *ArEB* 27 (Winter 1985): 10–18.

Outlines heuristic procedures and guidelines for writing and rewriting that emphasize audience.

2592. Mader, Diane C. "Speech: An Approach to Teaching Writing." *JTW* 4 (Fall 1985): 254–263.

Explains how a speaking/writing sequence and the videotaping and playing back of speeches can help students cultivate cognitive skills needed in writing.

2593. Magistrale, Tony. "Measuring Reality: Critical Writing and Television Analysis." *ExEx* 30 (Fall 1984): 20–21.

Uses soap operas as a stimulus for teaching critical judgments.

2594. Marik, Ray. "Discovering Computer Programming Basics in Expository Writing." *WaEJ* 7 (Fall 1984): 18–20.

Using flow charts and computer programming format in expository writing promotes analytical thinking and revision.

2595. Markhan, Marsha C. "Teaching Student Dialogue Writing in a College Composition Course: Effects upon Writing Performance and Attitudes." *DAI* (December 1984): 1607A.

Finds no statistically significant improvement in writing skills in the treatment group, although a questionnaire revealed improvement in attitudes toward writing.

2596. McCarron, William, and Thomas Keating. "Teaching What Writers Really Do." *Statement* 20 (October 1984): 4–9.

Suggests assignments and strategies to help students write as professional writers do, not as English textbooks prescribe.

2597. McCarthy, Lucille. "Situated Protocols: Studying a College Student's Writing in Classroom Contexts." Paper given at the CCCC Convention, Minneapolis, March 1985. ERIC ED 255 928 [12 pages]

Gathers writing protocols and ethnographic data from three freshman-sophomore students, finding writing concerns "situated" in course contexts.

2598. McCleary, William J. "Beyond Critical Thinking: Teaching Students to Use Their Knowledge in Academic Writing." Paper given at the Northeastern Conference on English in the Two-Year College, Atlantic City, N.J., October 1983. ERIC ED 237 999 [36 pages]

Advises teachers on how to use a case approach to writing.

2599. Meyers, G. Douglas. "Freedom through Language: Applications of the Ideas of Carl Rogers to the Teaching of Composition." Paper given at the CCCC Convention, New York, March 1984. ERIC ED 243 120 [14 pages]

Describes a student-centered approach to writing instruction based on the work of a clinical psychologist.

2600. Mohr, Marian M. *Revision: The Rhythm of Meaning.* Upper Montclair, N.J.: Boynton/Cook, 1984. 248 pages

Presents hundreds of student comments and dozens of examples of professional and student work to answer the question: "What are the characteristics of a writing classroom where change is expected and where writers experiment with revision?"

2601. Moneyhun, Clyde, and Marvin Drogenis. "Aristotle." *ArEB* 26 (Winter 1984): 50–56.

Describes a freshman composition class that uses Aristotle's *Rhetoric.*

2602. Moore, Wayne, Jr. "Word Processing in First-Year Comp." *CC* 3 (November 1985): 55–60.

Describes a freshman composition class using microcomputers and word processing. Concludes that students were successful in their writing, though not necessarily more so than other students.

2603. Moran, Michael G. "Lockean Epistemology and the Freshman Research Paper." Paper given at the CCCC Convention, New York, March 1984. ERIC ED 243 125 [10 pages]

Discusses the application of probabilistic reasoning to research paper writing.

2604. Morse, Donald E. "Letters to the Editor." *ArEB* 27 (Fall 1984): 99–100.

Describes an assignment for writing letters to the editor. [Reprinted from *Michigan English Teacher* (January–February 1984).]

2605. Murphy, Christine, and Bonnie Dickinson. "If You Meet the Buddha on the Road with a Rosetta Stone: A Dialogue on Strategies of Inquiry and the New Rhetoric." *FEN* 14 (Spring 1985): 13–18.

Explains both classical and romantic notions about inquiry.

2606. Murray, Donald M. "The Writer's I." Paper given at the CCCC Convention, Minneapolis, March 1985. ERIC ED 258 265 [10 pages]

Argues for the importance of first-person writing in the college composition course.

2607. Nelson, David C. "Fringe Benefits." *ArEB* 27 (Fall 1984): 49–50.

Offers a sample of student bloopers from freshman composition courses.

2608. Nickell, Samila S. "The Best of Both Worlds: Writing Conferences on the Computer." Paper given at the CCCC Convention, Minneapolis, March 1985. ERIC ED 258 195 [13 pages]

Discusses the advantages of combining conferences and computers.

2609. Nickell, Samila S. "Composition Students Experience Word Processing." *CC* 2 (November 1984): 11–14.

Describes experiences securing computers for students. Reports that students became comfortable revising and had a good attitude toward writing.

2610. Nystrand, Martin. *Learning to Write by Talking about Writing: A Summary of Research on Intensive Peer Review.* Madison, Wis.: University of Wisconsin, 1984. ERIC ED 255 914 [14 pages]

Describes the peer review component of the freshman program, noting its values.

2611. Olson, Gary A. "Diagnosing Problems with Invention." *JTW* 4 (Fall 1985): 194–202.

Reports on two diagnostic models developed and tested to determine students' problems with invention.

2612. Onore, Cynthia. *The Transaction between Teachers' Comments and Students' Revisions.* Urbana, Ill.: ERIC/RCS, 1984. ERIC ED 258 174 [27 pages]

Offers case studies of three college students, noting that the cyclical nature of revision may include unsuccessful changes.

2613. Oplt, Toni. "Caroline Gordon's 'A Last Day in the Field': Reading, Thinking, and Writing." *IlEB* 72 (Spring 1985): 25–30.

Illustrated with specific writing tasks related to this short story, argues that "literature does have its place in the college composition classroom."

2614. Oram, Virginia White. "The Freshman Decomposition (or D Composition)." *ET* 15 (Summer 1984): 42–43.

Examines why college freshmen seem to dislike freshman composition. Concludes that teacher reinforcement in elementary school apparently turns to teacher apathy in high school.

2615. Oram, Virginia White. "Modes Revisited." *ArEB* 27 (Winter 1985): 51–53.

Argues for the use of modes in composition classes.

2616. Page, Mirian Dempsey. "A Place for the Major Field in Freshman Composition: The First-Semester Course." *PCTEB* 49 (April 1984): 23–28.

Argues that a student's major is a "viable heuristic" for discovery.

2617. Parris, Peggy. "Helping Snoopy through the Dark and Stormy Night: Heuristics for Creative Writing." *IaEB* 33 (1984): 26–30.

Discusses the usefulness of Burke's pentad, Young, Becker, and Pike's tagmemic matrix, and Macrorie's freewriting as heuristics in creative writing.

2618. Parris, Peggy. "Prewriting Invention without Special Software." *CC* 2 (February 1985): 1–2.

Presents ways to use computers for inventing nonfiction, fiction, and poetry without special software programs.

2619. Paxman, David B. "Reinventing the Composition/Literature Course." *RR* 2 (January 1984): 124–132.

Suggests ways to use literature to enhance all phases of writing. Gives model assignments and audience exercises.

2620. Penfield, Elizabeth F. "Process, Product, and the Administration of the English Department." Paper given at the CCCC Convention, New York, March 1984. ERIC ED 244 259 [18 pages]

Discusses contextual factors impeding change in college writing instruction.

2621. Penfield, Elizabeth F., and Mary K. Ruetten. "A Survey of Freshman English in Louisiana." *LaEJ* 23 (Fall 1984): 1–41.

Reports on placement, support services, advanced standing, proficiency examinations, courses, and textbooks. Draws conclusions about the role of freshman programs.

2622. Peroni, Patricia. "A Book Review Assignment to Introduce Freshmen to the College Library." *ExEx* 30 (Fall 1984): 26–28.

Describes a method of introducing minority freshmen to the library and to book reviews. Uses *Autobiography of Malcolm X* and reviews of texts.

2623. Phillips, Lea. "A Model for the Teaching of Writing in the English Classroom." *EQ* 17 (Summer 1984): 38–41.

Describes a course in which students choose their own best work for grading.

2624. Pilarcik, Marlene A. "Language and Choice: Using a Chinese Perspective." *MLJ* 69 (Summer 1985): 143–146.

Describes an exercise in translating Chinese poetry that reveals relationships between language and thought and that demonstrates to students how they control language.

2625. Polanski, Virginia G. "Freshmen Comp Students Increase Heuristic Use of Early Drafts." *EQ* 18 (Summer 1985): 97–106.

As freshmen composition students write and develop their writing skills, more students use their early drafts more frequently.

2626. Polin, Linda G., and Edward M. White. "Patterns of Composition Instruction." *WPA* 8 (Spring 1985): 25–33.

Identifies preferences and differences in instructional practices between contract and tenure track faculty in the California State University system.

2627. Polin, Linda G., and Edward M. White. "Speaking Frankly: Writing Program Administrators Look at Instructional Goals and Faculty Retraining." *WPA* 9 (Fall-Winter 1985): 19–30.

Identifies writing program goals and faculty retraining practices in the California State University system.

2628. Pradl, Gordon M. "Discovering Our Own Composing Processes." *CEJ* 15 (Spring 1984): 104–105.

Argues that teachers who discover and know themselves as writers can better help students.

2629. Pytlik, Betty P. "Writing Assignments that Prepare Students for Writing on the Job." *ExEx* 30 (Spring 1985): 22–24.

Presents 10 writing assignments focusing on reports, letter writing for future positions, using library resources, and summary writing.

2630. Quinn, Karen B., and Ann Matsuhashi. "Stalking Ideas: The Generation and Elaboration of Arguments." Paper given at the AERA Convention, Chicago, April 1985. ERIC ED 257 043 [27 pages]

Reports on case studies of college students using reading to generate argumentative essays.

2631. Reavley, Katharine R. "Writing as a Way of Knowing: Expressive Discourse as a Means of Inquiry and Response in College Composition." *DAI* 45 (August 1984): 442A.

Argues for the epistemological function of expressive discourse and, thus, for beginning writing instruction with the self as both subject and audience.

2632. Reed, W. Michael. "The Effects of Writing Ability and Mode of Discourse on Cognitive Capacity Engagement." *DAI* 45 (January 1985): 1979A.

College freshmen of varying writing abilities received descriptive, narrative, or persuasive writing treatments. Concludes that writing ability affected cognitive engagement across mode and that, as words per clause increased, so did engagement.

2633. Reiter, David P. "Making Workshops Work." *EQ* 18 (Summer 1985): 38–43.

Advocates a balance between a student-oriented workshop and an instructor-oriented lecture/ discussion.

2634. Rex-Kerish, Lesley. "Focusing Twice Removed." *FEN* 14 (Spring 1985): 2–4, 8.

Explains an essay assignment designed to help students write and read personal analyses.

2635. Reynolds, Mark. "Expanding the Freewriting Heuristic." *TETYC* 11 (October 1984): 23–28.

Discusses integrating focused, sequenced freewriting assignments into traditional instruction.

2636. Riley, Katherine. "The Workshop Method: Potential Problems, Tested Solutions." *EngR* 35 (Fourth Quarter 1984): 14–16.

Argues that, despite gaps between theory and practice, workshops are one good way to teach proofreading and revision.

2637. Roemer, Kenneth M. "Inventive Modeling: Rainy Mountain's Way to Composition." *CE* 46 (December 1984): 767–782.

Although composition models are unfashionable, "if [writing] teachers select models carefully and present them...as paradigms of dynamic processes...then modeling can...contribute significantly."

2638. Roen, Duane H. "Empirical Consideration of Episodic Perspective Taking." Paper given at the CCCC Convention, Minneapolis, March 1985. ERIC ED 257 062 [20 pages]

Assigns 65 college freshmen to three audience perspectives, finding that a sense of audience affects revision.

2639. Ronald, Katharine J., and Hephzibah Roskelly. "Listening as an Act of Composing." Paper given at the CCCC Convention, Minneapolis, March 1985. ERIC ED 257 094 [12 pages]

Describes three listening exercises designed to make students sensitive to "voice" in writing.

2640. Rosen, Joan G. "A Model for Teaching Is a Model for Writing." *TETYC* 12 (December 1985): 274–279.

A composition teacher applies the stages of Kuhn's *Structure of Scientific Revolution* to her assumptions about her students and thereby generates new strategies.

2641. Rosenberg, Ruth. "The Uses of Incompatibility: Or, Why I Gave Up Gambling." *LaEJ* 23 (Winter 1984): 30–32.

Advocates forming peer groups according to dissimilar interests, thereby generating more and better detail for papers.

2642. Rosenberg, Ruth. "'Wadaya Mean?' Toward an Exploration of Purpose and Audience." *LaEJ* 23 (Fall 1984): 42–48.

Describes a writing assignment that leads peer groups to an inductive understanding of purpose and audience.

2643. Ross, William T. "Self and Audience in Composition." *FEN* 13 (Spring 1984): 14–16.

Argues that students must search for "acceptable roles" for themselves as writers and learn to maintain a chosen role throughout a composition.

2644. Roth, Lorie. "Introducing the Word Processor in Composition Classes." *CC* 2 (November 1984): 10–11.

Describes introducing students to word processing and making them comfortable using an "ally in the writing process."

2645. Roth, Richard. "Barriers to Discourse: Tautologies in Student Essays." Paper presented at the CCCC Convention, Minneapolis, March 1985. ERIC ED 259 374 [10 pages]

Identifies three kinds of tautologies found in student essays and suggests ways of helping students recognize and revise them.

2646. Rubinstein, S. Leonard, and Robert G. Weaver. "Talk to Me." *JTW* 4 (Spring 1985): 123–126.

A dialogue between a hypothetical student and teacher. Discusses topic selection, reasons for writing, and the relationship between writer and reader.

2647. Ruddell, Robert, and Owen Boyle. *A Study of the Effects of Cognitive Mapping on Reading Comprehension and Written Protocols.* Technical Report, no. 7. Riverside, Calif.: Learning from Text Project, 1984. ERIC ED 252 811 [32 pages]

Studies how cognitive mapping, a prewriting technique, assists college students in gathering information from prose and organizing it in subsequent writing.

2648. Salerno, Douglas. "Implications of Cognitive Complexity Research on the Teaching of Perspective Taking in Writing Courses." Paper given at the CCCC Convention, Minneapolis, March 1985. ERIC ED 255 927 [29 pages]

Discusses assignments that ask students to become involved in the construction of audiences.

2649. Schell, John F. "A Heuristic for the Teaching of Persuasion." Paper given at the MLA Convention, Los Angeles, December 1982. ERIC ED 234 397 [12 pages]

Applies Aristotle to analyze writing style, organization, and content.

2650. Schiff, Jeff. "Toward a Human Geography: Thoughts about In-Class Writing Environments." *JTW* 4 (Fall 1985): 162–169.

Emphasizes the importance of place on students' ability to write in class and the need for "at-homeness" for engendering effective writing.

2651. Schiff, Jeff. "Who's Reading Whom?: An Audience Analysis Primer." *ArEB* 27 (Winter 1985): 19–24.

Explains "audience-dominated writing pedagogy," including the use of an "audience journal."

2652. Sedgwick, Ellery. "Using Peer Rebuttals to Develop Skill in Argumentative Writing." *ExEx* 30 (Fall 1984): 6–7.

Describes a method for developing a sense of "the skeptical audience in argumentative writing and tactics for deflecting its counter arguments."

2653. Shapiro, Nancy S. *Rhetorical Maturity and Perry's Model of Intellectual Development.* Urbana, Ill.: ERIC/RCS, 1985. ERIC ED 258 180 [29 pages]

Studies college students' writing, finding a significant correlation between quality and a measure of intellectual maturity.

2654. Sharplin, Wanda S. "The Cooperative Theme." *LaEJ* 23 (Winter 1984): 28–30.

Describes how to use groups of two to develop an out-of-class paper.

2655. Shelden, Michael. "Orwell, Writing, and Moral Obligation." *IE* 8 (Fall 1984): 3–6.

Dishonesty in writing is a "failure to communicate in a natural and authentic voice." Reviews "Politics and the English Language."

2656. Shook, Ronald. "Let's Not Write about Ourselves." *TETYC* 12 (October 1985): 203–206.

Argues that mature students should not be asked for specifically personal writing but are ready to move into more objective types.

2657. Simpson, Jeanne H. "Invention Again; or, How the Skeptic Got into Hot Water." *JTW* 4 (Fall 1985): 184–192.

Calls for a metatheory "for identifying the kind of heuristic needed and the quality of the one chosen." Encourages "reusable and reliable methods" as the best heuristics.

2658. Singer, Martha M. L. "An Integrative Model of Competent Writing." *DAI* 45 (February 1985): 2427A.

Analyzes college students' essays according to a model based on ideational units of meaning. Describes the organization of a text in terms of structure, density, and meaning, with meaning as the strongest predictor of writing quality.

2659. Slattery, Pat. "Helping Students Develop a Sense of Audience." *Leaflet* 84 (Winter 1985): 45–49.

Describes an approach for encouraging students to write for a range of audiences, from "self" to "unknown."

2660. Small, Sharon. "Thematic Sequences: Another Approach." *IaEB* 33 (1984): 20–21.

Suggests that writing assignments be arranged thematically so that students will have more time to explore a topic.

2661. Smith, Charles R., Kathleen E. Kiefer, and Patricia S. Gingrich. "Computers Come of Age in Writing Instruction." *CHum* 18 (July–December 1984): 215–224.

Describes and evaluates the use of textual analysis software, principally the Writer's Workbench, in composition instruction at Colorado State University.

2662. Smith, Eugene. *Conducting a Followup Study of Students in Writing Courses.* Urbana, Ill.: ERIC/RCS, 1984. ERIC ED 247 596 [17 pages]

Studies 11 upper-division college students to determine the long-term effect of composition courses. Finds that students had more structured writing habits, more self-discipline, and more curiosity.

2663. Smith, Louise Z. "Composing Composition Courses." *CE* 46 (September 1984): 460–469.

Surveys invention techniques.

2664. Snyder, Carol. "Analyzing Classifications: Foucault for Advanced Writers." *CCC* 35 (May 1984): 209–216.

Devises a method of teaching classification using Foucault's principles of and questions about discourse.

2665. Sommers, Jeffrey. "Listening to Our Students: The Student-Teacher Memo." *TETYC* 11 (December 1984): 29–34.

Describes a project in which students submit memos on their own writing. Emphasizes the importance of listening carefully to student comments.

2666. Sosnowski, David, and Russell E. Stratton. "The Camera's Eye and Two Freshman Writers." *ArEB* 26 (Spring–Summer 1984): 50–56.

Explores the relationship between photography and writing, using two photographers/writers as evidence.

2667. Speck, Bruce W. "Going from Speaking to Writing: A Guided Exercise for Composition Students." *NebEC* 29 (Spring 1984): 8–16.

Presents six assignments to identify differences between speaking and writing and to evaluate discrepancies between what students hear and their transcriptions of what they hear.

2668. Stephens, Gary. "Computer Debating." *CC* 1 (August 1984): 7–8.

Describes having students engage in writing debates by using word processors and by responding to the writing of others in class.

2669. Sweedler-Brown, Carol. "Generating Structural Revision from the Freewriting of Basic Writers." *RR* 2 (January 1984): 92–100.

Argues against premature outlining. Suggests instead that writing generate thesis and outline.

2670. Tashlik, Phyllis. "Exploring Literary Discourse." *EngR* 36 (1985): 7–9.

Student literary journals join reading and writing and allow students to understand and interpret literature.

2671. Taylor, Michael. "DRAW: A Heuristic for Expressive Writing." *JTW* 4 (Fall 1985): 210–214.

Presents a heuristic—delineate, ruminate, analogize, and write—to generate creative phrasing and vivid mental images.

2672. Thackeray, William. *Writing with the Right Brain: The Use of Semantic Organizers.* Urbana, Ill.: ERIC/RCS, 1985. ERIC ED 252 885 [52 pages]

Studies first-year college students using semantic (key word) organizers for prewriting. Finds strong general progress and increased attitude and motivation.

2673. Tookey, Mary. "According to Tom, Dick, and Mary." *IlEB* 71 (Spring 1984): 46–48.

Reviews college freshmen composition students' attitudes about the quality of their high school education as revealed in "causal analysis" themes.

2674. Torsney, Cheryl. "Teaching Students to Write Sensibly: 'Once More to the Lake,' *On Golden Pond,* and Magazine Advertisements." *ExEx* 30 (Fall 1984): 31–33.

Discusses sensory language, avoiding passive voice, and peer evaluation of papers on advertisements, contrasting visual images, and written description.

2675. Tracy, Gilman. "Writing Plays in the Composition Classroom." *RR* 3 (September 1984): 65–68.

Suggests that writing and performing dramas in class can raise students' awareness of audience and help them learn that they have something to say.

2676. Walter, Otis M. "Plato's Idea of Rhetoric for Contemporary Students: Theory and Composition Assignments." *CCC* 35 (February 1984): 20–30.

Uses Plato's theory of ideas to develop assignments based upon values and definitions.

2677. Ward, Jay A. "Speaking, Writing, and the Making of Meaning." Paper given at the CCCC Convention, Minneapolis, March 1985. ERIC ED 255 931 [8 pages]

Discusses speaking/writing relationships, noting the need to take students from the context-dependence of speech to the context-independence of writing.

2678. Washington, Gene. "A Classical Q. Procedure." *EngR* 36 (1985): 2–4.

Discusses teaching students to use the questions of classical rhetoric to generate information on a topic.

2679. Washington, Gene. "Information and Visual Properties: A Matrix Representation." *ArEB* 27 (Fall 1984): 35–39.

Outlines questions about visual objects to help writers define them.

2680. Washington, Gene. "Yes-No Questions in Teaching Writing." *JTW* 4 (Fall 1985): 204–209.

"Answering a yes-no question is a major way of representing knowledge, in correlating a subject with a Concern, or Concerns."

2681. Weaver, Barbara. "The Role of Literature in Teaching Freshman Composition." *DAI* 45 (November 1984): 1322A.

Argues that including literature in freshman composition courses is "both desirable and possible."

2682. Webb, Agnes J. "Teaching Writing in a Video Studio." *MM* 20 (September 1984): 12–14.

Presents a nine-step process for developing a term paper through the production of a videotaped documentary.

2683. Weiner, Linda. "The Composition Class: Outward Bound." *FEN* 13 (Winter 1984): 1–4.

Discusses writing assignments related to the goals of wilderness experiences: discovering the self, extending of perspectives, appreciating choices, making personal commitments, and working as a team.

2684. Wess, Robert C. "Creativity and Composing: The Composition Teacher as Student." *TETYC* 12 (October 1985): 191–196.

Argues, using his teaching and writing experiences, for stressing Maslow's primary and secondary patterns of creativity and insight.

2685. Wess, Robert C. "Using Literature to Teach the Nonliterary Research Essay." Paper given at the CCCC Convention, Minneapolis, March 1985. ERIC ED 257 093 [19 pages]

Sketches an approach using a novel and readings about it.

2686. Wilson, Allison. "Writing with a Purpose: Inhibiting Effects of Prescriptive Alternatives." *FEN* 14 (Fall 1985): 17–19.

Disagrees with Hashimoto [*FEN* 13 (Winter 1984)]. Presents "paralyzing" mechanistic rules but argues that current generalizations also must be used in the classroom.

2687. Wilson, Robert L. "Building Trust...and Vocabulary." *ExEx* 30 (Fall 1984): 44–45.

Shows how to help students use context to determine the meaning of words.

2688. Wilson, Robert L. "Writing: A Matter of Processing." *IE* 8 (Winter 1985): 11–12.

Argues that teachers must teach the entire process of writing.

2689. Wilson, Steven. "High School, College, and the Job of the Freshman Writing Teacher." *ET* 15 (Summer 1984): 28–29.

An adaptation of a first-day lecture to a freshman writing class. Discusses the differences between high school and college and looks at the students' and teacher's roles.

2690. Woods, William F. "The Cultural Tradition of Nineteenth-Century 'Traditional' Grammar Teaching." Paper given at the CCCC Convention, Minneapolis, March 1985. ERIC ED 258 267 [21 pages]

Examines the myth of "grammar as a cultural heritage" and explores alternatives at the college level.

2691. Worthington, Pepper. "A Dilemma in Teaching Composition: How the Written Word Can/ Cannot Manifest the Unwritten Word." *ArEB* 28 (Fall 1985): 40–44.

Questions whether written words manifest inner concerns or hide them, offering guidelines for classroom discussion.

2692. Yerkes, Barbara H. "The Nominal Style: Why Writers Use It, Why They Should Revise It, and How We Can Teach Them to Do So." *DAI* 46 (August 1985): 411A.

Argues that the nominal style may be a natural way to express abstract thought and suggests ways to help students revise for a more flexible style.

2693. Zarry, Len. "A Case for Early Reading." *EQ* 17 (Summer 1984): 45–53.

Makes suggestions for stimulating growth in student writing based on findings about prewriting.

See also 23, 24, 61, 62, 67, 78, 116, 153, 159, 191, 307, 317, 342, 343, 401, 471, 496, 500, 524, 627, 1163, 1214, 1309, 1357, 1364, 1651, 1660, 1717, 1735, 1769, 1924, 2178, 2205, 2209, 2229, 2231, 2269, 2277, 2294, 2295, 2309, 2311, 2318, 2322,

2328, 2355, 2363, 2391, 2402, 2410, 2412, 2419, 2423, 2463, 2467, 2468, 2473, 2698, 2711, 2717, 2722, 2744, 2824, 2860, 2903, 3088, 3147, 3537, 3573, 3816

ADVANCED COMPOSITION

2694. Adams, Katherine H. "Bringing Rhetorical Theory into the Advanced Composition Class." *RR* 3 (January 1985): 184–189.

To engage writers and "sharpen their writing skills," readings on the writing process, heuristics, and style are suggested for classroom discussion.

2695. Adams, Katherine H., and John L. Adams. "Sentence Combining for Advanced Writers." *JTW* 3 (Spring 1984): 99–107.

Using sentence combining in out-of-class assignments to facilitate revision led to improvement in writing.

2696. Bloom, Lynn Z. "Diving into the Mainstream: Configurations of Advanced Composition." Paper presented at the CCCC Convention, New York, March 1984. ERIC ED 243 114 [13 pages]

Describes a variety of possible approaches to teaching advanced composition.

2697. Burns, Rex. "Description: How Much Is Enough?" *Writer* 97 (March 1984): 13–15.

Discusses ways in which description unifies fiction: to support a theme, to further action, to pace action, to modulate mood, and to reveal character.

2698. Caras, Roger. "The Small Matter of the Truth." *Writer* 97 (May 1984): 7–9, 44.

Argues that "the most difficult thing for the writer to achieve is accuracy." Discusses the problems associated with using facts, statistics, and opinions.

2699. Coe, Richard M. "A Heuristic for Analyzing a Particular Type of Writing Prior to Learning How to Produce It." Paper presented at the CCCC Convention, New York, March 1984. ERIC ED 257 105 [20 pages]

Describes an advanced composition assignment that asks students to develop a heuristic for analyzing a type of writing before producing it.

2700. Cohen, Alan S. "The Viking Portable." *ExEx* 30 (Fall 1984): 24–25.

Provides an assignment for an end-of-the-term paper involving reviewing, editing, and evaluating students' "selected works."

2701. Earley, George W. "Writing the Op-Ed Article." *Writer* 98 (March 1985): 14–17.

Describes a format for op-ed pieces and the process of submission. Includes an annotated listing of 26 op-ed markets.

2702. Field, Thomas T., Lawrence H. Freeman, and Angela B. Moorjani. "Introducing *The World of Language:* A Linguistic Basis for Language Study." *MLJ* 68 (Autumn 1984): 222–229.

Describes the development of a team-taught interdisciplinary course on language and communication (verbal and nonverbal) with an international perspective.

2703. Goforth, Caroline, and Don Latham. "Introductions and Conclusions in Popular Magazines." *ArEB* 27 (Winter 1985): 29–38.

Reports on a study of introductions, conclusions, and their relationship to the whole essay in professional writing.

2704. Hairston, Maxine. "Working with Advanced Writers." *CCC* 35 (May 1984): 196–208.

Notes that advanced writers initially rely upon wordy, impersonal, formulaic prose. Advocates taking risks as a way to promote growth in writing.

2705. Hansen, J. T. "Using Journals in Upper-Division Literature Courses." *WaEJ* 6 (April 1984): 25–26.

Journals help students read actively and carry out a dialogue with instructors of advanced literature classes.

2706. Keen, Nadene A. "The Research Proposal." *IE* 9 (Winter 1985): 10–12.

Describes research as a process and gives examples of forms for Research Project Guidelines, Research Proposal Contents, and a Research Proposal Checklist.

2707. Keene, Nadene. "Composition, Revision, and Word Processing." *IlEB* 73 (Fall 1985): 36–41.

Describes the expectations, presentation, and results of using word processing as a tool to revise and edit in an advanced composition course at Illinois State University.

2708. Kilpatrick, James J. "The Watched Pot of Language." *Writer* 97 (December 1984): 10–12.

A general discussion of the ever-changing pool of new words available to writers.

2709. L'Engle, Madeleine. "Don't Think: Write!" *Writer* 98 (July 1985): 9–11.

Discusses audience and concludes: "Give yourself the pleasure of forgetting earnestly to remember your audience at all times."

2710. Murray, Donald M. "Tricks of the Nonfiction Trade." *Writer* 98 (July 1985): 15–17, 45.

Offers advice about preparing to write, developing leads and endings, finding the right voice, and editing.

2711. Murray, Donald M. "Writing and Teaching for Surprise." *CE* 46 (January 1984): 1–7.

The writing process continually produces unexpected topics and development.

2712. Nilsen, Don L. F. "Epiphany: The Language of Sudden Insight." *ExEx* 30 (Fall 1984): 13–16.

Discusses the application of the religious term "epiphany" to rhetorical situations. Focuses on the "epiphanal metaphor."

2713. Ogilvie, Elisabeth. "The Practice and the Passion." *Writer* 98 (April 1985): 17–19.

Discusses the writer's power of observation, imagination, and love of words and their relationship to creating background in narrative.

2714. Papomchak, Robert Allen. "Beyond the Classroom with Computers." *CC* 2 (November 1984): 8–10.

Describes assigning, with positive results, a computer-generated essay to students in an advanced writing class.

2715. Perrin, Robert. "Preparing Professional Teacher-Writers." Paper presented at the NCTE Spring Conference, Columbus, April 1984. ERIC ED 243 133 [11 pages]

Describes an advanced college writing course for public school teachers designed to encourage professional writing.

2716. Peters, Elizabeth. "'Where Do You Get Your Ideas?'" *Writer* 98 (September 1985): 9–12.

Discusses the concept of ideas, how to recognize a usable idea, and how to develop one once identified.

2717. Porterfield, Kay Marie. "Phone Interviewing." *Writer* 97 (April 1984): 18–20.

Describes ways to prepare for telephone interviews and suggests strategies for conducting interviews that generate usable quotations.

2718. Schneider, Larissa A. "The Role of Public Relations in Four Organizational Types." *JQ* 62 (Autumn 1985): 567–576.

Finds that communication within and between organizations consisted of writing speeches, writing press releases, counseling management, holding press conferences, and conducting informal research before beginning new projects.

2719. Schuster, Charles I. "The Un-Assignment: Writing Groups for Advanced Expository Writers." Paper presented at the Wyoming Conference on Freshman and Sophomore English, Laramie, Wyo., June 1983. ERIC ED 234 409 [24 pages]

Offers a course plan.

2720. Schuster, Charles I. "The Un-Assignment: Writing Groups for Advanced Expository Writers." *FEN* 13 (Winter 1984): 4, 10–14.

Explains the use of writing groups in advanced composition classes. Includes policy statement, guidelines, and advice for writers and listeners.

2721. Teich, Nathaniel. "Rhetoric and Problem-Solving Strategies in Advanced Composition: A Pluralistic Approach." Paper presented at the CCCC Convention, New York, March 1984. ERIC ED 247 555 [12 pages]

Describes an advanced composition course that combines arguing-for-consensus proposals with functional, not formalistic, rhetoric.

2722. Winn, Joni. "The Perfect Interview." *Writer* 97 (August 1984): 15–17, 45.

Explains how to conduct an interview. Discusses appointments, preparing questions, making tapes and notes, and getting useful quotations.

2723. Witt, Brad. "Why I Don't Write." *ArEB* 28 (Fall 1985): 1–3.

An undergraduate writer takes writing teachers to task for their focus on conformity.

See also 342, 1160, 1349, 1609, 1720, 1770, 2212, 2257, 2494, 2514, 2525, 2552, 2618, 2663, 2764

BUSINESS COMMUNICATION

2724. Alexander, Clara. "Teaching Technical and Business Writing: Strategies and Evaluation." *TETYC* 12 (May 1985): 113–117.

Describes a course called "Writing for the World of Work," which includes oral communication, business writing, and preparing visuals, reports, and proposals.

2725. Andera, Frank. "Important Implications of Letter Mail Automation and Word Processing on Today's Written Communication." *ABCAB* 48 (September 1985): 45–49.

Explains techniques for reducing the cost of business correspondence by attending to letter and envelope fraud.

2726. Anderson, W. Steve. "The Rhetoric of the Resume." Paper presented at the College English Association Meeting, Clearwater Beach, Fla., April 1984. ERIC ED 249 537 [10 pages]

Advocates using Kinneavy's discourse model to teach students the concept and context of resumes.

2727. Arnold, Vanessa Dean. "The Importance of *Pathos* in Persuasive Appeals." *ABCAB* 48 (December 1985): 26–27.

Explains how instructors can illustrate the importance of *pathos* when discussing letter writing.

2728. Barkman, Patricia. "The Storyboard Method: A Neglected Aspect of Organizational Communication." *ABCAB* 48 (September 1985): 21–23.

Defines the storyboard method of organizing information and explains how it can be used in organizational communication.

2729. Bly, Robert W. "Wanted: 'Industrious' Writers." *WD* (February 1984): 38–41.

A successful freelance writer tells how to write industrial promotions and publicity. Includes tips and a job directory/pay scale.

2730. Bogert, Judith. "In Defense of the Fog Index." *ABCAB* 48 (June 1985): 9–12.

Explains that readability indexes, like the Gunning Fog index, can be beneficial in writing classes if used properly.

2731. Butler, Marilyn. "A Reassessment of the Case Approach: Reinforcing Artifice in Business Writing Courses." *ABCAB* 48 (September 1985): 4–7.

Argues that case assignments in business writing courses are ineffective because they are inherently artificial and do not teach students to write in complex situations.

2732. Casady, Mona J. "Practice What You Preach about Goodwill Messages." *ABCAB* 48 (December 1985): 6–9.

Explains that goodwill messages are effective first assignments in business communications

courses and that instructors should practice such writing assignments with their classes.

2733. Catron, Douglas M. "A Case for Cases." *ABCAB* 47 (May 1984): 21–25.

Discusses the value of the case study in business communication courses and applies the principles of case study design to one sample assignment.

2734. Clinkscale, Bella G. "Model for Multi-Faceted Assignment Planning in Oral Communication." *ABCAB* 47 (June 1984): 27–31.

Presents written and oral assignments to help business communication students bridge the gap between the classroom and the corporate world.

2735. David, Carol, and Donna Stine. "Measuring Skill Gains and Attitudes of Adult Writers in Short Courses." *ABCAB* 47 (May 1984): 14020.

Reports on a study to determine if a business writing short course offered to employees in industry, business, and government improves participants' writing skills.

2736. Dieterich, Daniel J. "Real Readers for Real Writers." Paper presented at the CCCC Convention, Minneapolis, March 1985. ERIC ED 258 234 [5 pages]

Offers a business writing assignment.

2737. Ede, Lisa S., and Andrea A. Lunsford. "Research on Co- and Group Authorship in the Professions: A Preliminary Report." Paper presented at the CCCC Convention, Minneapolis, March 1985. ERIC ED 257 086 [12 pages]

Reports on a survey and case studies, noting the frequency of collaborative writing in the professions.

2738. Ewald, Helen R. "The Me in You-Attitude: Business Communication in Transaction." *ABCAB* 48 (May 1985): 7–11.

Argues that business communication should be taught as a transaction, with emphasis on both the reader and author and his or her purpose.

2739. Feldman, Paula R. "Using Microcomputers for College Writing: What Students Say." Paper presented at the Spring Conference of the Delaware Valley Writing Council, Villanova, Pa., February 1984. ERIC ED 244 298 [11 pages]

Reports on course evaluations of a business writing class that used word processing.

2740. Flatley, Marie. "Improve Business Writing Skills with Reactive Writing." *ABCAB* 47 (May 1984): 25–26.

Describes a "journal write," a written reaction to an article the student has read.

2741. Frazer, Cynthia Lynch. "Problem-Solving Topics for 'Real World' Research." *IE* 9 (Winter 1985): 15–17.

Presents 6 situations as the bases for problem-solving papers and 13 guidelines for writing the paper. Emphasizes primary sources.

2742. Friedman, Paul G. "Hassle Handling: Front-Line Diplomacy in the Workplace." *ABCAB* 47 (May 1984): 30–34.

Discusses principles of handling oral communication problems for those who are "flak-catchers" or "enforcers" of organizational rules.

2743. Garver, Eugene. "Demystifying Classical Rhetoric." *ABCAB* 47 (September 1984): 24–26.

Discusses the uses of classical rhetoric in teaching invention in the business writing classroom.

2744. Gieselman, Robert D. "Megatrends: The Future of Business Writing, Technical Writing, and Composition." *ABCAB* 48 (December 1985): 2–6.

Outlines trends in university courses in business writing, technical writing, and composition and discusses future directions in research and educational programs.

2745. Goldstein, Jone R., and Elizabeth L. Malone. "Using Journals to Strengthen Collaborative Writing." *ABCAB* 48 (September 1985): 24–28.

Explains how instructors can use journals to handle collaborative writing assignments in business communication.

2746. Golen, Steven P., and David Lynch. "Preparing Visual Aids from Financial Periodicals." *ABCAB* 48 (December 1985): 24–25.

Describes a business communication assignment to create a visual aid and a written introduction that present data found in a financial periodical.

2747. Gould, John W. "Quotations that Liven a Business Communication Course." *ABCAB* 48 (December 1985): 27–33.

Explains how using relevant quotations can add interest to a business communication course.

2748. Hagge, John. "Strategies for Verbal Interaction in Business Writing." Paper presented at the CCCC Convention, New York, March 1984. ERIC ED 246 473 [18 pages]

Discusses interaction strategies in business writing, especially linguistically polite forms.

2749. Harty, Kevin J. "Campus Issues: A Source for Research in Business and Technical Writing Courses." *TETYC* 12 (October 1985): 221–224.

Shows how students can learn the skills required in business and industry by writing group projects based on campus-related issues.

2750. Herbert, Mellanie, and Mary Margaret Hosler. "Office Style Dictation Simulation – Both Sides Can Benefit." *ABCAB* 47 (May 1984): 26–28.

Describes an assignment simulating dictation that pairs business communication students with advanced shorthand students.

2751. Herndl, Carl G. "Hierarchies of Audiences and Texts." Paper presented at the CCCC Convention, New York, March 1984. ERIC ED 243 128 [9 pages]

Reports on interviews with business executives about the writing problems of young professionals.

2752. Hughes, Robert S., Jr. "Developing Business Communication Skills with the Overhead Projector: Student-Centered Techniques That Work." *ABCAB* 47 (June 1984): 21–24.

Describes student-centered classroom strategies for using overhead projectors.

2753. Jablin, Fredric M., and Kathleen Krone. "Characteristics of Rejection Letters and Their Effects on Job Applicants." *WC* 1 (October 1984): 387–406.

Finds that typical rejection letters follow the formula for a bad news letter, contain fewer than 90 words, and offer two reasons for the rejection.

2754. Johnson, Betty S., and Jeannette W. Vaughn. "Time Management and Communication: Integrating Skills for Higher Productivity." *JTWC* 15 (1985): 267–277.

Describes principles and practices of time management that should be taught to students in business communications courses.

2755. Johnson, J. Lynn, and John D. Pettit, Jr. "A Communication Skills Training Program for the Multinational Corporation." *ABCAB* 48 (September 1985): 33–38.

Describes a business and communication skills program designed for a multinational corporation. Discusses philosophy, topic, and techniques.

2756. Kelly, Kathleen. "Analyze a Communication Problem in the Workplace: A Report Assignment for the Part-Time MBA Student." *ABCAB* 48 (September 1985): 30–33.

Describes a business communication assignment in which part-time MBA students write a formal report analyzing a communication problem in the companies that employ them.

2757. Locker, Kitty O. "Arranging Victories for One's Students: A Legacy from Fran Weeks and Quintilian." *ABCAB* 47 (December 1984): 8–9.

Explains how Quintilian's quotation, "The job of the teacher is to arrange victories for his students," applies to the classroom.

2758. McGinty, Susan L., and Robert L. McGinty. "Systematic Thinking as a Prerequisite to Clarity of Expression in Business Writing." *JTWC* 14 (1984): 35–42.

A method for teaching students to think systematically and write clearly by applying a four-step problem-solving procedure.

2759. McLaren, Margaret C. "Useful Reporting: Linkspan between University and Employment." *ABCAB* 47 (September 1984): 47–49.

Describes a report writing assignment at a New Zealand university, where business and government organizations sponsor student reports.

2760. Merrill, Stephen M. "Stases, Common Topics, and Lines of Argument for the Letter of Application." Paper presented at the CCCC Convention, Minneapolis, March 1985. ERIC ED 254 866 [12 pages]

Suggests a reader-centered heuristic for application letters.

2761. Meyers, G. Douglas. "Adapting Zoellner's 'Talk-Write' to the Business Writing Classroom." *ABCAB* 48 (June 1985): 14–16.

Applies Zoellner's theory of connecting speaking and writing to business communication classes.

2762. Moran, Michael G. "Writing Business Correspondence Using the Persuasive Sequence." *ABCAB* 47 (June 1984): 24–27.

Applies the theory of eighteenth-century scientist Priestley's "persuasive sequence" to the writing of business correspondence.

2763. Myrsiades, Linda S. "Goal-Oriented Communication: A CBO Technique with High Management Payback." *ABCAB* 47 (June 1984): 10–14.

Describes the Communication by Objectives approach to corporate communication problems and explains how to use this strategy in case studies in the classroom.

2764. Palumbo, Roberta M. "Professional Writing for the Liberal Arts Student: An Untapped Resource." Paper presented at the ABCA Convention, Hammond, La., April 1984. ERIC ED 243 110 [11 pages]

Describes an advanced composition course that links business writing and the liberal arts.

2765. Pearson, Patricia, ed. *Bridging the Gap: From Ivory to Corporate Towers.* Urbana, Ill.: American Business Communication Association, 1974. ERIC ED 246 474 [220 pages]

A collection of 21 papers presented at the American Business Communication Association's Midwest Regional Conference, Ames, Iowa, April 1984.

2766. Pomerenke, Paula J. "Rewriting and Peer Evaluation: A Positive Approach for Business Writing Classes." *ABCAB* 47 (September 1984): 33–36.

Compares revision needs and strategies of composition and business writing students.

2767. Posey, Della Rose. "Skills Which Facilitate and Skills Which Inhibit Career Success for Women in Management as Perceived by Women." *DAI* 46 (December 1985): 1756A.

Classifies the effect of 25 skills, including written and oral communication, on the success of women managers, as perceived by 86 successful women managers.

2768. Posselt, Nancy. "A Case of Reality: Business Report Writing Based on Actual Events." *CET* (1984): 23–24.

Describes how a real-life business venture in a business writing class generates the types of reports needed to satisfy multiple purposes and audiences.

2769. Reep, Diana C. "The Manager's Message — Teaching the Internal Memo." *ABCAB* 47 (May 1984): 11–13.

Advocates writing internal memos in business communication courses and outlines methods for instruction.

2770. Rothwell, William J. "The Business Writing Instructor as Counselor." *ABCAB* 47 (September 1984): 49–52.

Explains how instructors function as counselors in their work with students, and discusses how counseling theories may be applied.

2771. Rothwell, William J. "A Career Planning Questionnaire." *ABCAB* 47 (June 1984): 15.

Presents a questionnaire to assist students with the job search unit of a business writing course.

2772. Schwartz, Helen J. "Data Bases in Writing: Method, Practice, and Metaphor." *ABCAB* 48 (September 1985): 11–16.

Explains how to incorporate instruction about data bases in business communication classes. Describes an assignment in which students construct their own data bases.

2773. Scott, James Calvert. "My Favorite Assignment: The Pictogram." *ABCAB* 47 (September 1984): 42–43.

Describes how to construct pictograms in a business communications course.

2774. Shelby, Annette. "A Teaching Module: Corporate Advocacy." *ABCAB* 47 (June 1984): 16–19.

Describes a classroom approach to teaching written and oral strategies of advocacy for organizations facing media attacks.

2775. Sherman, Dean. "The Binder Method: A Spatial, Conceptual Approach to Teaching Business Report Writing." *ABCAB* 48 (June 1985): 26028.

Describes a spatially oriented method of teaching organization in business reports through the use of three-ring binders.

2776. Sigband, Norman B. "The Changing Role of the CEO." *ABCAB* 48 (June 1985): 1–8.

A survey examining communication functions of Chief Executive Officers concludes that graduate and undergraduate business students need more communications courses.

2777. Sills, Caryl Klein. "Adapting Freewriting Techniques and Writing Support Groups for Business Communication." *ABCAB* 48 (June 1985): 12–14.

Discusses the application of freewriting and peer workshops to business communication classes.

2778. Sills, Caryl Klein. "Designing Forms for the Electronic Age." *ExEx* 29 (Spring 1984): 36–40.

Describes an assignment in form design for business, professional, and technical writing courses.

2779. Simcox, William A. "A Design Method for Graphic Communication." *ABCAB* 47 (May 1984): 3–7.

Outlines a method of designing computer graphics for business communication.

2780. Smeltzer, Larry R. "An Analysis of Communication Course Content for MBA Students." *ABCAB* 47 (September 1984): 28–33.

Presents the results of a study of appropriate course content for an MBA communication course.

2781. Smeltzer, Larry R., and Kittie W. Watson. "Listening: An Empirical Comparison of Discussion Length and Level of Incentive." *CSSJ* 35 (Fall 1984): 166–170.

Compares strategies used to improve listening skills in business and communication settings.

2782. Smith, Herb. "A Vehicle for Structuring Multiple Business Communications Assignments: The Annual Report." *ABCAB* 48 (December 1985): 22–24.

Describes an annual report assignment, discusses its benefits, and presents a strategy for using it in a business communications course.

2783. Soares, Eric J. "The Portfolio Approach to Business Communication." *ABCAB* 48 (September 1985): 17–21.

Describes an assignment in which business communication students construct portfolios to demonstrate writing and oral competence to potential employers.

2784. Steffey, Marda Nicholson. "A Case for Lawyers." *ABCAB* 47 (June 1984): 3–8.

Presents a case assignment designed to engage the interest of lawyers enrolled in a writing course.

2785. Stern, Barbara B. "A Philosophy of Communication for the Marketing Manager: Three 'T's' in an MBA Course." *ABCAB* 47 (May 1984): 28–30.

Argues that a formulaic approach to communications, with emphasis on time, tone, and transitory truths, be adopted to meet the needs of marketing managers.

2786. Stoddard, Ted D. "My Favorite Assignment: The 'Real Letter.'" *ABCAB* 48 (June 1985): 28–29.

Describes an assignment in which business communication students write and mail a letter about a current issue.

2787. Strickland, Robbie W. "A Case Study Examination of Reader Awareness and the Composing Process of Undergraduate Business Students." *DAI* 45 (November 1984): 1321A.

Case studies of students in a university finance course reveal that more skillful writers had greater audience awareness and less writing anxiety and were better able to plan, organize, and develop their writing.

2788. Suchan, James. "Managing the Business Communication Classroom's Organizational Environment." *ABCAB* 47 (December 1984): 13–15.

Applies principles of organizational behavior to the instructor's management of the business communication classroom.

2789. Tebeaux, Elizabeth. "Redesigning Professional Writing Courses to Meet the Communication Needs of Whites in Business and Industry." *CCC* 36 (December 1985): 419–428.

Makes eight suggestions for transforming pragmatic, discrete business and technical courses into one emphasizing the diversity of rhetorical skills needed for on-the-job communication.

2790. Thompson, Isabelle. "My Favorite Assignment." *ABCAB* 48 (September 1985): 29–30.

Describes an assignment in which students write a memo report about one position and two companies that interest them.

2791. Tibbetts, Arn M. "What Are the Most Useful Principles for Teaching Business Writing?" *ABCAB* 47 (September 1984): 18–21.

Outlines 10 principles taught in a basic course in business writing.

2792. Trace, Jacqueline. "Teaching Resume Writing the Functional Way." *ABCAB* 48 (June 1985): 34–41.

Explains why resume writing has a place in a business writing course and describes the steps for writing a functional or skill-centered resume.

2793. Varner, Iris I., and Patricia Marcum Grogg. "Using Microcomputers in Your Classes without a Lab." *ABCAB* 48 (September 1985): 9–11.

Outlines the process of introducing microcomputers into a business communication class.

2794. Waltman, John L., and Steven P. Golen. "Resolving Problems of Invention in Persuasive Letters." *ABCAB* 47 (June 1984): 19–20.

Describes persuasive letter assignments that are linked to formal reports on specific companies.

2795. Wilkinson, A. M. "Organizational Writing Vs. Business Writing." *ABCAB* 47 (September 1984): 37–39.

Describes a course in organizational writing and explains how it is broader than a business writing course.

2796. Wolf, Morris Philip. "S. I. Hayakawa's Scholarship and the Teaching of Business Communication." *ABCAB* 48 (May 1985): 5–7.

Discusses how Hayakawa's scholarship applies to business communication courses.

See also 15, 201, 345, 1068, 1383, 1647, 1821, 2800, 2808, 2814, 2817, 2841, 2844, 2847, 2849, 2853, 2856, 2861, 2872, 2874, 2881, 2976, 3406, 3631, 3655, 3763, 3769, 3790

SCIENTIFIC AND TECHNICAL COMMUNICATION

2797. Abshire, Gary M., and Dan Culberson. "'Editing is Editing is Editing'; or, by Any Other Name, the Smell Is Sweet." *JTWC* 15 (1985): 279–282.

Describes the duties and joys of editing.

2798. Amsden, Dorothy Corner, and Scott P. Sanders. "Developing Taste and Judgment: Correctness and the Technical Editor." *TWT* 12 (Fall 1985): 111–114.

Describes a brief exercise to demonstrate how technical editors make editorial decisions.

2799. Annett, Clarence H. "Improving Communication: Eleven Guidelines for the New Technical Editor." *JTWC* 15 (1985): 175–179.

Presents ways in which a technical editor can communicate effectively with the author of a manuscript.

2800. Arms, Valerie M. "The Computer: An Aid to Collaborative Writing." *TWT* 11 (Spring 1984): 181–185.

Describes how collaborative writing, "a common practice in industry," can be taught through the use of the computer.

2801. Barton, Ben F., and Marthalee S. Barton. "Toward a Rhetoric of Visuals for the Computer Era." *TWT* 12 (Fall 1985): 126–145.

Concludes that present methods and materials for teaching visual communication are deficient. Offers some pedagogical and research suggestions.

2802. Bielaski, Larry. "Process Writing as an Ice-Breaker." *TWT* 11 (Winter 1984): 120–121.

Uses process description to introduce students to some of the principles taught in a technical writing course.

2803. Bostian, Lloyd, and Tomas E. Byrne. "Comprehension of Styles of Science Writing." *JQ* 61 (Autumn 1984): 676–678.

Argues that an active style of science writing is preferred over a nominal, passive technical style.

2804. Brockmann, R. John, and Rebecca J. McCauley. "The Computer and the Writer's Craft: Implications for Teachers." *TWT* 11 (Winter 1984): 125–135.

Describes some ways to prepare students for the increasingly sophisticated uses of computers as communication tools.

2805. Brown, Ann E. "A Practicum for the Technical Writing Classroom." *TWT* 12 (Fall 1985): 102–106.

Describes how an in-house memo that played a part in the Three Mile Island nuclear reactor accident is used to demonstrate communication principles.

2806. Bump, Jerome. "Metaphor, Creativity, and Technical Writing." *CCC* 36 (December 1985): 444–453.

Urges increased attention to metaphorical thinking in technical writing since metaphors served as models and tools for scientists like Kepler, Bohr, Smeaton, Darwin, and Einstein.

2807. Carson, David L. "Technical Writing Is Writing." *CEJ* 15 (Spring 1984): 94.

Argues that technical writing is governed by the same principles of grammar, syntax, and organization evident in all good writing.

2808. Catron, Douglas M., ed. *Proceedings in Technical and Business Communication.* Ames, Iowa: Iowa State University Press, 1985.

Annotation not available.

2809. Chadwick, Kent. "The Professional Communications Network: A Research Process for Technical Writers." *TWT* 11 (Spring 1984): 210–220.

Describes an approach to teaching research and writing skills.

2810. Cheney, Patrick, and David Schleicher. "Redesigning Technical Reports: A Rhetorical Editing Method." *JTWC* 14 (1984): 317–337.

Advocates revising reports for selection and arrangement of ideas according to an author's goal and purpose before editing for correctness and style.

2811. Coney, Mary B., Judith A. Ramey, and James W. Souther. "Technical Writing in the English Department: An Outside Perspective." *BADE* 79 (Winter 1984): 40–42.

Defines technical writing and outlines conditions and five steps necessary to strengthen programs in English departments.

2812. Connor, Jennifer J. "Submissions in the Technical Writing Course: Towards Ensuring Their Originality." *EQ* 18 (Summer 1985): 53–56.

Suggests methods for ensuring the submission of original writing in a required course.

2813. Constantinides, Janet C. "Technical Writing for ESL Students." *TWT* 11 (Winter 1984): 136–144.

Describes a sequence of assignments that "allows ESL students to practice real forms and formats of technical writing as they are used in English."

2814. Costigan-Eaves, Patricia James. "Data Graphics in the Twentieth Century: A Comparative and Analytic Survey." *DAI* 45 (February 1985): 2632A.

Reviews methodologies and writing about data graphics in the twentieth century.

2815. Covington, David H. "Making Team Projects Work in Technical Communication Courses." *TWT* 11 (Winter 1984): 100–104.

Presents ways to organize and evaluate team projects.

2816. Cramer, Carmen. "Go Out and Prosper, Technocrats: Technical Writing and Rhetorical Translations." Paper presented at the CCCC Convention, Minneapolis, March 1985. ERIC ED 257 060 [11 pages]

Describes the undergraduate English major in technical writing at Southwestern Louisiana University.

2817. Dillon, Linda S. "Three Approaches to Writing for Group Acceptance." *TWT* 11 (Spring 1984): 186–189.

Describes three methods for gaining consensus in group projects.

2818. Dobrin, David N. "Is Technical Writing Particularly Objective?" *CE* 47 (May 1985): 237–251.

Argues that it is a mistake to teach students to use certain linguistic devices on the assumption that they make technical writing objective.

2819. Donnellan, LaRae M. "Technical Writing Style: Preferences of Scientists, Editors, and Students." Paper presented at the CCCC Convention, Minneapolis, March 1985. ERIC ED 258 262 [11 pages]

Reports survey results; for a fuller report, see Sandra S. Newton, *Computer Resources for Writing* ERIC ED 258 261.

2820. Dowdey, Diane. "Bridging the Gap: Science for a Popular Audience." Paper presented at the CCCC Convention, Minneapolis, March 1985. ERIC ED 258 266 [20 pages]

Examines the popular writing of six scientists.

2821. Dragga, Sam. "Technical Writing and Library Research: Pairing Objectives." *TWT* 12 (Fall 1985): 107–110.

Describes a series of assignments that require technical writing students to analyze and evaluate library resources in their fields.

2822. Durfee, Patricia B. "Writing in a High Tech World." *ICUT* 32 (Fall 1984): 180–184.

Results of a questionnaire sent to eight companies show technical writing students the importance of writing in the business world.

2823. Farkas, David K. "The Concept of Consistency in Writing and Editing." *JTWC* 15 (1985): 353–364.

Defines and analyzes consistency as a communication concept and sets forth "guidelines for establishing the most desirable patterns of consistency."

2824. Foster, Gretchen. "Technical Writing and Science Writing: Is There a Difference and What Does It Matter?" Paper presented at the CCCC Convention, New York, March 1984. ERIC ED 244 288 [16 pages]

Describes a two-semester technical writing course for freshman science majors.

2825. Goldstein, Jone R., and Elizabeth L. Malone. "Journals on Interpersonal and Group Communication: Facilitating Technical Project Groups." *JTWC* 14 (1984): 113–131.

Journals kept by technical writing students during group projects help develop oral and written communication skills as well as interpersonal skills.

2826. Halloran, S. Michael. "What Every Department Chair Should Know about Scholarship in Technical Communication." *BADE* 79 (Winter 1984): 43–47.

Mentions two books that provide background and presents four points of contrast between technical writing courses and traditional English studies.

2827. Harrington, Henry R., and Richard E. Walton. "The Warnier-Orr Diagram for Designing Essays." *JTWC* 14 (1984): 193–201.

A method of designing computer programs can be used in place of the serial outline to clarify development and organization in exposition.

2828. Hays, Robert. "Quirk Topics Enliven Technical Writing Classes." *JTWC* 14 (1984): 43–48.

Presents 20 topics deriving from some paradox in science or technology to challenge students to focus on a reader and to gather, interpret, and report data.

2829. Hays, Robert. "The Trade Jargon of Proposal Writing: A Brief Glossary." *TWT* 11 (Winter 1984): 94–99.

Defines terms used in proposal writing that are most useful for teachers of technical writing.

2830. Hensley, Dennis E. "Down to Cases." *WD* (December 1985): 30–31.

A freelance writer explains how to write technical case histories for trade or professional publications.

2831. Henson, Leigh. "Identifying Effective Writing Exercises for Lower-Division Technical Writing Courses." *JTWC* 14 (1984): 307–316.

Concludes that lower-division technical writing classes should prepare students for academic writing, while upper-division courses should prepare them for professional writing.

2832. Henson, Leigh. "A Note on the Status of Lower-Division Technical Writing." *TWT* 11 (Winter 1984): 89–93.

Presents results of a survey to determine if lower-division technical writing courses were offered, what the goals of such courses were, and how they related to freshman composition courses.

2833. Herrington, Anne J. "Writing in Academic Settings: A Study of the Rhetorical Contexts for Writing in Two College Chemical Engineering Courses." *DAI* 45 (July 1984): 104A.

Investigates contexts for writing and lines of reasoning in a chemical engineering lecture and lab class. Finds different expectations for each classroom community.

2834. Holdstein, Deborah H. "Computerized Instruction in Writing at the Illinois Institute of Technology: Practice, Editing, and Motivation for the Engineering Student." *WLN* 8 (March 1984): 6–8.

Describes a program designed for the technically oriented engineering student.

2835. Holloway, Watson L. "Looking for Mr. Jones: The Ideal of the American *Artifex*." *TWT* 12 (Winter 1985): 23–27.

Concludes that his vocational and technical students desire to interact with others and to engage in intellectual activities.

2836. Iysere, Marla M. "Teaching Technical Writing: Coping with Students' Misconceptions and Evaluation Anxieties." *JTWC* 15 (1985): 259–266.

Suggests ways to motivate and involve students enrolling in technical writing sections who would not ordinarily have taken an upper-division writing course.

2837. Jones, David R. "A Rhetorical Approach for Teaching the Literature of Scientific and Technical Writing." *TWT* 12 (Fall 1985): 115–125.

Describes numerous sources that can be used to teach students to analyze scientific and technical writing from a rhetorical point of view.

2838. Jordan, Mary K. "The Effects of Cooperative Peer Review on College Students Enrolled in Required Advanced Technical Writing Courses." *DAI* 45 (November 1984): 1319A.

Finds that cooperative peer review resulted in increased revisions and deletions and in improved attitudes toward revision.

2839. Josifek, Jami L. "Toward a Descriptive Analysis and ESP Pedagogy of Infinitival and Gerundive Complements to Nouns." *DAI* 44 (March 1984): 2751A.

Analyzes infinitival and gerundive complements and suggests their usefulness in teaching writing to science and technology students.

2840. Kellner, Robert Scott. "The Lexicon of Science: A Course in Technical Terminology." *JTWC* 15 (1985): 55–61.

Suggests that a course in technical terminology become an adjunct to the technical writing curriculum.

2841. Kies, Daniel. "Some Stylistic Features of Business and Technical Writing: The Functions of Passive Voice, Nominalization, and Agency." *JTWC* 15 (1985): 299–308.

Concludes that instructors should not condemn too quickly the use of passives and nominalizations because they can serve important functions of cohesion, emphasis, and style.

2842. Larson, Celia O. "Technical Training: An Application of a Strategy for Learning Stuctural and Functional Information." *DAI* 45 (April 1985): 3359B.

Finds that cooperative learning was effective for acquiring structural and functional information.

2843. Levine, Leslie. "Interviewing for Information." *JTWC* 14 (1984): 55–58.

Describes how to teach technical writing students to develop interviewing skills for gathering information.

2844. Marshall, Stewart. "Computer-Assisted Feedback on Written Reports." *CompEd* 9 (1985): 213–220.

Outlines a way of teaching report writing using the microcomputer to generate feedback.

2845. Mathes, J. C. "Good Engineering + Poor Communication = Three Mile Island." Paper presented at the American Society for Engineering Education Meeting, Washington, April 1984. ERIC ED 253 903 [23 pages]

Details the communication failures that led to the Three Mile Island nuclear accident.

2846. Matulich, Loretta. "Contract Learning in the Traditional Technical Writing Class." *TWT* 11 (Winter 1984): 110–115.

Presents a method for individualizing learning in a community college technical writing class.

2847. McCoy, Joan, and Harlan Roedel. "Drama in the Classroom: Putting Life in Technical Writing." *TWT* 12 (Winter 1985): 11–17.

Describes a series of dramatic situations used to demonstrate what oral and written communication is like in business and industry.

2848. McLean, James I. "Formative Evaluation of the Comprehensibility of Written Instruction." Paper presented at the CCCC Convention, Minneapolis, March 1985. ERIC ED 254 828 [19 pages]

Asks 150 experienced writers to revise a passage and then tests the comprehensibility of the original and revised passages, finding little difference.

2849. Moran, Michael G. "Using Student Experience to Teach the Technical Proposal." *TWT* 11 (Spring 1984): 199–200.

Describes a method for teaching proposal writing by having students prepare group proposals "for a fraternity bash" for a hypothetical fraternity, Phi Kappa Zero.

2850. Norman, Rose, and Marynell Young. "Using Peer Review to Teach Proposal Writing." *TWT* 12 (Winter 1985): 1–9.

A sequence of assignments that uses "students working in groups as review teams" to "inductively teach themselves the basics of successful proposal writing."

2851. O'Donoghue, R. "Incorporating the Principles of Good Writing into an Engineering Curriculum." *EnEd* 74 (April 1984): 664–665.

Describes the methods used and results achieved by a writing program delivered within sophomore engineering classes.

2852. O'Keefe, Katherine O'Brien, and Alan R. P. Journet. "A Hypothetico-Deductive Model for Teaching the Research Paper." *JTWC* 15 (1985): 339–352.

Advocates teaching students to "frame a workable research question" and then test it, as a way of teaching the intellectual process of research.

2853. Orth, Michael, and Carl R. V. Brown. "Computer-Generated Rhetorical Simulations for Business and Report Writing Courses." *JTWC* 14 (1984): 29–34.

By using commercially available computer simulations to create writing cases, two teachers help students understand data, audience, and objectives for report writing.

2854. Pearsall, Thomas E., Frances Sullivan, and Earl E. McDowell. *Academic Programs in Technical Communications.* Washington, D.C.: Society for Technical Communication, 1985. 114 pages

Gives program descriptions and information on 56 American colleges and universities offering undergraduate and graduate programs in technical communication.

2855. Porter, James E. "'Instructions' to Introduce Technical Writing." *TWT* 11 (Winter 1984): 116–119.

Shows how to use a class analysis of a set of poorly written instructions to demonstrate rhetorical principles to students.

2856. Potvin, Janet H. "The Simulated Professional Meeting: A Context for Teaching Oral Presentation in the Technical Communication Course." *JTWC* 14 (1984): 59–68.

Describes a method for developing oral presentation skills by having students present the results of their research at a simulated professional meeting.

2857. Price, A. Rae. "Teaching Word Analysis with Math and Engineering Terms." *JTWC* 14 (1984): 49–53.

Describes how to help science and engineering students appreciate words by analyzing etymology, word parts, and assimilation in technical language.

2858. *Proceedings of the Thirty-First International Technical Communication Conference.* Washington, D.C.: Society for Technical Communication, 1984. 589 pages

A collection of 214 papers presented at the thirty-first conference in Seattle, May 1984. Subjects include advanced technology applications; management and professional development; research, education, and training; visual communication; and writing and editing. Includes author and subject indexes. Authors are not indexed in this volume.

2859. *Proceedings of the Thirty-Second International Technical Communication Conference.* Washington, D.C.: Society for Technical Communication, 1985. 392 pages

A collection of papers presented at the thirty-second conference in Houston, May 1985. Subjects include advanced technology applications; management and professional development; research, education, and training; visual communication; and writing and editing. Includes subject and author indexes. Authors are not indexed in this volume.

2860. Raisman, Neal A. "Technical Writing Reduces Writing Anxiety: Results of a Two-Year Study." *TWT* 11 (Winter 1984): 145–156.

Concludes that teaching freshman composition using technical writing was 200 percent more effective in lowering student writing anxiety than using the literary-essay rhetorical approach.

2861. Raymond, Richard C. "Oral Communication and the Recommendation Report." *TWT* 11 (Winter 1984): 105–109.

Presents a way to modify a traditional writing assignment to include speaking and listening skills.

2862. Roberts, David D., and Patricia A. Sullivan. "Beyond the Static Audience Construct: Reading Protocols in the Technical Writing Class." *JTWC* 14 (1984): 143–153.

Describes the use of reading protocols to help technical writing students experience how readers come to understand prose.

2863. Rothwell, William J. "Administering the Climate Survey: A Toolkit." *JTWC* 15 (1985): 323–338.

Describes the steps to follow in administering a survey that measures the psychological climate of an organization.

2864. Roundy, Nancy. "The Heuristics of Pedagogy: Approaches to Teaching Technical Writing." Paper presented at the CCCC Convention, Minneapolis, March 1985. ERIC ED 257 095 [19 pages]

Offers a framework for pedagogies, dividing their heuristics into form, context, and method.

2865. Roundy, Nancy. "Revision Pedagogy in Technical Writing." Paper presented at the CCCC Convention, New York, March 1984. ERIC ED 243 119 [13 pages]

Describes methods of encouraging revision.

2866. Rude, Carolyn D. "Word Processing in the Technical Editing Class." *JTWC* 15 (1985): 181–190.

Presents assignments based on word processing that can be used to help students learn the content of a technical editing class.

2867. Ruehr, Ruthann. "Some Characteristics and Writing Problems of Technically Oriented Students." Paper presented at the CCCC Convention, New York, March 1984. ERIC ED 243 126 [12 pages]

Describes college students in technical disciplines at Michigan Technological University.

2868. Rutter, Russell. "Poetry, Imagination, and Technical Writing." *CE* 47 (November 1985): 698–712.

Argues that advanced literary study is central to teaching technical writing and that technical writing is a poetic endeavor.

2869. Santleman, Patricia Kelly. "Teaching Technical Writing: Focusing on Process." Paper presented at the CCCC Convention, Minneapolis, March 1985. ERIC ED 258 190 [10 pages]

Offers a case assignment.

2870. Sawyer, Thomas M. "Explanation." *JTWC* 15 (1985): 131–141.

Suggests a number of methods technical writers can use to explain "special scientific and engineering concepts."

2871. Sherrard, Carol A. "The Psychology of Summary Writing." *JTWC* 15 (1985): 247–258.

Draws implications for the teaching of summary writing from current research in cognitive psychology.

2872. Skelton, Terrance, and Deborah C. Andrews. "An Advanced Course in Business and Technical Publications." *JTWC* 15 (1985): 215–225.

Describes a course at the University of Delaware that teaches students to manage document production, asks them to work with other writers, and requires an internship.

2873. Southard, Sherry. "Humanistic Research Projects: The Basis for a Technical Report." Paper presented at the Midwest Section of the American Society for Engineering Education Meeting, Wichita, Kans., March 1984. ERIC ED 243 121 [10 pages]

Describes using literature as a basis for practicing technical report writing.

2874. Speck, Bruce W. "Assumptions and Pointing in Relation to Recommendations." *TWT* 11 (Spring 1984): 195–198.

Describes an exercise used to demonstrate that data should be structured so that they logically point toward conclusions and recommendations.

2875. Speck, Bruce W. "Teaching Technical Writing to Influence Potential Technocrats." *ArEB* 26 (Spring–Summer 1984): 1–7.

Suggests that the English teacher can emphasize the power of effective language in the technical writing class.

2876. Staley, R. Eric. "The Coming Revolution in Graduate Writing Programs." *CHE* 29 (29 August 1984): 80.

Market demand will continue to rise for graduates from vocational/technical writing programs but not for those from traditional programs in creative writing and literature.

2877. Stephens, Judith L., and Arthur J. Marsicano. "Adapting the Basic Speech Communication Course for Engineering and Engineering Technology Majors." *JTWC* 14 (1984): 133–142.

Describes and evaluates an experimental class in speech communication that focused on a topic of interest to engineering students.

2878. Sullivan, Dale. "Connections with Industry and the Liberal Arts: Attempts to Legitimize Teaching Technical Writing." Paper presented at the CCCC Convention, Minneapolis, March 1985. ERIC ED 254 859 [18 pages]

Reviews defenses of technical writing as a profession. See also the author's related 82-item, annotated bibliography ERIC ED 254 860.

2879. Swaino, Jean M. "Teaching Illustration *Throughout* the Technical Writing Course." *TWT* 12 (Winter 1985): 29–32.

Describes a method for teaching students to design and integrate relevant visual aids.

2880. Thierfelder, William R., III. "The Misused Memo: Diagnosis and Treatment." *JTWC* 14 (1984): 155–162.

Describes a question-asking technique to help writers plan, draft, and revise their memos.

2881. Thompson, Isabelle. "The Given/New Contract and Cohesion: Some Suggestions for Classroom Practice." *JTWC* 15 (1985): 205–214.

Describes ways to teach students the conclusions drawn from these two topics of current research.

2882. Vaughn, Jeannette W. "The Basics of English: Foundation for Success in Technical Communication." *TWT* 12 (Winter 1985): 19–22.

Suggests techniques to be used in a technical writing class to improve students' basic grammatical and punctuation skills.

2883. Weber, Barbara. "Technical Writing Skills: A Question of Aptitude or Interest." *JTWC* 15 (1985): 63–68.

Concludes that a growing number of employers are hiring technical writers and suggests some ways in which students can prepare themselves.

2884. Woolston, Donald C. "Incorporating Microcomputers into Technical Writing Instruction." *EnEd* 75 (November 1984): 88–90.

When students prepared eight standard assignments using the Apple IIe, both instructor productivity and the quality of student work improved.

2885. Zappen, James P. "Writing the Introduction to a Research Paper: An Assessment of Alternatives." *TWT* 12 (Fall 1985): 93–101.

An analysis of three methods for introducing scientific or technical research papers and a description of the advantages and disadvantages of each.

2886. Zeider, Martin A. "Runaway Adjectives." *EngR* 36 (1985): 8.

Urges educating students and teachers to use modifier plus noun structures carefully.

See also 34, 54, 82, 108, 199, 202, 288, 299, 470, 533, 564, 574, 603, 998, 1310, 1328, 1361, 1647, 1821, 2211, 2737, 2744, 2749, 2754, 2758, 2789, 2904, 2906, 2918, 2940, 3015

COMMUNICATION IN OTHER DISCIPLINES

2887. Adams, Barbara, Olivia Bissell, Angela Bodino, and Myrna Smith. "Writing for Learning: How to Achieve a Total College Commitment." Paper given at the American Association of Community and Junior Colleges Convention, San Diego, April 1985. ERIC ED 258 666 [38 pages]

Presents four papers describing aspects of the writing across the curriculum program at Somerset (N.J.) Community College.

2888. Alexander, James D. "Creative Writing across the Curriculum." Paper given at the Midwestern Conference on English in the Two-Year College, Milwaukee, February 1984. ERIC ED 241 946 [7 pages]

Discusses using elements of literary style in expository writing.

2889. Association of American Medical Colleges. "Physicians for the Twenty-First Century: Report of the Project Panel on the General Professional Education of the Physician and College Preparation for Medicine." *JMEd* 59 (November 1984).

Lists writing, reading, and communicating as "perhaps the most fundamental skills" for physicians. Encourages emphasis on these skills in premedical and medical curricula.

2890. Barker, Thomas T. "Video Field Trip: Bringing the Real World into the Technical Writing Classroom." *TWT* 11 (Spring 1984): 175–179.

Describes the use of instructor-produced videotapes to motivate and tutor students in a technical writing class.

2891. Barton, John. "A Physics Journal." *WaEJ* 6 (Spring 1984): 23–25.

Journals kept in a physics class may be used during exams. Argues that they increase learning significantly.

2892. Beck, James P. "'Writing-to-Learn?' But We've Scarcely Begun." *ArEB* 27 (Fall 1984): 71–79.

Discusses model content-area writing assignments that encourage thinking.

2893. Benbassat, J. "Common Errors in the Statement of the Present Illness." *MedEd* 18 (1984): 417–422.

Written case histories using narratives, objective language, and meticulous descriptions helped students better establish the diagnosis, prognosis, and therapy for their patients.

2894. Berger, Jeffrey. "Beyond the Workshop: Building Faculty Develoment into the WAC Program." Paper given at the CCCC Convention, Minneapolis, March 1985. ERIC ED 257 079 [19 pages]

Describes the program, which stresses revision, at the Community College of Philadelphia.

2895. Bernhardt, Stephen A. "Writing across the Curriculum at One University: A Survey of Fac-ulty Members and Students." *BADE* 82 (Winter 1985): 55–59.

Finds more support for writing than anticipated and concludes that colleagues in other disciplines are allies with whom English teachers can work toward a common goal.

2896. Bertch, Julie. "Writing for Learning in the Community College." Paper given at the Models for Excellence Conference, Cedar Rapids, Iowa, May 1985. ERIC ED 256 458 [15 pages]

Describes the "Writing for Learning" program at South Mountain (Ariz.) Community College.

2897. Best, Judith A. "Teaching Political Theory: Meaning through Metaphor." *ICUT* 32 (Fall 1984): 165–168.

Gives examples of metaphors a professor of political science uses to engage students and to develop their critical reasoning.

2898. Blanchard, Margaret A. "North Carolina Standardizes Newswriting Course Sections." *JourEd* 39 (Summer 1984): 18–22.

Describes how the School of Journalism at The University of North Carolina at Chapel Hill altered its initial newswriting course to provide a common syllabus, a series of competency tests, and a common numerical grading scale.

2899. Blatt, Gloria T., and Lois Matz Rosen. "The Writing Response to Literature." *JR* 28 (October 1984): 8–12.

Using expressive writing in literature courses helps focus ideas and lead from response to text. Using journals helps shape and record the learning experience.

2900. Bobb, Victor. "Cather, Chopin, and Frost: Discovering What to Make of a Diminished Thing." *IIEB* 72 (Spring 1985): 20–24.

Describes writing assignments based on the "conflict between what one expects and what one finds" in five works.

2901. Buerk, Dorothy. "The Voices of Women Making Meaning in Mathematics." *JEd* 167 (1985): 59–70.

Offers strategies to enhance mathematics learning for women. Journal writing is recommended as one strategy.

2902. Cassara, Ernest. "The Student as Detective: An Undergraduate Exercise in Historiographical Research." *HT* 18 (August 1985): 581–592.

Discusses a project in which history students learned to read and write critically as historians by following a particular practitioner.

2903. Clymer, Diane, and Duane H. Roen. "Writing across the Curriculum at the University of Arizona." *ArEB* 27 (Fall 1984): 11–19.

Describes a three-phase writing program, focusing on the development of writing-emphasis courses in the content areas.

2904. Covington, David H., Ann E. Brown, and Gary B. Blank. "A Writing Assistance Program for Engineering Students." *EnEd* 75 (November 1984): 91–94.

A program located within the School of Engineering delivers teaching, tutoring, workshops on numerous special topics, and advising services to faculty and students.

2905. Cullen, Robert J. "Writing across the Curriculum: Adjunct Courses." *BADE* 79 (Winter 1984): 15–17.

Reviews Kinneavy's three program models and argues for the superiority of a fourth model, adjunct courses as developed at UCLA and the University of Washington.

2906. Dorman, W. Wade, and James M. Pruett. "Engineering Better Writers: Why and How Engineers Can Teach Writing." *EnEd* 75 (April 1985): 656–658.

Argues that writing as a way of thinking is part of the engineering process as well as a professional necessity.

2907. Dudley, H. A. F. "Educational Semantics." *MedEd* 19 (1985): 423–424.

Defines terms used for staff appointments in medicine and lists British and American equivalents for each.

2908. Duke, Charles R., and Ruth Ann Futrell. "Myth or Reality: The Value of English in the Working World." *ArEB* 27 (Fall 1984): 88–98.

Interviews people in farming, manufacturing, auto clean-up, nursing, religion, and law enforcement about the value of their English classes. [Reprinted from *IE* 7 (Winter 1984).]

2909. Faigley, Lester, and Kristine Hansen. "Learning to Write in the Social Sciences." *CCC* 36 (May 1985): 140–149.

Urges teachers of writing courses directed toward specific disciplines to learn how those disciplines create and transmit knowledge.

2910. Fulwiler, Toby. "How Well Does Writing across the Curriculum Work?" *CE* 46 (February 1984): 113–125.

Describes the successes and failures learned in conducting over 40 writing across the curriculum workshops.

2911. Gambell, Trevor J. "Attitudes and Perceptions of University Education Professors to Student Writing." Paper given at the CCCC Convention, New York, March 1984. ERIC ED 244 294 [80 pages]

Studies attitudes toward student writing in education courses.

2912. Gambell, Trevor J. "The Great Demise?: Students' Writing in a College of Education." *EQ* 16 (Winter 1984): 23–25.

Offers three suggestions for improving student writing: vary types of assignments, use self- and peer grading, and use more essay examinations.

2913. George, Diana. "The Writing Center as Center in Writing across the Curriculum." *ArEB* 27 (Fall 1984): 20–25.

Discusses the role of the writing center in reinforcing a writing across the curriculum program.

2914. Gerdes, Marti. "Becoming a Newspaper 'Stringer.'" *Writer* 98 (April 1985): 14–16.

Gives advice to college graduates wanting to pursue a career in journalism.

2915. Griffin, C. W. "Programs for Writing across the Curriculum: A Report." *CCC* 36 (December 1985): 398–403.

Surveys writing across the curriculum programs. Discusses writing centers, faculty workshops, and curriculum changes.

2916. Hanrahan, Calvin M. "A Comparison of Two Approaches to Using Writing across the Curriculum." *DAI* 45 (February 1985): 2424A.

Compares a single-subject approach with a dual-subject approach to writing across the curriculum. Finds significant differences in the attitude surveys of the dual-subject group.

2917. Harris, Jeanette, and Christine Huit. "Using a Survey of Writing Assignments to Make Informed Curricular Decisions." *WPA* 8 (Spring 1985): 7–14.

Presents findings and curricular implications of a survey of the types of writing assigned by faculty across the curriculum.

2918. Herrington, Anne J. "Classrooms as Forums for Reasoning and Writing." *CCC* 36 (December 1985): 404–413.

A naturalistic study of writing in engineering courses suggests that teachers consider the intellectual and social conventions of disciplines and the classroom communities that facilitate learning these conventions.

2919. Hoffman, Eleanor M. "Make the Term Paper Viable." *IE* 9 (Winter 1985): 18–21.

Presents a sequence of three papers to teach research. Suggests a possible timetable.

2920. Jensen, Marvin D. "Memoirs and Journals as Maps of Intrapersonal Communication." *ComEd* 33 (July 1984): 237–242.

Advocates using memoirs and journals to understand "selective memory" and the "pattern of habitual thinking" that verifies self-identity.

2921. Jenseth, Richard. "Finding the Center: The Expressive Reading Journal in the College Classroom." Paper given at the CCCC Convention, New York, March 1984. ERIC ED 246 479 [11 pages]

Describes using journals in all subjects to improve reading and writing.

2922. Joorabchi, Bahman. "A Problem-Based Journal Club." *JMEd* 59 (September 1984): 755–757.

Using written summaries, excerpts, and discussion-provoking questions improved the discussion of journal articles by medical personnel and contributed to retaining content.

2923. Katula, Richard A., and Celest A. Martin. "Teaching Critical Thinking in the Speech Communication Classroom." *ComEd* 33 (April 1984): 160–167.

Discusses the need for speech communication teachers to emphasize invention. Presents a method for teaching critical thinking based on D'Angelo's conceptual theory of rhetoric.

2924. Kneeshaw, Stephen. "Kissing in History; or, Designing Sequential Writing Assignments." *WaEJ* 7 (Winter 1985): 9–12.

Twenty-five word précis, microthemes, and four-page papers can be used repeatedly in a history class.

2925. MacKenzie, Nancy. "Subjective Criticism in Literature Courses: Learning through Writing." *TETYC* 12 (October 1985): 228–234.

Advocates having students keep response journals in literature courses.

2926. Mallonee, Barbara C., and John R. Breihan. "Writing across the Curriculum, Phase Two: Beyond the Workshop — Empirical Rhetoric at Loyola." Paper given at the CCCC Convention, New York, March 1984. ERIC ED 248 515 [17 pages]

Describes Loyola (Baltimore) College's model of writing across the curriculum, including paired teaching, teacher training, departmental writing coordinators, and an evaluation survey.

2927. McCarthy, Lucille. "A Proposal for Dr. Marquardt, PhD." *MarylandJ* 19 (1984): 15–18.

Advocates using writing to record students' reactions to literary texts, then using these records to develop literary/critical skills.

2928. McLean, Deckle. "Reduce Obstacles Hindering Students' Learning to Write." *JourEd* 39 (Summer 1984): 33–36.

Identifies obstacles to learning newswriting and discusses ways to surmount them.

2929. McLean, James I. "Writing for Learning: Practical Application of Research Findings." Paper given at the Association for Educational Communications and Technology Meeting, Dallas, January 1984. ERIC ED 243 106 [32 pages]

Describes a plan for improving content-area writing instruction.

2930. McMahon, Christine. "Writing across the *English* Curriculum: Using Journals in Literature Classes." *TETYC* 12 (December 1985): 269–271.

Suggests that composing techniques developed for writing across the curriculum projects can also be employed in literature classes.

2931. Metteer, Christine. "Achieving Plain English: An Exercise in Legal Style." Paper given at the CCCC Convention, Minneapolis, March 1985. ERIC ED 255 938 [12 pages]

Describes the interdisciplinary writing program at Southwestern University School of Law.

2932. Miller, Frankie F. "Legal Writing Perspectives: Delaware Research." *DAI* 46 (October 1985): 916A.

Interviews with members of the Delaware legal community reveal an emphasis on brevity, clarity, and organization. Calls for more writing courses before and during law school.

2933. Moreland, Kim. "The Writing Center: A Center for Writing across the Curriculum Activities." *WLN* 10 (November 1985): 1–4.

Describes how tutors can work with teachers to improve the quality of writing in courses other than composition.

2934. Nakamura, Caroline, Robert Fearrien, and Sheldon Hershinow. "Write to Learn: Writing across the Curriculum at Kapiolani Community College." Paper given at the Pacific Western Division Conference of the Community College Humanities Association, San Diego, November 1984. ERIC ED 252 252 [14 pages]

Three papers on a writing across the curriculum program: its background/context, a case study, and a model for designing the program.

2935. Nees-Hatlen, Virginia. "Coherence and Commitment: Responding to Student Writing in the Disciplines." *ArEB* 27 (Fall 1984): 26–34.

Outlines the roles of reader, rhetorical critic, editor, and critic in assignments using writing as a way of learning.

2936. O'Reilly, Mary Rose. "The Peaceable Classroom." *CE* 46 (February 1984): 103–112.

Using experiences teaching war literature, argues for classroom techniques that combine ethical issues with intellectual rigor.

2937. Otto, Paul B. "Writing as a Process in a University Physical Science Class." Paper given at the National Association for Research in Science Teaching Meeting, French Lick Springs, Ind., April 1985. ERIC ED 254 405 [11 pages]

Reports on a study of a process approach to writing, finding no significant differences in writing quality between experimental and control groups.

2938. Parker, Robert. "The 'Language across the Curriculum' Movement: A Brief Overview and Bibliography." *CCC* 36 (May 1985): 173–177.

Advocates that the American writing across the curriculum movement shift to British principles, viewing language as an instrument of learning and seeing interconnenctions among language uses and underlying theory. Includes a bibliography.

2939. Parr, Gerald D., and Arlin V. Peterson. "Friendly Persuasion: When Everyone Talks at the Same Level, Classroom Communication Is More Effective. You and Your Students Will Both Learn to Listen." *ST* 52 (January 1985): 39–40.

Advocates using behavioral communication techniques to persuade students to attend to and learn subject matter.

2940. Postlethwait, S. N. "Using Science and Technology to Teach Science and Technology." *EnEd* 74 (January 1984): 204–209.

Argues that all faculty must teach communication. Describes an audio-tutorial system that gives botany students practice in taking assignments, writing succinct reports, and making oral presentations.

2941. Povar, Gail J., and Karla J. Keith. "The Teaching of Liberal Arts in Internal Medicine Residency Programs." *JMEd* 59 (September 1984): 714–721.

Describes efforts to include literature and writing (among other liberal arts subjects) in curricula for residents in internal medicine.

2942. Preston, James. *Writing across the Curriculum: Some Questions and Answers and a Series of Eleven Writing Projects.* Miami: Miami-Dade Community College, 1982. ERIC ED 256 414 [114 pages]

Reviews writing across the curriculum in question-answer format and offers 11 assignments for general education core courses.

2943. Rebhorn, Marlette. "What Does 'Writing across the Disciplines' Mean to Historians?" *TETYC* 12 (December 1985): 265–268.

Argues that, since professional historians write argument and persuasion, students should be trained in these modes.

2944. Richard, Jeremy. "Rhetorical Strategies for Music Criticism." Paper given at the CCCC Convention, New York, March 1984. ERIC ED 247 200 [17 pages]

Describes a writing assignment for music classes.

2945. Robillard, Douglas, Jr. "Teaching Robert Coover's 'The Babysitter': Writing to Unlock Meaning." *IlEB* 72 (Spring 1985): 62–65.

By using numbered paragraphs, students trace narrative lines, deal with viewpoint and consistency of plot and action, and examine the role television plays in a story.

2946. Saffran, Murray, and Richard A. Yeasting. "A First-Year, Student-Managed Course to Correlate Basic Sciences with Clinical Medicine." *JMEd* 60 (October 1985): 793-797.

Reports on a first-year course that required medical students to read and write to connect classroom learning with clinical practice.

2947. Scott, Norval, and Myron F. Weiner. "'Patientspeak': An Exercise in Communication." *JMEd* 59 (November 1984): 890-893.

Creating a "Patientspeak" dictionary of commonly misused or misunderstood terms improved communication between medical personnel and patients.

2948. Scott, Robert L. "Focusing Rhetorical Criticism." *ComEd* 33 (April 1984): 89-96.

Explains a model of rhetorical criticism.

2949. Sigman, Stuart J. "Some Common Mistakes Students Make When Learning Discourse Analysis." *ComEd* 34 (April 1985): 119-127.

Provides sample assignments and a syllabus for teaching discourse analysis to speech students. Explains four problems that beginning students often encounter.

2950. Smith, Eugene. "Student Writing in the Foreground of a Literature Class." *ExEx* 30 (Fall 1984): 34-39.

Presents a guide sheet for encouraging student responses to literary works. Involves students in developing reactions to literary works in writing and in discussion.

2951. Snodgrass, Sara E. "Writing as a Tool for Teaching Social Psychology." Paper presented at the APA Convention, Toronto, August 1984. ERIC ED 251 372 [43 pages]

Describes practical ways writing was used in a college social psychology course that included a course log, analyses of articles, and a research proposal.

2952. Soskin, Mark D., and Nancy Eldblom. "Integrating the Term Paper into Economics Courses at Liberal Arts Colleges: Industry Case Study Papers at SUNY—Potsdam. A Preliminary Study." Paper given at the New York State Economic Association Meeting, Syracuse, N.Y., April 1984. ERIC ED 246 732 [30 pages]

Reports on a study using research papers in upper-level economics courses.

2953. Sticht, Thomas G., and Larry Mikulecky. *Job-Related Basic Skills: Cases and Conclusions.* Columbus, Ohio: National Center Publications, 1984. ERIC ED 246 312 [54 pages]

Describes skills required for work and explores ways of improving the reading, writing, and computational abilities of workers.

2954. Strenski, Ellen. "The Write Stuff: Have Your Students Write in Science Class — Not Simply to Regurgitate Data, but to Support Their Opinions." *ST* 51 (May 1984): 58-61.

Advocates using writing, which forces students to collect, manipulate, and test factual data, as a way of helping them actively learn science.

2955. Thaiso, Christopher. "Language across the Curriculum." *ArEB* 27 (Fall 1984): 51-56.

Describes faculty workshops designed "to increase or vary the language experiences" of students in various subjects.

2956. Vukuvich, Diane. "Ideas in Practice: Integrating Math and Writing through the Math Journal." *JDEd* 9 (1985): 19-20.

Explains a University of Akron program incorporating writing into basic mathematics through personal math journals. Reports positive results.

2957. Walter, James A. "Paired Classes: Write to Learn and Learn to Write." Paper given at the Community College Humanities Association Meeting, Kalamazoo, Mich., October 1984. ERIC ED 248 933 [8 pages]

Describes a paired humanities and writing course format for writing in the disciplines.

2958. Walvoord, Barbara Fassler, and Daniel Singer. "Process-Oriented Writing Instruction in a Case-Method Class." Paper given at the American Management Association Meeting, Boston, August 1984. ERIC ED 249 500 [16 pages]

Studies three college business management courses, finding that response to the draft followed by revision produced the best results on case analyses.

2959. Walzer, Arthur E. "Articles from the 'California Divorce Project': A Case Study of the Concept of Audience." *CCC* 36 (May 1985): 150-159.

An analysis or research articles for three audiences concludes that students should analyze the discourse of their intended discipline for its purpose, rationale, and form.

2960. Webb, Judith. "The Public Speech as Model: Course Design for Patterns of Organization in Persuasive Writing." *DAI* 45 (September 1984): 851A.

Proposes a writing course based on the study of public speeches to give students a sense of how writers use audience.

2961. Westerfield, Michael W. "The Behaviors and Attitudes of the Non-English Faculty at York College toward the Teaching of Writing." *DAI* 45 (January 1985): 2019A.

Surveys of faculty members and students reveal that non-English courses rarely used prewriting, in-class writing, revision, or publication of student work. Faculty members were uninterested in receiving training in writing instruction, and they evaluated papers by marking errors and judging content.

2962. Whyte, Douglas A. "Teaching the Matching of Speech Rate to Community College Students." *DAI* 45 (November 1984): 1531A.

Tests the effectiveness of teaching social work students to match the paralanguage of clients as an aid to developing relationships.

2963. Williamson, Michael M. "The Function of Writing in Three College Curricula: Modes and Registers." Paper given at the NCTE Convention, Detroit, November 1984. ERIC ED 252 884 [16 pages]

Studies six college teachers of biology, English, and sociology through interviews and course artifacts. Finds that the teacher's reading of student writing is structured around registers.

2964. Yarrington, Roger. "J-Schools Should Encourage Higher Education Writers." *JourEd* 40 (Winter 1985): 11–12.

Describes how journalism schools can help to improve the press coverage of higher education.

See also 204, 280, 316, 445, 515, 726, 1130, 1329, 1331, 1332, 1335, 1342, 1347, 1348, 1353, 1360, 1394, 1405, 1429, 1439, 1440, 1446, 1492, 1506, 1524, 1532, 1670, 1673, 1686, 1706, 1725, 1815, 1941, 1951, 2169, 2221, 2260, 2292, 2299, 2317, 2327, 2589, 2668, 2784, 2814, 2985, 3748, 3817

ADULT EDUCATION

2965. Barbour, James, Barry Gaines, and Michael J. Hogan. "Language Requirements in English

Graduate Programs." *BADE* 79 (Winter 1984): 46–51.

Reports the results of a survey of 81 schools, listing languages required and means of satisfying requirements.

2966. Belz, Elaine. "Educational Therapy: A Model for the Treatment of Functionally Illiterate Adults." *AdEd* 35 (Winter 1984): 96–104.

Describes four phases of "instructional encounters," which address a student's negative self-image about learning ability and literacy.

2967. Blanchard, Jay S. "U.S. Armed Services Computer-Assisted Literacy Efforts." *JR* 28 (December 1984): 262–265.

Describes attempts by the military to teach vocabulary, problem solving, study skills, reading comprehension, sentence arrangement, and paragraph organization by using microcomputers, computers, and videodiscs.

2968. Duffy, Karen Louise, and Paul F. Fendt. "Trends in Adult Learning: Implications for Community College Education." *CCR* 12 (Summer 1984): 41–47.

Describes five major trends in adult learning. Notes that community college adult educators of the 1980s and 1990s need communication skills.

2969. Hildebrand, Janet E. "Writing Skills for the Preprofessional Student." *JTW* 3 (Fall 1984): 263–268.

Describes a comprehensive program for students planning to enter medicine, law, and graduate school.

2970. Hoffman, Eleanor M. "Corrections Personnel: Individualizing the Workshop." *ArEB* 27 (Fall 1984): 82–87.

In working with probation officers to improve their writing, advocates finding out their "wants and needs" to conduct a successful workshop.

2971. Kazemek, Francis E. "Adult Literacy Education: An Ethical Endeavor." *AdLBEd* 8 (1984): 61–72.

Asserts that ethics requires teachers to reach beyond functional skills and to approach students as equals in a dialogue about genuine ideas.

2972. Kazemek, Francis E. "'I wauted to be a Tencra to Help penp to L': Writing for Adult Beginning Learners." *JR* 27 (April 1984): 614–619.

Reports on a method of teaching illiterate adults

to write by integrating writing into each lesson, focusing on its practical uses, writing extensively with students, and building on strengths.

2973. Koring, Heidi. "Writing and Career Development." *ExEx* 30 (Fall 1984): 46–48.

Integrates job-seeking skills within the composition course. Describes the Haldane System for Identifying Motivated Skills.

2974. Kozol, Jonathan. "Benjamin's Story." *JEd* 167 (1985): 42–49.

A narrative asserting that fragmented skills instruction in the military produces a poor type of literacy.

2975. Nickerson, Raymond S. "Adult Literacy and Technology." *VLang* 19 (Summer 1985): 311–355.

The Chair of the Adult Literacy Initiative of the U.S. Department of Education reports on a workshop examining how technology might be used to teach reading, writing, and related skills to adults.

2976. Pfeiffer, William S. "Intensive Consulting: Watching Your Vegetables Grow." *ABCAB* 48 (March 1985): 11–14.

Describes consulting experiences helping an engineering firm begin a program of in-house writing courses.

2977. Ratner, Rochelle. "Critiquing the Writing of Older Adults." *TWM* 16 (May–June 1985): 6–8.

Describes a method of using workshops to encourage older students and senior citizens to write and revise their work.

2978. Siegel, Gerald. "Teaching College English to Nontraditional Students: A Survey of Research." Paper given at College English Association, Clearwater Beach, Fla., April 1984. ERIC ED 247 597 [17 pages]

Reviews the preferences of adult students about aspects of writing and literature they wish to study.

2979. Smith, Terry. "Assignment – Keep a Journal: Uses in Therapy." *WaEJ* 6 (Spring 1984): 27.

Therapists use journals because they give adults more objectivity about their lives.

2980. Wangberg, Elaine G., Bruce Thompson, and Justin E. Levitov. "First Steps toward an Adult Basic Word List." *JR* 28 (December 1984): 244–247.

Presents a 385-word spelling list for use by illiterate adults as they learn to write using interactive computers.

See also 20, 1567, 1838, 2422, 2656, 2755, 2908, 2995, 3464

ENGLISH AS A SECOND LANGAUGE

2981. Abraham, Roberta G. "Field Independence – Dependence and the Teaching of Grammar." *TESOLQ* 19 (December 1985): 689–702.

A study of 61 students indicates "that field-independent subjects performed better with the deductive lesson," and "field-dependent subjects performed better with the example lesson."

2982. Allison, Desmond, and Richard Webber. "What Place for Performative Tests?" *ELTJ* 38 (July 1985): 199–203.

Examines the use of performance tests and exercises, including lecture notes and library skills.

2983. Bailey, Lucille M. "A History of American Attitudes toward Black English." *IE* 7 (Spring 1984): 6–12.

A historical discussion of views toward black English. Argues that all languages have logic and positive qualities.

2984. Baumhover, Mary J. "The Intercultural Class: A Challenge for English Composition Teachers." *DAI* 44 (February 1984): 2459A.

Shows that ESL students can write effectively given the right motivation and situation.

2985. Brink, Daniel. "Word Processing with Nonstandard Alphabets." *CollM* 2 (Summer 1984): 147–150.

Suggests strategies for using the computer for word processing with non-English scripts.

2986. Broom, Mary Jo. "Something to Carry Along: A Student-Produced Writing Handbook." *UEJ* (1984): 27–31.

Describes a writing and reading curriculum for junior high ESL students.

2987. Brown, Tracey, and Margot Haynes. *Learning to Read English as a Second Language: Effects of Script System.* Urbana, Ill.: ERIC/RCS, 1983. ERIC ED 249 759 [19 pages]

Studies the script carryover effect, finding it to be characteristic of Japanese students learning English.

2988. Campbell, Donald, Carolyn Clark, and James D. Rowoth. *The Research Paper for Advanced ESL Students.* Urbana, Ill.: ERIC/RCS, 1984. ERIC ED 246 672 [29 pages]

A teaching guide.

2989. Carr, Marion. "A Five-Step Evaluation of a Holistic Essay-Evaluation Process." Paper given at the Summer TESOL Meeting, Toronto, July 1983. ERIC ED 238 263 [19 pages]

Describes how an intensive ESL program developed new evaluation criteria for essays.

2990. Carrell, Patricia. "Schema Theory and ESL Reading: Classroom Implications and Applications." *MLJ* 68 (Winter 1984): 332–343.

Recommends teaching ESL reading as the combination of text comprehension and the accumulation and activation of appropriate background information about the text's content and rhetoric.

2991. Carrell, Patricia. "Text as Interaction: Some Implications of Text Analysis and Reading Research for ESL Composition." Paper given at the TESOL Meeting, Houston, March 1984. ERIC ED 243 313 [20 pages]

Discusses applications to teaching ESL.

2992. Chalker, Sylvia. "Why Can't Someone Write a Nice, Simple Grammar?" *ELTJ* 38 (April 1984): 79–85.

Comments on readers' expectations for grammar books and makes suggestions for improvements.

2993. Clarke, Mark A. "On the Nature of Technique: What Do We Owe the Gurus?" *TESOLQ* 18 (December 1984): 577–594.

Describes "the Blackboard Composition," a technique for teaching ESL writing, and explores sources for that technique, citing Kaplan, Christensen, Fader, Murray, and Stevick.

2994. Cohen, Andrew D. "Reformulation: Another Way to Get Feedback." *WLN* 10 (October 1985): 6–10.

Reformulating, or having a native speaker rewrite a student's work, can help nonnative writers improve their style.

2995. Comings, John Kahler David. *Peace Corps Literacy Handbook.* Washington, D.C.: Peace Corps, 1984. ERIC ED 251 696 [176 pages]

Provides an introduction to literacy work, presenting information for planning, presenting, and guiding a literacy project.

2996. Cone, Dennis. "EFL Plagiarism: A Pound of Prevention." *IE* 7 (Spring 1985): 23–30.

Explores three reasons for plagiarism in EFL student writing and suggests ways to curtail it, especially through instruction in paraphrasing.

2997. Cortese, Guiseppina. "From Receptive to Productive in Post-Intermediate EFL Classes." *TESOLQ* 19 (March 1985): 7–25.

Describes a linguistically integrated, content-based, interactive class project that used reading to improve speaking and writing. Suggests reversing the "canonical sequence of skills."

2998. Dalgish, Gerard M. "Computer-Assisted ESL Research and Courseware Development." *CC* 2 (August 1985): 45–62.

Describes computer applications in a program for ESL students. Determining the kinds of errors common to the students led to developing courseware for a CAI writing program.

2999. Dalgish, Gerard M. *Microcomputers and Teaching English as a Second Language.* Research Monograph, no. 7. New York: CUNY, 1984. ERIC ED 253 213 [58 pages]

Critiques software for teaching ESL at the college level and outlines programs at CUNY.

3000. Davidson, Fred. "Teaching and Testing ESL Composition through Contract Learning." Paper given at the TESOL Meeting, Houston, March 1984. ERIC ED 245 560 [18 pages]

Describes using contracts to reduce repeated errors in ESL students' papers.

3001. De Jesus, Socorro. "Predictors of English Writing Performance of Native Spanish Speaking College Freshmen." Paper given at the CCCC Convention, New York, March 1984. ERIC ED 256 184 [13 pages]

Reports, among other findings, that integratively motivated students outperform instrumentally motivated students.

3002. Drobnic, Karl, and Kathryn Michaels, eds. *English for Specific Purposes* 1–8 (1977–1985). ERIC ED 258 442 [731 pages]

Makes available, in ERIC, the first eight volumes of an ESL journal containing bibliographies, notes, and book reviews.

3003. Edge, Julian. "Do TEFL Articles Solve Problems?" *ELTJ* 39 (July 1985): 153–157.

Discusses a rhetorical pattern in EFL journal articles and provides a framework for taking notes from and writing about these articles.

3004. Edge, Julian. "Structuring the Information Gap." *ELTJ* 38 (October 1984): 256–261.

Describes a communication procedure that moves from searching for information through writing and suggests ways of adapting it to various classes.

3005. Eggington, William, and Thomas Ricento. "Discourse Analysis as a Pedagogical Tool." Paper given at the CATESOL Meeting, Sacramento, March 1982. ERIC ED 236 938 [13 pages]

Finds that discourse bloc analysis overcomes transfer by nonnative writers of their culturally based native language rhetorical norms. [Reprinted in *CATESOL Occasional Papers* 9 (Fall 1983).]

3006. Elsasser, Nan, and Patricia Irvine. "English and Creole: The Dialectics of Choice in a College Writing Program." *HER* 55 (November 1985): 399–415.

Documents an experimental writing program that involved linguistic analyses of Creole and English and writing in and about both languages.

3007. England, Lizabeth. "The Use of Basic Writing Materials in ESL Writing Classes." Paper given at the CCCC Convention, New York, March 1984. ERIC ED 246 418 [13 pages]

Suggests that materials developed for basic writers are appropriate in ESL classes.

3008. Fillmore, Lily Wong, Paul Ammon, Barry McLaughlin, and Mary Sue Ammon. *Learning English through Bilingual Instruction.* Washington, D.C.: NIE, 1985. ERIC ED 259 579 [484 pages]

Offers ethnographic observations of a bilingual elementary school, stressing the social nature of language learning.

3009. Flanagan, Michael J. "A Study of a Half-Day ESOL Program for Second Language Learners in Grades One through Six." *DAI* 45 (September 1984): 831A-832A.

Examines differences in English language proficiency between groups of second-language learners in different programs.

3010. Franklin, Elizabeth Anne. *A Naturalistic Study of Literacy in Bilingual Classrooms.* Urbana, Ill.: ERIC/RCS, 1984. ERIC ED 258 179 [25 pages]

Studies two first-grade classrooms, finding that teachers' attempts to simplify English literacy make its acquisition more difficult for Hispanic students.

3011. Grubb, Melvin H. "The Writing Proficiency of Selected ESL and Monolingual English Writers at Three Grade Levels." *DAI* 45 (July 1984): 103A.

Compares the writing of monolingual students and students with limited proficiency in English in grades five, eight, and nine. Examines "organizational type" and level of content.

3012. Guerra, Veronica A. "Predictors of Second Language Learners' Error Judgments in Written English." *DAI* 45 (November 1984): 1381A.

Investigates the ability of Hispanic speakers to recognize and correct errors in their second language.

3013. Gutstein, Shelley P., Henry Batterman, Carol Harmatz-Levin, Joy Kreeft, and Christine Meloni. "Using REAL English: Writing a Dialogue Journal." Paper given at the TESOL Meeting, Toronto, March 1983. ERIC ED 256 155 [24 pages]

Discusses the value of dialogue journals in ESL classes, noting that they promote authentic, natural written language.

3014. Hoekje, Barbara. "Processes of Repair in Nonnative Speaker Conversation." Paper given at the TESOL Meeting, Houston, March 1984. ERIC ED 250 922 [26 pages]

Studies the efforts of 26 nonnative speakers to repair breakdowns in conversation. Finds that speakers have a variety of repair strategies.

3015. Holland, V. Melissa, Harvey Rosenbaum, Susan Stoddart, Janice C. Redish, Joan Harman, and Rebecca L. Oxford-Carpenter. *English-as-a-Second-Language Programs in Basic Skills: Education Program I.* Washington, D.C.: American Institutes for Research, 1984. ERIC ED 254 097 [125 pages]

An Army research report reviews the needs of ESL speakers and assesses the effectiveness of basic skills programs.

3016. Howard, Rebecca M. "Language Philosophy in Composition Theory and Its Pedagogical Implications for Native and Nonnative Speakers of English." *DAI* 45 (December 1984): 1737A.

Proposes that native and nonnative speakers work together in group inquiry classes.

3017. Huck, Sharon. "Setting Up a High School ESL Program." *EJ* 73 (September 1984): 41–45.

Discusses some common problems in setting up an ESL program and lists resources for the teacher.

3018. Huckin, Thomas N., and Leslie A. Olsen. "The Need for Professionally Oriented ESL Instruction in the United States." *TESOLQ* 18 (June 1984): 273–294.

Maintains that the level of English required to succeed academically is not sufficient to succeed professionally. Argues that writing and speaking need specialized attention.

3019. Jacoby, Jay. "Training Writing Center Personnel to Work with International Students: The Least We Need to Know." *WLN* 10 (October 1985): 1–6.

Discusses problems in tutoring ESL students. Includes a bibliography.

3020. James, Chris. "Acculturation in the ESL Curriculum." *EQ* 17 (Winter 1984): 37–47.

Explores the use of group discussions and journal entries to enable students to take the risks necessary to practice a new language.

3021. Kaplan, Robert B. "Bilingual/Bicultural Students and Competency Testing." *SLATE* 9 (February 1984).

Reviews the issues, surveys popular competency tests, highlights problems in testing, and provides four strategies for action. Includes bibliography.

3022. Kaplan, Robert B. "The Forum: Comments on Mark A. Clarke's 'On the Nature of Technique: What Do We Owe the Gurus?' [*TESLOQ* 18 (December 1984)]." *TESLOQ* 19 (September 1985): 613–616.

Maintains that Clarke had "the ill fortune to have had a good idea 20 years ago" and that his teaching techniques are not necessarily new.

3023. Kenney, Donald. "Teaching the Research Paper the Right Way." *VEB* 35 (Spring 1985): 49–53.

Describes research from a librarian's perspective, which includes finding, evaluating, and summar-

izing information, which leads to drawing conclusions and writing up findings.

3024. Kessler, Carolyn, and Mary Ellen Quinn. "Second Language Acquisition in the Context of Science Experiences." Paper given at the TESOL Meeting, Houston, March 1984. ERIC ED 248 713 [35 pages]

Studies the improved language use of an ESL student in a high school physical science class using the inquiry approach.

3025. Khalil, Aziz M. "Communicative Error Evaluation: A Study of American Native Speakers' Evaluations and Interpretations of Deviant Utterances Written by Arab EFL Learners." *DAI* 45 (May 1985): 3339A.

Discusses the pedagogical implications of grammatically deviant utterances of Arab EFL learners.

3026. Kobayashi, Hiroe. "Rhetorical Patterns in English and Japanese." *DAI* 45 (February 1985): 2425A.

Finds that cultural preferences for certain rhetorical patterns exist and that second-language learners use first-language rhetorical patterns when writing in English.

3027. Kossoudji, Sherrie Ann. "Language and Labor Markets: The Effect of English Language Ability on the Labor Market Outcomes of Immigrants." *DAI* 45 (August 1984): 580A.

Uses econometric models to investigate relationships between Asian and Hispanic men's English ability, expected earnings, and occupation. Contrasts with similar data for native born Americans.

3028. Kreeft, Joy, and Roger W. Shuy. *Dialogue Writing: Analysis of Teacher-Student Interactive Writing in ESL.* Washington, D.C.: Center for Applied Linguistics, December 1984. ERIC ED 252 097 [435 pages]

Reports on a study of sixth graders writing dialogue journals. Describes their use in class and the linguistic characteristics of journal entries.

3029. Kroll, Barbara. *What Does Time Buy? Syntactic Accuracy and Discourse Fluency in ESL Composition.* Urbana, Ill.: ERIC/RCS, 1982. ERIC ED 257 075 [31 pages]

Examines 50 in-class and 50 out-of-class ESL compositions, finding no significant difference in correctness and no relationship between correctness and discourse fluency.

3030. Larter, Sylvia, and Maisy Chang. *Bilingual Education and Bilingualism: A Review of Research.* Research Report, no. 175. Toronto: Toronto Board of Education, 1984. ERIC ED 250 925 [176 pages]

Reviews 110 studies of bilingualism, focusing on the effects of bilingual education on the academic and cognitive development of children and adults.

3031. Longfield, Diane M. "Teaching ESL to Adults: State of the Art." Paper given at the National Adult Literacy Conference, Washington, D.C., January 1984. ERIC ED 240 297 [43 pages]

A review of research.

3032. McGroarty, Mary. "The Forum: Some Meanings of Communicative Competence for Second Language Students." *TESOLQ* 18 (June 1984): 257–272.

Explains that communicative competence is complex, varies widely, and must be explored as the basis for a competence-based ESL curriculum.

3033. McGroarty, Mary. "High School Competency Tests and ESL Students." Paper given at the CATESOL Meeting, Los Angeles, April 1983. ERIC ED 253 066 [9 pages]

Results of competency tests of 27 tenth and twelfth graders correlated positively with oral English proficiency.

3034. McKee, Macey Blackburn. "Academic Writing *Vs.* Composition." *MEXTESOL Journal* 8 (October 1984). ERIC ED 249 807 [8 pages].

Argues that, since academic writing is different from the writing usually done in composition classes, ESL teachers should prepare students for academic writing.

3035. Oster, Judith. "The ESL Composition Course and the Idea of a University." *CE* 47 (January 1985): 66–76.

Discusses an ESL course at Case Western Reserve University that introduces foreign students to the idea of a university through reading, writing, and discussion.

3036. Parla, JoAnn. "The Written Spanish of Puerto Rican Bilinguals in a Situation of Language Contact: An Error Analytic Study." *DAI* 45 (February 1985): 2512A.

Examines written errors of monolingual and bilingual students in a Spanish-as-a-second-dialect course and discusses the pedagogical and epistemological implications for learning.

3037. Patton, Vicki. "Mini Course: How to Use the Dictionary." *WLN* 8 (April 1984): 1–4.

Describes an approach for teaching ESL and unskilled native speakers how to understand and use the information in a dictionary.

3038. Prabhu, Lalita. "My Aunt, My School to Come, Loves: A Tutoring Program for the Advanced ESL Student." *WLN* 10 (November 1985): 10–12.

Describes ways to increase the fluency and competency of ESL students. Argues that ESL students can be effective tutors.

3039. Qoqandi, Abdulaziz M. Y. "Measuring the Level of Syntactical Growth of Saudi Twelfth Graders in EFL Writing Using T-Unit Analysis." *DAI* 46 (October 1985): 916A.

Findings indicate that the type of program (science or humanities) did not have a significant effect on Arab EFL students' syntactic development, but that the mode of writing did have an impact.

3040. Ramos de Perez, J. Maria. "An Exploratory Study of Adjustment Difficulties of Spanish-Speaking International Students to Study at an American University." *DAI* 46 (December 1985): 1676A.

A survey based on interviews of 51 Spanish ESL students. Makes recommendations for improving language instruction and social integration for international students.

3041. Rice, Donna Steed. "Communication Problems of Immigrants and Refugees in Higher Education Whose Dominant Language Is Other Than English." *DAI* 46 (September 1985): 555A.

Analyzes written and oral language problems as perceived by Asian Pacific or Hispanic students at SUNY–Buffalo.

3042. Richmond, Kent C. "Teacher-Induced Errors." Paper given at the California Association of Teachers of English, San Jose, March 1984. ERIC ED 244 516 [17 pages]

Describes ESL writers' inaccurate assumptions about English and the writing process that result from inappropriate instruction.

3043. Schwab, Patricia N., and Charles R. Coble. "Reading, Thinking, and Semantic Webbing: Here's a New Way to Strengthen Reading Comprehension." *ST* 52 (May 1985): 68–71.

Recommends using semantic webbing, a visual outlining technique, to help students understand chapters in science textbooks.

3044. Skelton, John. "Dependence Relations in Language Teaching." *ELTJ* 38 (April 1984): 135–138.

Suggests ways to help teachers better explain the correct use of gerunds and infinitives after certain verbs.

3045. Snow, Marguerite, and Donna M. Brinton. "Linking ESL Courses with University Content Courses: The Adjunct Model." Paper given at the California Association of Teachers of English, San Jose, March 1984. ERIC ED 244 515 [40 pages]

Describes integrating ESL writing with other university courses.

3046. Soria, Andrew M. "Computer-Assisted Instruction for Learners of English as a Second Language: Design and Field Test of a Program to Review Word Order in a Sentence." *DAI* 46 (November 1985): 1266A.

Presents a program simulating instructor knowledge of English sentence structure, discusses field test results, and suggests future directions.

3047. Spack, Ruth. "Literature, Reading, Writing, and ESL: Bridging the Gaps." *TESOLQ* 19 (December 1985): 703–725.

Describes the benefits of using literature in ESL instruction and discusses how to integrate skills through literature. Gives examples of writing/reading assignments.

3048. Stevens, Vance. "Brief Reports and Summaries: The Effects of Choice and Control in Computer-Assisted Language Learning in Teaching Supplementary Grammar to Intermediate Student of ESL and to Remedial English Students at the College Entry Level." *TESOLQ* 18 (March 1984): 141–143.

Results do not empirically support that choice and control increase the effectiveness of computer-assisted instruction.

3049. Teich, Nathaniel. "Transfer of Writing Skills: How the Concept of Transfer Can Help Teachers of ESL and Basic Writing." Paper given at the CCCC Convention, Minneapolis, March 1985. ERIC ED 257 057 [11 pages]

Argues that assignments for ESL and basic writing students must be student centered, recognizing both the audience and the students' prior knowledge.

3050. Thabet, Ahmed A. "Cohesion in EFL Programs: A Computational Linguistics Approach." *DAI* 44 (April 1984): 3053.

Concludes that lack of cohesion in Egyptian EFL textbooks and programs contributes to student weaknesses in writing.

3051. Thomas, Helen. "Developing the Stylistic and Lexical Awareness of Advanced Students." *ELTJ* 38 (July 1984): 187–191.

Describes three text-analysis and revision exercises, working with material translated from Hungarian into English.

3052. Thomas, Jacqueline. "A Study to Determine the Role of Prior Linguistic Experience in Second and Third Language Learning." *DAI* 44 (April 1984): 3053A.

Concludes that bilingual English-speaking students master both oral and written French with more facility than monolingual English speakers.

3053. Timm, Lenora A. "Bilingualism and Bilingual Education in the United States." *AmA* 87 (June 1985): 334–342.

Reviews four books published from 1980 to 1982 on bilingual language learning and use (mainly Spanish-English), providing an overview of research, practice, and politics.

3054. Tregidgo, P. S. "'I Wish I Was Dead.'" *ELTJ* 38 (January 1984): 48–50.

Analyzes the subjunctive, comparing variations of meaning.

3055. Trueba, Henry T., Luis C. Moll, Stephen Diaz, and Rosa Diaz. *Improving the Functional Writing of Bilingual Secondary School Students.* Urbana, Ill.: ERIC/RCS, 1984. ERIC ED 240 862 [220 pages]

Describes a junior high school writing curriculum.

3056. Verts, Lita J. "Integration of ESL/LEP Students into the University." Paper given at the

TESOL Meeting, Corvallis, Oreg., July 1984. ERIC ED 248 725 [24 pages]

Describes a program of placement testing, advising, personal counseling, tutoring, and developmental coursework to ease ESL students into the university.

3057. Wallace, Ray B. "English for Specific Purposes in ESL Undergraduate Composition Classes: Rationale." *DAI* 46 (November 1985): 1218A.

A modified English for Specific Purposes course "was found to be an effective way of preparing students for their future academic and career needs."

3058. Wilcoxson, Barbara Marie. "Some Common Concerns of Reading and Writing for ESL Students." *ArEB* 27 (Winter 1985): 125–128.

Urges teaching reading and writing to ESL students as complementary skills.

3059. Wyatt, David H. *Computers and ESL.* Language in Education: Theory and Practice, no. 57. Washington, D.C.: ERIC Clearinghouse on Foreign Languages and Linguistics, 1984. ERIC ED 246 694 [129 pages]

Reviews computer applications in ESL instruction. Includes sections on writing.

See also 6, 75, 149, 344, 411, 492, 493, 497, 498, 499, 527, 565, 585, 603, 626, 757, 769, 797, 841, 847, 856, 870, 892, 902, 912, 920, 947, 964, 993, 1000, 1010, 1015, 1016, 1042, 1055, 1065, 1074, 1087, 1371, 1471, 2389, 2392, 2407, 2435, 2457, 2813, 3079, 3087, 3672, 3680, 3694, 3741, 3777, 3801, 3814, 3824

RESEARCH AND STUDY SKILLS

3060. Anderson, Nina L. "Say What?" *ExEx* 30 (Fall 1984): 29–30.

Uses vocabulary from popular television shows to teach vocabulary development to community college students.

3061. Andrews, Katherine A. "Using the Library for Individual Research." *IE* 9 (Winter 1985): 45–47.

Shows the similarity of teaching research then and now. [Reprinted from *EJ* 28(1939):378–382.]

3062. Ashley, Leonard R. N. "Upscale Synonyms." *WWays* 17 (August 1984): 177.

Presents a synonym quiz of 50 words.

3063. Benson, Barbara. "Research Papers: How to Help Students Learn the Process and Love the Product." *CET* (1984): 18–22.

Describes a three-week unit that features the process of discovery, problem solving, and the production of a finished research paper. Suggested topics included.

3064. Blackmon, Margaret Van Deman. "Real Research for Student Writers." *ExEx* 29 (Spring 1984): 31–33.

Presents an activity for teaching research skills, including Macrorie's "I-Searching," skimming and notetaking, and interviewing.

3065. Bryant, JoAnne Raiford, and Howard I. Berrent. "Open to Suggestion: OH RATS—A Notetaking Technique." *JR* 27 (March 1984): 548–50.

Acronym describes a notetaking system: take Overview, study Headings, Read to find information, Answer heading questions, self-Test, and Study. Imitates SQ3R method.

3066. Carino, Peter A. "The College Research Paper *Vs.* the High School Research Paper." *IE* 7 (Winter 1984): 6–11.

Encourages instructors to teach students to develop college research paper topics from their high school papers to support research as a continuing process of discovery.

3067. Carroll, Joyce Armstrong. "TV and Term Papers." *EJ* 74 (October 1985): 85–86.

Discusses using investigative and informational television shows to help students choose research topics, conduct research, and write term papers.

3068. Christenson, Eric H. "A Searching Question." *EJ* 74 (February 1985): 81.

Secondary students' informally surveyed teachers, professors, psychologists, authors, students, and curriculum specialists to determine when students should write research papers.

3069. Crowley, Ann V. "Using Journal Writing to Monitor Study Skills." *JDEd* 7 (Spring 1984): 21–23.

Describes procedures for applying journal writing to learning study skills. Discusses some advantages of using journals for self-monitoring and communication.

3070. Dazey, Mary Ann. "Teaching the Tools of Research." *CET* (1984): 12–17.

Describes using minipapers to teach research skills and writing.

3071. Downing, John, and Bert Morris. "An Australian Program for Improving High School Reading in Content Areas." *JR* 28 (December 1984): 237–243.

Describes a four-stage method for using writing to improve reading. Students identify organizational patterns, consider the implications of materials, extract relevant information, and "translate ideas for other readers."

3072. Frager, Alan M. "An 'Intelligence' Approach to Vocabulary Teaching." *JR* 28 (November 1984): 160–164.

Advocates using a combination of overt (structured overview, word lists, vocabulary cards) and covert (modeling enjoyment and use of unusual words, etymologies) methods for teaching vocabulary.

3073. Garner, Ruth. "Rules for Summarizing Texts: Is Classroom Instruction Being Provided?" *JEdR* 77 (May–June 1984): 304–308.

Finds that teachers did not give students adequate instructions in text-summarizing techniques.

3074. Grosskurth, Phyllis. "Search and Psyche: The Writing of Biography." *ESC* 11 (June 1985): 145–156.

Narrates her development as a biographer and discusses the "attitude" a biographer must maintain in researching and writing.

3075. Henrick, John. "Limits of the Human Life Cycle." *WWays* 17 (August 1984): 175.

Discusses the reconditioning of familiar phrases such as "From Birth to Death," using "metonymy, metaphor, alliteration, and rhyme."

3076. Hobbs, Richard. "'Wordo.'" *ExEx* 30 (Spring 1985): 25.

Provides a vocabulary development game to teach definitions of previously studied words.

3077. Hodges, Richard E. "Vocabulary: A Digest of Current Theory and Practice." *IlEB* 72 (Fall 1984): 30–33.

Summarizes the educational implications of vocabulary studies on "listening, speaking, reading, and writing." Suggests resources for further reading.

3078. *Interdisciplinary Studies Program. Teacher's Guide: Part IV.* Orlando: Valencia Community College, 1984. ERIC ED 245 772 [119 pages]

A teacher's guide to a content-centered course on the college research paper. Funded by National Endowment for the Humanities.

3079. Johnston, Sue Ann. "An Approach to the Teaching of Academic Writing." *ELTJ* 39 (October 1985): 248–252.

Describes a research paper project in China using alternate research sources, particularly interviews, to compensate for scanty library materials.

3080. Johnston, Sue Ann. "From Shakespeare to the Nuts and Bolts of Writing." *EQ* 16 (Winter): 26–28.

Suggests that students design their own formal reports.

3081. Kiewra, Kenneth A. "Acquiring Effective Notetaking Skills: An Alternative to Professional Notetaking." *JR* 27 (January 1984): 299–302.

Reviews research on notetaking. Concludes that students should attend class to understand content, take many notes, summarize, revise, and review all materials, including notes.

3082. Knight, Cynthia. "Come Wade, Dear Maid." *WWays* 17 (May 1984): 75.

Uses post office abbreviations for states to create a dialogue.

3083. Kollmeier, Harold H., and Kathleen Henderson Staudt. *Composition Students On-Line: Data-Base Searching in the Undergraduate Research Paper Course.* Drexel University Microcomputer Working Paper, no. 94-F2. Philadelphia: Dexel University, 1984. ERIC ED 254 220 [17 pages]

Reports that on-line data-base searches help students think more clearly, while allowing instructors to monitor their progress.

3084. Lehr, Fran. "Promoting Vocabulary Development." *JR* 27 (April 1984): 656–658.

Summarizes techniques for building vocabulary: connecting words with direct experience, using categorization to connect new words with known words, and using humor to foster memorization.

3085. McCartney, Robert. "The Cumulative Research Paper." *TETYC* 12 (October 1985): 198–202.

Describes a "cumulative research paper" assignment that the author developed. Five library assignments are evaluated separately and are then combined for the final paper, which is evaluated.

3086. McClearey, Kevin. "Hanging Around Words." *TETYC* 12 (December 1985): 281–286.

Students use a "keywords" journal to identify and study personally significant words.

3087. McDonough, Steven. "Academic Writing Practice." *ELTJ* 39 (October 1985): 244–247.

Discusses aids to helping postgraduate students write and answer their own essay exams. Describes methods of sequencing, grading, and assessing the task.

3088. Moran, Michael G. "Lockean Epistemology and the Freshman Research Paper." *FEN* 13 (Winter 1984): 17–19.

Probabilistic reasoning provides a framework for research paper courses that emphasize direct experience and involvement rather than generalized curiosity.

3089. Morton, Mike, and A. Ross Eckler. "Reaganagrams." *WWays* 17 (May 1984): 101–105.

llustrates how to form anagrams from Ronald Reagan's name.

3090. Phillips, Louis. "The Apple-Sauce Chronicles." *WWays* 17 (May 1984): 106–109.

Presents word play humor, knock-knock jokes, and inferences based on "some sort of weirdly logical question."

3091. Ratman, Nancy, and David Taylor. "Writing the OED in Poetry Class: A Sneak Attack." *EngR* 36 (1985): 9–11.

Advocates creating assignments in which students research layers of a word's meaning.

3092. Richgels, Donald J., and Ruth Hansen. "Gloss: Helping Students Apply Both Skills and Strategies in Reading Content Texts." *JR* 27 (January 1984): 312–317.

Glosses, or teacher's marginal questions, encourage students to read actively and to integrate new information about processes and content with the familiar.

3093. Richgels, Donald J., and John A. Mateja. "Gloss II: Integrating Content and Process for Independence." *JR* 27 (February 1984): 424–431.

Describes how teachers can model self-directed glossing (specialized marginal notations) in stages, including demonstration gloss, development gloss, internalization, and fading.

3094. Rogal, Samuel J. "The Library Research Paper: For the Term, during the Term, and throughout the Term." *ArEB* 27 (Fall 1984): 40–45.

Describes an approach to the research paper that asks students to assemble it over the course of the term.

3095. Simpson, Michele, and Sherrie L. Nist. "PLAE: A Model for Planning Successful Independent Learning." *JR* 28 (December 1984): 218–223.

Describes a four-stage cognitive method for improving students' studying. Emphasizes preplanning for tests, listing relevant techniques, activating the plan, and evaluating the results.

3096. Spring, Karen Strom. "Reading Faster: An Aid to Comprehension." *JDEd* 7 (Winter 1984): 22–23.

Recommends teaching reading to increase speed as a powerful reading aid and motivator. Notes three misconceptions about reading and several speed-reading techniques.

3097. Stiffler, Randall. "Writing within Limits, Writing without *N*'s." *ExEx* 30 (Spring 1985): 28–29.

Presents an exercise for writing a paper without using the letter encourages vocabulary development.

3098. Vargas, Marjorie Fink. "Developing an Immunity to Sophomoric Plagiarism: Notetaking Skills." *EJ* 74 (February 1985): 42–44.

Explores four types of notetaking to reduce plagiarism and to develop study skills.

3099. Viera, Carroll. "Teaching the Research Paper." *CET* (1984): 7–11.

Describes a laboratory process for enabling inexperienced students to write "tightly focused, impeccably documented papers, which are interesting, coherent, and worth reading."

See also 1256, 1300, 1354, 1722, 1739, 1755, 2009, 2086, 2128, 2247, 2272, 2382, 2434, 2452, 2506, 2538, 2554, 2647, 2682, 2706, 2741, 2809, 2821, 2852, 2885, 2919, 2927, 2982, 3003, 3436, 3796

OTHER

3100. Allred, Ruel A. *Spelling Trends, Content, and Methods.* Washington, D.C.: NEA, 1984. 32 pages

Reviews research on spelling and its instruction.

3101. Appleman, Philip. "200 Million Poets." *CE* 46 (September 1984): 455–457.

MFA programs are burgeoning, educating more poets than can be published and recognized. Being a poet, however, is one way of getting "rich quick."

3102. Betts, Doris. "Undergraduate Creative Writing Courses." *BADE* 79 (Winter 1984): 34–36.

Discusses the courses' rise in popularity and different ways to teach them. Analyzes the expectations of students and teachers.

3103. Bogart, Quentin J., and Sue I. Murphey. "Articulation in a Changing Higher Education Environment." *CCR* 13 (Fall 1985): 17–22.

Reviews articulation efforts between community colleges and the baccalaureate institutions to which their students transfer. Recommends uniform validation for the Associate of Arts degree curriculum.

3104. Brooks, Charlotte K. "Verbal Giftedness in the Minority Student: A NEWT Questions a SOT." *ET* 15 (Winter 1984): 13–20.

A dialogue between a new English teacher and a seasoned English teacher. The seasoned teacher presents techniques for teaching gifted students and urges viewing students as individuals.

3105. Carter, John Marshall. "Writing Games in the Bayeaux Tapestry." *EJ* 74 (November 1985): 31–34.

Gives examples of writing assignments designed for different disciplines and focusing on the Bayeaux Tapestry.

3106. Clark, Beverly L. *Talking about Writing: A Guide for Tutor and Teacher Conferences.* Ann Arbor, Mich.: University of Michigan Press, 1985. 240 pages

Provides suggestions for those who work with high school and college students seeking to improve writing skills in tutorial and conference settings.

3107. Clark, Roger, and Irvin Y. Hashimoto. "A Spelling Program for College Students." *TETYC* 11 (October 1984): 34–38.

Describes a spelling project in which students test themselves, analyze mistakes, and create individual reference dictionaries. The program is suitable for computer-assisted instruction.

3108. Donelson, Ken. "Some Worries about English for the Verbally Gifted." *ET* 15 (Winter 1984): 5–6.

Examines English education for the verbally gifted, argues that education should emphasize similarities and differences among students, and concludes that verbally gifted students may be difficult to teach and to control.

3109. DuBois, Barbara. "Lapsed Logic." *TETYC* 11 (December 1984): 53–55.

A humorous essay with examples of language misused in student papers and in popular media.

3110. Englert, Carol S., Elfrieda H. Hiebert, and Sharon R. Stewart. "Spelling Unfamiliar Words by an Analogy Strategy." *JSEd* 19 (Fall 1985): 291–306.

Reports on a study that investigated the effects of instructing mildly handicapped students in a strategy for spelling new words by using spelling patterns from known words.

3111. Ersek, Allen J. "The Effectiveness of Spelling Activities on First- and Second-Grade Students' Spelling Achievement." *DAI* 45 (July 1984): 79A.

A 12-week study reveals slight support favoring spelling activities for short-term achievement but no support favoring these activities for long-term achievements.

3112. Fortune, Ron, and Janice Neuleib. "Integrating Secondary and Postsecondary Writing Instruction through Collaborative Teaching." Paper presented at the CCCC Convention, New York, March 1984. ERIC ED 245 229 [30 pages]

Describes a National Endowment for the Humanities Project.

3113. Glanschow, Lenore. "Diagnosing and Remediating Writing Problems of Gifted Students with Language Learning Disabilities." *JEdG* 9 (Fall 1985): 25–45.

Three case studies point to an individualized approach to meet specific developmental, remedial, and adaptive needs of learning-disabled writers.

3114. Harada, Janet Louise. "Peer Tutoring as a Social Process." *DAI* 44 (March 1984): 2897A.

A case study of eight tutoring dyads revealed four distinct developmental phases for successful tutors.

3115. Hermann, Beth Ann. "Reading Instruction: Dealing with Classroom Realities." *CCR* 13 (Summer 1985): 28–34.

Reports on a study examining reading instruction in one community college. Concludes that reading instruction and teacher training should be improved.

3116. Hudson, Carolyn K. "Effects of Proximal Goals and Feedback on Spelling Achievement and Self-Efficacy in Learning Disabled Children." *DAI* 45 (January 1985): 2040A.

Short-term goals and progress feedback were speculated to have positive effects on spelling achievement and perceptions of self-efficacy for 40 eight- to 11-year-old children with learning disabilities.

3117. Hull, A. M. "New Classics for Old." *IE* 9 (Fall 1985): 17–20.

Demonstrates the recurring call for using modern as well as classical literature. [Reprinted from *EJ* 6 (1917): 542–550.]

3118. Jeffree, Dorothy, and Margaret Skeffington. *Reading Is for Everyone: A Guide for Parents and Teachers of Exceptional Children.* Englewood Cliffs, N.J.: Prentice-Hall, 1985. 154 pages

A guide for parents and teachers to help handicapped and developmentally disabled children and those with language difficulties learn to read. Includes advice on teaching levels and encouraging an interest in books.

3119. Keller, Christa. "Differentiated Reading Instruction for the Gifted." *ELAB* 25 (Spring 1984): 13–15.

Suggests modifying curricular materials and types of instruction to respond to the special learning characteristics of the gifted.

3120. Kinlock, A. M., W. Davey, F. Cogswell, R. Geierin, D. Rowan, and K. Pader. "A Hot Line for Grammar." *EQ* 18 (Summer 1985): 75–81.

Explains how to establish a campus "hot line" for questions about grammar and mechanics.

3121. Kuykendall, Carol. "Language: A Thinking Experience." *Statement* 20 (May 1985): 14–21.

Addresses the new educational mandates to teach thinking and argues that thinking is a constructionist activity that makes meaning, with language as an instrument of thought.

3122. Lang, Charles J., and Jackie Ireland. "Oral History Center: A Model for Minority Student Instruction." *CCR* 12 (Winter 1984–85): 21–24.

Describes the development of the Oral History Center at West Los Angeles College and discusses its contribution to the instructional program and to minority students.

3123. Lehr, Fran. "ERIC/RCS Report: Help for the Verbally Gifted." *ET* 15 (Winter 1984): 7–12.

Gives possible reasons why gifted students are neglected, lists four areas of concentrated studies for these students, and suggests ways of organizing special instruction.

3124. Luvaas-Briggs, Linda. "Integrating Basic Skills with College Content Instruction." *JDEd* 7 (Winter 1984): 6–9, 31.

Explains a program for high-risk students at Sacramento City College that integrates reading, writing, study skills, and content instruction in the classroom.

3125. McPherson, Elisabeth. "Spelling Revisited." *SLATE* 9 (January 1984).

Cautions against overemphasizing spelling, summarizes current classroom practice, and provides 10 teaching suggestions. Includes bibliography.

3126. Newlin, Peter. "Creating Creative Writing in a Traditional English Department." *BADE* 78 (Summer 1984): 24–27.

Traces the development of graduate creative writing programs, identifies present problems, and argues for a reappraisal.

3127. Nickerson, Raymond S., David N. Perkins, and Edward E. Smith. *The Teaching of Thinking.* Hillside, N.J.: Lawrence Erlbaum, 1985. 400 pages

Attempts to identify concepts, courses, and experiences likely to enhance intellectual development. Offers teaching strategies to "ease the transition from concrete to formal thinking."

3128. Paulenich, Fred F., and Barbara Singleton. "Reading at Home." *ELAB* 25 (Spring 1984): 15–17.

Offers suggestions to parents and teachers about how to foster reading.

3129. Plattor, Emma. "Listening and Speaking: Research Implications for Curriculum Development." *EQ* 17 (Spring 1984): 3–20.

Reviews research to suggest steps for developing a curriculum in listening and speaking.

3130. Powell, Philip M. "Teaching Writing to the Verbally Gifted." *ET* 15 (Winter 1984): 22–30.

Examines good writing, creativity as intelligence, and teaching writing to verbally gifted students.

3131. Roark, Dennis. "Integrating General Education with Vocational Studies." *CCR* 12 (Winter 1984–85): 30–37.

Reviews the rationale for integrating general education with vocational courses in community colleges, cites examples of successful programs, and suggests strategies for program development.

3132. Schmidt, John L. "The Effects of Four Generalized Conditions on Learning Disabled Adolescents' Written Language Performance in the Regular Classroom." *DAI* 45 (November 1984): 1367A.

Findings indicate that acquiring writing strategies did not ensure that students would transfer skills to the regular classroom.

3133. Suhor, Charles. "Thinking Skills." *SLATE* 9 (March 1984).

Summarizes issues and research and presents eight guidelines for teaching thinking skills. Includes bibliography.

3134. Taylor, David. "Identifying and Helping the Dyslexic Writer." *JDEd* 9 (1985): 8–11, 31.

Discusses the definition, identification, and treatment of dyslexia. Suggests ways to help the dyslexic writer. Provides a bibliography of tests and materials.

3135. Theisz, R. D. "Issues in Teaching Composition to Native American Students." *EN* 6 (1984): 33–44.

Discusses problems to be overcome in teaching writing to native Americans.

See also 769, 913, 1268, 1269, 1284, 1296, 1407, 1694, 1808, 2166, 2701

5

TEXTBOOKS AND INSTRUCTIONAL MATERIALS

GENERAL DISCUSSIONS

3136. Armbruster, Bonnie B., and Thomas H. Anderson. *Producing "Considerate" Expository Text; or, Easy Reading Is Damned Hard Writing.* Urbana, Ill.: University of Illinois Center for the Study of Reading, 1984. ERIC ED 240 510 [66 pages]

Describes an approach to constructing textbook materials.

3137. Chrismore, Avon. *The Rhetoric of Social Studies Textbooks: Metadiscourse.* Urbana, Ill.: ERIC/RCS and NCTE, 1983. ERIC ED 239 226 [35 pages]

Compares nine social studies textbooks and nine nontextbooks representing elementary through college levels.

3138. de Beaugrande, Robert. "Composition Textbooks: Ethnography and Proposal." *WC* 2 (October 1985): 391–413.

Suggests criteria for producing 22 textbooks that reflect recent insights on language and discourse.

3139. DeVito, Joseph A. *The Communication Handbook.* New York: Harper & Row, 1985. 337 pages

Contains over 2000 brief definitions and more than 100 essays pertaining to practical communication skills. An alphabetical dictionary lists communication terms.

3140. Edwards, Bruce L., Jr. "Deconstructing Composition Textbooks." Paper presented at the CCCC Convention, New York, March 1984. ERIC ED 243 130 [10 pages]

Criticizes college rhetoric texts for giving poor advice to writers.

3141. Faery, Rebecca Blevins. "Writing for Teachers." *EJ* 74 (April 1985): 80–82.

Reviews 18 books published in 1983 and 1984 that focus on the teaching of writing.

3142. Gere, Anne Ruggles. "Teaching Writing Teachers." *CE* 47 (January 1985): 58–65.

Surveys several books on composition instruction, focusing on Graves' *Rhetoric and Composition,* Second Revised Edition (1984).

3143. Goodman, Kenneth S., and Lois Bridges Bird. "On the Wording of Texts: A Study of Intra-Text Word Frequency." *RTE* 18 (May 1984): 119–145.

Examines word choice and frequency in six textbooks. Questions teachers' use of decontextualized vocabulary studies and authors' and editors' use of artificially controlled vocabulary.

3144. Grambs, David. *Words about Words: A Dictionary of 2000 Words—Old, New, and Surprising—for the Styles, Devices, Defects, and Oddities of the Craft of Prose Writing*. New York: Random House, 1984. 322 pages

A guide to enlivening prose through the use of more varied vocabulary. Intended to entertain as well as instruct.

3145. Phelan, James. "Review: Pluralism and Its Powers: Metapluralism and Its Problems." *CE* 46 (January 1984): 63–73.

Reviews Booth's *Critical Understanding: The Power and Limits of Pluralism* and discusses pluralism in general.

3146. Stillman, Peter. "Books That Don't Stack Up." *IaEB* 33 (1984): 18–19.

Critiques the form and content of contemporary grammar books.

3147. Sullivan, Phil. "Throwing Away Textbooks." *UEJ* (1985): 31–33.

Argues against using textbooks in a writing class. Instead, teachers should find their own voices in writing and teaching.

3148. Weinburg, Francine. "Is There a Missing Link?" Paper presented at the CCCC Convention, New York, March 1984. ERIC ED 243 143 [19 pages]

Discusses the time lag between developments in composition research and theory and their application in textbooks and instructional materials.

See also 1797, 1836

ELEMENTARY MATERIALS (K–8)

3149. Barnes, Donald L., and Arlene Burgdorf. *Reading and Critical Thinking*. New York: Educational Design, 1985. 96 pages

Presents 40 reading selections that isolate and teach 10 critical thinking skills. Each selection is followed by exercises and questions on material covered. Includes teacher's guide and answer key.

3150. *Basic Drills in English Skills: Books One through Four*. San Diego: Harcourt Brace Jovanovich, 1984.

A series of four workbooks dealing with grammar, usage, and mechanics. Each comes in a workbook or a duplicating master form with an answer key; for grades three through six.

3151. Coon, George E., Barbara B. Cramer, H. Thompson Fillman, Ann Lefcourt, Jerome Martin, and Neil C. Thompson. *Heath English: Grades Seven and Eight*. Lexington, Mass.: Heath, 1984.

A grammar and composition series that also includes two resource units dealing with research and library skills. A teacher's edition and supplementary materials are available.

3152. Cox, Nancy, Barbara Pettegrew, and Robert McBaine. *Grammar and Composition, Books One, Two, and Three*. Columbus, Ohio: Merrill, 1984. 172 pages

Three workbooks for grades seven through nine. Each book includes 15 units providing practice and reinforcement in principles of grammar, usage, mechanics, composition, and diction through explanatory materials, exercises, and review lessons. Books contain identically titled general units covering increasingly complex mechanical and rhetorical concepts. Teachers' annotated edition includes mastery tests.

3153. *Developing Key Concepts in Composition*. Baldwin, N.Y.: Barnell Loft, 1985.

In softcover, this series for grades three through six is designed to incorporate all communication skills into the writing process.

3154. Donsky, Barbara V. "Trends in Written Composition Instruction in Elementary School Textbooks, 1900–1959." *DAI* 45 (December 1984): 1636A.

Concludes that textbooks provided accurate guides to educational trends, as influenced by changing times and preferences.

3155. *Follett Spelling Program*. Columbus, Ohio: Ginn, 1984.

Weekly units highlight one or two basic spelling principles and provide practice in dictionary, handwriting, proofreading, and language arts skills. Text, teacher's edition, and teacher's resource materials are available.

3156. *Ginn English Program*. Rev. ed. Columbus, Ohio: Ginn, 1986.

A process writing program emphasizing functional and creative writing. Practice units stress grammar, usage, and mechanics in rewriting. Text, teacher's edition and resource book, and supplementary materials are available.

3157. Granowski, Alvin, and John Dawkins. *Writing Sentences, Paragraphs, and Compositions.* Cleveland: Modern Curriculum Press, 1984.

Workbooks for grades two through six support a process approach to composition and give practice in prewriting, composing, editing, and revising. Designed to correlate with most basic language arts programs.

3158. Gray, Betty G., Nancy N. Ragno, and Marian Davis Toth. *Silver Burdett English K–8.* Morristown, N.J.: Silver Burdett, 1985.

A series of textbooks providing instruction in the writing process, grammar, usage, and mechanics at the sentence level. Teacher resource materials and student writing folders are also available.

3159. Kalupa, Nancy Elizabeth Pruitt. "The Making of a Chinese Citizen, Post-Mao: Political Socialization Content in Chinese Elementary Language Textbooks." *DAI* 45 (August 1984): 626A.

A content analysis of 10 elementary Chinese language readers, analyzing the political and cultural values presented since Mao's death.

3160. Kirby, Dan, and Carol Kuykendall. *Thinking through Language, Book 1.* Urbana, Ill.: NCTE, 1985. 114 pages

Developed to teach thinking through language skills. Has a nonverbal/holistic emphasis, is aimed at junior high and middle school students, and is designed for integration into the English curriculum. Units include experiencing the arts, exploring possibilities, investigating the issues, and probing the future. Teacher's guide available.

3161. Kuhlman, Yvonne, and Joyce Bartky. *Glencoe English, Grades 7–8.* Encino, Calif.: Glencoe, 1984.

A developmental program in composition, speech, and grammar, with step-by-step application of writing and grammar skills. Supplementary materials available.

3162. Littell, Joy, ed. *Basic Skills in English.* Evanston, Ill.: McDougal, Littell, 1985.

A composition and grammar series for students in grades seven and eight reading below grade level. Series contains, in addition to student editions, teacher's editions, practice books, duplicating masters, and diagnostic and mastery tests.

3163. Murphy, Lackamp, and Janeta Himes. *Success in Spelling.* 2d ed. River Forest, Ill.: Laidlaw, 1985.

Designed to help students in grades one through eight master basic vocabulary and develop word building skills. Applies spelling knowledge to functional and creative writing. Teacher's edition and activities masters available.

3164. *Persona: Books I and II.* Littleton, Mass.: Sundance, 1985.

Each book contains 88 activity sheets using poems, news clippings, anecdotes, questions, historical facts, or excerpts from plays and novels as a starting point for writing. Students must assume, in writing, the personalities of the characters in the readings. Book I is intended for grades 6 to 9; Book II, grades 9 through 12.

3165. Thoburn, Tina, Virginia Arnold, Ann Terry, Rita Schlatterbeck, and Donna Townsend. *Macmillan English K–8, Series E.* New York: Macmillan, 1984.

Designed to teach children to use language effectively in oral and written communication. Offers structured activities in grammar and related language skills as a foundation for effectively written sentences.

3166. Woodruff, G. Willard, George N. Moore, and Frank E. Ferguson. *Language Skills Series.* North Billerica, Mass.: Curriculum Associates, 1985.

For students in grades one through six. Each textbook covers sentences, paragraphing, study skills, capitalization and punctuation, and grammar and usage. A reference section includes word lists.

3167. *Write It Down: The Second "R."* Baldwin, N.Y.: Barnell Loft, 1985.

A softcover series for grades four through six that emphasizes the reading and writing connection. Guides students through the writing process with story starters, illustrations, prewriting questions, extensive revision techniques, and personal evaluation methods.

See also 32, 2014, 2047, 3174, 3183, 3184

SECONDARY MATERIALS (9-12)

3168. Addison, Alice A. "A Discourse Analysis of Secondary School Science Textbooks with a Comparison of Text Features and Reading Comprehension for Native and Nonnative English Speakers." *DAI* 44 (April 1984): 3045A.

Compares features of secondary school science textbooks and concludes that textbooks for vocational courses are not necessarily less complex than those for academic courses.

3169. *Building English Skills.* Evanston, Ill.: McDougal, Littell, 1985. 250 pages

A series that instructs students in the process of writing, other language skills, grammar, usage, and mechanics. A teacher's edition is provided as well as a skills practice book, tests, and duplication masters.

3170. *Composition and Grammar: Steps in the Writing Process.* The Laidlaw English Series. River Forest, Ill.: Laidlaw, 1985.

A series of composition textbooks that includes a grammar and usage handbook. Composition chapters stress process method, peer response, and holistic evaluation. Students' and teacher's editions.

3171. Duda, Phyllis, and Patrick Sebranek. *Basic English Revisited: A Study Skills and Writing Process Workbook.* Burlington, Vt.: Basic English Revisited, 1985. 156 pages

A workbook to accompany *Basic English Revisited* (5th ed., 1985). Includes exercises on adapting the writing process to a variety of writing assignments.

3172. *English Ninety-Three: Lessons in Basic Writing Skills.* River Forest, Ill.: Laidlaw, 1984.

A consumable text for drill in writing and language skills. Includes student's and teacher's editions.

3173. Hughes, Donna M., Louise K. Lowry, Richard W. Clark, Yvonne Kuhlman, and Joyce Bartky. *Glencoe English, Grades Nine through Twelve.* 2d ed. Encino, Calif.: Glencoe, 1985.

A series of textbooks, each organized in six major sections: composition, composition handbook, speech, speech handbook, grammar handbook, and challenge materials. Composition chapters emphasize process. Supplementary materials available.

3174. Kelly, Patricia P. "Teaching the Process of Writing." *EJ* 73 (November 1984): 94-95.

Reviews four series of textbooks for teaching composition, language skills, and literature interpretation.

3175. Kelly, Patricia P. "Writing Texts for Special Uses." *EJ* 74 (September 1985): 80-81.

Reviews of four textbooks helpful to secondary students.

3176. O'Hare, Frank. *Sentencecraft.* Columbus, Ohio: Ginn, 1985.

A sentence-combining program using 18 sentence-set lessons to practice syntactic structures. Eight writing workshop lessons prompt original student compositions. Teacher's guide available.

3177. Perrin, Robert. "Diary of a Mad Textbook Reviewer; or, What I Learned about High School Composition Texts." *EJ* 73 (September 1984): 48-51.

An experienced reviewer bemoans the emphasis on grammar and mechanics and insufficient attention to the composing process in composition textbooks.

3178. Sebranek, Patrick. *Basic English Revisited: A Practical Writing Skills Workbook.* Burlington, Vt.: Basic English Revisited, 1984. 172 pages

A workbook to accompany *Basic English Revisited* (5th ed., 1985). Provides writing exercises and exercises on punctuation, sentence correctness, and sentence combining.

3179. Sebranek, Patrick, and Verne Meyer. *Basic English Revisited: A Student Handbook.* 5th ed. Burlington, Vt.: Basic English Revisited, 1985. 218 pages

A grammar handbook that includes sections on the writing process, the research paper, library skills, speech skills, the use of maps, and study skills.

3180. Stanford, Barbara Dodds, and Gene Stanford. *Thinking through Language, Book Two.* Urbana, Ill.: NCTE, 1985. 104 pages

Developed to teach thinking through language skills. Intended for high school students, discusses distinctions between linear and holistic thinking processes. Can be integrated into the English curriculum. Units include perception, relationships and connections, problem solving, and the creative imagination. Teacher's guide available.

3181. Suhor, Charles. "English Textbooks Based on Research and Theory: A Possible Dream." *CEJ* 15 (Spring 1984): 24–27, ERIC ED 249 530.

Applauds the National Council of Teachers of English's Student Guide Series (1985) as supplemental material for classroom use that is based on current theory and research.

3182. Vanderlaan, Eunice. *Basic English Revisited: A Basic Grammar and Writing Workbook.* Burlington, Vt.: Basic English Revisited, 1984. 140 pages

A grammar workbook to accompany *Basic English Revisited* (5th ed., 1985). Includes exercises on grammar, usage, and mechanics.

3183. Winterowd, W. Ross, and Patricia Y. Murray. *English: Writing and Skills.* San Diego: Coronado, 1985.

A series of textbooks for students in grades 7 through 12. Approaches writing as process, provides literary models for reinforcement, offers practice with sentence combining, and combines traditional, structural, and transformational approaches to grammar.

3184. *Words and Sentences.* Columbus, Ohio: Ginn, 1984.

A cumulative program for students in grades 7 through 12. Reinforces and reviews skills in grammar, usage, mechanics, composition, and word study. Supplementary materials are available.

See also 1, 1756, 2240, 3164

HIGHER EDUCATION MATERIALS

DEVELOPMENTAL WRITING

Handbooks

3185. Dornan, Edward A., and Charles W. Dawe. *The Brief English Handbook.* Boston: Little, Brown, 1984. 400 pages

A reference guide that provides an overview of grammar, coverage of sentence clarity and variety, and material on diction and logic. Includes a major section on composition.

3186. Shaw, Henry. *Errors in English and Ways to Correct Them.* 3d ed. New York: Harper & Row, 1985. 272 pages

A reference book that suggests ways to correct errors in sentences, usage, spelling, punctuation, and grammar.

3187. Sullivan, Sally. *Helpbook for Student Writers.* New York: Random House, 1984. 272 pages

Uses an inductive approach to help students correct usage, punctuation, and diction errors. Includes at least two freewriting assignments per section and three chapters on improving style.

See also 3673

Rhetorics

3188. Agee, Ann, and Gary Kline. *The Basic Writer's Book.* 2d ed. Englewood Cliffs, N.J.: Prentice-Hall, 1985. 448 pages

Presents basic sentence and paragraph strategies in a rhetorical context. Includes a special study of verbs.

3189. Bander, Robert G. *Writing: Basics and Beyond.* Glenview, Ill.: Scott, Foresman, 1985. 307 pages

Four-part writing text uses a skills approach to grammar, sentence writing, and paragraph construction. Concept-and-practice format provides controlled and freewriting practice.

3190. Bator, Robert. *Shared Prose.* New York: Holt, Rinehart and Winston, 1985. 335 pages

A rhetoric and workbook that presents a six-stage approach to the writing process. Use of mechanics provides formulas for writing.

3191. Betts, Irene D., and Carol C. Howell. *The Writing Plan.* Englewood Cliffs, N.J.: Prentice-Hall, 1984. 288 pages

A partly self-instructional basic writing program based on mastery skills. Provides lessons in the process of writing paragraphs, essays in rhetorical modes, and research papers.

3192. Blum, Jack, Carolyn Brinkman, Elizabeth Hoffman, and David Peck. *A Guide to the Whole Writing Process.* Boston: Houghton Mifflin, 1984. 262 pages

Presents the writing process from first ideas to final editing. Emphasizes the recursive nature of writing. Students keep journals recording ideas and experiences, and use techniques, strategies, and concepts in the text to develop their ideas into structured papers.

3193. Brown, Daniel J., and William E. Burnette. *Connections: A Rhetoric/Short Prose Reader.* Boston: Houghton Mifflin, 1984. 339 pages

A rhetoric and reader that provides instruction and practice in paragraph and essay writing. Emphasizes invention and thinking skills but gives detailed treatment to the rhetorical modes of informing, explaining, and persuading. Includes 34 readings, grouped by modes.

3194. Collins, Carmen. *Read, Reflect, Write: The Elements of Flexible Reading, Fluent Writing, Independent Learning.* Englewood Cliffs, N.J.: Prentice-Hall, 1984. 159 pages

A brief textbook designed to develop metacognitive strategies by integrating reading, analytical thinking, and writing skills. Presents these skills as interactive learning strategies.

3195. Fawcett, Susan, and Alvin Sandberg. *Evergreen: A Guide to Writing.* 2d ed. Boston: Houghton Mifflin, 1984. 414 pages

A guide for writing paragraphs, short essays, and essay examinations. Extensive unit on grammar with practice to reinforce and build upon each skill presented.

3196. Gorrell, Donna. *Bridges.* Boston: Little, Brown, 1985. 300 pages

Model readings that exhibit observable structures. Patterning and copying exercises form a "bridge" between readings and writing assignments.

3197. Guilford, Charles. *Beginning College Writing.* Boston: Little, Brown, 1985. 300 pages

A process-oriented rhetoric that takes students through sequenced stages. Analyzes grammatical and mechanical errors in the context of writing. Covers writing/thinking relationships.

3198. Kantorowitz, Thelma D., and Catherine R. Ott. *Effective Writing for the Business World.* Boston: Little, Brown, 1984. 268 pages

Emphasizes practical rather than theoretical knowledge of effective communication in the business world. Nine chapters on letter and memo writing. Includes examples, exercises, and a checklist of points covered in each chapter.

3199. Langan, John. *College Writing Skills with Readings.* New York: McGraw-Hill, 1984. 448 pages

A rhetoric and reader emphasizing the five-paragraph essay, sentence construction, and principles of unity, support, and coherence.

3200. Lorch, Sue. *Basic Writing: A Practical Approach.* 2d ed. Boston: Little, Brown, 1984. 384 pages

Presents the writing process in three stages: generating material, shaping for the reader, and revising and editing. Discusses presenting a supported argument to a specific audience and includes a chapter on revising.

3201. Lyons, Chopeta. *Discover Writing: A Rhetoric/Workbook for the Beginning Writer.* Englewood Cliffs, N.J.: Prentice-Hall, 1984. 268 pages

Designed to help students discover their own writing processes through practice in drafting, revising, editing, and proofreading. Presents classic patterns and addresses grammar problems.

3202. McKoski, Martin M., and Lynne C. Hahn. *The Developing Writer: A Guide to Basic Skills.* 2d ed. Glenview, Ill.: Scott, Foresman, 1984. 336 pages

Uses a process approach to sentences, paragraphs, and brief essays. Edition includes a new chapter on the brief essay and increased coverage of topic sentences.

3203. Meyers, Alan. *Writing with Confidence.* 2d ed. Glenview, Ill.: Scott, Foresman, 1984. 336 pages

Fifteen chapters feature grammatical discussions and exercises that begin with writing complete sentences and end with writing paragraphs. Chapters 10 through 14 are designed to help nonnative English speakers.

3204. Nordquist, Richard. *Writing Exercises: Building, Combining, and Revising.* New York: Macmillan, 1985. 367 pages

Integrates sentence combining with examples of student and professional essays. Treats syntactic strategies together with rhetorical strategies. Instructor's manual.

3205. Parks, A. Franklin, James A. Levernier, and Ida Masters Hollowell. *Structuring Paragraphs: A Guide to Effective Writing.* 2d ed. New York: St. Martin's Press, 1985. 224 pages

Presents a structured approach to planning, organizing, writing, and revising paragraphs and short essays. Also treats sentence combining, essay questions, and several methods of development. Instructor's manual.

3206. Sharpe, Pamela J. *Talking with Americans: Conversation and Friendship Strategies for*

Learners of English. Boston: Little, Brown, 1984. 204 pages

Designed to encourage communicative competence through sociolinguistic activities. Readings on interpersonal relationships. Writing exercises include summary writing, list making, and journal writing.

3207. Sieben, J. Kenneth, and Lillian Small Anthony. *Composition Five: Skills for Writing*. 2d ed. Glenview, Ill.: Scott, Foresman, 1985. 446 pages

This edition presents five skills in each chapter — reading, writing, grammar, mechanics, and spelling/vocabulary — by asking students to read and analyze essays from popular magazines.

3208. Stillman, Peter. *Writing Your Way*. Upper Montclair, N.J.: Boynton/Cook, 1984. 158 pages

Twenty-six chapters emphasize self-initiated writing rather than skills, drills, steps, or stages.

3209. Sullivan, Kathleen E. *Paragraph Practice*. 5th ed. New York: Macmillan, 1984. 220 pages

The first half of the book treats topic sentences and paragraphs; the second half, thesis sentences and short compositions. Edition presents new chapters on coherence and continuity, new models on updated topics, and expanded rhetorical material.

3210. Tucker, Amy, and Jacqueline Costello. *The Random House Writing Course for ESL Students*. New York: Random House, 1984. 452 pages

Designed to prepare ESL students for freshman composition. Uses a process approach to discuss rhetorical strategies, reading skills, and grammar.

3211. Tyner, Thomas E. *Writing Voyage: An Integrated Process Approach to Basic Composition*. Belmont, Calif.: Wadsworth, 1985. 380 pages

Five units move students through the stages of writing. Units contain progressive assignments with a four-part structure: beginnings, revisions, final corrections, and a summary section with readings.

3212. Webb, Suzanne S. "A Plea for More Comprehensive Remedial Textbooks." *ET* 16 (1984): 11–15.

Urges changes in remedial textbooks, which should include instruction in reading, invention, drafting, revision, aims of discourse, and surface features.

3213. Webb, Suzanne S., and William E. Tanner. *A Writer's Plan*. San Diego: Harcourt Brace Jovanovich, 1985. 256 pages

A structured composition textbook that emphasizes writing instruction rather than mechanical corrections. A common organizational format in all eight chapters focus on instruction and practice in reading and writing.

Readers

3214. Barnwell, William H., and Julie Price. *Reflections: A Thematic Reader*. Boston: Houghton Mifflin, 1985. 489 pages

A thematic reader offering 33 selections with questions, vocabulary, and writing assignments. "Writing Notes" treat rhetorical modes, audience, and writing summaries. Appendixes cover the library, grammar, and mechanics.

3215. Conlin, Mary Lou. *Patterns Plus: A Short Prose Reader with Argumentation*. Boston: Houghton Mifflin, 1984. 409 pages

A rhetorically organized reader covering traditional rhetorical modes, including argumentation and persuasion. Contains professional and student paragraphs and short essay selection.

3216. Donald, Robert B., Betty R. Morrow, Lillian G. Wargetz, and Kathleen Werner. *Models for Clear Writing*. Englewood Cliffs, N.J.: Prentice-Hall, 1984. 400 pages

Student and professional essays illustrate each rhetorical pattern and the structure of expository prose. Provides an overview of the writing process for each pattern. Includes questions on technique and content and sections on reading, writing, and vocabulary.

3217. Field, John P., and Robert H. Weiss. *Cases for Composition*. 2d ed. Boston: Little, Brown, 1984. 352 pages

Presents a case approach to teaching writing skills. Fifty-three cases focus on audience, problem solving, and persuasion. Three new introductory chapters on the techniques of case instruction.

3218. Gillespie, Sheena, and Linda Stanley. *Someone Like Me: Images for Writing*. 5th ed. Boston: Little, Brown, 1984. 384 pages

A multigenre, thematically organized reader that progresses from personal and subjective experiential approaches to objective evaluation. Uses essay models to suggest writing techniques. This edition adds works by Angelou and Orwell, Hemingway and Cather, Rich and Levertov.

3219. Jacobus, Lee A. *Developing College Reading.* 3d ed. San Diego: Harcourt Brace Jonaovich, 1984. 352 pages

A collection of 36 selections meant to be typical of the kind of reading and levels of difficulty students will encounter in other college courses. Exercises measure recall of information, inferences, and vocabulary development.

3220. Moss, Andrew. "Readers for Basic Writing Courses: A Selective Survey." *TETYC* 12 (May 1985): 164–169.

Reviews nine readers classified as reader/rhetorics, readers for basic writing, and readers for basic writing and freshman composition courses.

3221. Rogers, Glenn C., and Judy R. Rogers. *Patterns and Themes: A Basic English Reader.* Belmont, Calif.: Wadsworth, 1985. 240 pages

Presents brief reading selections organized around nine theme topics. Examples range from short stories to popular journalism to student essays.

3222. Smith, Brenda. *Bridging the Gap: College Reading.* 2d ed. Glenview, Ill.: Scott, Foresman, 1985. 376 pages

Presents reading and study skills through textbook selections arranged according to three levels of readability. Edition includes new chapters on study skills and reading flexibility. Readings range from grade levels 7 to 14.

3223. Smith, Brenda. *Picking up the Pace: Efficient Reading for Life.* Glenview, Ill.: Scott, Foresman, 1984. 352 pages

Combines classroom practice with everyday reading by using Lifetime Reinforcement exercises. Students learn to match reading rate with reading purpose.

3224. Wassman, Rose, and Anne Paye. *A Reader's Handbook.* Glenview, Ill.: Scott, Foresman, 1985. 414 pages

Emphasizes continual reinforcement and integration of reading skills. Selections drawn from magazines, newspapers, textbooks, and literature are graded in complexity from grade 8 through 11.

See also 3448

Workbooks

3225. Adams, Royce W. *Think, Read, React, Plan, Write, Rewrite.* 4th ed. New York: Holt, Rinehart and Winston, 1985. 347 pages

Students develop expository writing skills by following six consecutive steps, beginning with thinking about a subject and proceeding through revision.

3226. Burhans, Clinton S., Michael J. Steinberg, and Jean Strandness. *The Writer's Way: A Process-to-Product Approach to Writing.* 7th ed. East Lansing, Mich.: Spring Publishing, 1985. 382 pages

A text/workbook for basic writing courses. Includes advice on journals and peer editing, practice exercises in mechanics and style, an editing-revising handbook, and academic and other writing assignments. Instructor's guide.

3227. Campbell, Dianna S., and Terry Ryan Meier. *Easy Writer: Basic Sentence Combining and Comprehensive Skills.* 2d ed. New York: Harper & Row, 1984. 267 pages

Six chapters provide exercises in sentence combining and revision techniques.

3228. Choy, Penelope, and James R. McCormick. *Basic Grammar and Usage.* 2d alternate ed. Englewood Cliffs, N.J.: Prentice-Hall, 1985. 256 pages

A grammar textbook that emphasizes problems like subject-verb agreement, pronoun usage, fragments, run-on sentences, and incorrect punctuation of clauses.

3229. Dick, John A. R. "Basic Writing Workbooks, Sentence Style Books, and Copybooks: A Review." *TETYC* 12 (May 1985): 140–153.

Mentions about 100 textbooks published since 1980 in the categories of workbooks of grammar and usage, sentence style books, and copybooks and others.

3230. Dunn-Rankin, Patricia. *Vocabulary.* 2d ed. New York: McGraw-Hill, 1984. 215 pages

Emphasizes vocabulary building by offering a variety of methods, including word recognition drills, the keyword method, and structural analysis. Organized around 130 words often found in college reading material.

3231. Eisenberg, Nora, and Harvey S. Wiener. *Stepping Stones: Skills for Basic Writers.* New York: Random House, 1984. 256 pages

Guides students from writing sentences to drafting and revising short essays. Extensive exercises, especially on verb forms and tenses.

3232. Emery, Donald W., John M. Kierzek, and Peter Lindblom. *English Fundamentals, Form B.* 8th ed. New York: Macmillan, 1985. 333 pages

A basic writing skills workbook that treats principles of grammar and usage. Tear-out exercises after each chapter. Answer key.

3233. Ezor, Edwin, and Jill Lewis. *From Paragraph to Essay: A Process Approach for Beginning College Writing.* New York: McGraw-Hill, 1984. 448 pages

A process-oriented workbook that emphasizes the paragraph in preparation for essay writing. Principal feature is a questioning technique to help students generate paragraphs, then essays.

3234. Farbman, Evelyn. *Signals: A Grammar and Guide for Writers.* Boston: Houghton Mifflin, 1985. 475 pages

A grammar and writing workbook that covers descriptive grammar, error analysis and correction, and the writing process. Emphasizes student writing as a basis for studying grammar and usage.

3235. Feinstein, George W. *Programmed Spelling Demons.* 2d ed. Englewood Cliffs, N.J.: Prentice-Hall, 1984. 240 pages

A workbook for overcoming common spelling problems. Uses a phonics approach and stresses drill. Programmed format allows for individualized study.

3236. Fitzpatrick, Carolyn H., and Marybeth Ruscica. *The Complete Sentence Workout Book.* Lexington, Mass.: Heath, 1985. 336 pages

Covers basic sentence elements before moving to more complex writing tasks. Each chapter contains objectives, grammar rules, and practical applications with sentence exercises and paragraphs for proofreading.

3237. Frew, Robert, Richard Guches, and Robert Mehaffy. *A Writer's Guidebook.* 2d ed. Palo Alto, Calif.: Peek, 1985. 270 pages

A workbook offering instruction and practice in grammar and style.

3238. Frew, Robert, Richard Guches, and Robert Mehaffy. *Writer's Workshop: A Self-Paced Program for Composition Mastery.* 3d ed. Palo Alto, Calif.: Peek, 1984. 282 pages

Provides a sequenced approach to writing skills, beginning with simple sentences and ending with the complete composition. Written for use in freshman English courses.

3239. Gallo, Joseph D., and Henry W. Rink. *Shaping College Writing.* 4th ed. San Diego: Harcourt Brace Jovanovich, 1985. 166 pages

Covers elements of effective essay and paragraph construction (topic sentences, unity, support, coherence, organization). Presents six methods of paragraph development.

3240. Harris, Jeanette, and Ann Moseley. *Contexts: Writing and Reading.* Boston: Houghton Mifflin, 1985. 391 pages

Emphasizes the integration of writing and reading, including paragraph and sentence writing. Exercises throughout. Reading and writing assignments include essays and apparatus. The appendix covers capitalization, spelling, vocabulary.

3241. Kinsella, Paul. *The Techniques of Writing.* 4th ed. San Diego: Harcourt Brace Jovanovich, 1985. 479 pages

A text and workbook covering grammar, usage, organization, and style. Edition includes new discussions, revised content, new material, a glossary of grammatical terms, and 10 sets of exercises on parts of speech.

3242. Langan, John. *College Writing Skills.* New York: McGraw-Hill, 1984. 416 pages

Based on *English Skills* (3d ed., 1984) but stresses the writing of expository essays. Uses student and professional models.

3243. Langan, John. *English Skills.* 3d ed. New York: McGraw-Hill, 1984. 448 pages

A combined composition and grammar textbook with a new chapter on study skills. Emphasizes clear thinking as the key to clear writing and balances personal and objective writing.

3244. Langan, John. *Reading and Study Skills, Form B.* 2d ed. New York: McGraw-Hill, 1984. 448 pages

Presents activities, tests, and reading selections to improve reading rate and comprehension and study skills. An alternate version of *Form A* (1982).

3245. Langan, John. *Sentence Skills, Form B.* 2d ed. New York: McGraw-Hill, 1984. 420 pages

Alternate version of *Form A* (1983). Presents exercises, examples, and tests for improving sentence structure.

3246. Mackie, Benita, and Shirley Rompf. *Building Sentences.* Englewood Cliffs, N.J.: Prentice-Hall, 1985. 342 pages

A workbook designed to help students write clear and correct simple, compound, and complex sentences. Emphasizes sentence construction, not analysis.

3247. Matthew, Marie-Louise, and Laraine Fergenson. *All in One: Basic Writing Skills Workbook and Reader.* 2d ed. Englewood Cliffs, N.J.: Prentice-Hall, 1985. 448 pages

Comprehensive workbook includes reading selections with exercises and vocabulary instruction. Edition presents new material on paragraph and essay writing.

3248. Myers, Alan, and Ethel Tiersky. *Toward American English: Workbook to Accompany Moving Ahead.* Glenview, Ill.: Scott, Foresman, 1984. 192 pages

Provides instruction and practice in paragraph writing for ESL students.

3249. Myers, Alan, and Ethel Tiersky. *Toward American English: Workbook to Accompany Starting Line.* Glenview, Ill.: Scott, Foresman, 1984. 192 pages

Emphasizes writing skills at the sentence level. Includes grammar drills and substitution, transformation, and role-playing exercises. For ESL students.

3250. Raygor, Alton, and Robin Raygor. *Effective Reading: Improving Reading Rates and Comprehension.* New York: McGraw-Hill, 1984. 320 pages

To improve reading rates and comprehension, presents reading selections excerpted from college textbooks.

3251. Smith, Elliott L. *Contemporary Vocabulary.* 2d ed. New York: St. Martin's Press, 1985. 384 pages

A vocabulary improvement textbook with exercises to facilitate academic study. Treats Latin and Greek roots, prefixes, suffixes, action and descriptive words, foreign expressions, and words from the classroom. Instructor's manual.

3252. Steele, Gary G. *Shortcuts to Basic Writing Skills.* 2d ed. New York: Holt, Rinehart and Winston, 1985. 334 pages

A workbook that focuses on writing problems while minimizing grammatical terminology.

3253. Tollefson, Stephen K. *Shaping Sentences: Grammar and Context.* San Diego: Harcourt Brace Jovanovich, 1985. 255 pages

Emphasizes basic problems in grammar and usage, including subject-verb agreement, pronoun usage, fragments, run-on sentences, and incorrect punctuation of clauses.

3254. Wiener, Harvey S. *Creating Compositions.* 4th ed. New York: McGraw-Hill, 1984. 560 pages

Brings together all the components involved in writing paragraphs and essays.

See also 3190

Special Texts

3255. Chaffee, John. *Thinking Critically.* Boston: Houghton Mifflin, 1985. 468 pages

Engages students in examining and developing how they think critically. Covers problem solving, perceiving, conceptualizing, composing, and constructing arguments. Exercises involve reading, writing, speaking, and listening.

3256. Hashimoto, Irvin Y., and Roger Clark. "College Spelling Texts: The State of the Art." *WCJ* 5 (Fall–Winter 1984): 1–13.

Reviews 12 college spelling textbooks, finding significant shortcomings, ranging from a patronizing tone to inadequate research support. Concludes that "there is room for decent spelling textbooks."

3257. Moberg, Goran. *Writing in Groups.* 4th ed. Dubuque: Kendall/Hunt, 1985. 200 pages

A textbook designed to turn writing classes into small workshops in which students write, edit, and revise their work in groups. Covers the writing of journals, fables, verse, short fiction, argumentation, and documented essays. Includes a handbook section and sample student writing.

3258. Myers, Alan, and Ethel Tiersky. *Toward American English: Starting Line.* Glenview, Ill.: Scott, Foresman, 1984. 240 pages

Presents a course of instruction for ESL students. Includes a textbook, workbook, instructor's manual, and audiocassettes.

3259. Myers, Alan, and Ethel Tiersky. *Toward American English: Moving Ahead.* Glenview, Ill.: Scott, Foresman, 1984. 256 pages

Integrates speaking, listening, reading, and writing within a structured, notional-functional context for intermediate ESL students.

3260. Rubin, Dorothy. *Gaining Word Power*. 2d ed. New York: Macmillan, 1985. 416 pages

A vocabulary improvement text that presents words in graduated levels of difficulty. Each chapter contains exercises, a check-up test, and true/false and analogy activities. Instructor's manual.

3261. Staitz, Robert L., Francine B. Steiglitz, and Maureen Dezell. *Contemporary Perspectives: An Advanced Reader/Rhetoric in English*. Boston: Little, Brown, 1984. 215 pages

Twenty-eight selections from contemporary books, journals, and newspapers are grouped thematically into seven chapters, each with a dual focus on rhetoric and reading.

3262. Staitz, Robert L., Francine B. Steiglitz, and Nancy H. Goulde. *Stimulus: A First Reader/Workbook in English*. Boston: Little, Brown, 1984. 210 pages

Intensive reading, syntax, and vocabularly for beginning ESL students. Forty brief readings grouped in 10 chapters. Includes a variety of language activities.

3263. Stotsky, Sandra. "A Review of Vocabulary Texts for Developmental Writing Courses." *TETYC* 12 (May 1985): 154–163.

Reviews vocabulary texts that teach selected groups of words and those that also teach strategies for learning vocabulary.

FRESHMAN COMPOSITION

Handbooks

3264. Branchaw, Bernadine. *English Made Easy*. 2d ed. New York: McGraw-Hill, 1985. 208 pages

Fifty lessons cover "the essentials of grammar, usage, punctuation, style, capitalization, and number usage." Includes practice exercises.

3265. Corbett, Edward P. J. *The Little English Handbook: Choices and Conventions*. 4th ed. Glenview, Ill.: Scott, Foresman, 1984. 288 pages

A reference handbook that covers 50 problem areas in grammar, style mechanics, paragraphing, and punctuation. Provides models for research papers, footnotes and bibliography, business letters, and resumes.

3266. Corder, Jim W., and John J. Ruskiewicz. *Handbook of Current English*. 7th ed. Glenview, Ill.: Scott, Foresman, 1985. 737 pages

Presents grammar, mechanics, and rhetoric from a contemporary theoretical base. Includes a workbook, two test packages, a portfolio of teaching ideas, and a handbook for essay examinations.

3267. Crews, Frederick, and Sandra Schor. *The Borzoi Handbook for Writers*. New York: Knopf, 1984. 592 pages

Focuses on problems students have in writing clear, correct prose. Includes material on writing the research paper. Instructor's manual and diagnostic test package.

3268. Flynn, James, and Joseph Glaser. *Writer's Handbook*. New York: Macmillan, 1984. 640 pages

Covers grammar, punctuation, mechanics, and research. Includes exercises, student writing samples, a glossary, and sections on special writing forms and research papers.

3269. Frew, Robert, Richard Guches, and Robert Mehaffy. *Survival: A Sequential Program for College Writing*. 2d ed. Palo Alto, Calif.: Peek, 1985. 336 pages

A guide to college writing skills. Includes chapters on essays, sentence structure, the library research paper (and the new MLA style), and the essay exam.

3270. Gula, Robert J. *Precision: A Reference Handbook for Writers*. Lanham, Md.: University Press of America, 1984. 290 pages

Originally published in 1980, a handbook of traditional grammar with recommendations on changing usage. Also covers style, letter writing, footnoting, and bibliographical forms.

3271. Guth, Hans P. *New English Handbook*. 2d ed. Belmont, Calif.: Wadsworth, 1985. 608 pages

A comprehensive handbook intended to encourage effective writing rather than focus on errors. Provides a reference guide to modern usage.

3272. Hacker, Diana. *Rules for Writers: A Brief Handbook*. Boston: Bedford Books, 1985. 437 pages

A compact guide to the conventions of grammar, usage, and the writing process. Hand-edited sentences illustrate revision. Answers to some exercises are included. Instructor's manual.

3273. Hibbison, Eric. *A Handbook for Student Writers and Researchers*. Englewood Cliffs, N.J.: Prentice-Hall, 1984. 384 pages

A brief paperback handbook offers instruction in the process of writing and revising for style. Also covers research writing.

3274. Kirkland, James W., and Collett B. Dilworth. *Concise English Handbook.* Lexington, Mass.: Heath, 1985. 400 pages

A rhetorically based handbook includes strategies for composing, revising, and editing. Presents a reader-centered approach to paragraph development and covers writing about literature, essay tests, business letters, and research papers. Annotated teacher's edition and student workbook.

3275. Kolln, Martha. *Language and Composition: A Handbook and Rhetoric.* New York: Macmillan, 1984. 512 pages

The handbook treats sentence grammar, diction, usage, punctuation, and spelling; the rhetoric approaches essays through traditional modes and covers the research paper as well as specialized writing situations. Instructor's manual with tests, workbook, and answer key.

3276. Leggett, Glenn, C. David Mead, and Melinda Kramer. *Prentice-Hall Handbook for Writers.* 9th ed. Englewood Cliffs, N.J.: Prentice-Hall, 1985. 576 pages

Presents writing as a decision-making process and gives strategies for satisfying an audience's needs while accomplishing the writer's goals. Treats research across the curriculum. Presents the new MLA styles, student and professional examples, and new exercises.

3277. Marius, Richard, and Harvey S. Wiener. *The McGraw-Hill College Handbook.* New York: McGraw-Hill, 1985. 637 pages

A process-oriented handbook presents options for prewriting, organizing essays, developing theses, and drafting. Covers both old and new MLA styles.

3278. Roberts, William H. *The Writer's Companion.* Boston: Little, Brown, 1985. 250 pages

A brief reference handbook that alphabetically organizes persistent writing problems. Includes new MLA documentation guidelines.

3279. Robey, Cora, Alice Hedrick, and Ethelyn Morgan. *New Handbook of Basic Writing Skills.* 2d ed. San Diego: Harcourt Brace Jovanovich, 1984. 400 pages

A handbook of grammar, usage, and composition that gives intensive coverage of common writing problems.

3280. Winkler, Anthony C., and Jo Ray McCuen. *Writing the Research Paper: A Handbook.* 2d ed. San Diego: Harcourt Brace Jovanovich, 1985. 304 pages

A comprehensive student handbook for writing research papers.

See also 3185

Rhetorics

3281. Adams, Michael. *The Writer's Mind: Making Writing Make Sense.* Glenview, Ill.: Scott, Foresman, 1984. 336 pages

A rhetoric with an emphasis on revision and argumentation. Includes writing and editing exercises, annotated essays, and illustrative examples.

3282. Adelstein, Michael E., and Jean G. Pival. *The Writing Commitment.* 3d ed. San Diego: Harcourt Brace Jovanovich, 1984. 565 pages

Emphasizes the writing process, presenting prewriting strategies at the beginning of each major section and providing examples of actual revisions at the end of each section.

3283. Alvarez, Joseph A. *The Elements of Composition.* San Diego: Harcourt Brace Jovanovich, 1985. 256 pages

A comprehensive rhetoric intended for students in regular, not remedial, composition classes. Covers all aspects of the writing process and includes 200 examples from works of published writers.

3284. Axelrod, Rise B., and Charles R. Cooper. *The St. Martin's Guide to Writing.* New York: St. Martin's Press, 1985. 687 pages

A comprehensive rhetoric with full-length readings and a complete handbook. Nine writing guides lead students through the composing process, from invention to drafting to peer critiquing and revising. Instructor's manual.

3285. Axelrod, Rise B., and Charles R. Cooper. *The St. Martin's Guide to Writing.* Short ed. New York: St. Martin's Press, 1985. 576 pages

Covers major forms of nonfiction prose and standard rhetorical strategies, each form exemplified by readings. Guides to writing provide sequences of activities. Instructor's manual.

3286. Bailey, Edward P., Jr., Phillip A. Powell, and Jack M. Shuttleworth. *The Practical Writer.* 3d ed. New York: Holt, Rinehart and Winston, 1985. 290 pages

A rhetoric that progresses step by step from a one-paragraph through a five-paragraph essay.

3287. Bazerman, Charles. *The Informed Writer: Using Sources in the Disciplines.* Boston: Houghton Mifflin, 1985. 518 pages

Emphasizes using reading to write well. Treats the research paper and includes a new five-chapter unit on writing in the disciplines. Over 40 essays or excerpts.

3288. Berke, Jacqueline. *Twenty Questions for the Writer: A Rhetoric with Readings.* 4th ed. San Diego: Harcourt Brace Jovanovich, 1985. 630 pages

A reader, rhetoric, and handbook. Includes principles of paragraph construction, revision, and editing. Covers diction and sentence combining as well as grammar, punctuation, and mechanics.

3289. Biddle, Arthur W. *Writer to Writer.* New York: McGraw-Hill, 1984. 256 pages

A process-oriented rhetoric that emphasizes product-centered writing. Treats prewriting, drafting, and rewriting with writing assignments sequenced in that order within each chapter.

3290. Bruffee, Kenneth A. *A Short Course in Writing.* 3d ed. Boston: Little, Brown, 1985. 270 pages

Designed to be used in a collaborative learning setting. Provides a sequence of argumentative and explanatory essay exercises focused on improving organization and coherence.

3291. Crews, Frederick. *The Random House Handbook.* 4th ed. New York: Random House, 1984. 528 pages

A handbook and rhetoric covering grammar and usage as well as providing students with guidance in writing the whole essay and research papers.

3292. D'Angelo, Frank. *Process and Thought in Composition with Handbook.* 3d ed. Boston: Little, Brown, 1985. 560 pages

Presents principles common to thinking and writing and emphasizes the process of putting thoughts into written form. Includes new material on audience, sentence structure, and word choice. A revised research paper chapter presents APA and new MLA styles.

3293. DiYanni, Robert. *Connections: Writing, Reading, and Thinking.* Upper Montclair, N.J.: Boynton/Cook, 1985. 320 pages

Treats writing as the making of connections or relationships. Also emphasizes reading and writing about literature.

3294. Duncan, Jeffrey L. *Writing from Start to Finish: A Rhetoric with Readings.* San Diego: Harcourt Brace Jovanovich, 1985. 592 pages

Integrates process essays and finished pieces to show the relationship between a writer's conscious process and a writer's actual product. Discusses prewriting, writing, rewriting, and editing.

3295. Flower, Linda S. *Problem-Solving Strategies for Writing.* 2d ed. San Diego: Harcourt Brace Jovanovich, 1985. 256 pages

A process-oriented writing textbook suitable for any composition course. Applies a problem-solving approach to writing, breaking the process into component parts.

3296. Gefvert, Constance J. *The Confident Writer: A Norton Handbook.* New York: Norton, 1985. 648 pages

Both a reference handbook and writing textbook in seven parts. Covers writing as process, paragraphs, sentence grammar, writing and revising sentences, words, punctuation and mechanics, and special writing assignments. Advice on usage is based on survey data from a variety of professions.

3297. Gere, Anne Ruggles. *Writing and Learning.* New York: Macmillan, 1985. 544 pages

A comprehensive rhetoric and handbook that stresses connections between the writing course and other college courses. Emphasizes revision. Instructor's manual.

3298. Hacker, Diana, and Betty Renshaw. *Writing with a Voice: A Rhetoric/Handbook.* Boston: Little, Brown, 1985. 432 pages

Formerly *A Practical Guide for Writers,* illustrates writing principles with more than 30 student essays, many with multiple drafts. Revised handbook section treats grammar and usage and includes a section on dialect interference.

3299. Hall, Donald. *Writing Well.* 5th ed. Boston: Little, Brown, 1985. 450 pages

A comprehensive rhetoric. "The Whole Essay" has been moved to Part I to accommodate a new philosophy of teaching the essay first. Expanded coverage of argument and a revised research chapter.

3300. Hammond, Eugene R. *Informative Writing.* New York: McGraw-Hill, 1984. 416 pages

Asks students to find the facts, draw inferences from those facts, and decide on a thesis incorporating those inferences. Contains 11 student papers.

3301. Harrington, John, and Michael Wenzl. *A Suitable Design: How to Organize Your Writing.* New York: Macmillan, 1984. 225 pages

Offers an inventory of designs that present principles of effective organization in writing. Covers business writing and traditional modes and includes examples and summary boxes.

3302. Hockheiser, Robert M. *Don't State It... Communicate It.* Woodbury, N.Y.: Barron's, 1985. 178 pages

Ten chapters cover the importance of writing, strategies for adapting writing to fit an audience, techniques for persuasion, and editing.

3303. Irmscher, William F., and Harryette Stover. *The Holt Guide to English.* Alternate ed. New York: Holt, Rinehart and Winston, 1985. 397 pages

A compact version of *The Holt Guide to English,* designed to be more accessible.

3304. Keating, Rod. *Guidelines: Composing and Responding to Essays.* New York: Macmillan, 1984. 300 pages

Organized around composing guidelines, short statements about what to do and when to do it. Includes practical advice section, suggestions for responding to and giving criticism, and student examples.

3305. Kirszner, Laurie, and Stephen Mandell. *Writing: A College Rhetoric.* Brief ed. New York: Holt, Rinehart and Winston, 1985. 448 pages

A paperback edition of the 1984 hardcover edition that omits the handbook section.

3306. Macrorie, Ken. *Telling Writing.* 4th ed. Upper Montclair, N.J.: Boynton/Cook, 1985. 300 pages

A student-centered approach to teaching writing. Concentrates on such techniques as freewriting, reader-based prose, and revising.

3307. Macrorie, Ken. *Writing to Be Read.* 3d ed. Upper Montclair, N.J.: Boynton/Cook, 1984. 287 pages

Focuses on student writing. Includes a section on reading one's writing aloud and a chapter on interviewing.

3308. Martin, Lee J., and Harry P. Kroitor. *The Five-Hundred Word Theme.* 4th ed. Englewood Cliffs, N.J.: Prentice-Hall, 1984. 384 pages

Offers guidance for writing short papers that are unified, coherent, and adequately developed. Also covers the research paper and includes a short section on mechanics and style.

3309. McClelland, Ben W. *Writing Practice: A Rhetoric of the Writing Process.* White Plains, N.Y.: Longman, 1984. 304 pages

Presents a practice-oriented approach to the writing process. Includes examples of student writing and developmentally organized exercises.

3310. McCrimmon, James M. *Writing with a Purpose.* 8th ed. Edited by Joseph F. Trimmer and Nancy Sommers. Boston: Houghton Mifflin, 1984. 752 pages

A comprehensive rhetoric with an emphasis on the writer's purpose. Edition includes a new presentation of the writing process with discussions of planning, drafting, and revising. Instructor's manual.

3311. McGuire, John F. *Words in Action: The 5 C's Approach to Good Writing.* Lanham, Md.: University Press of America, 1984. 226 pages

Presents instruction and exercises for achieving the "5 C's," "clear, concise, coherent, considerate, and correct writing." Emphasizes logic and human relationships involved in the communication process.

3312. Podis, Leonard, and JoAnne M. Podis. *Writing: Invention, Form, and Style.* Glenview, Ill.: Scott, Foresman, 1984. 576 pages

Twelve chapters divided into four parts that treat traditional rhetorical patterns through a process approach. Exercises and writing suggestions follow each chapter. Special assignments section includes business writing and writing for other disciplines.

3313. Ponsot, Marie, and Rosemary Deen. *The Common Sense: What to Write, How to Write It, and Why.* Upper Montclair, N.J.: Boynton/Cook, 1985. 176 pages

Offers directions for four sequential ways into exposition and analysis. Based on the rationale presented in the authors' *Beat Not the Poor Desk* (1982).

3314. Ruggiero, Vincent Ryan. *Composition: The Creative Response.* Belmont, Calif.: Wadsworth, 1985. 480 pages

A comprehensive rhetoric and handbook that emphasizes creativity and critical thinking in writing. Covers prewriting, drafting, and revising.

3315. Scholes, Robert, and Nancy R. Comley. *The Practice of Writing.* New York: St. Martin's Press, 1985. 362 pages

Emphasizes learning by doing. Discusses forms of writing only briefly, devoting space instead to writing practice. Sixty-three exercises and assignments are all preceded by readings.

3316. Skwire, David. *Writing with a Thesis.* 4th ed. New York: Holt, Rinehart and Winston, 1985. 323 pages

A rhetoric and reader based on principles of persuasion.

3317. Skwire, David, and Frances Chitwood Beam. *Student's Book of College English.* New York: Macmillan, 1985. 560 pages

A comprehensive textbook that combines a rhetoric with readings and a handbook. Instructor's manual.

3318. Stanley, Linda C., David Shimkin, and Allen H. Lanner. *Ways to Writing: Purpose, Task, and Process.* New York: Macmillan, 1985. 448 pages

A process-oriented rhetoric that includes a handbook of grammar and usage. Each chapter discusses the purpose, invention, audience, arrangement, revision, and style of a specific writing task. Instructor's manual.

3319. Tibbetts, Charlene, and Arn M. Tibbetts. *Strategies: A Rhetoric and Reader.* 2d ed. Glenview, Ill.: Scott, Foresman, 1984. 368 pages

Seven chapters provide instruction in writing, from generating ideas to revising and editing. Ten chapters offer 3 student and 36 professional essays categorized by rhetorical strategy.

3320. Walvoord, Barbara Fassler. *Writing: Strategies for All Disciplines.* Englewood Cliffs, N.J.: Prentice-Hall, 1985. 480 pages

Offers strategies for effective writing and illustrates their application in writing for various disciplines. Covers the writing process, modes for thinking and organizing, research, and research writing.

3321. White, Fred D. "Reconsidering the Usefulness of Rhetoric Textbooks in Freshman Composition Courses." Paper presented at the CCCC Convention, New York, March 1984. ERIC ED 250 684 [15 pages]

Argues for textbooks that demonstrate to students that personal composing processes rather than the traditional rhetorical modes are the central issue in learning to write.

3322. Winkler, Anthony C., and Jo Ray McCuen. *Rhetoric Made Plain.* 4th ed. San Diego: Harcourt Brace Jovanovich, 1984. 448 pages

A guide to English composition. Each chapter is based on a question students should ask themselves at each stage of the composing process.

3323. Woodman, Leonora, and Thomas P. Adler. *The Writer's Choices.* Glenview, Ill.: Scott, Foresman, 1985. 510 pages

Stresses editing and revising skills with peer editing exercises in every chapter. Provides fifty student essays. Includes a handbook.

3324. Yarber, Robert E. *Writing for Colleges: A Practical Approach.* Glenview, Ill.: Scott, Foresman, 1985. 347 pages

A process-oriented rhetoric covers expository modes, persuasion, research papers, essay examinations, business letters, and resumes. Includes a handbook of grammar, usage, and mechanics as well as checklists and student examples.

Readers

3325. Aaron, Jane E. *The Compact Reader.* Boston: Bedford Books, 1984. 384 pages

A rhetorically arranged reader with 26 essays and full editorial apparatus. Each section's introduction explains one method of development, illustrates the use of the method in writing essays, and analyzes two professionally written paragraphs. Instructor's manual.

3326. Barnet, Sylvan, Morton Berman, and William Burto. *Literature for Composition.* Boston: Little, Brown, 1984. 832 pages

A thematically arranged anthology of essays, fiction, poetry, and drama that approaches composition skills through the analysis of literature.

3327. Behrens, Lawrence, and Leonard Rosen. *Writing and Reading across the Curriculum.* 2d ed. Boston: Little, Brown, 1985. 610 pages

A thematically organized cross-curricular anthology that emphasizes synthesis, analysis, and criticism. New chapter is devoted to a casebook study of Orwell's *Animal Farm.*

3328. Brent, Harry, and William Lutz. *Rhetorical Considerations.* 4th ed. Boston: Little, Brown, 1984. 496 pages

Presents 81 brief selections, thematically arranged, on traditional and contemporary concerns. Apparatus emphasizes writing as a process.

3329. Burt, Forrest D., and E. Cleve Want. *Invention and Design: A Rhetorical Reader.* 4th ed. New York: Random House, 1984. 416 pages

Fifty-six essays. Text emphasizes inventing ideas and designing effective prose. Includes revised and new exercises and applications after each essay. Instructor's manual.

3330. Coles, William E., Jr., and James Vopat. *What Makes Writing Good.* Lexington, Mass.: Heath, 1984. 360 pages

Forty-eight student essays chosen by prominent writing teachers who comment on each selection. Study questions follow each assignment. Each chapter builds sequentially on the others.

3331. Comley, Nancy R., David Hamilton, Carl Klaus, Robert Scholes, and Nancy Sommers. *Fields of Writing: Readings across the Disciplines.* New York: St. Martin's Press, 1984. 771 pages

A cross-curricular reader offering 92 selections drawn from arts and humanities, social sciences and public affairs, and natural sciences and technologies. Organized in four categories: reporting, explaining, arguing, and reflecting. Instructor's manual.

3332. Decker, Randall E. *Patterns of Exposition.* 9th ed. Boston: Little, Brown, 1984. 480 pages

Each of the 11 sections illustrates a different rhetorical technique. Includes a new section, "Reasoning by Use of Argument," and new selections by well-known authors.

3333. Eastman, Athur, Caesar Blake, Hubert English, Jr., Joan Hartman, Alan Howes, Robert Lenaghan, Leo McNamara, and James Rosier. *The Norton Reader.* 6th ed. New York: Norton, 1984. 1300 pages

A reader emphasizing depth and breadth of selection, includes 218 selections, 65 of them new to this edition.

3334. Eden, Rick A. "Against Language Readers." *FEN* 13 (Spring 1984): 4–5, 10–11.

Argues that most language readers are anti-process, are too concerned with the limitations of language, and offer misleading essay samples.

3335. Eschholz, Paul A., and Alfred F. Rosa. *Subject and Strategy.* 3d ed. New York: St. Martin's Press, 1985. 611 pages

A rhetorically arranged collection of 64 essays stressing the relationship between reading and writing. Each of 10 rhetorical selections includes an introduction, apparatus, and a student essay accompanied by an interview with the writer. Instructor's manual.

3336. Fahnestock, Jeanne, and Marie Secor. *Readings in Argument.* New York: Random House, 1985. 654 pages

A cross-disciplinary collection of readings chosen to illustrate principles of argument. Section introductions treat invention and analysis. Includes reading questions and writing assignments.

3337. Goshgarian, Gary. *The Contemporary Reader.* Boston: Little, Brown, 1984. 500 pages

A thematically organized anthology of essays by prominent American writers representing a diversity of styles and strategies.

3338. Hall, Donald. *The Contemporary Essay.* Boston: Bedford Books, 1984. 488 pages

Selections by 34 major living American writers of nonfiction prose, arranged chronologically. Apparatus includes a general introduction, headnotes, questions, assignments, and a rhetorical index. Instructor's manual.

3339. Hall, Donald, and D. L. Emblem. *A Writer's Reader.* 4th ed. Boston: Little, Brown, 1985. 530 pages

A companion to *Writing Well* (5th ed., 1985). Includes selections chosen for brevity, quality, and varieties of tone. Alphabetical arrangement.

3340. Heffernan, William A. *The Harvest Reader.* San Diego: Harcourt Brace Jovanovich, 1984. 592 pages

A rhetorical reader with 74 contemporary model essays. Progresses from a focus on the speaker to a focus on the subject to a focus on the audience.

3341. Howard, Maureen, ed. *The Penguin Book of Contemporary American Essays.* New York: Penguin, 1984. 282 pages

Contains 26 selections representing major authors and major essay types. Introduction presents brief commentaries on the rhetorical purpose of each essayist. Instructor's guide.

3342. Kennedy, X. J., and Dorothy M. Kennedy. *The Bedford Reader.* Boston: Bedford Books, 1984. 594 pages

Forty-nine essays (26 new to this edition) in 10 rhetorical sections. Each section features a "postscript on process" by a professional writer describing how he or she wrote the essay included. Instructor's manual.

3343. Klammer, Enno. *Writing: Readings and Advice.* San Diego: Harcourt Brace Jovanovich, 1984. 336 pages

A collection of 58 essays combined with extensive rhetorical materials. Illustrates through precept and example how to write essays using the traditional modes of development.

3344. Loewe, Ralph E. *A Reader for College Writers.* 2d ed. Englewood Cliffs, N.J.: Prentice-Hall, 1985. 368 pages

A rhetorically organized reader with a thematic table of contents. Models progress from simple to more complex. This edition expands the treatment of reading and writing processes and adds a chapter on argumentation and persuasion.

3345. Loy, Sandra. *The Writer's Voice.* New York: Holt, Rinehart and Winston, 1985. 365 pages

Presents contemporary and traditional readings from many cultures and eras.

3346. Maimon, Elaine P., Gerald L. Belcher, Gail W. Hearn, Barbara F. Nodine, and Finbarr W. O'Connor. *Reading in the Arts and Sciences.* Boston: Little, Brown, 1985. 406 pages

An anthology of cross-disciplinary selections. Offers strategies for reading and writing in academic disciplines and emphasizes developing skills in assessing audience and purpose.

3347. Muller, Gilbert H. *The McGraw-Hill Reader.* 2d ed. New York: McGraw-Hill, 1984. 572 pages

Presents 120 thematically arranged essays by contemporary and classical writers. Includes an alternate table of contents and two new sections of writings on education and business.

3348. Muller, Gilbert H., and John A. Williams. *The McGraw-Hill Introduction to Literature.* New York: McGraw- Hill, 1984. 800 pages

Chapter introductions discuss themes and techniques. Provides biographical information for each author and exercises for each section.

3349. Muscatine, Charles, and Marlene Griffith. *The Borzoi College Reader.* 5th ed. New York: Knopf, 1984. 756 pages

A thematically organized reader that emphasizes critical thinking and effective writing and reading across the curriculum. Instructor's manual.

3350. Nicholas, J. Karl, and James R. Nicholl. *Rhetorical Models for Effective Writing.* 3d ed. Boston: Little, Brown, 1985. 464 pages

Treats writing skills and reading effectiveness through a range of models. Edition features new essay on rhetoric and writing process. One-third of the selections are new.

3351. Penfield, Elizabeth F., and Nancy Wicker. *The Writer's Roles: Readings with Rhetoric.* Glenview, Ill.: Scott, Foresman, 1985. 508 pages

A process-oriented reader and rhetoric. Readings from many disciplines emphasize different roles for writers. Writing assignments suggest an audience and purpose.

3352. Rottenberg, Annette T. *Elements of Argument: A Text and Reader.* Boston: Bedford Books, 1985. 474 pages

Presents concepts of argument by adapting Toulmin's model. Includes both good and bad examples, 71 readings, and an appendix on writing an argumentative paper. Instructor's manual.

3353. Schorer, Mark, Everett Jones, Philip Durham, and Mark Johnston. *Harbrace College Reader.* 6th ed. San Diego: Harcourt Brace Jovanovich, 1984. 526 pages

Contains 73 selections designed to instruct and to stimulate deeper thinking and better writing. Organization blends three approaches: rhetorical, thematic, and chronological. Includes biographical headnotes.

3354. Schwegler, Robert. *Patterns in Action.* Boston: Little, Brown, 1985. 460 pages

A rhetorically organized reader that presents rhetorical patterns as active techniques for effective writing. Each chapter covers one pattern and contains four to six essays varying in length, aim, and strategy.

3355. Shrodes, Caroline, Harry Finestone, and Michael Shugrue. *The Conscious Reader.* 3d ed. New York: Macmillan, 1985. 815 pages

A thematic reader that includes essays, short stories, and poetry. This edition contains readings from a broader range of academic disciplines. Instructor's manual.

3356. Smart, William. *Eight Modern Essayists.* 4th ed. New York: St. Martin's Press, 1985. 299 pages

Presents the work of Woolf, Orwell, White, Thomas, Baldwin, Hoagland, Didion, and Walker. Each writer is represented by four to six essays. Instructor's manual.

3357. Sommers, Nancy, and Donald McQuade. *Student Writers at Work: The Bedford Prizes.* New York: St. Martin's Press, 1984. 289 pages

Presents the work of 31 winners of the publisher's 1982 national freshman essay contest. Includes headnotes and questions on revision for each essay. Supporting chapters present drafts of winning essays and samples of editing done by peers and professionals. Instructor's manual.

3358. Steward, Joyce. *Contemporary College Reader.* 3d ed. Glenview, Ill.: Scott, Foresman, 1985. 493 pages

Presents 53 contemporary readings from a variety of disciplines. Includes writing assignments and three essays on one topic to illustrate several ways of writing arguments.

3359. Steward, Joyce, and Marjorie Smelstor. *Writing in the Social Sciences.* Glenview, Ill.: Scott, Foresman, 1984. 368 pages

A guide for students and professionals writing in the fields of psychology, sociology, history, anthropology, and economics. Part I surveys the writing process, and Part II treats the purposes for writing.

3360. Taylor, Ann. *Short Model Essays: Patterns and Subjects for Writing.* Boston: Little, Brown, 1984. 340 pages

A collection of student and professional essays short enough to be read closely in one class period.

3361. Trimmer, Joseph F., and Maxine Hairston. *The Riverside Reader, Vol. 1.* 2d ed. Boston: Houghton Mifflin, 1985. 576 pages

A rhetorically organized collection of 51 essays, 19 new to this edition. Includes an introduction and guidelines for reading, an alternate thematic table of contents, headnotes, study questions, and writing topics.

3362. Wasson, John M. *Subject and Structure: An Anthology for Writers.* 8th ed. Boston: Little, Brown, 1984. 448 pages

Reader organized by both topic and rhetorical mode. Eighteen of the 66 selections are new. Includes classic and contemporary essays with stories, six poems, discussions of rhetorical techniques, discussion questions, and writing suggestions.

3363. Winterowd, W. Ross, and Charlotte Preston. *Themes and Variations: A College Reader.* San Diego: Harcourt Brace Jovanovich, 1985. 448 pages

An anthology of 56 essays and 18 poems representing a broad range of writing styles.

See also 3316

Workbooks

3364. Benzel, Kathryn, Janne Goldbeck, and Michael Benzel. *The Little English Workbook.* 2d ed. Glenview, Ill.: Scott, Foresman, 1984. 304 pages

Provides explanations of writing terms with exercises focusing on common writing problems. Includes a new section on developing research skills. Designed to complement *The Little English Handbook* (4th ed., 1984) or to be used independently.

3365. de Beaugrande, Robert. *Writing Step by Step: Easy Strategies for Writing and Revising.* San Diego: Harcourt Brace Jovanovich, 1985. 382 pages

Emphasizes self-reliance and critical judgment in relation to writing skills. Covers problem areas in grammar, usage, spelling, and punctuation.

3366. Graham, Sheila Y. *Harbrace College Workbook, Form 9B.* San Diego: Harcourt Brace Jovanovich, 1984. 337 pages

Follows the organization and numbering system of the *Harbrace College Handbook* (9th ed., 1982). Combines self-contained exercises and explanations with a functional approach to grammar, punctuation, mechanics, and writing.

3367. Harris, Muriel. *Practice for a Purpose: Writing Activities for Classroom, Lab, and Self-Study.* Boston: Houghton Mifflin, 1984. 448 pages

Practice exercises in planning, drafting, revising, and using argument for essay examinations, literary papers, research papers, and business writing. Includes writing topics and student and professional examples. Can be used independently or to supplement *Writing with a Purpose,* (8th ed., 1984).

3368. Hennessey, Michael. *The Borzoi Practice Book for Student Writers.* New York: Knopf, 1985. 225 pages

Exercises for practice in writing, revising, and editing. Also includes exercises in grammar and usage.

3369. Kolln, Martha. *Language and Composition: A Workbook.* New York: Macmillan, 1984. 512 pages

Treats sentence grammar, punctuation, usage, diction, the paragraph, and the essay. Supplements *Language and Composition: A Handbook and Rhetoric* (1984). Answer key.

3370. Kramer, Melinda G. *Prentice-Hall Workbook for Writers.* 4th ed. Englewood Cliffs, N.J.: Prentice-Hall, 1985. 352 pages

A workbook covering both the functions and applications of grammar, sentence construction, and composition. Includes new exercises on immigrants' contributions to America.

3371. Lester, James D. *Study Guide for Writing Research Papers.* 4th ed. Glenview, Ill.: Scott, Foresman, 1984. 298 pages

Self-paced workbook provides practice exercises and drills to sharpen students' research skills. Seven chapters with a glossary and answer key. Designed to accompany *Writing Research Papers* (4th ed., 1983).

3372. Mahaney, William E. *Workbook of Current English.* 3d ed. Glenview, Ill.: Scott, Foresman, 1985. 400 pages

Companion to *Handbook of Current English* (7th ed., 1985). Edition places increased emphasis on student writing and sentence combining. Includes end-of-chapter review exercises.

3373. Robey, Cora, Helen Mahoney, Alice Hedrick, Ethelyn Morgan, and Sarah Krebs. *New Workbook of Basic Writing Skills.* 2d ed. San Diego: Harcourt Brace Jovanovich, 1984. 304 pages

Parallels the organization and coverage of the *New Handbook of Basic Writing Skills* (2d ed., 1984). Contains supplementary exercises to reinforce material in each of the *Handbook's* 29 chapters.

3374. Van Sant, Ann Jessie. *The Random House Workbook.* 4th ed. New York: Random House, 1984. 256 pages

Supplements *The Random House Handbook* (4th ed., 1984). Begins with a review of sentence structure and concludes with writing and revising the paragraph.

Special Texts

3375. Costanzo, William. *Double Exposure: Composing through Writing and Film.* Upper Montclair, N.J.: Boynton/Cook, 1984. 272 pages

Draws on the relationship between composing through film techniques and composing through language. Includes many film-making activities as well as writing activities.

3376. Dawe, Charles W., and Edward A. Dornan. *One to One: Resources for Conference-Centered Writing.* 2d ed. Boston: Little, Brown, 1984. 400 pages

A guide for self-paced, conference-centered writing instruction emphasizing the composing process. Edition includes 20 percent more writing assignments and an expanded index for writers.

3377. DeWitt-Spurgin, Sally. *The Power to Persuade.* Englewood Cliffs, N.J.: Prentice-Hall, 1985. 352 pages

Covers reasoning and finding evidence in constructing arguments. Attends to the writer/reader relationship and emotional appeals as well as to logical appeals. Forty-five readings. Discussion of the new MLA style.

3378. Halpern, Diane F. *Thought and Knowledge: An Introduction to Critical Thinking.* Hillside, N.J.: Erlbaum, 1984. 424 pages

A textbook that applies theories of cognitive psychology to the development of thinking skills. Discusses the influence of language on thought, strategies for problem solving, valid reasoning and decision making, and memory skills.

3379. Howard, C. Jeriel, and Richard F. Tracz. *Contact: A Textbook in Applied Communication.* 4th ed. Englewood Cliffs, N.J.: Prentice-Hall, 1984. 320 pages

Intended to develop an awareness of and aptitude in the basic oral and written communication skills necessary for career success.

3380. Kail, Harvey, and Ronda Dubay. "Texts for Tutors and Teachers." *WCJ* 5 (Fall–Winter 1984): 14–29.

Reviews textbooks written specifically for tutors and tutor supervisors, including works by Bruffee and Elbow.

3381. Koch, Arthur E., and Stanley B. Felber. *What Did You Say?* 3d ed. Englewood Cliffs, N.J.: Prentice-Hall, 1985. 384 pages

Treats effective communication by focusing on practical skills for writing, listening, and job interviews. New handbook section.

3382. Lang, Gerhard, and George D. Heiss. *A Practical Guide to Research Methods.* 3d ed. Lanham, Md.: University Press of America, 1984. 206 pages

An introduction to research methods. Covers the selection and formulation of a research problem, the use of previous research, statistical analysis and data processing, measurement in research, types of research, research methods and tools, and writing the research report.

3383. Moffett, James, Miriam Baker, and Charles R. Cooper. *Active Voices IV.* Upper Montclair, N.J.: Boynton/Cook, 1985. 368 pages

A collection of student writings based on the assignment sequences in *Active Voice* (1981). Can be used alone or with Moffett's *Points of Departure* (1985) and *Points of View* (1966).

3384. Myers, Doris T. *Understanding Language.* Upper Montclair, N.J.: Boynton/Cook, 1984. 240 pages

Can be used for introducing students to language through writing or for teaching composition through an introduction to language.

3385. Roth, Audrey J. *The Research Paper: Process, Form, and Content.* 5th ed. Belmont, Calif.: Wadsworth, 1985. 303 pages

Discusses the process of creating a report from library and other sources. Treats documentation, the preparation and presentation of research papers, the use of computers, the new MLA style, and nonprint sources. Instructor's manual.

3386. Sears, Donald. *The Harbrace Guide to the Library and the Research Paper.* 4th ed. San Diego: Harcourt Brace Jovanovich, 1984. 154 pages

A guide in workbook format for self-instruction in the preparation of the research paper. Includes and annotates student research papers and provides examples of the 1977 and 1984 MLA styles and the 1983 APA style.

3387. Walker, Melissa. *Writing Research Papers: A Norton Guide.* New York: Norton, 1984. 224 pages

A guide to the process of research writing with a full treatment of the 1984 MLA and the 1983 APA styles, as well as scientific documentation. Includes an annotated bibliography of reference sources.

3388. Weidenborner, Stephen, and Domenick Caruso. *Writing Research Papers: A Guide to the Process.* 2d ed. New York: St. Martin's Press, 1985. 225 pages

Treats the process of producing a research paper. Describes the new MLA guidelines, covers documentation systems in different disciplines, and presents sample research papers illustrating MLA, APA, and traditional endnote styles.

See also 3280

ADVANCED WRITING

Rhetorics

3389. Bloom, Lynn Z. *Fact and Artifact: Writing Nonfiction.* San Diego: Harcourt Brace Jovanovich, 1985. 337 pages

Emphasizes style and revision. Examples of professional and student writing focus on the processes of writing about people, places, performance, controversy, process, science, and humor.

3390. Dougherty, Barbey N. *Composing Choices for Writers.* New York: McGraw-Hill, 1985. 350 pages

Addresses the need to organize ideas clearly and to map the organization for readers. Features prewriting, argument, and choices governing the writing process.

3391. Marius, Richard. *A Writer's Companion.* New York: Knopf, 1984. 256 pages

A brief guide to writing essays. Emphasizes style and process and provides extensive treatment of argument and figurative language.

3392. Ruggiero, Vincent Ryan. *Enter the Dialogue: A Dramatic Approach to Critical Thinking.* Belmont, Calif.: Wadsworth, 1984. 171 pages

Treats critical thinking in the context of composition through the use of dialogue. Each chapter contains a writing tip, annotated essays, and a set of dialogues. Includes a brief handbook and glossary.

3393. Smith, H. Wendell. *Readable Writing.* Belmont, Calif.: Wadsworth, 1984. 307 pages

Offers techniques for improving style through revision. Identifies eight qualities of good writing: substance, order, economy, emphasis, variety, clarity, consistency, and appearance.

Readers

No entries for 1984 and 1985 in this section.

See also 497

Composition and Literature Texts

3394. Daiker, Donald, Mary F. Hayes, and Jack E. Wallace. *Literature: Options for Reading and Writing.* New York: Harper & Row, 1985. 1108 pages

An anthology that treats literary comprehension, strategies for writing about literature, and elementary literary criticism. Offers preliminary writing exercises, paragraph assignments, and sentence-combining exercises for every work anthologized.

3395. Grassi, Rosanna, and Peter DeBlois. *Composition and Literature: A Rhetoric for Critical Writing.* Englewood Cliffs, N.J.: Prentice-Hall, 1984. 326 pages

Discusses the composition of a critical essay from invention through organizing, developing, and revising. Also introduces the basic literary elements of fiction, drama, and poetry.

3396. Knickerbocker, K. L. *Interpreting Literature.* New York: Holt, Rinehart and Winston, 1985. 1184 pages

An anthology for five literary genres, including essays and biography.

3397. Laff, Ned Scott. "Review: Teaching the Text in Class." *CE* 46 (September 1984): 493–502.

Reviews *Rhythms of English Poetry* and *Style in Fiction.* Discusses methods for using a textbook to teach poetry and other forms of literature.

Business and Technical Writing

3398. Batteiger, Richard P. *Business Writing: Process and Forms.* Belmont, Calif.: Wadsworth, 1985. 496 pages

Features chapters on persuasion, editing, and resume writing with a series of examples and exercises. Four appendixes offer resources and references.

3399. Clements, Wallace, and Robert Berlo. *The Scientific Report: A Guide for Authors.* Washington, D.C.: Society for Technical Communication, 1984. 46 pages

A guide for writers of scientific reports. Contains an annotated bibliography of reference works.

3400. Couture, Barbara, and Jone R. Goldstein. *Cases for Professional and Technical Writing.* Boston: Little, Brown, 1985. 288 pages

Collection of 31 original cases describing on-the-job writing assignments. Each case provides information necessary for students to write documents typically faced by entry-level employees.

3401. Dumont, Raymond, and John Lannon. *Business Communications.* Boston: Little, Brown, 1984. 700 pages

Emphasizes the writing process. Covers outlining, readability, summarizing, and persuasion and integrates technology-related topics throughout.

3402. Fruehling, Rosemary, and Sharon Bouchard. *Business Correspondence.* 4th ed. New York: McGraw-Hill, 1985. 224 pages

Discusses principles of writing letters, memos, and reports. Contains a section on grammar and usage.

3403. Gelderman, Carol. *Better Writing for Professionals: A Precise Guide.* Glenview, Ill.: Scott, Foresman, 1984. 116 pages

Provides examples of professional writing and techniques for writing reports, letters, articles, and speeches.

3404. Glatthorn, Allan A. *Writing for Success.* Glenview, Ill.: Scott, Foresman, 1985. 134 pages

A guide to help business managers write effectively. Includes chapters on writing to project a successful image and on organizing and formatting writing. Last section features examples of "difficult messages."

3405. Goodman, Michael. *Write to the Point: Effective Communication in the Workplace.* Englewood Cliffs, N.J.: Prentice-Hall, 1984. 372 pages

Emphasizes strategies for writing in the workplace. Covers brainstorming techniques, word choice, audience analysis, organization, grammar, sentence and paragraph construction, and the use of illustrations.

3406. Hamon, Keith W. "Text and Context: A Study of Business Writing Strategies." *DAI* 45 (October 1984): 1107A.

Surveys business and industrial employees about writing strategies suggested by recent business writing texts.

3407. Houp, Kenneth, and Thomas E. Pearsall. *Reporting Technical Information.* 5th ed. New York: Macmillan, 1984. 544 pages

A process-oriented text with examples from the professional world. Includes a reference grammar handbook, exercises, appendixes on research. A new chapter on getting started and updated chapters on proposals and empirical research report. Instructor's manual.

3408. Journet, Debra, and Julie Lepick Kling. *Readings for Technical Writers.* Glenview, Ill.: Scott, Foresman, 1984. 384 pages

A collection of 36 selections by professional technical writers. Arranged by genre and intended to represent a range of styles and formats.

3409. Kolin, Philip C., and Janeen L. Kolin. *Models for Technical Writing.* New York: St. Martin's Press, 1985. 480 pages

A collection of more than 65 model reports, memos, letters, proposals, feasibility studies, and other documents written for business, industry, and government. Includes chapters on audience analysis, techniques, and types of technical writing. Instructor's manual.

3410. Lannon, John. *Technical Writing.* 3d ed. Boston: Little, Brown, 1985. 640 pages

Edition emphasizes the writing process and persuasion, gives greater attention to models in the world of work, and includes a new chapter on paragraphs.

3411. Larkin, George. *Working Writing.* Columbus, Ohio: Merrill, 1985. 480 pages

A comprehensive textbook for business or technical writing courses. Designed to help students learn not only about writing and technical formats, but also about the contexts shaping communication in business.

3412. Markel, Michael H. *Technical Writing: Situations and Strategies.* New York: St. Martin's Press, 1984. 538 pages

Provides comprehensive coverage of topics usually treated in technical writing courses. Emphasizes the writing situation and the sequential process of technical writing. Includes examples—many annotated—and exercises throughout. A writer's checklist concludes each chapter. Instructor's manual.

3413. Moore, Nick, and Martin Hesp. *The Basics of Writing Reports Et Cetera.* London: Clive Bingley (distributed in the U.S. by The Shoe String Press), 1985. 120 pages

A manual for writing business reports, including annual reports, press releases, leaflets, committee papers, and minutes. Advocates revising for clarity and offers advice on working with printers.

3414. Oliu, Walter E., Charles T. Brusaw, and Gerald J. Alred. *Writing That Works: How to Write Effectively on the Job.* 2d ed. New York: St. Martin's Press, 1984. 575 pages

An introduction to writing for business, industry, and the professions. Treats planning, drafting, and revising in an occupational context and provides examples, exercises, and assignments throughout. Comprehensive handbook section. Instructor's manual.

3415. Olson, Gary A., James DeGeorge, and Richard E. Ray. *Style and Readability in Business Writing.* New York: Random House, 1984. 228 pages

A brief text that uses sentence-combining techniques to improve the clarity, economy, style, and readability of business writing. Exercises in each chapter. Instructor's manual.

3416. Robinson, Patricia A. *Fundamentals of Technical Writing.* Boston: Houghton Mifflin, 1985. 299 pages

Nine inductively developed chapters present realistic situations requiring students to plan or evaluate job-related writing. Emphasizes both process and written products. Includes handbook and separate instructor's manual.

3417. Ross-Larson, Bruce. *Edit Yourself: A Manual for Everyone Who Works with Words.* New York: Norton, 1985. 128 pages

A guide for business and professional writers. Addresses common writing problems, style, and mechanics.

3418. Roundy, Nancy, and David Mair. *Strategies for Technical Communication.* Boston: Little, Brown, 1985. 480 pages

Focuses on the writing process. Each chapter presents the steps necessary to produce a particular kind of document and emphasizes decision-making strategies.

3419. Sigband, Norman B., and David N. Bateman. *Communicating in Business.* 2d ed. Glenview, Ill.: Scott, Foresman, 1985. 590 pages

Five parts focus on general principles of business writing, business letters, business reports, oral communications, and resumes. Includes examples throughout, exercises, and end-of-chapter reviews.

3420. Starczyk, Lawrence J., and John R. Jewell. *Effective Business Writing.* New York: Macmillan, 1984. 320 pages

Covers grammar, style, and rhetoric as they apply to business forms. Includes examples, exercises, and a reference grammar. Instructor's manual.

3421. VanAlstyne, Judith. *Professional and Technical Writing Strategies.* Englewood Cliffs, N.J.: Prentice-Hall, 1985. 384 pages

Treats strategies for professional and technical writing, including prewriting, correspondence, reports, manuals, research and documentation, and oral communication.

3422. Warren, Thomas L. *Technical Writing: Purpose, Process, and Form.* Belmont, Calif.: Wadsworth, 1984. 358 pages

Emphasizes the collection, analysis, and organization of data. Includes exercises to prepare for writing in careers and a handbook of grammar, mechanics, and sentence style.

3423. Weisman, Herman. *Basic Technical Writing.* 5th ed. Columbus, Ohio: Merrill, 1985. 600 pages

Presents techniques for writing about science and technology against a background meant to help students understand the process of technical communications. Appendix offers examples of technical writing.

See also 2780

Special Texts

3424. Achtert, Walter S., and Joseph Gibaldi. *The MLA Style Manual.* New York: MLA, 1985. 271 pages

A guide for the scholar and graduate student on preparing theses, dissertations, and manuscripts. Also discusses publishing procedures.

3425. Behling, John H. *Guidelines for Preparing the Research Proposal.* Rev. ed. Lanham, Md.: University Press of America, 1984. 88 pages

Revised and updated edition of the 1978 original. Designed to facilitate the preparation of research proposals in the social sciences.

3426. Bizzell, Patricia, and Bruce Herzberg. "Writing across the Curriculum Textbooks: A Bibliographic Essay." *RR* 3 (January 1985): 202–217.

Stresses a process approach to writing as a way to learn and reviews eight textbooks for writing across the curriculum courses.

3427. Bornstein, Diane D. *An Introduction to Transformational Grammar.* Lanham, Md.: University Press of America, 1984. 272 pages

Originally published in 1977, presents transformational grammar in relation to traditional and structural grammar and suggests applications to writing, reading, literary criticsm, and dialect study.

3428. Brooks, Brian S., George Kennedy, Daryl R. Moen, and Don Ranly. *News Reporting and Writing.* New York: St. Martin's Press, 1985. 548 pages

Covers basic journalistic skills, elements and techniques of good writing, specialized reporting, and the rights and responsibilities of journalists. Includes a new chapter on using electronic data bases. Instructor's manual and workbook.

3429. Capassila, Toni Lee. "Academic Discourse: At the Movies." *EngR* 36 (1985): 8–11.

Discusses movies as starting points for research and writing about social themes and social criticisms.

3430. Clark, Virginia, Paul A. Eschholz, and Alfred F. Rosa. *Language: Introductory Readings.* 4th ed. New York: St. Martin's Press, 1985. 740 pages

Forty readings, more than half new to this edition, represent a balance between classic theoretical statements or research reports and recent research reports and articles.

3431. Cook, Claire Kehrwald. *Line by Line: How to Edit Your Own Writing.* Boston: Houghton Mifflin, 1985. 220 pages

A guide to clear writing, with hundreds of before-and-after examples demonstrating how to analyze and repair common errors using professional copyeditors' techniques. Includes advice on basic grammar and usage.

3432. Fitzgerald, Sallyanne H. "Audiovisual and the Basic Writer." *ArEB* 26 (Spring–Summer 1984): 31–33.

Advocates providing content for basic writing through tapes and slides.

3433. Gibaldi, Joseph, and Walter S. Achtert. *The MLA Handbook for Writers of Research Papers.* New York: MLA, 1984. 222 pages

Discusses the mechanics of research writing and documentation. Presents the new MLA style.

3434. Lancombe, Joan, Dorothy Neal, and Joseph Cleary. *English Style Skill-Builders.* New York: McGraw-Hill, 1985. 312 pages

A self-paced program with modules devoted to style, mechanics, and usage.

3435. Lomask, Milton. *The Biographer's Craft.* New York: Harper & Row, 1985. 244 pages

An anecdotal primer that includes sections on how to select, test, and "reveal" a subject and how to find the best mode of development, style, and tone. Includes chapters on autobiography, regional biography, and psychobiography.

3436. McCormick, Mona. *The New York Times Guide to Reference Materials.* Rev. ed. New York: Times Books, 1984. 224 pages

Gives advice on locating and using almanacs, encyclopedias, atlases, indexes, anthologies, language handbooks, government pamphlets, bibliographies, data bases and on-line catalogs, as well as card catalogs and research sources for specific subjects.

3437. Mitchell, Catharine C. "'Little Books' Aid Teaching of Writing." *JourEd* 39 (Autumn 1984): 21–24.

Briefly reviews books on style by Zinsser, Trimble, Strunk and White, Flesch, and others. Shows how they may be used in teaching newswriting.

3438. Schwartz, Mimi, Donald M. Murray, Mary Ann Waters, Toby Fulwiler, and Valerie M. Arms. *Writing for Many Roles.* Upper Montclair, N.J.: Boynton/Cook, 1984. 230 pages

A cross-curricular textbook that emphasizes roles appropriate to any course or field of study. Treats journal writing, letter writing, essay writing, rewriting, newswriting, poetry, technical writing, and research writing.

3439. Smith, Michael Holley. *The Resume Writer's Handbook.* 2d ed. New York: Barnes & Noble Books, 1985. 208 pages

A comprehensive handbook on resume writing for college students and adults; includes sample resumes.

3440. Williams, Joseph M. *Style: Ten Lessons in Clarity and Grace.* 2d ed. Glenview, Ill.: Scott, Foresman, 1985. 251 pages

Offers a systematic presentation of style for mature writers and specific ways to revise unclear writing into clear, readable prose. Exercises are drawn from many disciplines.

3441. Zinsser, William. *On Writing Well: An Informal Guide to Writing Nonfiction.* 3d ed. New York: Harper & Row, 1984. 224 pages

An informal guide to nonfiction writing for adults with new chapters on nonfiction as the new American literature, writing with a word processor, and voice.

See also 520, 1050, 3145

VIDEOTAPES, FILMS, AND FILMSTRIPS

3442. *Basic Writing Skills for Everyday Life.* New Rochelle, N.Y.: Spoken Arts, 1985.

Discusses how to organize thoughts, write succinctly, and edit work. Includes four filmstrips, a teacher's guide, a resource booklet, and 16 duplicating masters. For grades 7 through 12.

3443. Boomer, Garth, and Sheila Fitzgerald. *General Session: 1984 Convention.* 1984 NCTE Convention Speeches. Urbana, Ill.: NCTE, 1984.

Advocates a search for a theory of teaching and examines interactions between students and teachers. Argues against prepackaged instruction, objective testing, and "deskilling" practices. Forty-minute cassette.

3444. *Building Better Sentences.* Niles, Ill.: United Learning, 1984.

Cartoon characters and stories introduce students in primary and intermediate grades to sentence types, sentence punctuation, word order, and ways of solving sentence problems. Four filmstips and cassettes, duplicating masters, and teacher's guide.

3445. Burmester, David. "Films about Writing." *EJ* 74 (March 1985): 99–100.

Reviews two film series for classroom use: *Before the First Word* and *Teachers Teaching Writing.*

3446. *Business Correspondence That Works.* New Rochelle, N.Y.: Spoken Arts, 1985.

Analyzes business correspondence for purpose, tone, and clarity and emphasizes writing techniques for effective communication. Six cassettes, a teacher's guide, and 30 student response books. For grades 7 through 12.

3447. *Composition Skills.* Essential Writing Skills Series. Niles, Ill.: United Learning, 1984.

A program intended to present writing as a process applicable to all writing forms. Focuses on the essay, exposition, the report, the story, and poetic writing. Five filmstrips and cassettes, duplicating masters, and teacher's guide. For high school students.

3448. Costanzo, William. "Visual Resources for Basic Writers: A Sampling of Films, Videotapes, Texts, and Methods." *TETYC* 12 (May 1985): 130–139.

Reviews six films on writing and a television course on writing. Also includes a section on writing textbooks for the thinking eye.

3449. *Creative Writing.* Essential Writing Skills Series. Niles, Ill.: United Learning, 1984.

Provides high school students information and guidelines for writing stories and poems. Presents various poetic forms and discusses major fictional elements and literary devices. Four filmstrips and cassettes, duplicating masters, and teacher's guide.

3450. *Everyday Writing Skills.* LifeSkills Program. New Rochelle, N.Y.: Spoken Arts, 1985.

Presents writing skills necessary for filling out forms, writing letters, and completing applications. Four filmstrips, four cassettes, a teacher's guide, and 28 skill extenders. For grades 7 through 12.

3451. *Expanding Your Vocabulary.* LifeSkills Program. New Rochelle, N.Y.: Spoken Arts, 1985.

Demonstrates how students can build a working vocabulary for reading and writing. Includes four filmstrips, four cassettes, a teacher's guide, and 25 skill extenders. For grades 7 through 12.

3452. Harste, Jerome. *The Authoring Cycle: Read Better, Write Better, Reason Better.* Portsmouth, N.H.: Heinemann, 1985.

A series of eight 30-minute videotapes presenting alternatives to improving the teaching of reading and writing in elementary schools. Reviews current literacy research, outlines a model curriculum, suggests how classrooms can be made compatible with varied learning styles, encourages students to take ownership of texts and share their writing, shows how children can become editors, and explains how teachers can plan exercises to place literacy at the center of the curriculum.

3453. Herrmann, Andrea W., and Brian Gallagher. *Using the Computer in the Classroom: Approaches and Issues.* Urbana, Ill.: NCTE, 1984.

Describes the benefits and difficulties of introducing word processors to high school students. Identifies advantages in working with basic writers in a community college. Sixty-minute cassette.

3454. *Introduction to Parts of Speech.* Niles, Ill.: United Learning, 1985.

Lessons use characters and situations to provide an overview of nouns, verbs, adjectives, and pronouns. Four filmstrips and cassettes, duplicating masters, teacher's guide, and an optional two-disk software package. For primary grades.

3455. Koch, Kenneth. *Wishes, Lies, and Dreams.* New Rochelle, N.Y.: Spoken Arts, 1985.

A poet instructs children on ways to write their own poetry. Two cassettes.

3456. *Mastering Problems of English Usage.* New Rochelle, N.Y.: Spoken Arts, 1985.

Reviews the elements of grammar through students' written responses. Includes six filmstrips, six cassettes, and a teacher's guide. For grades 7 through 12.

3457. Mikulec, Patrick B. "Video-English." *EJ* 73 (January 1984): 60–62.

Describes several ways to use video for reading and writing video histories, yearbooks, essays, and poetry.

3458. Osenlund, Kathryn. "Speech Videotaping." *ExEx* 29 (Spring 1984): 41–42.

Introduces nonthreatening videotaping on unrestricted topics for speeches. Describes "screen and crit" activities.

3459. *Practical Writing.* Essential Writing Skills Series. Niles, Ill.: United Learning, 1984.

Introduces high school students to the philosophy and techniques of business writing. Includes strategies for writing positively and decisively as well as advice on composing letters, directions, job applications, and resumes. Four filmstrips and cassettes, duplicating masters, and teacher's guide.

3460. *Punctuation through Proofreading.* LifeSkills Program. New Rochelle, N.Y.: Spoken Arts, 1985.

In four work situations, students see the interconnection between proofreading and correct punctuation. Includes four filmstrips, four cassettes, a teacher's guide, and 26 skill extenders. For grades 7 through 12.

3461. *The Research Paper.* LifeSkills Program. New Rochelle, N.Y.: Spoken Arts, 1985.

Presents steps for gathering, interpreting, and organizing information for reseach papers. Includes four filmstrips, four cassettes, a teacher's guide, and 25 skill extenders. For grades 7 through 12.

3462. *Sentence Structure I.* Essential Writing Skills Series. Niles, Ill.: United Learning, 1985.

Lessons cover what sentences are, sentence patterns, the use of modifiers and pronouns, and verbal phrases. Four filmstrips and cassettes, duplicating masters, and teacher's guide. For high school students.

3463. *Sentence Structure II.* Essential Writing Skills Series. Niles, Ill.: United Learning, 1985.

Lessons discuss and illustrate sentence types, dependent and independent clauses, the role of coordination and subordination, and common sentence problems. Four filmstrips and cassettes, duplicating masters, and teacher's guide. For high school students.

3464. Stover, Harryette. "Reaching Adult Learners through Public Television." Paper presented at the CCCC Convention, Minneapolis, March 1985. ERIC ED 257 104 [8 pages]

Describes a videotape program prepared by a Texas community college for nontraditional adult students.

3465. Tornow, Joan. *Every Child Is a Writer.* Portsmouth, N.H.: Heinemann, 1984.

A 20-minute filmstrip documenting how a New Hampshire elementary school uses Graves's process approach to teach writing.

3466. *Vocational English.* New Rochelle, N.Y.: Spoken Arts, 1985.

Young adults discuss the speaking, reading, and writing skills needed in the workplace. Includes four filmstips, four cassettes, a teacher's guide, and eight reproducible worksheets. For grades 9 through 12.

3467. *The Write Course: An Introduction to College Composition.* New York: CBS College Publishing, 1984.

A telecourse of 30 half-hour lessons covering topics customarily treated in college writing courses. Produced by the Center for Telecommunications of the Dallas County Community College District, with a study guide prepared by Harryette Stover.

3468. *Writers Writing.* Chicago: Encyclopaedia Britannica Educational, 1985.

A series of three documentary films — *Before the First Word, Telling an Old Story,* and *Pieces of a Puzzle* — produced by Learning Designs and WNET. Each film follows a professional journalist as he or she gathers information and writes a story. Emphasizes seeing, forming, and revision as essential dimensions of the writing process.

3469. *Writing Basics: The Effective Paragraph.* New Rochelle, N.Y.: Spoken Arts, 1985.

Presents a learning by doing method for writing organized, fully developed, and coherent paragraphs. Includes three filmstrips, three cassettes, 32 worksheets, and a teacher's guide. For grades 7 through 12.

3470. *Writing Compositions.* New Rochelle, N.Y.: LifeSkills Program, 1985.

Students help each other write a term paper. Includes four filmstrips, four cassettes, a teacher's guide, and 32 skill extenders. For grades 7 through 12.

3471. *Writing Reports and Letters.* New Rochelle, N.J.: Spoken Arts, 1985.

Explains principles of writing paragraphs, book reports, research reports, and letters. Includes four filmstrips, four cassettes, 16 activity masters, and a teacher's guide. For grades 7 through 12.

3472. *Writing the Expository Essay.* New Rochelle, N.Y.: Spoken Arts, 1985.

Explains the steps for writing an expository essay and reviews the fundamentals of clear writing. Four filmstrips, four cassettes, a teacher's guide, and 24 Skill Extenders. For grades 7 through 12.

See also 2447, 2682, 2890

RECORDINGS

3473. Clark, Irene Lurkis. "Audiotapes and the Basic Writer: A Selected Survey of Useful Materials." *TETYC* 12 (May 1985): 120–129.

Describes six tapes on "Editing: Grammar and Mechanics" and three tapes on the "Composing Process."

See also 26, 3778

COMPUTER PROGRAMS AND OTHER MATERIALS

3474. ALPS Writing Lab. Provo, Utah: Automated Language Processing Systems. For Apple Macintosh.

Consists of three groups of programs: a word processor, text-analysis programs (MacProof), and programming and shared resources to support network communication and make reference materials available to the writer. MacProof programs help students identify and correct problems of spelling, usage, grammar, and structure.

3475. Analysis of Writing. Miami: Miami-Dade Community College. For IBM PC/XT.

Enables teachers to evaluate the mechanics and organization of students' writing. Generates individualized letters discussing problems and produces a status report on each student's progress.

3476. Anderson, Philip M., ed. "Electronic English." *Leaflet* 82 (Special Issue, 1983). ERIC ED 259 388 [48 pages].

Makes available in ERIC a special issue on computers and English instruction.

3477. Appleby, Bruce C., Mim Baker, Owen Thomas, and Stephen A. Bernhardt. "Print, Nonprint, and Computers." *EJ* 74 (October 1985): 87–89.

Reviews a word processing program, a newsletter for teachers who use computers to teach writing, and a software program published together with a textbook.

3478. Ashley, Leonard R. N. "IBmphasis on Jargon." *WWays* 17 (February 1984): 55.

Lists computer terms and invites readers to use their "wetware" (brains) to solve a 15-question quiz.

3479. Ashmore, Timothy M. "Evaluating CAI Material for the Microcomputer." Paper given at the Speech Communication Association, Chicago, November 1984. ERIC ED 252 180 [180 pages]

Describes nine published evaluation forms and develops a combined version based on 22 criteria.

3480. Ashwell, Jonathan D. Bookends. Birmingham, Mich.: Sensible Software. For Apple II.

A bibliographic program that records, stores, edits, and searches for references by author, keyword, and title categories. Rearranges and prints reference data in any format specified. Chains reference files to expand the estimated 900 references that can be stored on each diskette.

3481. AT&T Technologies and AT&T Bell Laboratories. UNIX Instructional Workbench. Greensboro, N.C.: AT&T Technology System. For AT&T 3B, DEC VAX-class.

A set of programs containing an authoring system, a delivery system, and courseware. Helps teachers create courses, design course materials, and maintain records on students' progress.

3482. Auten, Anne. "Computers in English: How and Why?" *EJ* 73 (January 1984): 54–56.

Surveys ERIC and NCTE software, resources, and reports on computer-assisted writing instruction. Includes references, addresses.

3483. Bali, Mrinal. "A Writer's Guide to Buying a Word Processor." *Writer* 97 (April 1984): 5–8.

Provides information about microcomputer word processors, including programs, computers and memory, storage, printers, and monitors.

3484. Bank Street College of Education, Franklin E. Smith, Intentional Educations, and Scholastic. Bank Street Writer II. New York: Scholastic Software. For Apple II, IBM PC.

An enhanced version of Bank Street Writer, includes full cursor movement on the "write" screen, printer format commands such as boldface and underlining, and the option of 40- or 80-column display. Other features include a calculator function, expanded find and replace capabilities, and a copy function.

3485. Bank Street Storybook. Northbrook, Ill.: Mindscape. For Apple II.

An interactive computer program that permits students in grades three to nine to create stories with text, illustrations, and animation. Students use a built-in word and graphics processor, and finished stories can be printed in black and white or color.

3486. Barker, Thomas T. Comment. Lubbock, Tex.: Texas Tech University. For DEC Rainbow 100, IBM PC.

A computer-assisted revision aid used in conjunction with GRAMMATIK. Calculates surface elements, compares percentages to standards set by the teacher, and prints out advice on content, prepositions, continuity, vagueness, and sentence variety.

3487. Barry, Lois. "Notes from a North Star." *WaEJ* 7 (Fall 1984): 25–28.

Cites advantages for teachers who own and use word processors. Offers suggestions to first-time buyers.

3488. Basic Composition. Montrose, Ala.: The Software Teacher. For Apple II, IBM PC.

A four-disk computer program of exercises and examples designed to help students write and revise sentences, improve diction, and organize and write an expository essay.

3489. Bell, Arthur H., and Sharon R. Anderson. English MicroLab. Boston: Houghton Mifflin. For Apple II.

A series of modules that provide explanations, exercises, and diagnostic and mastery tests. Covers sentence construction, grammar, and punctuation.

3490. Biagi, Shirley. *A Writer's Guide to Word Processors.* Englewood Cliffs, N.J.: Prentice-Hall, 1984. 160 pages

A guide to help writers choose word processors. Provides information on costs, uses, advantages, and disadvantages.

3491. Black's Law Dictionary for the Sensible Speller. Birmingham, Mich.: Sensible Software. For Apple and compatible computers.

Supplements Sensible Speller with 20,000 words from *Black's Law Dictionary* and 15,000 words from the *Random House Dictionary.* Combines legal terms and words in common usage.

3492. Bodmer, George R. "The Apple Ate My Paper." *CE* 46 (October 1984): 610–611.

Predicts new student excuses made possible with word processing.

3493. Bolt Bernak and Newman. QUILL: Grades Three through Twelve. Lexington, Mass.: Heath. For Apple.

An integrated package of computer programs. Includes a word processing program, the Writer's Assistant, the Planner, the Library, and the Mailbag.

3494. Booth, Wayne. "Catching the Overflow." *CE* 46 (February 1984): 140–142.

Suggests that word processors allow writers to write faster but not necessarily say more.

3495. Brackett, George. Storytree. New York: Scholastic Software. For Apple II, Commodore 64/128, IBM PC.

A word processing program that enables users to create interactive stories that branch according to choices the writer makes.

3496. Bray, David, Russ Nelson, and Dennis Horn. Lancelot. Potsdam, N.Y.: Clarkson Univeristy. For IBM PC, Zenith Z-100 and Z-150, DEC Rainbow, TI professional.

Contains a spelling checker and programs to analyze language for problems of diction, usage, prepositions, word length, sentence length, and passive constructions. Gives students advice and reports a style index and histogram.

3497. Brigham Young University, Mitre Corporation, and National Science Foundation. TICCIT English Program. Provo, Utah: Brigham Young University. For Hazeltine TICCIT or MicroTICCIT systems.

TICCIT (Time-Shared Interactive Computer-Controlled Information Television) is a system of integrated hardware, software, and courseware. Seventeen English course units cover grammar and mechanics and provide instruction in reasoning, interpretation, and effective essay writing. Also provides diagnostic and mastery tests.

3498. Brooker, Gerard T. "High Tech and the Modern English Department: A Crisis in the Making." *EJ* 73 (January 1984): 31.

Examines the ethics of student writers hiring professional "editor-consultant-word processors."

3499. Bruce, Bertram, Bolt Bernak and Newman, Sarah Michaels, and Karen Watson-Gegeo. *Reviewing the Black History Show: How Computers Change the Writing Process.* Technical Report, no. 320. Urbana, Ill.: University of Illinois Center for the Study of Reading, 1984. ERIC ED 247 544 [20 pages]

Reports on the use of Quill, a software system that includes tools for writing and new environments for communication. Concludes that Quill can produce changes in both writing and the classroom's social structure.

3500. Bruce, Bertram, Sarah Michaels, and Karen Watson-Gegeo. "How Computers Can Change the Writing Process." *LArts* 62 (February 1985): 143–149.

Argues that using the Quill system may facilitate interaction in composing and revising and encourage students to develop a sophisticated sense of audience.

3501. Bryner, Paula. "The Word Processor in the Composition Classroom." *ELAB* 25 (Spring 1984): 6–7.

Presents a general overview of the impact of computers on writing instruction.

3502. Build a Book. New York: Scarborough Systems. For Apple II, Commodore 64.

A book publishing program that permits children to create a data file of names, dates, and other personal information that is then merged with a prewritten story. Detailed instructions guide the child through the printing and binding of the resulting book.

3503. Building Vocabulary Skills. Bridgeport, Conn.: Intellectual Software. For Apple II.

A drill and practice program of randomly generated exercises covering 500 words, arranged cumulatively in ascending order of difficulty. Treats synonyms, antonyms, analogies, and sentence completions.

3504. Burns, Hugh. Burke. Austin, Tex.: University of Texas. For Apple II.

Designed to aid students in prewriting informative or journalistic compositions. Questions asked in the program are based on Burke's dramatistic pentad.

3505. Burns, Hugh. "The Challenge for Computer-Assisted Rhetoric." *CHum* 18 (July–December 1984): 173–181.

Suggests ways that word processors could help with brainstorming, style, and other aspects of writing. Presents sample human/computer dialogue.

3506. Burns, Hugh. "Knowledge and Imagination." *ArEB* 26 (Spring–Summer 1984): 79–85.

Discusses how computers can assist in invention, arrangement, style, memory, and delivery.

3507. Burns, Hugh. Tagi. Austin, Tex.: University of Texas. For Apple II.

An invention program, especially useful for exploratory and informative writing. Based on Young, Becker, and Pike's tagmemic matrix.

3508. Burns, Hugh. Topoi. Austin, Tex.: University of Texas. For Apple II.

An invention program, especially useful for persuasive writing. Based on Aristotle's 28 *topoi.*

3509. Business Writing. Montrose, Ala.: The Software Teacher. For Apple II, IBM PC.

A two-disk computer program designed to teach students to write various forms of internal and external business communications.

3510. Capitalization Skills. Boca Raton, Fla.: IBM Software Publishing Division. For IBM PC.

Runs under Private Tutor 20. Seven lessons help students review and test their mastery of capitalization.

3511. Case, Donald P. "Processing Professorial Words: Personal Computers and the Writing Habits of University Professors." *CCC* 36 (October 1985): 317–322.

Interviews with 60 faculty members indicate, with some qualifications, a positive attitude toward microcomputers as motivators and as aids to revision.

3512. Cohen, Michael, and Richard A. Lanham. Homer. New York: Scribner. For Apple II and III.

Offers guidance in revising by analyzing texts for sentence length, prepositional phrases, forms of the verb "to be," possible nominalizations, and vague words. Based on Lanham's "Paramedic Method," presented in *Revising Prose* (1979).

3513. Collymore, J. C., M. L. Fox, L. T. Frase, P. S. Gringrich, S. A. Neenan, and N. M. MacDonald. UNIX Writer's Workbench. Greensboro, N.C.: AT&T Technology System. For AT&T 3B, DEC PDP 11/70, DEC VAX-class.

A set of programs that analyze prose documents for problems in organization, paragraph development, reliance on the verb "to be," diction, vagueness, spelling, punctuation, split infinitives, misused articles, and style. Can compare students' papers with teacher-selected writing samples. Students receive printed comments and suggestions.

3514. Composition Strategy. Scotts Valley, Calif.: Behavioral Engineering. For Apple II.

Uses special words and cues to direct a writer's thinking. Puts keywords and connectives at the end of a sentence being typed to prompt the writer to consider what to write next. Also instructs writers how to move their eyes to organize "mental maps" of the text.

3515. *Computer-Based Sentence-Combining Instruction.* Los Alamitos, Calif.: Southwest Regional Laboratory for Educational Research and Development, 1982. ERIC ED 239 307 [390 pages]

Provides sentence-combining courseware, an operating manual, and specifications for instruction and content for intermediate grades.

3516. Cramer, Carmen. "Selling the Skeptic: Computers in the Humanities." *CC* 1 (August 1984): 2–3.

Suggests ways to help humanities teachers overcome their suspicions about using computers.

3517. Crossword Magic. Northbrook, Ill.: Mindscape. For Apple II.

A computer program that allows users to arrange, edit, and print crossword puzzles. The program accepts numbers and operation symbols as clues or as answers so that cross-number puzzles can be created.

3518. Daiute, Colette. *Writing and Computers.* Reading, Mass.: Addison-Wesley, 1985. 346 pages

A book for teachers and parents that suggests methods for using computers in writing instruction. Thirteen chapters in four sections: demystifying the writing process, writers of different ages, and setting up compuer writing environments.

3519. Danielson, Wayne A. "The Writer and the Computer." *CHum* 19 (April–June 1985): 85–88.

Describes typical features of existing word processors, suggests other tasks that such programs could perform, and raises questions about their effect on writing quality.

3520. Definitions Review. Raleigh, N.C.: North Carolina State University. For Apple II, IBM PC.

A drill and practice program that teachers can modify. Students can choose definitions and furnish the word, or choose words and furnish the definitions.

3521. Developing Writing Skills. Bridgeport, Conn.: Intellectual Software. For Apple II.

A three-disk program covering word choice, sentence structure, and paragraph construction. Includes explanations, exercises, and self-tests on such problems as abstract language, fragments, run-on sentences, transitions, and clichés.

3522. The Devil and Mr. Webster. Stony Brook, N.Y.: Krell Software. For IBM PC, Apple II, AT&T, Commodore 64, Franklin.

Provides a vocabulary tutorial in a game format. Features over 9000 words.

3523. Dixson, Robert J. Essential Idioms in English. New York: Regents/ALA. For Apple II.

A computer program of 13 lessons on English idioms. For ESL students.

3524. Dorgan, Virginia, and Irene McDonald. High School Composition I and II. Porter, Tex.: Texas Courseware. For IBM PC, Apple II.

A computer program that reviews composition skills. Part I emphasizes sentence structure, methods of revision, and diction and introduces students to the paragraph. Part II continues the study of paragraphs and treats logical theme development, including how to develop and support a thesis.

3525. Edwards, Bruce L., Jr. "The Functions of Literacy: The Past as Future/The Future as Past." Paper given at the CCCC Convention, Minneapolis, March 1985. ERIC ED 259 376 [11 pages]

Criticizes the mistrust of computers.

3526. Elias, Richard. "Will Computers Liberate the Comp Drudge?" Paper given at the Spring Conference of the Delaware Valley Writing Council, Villanova, Pa., February 1984. ERIC ED 241 954 [10 pages]

Discusses setting limits on objectives for computer use in composition.

3527. Elias, Richard. Writer. Delaware, Ohio: Ohio Wesleyan University. For DEC VAX-class.

A shell that allows users to chain into a resident text editor and formatter and into style- and error-checking programs. Intended to help writers discover their message as they move from draft to draft.

3528. English: Basic Mechanics. Dubuque, Iowa: Educulture. For Apple II.

A series of five modules provides 100 lessons on grammar, basic sentence patterns, modifiers, independent clauses, subordinate clauses, and subordinate phrases. Diagnostic tests determine which exercises students need.

3529. Essay Writer. Port Chester, N.Y.: Microcomputer Workshops Courseware. For Apple II, Commodore 64, Radio Shack, IBM PC.

A word processing program for young writers. Editing can be done on the same screen as text entry, and menus and other directions guide users through the features of the word processor.

3530. Etchison, Craig. "Who's Making the Decisions — People or Machines?" *CC* 2 (August 1985): 17–26.

Argues that microcomputers be viewed and used as a tool in a holistic method of teaching writing rather than as a technology that controls the classroom.

3531. Falk, Carol J. "English Skills Tutorials for Sentence-Combining Practice." *CC* 2 (February 1985): 2–4.

Describes remedial, tutorial computer programs written by the author.

3532. Fiction Writing. Montrose, Ala.: The Software Teacher. For Apple II, IBM PC.

Presents six modules of computer instruction covering characterization, plotting, point of view, detail, and questions about marketing fiction.

3533. Film Writing. Montrose, Ala.: The Software Teacher. For Apple II, IBM PC.

Presents three modules of computer instruction to help users write for visual production, develop scripts, and format them.

3534. Fischer, Olga Howard, and Chester A. Fischer. "Electrifying the Composing Process: Electronic Workspaces and the Teaching of Writing." *JTW* 4 (Spring 1985): 113–121.

Surveys electronic prewriting, drafting, revision, proofreading, publishing, and evaluation.

3535. Friedman, Morton, Earl Rand, Ruth Von Blum, Michael Cohen, Lisa Gerrard, Andrew Magpantay, Susan Cheng, Arturo Pisano, and Louisa Mak. HBJ Writer (formerly WANDAH). San Diego: Harcourt Brace Jovanovich. For IBM PC.

A self-contained program that includes a word processor, four prewriting aids, and aids for revising mechanics, style, and organization.

3536. Galahad. Potsdam, N.Y.: Clarkson University. For IBM PC, Zenith Z-100 and Z-150, DEC Rainbow, TI Professional.

A word processor and screen editor designed for scientific writing.

3537. Gardner, Ruth. "The Computer and the College Composition Class: Projections." *ArEB* 26 (Spring–Summer 1984): 64–68.

Presents a nine-point rationale for using word processing in freshman composition. Suggests that such a program produces "more playful and productive writers and thinkers."

3538. Gere, Anne Ruggles. "Practice to Theory: Computers in Composition Classes." *WaEJ* 7 (Fall 1984): 33–34.

Preliminary research indicates that word processors increase fluency but may lead to decreased coherence in writing.

3539. Gordon, Karen Elizabeth. *The Transitive Vampire: A Handbook of Grammar.* New York: Times Books, 1984. 144 pages

An illustrated handbook. Humorous sample sentences demonstrate grammatical principles.

3540. Graham, Sheila Y., and Eileen B. Evans. The Caret Patch. San Diego: Harcourt Brace Jovanovich. For Apple II, IMB PC.

Designed to accompany the *Harbrace College Handbook.* Provides diagnostic tests, practice exercises, and competitive two-student games that require students to recognize and repair errors appearing in sequences of sentences.

3541. Grammar Examiner. San Francisco: Designware. For Apple II, IBM PC, Commodore 64, Atari.

A game of grammar skills in which players climb from cub reporter to editor in chief through skill in punctuation, capitalization, verb tense, subject-verb agreement, adverb and adjective usage, and homonyms.

3542. Grammar Mastery. New York: Regents/ALA. For Apple II.

Three sets of programs review basic verb tenses, nouns and pronouns, yes/no and *wh* questions, clauses, prepositions, adjectives, and adverbs.

3543. Grammar, What Big Teeth You Have! Stony Brook, N.Y.: Krell Software. For IBM PC, Apple II, AT&T, Commodore 64, Franklin.

Provides drill and practice grammar instruction. Diagnoses usage problems commonly encountered on standardized exams.

3544. Graphics Department. Birmingham, Mich.: Sensible Software. For Apple II.

Creates drawings, diagrams, charts, and lettering by entering data on the keyboard. Features include "overlay" options, 100 colors, 40 lettering styles, and a slide projector module.

3545. Halpern, Jeanne W., and Sarah Liggett. *Computers and Composing: How the New Technologies Are Changing Writing.* Studies in Writing and Rhetoric. Carbondale, Ill.: Southern Illinois University Press, 1984. 152 pages

After examining several "new communication systems," proposes methods for introducing them in college writing classes. Discusses how the choice of medium affects the composing process as well as classroom experiments in which instructional units were tested.

3546. Hammer, Cary, and Mitchell Balsam. Story Maker. New York: Scholastic Software. For Apple II.

Program permits users to create pictures with the keyboard, a mouse, KoalaPad, or joystick as a prompt for writing. Or they can write a story and then draw the illustrations or select from preprogrammed pictures. Printouts, a variety of typefaces, and midpage illustrations are possible.

3547. Hansen, Craig, and Lance Wilcox. "Adapting Microcomputers for Use in College Composition." Paper given at the Spring Conference of the Delaware Valley Writing Council, Villanova, Pa., February 1984. ERIC ED 247 609 [11 pages]

Discusses problems of software availability and outlines the development of Access.

3548. Hansen, Craig, and Lance Wilcox. "An Authoring System for Use by Teachers of Composition." *CC* 1 (May 1984): 3–4.

Explains a three-year project at University of Minnesota to develop a computer authoring system so that teachers can write own instructions, guides, and materials for writing courses.

3549. Hartley, Charles. Sensible Speller. Birmingham, Mich.: Sensible Software. For Apple II.

A spelling checker that finds misspellings by high-speed word comparison with the 85,000-word *Random House Dictionary.* Shows misspelled words in context, locates potential misspellings in the text, permits adding words to the dictionary, and prints misspelled and corrected words.

3550. Hassett, James. "Hacking in Plain English." *PsyT* 18 (June 1984): 38–39, 42–45.

Explains the work being done with conversational programs like Intellect and Explorer so that computers can understand English as easily as young children.

3551. Hayes, Tom. "Computers and the Elementary School Student: A Comparison of Story Maker and Bank Street Writer." *WaEJ* 7 (Fall 1984): 14–17.

Selecting software for elementary school writers requires evaluating menus, directions on screens, tutorials, documentation, error detection features, and how easy the program is to use.

3552. Holdstein, Deborah H., and Tim Redman. "Empirical Research in Word-Processing: Expectations *Vs.* Experience." *CC* 3 (November 1985): 43–54.

An experimental group of students doing compositions on VAX with the Runoff program reported a variety of difficulties and dissatisfactions, many extraneous to the choice of software.

3553. Holmes, Leigh Howard. "Word Processing Theme Comments in the Writing Lab." *WLN* 8 (January 1984): 6–7.

Describes the development of a computer program that explains theme annotations and directs students to appropriate corrective exercises.

3554. Horn, William D. The Proposal Writer. Potsdam, N.Y.: William D. Horn. For IBM PC.

Leads users by prompts through the process of writing grants and proposals.

3555. How to Do Research. Bridgeport, Conn.: Intellectual Software. For Apple II, IBM PC.

An interactive tutorial program that provides instruction in notetaking, making an outline, consulting bibliographies, and using card catalogs and computerized data bases.

3556. Institute of Educational Research. Activity Files for the Bank Street Writer, Vol. 2. New York: Scholastic Software. For Apple II, Atari, Commodore 64/128, IBM PC.

Runs in conjunction with Bank Street Writer and Bank Street Writer II. Consists of 40 lessons that provide practice in writing tasks such as punctuating business letters, using third-person narration, writing complete instructions, and using semicolons.

3557. Intellectual SAT Vocabulary. Bridgeport, Conn.: Intellectual Software. For Apple II and IBM PC.

A drill and practice program for high school students. Focuses on antonyms.

3558. Jaech, Sharon. "The Process of Writing and Writing with a Word Processor." *WaEJ* 7 (Fall 1984): 3–7.

Reduced physical effort, immediacy, ease or revision, and the power of the machine make word

processing attractive. Problems include confusion of technique with coherence, time-consuming formatting, and a lack of intimacy.

3559. Jobst, Jack. "Computer-Assisted Grading: The Electronic Handbook." *JTW* 3 (Fall 1984): 225–235.

Describes the advantages, features, and positive student response to computer-assisted grading.

3560. Just Imagine. West Chester, Pa.: Commodore Electronics. For Commodore 64.

A computer program that enables young writers to choreograph a scene, selecting among 9 backgrounds (some with moving elements), 48 stationary objects, and 25 animated characters. Then they write a story to accompany the completed scene.

3561. Language Skills. Boca Raton, Fla.: IBM Software Publishing Division. For IBM PC.

Runs under Private Tutor 20. Six lessons cover parts of speech and grammatical problems, including sentence construction, noun and verb confusion, subject-verb agreement, adjective and adverb confusion, pronoun cases, and pronoun-antecedent agreement.

3562. Lawrence, John S. "ThinkTank for the Apple IIe." *CHum* 19 (July–September 1985): 194–196.

Describes ThinkTank, software that allows the simultaneous creation of outlines and related text.

3563. Leahy, Ellen K. "A Writing Teacher's Shopping and Reading List for Software." *EJ* 73 (January 1984): 62–65.

Suggests software for six categories of computer-assisted writing instruction. References include "most promising current software."

3564. Learning Parts of Speech. Bridgeport, Conn.: Intellectual Software. For Apple II, IBM PC.

A collection of interactive tutorials with drill and practice exercises. For elementary students.

3565. Learning Ways, Inc. MasterType's Writer (formerly Writing Wizard). Tarrytown, N.Y.: Scarborough Systems and Collamore Educational Publishing. For Apple II, Commodore 64/128.

A word processor that offers the option of split-screen writing, illustration, and animation as well as the standard features of search and replace, page formatting, and underlining.

3566. Lebowitz, Michael. "Creating Characters in a Story-Telling Universe." *Poetics* 13 (June 1984): 171–193.

Describes Universe, a program that generates fictional characters with consistency and coherence and will eventually create soap-opera style narratives.

3567. Lesgold, Alan M., and Frederick Reif, eds. *Computers in Education: Realizing the Potential. Report of a Research Conference, Pittsburgh, Pa., 20–24 November 1982.* Washington, D.C.: Office of Educational Research and Improvement, 1983. ERIC ED 235 784 [265 pages]

Proceedings include three papers on the future of computers in writing education.

3568. Lessons in Reading and Reasoning. Bridgeport, Conn.: Intellectual Software. For Apple II, IBM PC.

A computer program of five disks containing lessons in fallacies, including loaded words, false analogies, stereotyping, and rationalizations.

3569. Levin, Barbara B. "A Dozen Ways to Put Your Classroom Computer to Work...At Last." *CurrR* 25 (September–October 1985): 40–45.

Describes 12 ways of getting maximum use from computers during the school day, including individualized feedback, cooperative and discovery learning, and creative writing. Also identifies "classroom software that works."

3570. Lindenau, Suzanne E. "The Teacher and Technology in the Humanities and Arts." *MLJ* 68 (Summer 1984): 119–124.

Calls for humanities and arts teachers to improve their teaching by embracing computer technology, particularly within a language lab.

3571. Louth, Richard H. "Learning, Teaching, and Writing: A Workshop Using Transparencies." *DAI* 45 (February 1985): 2523A.

Concludes that whole-class workshops are practical for teaching writing to large classes.

3572. Lucking, Robert. "Marking Papers and Record Keeping for Apple Users." *CC* 2 (February 1985): 6.

Recommends that Apple computer users explore AppleWriter II and Appleworks as tools for commenting on student papers and for record keeping.

3573. Lund, Donna D. "A Computer-Aided Instruction Program in Sentence Rhetoric: Theory and Application." *DAI* 44 (February 1984): 2459A.

Finds that writing at the computer can improve college students' motivation, self-confidence, and understanding of revision.

3574. Marcus, Stephen. Activity Files for the Bank Street Writer, Vol. 1. New York: Scholastic Software. For Apple II, Atari, Commodore 64/128, IBM PC.

Computer-based activities teach and reinforce the fundamentals of the writing process, including writing and revising skills. Activities also provide writing practice in a variety of modes.

3575. Marcus, Stephen. Compupoem. Woodcliff Lake, N.J.: K–12 MicroMedia. For Apple II, TRS-80.

A software program designed to help students study and write poetry. Asks students for parts of speech that the program then assembles into a haiku-like poem.

3576. Marcus, Stephen. pfs: Write Activity Files. New York: Scholastic Software. For Apple II.

Computer-based writing activities provide practice in prewriting through revising and writing in a variety of modes.

3577. Marling, William. "Grading Essays on a Microcomputer." *CE* 46 (December 1984): 797–810.

Describes a system in which students write and the teacher grades and manages a writing class — all using computers.

3578. Marling, William, and Cynthia Marling. Grader. Cleveland, Ohio: Case Western Reserve University. For IBM PC.

Enables teachers to mark papers submitted on disk with 18 mnemonics and as much marginal and final commentary as desired. Saves all errors and comments noted in its "gradebook."

3579. Marling, William, and Cynthia Marling. Reader. Cleveland, Ohio: Case Western Reserve University. For IBM PC.

Works with Grader. Allows students to scroll through compositions and print out corrections to over 70 possible problems. Separate "university" and "junior college" versions are available.

3580. Marling, William, and Cynthia Marling. Writer. Cleveland, Ohio: Case Western Reserve University. For IBM PC.

A text editor that works with the Marlings's Grader and Reader programs.

3581. MaxThink. Piedmont, Calif.: Neil Larson. For Apple Macintosh, IBM PC.

Helps users create outlines by organizing ideas, establishing linear and hierarchical relationships, and displaying information in text and graphic formats.

3582. McAllister, Carole. "The Effects of Word Processing on the Quality of Writing: Fact or Illusion?" *CC* 2 (August 1985): 36–44.

Describes a study in which 30 university composition teachers rated compositions written on a word processor higher than the same composition written by hand or typed.

3583. McCann, Thomas M. "Sentence Combining for the Microcomputer." *CC* 1 (May 1984): 1–2.

Describes sentence-combining exercises, based on the Christensen program and directed toward subordinating ideas through the use of free modifiers.

3584. McCarley, Barbara. "Why Teach Word Processing to Young Writers?" *CurrR* 25 (November–December 1985): 49–50.

Describes educators' objections to teaching word processing and discusses potential means of overcoming these "roadblocks."

3585. McKenzie, Jamieson. "Accordion Writing: Expository Composition with the Word Processor." *EJ* 73 (September 1984): 56–58.

Describes the composing process on a word processor, concluding that its primary value is to remove anxiety, not facilitate editing.

3586. McMahon, Marilyn, Sara Hoover, and William Popp. *Report Writing in dBase II.* Englewood Cliffs, N.J.: Prentice-Hall, 1985. 137 pages

Concentrates on dBase II's report writing command, with explanations of editing, using memory variables and string functions, using data files, and using the printer.

3587. Meeker, Michael W. "Word Processing and Writing Behavior." Paper given at the Minnesota Council of Teachers of English Meeting, Mankato, Minn., October 1984. ERIC ED 250 686 [29 pages]

Argues that word processors encourage prewriting, drafting, and revison and create a new objectivity and sense of control.

3588. Micro Teacher. San Francisco: Eduware. For Apple II, IBM PC.

A five-volume tutorial and practice program that teaches parts of speech and correct usage. Includes mastery tests and remedial help.

3589. Milner, Joseph O., ed. "Micro to Main Frame Computers in English Education." *NCET* 39 (Special Issue, Winter 1982). ERIC ED 255 915 [45 pages].

Makes available in ERIC a special issue on computers and the language arts.

3590. Monroe, Rick. "Computers and Composition." *WaEJ* 7 (Fall 1984): 30–32.

Acknowledges that computers increase motivation and ease of revision but warns of their limitations.

3591. Mott, Tim, Steve Hayes, Norm Lane, David Maynard, Jerry Morrison, Steve Shaw, and Dan Silva. Cut and Paste. Northbrook, Calif.: Mindscape. For Apple II.

A word processor for young students in grades four and higher. Uses on-screen commands to write, edit, and print.

3592. Mountain, Lee. "Wanted: Software by English Teachers." *EJ* 73 (January 1984): 57–59.

A survey of 64 replies from software companies. Provides tips to English teachers interested in developing microcomputer programs. Includes references.

3593. Nageley, John, and Irene D. Hays. "Using Computers to Simplify the Writing Process." *WaEJ* 7 (Fall 1984): 8–9.

Computers eliminate recopying and introduce an element of play. Writers can use them without understanding how they work.

3594. Narcissus. Potsdam, N.Y.: Clarkson University. For IBM PC, Zenith Z-100 and Z-150, DEC Rainbow, TI Professional.

A computer authoring system designed to create computerized quizzes and study guides.

3595. Neuwirth, Christine M., David S. Kaufer, and Cheryl Geisler. "What Is EPISTLE?" *CC* 1 (August 1984): 1–2.

Epistle is a grammar and stylistic analysis program developed by IBM. Carnegie-Mellon is assessing its capabilities, its effects on revision, and its potential as a teaching tool.

3596. Newman, Judith M. "Language Learning and Computers." *LArts* 61 (September 1984): 494–497.

Argues that, because people control machines, the word processor can become a means for students and teachers to make meaning collaboratively.

3597. The Newsroom. Minneapolis: Springboard Software. For Apple II, IBM PC, Commodore 64/128.

Assists users to design, write, and print newspapers or newsletters. Designed to be used with the Clip Art Collection, a library of 600 pieces of commerical art.

3598. Newton, Sandra S. *Computer Resources for Writing.* Urbana, Ill.: ERIC/RCS, 1984. ERIC ED 254 262 [36 pages]

Reviews a number of uses of computers in two-year college writing classes — for grammar drill, as word processors, and for special invention and editing programs.

3599. Noble, David F., and Virginia D. Noble. *Improve Your Writing with Word Processors.* Indianapolis: Que, 1984. 275 pages

Explains how to improve writing skills by using the text-handling and editing capabilities of word processors. Focuses especially on restructuring and revising paragraphs and sentences.

3600. Nota Bene. New York: MLA. For IBM PC.

A word processing program designed for scholars and teachers in the humanities.

3601. Ostrom, Hans. "Hardware and Hard Questions: A Conference on Computers and Writing." *WaEJ* 7 (Fall 1984): 8–9.

Summarizes trends, accomplishments, and unanswered questions evident at the first annual Western States Conference on Computer-Assisted Instruction, May 1984.

3602. Panda Learning Systems. The Writing Adventure. Allen, Tex.: DLM Teaching Resources. For Apple II, Commodore 64/128.

A computer program that asks students to write a story by presenting scenes, questions, and "notecards" for recording story ideas. A "proofing aid" highlights potential problems of style, punctuation, and diction in the student's draft.

3603. Pea, Roy D. *Prospects and Challenges for Using Microcomputers in School.* Technical Report, no. 7. New York: Bank Street College of Education, 1984. ERIC ED 249 927 [23 pages]

Discusses problems and prospects for integrating microcomputers in schools. Details six aspects of successful integration.

3604. Penroe, John M. "Computer Software Review." *ABCAB* 47 (September 1984): 22–24.

Review article on computer software of interest to business writers, including Grammatik, Punctuation & Style, The Random House Proofreader, and The Word Plus.

3605. The Perfect Score. Northbrook, Ill.: Mindscape. For Apple II, Commodore 64/128, IBM PC.

An interactive computer program designed to help students in grades 10 to 12 prepare for SAT exams. A timed SAT and Test of Standard Written English is included, and a listing of printed scores is available.

3606. Persuasive Essay. Bridgeport, Conn.: Intellectual Software. For Apple II, IBM PC.

A five-disk program for remedial and average high school students. Includes explanations, exercises, and self-tests to help students select appropriate topics, develop support for opinions, and write effective conclusions. A version for junior high school students is also available.

3607. Practical Composition Series. Bridgeport, Conn.: Intellectual Software. For Apple II, Macintosh, IBM PC.

A collection of programs that include explanations, exercises, and self-tests for selecting correct words, constructing accurate sentences, and developing an effective strategy and style for writing the essay.

3608. Practical Grammar I, II, and III. Bridgeport, Conn.: Intellectual Software. For Apple II, TRS-80 Models III and IV.

Several interactive programs containing lessons on sentence patterns, parts of speech, case and gender, clauses, and phrases. Provide extensive drills, automatic scoring, immediate feedback, and branching.

3609. Practical Spelling. Bridgeport, Conn.: Intellectual Software. For Apple II, IBM PC.

Contains suggestions for improving spelling. Gives spelling rules, advice about forming plurals, possessives, and contractions. Lists 100 spelling demons.

3610. Practical Vocabulary. Bridgeport, Conn.: Intellectual Software. For Apple II, IBM PC.

A vocabulary drill and practice program that includes definitions, antonyms, synonyms, word roots, and prefixes. Tests students, scores tests, and keeps track of scores.

3611. Punctuation Skills. Boca Raton, Fla.: IBM Software Publishing Division. For IBM PC.

Runs under Private Tutor 20. Six lessons help students review and test their mastery of periods, exclamation points, commas, apostrophes, quotation marks, colons, and semicolons.

3612. Rabin, Joseph. "Advent of the Post-Gutenberg University." *ArEB* 26 (Spring–Summer 1984): 58–63.

Discusses the possible effects of computers on scholarship and instruction.

3613. The Reading Workshop. Northbrook, Ill.: Mindscape. For Apple II.

An interactive computer program that presents 10 activities reinforcing concepts in reading and language arts. Skill with sequencing, comprehension, context clues, spelling, punctuation, parts of speech, decoding, reading, and writing are developed in the context of literature.

3614. Redmond, Claire, Cheryl Lawrence, and Frank Villani. "User-Friendly Software." *CC* 3 (November 1985): 7–12.

Examines the "user-friendly" wording in CAI instruction. Concludes that the computer should be viewed as a tutor, not a teacher.

3615. Report Card. Birmingham, Mich.: Sensible Software. For Apple II, IBM PC.

A grading system that stores up to 300 students' names and grades from 12 classes. Compiles grades according to class averages, letters, individuals, results of an activity. Weights assignments to reflect different values and allows "no grade" marks. Sorts by names, grades, codes, and activities.

3616. RightWriter. Longboat Key, Fla.: Decisionware. For IBM PC.

Analyzes documents for errors in grammar, usage, punctuation, style, and spelling.

3617. Rodrigues, Dawn. "Sounding the Depths: Computers and Basic Writers." Paper given at the CCCC Convention, New York, March 1984. ERIC ED 248 505 [17 pages]

Argues that specific word processing skills should be taught when an individual student needs them during a given composing task.

3618. Rodrigues, Raymond J., and Dawn Rodrigues. "Computer-Based Invention: Its Place and Potential." *CCC* 35 (February 1984): 78–87.

Describes two kinds of computer programs for invention: guides for sequential learning and questions to generate and stucture ideas or assist open-ended inquiry.

3619. Rodrigues, Raymond J., and Dawn Rodrigues. Creative Problem Solving. Las Cruces, N.M.: New Mexico State University. For Apple II, IBM PC.

A two-part prewriting program intended to create analogies leading to insights into a topic: Visual Synectics asks students to compare their topics to objects, and Comparing Subtopics asks students to list and compare subtopics.

3620. Roen, Duane H., and Margaret Fleming. "The CIA and CAI: A Dialogue on Some Pedagogical Issues." *IIEB* 73 (Fall 1985): 11–21.

Debates the efficacy of computers as tools for writing.

3621. Ross, Donald, and Robert Rasche. Eyeball: A Program for Stylistic Descriptions. Minneapolis: University of Minnesota. For CDC and IBM mainframes.

Produces descriptions of word length, vocabulary structure, syntactic categories, and sentence length from a tagged file that can be explored for a wide range of statistical measures of style.

3622. Roth, Audrey J. "Babes in Toyland; Or, How I Stopped Looking and Learned to Start Living with a Computer." Paper given at the Southeastern Conference on English in the Two-Year College, Arlington, Va., February 1984. ERIC ED 240 595 [11 pages]

Describes the experience of learning to use a word processor.

3623. Rubin, Andee, and Bertram Bruce. *Quill: Reading and Writing with a Microcomputer.* Urbana, Ill.: University of Illinois Center for the Study of Reading, 1984. ERIC ED 240 516 [44 pages]

Studies software for teaching language arts.

3624. SAT/GRE Vocabulary. Bridgeport, Conn.: Intellectual Software. For Apple II.

Designed to improve vocabulary skills of high aptitude students. Includes antonyms and analogies disks, as well as lessons on taking tests.

3625. Schwartz, Helen J. *Issues of Integrating Computers into Writing Instruction.* Urbana, Ill.: ERIC/RCS, 1984. ERIC ED 244 274 [17 pages]

Discusses computers in the writing classroom.

3626. Schwartz, Helen J. Prewrite. Upper Montclair, N.J.: Boynton/Cook. For Apple II.

A companion to *Writing for Many Roles* (1985). Helps students find and shape topics through a series of interactive questions. Prints the student's notes.

3627. Schwartz, Helen J. SEEN. Rochester, Mich.: Helen J. Schwartz. For Apple II.

An interactive program that guides students in testing opinions about literature.

3628. Selfe, Cynthia L., and Billie J. Wahlstrom. *The Benevolent Beast: Computer-Assisted Instruction for the Teaching of Writing.* Urbana, Ill.: ERIC/RCS, 1982. ERIC ED 234 398 [17 pages]

Reports on the development of interactive software at Michigan Technological University for supplementing process-based instruction.

3629. Selfe, Cynthia L., and Billie J. Wahlstrom. "Fighting in the Computer Revolution: A Field Report from the Walking Wounded." *CC* 2 (August 1985): 63–68.

Argues that the cultures of computer scientists and of traditional humanists are separated by metaphors that inform their realities.

3630. Selfe, Cynthia L., and Billie J. Wahlstrom. WordsWork (formerly Wordsworth II). Houghton, Mich.: Michigan Tech Software. For IBM PC.

Eight modules of supplemental instruction in description, narration, personal writing, classification, evaluation, persuasion, and writing about literature. Each module contains a "planning"

and "polishing" program to guide students in developing and revising their drafts.

3631. Sensible Technical Dictionary for the Sensible Speller. Birmingham, Mich.: Sensible Software. For Apple II.

Supplements Sensible Speller with a two-disk set of technical terms. The "Life Sciences" disk contains over 22,000 words from the fields of anatomy, biology, medicine, and psychology. The "Physical Sciences" disk contains over 25,000 words from the fields of astronomy, aviation, electronics, engineering, geology, math, meterology, mineralogy, optics, photography, and physics.

3632. Shostak, Robert. *Computers in Composition Instruction.* Eugene, Oreg.: International Council for Computers in Education, 1984. ERIC ED 240 702 [89 pages]

A collection of nine essays focusing on the use of microcomputers in writing instruction, especially as an aid to prewriting, and on the design and selection of courseware.

3633. Show Director. Northbrook, Ill.: Mindscape. For Commodore 64/128, IBM PC.

An interactive computer program designed to assist students in grades two to six to create theatrical presentations. Students use a word processor to type their texts and then choose among 12 settings, 40 characters, music, and sound effects to complete their story scripts.

3634. Shuman, R. Baird. "A Dozen Ways for English Teachers to Use Microcomputers." *EJ* 74 (October 1985): 37–39.

Divides 12 simple uses of the microcomputer into administrative uses and combined administrative and instructional uses.

3635. Smith, John B. ARRAS. Chapel Hill, N.C.: Conceptual Tools. For IBM or look-alike mainframe 43XX, 30XX, etc.

A full-text retrieval and analysis system that provides interactive access to lexical information, interactive concordances, and graphical distribution. Program searches for contextual patterns and has facilities for defining and maintaining analytic categories.

3636. Smye, Randy. "Computer Innovations for Teaching the Writing Process." *EQ* 17 (Summer 1984): 27–37.

Suggests three ways to help teachers deal with computer technology.

3637. Software Publishing Corporation. pfs: Write. New York: Scholastic Software and Software Publishing Corporation. For Apple II, IBM PC.

A word processing program that includes such options as search and replace, block editing, and line formatting. The version distributed by Scholastic includes a learning activites disk and teaching guide.

3638. Sommers, Elizabeth A., and James L. Collins. "Microcomputers and Writing." *CC* 2 (August 1985): 27–35.

Argues that many computer programs do not make adequate use of the microcomputer's capabilities to assist students in writing. Identifies several that do.

3639. Sommers, Elizabeth A., and James L. Collins. "What Research Tells Us about Composing and Computing." Paper given at the Computer Educators League, Buffalo, September 1984. ERIC ED 249 497 [22 pages]

Reviews research and concludes that computers are helpful when integrated into teaching.

3640. Southwell, Michael G. GrammarLab. Boston: Little, Brown. For Apple II, IBM PC.

Five units of computer-assisted instruction in sentence structure, nouns, present-tense verbs, past-tense verbs, and the verb "to be." Emphasis is on instruction rather than drill or testing.

3641. Spelling Skills. Boca Raton, Fla.: IBM Software Publishing Division. For IBM PC.

Runs under Private Tutor 20. Eight lessons help students review and test their mastery of spelling principles, including the formation of plurals, suffixes, words with "silent" letters, homophones, and words using *i* and *e*.

3642. Spell It! Torrance, Calif.: Davidson and Associates. For Apple II, IBM PC, Commodore 64/128, Atari.

An interactive computer program presents rules for 1000 commonly misspelled words and four activities, including a word scramble and arcade game. Lists of 20 words are grouped in ascending order of difficulty, and an editor allows the entry of additional words.

3643. Stedman's Medical Dictionary for the Sensible Speller. Birmingham, Mich.: Sensible Software. For Apple II.

Supplements Sensible Speller with a three-disk set of over 65,000 medical terms.

3644. Steele, Louise W. "The Least You Should Know about Office Machines (A Talk to Students)." *ABCAB* 47 (September 1984): 10–17.

Explains the types and uses of equipment that business communication students will find in the modern office.

3645. Sticky Bear Reading. Columbus, Ohio: Weekly Reader Family Software. For IBM PC, Apple II, Commodore 64.

An educational game that builds reading comprehension and vocabulary. For children ages five to eight.

3646. Sticky Bear Spellgrabber. Columbus, Ohio: Weekly Reader Family Software. For Apple II, Commodore 64.

Builds vocabulary and spelling skills with three games. Draws from a 4000-word list or an optional customized list. For children ages six to nine.

3647. Strickland, James. Quest. Slippery Rock, Pa.: Slippery Rock University. For Apple II, IBM PC.

An interactive program that asks writers questions about their topics. Applies classical rhetorical invention, tagmemics, and Burke's pentad.

3648. Stultz, Russell. *Writing and Publishing on Your Microcomputer*. Englewood Cliffs, N.J.: Prentice-Hall, 1984. 165 pages

A guide for home and business uses of microcomputers. Offers advice on creating professional-quality documents for publication, with discussions of word processing, telecommunications, and typesetting.

3649. Sudol, Ronald A. "Applied Word Processing: Notes on Authority, Responsibility, and Revision in a Workshop Model." *CCC* 36 (October 1985): 331–335.

Argues that teaching writing in a computer laboratory provides a setting for collaborative learning, changes teacher roles, allows students to maintain authority over their texts, and leads to an alternative conception of revision.

3650. Television Writing. Montrose, Ala.: The Software Teacher. For Apple II, IBM PC.

Presents six modules of computer instruction in writing for television. Covers television techniques, building a script, plotting, writing for a market, and rewrites.

3651. Theismeyer, Elaine, and John Theismeyer. Editor. Penn Yan, N.Y.: Serenity Software. For TRS-80 Models III and IV.

A text-analysis system that checks a text created on a word processor for mistakes and questionable decisions in usage and mechanics.

3652. Theismeyer, John. "Teaching with Text Checkers." Paper given at the Spring Conference of the Delaware Valley Writing Council, Villanova, Pa., February 1984. ERIC ED 246 469 [11 pages]

Discusses the use of Editor, a computerized system to monitor errors in writing, in the college composition class.

3653. Thomas, P. G. "Text Processing in a Student Environment." *CompEd* 9 (1985): 21–30.

Presents a technical assessment describing "the need for an increased awareness of string processing facilities."

3654. Thrush, Jo Ann, and Randolph S. Thrush. "Microcomputers in Foreign Language Instruction." *MLJ* 68 (Spring 1984): 21–27.

Reviews educational uses of computers and microcomputers in language instruction. Calls for teachers to use computers, design software, and learn how to apply this technology.

3655. Tink's Adventure. Northbrook, Ill.: Mindscape. For Apple II, Commodore 64/128, IBM PC.

Assists students in kindergarten through grade four to become familiar with the computer keyboard and to learn the alphabet.

3656. Versluis, Edward B. "Computer Simulations and the Far Reaches of Computer-Assisted Instruction." *CHum* 18 (July–December 1984): 225–232.

Describes several computer simulations used in writing instruction and suggests directions for their expanded use.

3657. Vocabulary Mastery Series A and B. New York: Regents/ALA. For Apple II.

A series of computerized lessons for studying 2000 English words.

3658. Waddell, Craig. "Word Processing in the Writing Class: Tutorials Can Help Break the Ice." *CC* 3 (November 1985): 61–70.

Presents a tutorial for Quicksoft's PC-Write Version 23 software.

3659. Wahlstrom, Billie J. "What Does User-Friendly Mean Anyway?" *CC* 3 (November 1985): 13–28.

Argues that "user-friendly" should be applied only to the format, not the content, of courseware. Calls for more research on the content and format issues of educational technology.

3660. Weathers, Winston, and Joe H. Nichols. The Quintilian Analysis. Tulsa: Joseph Nichols. For IBM PC, TRS-80 III and IV, Zenith Z-100, Tandy 1000 and 2000, Sperry PC.

Analyzes prose compositions against stylistic elements drawn from twentieth-century American and British essays. Prints a commentary and provides a lexicon of the vocabulary used in the composition.

3661. Winograd, Terry. "Computer Software for Working with Language." *SAm* 251 (September 1984): 130–145.

Surveys software for computer translation, word processing, question answering, and electronic mail.

3662. Winterbauer, Art. "Computer-Based Composition Aid for Writing." *CC* 1 (May 1984): 2–3.

Describes the development of a program for narrowing a topic, brainstorming it, and arranging material for a college essay.

3663. The Word Alert! Collection. New York: Regents/ALA. For Apple II.

A set of four computer word games designed for ESL or language arts classes.

3664. Word Attack! Torrence, Calif.: Davidson and Associates. For Apple II, IBM PC, Commodore 64/128, Atari.

A vocabulary building system with four exercises including an arcade style game for reinforcement. Sentences illustrate the use of 675 words on nine levels of difficulty from ages eight to adult. An editor allows the entry of additional words. Disks are available for lower grade levels, SAT preparation, and affixes.

3665. Working with Antonyms and Synonyms. Bridgeport, Conn.: Intellectual Software. For Apple II.

Uses a controlled vocabulary, words underlined in sentences, and randomly selected displays. Permits teacher to keep records, to control the rate of presentation, and to add material.

3666. Working with Sentences. Bridgeport, Conn.: Intellectual Software. For Apple II, IBM PC.

A collection of interactive tutorials reinforced by drill and practice exercises. Students receive immediate feedback and remediation in working with verbs, pronoun and verb agreement, punctuation, and usage concepts treated in the context of sentences.

3667. Worley, Lloyd. "Using Word Processing in Composition Classes." Paper given at the CCCC Convention, New York, March 1984. ERIC ED 243 127 [10 pages]

Describes the features of a good word processor and explores its effects on the writing process.

3668. Wresch, William. *The Computer in Composition Instruction: A Writer's Tool.* Urbana, Ill.: NCTE, 1984. 221 pages.

A collection of 13 articles that describe the role and effects of computers in writing instruction, especially as aids to prewriting and revision. Provides descriptions of the University of Minnesota's project, Burns's and the Rodrigues's prewriting programs, Homer, the Writer's Workbench, SEEN, Wordsworth II, Comp/Lab, Wandah, and other prewriting, text-analysis, and word processing programs. Includes an annotated bibliography.

3669. Wresch, William. Writer's Helper. Iowa City, Iowa: CONDUIT. For Apple II, IBM PC.

A collection of 22 programs arranged in two sections. Prewriting programs offer students several ways to find, explore, and organize topics, and text-analysis programs help students locate organizational, grammatical, and stylistic problems in drafts.

3670. The Write Approach I and II. Bridgeport, Conn.: Intellectual Software. For Apple II.

Includes a word processor and extensive writing exercises on separate data disks. Covers editing skills, sentence improvement, and paragraph revision on either the elementary or secondary level. Helps students practice proofreading for errors, combining sentences, and modeling and reorganizing scrambled paragraphs.

3671. Writing Is Thinking. Dallas: Kapstrom. For IBM PC, Apple II.

An interactive program to help students think through a topic, formulate a thesis, choose a structure, write a paragraph, and revise.

3672. Wyatt, David H. "ESL Applications of the Computer-Controlled Videodisc Player." *CHum* 18 (July–December 1984): 243–249.

Describes videodisc hardware and how it can be used to teach listening skills in ESL courses.

3673. Wye, Margaret Enright. *The Complete Guide to Punctuation: A Quick Reference Desk Book.* Englewood Cliffs, N.J.: Prentice-Hall, 1985. 181 pages

A basic guide to punctuation and its rationale, with exercises and a diagnostic test.

3674. Zimmer, JoAnn. "The Continuing Challenge: Computers and Writing." *CC* 2 (February 1985): 4–6.

Describes how one college has integrated commercial and original computer programs for prewriting, writing, and editing.

See also 2, 21, 30, 35, 37, 45, 71, 95, 158, 215, 237, 283, 381, 424, 451, 453, 454, 550, 576, 702, 706, 826, 854, 1370, 1389, 1622, 1676, 1711, 1717, 1739, 1749, 1750, 1755, 1875, 1897, 1899, 1904, 2062, 2073, 2076, 2081, 2107, 2116, 2124, 2185, 2197, 2210, 2262, 2270, 2305, 2321, 2324, 2351, 2356, 2375, 2384, 2389, 2391, 2423, 2425, 2427, 2445, 2461, 2477, 2498, 2507, 2512, 2608, 2661, 2668, 2725, 2728, 2746, 2772, 2800, 2804, 2827, 2834, 2853, 2884, 2975, 2998, 2999, 3048, 3059, 3107, 3453, 3735, 3775, 3851

6

TESTING, MEASUREMENT, AND EVALUATION

EVALUATION OF STUDENTS

3675. Allred, Ruel A. "Comparison of Proofreading-Type Standardized Spelling Tests and Written Spelling Test Scores." *JEdR* 77 (May–June 1984): 289–303.

Suggests that proofreading tests give information about students' general spelling ability.

3676. Arrasmith, Dean G., Daniel S. Sheehan, and Wayne Applebaum. "A Comparison of the Selected-Response Strategy and the Constructed-Response Strategy for Assessment of a Third-Grade Writing Test." *JEdR* 77 (January–February 1984): 172–177.

These two measures assess different tasks. Constructed-response scores were most linked to writing performance, but both measures were linked to teacher evaluation.

3677. Bamberg, Betty. "Assessing Coherence: A Reanalysis of Essays Written for the National Assessment of Educational Progress, 1969–1979." *RTE* 18 (October 1984): 305–319.

A "holistic coherence scale" indicates that 17-year-olds write more coherently than 13-year-olds and that coherence is an important factor in holistic ratings of essay quality.

3678. Barnes, Linda L. "Communicative Competence in the Composition Classroom: A Discourse Analysis." *DAI* 45 (March 1985): 2856A.

Finds that teachers' written comments often have an impact different from what the teacher intended and that students' responses to comments are shaped by the comments they receive.

3679. Benesch, Sarah. "Improving Peer Response: Collaboration between Teachers and Students." *JTW* 4 (Spring 1985): 87–94.

Advises "modeling, monitoring, and intervention" to improve peer response and discourages using teacher-generated guides before peer groups begin work.

3680. Bensoussan, Marsha, and Rachel Ramraz. "Testing EFL Reading Comprehension Using a Multiple-Choice Rational Cloze." *MLJ* 68 (August 1984): 230–239.

Recommends fill-in tests using the rational cloze procedure (with possible responses in a multiple-choice format) to evaluate reading comprehension.

3681. Blau, Andrea F., Margaret Lahey, and Adriana Oleksiuk-Velez. "Planning Goals for Intervention: Language Testing or Language Sampling?" *ExC* 51 (September 1984): 78–79.

Examines the diagnostic potential of the Carrow Elicited Language Inventory.

3682. Blee, Myron R., and John Nickens. "Point/ Counterpoint: Is Statewide Exit Testing for Community College Students a Sound Idea?" *CJCJ* 56 (October–November 1985): 52–53.

Presents positive and negative views of the Florida College Level Academic Skills Project and Test, a statewide sophomore exit test including subtests in English.

3683. Blok, H. "Estimating the Reliability, Validity, and Invalidity of Essay Ratings." *JEdM* 22 (Spring 1985): 41–52.

Tests two assumptions about true scores of essay ratings and discusses the implications of the resulting coefficients of reliability, validity, and invalidity.

3684. Boggs, George R. *The Effect of Basic Skills Assessment on Student Achievement and Persistence at Butte College: A Research Report.* Oroville, Calif.: Butte College, 1984. ERIC ED 244 686 [23 pages]

Studies reading and writing placement tests and their impact on student achievement.

3685. Borja, Francisco, and Peter H. Spader. "AWK: Codes in Grading Essays." *CollT* 33 (Summer 1985): 113–116.

Proposes the coherent use of marginal codes to mark students' writing problems.

3686. Breland, Hunter M., and Robert J. Jones. "Perceptions of Writing Skills." *WC* 1 (January 1984): 101–119.

Reports that raters using holistic scoring and raters using criteria-based scoring agree and disagree on the importance of discourse skills and mechanics.

3687. Brenner, Kenneth. "The Psychological Impact of Grade Norms on Children." *Psychology* 21 (1984): 50–51.

Discusses the "inadequacies" of grade norms and the potential psychological harm of misinterpreting the norms.

3688. Bullock, Richard. "Zen and the Art of Evaluating Writing." *Leaflet* 83 (Fall 1984): 35–39.

Describes a technique for responding to student writing nonjudgmentally.

3689. Burkland, Jill, and Nancy Grimm. "Students' Responses to Our Response, Parts I and II." Paper given at the CCCC Convention, New York, March 1984. ERIC ED 245 241 [21 pages]

Studies college students' responses to teachers' written comments on freshman English essays.

3690. Burry, James, and Edys Quellmalz. *Assessing Students' Writing Skills: The CSE Expository and Narrative Rating Scales.* Washington: NIE, 1983. ERIC ED 238 942 [59 pages]

Gives features, uses, and purposes of expository and narrative analytic rating scales for assessing students' writing.

3691. Butler, Sydney J. "New Bottles for New Wine." *EQ* 18 (Summer 1985): 57–68.

Describes a grading system to accommodate a modern approach to the teaching of written composition.

3692. Carlman, Nancy. "The Effects of Scoring Method, Topic, and Mode on Grade Twelve Students' Writing Scores." *DAI* 46 (August 1985): 367A.

Concludes that holistic and primary-trait scoring methods should not be compared without qualification.

3693. Carlman, Nancy. "Topic Choice: There Failure Lurks." *EJ* 74 (September 1985): 56–59.

Concludes that students' writing ability should not be based on one piece of writing. Briefly discusses alternatives for writing tests.

3694. Carlson, Sybil B., and Roberta Camp. "Relationships between Direct and Indirect Measures of Writing Ability." Paper given at the National Council on Measurement in Education Meeting, Chicago, April 1985. ERIC ED 255 543 [23 pages]

Summarizes Educational Testing Service's studies of native and nonnative speakers.

3695. Carr, Bert. "Evaluation: The Holistic Scoring Approach." *VEB* 34 (Spring 1984): 5–11.

Argues that holistic evaluation is the best way to reduce the paper load. Establishes a rubric to determine scores.

3696. Charney, Davida. "The Validity of Using Holistic Scoring to Evaluate Writing: A Critical Overview." *RTE* 18 (February 1984): 65–81.

Warns that holistic scoring may achieve reliability only in artificial reading environments and suggests that conditions imposed on holistic rating sessions work at cross purposes.

3697. Clark, Beverly L. "Ughs, Awks, and Ahas." *ICUT* 32 (Fall 1984): 169–172.

Proposes responding to student writing with positive reinforcement, including questions, responses, and solutions to problems.

3698. Clark, Irene Lurkis. "Listening to Writing: Implications for Evaluation and Pedagogy." Paper given at the CCCC Convention, Detroit, March 1983. ERIC ED 236 625 [29 pages]

Argues that content, structure, and task fulfillment can be evaluated reliably by listening to student essays.

3699. Clifton, Linda. "What If the Kids Did It?" *WaEJ* 7 (Winter 1985): 12–16.

Students develop evaluation criteria before writing and meet in small groups to assess work and assign grades.

3700. Condrey, Leroy J. *Evaluation of the Skills Prerequisite System at Fullerton College: A Two Year Followup.* Fullerton, Calif.: Fullerton College, 1984. ERIC ED 244 663 [99 pages]

Discusses the results of a follow-up study of entrance testing, including tests of writing ability.

3701. Cooper, Peter L. *The Assessment of Writing Ability: A Review of Research.* Princeton, N.J.: ETS, 1984. ERIC ED 250 332 [53 pages]

Argues that the essay test is more valid, that the objective test is more reliable, that objective tests overpredict for minorities, and that a test combining an essay and an objective section is best.

3702. Covino, William A. "Writing Tests and Creative Fluency." *RR* 3 (September 1984): 50–57.

Regards "creative fluency" and multiple viewpoints as alternatives to traditional writing samples to judge proficiency.

3703. Creeden, John E. "The Effect of High School Writing Experiences on Scores on the University of Wisconsin's English Placement Test." *DAI* 45 (June 1985): 3492A.

Findings indicate that the placement test did not detect important differences in high school writing experiences or comprehensively measure students' writing abilities.

3704. Cronin, Frank. "Rogerian Rhetoric and Teaching Composition." *WaEJ* 6 (Winter 1984): 20–23.

Recommends using Rogers's unconditional positive regard in responding to student writing, even when noting errors and problems. Recommends Rogerian rhetoric for persuasive writing.

3705. David, Carol, and Thomas Bubolz. "Evaluating Students' Achievement in a Writing Center." *WLN* 9 (April 1985): 10–14.

Describes and evaluates a program designed for remedial students.

3706. Dawe, Alan, Wendy Watson, and David Harrison. *Assessing English Skills: Writing. A Resource Book for Adult Basic Education.* Victoria, Canada: British Columbia Ministry of Education, 1984. ERIC ED 241 956 [89 pages]

A collection of 10 articles on writing assessment. Authors not indexed in this volume.

3707. Dorans, Neil J., and Neal M. Kingston. "The Effects of Violations of Unidimensionality on the Estimation of Item and Ability Paramenters and on Item Response Theory Equating of the GRE Verbal Score." *JEdM* 22 (Winter 1985): 249–262.

Examines the impact of violations of unidimensionality on the verbal scale of the GRE Aptitude Test.

3708. Dragga, Sam. "Praiseworthy Grading." *JTW* 4 (Fall 1985): 264–268.

Explains a practice in which the teacher comments only on the positive features of writing. The higher the number of positive features, the higher the grade and the fuller the explanation of the evaluation.

3709. Eidvson, Sandra, and Barbara Mitacek. "Assessing the Progress of Moderately Retarded Students in Applied Academic Skills." Paper given at the Council for Exceptional Children Meeting, Washington, April 1984. ERIC ED 245 480 [31 pages]

Suggests that currently available evaluation tools are not appropriate. Describes an appropriate evaluation tool for academic skills, including writing.

3710. Emig, Janet, and Barbara King. *Emig-King Attitude Scale for Students.* Urbana, Ill.: ERIC/RCS, 1979. ERIC ED 236 630 [12 pages]

Assesses students' preference for, perception of, and process of writing.

3711. Evans, Peter J. A. "Assessment in Ontario." *EQ* 17 (Summer 1984): 54–58.

Responds to the Minister of Education's announcement of testing in English and mathematics for the provinces. Describes possible tests.

3712. Evans, Peter J. A. "Canadian Activity in Large Scale Assessment of Writing." *EQ* 18 (Summer 1985): 23–37.

Argues that writing is necessary in any valid writing assessment program. Describes the program for the Canadian provinces.

3713. Evans, Peter J. A. "Writing, the English Program, and the Writing Folder." *EQ* 18 (Summer 1985): 44–52.

Suggests elaboration that can enrich the folder and its uses.

3714. Faigley, Lester, Roger D. Cherry, David A. Jolliffe, and Anna M. Skinner. *Assessing Writers' Knowledge and Process of Composing.* Edited by Marcia Farr. Writing Research: Multidisciplinary Inquiries into the Nature of Writing. Norwood, N.J.: Ablex, 1985. 288 pages

Develops a research-based theoretical framework for assessment. Describes methods of assessing text production skills through performance on controlled tasks, offers a direct approach to describing changes in composing processes by focusing on writers' awareness of their own strategies, and argues for a theory of assessment that accounts for both knowledge and strategies.

3715. Fischer, Robert A. "Testing Written Communicative Competence in French." *MLJ* 68 (Spring 1984): 13–20.

Recommends using principles of communicative competence to evaluate students' performance in a French class.

3716. Fishman, Judith. "Do You Agree or Disagree: The Epistemology of the CUNY Writing Assessment Test." *WPA* 8 (Fall-Winter 1984): 17–25.

Examines some of the questions and concerns about the writing assessment test explored at Queens College.

3717. Ford, Cecilia E. "The Forum: The Influence of Speech Variety on Teachers' Evaluation of Students with Comparable Academic Ability." *TESOLQ* 18 (March 1984): 25–40.

Using speech and writing samples by third and fourth graders, evaluated by 40 teachers, the study concludes that students' first language affects teachers' evaluations of writing.

3718. Frederiksen, Norman. "The Real Test Bias: Influences of Testing on Teaching and Learning." *AmP* 39 (1984): 193–202.

Supports the use of tests and teaching methods that reflect "the whole domain of educational goals" rather than "efficient" tests that leave important abilities unaddressed.

3719. Freedman, Sarah Warshauer. "The Evaluation of, and Response to, Student Writing: A Review." Paper given at the AERA Convention, New Orleans, April 1984. ERIC ED 247 605 [32 pages]

Argues that response is effective when given during the writing process and when it is text-specific, positive, and encouraging.

3720. Fuller, Davis G. "A Theory of Teacher Commentary: The Aims and Methods of Interactive Response to Student Writing." *DAI* 44 (February 1984): 2463A.

Proposes that reader commentary replace teacher evaluation and commentary as a response to writing.

3721. Greenberg, Karen L. "Writing Assessment Test Design: Response to Two *WPA* Essays." *WPA* 9 (Fall-Winter 1985): 31–40.

Responds to criticisms of topic design in the CUNY writing assessment test.

3722. Griffiths, Anne H. "Prospective Secondary Teachers' Responses to Student Use of Black English in Written Composition." *DAI* 45 (June 1985): 3570A.

Finds significant differences between white and black and between male and female prospective teachers' evaluation of students' writing.

3723. Harris, David P. "Some Forerunners of Cloze Procedure." *MLJ* 69 (Winter 1985): 367–376.

Contrasts Taylor's cloze procedures for testing language proficiency with completion tests devised earlier by Ebbinghaus and Trabue. Finds a substantial statistical relationship between these procedures.

3724. Hartnett, Carolyn. *Analyzing Cohesive Ties (ACT).* Urbana, Ill.: ERIC/RCS, 1980. ERIC ED 236 654 [15 pages]

Describes a tabulation sheet for recording all instances of cohesive ties in writing.

3725. Haviland, Mark G., Dale G. Shaw, and Carol P. Haviland. "Predicting College Graduation Using Selected Institutional Data." *Psychology* 21 (1984): 1–3.

Results show that high school rank is the "best single predictor" of graduation within five years of matriculation.

3726. Hayes, Mary F., and Donald Daiker. "Using Protocol Analysis in Evaluating Responses to Student Writing." *FEN* 13 (Fall 1984): 1-4, 10.

Concludes that students frequently misunderstand instructors' comments on papers, even when instructors follow approved methods and students put time and effort into understanding. Encouraging remarks are valued.

3727. Hayhoe, Mike. "The Current State of Assessment in English Education." *EQ* 17 (Summer 1984): 59-66.

Describes the revamping of the examination system in secondary schools.

3728. Head, L. Quinn. "The Effects of Trait Anxiety and Student Use of Objectives on State Anxiety and College Academic Performance." *Psychology* 21 (1984): 34-39.

Concludes that using objectives from class lectures did not significantly reduce test anxiety among students.

3729. Herman, Joan L. "Serving the Mutual Needs of Research and Practice: The Methodology Project Example." Paper given at the AERA Convention, New Orleans, April 1984. ERIC ED 244 984 [12 pages]

Describes how methodological research in writing assessment assisted teachers and administrators.

3730. Hilgers, Thomas L. "Toward a Taxonomy of Beginning Writers' Evaluative Statements on Written Compositions." *WC* 1 (July 1984): 365-384.

Identifies four categories of criteria that students in grades two through six used to evaluate compositions that they or anonymous peers had written.

3731. Hillerich, Robert L. "An Effort towards Improving the Spelling Pretest." *JEdR* 77 (May-June 1984): 309-311.

Finds little advantage to immediate feedback on spelling pretest errors.

3732. Homburg, Taco Justus. "Holistic Evaluation of ESL Compositions: Can It Be Validated Objectively?" *TESOLQ* 18 (March 1984): 87-107.

Compares scores on the Michigan writing test to those on the Michigan Test of English Language Proficiency and concludes that holistic evaluation can be reliable and valid.

3733. Horvath, Brooke K. "The Components of Written Response: A Practical Synthesis of Current Views." *RR* 2 (January 1984): 136-156.

Summarizes and evaluates research to suggest effective techniques for writing comments on student papers. Includes annotated bibliography.

3734. Hrach, Elaine. "The Influence of Rater Characteristics on Composition Evaluation." *DAI* 45 (August 1984): 440A.

Results reveal no patterns relating raters' judgments of writing quality to raters' experience with writing skills or to raters' tolerance of ambiguity.

3735. Hsiao, Frank S. T. "A Statistical Method of Grading: Theory and Practice." *CompEd* 9 (1985): 227-234.

Describes a method of grading students through microcomputer spreadsheet programs.

3736. Hughes, David C., and Brian Keeling. "The Use of Model Essays to Reduce Context Effects in Essay Scoring." *JEdM* 21 (Fall 1984): 277-281.

Investigates the effectiveness of providing scorers with model essays to reduce the influence of context.

3737. Iysere, Marla M. "Setting Standards in Multiple-Section Courses." *ICUT* 32 (Fall 1984): 173-179.

Describes the process and gives guidelines for faculty in English and other disciplines devising common standards for courses and student writing.

3738. Johnson, Berman E. "Valid Testing Model for Admissions Placement." *CCR* 12 (Fall 1984): 8-12.

Describes a required placement test in reading, composition, and mathematics at DeKalb Community College. Reports favorable correlations with the SAT.

3739. Jolly, Peggy. "Evaluating the Evaluator." Paper given at the CCCC Convention, Minneapolis, March 1985. ERIC ED 254 856 [10 pages]

Discusses the general problem of evaluation, offering suggestions for teachers in commenting on and grading student writing.

3740. Kearney, Lynn B. "Trusting the Process: Qualitative Data Analysis." *EngR* 36 (Fourth Quarter, 1985): 5–7.

Argues that, to overcome bias in ethnographic samplings, subsequent hypotheses must be tested.

3741. Khalil, Aziz M. "Communicative Error Evaluation: Native Speakers' Evaluation and Interpretation of Written Errors of Arab EFL Learners." *TESOLQ* 19 (June 1985): 335–351.

Study of 240 American undergraduates concludes that semantically deviant, rather than grammatically deviant, utterances are "judged to be less intelligible and interpretable."

3742. Kingsbury, Callie, and Mary M. Dupuis. "The Paper Load: Alternatives in Grading Compositions." *PCTEB* 51 (April 1985): 19–26.

Argues that assessment techniques should be determined by the purpose of the assignment. Illustrates by describing four techniques.

3743. Koffler, Stephen L. "Assessing Students' Writing Skills: A Comparison of Direct and Indirect Methods." Paper given at the AERA Convention, New Orleans, April 1984. ERIC ED 242 771 [19 pages]

Compares measurement techniques, recommending a combination of methods.

3744. Lalande, John F., II. "Reducing Composition Errors." *FLA* 17 (April 1984): 109–117.

A study of writing done in German classes suggests that comprehensive marking of errors for students to correct improves writing skills at the intermediate level. Originally appeared in *The Modern Language Journal,* 66 (1982).

3745. Larson, Jerry W., and Randall L. Jones. *Proficiency Testing for the Other Language Modalities.* Urbana, Ill.: ERIC/RCS, 1984. ERIC ED 238 268 [26 pages]

Discusses issues involved in extending foreign language proficiency testing to reading and writing.

3746. Larson, Richard L. "Tests of Minimum Competence in Writing." *SLATE* 10 (September 1985).

Examines definitions, forms of testing, problems of essay tests and how to address them, and procedures for scoring. Presents recommendations and a 16-item bibliography.

3747. Lutz, William. "What We Know and Don't Know: Needed Research in Writing Assessment." Paper given at the National Council on Measurement in Education Meeting, Montreal, April 1983. ERIC ED 236 242 [12 pages]

Reviews large-scale writing assessment research and suggests additional studies.

3748. Mallonee, Barbara C., and John R. Breihan. "Responding to Students' Drafts: Interdisciplinary Consensus." *CCC* 36 (May 1985): 213–231.

Four-year, cross-curricular collaborations on response to student writing resulted in four areas of consensus on errors, terminology, process, and worth of effort.

3749. Marsh, Herbert W., and Robert Ireland. *Multidimensional Evaluations of Writing Effectiveness.* Urbana, Ill.: ERIC/RCS, March 1984. ERIC ED 242 785 [33 pages]

Studies ratings of seventh-grade essays by student teachers and master teachers in Australia.

3750. Marsh, Robert. "A Comparison of Take-Home Vs. In-Class Exams." *JEdR* 78 (November–December 1984): 111–113.

Argues that college students learned far more from in-class than from take-home exams.

3751. Matthews, Frances D. "The Writing Assessment Program of Mercer University's College of Liberal Arts." *DAI* 46 (October 1985): 916A.

Describes a writing assessment model developed as Mercer University redesigned its general education program.

3752. McLeod, Alan M., ed. *Evaluation and Oral Communication.* N.p.: Virginia Association of Teachers of English, 1984. 50 pages

A collection of 16 articles on the evaluation of student writing and on strategies for teaching oral communication. Appeared as *Virginia English Bulletin* 34 (Spring 1984).

3753. McMorris, Robert F. "Effects of Incorporating Humor in Test Items." *JEdM* 22 (Summer 1985): 137–146.

Discusses two matched forms of a multiple-choice grammar test, one with and one without humorous items.

3754. Michaels, Sarah. "Hearing the Connections in Children's Oral and Written Discourse." *JEd* 167 (1985): 36–56.

A case study of teacher response to oral and written discourse and the influence it has on students' literacy development.

3755. Mier, Margaret. "ERIC/RCS Report: Teacher Commentary on Student Writing in the Process-Oriented Class." *Leaflet* 84 (Winter 1985): 30–34.

Discusses characteristics of effective writing evaluations. Suggests strategies for making teacher commentary count.

3756. Mier, Margaret. "Teacher Commentary on Student Writing in the Process-Oriented Class." *NCET* 42 (Fall 1984): 24–26.

Reports on ERIC studies that assess the effect of teacher response to student writing.

3757. Mier, Margaret. "Teacher Commentary on Student Writing in the Process-Oriented Class." *Statement* 20 (May 1985): 48–51.

A survey of ERIC materials that discuss the characteristics of effective writing evaluations and suggest strategies for making evaluations count.

3758. Miller, Leann R. *Pennsylvania's Public School Students: Caught in the Tide?* Urbana, Ill.: ERIC/RCS, 1984. ERIC ED 244 992 [9 pages]

Compares state achievement with national trends. Includes comparison of achievement in writing.

3759. Mitchell, Victoria. "Shared Grading: A Teaching Experiment." *EngR* 35 (Third Quarter 1984): 12–14.

Teachers serve as allies and coaches for their own students, then become objective graders and umpires for other teachers' students.

3760. Moorhead, Michael. "In Search of an English 101 Exit Exam." *TETYC* 11 (October 1984): 29–33.

Describes difficulties in developing a departmental exit examination. A grammar test was ineffective. A holistically scored essay was chosen.

3761. Morante, Edward A., Shari Faskow, and Irene Nomejko. "The New Jersey Basic Skills Assessment Program: Part I." *JDEd* 7 (Winter 1984): 2–4.

Explains the structure, results, and implications for teaching of the New Jersey College Basic Skills Placement Test. Calls for reinforcing reading and writing across the curriculum.

3762. Morgan, Margaret. "A Rhetorical Analysis of Teacher Commentary on Student Texts." *DAI* 46 (December 1985): 1546A.

Examines three types of teacher comments — informative, deliberative, and epideictic — and suggests that epideictic (personal response) has the greatest potential for effecting changes in student writing.

3763. Murphree, Carolyn T. "A Consideration of Competency Testing." *ABCAB* 48 (June 1985): 24–25.

Describes a writing competency testing program and how it can benefit a business communication course.

3764. Newkirk, Thomas. "Direction and Misdirection in Peer Response." *CCC* 35 (October 1984): 301–311.

Corroborates earlier studies finding that students and instructors frequently use different criteria and stances in judging written work.

3765. Newkirk, Thomas. "How Students Read Student Papers: An Exploratory Study." *WC* 1 (July 1984): 283–305.

Shows that instructors and peer readers use different criteria to evaluate student essays.

3766. O'Donnell, Holly. "Large Scale Writing Assessment." *ArEB* 28 (Fall 1985): 82–88.

Discusses the advantages and disadvantages of direct and indirect assessment and of three approaches to scoring. Indicates trends in writing assessment.

3767. O'Donnell, Holly. *Large Scale Writing Assessment: ERIC Digest.* Urbana, Ill.: ERIC/RCS, 1984. ERIC ED 250 691 [14 pages]

Explains approaches to, problems with, and trends in large-scale writing assessment.

3768. O'Neal, Marcia R., Helen I. Guttinger, and Chris M. Morris. "Validation of a Writing Attitude Scale." Paper given at the Mid-South Educational Research Association Meeting, New Orleans, November 1984. ERIC ED 252 577 [14 pages]

Describes nine tests used to validate the Florida Writing Project Student Survey, a 25-item writing attitude scale for grades 6 through 12.

3769. Ober, Scott. "The Influence of Selected Variables on the Grading of Student-Written Letters." *ABCAB* 47 (March 1984): 7–11.

Reports on a study to determine the influence of format, guidance, and the passage of time on instructors' evaluations of student-written business letters.

3770. Olson, Margot A., and Diane Martin. "Assessment of Entering Student Writing Skill in the Community College." Paper given at the AERA Convention, Boston, April 1980. ERIC ED 235 845 [35 pages]

Finds a holistically scored writing sample a more stringent placement instrument than the Nelson-Denny Reading Test, an objective English composition test, or a self-assessment.

3771. Olson, Miles C., and Marc Swadener. "Establishing and Implementing Colorado's Writing Assessment Program." *EEd* 16 (December 1984): 208–219.

Describes the instrument used to assess writing in Colorado.

3772. Onore, Cynthia. "Students' Revisions and Teachers' Comments: Toward a Transactional Theory of the Composing Process." *DAI* 45 (December 1984): 1671A.

Results indicate that "good teacher commentary demands reentry into the composing process without a necessary textual result," and that growth resides within that process.

3773. Page, Ellis B., and Helmuts Feifs. "SAT Scores and American States: Seeking for Useful Meaning." *JEdM* 22 (Winter 1985): 305–312.

Uses the 50-state SAT means as the criterion in a multivariate model to compare test performance by state.

3774. Parker, John Reed. "Undergraduate College Students' Use of Assertive Message Types and Perceptions of Communication Competence in Nonclassrooms." *DAI* 45 (February 1985): 2303A.

Investigates questions of assertiveness and gender in interactions of students and teachers outside the classroom.

3775. Pedersen, Elray L. "Computerized Personal Comments for Student Discourse." Paper given at the NCTE Convention, Detroit, November 1984. ERIC ED 253 882 [17 pages]

Describes Comments, a computer program to assist teachers commenting on student papers.

3776. Penfield, Elizabeth F., Adelaide McGuinnis, Isaac Brumfield, and Susan Halter. "Testing Writing in Louisiana Colleges and Universities." *LaEJ* 24 (Fall 1985): 1–17.

Describes proficiency examinations used in four courses at two institutions and as a graduation requirement at a third.

3777. Perkins, Kyle, and Charles Parish. "Direct *Vs.* Indirect Measure of Writing Proficiency: Research in ESL Composition." Paper given at the TESOL Meeting, Houston, March 1984. ERIC ED 243 306 [35 pages]

Compares two measurement techniques.

3778. Platek, Teri. "Using Cassettes to Respond to Essays." *EngR* 35 (Third Quarter 1984): 8–9.

Advocates recording responses to student writing on cassettes.

3779. Poirier-Bures, Simone. "Analyzing and Evaluating Argument." *VEB* 34 (Spring 1984): 43–44.

Describes four components of an argumentative paper that must be judged to arrive at a fair appraisal of the paper.

3780. Popplewell, Scott L. "A Comparative Study of the Writing and Reading Achievement of Children, Ages Nine and Ten, in Great Britain and the United States." *DAI* 45 (March 1985): 2823A.

Results indicate that writing achievement scores differ little between children in Great Britain and the United States when evaluated holistically.

3781. Powers, Donald E. "Effects of Coaching on GRE Aptitude Test Scores." *JEdM* 22 (Summer 1985): 121–136.

Relates the length and type of test preparation programs to GRE Aptitude Test scores for a large representative sample of test takers.

3782. Purves, Alan C. "In Search of an Internationally Valid Scheme for Scoring Compositions." *CCC* 35 (December 1984): 426–438.

Describes the development of a scoring scheme of 8 features for the study of writing in 17 countries undertaken by the International Association for the Evaluation of Educational Achievement.

3783. Purves, Alan C., A. Söter, Sauli Takala, and Anneli Vähäpassi "Towards a Domain-Referenced System for Classifying Composition Assignments." *RTE* 18 (December 1984): 385–416.

Develops a domain- or criterion-referenced system, consisting of 15 dimensions, to both describe and classify current writing assignments and to create new assignments.

3784. Quellmalz, Edys. *Scale for Evaluating Expository Writing* (*SEEW*). Urbana, Ill.: ERIC/RCS, 1982. ERIC ED 236 670 [18 pages]

Presents criterion-referenced, six-point scales for basic essay elements.

3785. Quellmalz, Edys. *Scale for Evaluating Narrative Writing* (*SENW*). Urbana, Ill.: ERIC/RCS, 1982. ERIC ED 236 653 [19 pages]

Presents a criterion-referenced, six-point rating scale for general competence in narrative essay writing.

3786. Rafoth, Bennett A., and Donald L. Rubin. "The Impact of Content and Mechanics on Judgments of Writing Quality." *WC* 1 (October 1984): 446–458.

Finds that raters placed more emphasis on mechanics than content in evaluating essays and followed preconceived criteria more often than specified criteria.

3787. Rasor, Richard A., and Tom Powell. *Predicting English Writing Course Success with Vocabulary and Usage Subtests.* Sacramento: American River College, 1984. ERIC ED 243 535 [34 pages]

Reports on the use of multiple-choice tests as placement instruments for college writers.

3788. Reed, W. Michael, and John K. Burton. "Effective and Ineffective Evaluation of Essays: Perceptions of College Freshmen." *JTW* 4 (Fall 1985): 270–283.

Advocates students' responding to evaluation techniques, giving feedback to all parts of the writing, negative and positive, peer evaluations, student-instructor conferences, and ungraded writing.

3789. Reigstad, Thomas J., Ann Matsuhashi, and Nina Luban. *Writing Center Tutorial Record Form* (*WCTRF*). Urbana, Ill.: ERIC/RCS, 1980. ERIC ED 236 631 [6 pages]

Reports on pre- and postconference forms that result in profiles of writers and conferencing activities.

3790. Rentz, Kathryn C. "Some Discouraging Words about Checkmark Grading." *ABCAB* 48 (June 1985): 20–23.

Discusses the disadvantages of using the "behavioral" or checkmark grading system in business communication courses.

3791. Richards, Amy. "College Composition: Recognizing the Learning Disabled Writer." *JBW* 4 (Fall 1985): 68–79.

Presents diagnostic guidelines related to spelling, punctuation, and sentence clarity. Briefly discusses ways to help disabled writers become more efficient.

3792. Rose, Mike. *Questionnaire for Identifying Writer's Block* (*QIWB*). Urbana, Ill.: ERIC/RCS, 1981. ERIC ED 236 652 [8 pages]

Describes a 24-item questionnaire for identifying five factors in students' attitudes toward writing.

3793. Rounds, Jeanine C., and Don Anderson. "Entrance Assessment and Student Success." *CCR* 12 (Winter 1984–1985): 10–15.

Reviews attitudes toward entry testing since 1900, reports on a 1982–1983 survey of assessment procedures in California community colleges, and makes eight recommendations for effective assessment.

3794. Rubin, Lois E. "How Student Writers Judge Their Own Writing." *DAI* 45 (September 1984): 829A.

Finds college students unable to judge their writing objectively. Students' satisfaction with their writing has little to do with textual qualities.

3795. Ruth, Leo, and Sandra Murphy. "Designing Topics for Writing Assessment: Problems for Meaning." *CCC* 35 (December 1984): 410–422.

Discusses topics designated for essay tests. Includes a model for a "writing assessment episode" and proposes four generalizations that have implications for conducting writing assessments.

3796. Samson, George E. "Effects of Training in Test-Taking Skills on Achievement Test Performance: A Qualitative Synthesis." *JEdR* 77 (May-June 1985): 261–266.

Training in test-taking skills produced higher test scores for elementary and secondary school students.

3797. Savage, David. "Scrutinize Students' Test Scores, and They Might Not Look So Rosy." *ASBJ* 171 (August 1984): 22.

Points out that improvement in test scores, which may be achieved in many ways, may not mean improved reading or language skills.

3798. Savale, Zoila A. "Statewide Minimum Competency Tests in Writing Skills: How Competent Are the Tests?" *DAI* 45 (December 1984): 1671A.

Examines the strengths and weaknesses of various kinds of minimum competency tests in writing. Discussion emphasizes holistic scoring.

3799. Savignon, Sandra J. "Evaluation of Communicative Competence: The ACTFL Provisional Proficiency Guidelines." *MLJ* 69 (Summer 1985): 129–134.

Argues that the ACTFL Guidelines do not take into account the view of language as communicative competence. Points to a tension between accuracy and communication.

3800. Semke, Harriet D. "Effects of the Red Pen." *FLA* 17 (May 1984): 195–202.

A study investigating four methods of correcting freewriting indicates that writing practice alone enhanced achievement. Having students correct their mistakes was least effective.

3801. Simmonds, Paul. "A Survey of English Language Examinations." *ELTJ* 39 (January 1985): 33–42.

Compares 23 British and American EFL/ESL examinations, including methods of testing writing skills.

3802. Sommers, Jeffrey. "Enlisting the Writer's Participation in the Evaluation Process." *JTW* 4 (Spring 1985): 95–103.

A student-teacher memo guides students' comments on drafts and helps a nonappropriating teacher respond to the revision.

3803. Stanton, H. E. "Improving the Quality of Written Work." *ICUT* 32 (Summer 1984): 138–139.

Presents evidence of improved ratings when students in various disciplines work in small groups to generate criteria and rate their papers.

3804. Stewart, Murray. "What Do High School Teachers across the Curriculum Think of Freshman Writing?" *EQ* 17 (Spring 1984): 97–101.

Identifies differences in quality ratings given samples of freshman writing by English and social studies, mathematics and science teachers.

3805. *Student Achievement in Illinois: An Analysis of Student Progress.* Springfield, Ill.: Illinois State Board of Education, 1984. ERIC ED 247 263 [103 pages]

The second annual report on student achievement in Illinois. Describes student performance in grammar and composition.

3806. Sweedler-Brown, Carol. "The Influence of Training and Experience on Holistic Essay Evaluations." *EJ* 74 (September 1985): 49–55.

Concludes that the level of experience and training significantly affects the reliability of a grader's evaluations.

3807. Swope, John W. "The Effect of a Second Invention Strategy on the Frequencies of Surface and Text-Based Changes in the Writing of College Freshmen." *DAI* 44 (June 1984): 3671A.

Quality ratings were affected by students' using a second invention strategy when revising.

3808. Takala, Sauli, and Anneli Vähäpassi. "International Study of Written Composition." Paper given at the International Writing Association Convention, Norwich, England, April 1985. ERIC ED 257 096 [20 pages]

Describes the goals of a collaborative project involving 15 countries.

3809. Texas Education Agency, Division of Educational Assessment. *Writing Objectives and Measurement Specifications, 1986: Grades Three, Five, and Nine—Texas Assessment of Basic Skills.* Austin, Tex.: Texas Education Agency, Division of Educational Assessment, 1984. ERIC ED 251 498 [49 pages]

Contains the writing objectives and measurement specifications used by teachers and test makers for the Texas Assessment of Basic Skills.

3810. Thompson, Edgar H., and John W. Swope. "Evaluation: Self-Evaluation Strategies for Prewriting and Rewriting." *VEB* 34 (Spring 1984): 9–12.

Presents sets of questions that direct students in evaluating their prewriting and rewriting.

3811. Tillinghast, B. S., John E. Morrow, and George E. Uhlig. "Validity of the PPVT-R Using Elementary School Academic Grades as Criteria." *Psychology* 21 (1984): 43–47.

Concludes that further research is required to test the consistent validity of the Peabody Pictoral Vocabulary Test—Revised as a sole grade predictor.

3812. Troyka, Lynn Quitman. *An A Posteriori: Examination of the Evaluation Scale of the Writing*

Assessment Test at CUNY. Research Monograph, no. 3. New York: CUNY Office of Academic Affairs, 1982. ERIC ED 236 267 [99 pages]

Reevaluating the Writing Skills Assessment Test resulted in refined descriptive criteria for the scores one through six.

3813. Troyka, Lynn Quitman. "The Phenomenon of Impact: The CUNY Writing Assessment Test." *WPA* 8 (Fall–Winter 1984): 27–36.

Responds to Fishman's criticism of the CUNY writing assessment test, [*WPA* 8 (Fall–Winter 1984)], asserting that the test is a valuable tool in CUNY's writing programs.

3814. Vann, Roberta J., Daisy E. Meyer, and Frederick O. Lorenz. "The Forum: Error Gravity: A Study of Faculty Opinion of ESL Errors." *TESOLQ* 18 (September 1984): 427–440.

A survey of 164 professors at Iowa State University indicates that faculty view sentence-level errors hierarchically, as influenced by professor's age and discipline.

3815. Wainer, Howard. "An Exploratory Analysis of Performance on the SAT." *JEdM* 21 (Summer 1984): 81–91.

Analyzes the performance of various ethnic groups on the SAT.

3816. Weber, Jerry. "Assessment and Placement: A Review of the Research." *CCR* 13 (Winter 1985–86): 21–32.

Reviews research on basic skills assessment and placement. Recommends procedures.

3817. Weinman, J. "A Modified Essay Question Evaluation of Preclinical Teaching of Communication Skills." *MedEd* 18 (1984): 164–167.

Modified essay questions enabled students to incorporate psychosocial factors into evaluations of medical problems and to address broader aspect of health care and physicians' roles.

3818. Westcott, Warren, and Phillip Gardner. "Holistic Scoring as a Teaching Device." *TETYC* 11 (December 1984): 35–39.

Students were trained to holistically score each others' papers. Analytic discussion followed the scoring.

3819. White, Edward M. "Holisticism." *CCC* 35 (December 1984): 400–409.

Chronicles the development of holisticism in English testing. Defines holistic scoring and discusses its strengths, limitations, misuses, and abuse.

3820. White, Edward M. "Poststructual Literary Criticism and the Response to Student Writing." *CCC* 35 (May 1984): 186–195.

Explains that a basic correspondence exists between poststructural criticism and the theories and practice of many writing teachers.

3821. White, Edward M. *Teaching and Assessing Writing.* San Francisco: Jossey-Bass, 1985. 304 pages

Presents recent research in the theory and practice of assessing writing. Provides guidance in assigning, responding to, and evaluating student writing.

3822. White, Kathryn F., and Betty S. Johnson. "Evaluation Criteria Used in Business Communication Courses Taught in Colleges of Business Affiliated with AACSB." *ABCAB* 47 (September 1984): 39–42.

Describes a study of grading criteria used by selected business communication instructors at schools accredited by the American Assembly of Collegiate Schools of Business.

3823. Wilson, Robert L. "Why All the Hoopla about SAT Scores?" *NebEC* 30 (Fall 1984): 5–6.

Examines relationships between SAT scores and changing emphases in education and learning styles.

3824. Zamel, Vivian. "Responding to Student Writing." *TESOLQ* 19 (March 1985): 79–101.

A study concludes that, by focusing on error correction, ESL teachers "view themselves as language teachers rather than writing teachers."

3825. Zasloff, Tela. "Diagnosing Student Writing: Problems Encountered by College Freshmen." *DAI* 45 (October 1984): 1108A.

Suggests that writing problems are closely tied to reading comprehension problems.

3826. *1984 TABS Final Report.* Austin, Tex.: Austin Independent School District Office of Research and Evaluation, 1984. ERIC ED 252 596 [56 pages]

Describes the results of the Texas Assessment of Basic Skills administered in grades three, five, and nine in mathematics, reading, and writing.

See also 29, 74, 332, 747, 971, 1267, 1306, 1318, 1386, 1570, 1595, 1644, 1673, 1773, 1777, 1798, 1892, 1926, 1929, 1933, 1949, 2088, 2138, 2300, 2312, 2369, 2373, 2443, 2455, 2460, 2623, 2935, 3021, 3036, 3590, 3594, 3612

EVALUATION OF TEACHERS

3827. Braskamp, Larry A., Dale C. Brandenburg, and John C. Ory. *Evaluating Teaching Effectiveness.* Sage, Calif.: Sage, 1984. 136 pages

A guide to designing, implementing, and critiquing teacher evaluation. Describes techniques for securing and interpreting information from students, colleagues, the teacher, alumni, and written records.

3828. Busch, John Christian, and Richard M. Jaeger. "An Evaluation of Methods for Setting Standards on the Essay Portion of the National Teacher Examinations." Paper given at AERA Convention, New Orleans, April 1984. ERIC ED 248 270 [20 pages]

Addresses seven questions about passing scores on the essay subtest of the National Teacher Examinations for the North Carolina State Board of Education. Describes the training of essay raters.

3829. Cahn, Dudley D. "Relative Importance of Perceived Understanding in Students' Evaluation of Teachers." *PMS* 59 (October 1984): 610.

Finds that "perceived understanding" was the most important factor in student evaluations of teachers. It correlated with "classroom presence," student-centered behavior, and democratic or participatory teaching style.

3830. Duke, Charles R. "Developing a Writing Assessment of Candidates for Admission to Teacher Education." *JTEd* 36 (March–April 1985): 7–11.

Outlines a procedure for developing, administering, and scoring a written assessment examination for education students.

3831. Emig, Janet, and Barbara King. *Emig-King Attitude Scale for Teachers.* Urbana, Ill.: ERIC/RCS, 1979. ERIC ED 236 629 [12 pages]

A revised version of a scale that measures the attitudes of pre- and in-service teachers toward writing.

3832. Gary, Melvin, and Sandra Brown. *Gary-Brown Writing Opinionnaire for College Instructors.* Urbana, Ill.: ERIC/RCS, 1981. ERIC ED 236 660 [11 pages]

Describes an instrument for assessing, through writing, teachers' attitudes toward teaching and evaluating writing and course content.

3833. Moore, Wayne, Jr. "Grading Scales in College Freshman Composition." *WC* 2 (October 1985): 492–497.

Finds that teachers' current interest in grading scales to evaluate written compositions did not correspond to their use.

3834. Poston, Lawrence. "Neither Bane nor Boon: External Reviewing in the Tenure and Promotion Process." *BADE* 77 (Spring 1984): 44–46.

Discusses how to select reviewers, provides a sample letter, and outlines guidelines for timely notice, appropriate payment, and protection following review.

3835. Rose, Janet S., and W. James Popham. "Developing a Defensible Language Skills Test for Teachers." Paper given at AERA Convention, New Orleans, April 1984. ERIC ED 247 292 [23 pages]

Describes a rationale for developing language competencey tests for teachers.

3836. Schlatter, Franklin D. "Questions about Merit Pay and Teacher Evaluation that Proponents Must Answer." *SLATE* 10 (March 1985).

Raises questions about who evaluates what, when, and by what standards to provide fair, reasonable, valid bases for merit pay. Includes bibliography.

3837. Sechrist, Paul W. "Oral Communication Competency for Teachers: Construct and Case Study." *DAI* 45 (June 1985): 3482A.

Proposes a construct for communication competence and suggests techniques for assessing such competence.

3838. Stevenson, Dwight W. "Evaluating Technical Communication Faculty: Some Empirically Based Criteria and Guidelines." Paper given at CCCC Convention, New York, March 1984. ERIC ED 243 115 [22 pages]

Describes faculty publication activity and suggests guidelines for evaluation.

See also 1025, 1281, 1554, 1619, 2106, 2441, 3705

EVALUATION OF PROGRAMS

3839. Bencich, Carole. "10,000 Opinions of the Writing Skills Enhancement Program." *FlaEJ* 21 (Fall 1985): 12–14.

Describes and summarizes 10,974 Brevard County high school students' essays about their skills, habits, and attitudes toward writing after participating in a statewide program.

3840. Froese, V. "Trends in Canadian Provincial Reading Assessments." *EQ* 16 (Winter 1984): 4–9.

Discusses the purposes of reading evaluation, trends in types of assessments used, and possible indicators of changes in literacy levels in the Canadian Provinces.

3841. Palmer, James C. "Do College Courses Improve Basic Reading and Writing Skills?" *CCR* 12 (Fall 1984): 20–28.

Reviews a study of 6000 urban community college students to determine if reading and writing courses improve ability. Reports no solid evidence of improvement.

3842. Poland, William E., and David Pierce. "Remedial Education in the States." *CCR* 12 (Winter 1984–1985): 16–20.

Reports on a 1983 study to ascertain the status of remedial education as perceived by state directors of community/junior colleges. Includes six recommendations.

3843. Presley, John. "Evaluating Developmental English Programs in Georgia." *WPA* 8 (Fall–Winter 1984): 47–56.

Concludes that the findings of reports and studies used in Georgia to evaluate developmental English curricula show encouraging results.

3844. Wesdorp, Hildo. "On the Identification of Critical Variables in Written Composition Instruction." Paper given at NCTE Convention, Washington, November 1982. ERIC ED 258 167 [24 pages]

Reports on an international survey.

3845. Witte, Stephen P., and Lester Faigley. *Evaluating College Writing Programs.* Studies in Writing and Rhetoric. Carbondale, Ill.: Southern Illinois University Press, 1983. 136 pages

Reviews evaluation studies conducted at four universities. Attempts to develop a comprehensive framework for evaluators.

3846. Yee, Nancy. "Writing Proficiency Examinations: A New Perspective on Writing Labs." *WLN* 10 (September 1985): 3–6.

Reports an increase in the number of writing proficiency examinations and recommends ways to assist students and faculty in preparing for them.

See also 1267, 1567, 1648, 1651, 1674, 1679, 2735, 2926, 3808

OTHER

3847. Camden, Carl, Howard Mims, and Michael T. Motley. "Convergent Validity of Three Communication Data Collection Techniques: An Analysis of Black American English Grammatical Usage." *WJSC* 49 (Summer 1985): 166–176.

Investigates grammatical style measured by naturalistic, laboratory interaction, and self-reporting methods.

3848. Dohaney, M. T. "In Praise of In-Depth Assessment of the Writing Assignment." *EQ* 16 (Winter 1984): 43–46.

Claims that in-depth assessment is the most effective base for grading and determining students' needs. Includes a scale.

3849. Hample, Dale. "Refinements on the Cognitive Model of Argument: Concreteness, Involvement, and Group Scores." *WJSC* 49 (Fall 1985): 267–285.

Evaluates two possible limits on the current cognitive model and attempts to resolve reliability problems suggested by previous work.

3850. McCroskey, James C., and Michael J. Beatty. "Communication Apprehension and Accumulated Communication State Anxiety Experiences: A Research Note." *ComM* 51 (March 1984): 79–84.

Tests PRCA-24 as a cross-situational predictive instrument by examining the relationship between trait communication and state anxiety in each of four contexts.

3851. NCTE Committee on Instructional Terminology. *Guidelines for Review and Evaluation of English Language Arts Software.* Urbana, Ill.: NCTE, 1984. 4 pages

Advocates considering teacher management, instructional strategies, content, and ease of operation in evaluating software.

3852. Rubin, Rebecca B. "The Validity of the Communication Competency Assessment Instrument." *ComM* 52 (June 1985): 173–185.

Examines the operational validity of the instrument.

3853. Shell, Kathy L. "The Validation of the Writing Assessment Test." *DAI* 45 (February 1985): 2501A.

A study to validate the Writing Assessment Test, used for diagnostic decisions about writing skill in fourth and fifth grades.

See also 397, 931, 1261, 1288, 2799

AUTHOR INDEX

Aaron, Jane E., 3325
Aarts, Jan, 854
Abbott, Robert D., 83, 249
Abelson, Robert P., 1206
Abraham, Roberta G., 2981
Abram, Robert E., 2193
Abruzzo, Craig, 2208
Abshire, Gary M., 2797
Achtert, Walter S., 3424, 3433
Acredolo, Linda P., 1088
Adams, A., 838
Adams, Alice B., 1824
Adams, Barbara, 2887
Adams, John C., 340
Adams, John L., 2695
Adams, Katherine H., 57, 2476, 2694, 2695
Adams, Michael, 3281
Adams, Royce W., 3225
Addison, Alice A., 3168
Addison, James C., Jr., 855, 2155
Adelstein, Michael E., 3282
Adler, Keith, 1073
Adler, Thomas P., 3323
Afek, Irene, 2288
Afflerbach, Peter, 1971
Afghari, Akbar, 856
Africk, Henry, 2389
Agee, Ann, 3188
Agee, Hugh, 1
Aghazarian, Aram A., 554
Akiyama, M. Michael, 857
Akst, Geoffrey, 2389
Alberghene, Janice M., 2156
Albritton, Tom, 1278
Alesandri, Kathryn Lutz, 1256
Alexander, Clara, 1836, 2724
Alexander, James D., 2888
Alfieri-Fenston, Gloria, 1089
Algeo, John, 858
Algren, Edith, 1365
Allegretti, Christine L., 756
Allen, Diane, 1779, 1780
Allen, Jo, 2211
Allen, R. R., 2138
Alley, Gordon R., 761

Allison, Desmond, 2982
Allred, Linda J., 2389
Allred, Ruel A., 3100, 3675
Almeida, Jose C., 859
Alpert, Bracha R., 1257
Alred, Gerald J., 3414
Altimore, Michael, 58
Alvarez, Joseph A., 3283
Amberg, Margaret, 1972
Ames, Jay, 860
Amiran, M., 1221
Ammon, Mary Sue, 3008
Ammon, Paul, 237, 3008
Amsden, Dorothy Corner, 2798
Anandam, Kamala, 2477
Anastasi, Ann, 1234
Andera, Frank, 2725
Andersen, Elaine S., 861
Andersen, Janis F., 1367
Andersen, Kenneth E., 1366
Andersen, Peter A., 1367
Anderson, Alonzo B., 1431
Anderson, Dan, 2460
Anderson, Don, 3793
Anderson, Edward, 1836
Anderson, Floyd D., 59
Anderson, Janice Walker, 1368
Anderson, Judi, 2157
Anderson, Kristine F., 1309, 2390
Anderson, Margaret A., 1973
Anderson, Nina L., 3060
Anderson, Norman A., 60
Anderson, Paul V., 916
Anderson, Philip M., 3476
Anderson, Richard C., 740, 812, 817, 838
Anderson, Sharon R., 3489
Anderson, Thomas H., 817, 3136
Anderson, W. Steve, 2726
Anderson, Wayne C., 628, 629
Andrews, Deborah C., 2872
Andrews, John D. W., 1258
Andrews, Katherine A., 3061
Angenot, Marc, 630
Annas, Pamela J., 61
Annett, Clarence H., 2799

Anson, Chris M., 62, 2478, 2479, 2480
Anthony, Gwendolyn, 1296
Anthony, Lillian Small, 3207
Aoun, Joseph, 862
Applebaum, Wayne, 3676
Applebee, Arthur N., 63, 318, 1835, 2261
Appleby, Bruce C., 95, 1781, 3477, 3668
Appleman, Philip, 3101
Apstein, Barbara, 515
Arakelian, Paul G., 863
Arca, Maria, 1090
Arib, Michael A., 1150
Ariel, Tsivia, 2288
Arkin, Marian, 2389, 2391
Arkle, Stephen, 2226
Armbruster, Bonnie B., 817, 1173, 1221, 3136
Armington, David, 1974
Armour, Maureen, 1548
Arms, Valerie M., 2800, 3438
Armstrong, Cherryl, 64
Arnett, Nancy Carol, 1369
Arnett, Robert, 778
Arnold, Kathy, 2158, 2159
Arnold, Linda K., 2160
Arnold, Richard, 631
Arnold, Vanessa Dean, 2727
Arnold, Virginia, 3165
Arons, Arnold B., 1825
Arrasmith, Dean G., 3676
Arrington, Phillip K., 65
Arrow, Ralph, 632
Asals, Heather, 567
Aschauer, Mary Ann, 1370
Ashby-Davis, Claire, 1975
Ashley, Leonard R. N., 864, 865, 866, 3062, 3478
Ashmore, Timothy M., 3479
Ashwell, Jonathan D., 3480
Askew, Lida, 2161
Association of American Medical Colleges, 2889
AT&T Bell Laboratories, 3481
AT&T Technologies, 3481
Atari, Omar F., 1371
Athey, I., 838
Athey, Irene, 1486
Atwater, Deborah F., 66
Atwell, Nancie, 400, 1976, 2046, 2162
Au, K., 817
Austin, Doris E., 67
Auten, Anne, 3482
Autrey, Ken, 2
Au-Yeung La, Winnie, 420
Avery, Carol S., 1977, 2046
Axelrod, Rise B., 3284, 3285

Aycock, Coleen K., 68

Babcock, John Gilbert Chittenden, 1372
Bachen, Christine M., 828
Bachtin, Nicholas, 867
Backman, Sven, 868
Bacon, Nora, 2481
Baddeley, Alan, 741
Baghban, Marcia, 69
Bahruth, Robert, 2046
Bailey, Adrienne Y., 2163
Bailey, Charles-James N., 869
Bailey, Dennis L., 340
Bailey, Edward P., Jr., 3286
Bailey, Lucille M., 2983
Bajuniemi, Lee E., 762
Baker, Anne, 1835
Baker, Carolyn D., 2090
Baker, Catherine, 778
Baker, Deborah Carol, 70
Baker, George A., III, 1822, 2459
Baker, L., 817
Baker, Linda, 742
Baker, Mim, 3477
Baker, Miriam, 3383
Baker, Temple, 1125
Bal, Mieke, 633
Balamore, Usha, 1091
Baldwin, Dean R., 2164
Bali, Mrinal, 3483
Balkema, Sandra J., 71
Ball, Carolyn, 563
Ballard, Leslie, 2165
Ballstaedt, S.-P., 1173
Balsam, Mitchell, 3546
Baltes, Paul B., 1106
Bamberg, Betty, 3677
Bander, Robert G., 3189
Bank, Stanley, 72
Bank Street College of Education, 3484
Banker, Stephen Robert, 1373
Bannister, Linda, 1741
Bannister-Wills, Linda, 1745
Barabas, Christine P., 73
Barber, Charles, 868
Barbour, James, 1675, 2965
Barker, Bill, 1596
Barker, Larry L., 1374
Barker, Thomas T., 1676, 2890, 3486
Barker, Wendy, 634
Barkman, Patricia, 2728
Barnes, Donald L., 3149
Barnes, Dorothy, 1799, 2166

Barnes, Douglas, 1799, 2166
Barnes, James A., 743
Barnes, Judith A., 1375
Barnes, Linda L., 74, 3678
Barnes, Sylvia, 1782
Barnet, Sylvan, 3326
Barnum, Carol M., 1310
Barnwell, William H., 3214
Baron, J., 1110
Baron, Marthalee S., 1783
Baron, Naomi S., 1376
Barrett, Harold, 340
Barrs, Myra, 1799
Barry, Francis J., 2167
Barry, Lois, 3487
Bart, Leslie A., 2193
Bartelo, Dennise, 75, 1978
Bartholomae, David, 33, 191, 260, 407, 513
Bartky, Joyce, 3161, 3173
Bartlett, Elsa J., 76
Bartley, Shirley, 1377
Bartman, Fred, 1596
Barton, Ben F., 1783, 2801
Barton, John, 2891
Barton, Marcia, 2482
Barton, Marthalee S., 2801
Baru, Ellen, 1979
Barzun, Jacques, 77
Basham, Charlotte, 870
Bateman, David N., 3419
Bates, Elizabeth, 1051
Bates, John, 2109, 2110
Bates, John E., 1189
Bates, Patricia T., 78
Bathke, Julia, 2168
Bator, Robert, 3190
Batteiger, Richard P., 3398
Batterman, Henry, 3013
Batty, Beauford R., 1836
Batty, Constance J., 1836
Baudin, Fernand, 79
Baum, Joan, 2389
Bauman, Gail A., 1980
Baumann, James F., 744
Baumhover, Mary J., 2984
Baumlin, James S., 80, 2169
Bayer, John George, Jr., 81
Bayles, Kathryn, 1189
Bazerman, Charles, 82, 3287
Beach, Richard, 83, 84, 842, 1311, 1549
Beachem, Michael T., 1981
Beam, Frances Chitwood, 3317
Beaman, Bruce, 2226

Bear, John, 1414
Beard, John, 3, 4
Beatty, Michael J., 1092, 1093, 3850
Beauzee[?], 871
Bebout, Linda, 745
Bechler, Pinchos, 2288
Beck, Isabel L., 746, 2089
Beck, James, 1826, 2483
Beck, James P., 2484, 2485, 2486, 2892
Beck, L., 817
Becker, A. L., 260
Becker, Joseph D., 85
Beckman, Judy, 1982
Bedetti, Gabriella, 2487
Beem, Beverly, 2488, 2575
Beem, Jane A., 2170
Been, Sheila, 2288
Beene, Lynn Diane, 33
Beers, Susan E., 2489
Beggs, James S., 33
Begin, John, 802
Behling, John H., 3425
Behm, Richard H., 9
Behnke, Ralph R., 1479
Behrens, Lawrence, 3327
Beiderwell, Bruce, 635
Beidler, Peter G., 1784
Belanger, Joe, 1087
Belcher, Gerald L., 3346
Belcher, Vivian, 243
Bell, Arthur H., 3489
Bell, Elizabeth, 1550
Bell, John, 2389
Bell, Kathleen L., 2490
Bell, Robert A., 963
Bell, T. H., 1785, 1786
Bellamy, Joe David, 636
Belz, Elaine, 2966
Benbassat, J., 2893
Bencal, Cynthia E., 2042
Bencich, Carole, 3839
Benedict, Susan, 2046
Benelli, Beatrice, 837
Benesch, Sarah, 2491, 3679
Ben-Meir, Dvora, 2288
Benner, Pamela, 1904, 2492
Bennett, Adrian T., 1350
Bennett, Bruce, 2171
Bennett, James R., 340
Bennett, Jo Ann, 872
Bennett, Robert A., 1259
Bennett, W. Lance, 1378
Bennett, William J., 1827

Bennett, Winfield S., 987
Benoit, William L., 5, 86
Benson, Barbara, 3063
Benson, Thomas W., 1379
Bensoussan, Marsha, 3680
Benton, Kay Hutchison, 2392
Benton, Stephen L., 87
Benzel, Kathryn, 3364
Benzel, Michael, 3364
Bereiter, Carl, 88, 157, 318, 568, 747, 1110, 1173, 1297, 1828
Berg, Anna, 2393
Berg, Temma F., 637
Berger, Allen, 1829
Berger, Jeffrey, 2894
Bergerson, Howard W., 873
Bergeson, Mary Alice, 1551
Berk, Laura E., 1094
Berke, Jacqueline, 3288
Berkenkotter, Carol, 89, 90
Berlin, James A., 91, 92, 340
Berlo, Robert, 3399
Berman, Louise M., 1620
Berman, Morton, 3326
Bernhardt, Stephen A., 93, 94, 95, 2895, 3477
Berrent, Howard I., 3065
Bertch, Julie, 2896
Berthoff, Ann E., 96, 97, 98, 120, 260, 407
Bertrand, Nancy, 1959
Berwick, Robert, 874
Besner, Neil, 99
Besser, Mary Pamela, 2394
Best, Judith A., 2897
Betts, Doris, 3102
Betts, Irene D., 3191
Bevilacqua, Vincent M., 100, 101
Biagi, Shirley, 3490
Bibb, Thomas Clifford, 1836
Biber, Douglas E., 875
Bichard, Sandra L., 1244
Bickel, Linda L., 2507
Bickhard, Mark H., 1095
Biddle, Arthur W., 3289
Bieke, Kathleen A., 102
Bielaski, Larry, 2802
Biggers, Thompson, 1380
Billman, Dorrit Owen, 876
Bird, Lois Bridges, 3143
Bird, Marlene, 747
Birdsong, Theda P., 1348, 2172
Birkmire, Deborah P., 748
Birnbaum, June, 1486
Birns, H. William, 34

Bisanz, G. L., 121
Bissell, Olivia, 2887
Bissex, Glenda L., 1431, 2063
Bitzer, Lloyd F., 340
Bizzell, Patricia, 407, 1096, 2395, 3426
Bjork, Robert E., 103
Black, Edwin, 1381
Black, J. B., 121, 838, 1173
Black, J. L., 749, 750
Black, James, 3752
Black, Janet K., 1552
Black, John B., 1206
Black, Kathryn N., 1176
Blackburn, Ellen, 1983, 2046
Blackmon, Margaret Van Deman, 3064
Blair, Carole, 104
Blair, Edward, 1363
Blake, Caesar, 3333
Blanchard, Jay S., 2967
Blanchard, Margaret A., 2898
Blank, Gary B., 1686, 2904
Blank, Marion, 754
Blatt, Gloria T., 2899
Blau, Andrea F., 3681
Blazer, Bonita, 105
Blee, Myron R., 3682
Bleeker, Gerrit, 2173
Block, Richard A., 1830
Blok, H., 3683
Bloom, Lynn Z., 33, 513, 2696, 3389
Bloome, David, 1984
Blow, F. C., 1201
Blue, Kay, 1831
Blum, Jack, 3192
Bly, Robert W., 2729
Bobb, Victor, 2900
Bodino, Angela, 2887
Bodmer, George R., 3492
Boesch, Ernst E., 1114
Bogart, Quentin J., 3103
Bogdan, Deanne, 2377
Bogert, Judith, 2730
Boggs, George R., 2396, 3684
Bohn, Willard, 7
Boiarsky, Carolyn, 1382, 1832, 1833, 2493
Boice, Robert, 106, 513, 1097
Boley, Tommy J., 2397
Bolotta, Rene L., 107
Bolt Bernak and Newman, 3493, 3499
Bond, Sandra J., 751
Bonitatibus, Gary J., 1098
Book, Cassandra L., 752
Books, Larry Wayne, 108

Booley, Heather A., 109
Boomer, Garth, 877, 1260, 1853, 3443
Booth, Jim, 2174
Booth, Wayne, 3494
Borchardt, Kathleen M., 783
Borgmann, Dmitri A., 878, 879, 880, 881, 882, 883, 884, 885, 886, 887, 888
Borja, Francisco, 3685
Bork, Alfred, 2389, 3632
Bormann, Dennis R., 110
Bornstein, Diane D., 3427
Borus, Dixie N., 1960
Boruta, Marcia J., 237
Bosco, Jay J., 1677
Bostian, Lloyd, 2803
Boswell, Bill, 638
Bouchard, Sharon, 3402
Boutin, Frances, 1985
Bovair, S., 121
Bower, G. H., 838
Bower, Judith A., 820
Bowerstock, G. W., 639
Bowman, Barbara, 2494
Bowman, Joel P., 1383, 2765
Boyd, Reta, 2098
Boyer, Ernest L., 1261
Boyer, James, 2098
Boyle, Owen, 2647
Brackett, George, 3495
Bradac, James, Jr., 1384
Bradford, Annette, 171, 2398
Bradford, Ernest, 1836
Braffman, Ellen J., 2085
Braig, Deborah E., 1986
Brainerd, C. J., 1099
Branchaw, Bernadine, 2765, 3264
Branco, David J., 111
Brand, Alice G., 112
Brandenburg, Dale C., 3827
Brandes, Paul D., 113
Brandt, Deborah, 114, 115, 116
Brandtstädter, Jochen, 1106
Branham, Robert J., 117
Brannon, Lil, 260, 343, 400, 916, 1553, 1745
Branscombe, Amanda, 237
Bransford, J. D., 838, 1221
Brasch, Walter M., 889
Braskamp, Larry A., 3827
Braun, Winnifred, 2046
Brause, Rita S., 392, 1987
Bray, David, 3496
Brazee, Phyllis, 1988
Bredin, Hugh, 118, 890

Breihan, John R., 2926, 3748
Breland, Hunter M., 3686
Brennan, Mark, 119
Brennan, Roslin E., 119
Brenner, Douglas Francis, 1385
Brenner, Kenneth, 3687
Brent, Douglas, 524
Brent, Harry, 1834, 3328
Brereton, John, 120
Brewster, Marty, 1989
Brezezinski, Evelyn J., 1386
Bridgeman, Brent, 2495
Bridges, Jean Bolen, 891
Bridgford, Kim, 2496
Bridwell, Lillian S., 35, 83, 237, 2507, 3668
Briggs, Charles L., 892
Briggs, John C., 33
Brigham Young University, 3497
Brill, Jane, 1756
Brink, Daniel, 2985
Brinkman, Carolyn, 3192
Brinton, Donna M., 3045
Briscoe, Mary Louise, 1641
Bristow, Margaret, 2497
Britton, B. K., 121
Britton, James, 122, 1596, 1799, 1835, 1853
Broad, Richard G., 3476
Broadhead, Glenn, 191, 2765
Brock, Bernard L., 123, 124
Brockmann, R. John, 2804
Brockriede, Wayne, 125, 229
Brodkey, Linda, 126
Brodner, Frederick, 893
Brodsky, Allen, 1387
Bromley, Karen D., 1990, 1991
Bronson, Barbara, 340, 2226
Brook, Robert, 237
Brooke, Maxey, 894, 895, 896
Brooke, Robert E., 897
Brooker, Gerard T., 3498
Brooks, Brian S., 3428
Brooks, Charlotte K., 1836, 3104
Brooks, Larry W., 1300
Broom, Mary Jo, 2986
Brostoff, Anita, 1813, 2175
Broughton, Bradford B., 127
Brown, A., 817
Brown, A. L., 838, 1110, 1173
Brown, Alan, 1678, 1679, 2176
Brown, Ann E., 1686, 2805, 2904
Brown, Betsy E., 1554
Brown, Carl R. V., 2853
Brown, Daniel J., 3193

Brown, Garth H., 2090
Brown, Jane L., 2498, 2499
Brown, Jean E., 128, 2377
Brown, Lawrence W., 2177
Brown, Margaret C., 2399
Brown, Margery, 1100
Brown, Mary Helen, 1388
Brown, Peggy Ann, 1642
Brown, Peter D., 1389
Brown, Sandra, 3832
Brown, Tracey, 2987
Browne, Beverly Ann, 753
Brownell, Tom, 3476
Brownstein, Marilyn L., 640
Bruce, Bertram, 3499, 3500, 3623
Bruffee, Kenneth A., 407, 1643, 1745, 1837, 2178, 3290
Bruflodt, Hank A., 258
Brumfield, Isaac, 3776
Brummett, Barry, 129, 130, 131
Bruner, J., 1110
Bruner, Jerome, 1431
Brusaw, Charles T., 3414
Bruskin, Carol, 754
Bryant, Coralie, 1262
Bryant, Deborah G., 132
Bryant, JoAnne Raiford, 3065
Bryant, John, 2500
Bryner, Paula, 3501
Bubolz, Thomas, 3705
Buckelew, Roy Edward, 1390
Buckler, Patricia Prandini, 2501
Buckley, William K., 1672
Buddemeier, Richard E., 133, 134
Buehler, Mary F., 135
Buerk, Dorothy, 2901
Bulgarella, Laurie, 376
Bullock, Mary, 1101
Bullock, Richard, 3688
Bulsys, Joseph Algirdas, 1391
Bump, Jerome, 2806
Buncombe, Marie H., 1836
Bunge, Nancy, 136
Burani, Cristina, 755
Burden, Denise, 1558
Burgchardt, Carl R., 1392
Burgdorf, Arlene, 3149
Burgess, Parke G., 124, 137
Burgess, Tony, 1799
Burhans, Clinton S., 3226
Burke, Carolyn L., 286, 952, 1277
Burke, Kenneth, 124, 138, 139
Burkhardt, Ross M., 140

Burkland, Jill, 3689
Burleson, Brant R., 141, 1393
Burmester, David, 3445
Burnette, William E., 3193
Burnham, Christopher, 33, 1555
Burns, Gerald Thomas, 1263
Burns, Hugh, 400, 3504, 3505, 3506, 3507, 3508, 3632, 3668
Burns, Rex, 2697
Burns, Robert Alan, 641
Burns, Thomas, 1394
Burris, Leslie, 1556
Burrows, Alvina Truet, 1992
Burry, James, 3690
Burt, Forrest D., 3329
Burto, William, 3326
Burtoff, Michele J., 142
Burton, John K., 496, 3788
Busch, John Christian, 3828
Bush, Sam, 1596
Bushman, John H., 2179
Butler, Andrea, 1993, 1994
Butler, Marilyn, 2731, 2765
Butler, Maureen, 143
Butler, Sydney J., 3691
Butters, Ronald S., 898
Buttny, Richard, 1395
Butturff, Douglas R., 916
Byrne, James P., 1190
Byrne, Tomas E., 2803

Cacha, Frances B., 1995, 1996
Cahn, Dudley D., 3829
Cain, William E., 642, 643
Cairns, P., 644
Calder, Robert L., 2377
Calfee, Robert C., 1865
Calhoun, Anga Windsor, 2180
Calhoun, Mary Lynne, 756
Calkins, Lucy McCormick, 400, 2063
Callaghan, Patricia, 144
Camden, Carl, 1473, 3847
Cameron, J. Camp, 1105
Camp, Roberta, 3694
Campbell, Anne, 1557
Campbell, Dianna S., 3227
Campbell, Don, 1596
Campbell, Donald, 2988
Campbell, Gracemarie, 2181
Campbell, James, 145
Campbell, Jane, 645
Campbell, Joann, 2400
Campbell, John Angus, 146

Camperell, K., 838
Campione, J. C., 1173, 1221
Capassila, Toni Lee, 3429
Capp, Diane, 1860
Cappella, J. N., 1352
Capps, Ronald Robert, 147
Capuzzi, Frank A., 296
Caramazza, Alfonso, 755, 1110
Caras, Roger, 2698
Carbaugh, Donal A., 1312
Carell, Patricia L., 757
Carey, Robert F., 646
Carey, S., 1110
Carino, Peter A., 2401, 2402, 3066
Carleton, Walter M., 148
Carlman, Nancy, 3692, 3693
Carlson, Greg N., 899
Carlson, Patricia, 2575
Carlson, Sybil, 1124
Carlson, Sybil B., 2495, 3694
Carmona, Ralph Chris, 900
Carmusin, Amy, 1680
Carnegie Foundation for the Advancement of
    Learning, 1261
Carpenter, Carol, 1102
Carpenter, P., 817
Carpenter, P. A., 838, 1173
Carpenter, Ronald H., 901
Carr, Bert, 3695, 3752
Carr, Marion, 2989
Carrell, Patricia, 149, 902, 2990, 2991
Carrier, Carol, 1103
Carrier, David, 647
Carroll, John B., 838, 1104
Carroll, John Joseph, 150
Carroll, Joyce Armstrong, 83, 2403, 3067
Carson, David L., 2807
Carter, James, 1608
Carter, John Marshall, 2182, 2183, 3105
Carter, Lu, 2404
Caruso, Domenick, 3388
Casady, Mona J., 2732
Cascardi, A. J., 648
Case, Donald P., 3511
Case, R., 1110
Casentino, Sue, 2208
Casmir, Fred L., 1396
Cassara, Ernest, 2902
Cassari, Laura E., 2765
Cassell, Richard M., 1313
Cassidy, Andrea, 1556
Cassidy, Frederic G., 903
Castaneda, Hecto-Neri, 904

Castellano, Rose Lynn, 151
Catron, Douglas M., 2733, 2808
Catroppa, Barbara, 1681
Caulfield, Peter J., 1397
Cavallari, Susan D., 1838
Cavedon, Adel, 758
Cavenaugh, John C., 1105
Cawelti, Scott, 2502
Cazden, Courtney B., 237, 838, 1486
Ceci, Stephen J., 1644
Cervero, Ronald M., 1264
Cetron, Marvin J., 1814
Chadburn, Bev, 2135
Chadwick, Kent, 2809
Chafe, Wallace, 237
Chaffee, John, 3255
Chalker, Sylvia, 2992
Chall, Jeanne S., 318, 759, 1839
Chamberlin, John, 2377
Chambers, Aidan, 649
Chang, Maisy, 3030
Chaplin, Miriam T., 1836
Chapman, Diane L., 1997
Chapman, Marcia, 2184
Chapman, Michael, 1106
Charischak, Ihor, 2389
Charland, Maurice Rene, 1398
Charney, Davida, 3696
Chase, Dennis, 2503, 2504
Chase, Geoffrey W., 1682, 1683
Check, Joseph W., 1558
Cheney, Patrick, 2810
Cheng, Patricia W., 1107
Cheng, Susan, 3535
Cherry, Roger D., 83, 3714
Cherwitz, Richard A., 152
Cheshire, Barbara W., 153
Chew, Charles R., 154, 2046, 2185, 2186
Chew, Timothy, 2185
Chi, Michelene T. H., 1108, 1110
Chinen, Allen B., 1109
Ching, Liu Mei, 1399
Ching, Marvin K. L., 33, 905
Chipman, S. F., 1110, 1221
Chiseri-Strater, Elizabeth, 155, 156
Chiteman, Michael D., 1684
Chittick, Kathryn, 650
Chopra, Raj K., 1787
Chou, Frank H., 1998
Choueka, Yaacov, 906
Choy, Penelope, 3228
Chrismore, Avon, 3137
Christensen, Francis, 260

Christensen, Linda, 1972
Christenson, Eric H., 1840, 3068
Chudy, Gladys L., 1999
Church, Elizabeth, 157, 318
Church, Susan M., 2000, 2098
Cianciolo, Patricia J., 1400
Ciner, Elizabeth, 2575
Cioffi, Grant, 83
Cisneros, Sandra, 2187
Clanchy, Michael T., 1499
Clark, Ann K., 907
Clark, Beverly L., 158, 3106, 3697
Clark, Carolyn, 2988
Clark, Christopher M., 237, 1841, 2001, 2206
Clark, Curtis L., 760
Clark, Frances L., 761
Clark, Irene Lurkis, 159, 1685, 3473, 3698
Clark, John R., 1842, 2002
Clark, Margaret M., 1431
Clark, Richard W., 3173
Clark, Roger, 3107, 3256
Clark, Ruth Anne, 2003
Clark, Thomas, 1559
Clark, Thomas L., 1843
Clark, Virginia, 3430
Clark, Wilma, 1844
Clark-Beattie, Rosemary, 651
Clarke, Mark A., 2993
Clarke, Robert, 1265
Clarke, Stephen, 2166
Cleary, Joseph, 3434
Clements, Wallace, 3399
Clifford, John, 160, 400, 407
Clifton, Linda, 2226, 3699
Clines, Raymond H., 2505
Clinkscale, Bella G., 2734
Clinton, DeWitt, 2188
Clymer, Diane, 2903
Cobb, Loretta, 1745
Cobb, Martha K., 1836
Coble, Charles R., 3043
Cochran-Smith, Marilyn, 1431
Cody, Michael J., 1479
Coe, Richard M., 2699
Cogswell, F., 3120
Cohen, Alan S., 2700
Cohen, Andrew D., 2288, 2994
Cohen, Jodi Rise, 161
Cohen, Michael, 3512, 3535
Cohen, Michael E., 3668
Cohn, Margot, 318
Colasurdo, Anthony P., 2189
Colavito, Joseph J., 2506

Colbert, Karen K., 1152
Colborne, R. Garnet, 2377
Coleman, Gerald, 2393
Coles, William E., Jr., 3330
Colligan, Robert C., 762
Collins, A., 817, 838, 1110
Collins, Carmen, 763, 3194
Collins, D. W. K., 749
Collins, James, 1401
Collins, James L., 83, 162, 2507, 3638, 3639
Collins, James P., 2004
Collins, Janay, 1073
Collins, Kathleen, 2190
Collins, Mary Evelyn, 163
Collins, W. K., 750
Collymore, J. C., 3513
Combs, Warren E., 916
Comings, John Kahler David, 2995
Comley, Nancy R., 3315, 3331
Commission on Reading, 740
Comprone, Joseph J., 164, 191, 652, 2508
Condravy, Joan C., 28, 2405
Condrey, Leroy J., 3700
Cone, Dennis, 2996
Coney, Mary B., 2811
Conference for Secondary School English Department Chairpersons, 1645
Conley, Thomas M., 165
Conlin, Mary Lou, 3215
Connor, Jennifer J., 2812
Connor, Ulla, 764
Connors, Robert J., 166, 167, 168, 169, 170, 171, 172, 407
Constantinides, Janet C., 2813
Cook, Claire Kehrwald, 3431
Cook, John Granger, 908
Cook, William W., 1836
Coombs, Marjorie, 2005
Coon, George E., 3151
Cooper, Charles R., 83, 260, 1318, 3284, 3285, 3383
Cooper, G. Robb, 2765
Cooper, Jan, 2509
Cooper, Lynn D., 2765
Cooper, Marilyn M., 83
Cooper, Martha D., 173
Cooper, Peter L., 3701
Cooper, Robert G., 1095
Cooper, Rose Marie, 1402
Copeland, Celia A., 1560
Copeland, Evelyn, 8
Copeland, Kathleen, 765, 1326
Copley, Barbara, 83
Corbett, Edward P. J., 174, 260, 407, 1845, 3265

Corbett, Marlene, 1646
Corbett, Stephen S., 1266
Corbin, Kyle, 909
Corder, Jim W., 175, 176, 177, 178, 179, 3266
Cordle, Virginia M., 821
Corley, Joseph Russell, 1403
Cormack, Phil, 1835
Cormier, Robert, 180
Cornoldi, Cesare, 758
Corona, Laurel, 2406
Corrito, Jo An, 2389
Cortese, Guiseppina, 2997
Costanzo, William, 3375, 3448
Costello, Jacqueline, 3210
Costigan-Eaves, Patricia James, 2814
Cotton, Helen D. S., 1561
Couture, Barbara, 1647, 3400
Covert, Laurie Anne Schmid, 1314
Covington, David H., 1686, 2815, 2904
Covington, M. V., 1221
Covino, William A., 3702
Cox, Bene Scanlon, 1745
Cox, Beverly, 181
Cox, Nancy, 3152
Craig, Randall, 653
Cramer, Barbara B., 3151
Cramer, Carmen, 2816, 3516
Cranley, Sharon J., 2006
Craven, Jerry, 2191
Cravens, Hamilton, 1111
Creeden, John E., 3703
Cresswell, M. J., 910
Cressy, David, 1499
Crews, Frederick, 3267, 3291
Crews, Ruthellen, 2007
Crisler, Jesse A., 2510
Crismore, Avon, 1633
Criswell, Dana, 2511
Croft, Mary K., 1745
Cromley, Janet S., 1546
Cronell, Bruce, 911, 912
Cronin, Frank, 537, 1220, 1846, 3476, 3704
Cross, John A., 2512
Crosson, Bruce, 1112
Crowe, Chris, 2192
Crowe, Michael R., 2193
Crowhurst, Marion, 182
Crowley, Ann V., 3069
Crowley, Sharon, 183, 184, 185, 2513
Crusius, Timothy W., 186
Culberson, Dan, 2797
Cullen, Robert J., 2905
Cullen, Roxanne M., 913

Culp, Mary Beth, 187, 766
Culver, Steven, 2194, 3752
Cunningham, Anne E., 840
Cunningham, Cliff C., 1963
Cunningham, Merrilee, 2377
Cureton, George O., 1836
Cureton, Richard D., 955
Curey, Bob J., 2512
Curl, David, 1596
Curran, Doris, 2008, 2009
Curran, Jane M., 2195, 2196
Curtice, Carolyn Ann, 2197
Curtis, Deborah, 1687
Curtis, Jan K., 914
Curtis, W. Scott, 1267
Cypert, Rick, 2198

Dahbi, Mohammed, 915
Dahl, Karin L., 190
Daiker, Donald, 191, 260, 407, 916, 3394, 3726
Dairs, Suzanne, 2407
Daiute, Colette, 83, 237, 3518, 3668
Dalgish, Gerard M., 2389, 2998, 2999
Daly, John A., 83, 513
D'amico, Deborah, 2042
D'Angelo, Frank, 33, 171, 189, 260, 340, 407, 3292
Danheiser, Thomas L., 2199
Daniel, Stephen H., 192
Danielewicz, Jane, 237
Daniell, Beth, 1404
Daniels, Harvey, 1562
Daniels, Tom D., 193
Danielson, Wayne A., 3519
Dansei, Marcel, 917
Dansereau, Donald F., 449, 1221, 1300
D'Arcy, Pat, 1698
Dascal, Marcelo, 329
Dasenbrock, Reed Way, 834
Dates, Jannette Lake, 1405
Däumer, Elisabeth, 188
Davey, W., 3120
David, Carol, 2735, 3705
Davidson, Fred, 3000
Davidson, Priscilla, 2575
Davis, Chuck, 2200
Davis, Elwyn H., 2389
Davis, Frances A., 1486
Davis, Frederica, 1847
Davis, Irma, 1689
Davis, James E., 2514
Davis, Ken, 2201
Davis, Kevin, 1690, 1691
Davis, Mary, 2515

Davis, Millie, 2202
Davis, Robert Murray, 654
Davis, Ruth, 2389
Davis, Vivian I., 1836
Dawe, Alan, 3706
Dawe, Charles W., 3185, 3376
Dawkins, John, 3157
Day, M. C., 1110
Day, Margaret M., 2010
Dazey, Mary Ann, 3070
deAvaila, E. A., 1110
de Beaugrande, Robert, 191, 194, 1173, 1848, 2203, 3138, 3365
DeBeni, Rossana, 758
DeBlois, Peter, 3395
De Bono, E., 1221
DeBrosse, James, 1563
DeCelles, Linda, 2423
Decker, Randall E., 3332
Decker, Sadie N., 794
Decker-Amos, Linda, 1521
Deen, Rosemary, 2516, 3313
Deese, Rebecca, 918
De Ford, Diane, 1835
DeGeorge, James, 3415
DeGraaff, Robert M., 655
De Jesus, Socorro, 3001
DeLacoste, Christine, 1125
Delgado, Joseph Figueroa, 1406
Dell, Gary S., 1129
Delmar, P. Jay, 2517
Dent, Cathy H., 195
Denton, Robert F., 16
DeRoach, J. N., 749, 750
DeRoller, Joseph, 2185
Deshler, Donald D., 761, 1268, 1269
Desmond, William, 196
DeStefano, Johanna S., 2063
Devereux, Robert, 919
DeVito, Joseph A., 3139
Devlin, Frank, 2518
DeVogler-Ebersole, Karen, 658
de Vries, Brian, 1244
DeVries, Rheta, 1104
DeWitt-Spurgin, Sally, 3377
Dezell, Maureen, 3261
Dial, Robert L., 916
Diamond, C. T. P., 1853
Diamond, Joan, 1982
Diaz, Rafael M., 1123
Diaz, Rosa, 3055
Diaz, Stephen, 3055
Dice, Laura, 2519

DiCecco, Joseph Vincent, 767
Dick, John A. R., 3229
Dicker, Susan, 920
Dickinson, Bonnie, 2605
Diefenbeck, James A., 1315
Dieterich, Daniel J., 9, 2736
Dietrich, Julia C., 472
Diffley, Kathleen Elizabeth, 197
Dillingham, Don, 2408
Dillon, Linda S., 2817
Dilworth, Collett B., 3274
DiMare, Lesley Ann, 198
Dingwaney, Anuradha, 656
Dionisopoulos, George N., 1316
Dismuke, Diane, 2011
DiStefano, Philip, 1270
Dittman, Trudy, 2575
Divas, Antonia, 1212
Dixon, Diane J., 2012
Dixon, John, 1853, 2377
Dixson, Robert J., 3523
DiYanni, Robert, 407, 3293
Doake, David B., 2063
Dobrin, David N., 199, 2818
Dobson, L. N., 200
Dodd, Anne Wescott, 2204
Dodd, Carley H., 1538
Doe, Sandra, 2520, 2575
Doe, Sue Rowe, 2521
Dohaney, M. T., 1849, 3848
Doheny-Farina, Stephen, 201, 202
Dolby-Stahl, Sandra K., 203
Dolinsky, Claudia, 921
Dollieslager, Rick, 2522
Dominguez, J., 1221
Donald, Robert B., 3216
Donaldson, Margaret, 1431
Donelson, Ken, 1407, 3108
Donlan, D., 838, 2344
Donlon, Edward T., 1267
Donnellan, LaRae M., 2819
Donohue, Christine, 2013
Donovan, Timothy R., 400, 2575
Donsky, Barbara V., 2014, 3154
Dorans, Neil J., 3707
Dorazio, Patricia, 2523
Dorgan, Virginia, 3524
Dorman, W. Wade, 2906
Dornan, Edward A., 3185, 3376
Doty, Ralph, 1271
Dougherty, Barbey N., 3390
Dougherty, Eleanor Donnelly, 922
Dougherty, Nan, 2765

Douglas, George, 1408, 1788
Douglas, Wallace, 120
Dovidio, John F., 1512
Dowdey, Diane, 204, 2820
Dowling, David, 657
Dowling, Ralph Edward, 1409
Downey, Bill, 205
Downey, Sharon Dee, 206
Downing, Carol Ann, 207
Downing, John, 3071
Dowst, Kenneth, 191, 208
Dragga, Sam, 2821, 3708
Drake, Dorothy A., 768
Drakeford, Carolyn, 1836
Dreher, M. J., 838
Drescher, Carolyn S., 2015
Drew, Dan G., 1410
Drobnic, Karl, 3002
Drogenis, Marvin, 2601
Dubay, Ronda, 3380
DuBois, Barbara, 2524, 3109
Duda, Phyllis, 3171
Dudley, H. A. F., 2907
Dudley, Pat, 1850
Dudley-Marling, Curtis C., 2016
Duffy, Gerald G., 752
Duffy, Karen Louise, 2968
Duggan, Tamia, 2017
Duin, Ann, 1851, 2205, 2507
Duke, Charles R., 1789, 1852, 2908, 3830
Dumont, Raymond, 3401
Dunbar, Nancy Reeve, 1411
Dunbar-Odom, Donna, 2409
Duncan, Jeffrey L., 3294
Duncan, Patricia H., 2018
Duncan, S., 1110
Dunham, Donald E., 563
Dunn, Saundra, 237, 2206
Dunn-Rankin, Patricia, 3230
Dupree, James Vincent, 1412
Dupuis, Mary M., 3742
Duran, Elva, 769
Duran, R. P., 1110
Durfee, Patricia B., 2822
Durham, Philip, 3353
Durst, Russel K., 10, 11
Duvall, Betty J., 2019
Dwyer, Barry, 2090
Dyson, Anne Haas, 12, 209, 210, 223, 318, 2020, 2021, 2022, 2023

Eagleson, Robert D., 1853, 2377
Eagney, Peggy, 1113

Earley, George W., 2701
Eastern Washington University Research Laboratory, 211, 1854
Eastman, Athur, 3333
Eaton, Sara, 83
Ebersole, Peter, 658
Eblen, Charlene, 1564
Eccles, Jacquelynne, 1234
Eckensberger, Lutz H., 1114
Eckler, A. Ross, 923, 924, 925, 926, 927, 928, 3089
Eckoff, Barbara, 318
Ede, Lisa S., 13, 171, 212, 380, 1115, 2737
Edelsky, Carole, 213
Eden, Rick A., 3334
Edge, Julian, 3003, 3004
Edie, William F., 1413
Ediger, Marlow, 2024, 3476
Edwards, Bruce L., Jr., 214, 3140, 3525
Edwards, Grace Toney, 2207
Edwards, Walter F., 1836
Egendorf, Arthur, 407
Eggington, William, 3005
Ehri, Linnea C., 768, 1961
Ehrlich, Diane B., 215
Eichorn, Dorothy H., 1815
Eidvson, Sandra, 3709
Einhorn, Hillel J., 1116
Eisenberg, Nora, 3231
Eiss, Harry, 929
Eizykman, Boris, 659
Eklof, Ben, 1499
Ekman, Paul, 1414
Elam, Ohakwe Temple, 1415
Elasser, Nan, 1835
Elbow, Peter, 191, 216
Eldblom, Nancy, 2952
Eldred, Janet, 2410
Elias, Kristina M., 2208
Elias, Richard, 3526, 3527
Elifson, Joan M., 1117
Elkhatib, Ahmad S., 930
Elledge, Elaine Kilgore, 1745
Ellicott, Abbie M., 1205
Ellinger, Robert S., 2765
Elliot, Brian A., 931
Elliot, Norman, 1416
Elliott, Appele Gan Marietta, 1417
Elliott, Carol, 1596
Ellis, A. W., 1418
Ellsworth, Elizabeth Ann, 1419
Elsasser, Nan, 3006
Emblem, D. L., 3339
Emery, Donald W., 3232

Emig, Janet, 260, 1486, 3710, 3831
Emmanuel, Lenny, 2525
End, Laurel J., 770
Endicott, Phyllis, 1590
Engel, Bernard F., 1855
Engel, Mary, 2526, 2527
England, Lizabeth, 3007
Englert, Carol S., 1118, 3110
English, Hubert, Jr., 3333
Englund, Carl E., 1505
Enos, Richard Leo, 217, 218
Enos, Theresa, 219
Enright, Robert D., 1119
Epes, Mary, 932, 2411
Epperson, Deborah, 2492
Epps, Janis, 1836
Erickson, Keith V., 220
Erickson, Lori, 1565
Ersek, Allen J., 3111
Erwin, Dan Roland, 1420
Eschholz, Paul A., 3335, 3430
Etchison, Craig, 3530
Ettlinger, George, 1007
Eubanks, Ralph T., 602
Evans, Christine Sobray, 2025
Evans, Eileen B., 15, 3540
Evans, John S., 2507
Evans, Mary Ann, 1120
Evans, Peter J. A., 1566, 3711, 3712, 3713
Evans, Peter O., 459
Evans, Rick, 2509
Evans, Vella Neil, 1317
Ewald, Helen R., 2209, 2528, 2738
Ewing, Charles Burgess, 1421
Ewing, Noreen J., 1692
Ezor, Edwin, 3233

Fabien, Miriam G., 2412
Facione, Peter A., 1272
Factor, June, 2090
Faery, Rebecca Blevins, 2575, 3141
Fagan, Bob, 221
Fagan, Edward R., 1856, 1857
Fagan, William T., 1318
Fagley, N. S., 222
Fahnestock, Jeanne, 340, 3336
Faigley, Lester, 83, 191, 260, 407, 916, 2909, 3714, 3845
Fairbrother, Helen Anne, 771
Fairburn, Jo, 2027
Fairchild, Steven H., 1959
Falk, Carol J., 3531
Farantini, Franca, 837

Farbman, Evelyn, 3234
Farkas, David K., 2823
Farnsworth, Briant J., 1790
Farr, Marcia, 223, 224, 1962, 2026, 2138, 3714
Farr, R., 817
Farrell, Pamela B., 2210
Faskow, Shari, 2443, 3761
Fauconnier, Gilles, 933
Fawcett, Susan, 3195
Fazio, Gene, 2529
Fearing, Bertie E., 1745, 2211
Fearn, Leif, 1858, 2212
Fearrien, Robert, 2934
Feasley, Florence G., 660
Feehan, Michael, 340
Feeman, Dorothy J., 840
Feezel, Jerry D., 1422
Feifs, Helmuts, 3773
Feingold, Carolyn, 2213
Feinstein, George W., 3235
Felber, Stanley B., 3381
Feldhusen, John F., 1210
Feldman, Paula R., 2739
Feldmeier, Linda, 191
Felten, Paul, 2214
Fendt, Paul F., 2968
Fenton, Mary C., 2530
Fergenson, Laraine, 3247
Ferguson, Anne M., 2027
Ferguson, Frank E., 3166
Ferguson, John, 2028
Ferreiro, Emilia, 1431
Ferris, Frank, 2185
Feuerstein, R., 1221
Field, John P., 3217
Field, Thomas T., 2702
Fillman, H. Thompson, 3151
Fillmore, Lily Wong, 3008
Filloy, Richard A., 661
Finch, Jacqueline Brice, 1836
Finestone, Harry, 3355
Fingrutd, Meryl Anne, 225
Finkel, Candida A., 226
Finkle, Sheryl L., 2531
Finn, Seth, 772, 1319
Fiore, Kyle, 1835
Fischer, Chester A., 3534
Fischer, Lucille, 2215
Fischer, Olga Howard, 3534
Fischer, P. M., 1173
Fischer, Robert A., 3715
Fish, Marjorie Jane, 1816
Fisher, Anita, 2216

Fisher, Bernice, 1121
Fisher, Walter K., 227
Fisher, Walter R., 228, 229
Fishman, Andrea R., 1423
Fishman, Judith, 3716
Fisk, William R., 1122
Fitting, Peter, 662
Fitzgerald, Jill, 1273
Fitzgerald, Sallyanne H., 2217, 3432
Fitzgerald, Sheila, 3443
Fitzpatrick, Carolyn H., 3236
Five, Cora, 2046
Flachmann, Kim, 2218
Flaherty, Gloria P., 2219
Flanagan, Michael J., 3009
Flatley, Marie, 2740
Flavell, John H., 1098
Fleischer, Stefan, 83
Fleming, Margaret, 773, 934, 3620
Flinn, Jane Zeni, 1859
Flood, James, 1860
Flores d'Arcais, Giovanni, 774
Florio, Susan, 2001
Florio-Ruane, Susan, 237, 1841, 2206
Flower, Linda S., 83, 230, 231, 260, 3295
Flynn, Elizabeth A., 2532
Flynn, James, 3268
Fogliani, Anne M., 775
Fogliani-Messina, Teresa M., 775
Fokerts, Jean, 1424
Fontaine, Sheryl I., 232, 233
Ford, Cecilia E., 3717
Ford, Sue, 1629
Fordyce, David J., 1491
Forrester, Kent, 2533, 2534
Forsman, Syrene, 2226
Fortune, Ron, 191, 3112
Foster, Dan, 935
Foster, David, 2535
Foster, Deborah Dene, 936
Foster, Gretchen, 2824
Foster, Michele, 2063
Fountas, Irene C., 2029
Fountoukidis, Dona Lee, 937
Fowler, Lois, 1861, 2536
Fowler, Robert J., 1836
Fox, Barry, 2537
Fox, Deborah, 46
Fox, M. L., 3513
Fox, Mary L., 237
Fox, Robert R., 1862
Fox, Ronda, 663
Fox, Sharon E., 234

Fox, Tom, 235
Frager, Alan M., 1946, 3072
Frandsen, Kenneth D., 193
Franenglass, Marni H., 1123
Frank, Alan, 938, 939
Franklin, A. J., 1110
Franklin, Christina C., 1119
Franklin, Elizabeth Anne, 3010
Franklin, Phyllis, 1863
Frase, L. T., 3513
Frase, Lawrence T., 237, 481
Frazer, Cynthia Lynch, 2413, 2538, 2741
Frederiksen, Norman, 1124, 3718
Fredin, Eric S., 236
Freebody, P., 838
Freebody, Peter, 2090
Freed, Richard C., 2765
Freedle, Roy O., 412
Freedman, Aviva, 2112
Freedman, Morris, 1864
Freedman, Sarah Warshauer, 83, 237, 1865, 2539, 3719
Freedman-Stern, Renee, 1125
Freeman, Donald, 407
Freeman, Douglas N., 340
Freeman, Lawrence H., 2702
Freeman, Mark, 1126, 1127
Freemer, Phillip T., 2030
Fregoe, David Harry, 238
French, Tita, 2540
Frentz, Thomas S., 239
Frese, Michael, 1128
Freund, Judy, 1952
Frew, Robert, 3237, 3238, 3269
Friday, Robert Andrew, 1425
Friedlander, Alexander, 1745
Friedman, Morton, 3535
Friedman, Paul G., 2742
Friedman, Sheila, 2031
Friedmann, Thomas, 2414
Friesen, Wallace V., 1414
Frisbie, Richard D., 2765
Frith, Greg H., 2220
Froese, V., 3840
Frow, John, 940
Fruehling, Rosemary, 3402
Fulkerson, Gerald, 240
Fulkerson, Richard, 340
Fulkerson, Tahita, 2541, 2542
Fuller, Davis G., 3720
Fuller, Frank, 1462
Fuller, Steven, 664
Fulmer, Hal W., 1320

Fulwiler, Toby, 260, 2032, 2221, 2910, 3438
Funt, Robert, 941
Furnas, Alfreda, 2046
Furth, Hans, 1114
Futrell, Ruth Ann, 1789, 2908

Gadomski, Kenneth E., 665
Gage, John T., 171
Gage, Thomas, 1567
Gaidis, William C., 1426
Gaines, Barney, 1675
Gaines, Barry, 2965
Gaines, Bette C., 1274
Gaines, Robert, 241
Galda, Lee, 83, 462, 463
Gale, Steven H., 1693
Gallagher, Brian, 2389, 2391, 3453
Gallagher, Margaret, 1633
Gallo, Joseph D., 3239
Gambell, Trevor J., 2222, 2377, 2911, 2912
Gambrell, Linda B., 2033
Gandy, Oscar, Jr., 1405
Gann, Marjorie, 1866
Ganz, Alice, 2034
Gaonkar, Dilip Parameshwar, 242
Garcia, Ione M., 1790
Gardner, Holly Frances, 1427
Gardner, Phillip, 3818
Gardner, Ruth, 3537
Gardner, Susan S., 1568
Garner, Cynthia, 2223
Garner, Ruth, 243, 3073
Garnes, Sara, 171, 1569
Garnsey, Susan M., 1129
Garrett, Mary Margaret, 244
Garrity, Patricia J., 2035
Garver, Eugene, 245, 2743
Garvey, William D., 1130
Garvin, Ruth A., 1094
Gary, Melvin, 3832
Gaspar, Dennis, 1867
Gassaniga, Michael S., 1131
Gati, Stamar, 1132
Gaudet, Marcia, 2415
Gay, John Franklin, 1428
Gay, Pamela, 246
Gayle, Margaret, 1814
Gaziano, Cecilie, 1429
Gebhardt, Richard, 191, 2543
Gee, James Paul, 1275
Gee, T. W., 247
Gefen, Rafael, 2288
Gefvert, Constance J., 3296

Geierin, R., 3120
Geiser, Patricia, 2224
Geisler, Cheryl, 248, 3595
Gelderman, Carol, 3403
Geller, Linda Gibson, 2036
Gelman, R., 1110
Genishi, Celia, 2063
George, Diana, 2225, 2544, 2913
Gerdes, Marti, 2914
Gere, Anne Ruggles, 83, 237, 249, 400, 1648, 1868, 2226, 2545, 3142, 3297, 3538
Gerlack, John, 666
Gernsbacher, Morton Ann, 776, 1133
Gerrard, Lisa, 3535
Gerrig, Richard Jay, 777
Gerrity, T., 1265
Gerson, Steven M., 2765
Gervickas, Vicki, 30
Ghadessy, Moshen, 250
Giannasi, Jenefer, 16
Giannelli, Gary, 1570
Gibaldi, Joseph, 3424, 3433
Gibbs, Vanita M., 778
Gibson, Claude L., 1571
Gibson, Dirk Cameron, 1430
Gibson, E. J., 838
Gibson, Walker, 120
Gieselman, Robert D., 2744
Gilbert, Edwyna C., 1973
Gildea, Patricia Mae, 779
Gilewski, Michael J., 1255
Gill, Margaret, 1835
Gillam-Scott, Alice, 251
Gillespie, Sheena, 3218
Gillespie, Tim, 2227
Gillinham, Robert G., 2389
Gills, Paula, 1694
Gingrich, Patricia S., 2661
Giora, Rachel, 942
Giordano, Gerard, 2037
Giroux, Henry A., 1321
Giv'on, Hanna, 2288
Giza, Marie, 2038
Glanschow, Lenore, 3113
Glaros, Alan, 1254
Glaser, Joseph, 3268
Glaser, R., 1110, 1221
Glaser, Robert, 1869
Glass, Tom, 2546
Glasser, William, 2228
Glassman, Steve, 1870
Glassman, Susan, 1695, 1696
Glatthorn, Allan A., 3404

Glauner, Jeffrey, 252, 1697
Gleeson, Kitty, 2229
Glenn, Sheila M., 1963
Glick, J., 1147
Globerson, Tamar, 1134
Glover, John A., 87
Goebel, George H., 253
Goelman, Hillel, 1431
Goerdt, Arthur L., 2547
Goforth, Caroline, 2703
Goldbeck, Janne, 3364
Goldberg, Marilyn K., 2416
Goldberg, Mark F., 1698, 1871, 2039
Golden, James L., 171
Golden, Joanne M., 2040
Golden, Peter, 1558
Goldsmith, James, 1699
Goldstein, Jone R., 2745, 2825, 3400
Goldstein, Richard M., 2548
Golen, Steven P., 1534, 2746, 2794
Gomez, Debra, 2417
Gonzalez, Laverne, 1596
Goodman, Jesse, 2041
Goodman, Kenneth S., 318, 838, 3143
Goodman, Lorraine, 559
Goodman, Michael, 3405
Goodman, S. M., 121
Goodman, Yetta, 254, 318, 1431, 1486, 2063, 2154
Goodwin, Pearl, 255
Goodwyn, Susan W., 1088
Gopen, George D., 1322, 1649
Gordon, Alice M., 1135
Gordon, Eleanor, 237
Gordon, Karen Elizabeth, 3539
Gordon, Naomi M., 2042
Gorman, Margaret, 1674
Gorman, Mike, 1674
Gorrell, Donna, 3196
Gorrell, Robert M., 256
Goshgarian, Gary, 3337
Goswami, Dixie, 83, 260
Gottfredson, Stephen D., 1130
Gough, P. B., 838
Gould, John W., 2747
Gould, June, 1572
Goulde, Nancy H., 3262
Gourevitch, Victor, 1038
Gowen, Brent, 2549
Grabe, Cindy, 2043
Grabe, Mark, 2043
Grabe, William P., 257
Graesser, Arthur C., 121, 258
Graham, Jean Bettis, 1650

Graham, Judith, 1799
Graham, Robert J., 667, 668
Graham, Sheila Y., 3366, 3540
Grambs, David, 3144
Granowski, Alvin, 3157
Grant, Jeff, 943, 944
Grant-Davie, Keith A., 780
Grasha, Anthony, 1167
Grassi, Ernesto, 259
Grassi, Rosanna, 3395
Grattan, Mary, 1700
Graves, Donald H., 318, 513, 1276, 1853, 2046, 2090
Graves, Michael F., 839
Graves, Richard L., 171, 260, 2550
Gray, Betty G., 3158
Gray, William M., 1136
Greeley, Andrew W., 1323
Green, Bert F., Jr., 1110, 2389
Green, Judith L., 2063
Green, Karen, 945
Green, Lawrence D., 669
Green, Michael, 946
Greenbaum, Joan, 2389
Greenbaum, Sidney, 1030
Greenberg, Karen L., 3721
Greenberg, Valerie D., 261
Greene, Jennifer, 223
Greene, John O., 262, 263, 1137
Greenfield, Adele, 1872
Greeno, James G., 1110, 1159
Greenspan, Steven L., 1138
Gregg, Lynn C., 2230
Gregg, Richard B., 264
Gregor, Margaret Ann Norville, 1701
Gregory, Gerald, 1799
Gregory, Marshall W., 265
Gremore, Robert, 1573
Grever, Jean K., 2765
Grieb, Kenneth J., 266
Griffin, C. W., 2915
Griffin, Charles James Grant, 1432
Griffin, Leland, 1433
Griffin, Margaret, 1552
Griffith, Marlene, 3349
Griffiths, Anne H., 3722
Grim, Patricia Ann, 1434
Grimm, Nancy, 1873, 3689
Grindal, Gracia, 2575
Grinds, Anne Bradstreet, 2389
Gringrich, P. S., 3513
Groff, Patrick, 1574
Grogg, Patricia Marcum, 1575, 2793
Groppe, John D., 267

Gross, Alan G., 268, 269
Gross, Alan M., 1435
Gross, Gerald, 1436
Grosskurth, Phyllis, 3074
Grossman, Florence, 1874
Grubb, Melvin H., 3011
Grunig, James E., 270, 1324
Guches, Richard, 3237, 3238, 3269
Guerra, Veronica A., 3012
Guffin, Jim, 1803
Guilford, Charles, 3197
Gula, Robert J., 3270
Gulesian, Mark G., 3752
Gundlach, Robert, 223
Gustafsson, Jan-Eric, 1139
Guth, Hans P., 3271
Guthrie, John T., 271, 272, 273, 274, 781, 838
Gutierrez, Felix, 1545
Gutstein, Shelley P., 3013
Guttinger, Helen I., 3768

Haan, Norma, 1140
Hacker, Diana, 3272, 3298
Hackworth, Robert, 1791
Haddad, Heskel M., 782
Hadley, David, 2551
Haggard, M. Rapp, 838
Hagge, John, 2748
Hahn, Lynne C., 3202
Hailey, Joy Lynn, 83
Hairston, Maxine, 260, 1576, 1577, 2704, 3361
Hake, Rosemary, 191, 916
Hakuta, Kenji, 947
Hall, Chris, 2231
Hall, Christine K., 2418
Hall, Donald, 3299, 3338, 3339
Hall, John D., 2765
Hall, Mary Pat, 2255
Hall, Phil, 2419
Hall, Susan E. M., 1964, 2044
Hall, W. S., 817
Halliday, M. A. K., 948
Halloran, S. Michael, 171, 275, 2826
Halpern, Diane F., 3378
Halpern, Jeanne W., 276, 1875, 3545
Halter, Susan, 3776
Hamann, Lori, 1972
Hamid, Abdel Rahim Nur Eldin, 1437
Hamilton, David, 3331
Hamilton, Gord, 2045
Hammar, Diane, 2185
Hammer, Cary, 3546
Hammond, Eugene R., 3300

Hamon, Keith W., 3406
Hample, Dale, 277, 2552, 3849
Hancock, Emily, 1205
Handel, Stephen, 1250
Handlen, Tom, 1578
Hanisko, SandraLee Mary, 1438
Hanna, Stanley, 1876
Hannan, Elspeth, 2045, 2107
Hanning, R. W., 1579
Hannon, Jody, 2232
Hannula, Joyce Jarosz, 2233
Hanrahan, Calvin M., 2916
Hansen, Craig, 3547, 3548
Hansen, J., 817
Hansen, J. T., 2705
Hansen, Jane, 318, 1039, 1580, 2046
Hansen, Kristine, 2909
Hansen, Ruth, 3092
Hansen, Tom, 670
Harada, Janet Louise, 3114
Harbert, Kathy Lynn, 278
Harder, John, 2377
Hardt, Ulrich H., 2047
Hardy-Brown, Karen, 1141
Hare, Victoria Chou, 783
Haring-Smith, Tori, 1581
Harker, Judith O., 2063
Harker, W. John, 671
Harman, David, 1445
Harman, Joan, 3015
Harman, Lesley Diana, 949
Harmatz-Levin, Carol, 3013
Harned, Jon, 279, 280
Harpine, William D., 281
Harrington, Henry R., 2827
Harrington, John, 3301
Harris, Adrienne, 1114, 1142
Harris, Catherine Mary, 2234
Harris, David P., 3723
Harris, Jeane, 2553
Harris, Jeanette, 282, 283, 916, 1702, 1745, 2420, 2554, 2917, 3240
Harris, John S., 950
Harris, Joseph, 284
Harris, Muriel, 260, 285, 513, 1703, 1877, 3367
Harris, Rochelle L., 1205
Harris, Roy, 951
Harris, Sharon, 3752
Harris, Wendell V., 1325
Harrison, David, 3706
Harrison, Ellen, 2555
Harrison, Sam, 2048
Harshaw (Hrushovski), Benjamin, 672

Harste, Jerome, 286, 952, 1277, 1835, 3452
Hart, Dabney, 1704
Hart, Mary, 1878
Hartley, Charles, 3549
Hartman, Diane M., 784
Hartman, Joan, 3333
Hartnett, Carolyn, 2421, 3724
Hartstein, Marc, 1705
Hartwell, Patrick, 191, 953, 954, 955, 1582, 1642, 1745
Harty, Kevin J., 2749
Hartzog, Carol P., 1651
Harvey, Irene E., 287
Harwick, John, 38
Harwood, John T., 1554
Haselkorn, Mark P., 288
Hashimoto, Irvin Y., 289, 290, 1583, 2422, 2556, 3107, 3256
Haskell, Dale E., 291
Haskins, Ethelbert W., 1143
Haskins, Jack B., 1439, 1440
Hassett, James, 3550
Hastak, Manoj, 1144
Hathaway, James, 2235
Hatta, Takeshi, 956
Hattenhauer, Darryl, 1145, 1879
Haugh, Jane A. M., 1146
Hauser, Gerard A., 292
Hausfeld, Steven Russel, 785
Haussler, Myna M., 786, 2063
Haviland, Carol P., 1706, 3725
Haviland, Mark G., 3725
Hawisher, Gail E., 2557
Hawkins, J., 1147
Hawley, Christopher S., 1880
Hawthorne, Joan, 293
Hay, John A., 1853
Hayes, Curtis, 2046
Hayes, David A., 1326
Hayes, Ira, 957
Hayes, John R., 83, 230, 231, 260, 751, 1110, 1162
Hayes, Mary F., 3394, 3726
Hayes, Steve, 3591
Hayes, Tom, 3551
Hayhoe, Mike, 3727
Haynes, Margot, 2987
Hays, Irene D., 3593
Hays, Robert, 2828, 2829
Head, L. Quinn, 3728
Heady, Stephen, 2538
Heald-Taylor, B. Gail, 294
Healy, David, 1672
Healy, Mary K., 2049

Hearn, Gail W., 3346
Heath, Robert L., 295
Heath, Shirley Brice, 237, 1431, 1835
Heavilin, Barbara A., 2558
Heckler, Edward, 2236
Hedrick, Alice, 3279, 3373
Heerman, Charles E., 836
Heffernan, William A., 3340
Heidegger, Martin, 296
Heidt, Donald, 333
Heinold, Henry Robert, 916
Heisel, Marsel, 787
Heiss, George D., 3382
Helberg, Paul J., 2185
Held, Nadine, 1707
Heller, Scott, 2559
Hellweg, Paul, 673, 958
Helmer, James E., 2765
Helstrom, Ward, 1584
Hemmeter, Thomas, 1708
Hemming, Heather, 2046
Henderson, Lola M., 1637
Hennelly, John, 1792
Hennessey, Michael, 3368
Hennings, Dorothy Grant, 318
Henrick, John, 297, 674, 959, 960, 3075
Henriksen, Leif, 1245
Henry, George H., 1709
Hensley, Dennis E., 2830
Henson, Leigh, 2237, 2831, 2832
Henzell-Thomas, Jeremy, 961
Herber, H., 1221
Herbert, Kim, 2208
Herbert, Mellanie, 2750
Herman, Joan L., 3729
Herman, Lewis M., 1148
Herman, Patricia A., 812
Hermann, Beth Ann, 3115
Hernandez-Ramos, Pedro, 828
Herndl, Carl G., 2751
Herrington, Anne J., 298, 299, 2833, 2918
Herrmann, Andrea W., 2238, 3453
Herrscher, Walter, 2560
Herrstrom, David Sten, 300
Hersh, Richard E., 901
Hershinow, Sheldon, 2934
Hershon, Robert, 2239
Herzberg, Bruce, 407, 3426
Hesp, Martin, 3413
Hess, Thomas M., 1149
Hester, Hilary, 2109, 2110
Hewer, Alexandra, 1168
Hewing, Pernell H., 2765

Hewitt, Geof, 2050
Heydorn, Bernard W., 788
Hibbison, Eric, 3273
Hickerson, Benny, 2240
Hickey, Linda S., 563
Hickman, Janet, 2063
Hiebert, Elfrieda H., 1118, 3110
Higgs, Rosalee O., 301
Higson, Verns, 1103
Hikins, James W., 152
Hildebrand, Janet E., 2969
Hilgers, Thomas L., 3730
Hill, Jane C., 1150
Hill, Margaret H., 2051
Hill-Lubin, Mildred A., 1836
Hillerich, Robert L., 3731
Hillocks, George, 675
Himes, Janeta, 3163
Himley, Margaret, 1965, 2109, 2110
Hindel, Lee J., 2241
Hines, Roger B., 1327
Hink, Kaye E., 2052
Hipple, Marjorie L., 1966
Hipple, Ted, 2242, 2243
Hirsch, E. D., Jr., 676, 1793
Hirsch, S. Carl, 2244
Hirst, William, 1151
Hitt, Valeria, 2245
Hoagland, Nancy L., 302
Hobbs, Richard, 3076
Hockheiser, Robert M., 3302
Hocks, Elaine, 1881
Hodges, Richard E., 2053, 3077
Hodges, V. Pauline, 1882
Hodgins, Audrey, 2246
Hodgins, Frank, 2561
Hoekje, Barbara, 3014
Hoetker, James, 1278
Hoffman, Eleanor M., 1883, 2919, 2970
Hoffman, Elizabeth, 3192
Hoffman, Paul, 962
Hoffman, Stevie, 303
Hofmann, Richard J., 916
Hogan, Homer, 304, 1884
Hogan, J. Michael, 305, 1441
Hogan, Michael J., 1675, 2965
Hogan, Michael Phinney, 1279
Hogan, Robert F., 1794
Hogarth, Robin M., 1116
Hoke, Diana L., 2247
Holbrook, Hilary Taylor, 17, 18, 1652, 1885, 3752
Holdaway, Don, 2054
Holden, Marjorie H., 2248

Holdstein, Deborah H., 2423, 2834, 3552
Holland, Norman N., 706, 796
Holland, V. Melissa, 3015
Hollinger, Robert, 306
Hollingsworth, Craig R., 1886
Holloway, Karla F. C., 1836
Holloway, Watson L., 2835
Hollowell, Ida Masters, 3205
Holmes, Elizabeth, 1710
Holmes, Ken, 2229
Holmes, Leigh Howard, 1711, 3553
Holt, Sue, 1302
Holt, Suzanne L., 318
Holyoak, Keith J., 1107
Homan, Margaret, 677
Homburg, Taco Justus, 3732
Homenick, Michael P., 1442
Hood, Michael Dennis, 307
Hooper, Frank H., 1152
Hooper, Judith O., 1152
Hoover, Judith D., 1443
Hoover, Sara, 3586
Hopkins, Richard L., 1153
Hopkinson, Patricia L., 258
Hopper, Robert, 963, 2092
Horn, Dennis, 3496
Horn, William D., 3554
Hornbeck, David E., 1328
Hornburger, Jane, 1836
Hornby, Melinda C., 828
Horning, Alice S., 2562
Horvath, Brooke K., 3733
Hosler, Mary Margaret, 2750
Houp, Kenneth, 3407
Houpt, Sheri, 2424
Housel, Thomas J., 1444
Howard, C. Jeriel, 3379
Howard, Maureen, 3341
Howard, Rebecca M., 3016
Howarth, Tony, 2185
Howell, Carol C., 3191
Howell, Sharon L., 308
Howes, Alan, 3333
Hrach, Elaine, 3734
Hrushovski, Benjamin, 309
Hsiao, Frank S. T., 3735
Hsu, Chen-chin, 1301
Hubbard, Frank, 2575
Hubbard, Marsha Owens, 3752
Hubbard, Ruth, 2046, 2055, 2056
Huber, Carole A., 1887
Huberman, Elizabeth, 1329
Huck, Sharon, 3017

Huckin, Thomas N., 3018
Hudelson, Sarah, 964
Hudgins, Nancy L., 2057
Hudson, Carolyn K., 3116
Hudson, Kathleen A., 2563
Hudson, Lynne, 1136
Hudson, Sally A., 310, 2058
Huffman, Suanne, 2249
Hughes, David C., 3736
Hughes, Donna M., 3173
Hughes, Robert S., Jr., 2752
Huit, Christine, 2917
Hull, A. M., 3117
Hull, Glynda A., 33, 191, 311, 312, 400, 563, 2507
Hult, Christine A., 313
Humes, Ann, 314
Hunt, Barbara, 1836
Hunt, Kellogg W., 916
Hunt, Maurice, 1585, 2564
Hunt, Peter, 1888
Hunt, Russell A., 191, 848, 2565
Hunter, Carman St. John, 1445
Hunter, Linda, 2425
Hurlow, Marcia, 1712, 2426
Hurt, Madeline, 2250
Husband, Robert L., 2765
Hutchings, Meredith, 2098
Hutchinson, Jean E., 965, 1175
Hutchinson, R. T., 1221
Hyde, Janet Shibly, 966
Hyde, Michael J., 1330
Hyler, Linda, 2251
Hynds, Ernest C., 1446
Hynds, Susan D., 789
Hythecker, Velma I., 449

Illinois Community College Board, 1889
Innis, Robert E., 967
Institute of Educational Research, 3556
Intentional Educations, 3484
Ireland, Jackie, 3122
Ireland, Robert, 3749
Irmscher, William F., 120, 1796, 3303
Irvine, Patricia, 3006
Isaacs, Nancy S., 782
Isaak, Mark, 968, 969
Iysere, Marla M., 2836, 3737

Jablin, Fredric M., 1469, 2753
Jacka, Brian, 2090
Jackson, Brian, 1280
Jackson, Doris C., 1992
Jackson, Douglas N., 1172

Jackson, Rex, 2059
Jacob, Evelyn, 1431
Jacob, Kay, 2252
Jacobi, Martin J., 315
Jacobs, Suzanne E., 316, 2060, 2061
Jacobs, Vicki A., 318
Jacobson, Beatrice, 2427
Jacobus, Lee A., 3219
Jacoby, Adrienne, 1586, 2062
Jacoby, Jay, 19, 3019
Jaech, Sharon, 2566, 3558
Jaeger, Richard M., 3828
Jager, M., 838
Jaggar, Angela, 2063
James, Chris, 3020
James, Janis, 1890
Jamieson, Barbara C., 317, 970
Janda, Mary Ann, 224
Jandreau, Steven, 811
Janke, Robert H., 1546
Japp, Phyllis M., 1447
Jaquette, D. S., 1110
Jason, G. James, 2567
Jefferson, Bonnie Sharp, 1448
Jefferson, Patricia Ann, 1449
Jeffree, Dorothy, 3118
Jeffries, R., 1221
Jeffries, Sophie, 971
Jeffries-Thaiss, Ann, 2138
Jensen, Julie M., 318, 1318
Jensen, Marvin D., 2920
Jenseth, Richard, 2921
Jewell, John R., 3420
Jobst, Jack, 3559
Johannesen, Richard L., 602
Johannessen, Larry R., 2254
Johansson, Stig, 319
Johns, B., 1265
Johnson, Barbara E., 790
Johnson, Berman E., 3738
Johnson, Betty S., 2754, 3822
Johnson, Fern L., 83
Johnson, Helen H., 1836
Johnson, J. Lynn, 2755
Johnson, Joann B., 1713
Johnson, John R., 1450
Johnson, Nan, 171, 320, 2377
Johnson, Neville, 2090
Johnson, Sabina Thorne, 2568
Johnson, Sue, 2064
Johnson, William, 1882
Johnson-Cohen, Lois R., 791
Johnson-Laird, P. N., 1110

Johnston, Brian, 1853
Johnston, Kenneth G., 678
Johnston, Mark, 3353
Johnston, Patricia, 2226
Johnston, Peter H., 792
Johnston, Sue Ann, 3079, 3080
Johnstone, Henry W., 321
Jolliffe, David A., 1331, 3714
Jolly, Peggy, 1745, 3739
Jones, B. F., 1221
Jones, David R., 2837
Jones, Everett, 3353
Jones, James Lyle, 679
Jones, Margaret B., 2065
Jones, Merrill Anway, 322
Jones, Michael P., 2253
Jones, Nancy, 2575
Jones, Randall L., 3745
Jones, Robert J., 3686
Jones, Stan, 513
Joorabchi, Bahman, 2922
Jordan, Mark D., 323
Jordan, Mary K., 2838
Joseph, John, 972
Joseph, Nancy, 2428
Josifek, Jami L., 2839
Journet, Alan R. P., 2852
Journet, Debra, 324, 3408
Juell, Pat, 2226
Julian, Kathy, 1587
Jung, M. A., 1817
Just, M. A., 817, 838, 1173

Kagan, Jerome, 1154
Kahan, Lisa D., 1451
Kahane, Henry, 973
Kahane, Renee, 973
Kahn, Elizabeth, 2254
Kai-Kee, Elliot, 325
Kail, Harvey, 1714, 3380
Kaiser, Marjorie M., 472
Kakela, Peter, 1596
Kalinevitch, Karen, 2429
Kalupa, Nancy Elizabeth Pruitt, 3159
Kane, Roberta, 974
Kantor, Kenneth J., 83, 2138
Kantor, Lida, 1242, 1243
Kantorowitz, Thelma D., 3198
Kantrowitz, Bruce Michael, 326
Kaplan, Robert B., 3021, 3022
Karagellis, Antigone, 1212
Karlin, Andrea R., 2067
Karlin, Robert, 2067

Karloff, Kenneth, 2569
Karpen, James, 327, 328
Kasten, Wendy C., 2068
Katims, M., 1221
Katriel, Tamar, 329
Katula, Richard A., 2923
Katz, Sandra, 2570
Kaufer, David S., 248, 2571, 3595
Kaus, Cheryl R., 1165
Kavanaugh, J. F., 838
Kay, Paul, 975
Kaye, Susan H., 540
Kaywell, Joan, 2243
Kazemek, Francis E., 20, 2971, 2972
Kean, Donald K., 330
Kean, John M., 1972
Kearney, Lynn B., 3740
Kearney, Patricia, 1281
Kearns, Edward A., 1588
Kearns, Michael S., 2572
Keating, Rod, 3304
Keating, Thomas, 2596
Keck, Judith W., 1797
Keech, Catharine L., 331
Keeling, Brian, 3736
Keen, Nadene A., 2706
Keenan, Stacey A., 793
Keene, Michael L., 400
Keene, Nadene, 2707
Kegley, Pamela H., 332
Kehl, D. G., 333, 407
Keitel, Bruce, 2406
Keith, Karla J., 2941
Keith, Philip M., 2575
Keller, Christa, 3119
Keller, Joseph, 334
Keller, Monika, 1155
Keller, Rodney D., 2573
Kellerman, Kathy, 1156
Kelley, Kathleen R., 2069
Kelley, William J., 3476
Kellner, Robert Scott, 2840
Kellner, Robert W., 2138
Kelly, Kathleen, 2756
Kelly, Lou, 260, 1589
Kelly, Patricia P., 496, 1891, 2255, 3174, 3175
Kempton, Willett, 975
Kendall, John, 2256
Kennedy, Dorothy M., 3342
Kennedy, George, 3428
Kennedy, Mary Lynch, 335
Kennedy, X. J., 3342
Kenney, Donald, 3023

Kent, Carolyn E., 976
Keran, Shirley, 3589
Kerek, Andrew, 191, 260, 407, 916
Kerns, Kimberley, 794
Kessel, Barbara, 2574
Kessler, Carolyn, 3024
Kevelson, Roberta, 336
Keville, Richard, 2070
Khalil, Aziz M., 3025, 3741
Kiah, Rosalie Black, 1836
Kibler, Robert, Jr., 1374
Kiefer, Barbara Z., 2063
Kiefer, Kathleen E., 237, 2661, 3668
Kieras, David E., 121, 795
Kierzek, John M., 3232
Kies, Daniel, 2841
Kiewe, Amos, 1452
Kiewra, Kenneth A., 1282, 3081
Killingsworth, M. Jimmie, 337
Killion, Jo Ellen, 1270
Kilpatrick, James J., 2708
Kim, Kyung J., 1157
Kimberley, Keith, 1799
Kimura, Doreen, 1158
Kincheloe, Joe, 1933
King, Andrew A., 338
King, Barbara, 3710, 3831
King, Chelle, 1985
King, Don, 2257
King, Jeffrey C., 977
King, Martha L., 1207, 2063, 2109, 2110
King, Mary, 2430
King, Robert L., 1453
King, Stephen W., 978
Kingma, J., 1099
Kingsbury, Callie, 3742
Kingsley, Ronald F., 2082
Kingston, Neal M., 3707
Kinkead, Joyce, 1715
Kinlock, A. M., 3120
Kinneavy, James L., 171, 407, 916
Kinney, Martha A., 2071
Kinsella, Paul, 3241
Kintgen, Eugene R., 796
Kintsch, Walter, 838, 1159
Kipnis, David, 1160
Kirby, Dan, 3160
Kirkland, James W., 3274
Kirkwood, William G., 680
Kirsch, Max, 2389
Kirszner, Laurie, 3305
Kitamura, Seiro, 1301
Kitchener, Robert F., 1161

Kjellmer, Goran, 868
Klammer, Enno, 3343
Klare, George R., 537, 1220
Klauk, E. Russell, 339
Klaus, Carl, 2575, 3331
Kleine, Michael, 2576
Klimoski, Victor, 1103
Kline, Charles R., Jr., 260
Kline, Gary, 3188
Kling, Julie Lepick, 3408
Klitgaard, Robert, 1798
Klumpp, James F., 1513
Knapp, John V., 1892
Kneeshaw, Stephen, 2924
Kneupper, Charles W., 340, 341, 342, 371
Knickerbocker, K. L., 3396
Knight, Cynthia, 3082
Knight, John H., 1283
Knight, Susan J., 1716
Knighten, Katherine Wells, 2072
Knoblauch, C. H., 260, 343, 400, 1745
Knodt, Ellen Andrews, 2577
Knot, G., 817
Kobayashi, Hiroe, 979, 3026
Koch, Arthur E., 3381
Koch, Barbara J., 344
Koch, Kenneth, 3455
Koening, Jeffrey L., 2073
Koffler, Stephen L., 3743
Kohlberg, Lawrence, 1104, 1168, 1233
Kohn, Meryle, 2389
Kolin, Janeen L., 3409
Kolin, Philip C., 3409
Kollar, Mary, 2258, 2259
Kollmeier, Harold H., 3083
Kolln, Martha, 260, 954, 2578, 3275, 3369
Koring, Heidi, 2579, 2580, 2973
Kornblueth, Ilana, 2288
Kornhuber, Hans-H., 1245
Kossoudji, Sherrie Ann, 3027
Kotker, Joan Garcia, 1717, 1718
Kotler, Janet, 345
Kotovsky, K., 1162
Kozicki, Henry, 346
Kozol, Jonathan, 2974
Kraft, Robert G., 1893
Kraftchick, Steven John, 347
Kramer, Deirdre A., 1105
Kramer, Melinda G., 3276, 3370
Kramsch, Claire, 797
Krebs, Sarah, 3373
Kreeft, Joy, 2074, 3013, 3028
Krell, David Farrell, 296

Kremers, Marshall N., 348
Kressel, Rikva, 2288
Krippendorff, Klaus, 349
Krishna, Valerie, 260
Kroitor, Harry P., 1894, 3308
Kroll, Barbara, 3029
Kroll, Barry M., 260, 350, 351, 352, 2075
Krone, Kathleen, 2753
Kronfeld, Sional, 2288
Krupa, M. P., 1110
Kucer, Stephen, 353, 980
Kuchinskas, Gloria, 3632
Kuczaj, Stan A., II, 1032
Kuhlman, Yvonne, 3161, 3173
Kuiper, Koenraad, 681
Kumi, Linda M., 1836
Kurfiss, Joanne, 1163, 1332
Kurland, Daniel J., 1333
Kurth, Ruth J., 2076
Kurzbard, Gary, 1454
Kushner, Marvin, 2389
Kussat, Reinhart G., 2389
Kuykendall, Carol, 3121, 3160
Kwak, Winnifred, 2098

Laba, Martin, 1455
LaBerge, S., 838
Labouvie-Vief, Gisela, 1164
Lackie, Joyce C., 1590
Lacy, Stephen, 1424
Laff, Ned Scott, 3397
Lahey, Margaret, 3681
Laib, Nevin K., 191, 355
Laine, Chet, 1895
Lake, Randall A., 356
Lalande, John F., II, 3744
Lally, Tim D. P., 172
LaMar, Helen J., 357
Lamaster, Ava, 1556
Lambert, Judith R., 2431
Lambiotte, Judith, 449
Lampert, Judy E., 2077
Lampert, Kathleen W., 2260, 2581
Lance, Mark Norris, 981
Lancombe, Joan, 3434
Land, Darren F., 1896
Land, Robert E., Jr., 358, 563
Lane, Harlan, 1284
Lane, Norm, 3591
Lang, Charles J., 3122
Lang, Gerhard, 3382
Lang, Helen S., 359
Langan, John, 3199, 3242, 3243, 3244, 3245

Langendoen, D. Terence, 2389
Langer, J., 817
Langer, Janet, 798
Langer, Judith A., 318, 360, 361, 362, 363, 1835, 2078, 2079, 2261
Langstaff, Janice J., 1256
Lanham, Richard A., 3512, 3668
Lanky, Edward, 1165
Lanner, Allen H., 3318
Lannon, John, 3401, 3410
Lansing, Margaret L., 21, 2262
La Point, Ray, 1972
Lapsley, Daniel K., 1119
Laqueur, Thomas W., 1499
Larkin, George, 3411
Larkin, J. H., 1110
La Roche, Mary G., 354
Larochelle, Therese, 2432
Larsen, Elizabeth K., 364
Larsen, Gordon, 787
Larsen, Richard B., 1897
Larson, Celia O., 449, 1300, 2842
Larson, Jerry W., 3745
Larson, Reed, 513
Larson, Richard L., 171, 407, 3746
Larson-Shapiro, Nancy, 1017
Larter, Sylvia, 3030
Lassner, Phyllis, 1719
Latham, Don, 2703
Lathrop, Ann, 3632
Latta, Susan, 2263
Latzer, Robert, 2389
Lauby, Jacqueline, 1720, 1721, 2433
Lauer, Janice M., 171, 365
Lauton, David, 982
Laverdiere, R., 1265
Lawlor, Joseph, 3632
Lawrence, Cheryl, 3614
Lawrence, John S., 3562
Lawrence, Renee, 1164
Lawrence, Robert, 2264
Laycock, Don, 983, 984
Lazarus, Peggy, 1552, 2109, 2110
Lazerson, Marvin, 1285
Leahy, Ellen K., 2389, 3563
Leahy, Richard, 1722, 1898
Learning Ways, Inc., 3565
LeBar, Barbara, 2265
Lebowitz, Michael, 3566
Lebowitz, Richard, 1596
Lebrun, Yvan, 1456
LeClair, Tom, 682
Lederer, Richard, 985, 986, 3476

Lederman, Marie Jean, 366, 1723, 2434, 2582
Ledford, Suzanne Y., 799
LeDoux, Joseph, 1151
Lee, Benjamin, 1114
Lee, Helen C., 1899
Lee, James F., 800
Lee, Joyce W., 1724
Lee, Shin-ying, 1301
Leech, Geoffrey, 1030
Lefcourt, Ann, 3151
Lefevre, Karen B., 367
Leff, Michael C., 368
Leggett, Glenn, 3276
Lehmann, W. P., 987
Lehnert, W. G., 1173
Lehr, Fran, 22, 23, 24, 3084, 3123
Leichter, Hope Jensen, 1431
LeMaster, R. Douglas, 1656
Lemert, James B., 1457
Lemieux, Jacques, 683
Lemons, Robert, 801
Lenaghan, Robert, 3333
L'Engle, Madeleine, 2709
Lent, John A., 1458
Lentz, Richard Glenn, 1459
Lentz, Tony M., 369
Lenz, B. Keith, 1268, 1269
Lerman, Evelyn, 2042
Lesgold, Alan M., 3567
Lesser, Ronnie, 1166
Lessl, Thomas M., 1460
Lester, James D., 3371
Lester, Nancy B., 814
LeTourneau, Mark S., 2435
Levernier, James A., 3205
Levi, Laurie S., 1167
Levin, Barbara B., 3569
Levin, Harry, 684
Levin, James A., 237
Levine, Charles, 1168
Levine, Denise Stavis, 2080
Levine, Josie, 1799
Levine, Leslie, 2843
Levitov, Justin E., 2980
Levitt, Renee, 2185
Levy, Betty Ann, 802
Levy, Beverly Sauer, 540
Levy, Jerre, 1169
Lewis, Clayton W., 370, 371, 2583
Lewis, Dorothy P., 372
Lewis, Eric W., 258
Lewis, Janice, 803
Lewis, Jill, 3233

Lewis, Ruby M., 2436
Leys, Margie, 845
Libby, Judith S., 2266, 2584
Lichtman, Sharon R., 2267
Lide, Barbara, 685
Lide, Francis, 685
Lieber, Justin, 686
Lieber, Michael D., 1335
Liebling, Cheryl R., 2109, 2110
Liebman-Kleine, JoAnne D., 84, 804
Liggett, Sarah, 25, 1556, 1875, 1900, 3545
Light, Leah L., 1255
Lima, Susan Diane, 988
Lindblom, Peter, 3232
Lindemann, Erika, 1591, 1592
Lindemann, Shirlee, 2507
Lindenau, Suzanne E., 3570
Lindfors, Judith Wells, 2063
Linell, Per, 868
Linn, Bill, 2585
Linn, Michael D., 26
Linville, William, 778
Lipman, M., 1221
Lipscomb, Delores, 1836
Lipson, Carol S., 373
List, Kathleen L., 374
Lithicum, Frances, 2268
Littell, Joy, 3162
Little, Greta D., 33
Little, Sherry Burgus, 2269
Littlefield, Robert Stephen, 375
Litvack, Mark, 1901
Lloyd-Jones, Richard, 120
Loar, David, 2586
Lochhead, J., 1221
Locker, Kitty O., 2757, 2765
Lockward, Diane, 1593
Loeb, Helen M., 1902
Loewe, Ralph E., 3344
Logan, Kenneth J., 1594
Loheyde, Katherine Jones, 2437
Lomask, Milton, 3435
Long, Roberta, 376
Long, Russell C., 2587
Longfield, Diane M., 3031
Longhorn, Ian, 1170
Lönroth, Lars, 1334
Lopez, Consuelo, 1461
Lopez, John Michael, 1336
Lopez, Richard L., Jr., 1196
LoPresti, Gene, 191
Lorch, Sue, 3200
Lorenz, Frederick O., 3814

Loris, Michelle Carbone, 1725
Losse, Deborah N., 687
Lott, Carolyn J., 2081
Lotto, Edward, 377, 378, 1903
Louth, Richard H., 3571
Lovelace, Martin John, 989
LoVerso, Marco, 688
Loving, Shelley, 3752
Lowie, Elie, 2389
Lowry, Louise K., 3173
Loy, Sandra, 3345
Luban, Nina, 3789
Lucariello, Joan, 1171
Lucas, Margery Marie, 805
Lucas, Ruth, 2575
Lucey, Wayne, 806
Lucker, G. William, 1301
Luckett, Clinton, 1726
Lucking, Robert, 1904, 3572
Ludlow, Larry, 675
Lumley, Dale, 1595
Lumsden, D. Barry, 1462
Lumsden, David, 990
Lund, Donna D., 3573
Lunsford, Andrea A., 171, 212, 379, 380, 400, 2737
Lunsford, Ronald F., 33
Lupack, Barbara T., 1654, 1727
Lusignan, Serge, 906
Lutz, Jean A., 381
Lutz, William, 3328, 3747
Luvaas-Briggs, Linda, 3124
Lycan, William B., 991
Lynch, Daniel, 2389
Lynch, David, 2746
Lyne, John, 382, 689
Lynn, Steven W., 2588
Lyons, Chopeta, 2438, 3201
Lyons, Mary Ethel, 1463
Lyons, Peter A., 2589
Lyons, Robert, 120, 407

Mabry, Phyllis, 2270
MacAllister, Joyce B., 2590
MacDonald, N. M., 3513
Mace, Patricia E., 1095
MacFarlane-Housel, Doreen, 1596
MacKenzie, Nancy, 2925
MacKenzie, Scott Bradley, 1464
MacKenzie-Keating, Sandra, 1197
Mackey, Gerald, 2271
Mackie, Benita, 3246
Maclean, Marie, 690
MacLennon, Richard N., 1172

Macrorie, Ken, 260, 1596, 3306, 3307
Madden, Thomas R., 2439
Maddox, Kathleen S., 2591
Maden, Thomas F., 383
Mader, Diane C., 2592
Madhubuti, Haki R., 1836
Madigan, Chris, 1905
Magistrale, Tony, 1597, 2593
Magpantay, Andrew, 3535
Mahaney, William E., 3372
Maher, Frances, 1286
Mahoney, Helen, 3373
Mailloux, Steven, 691
Maimon, Elaine P., 407, 916, 1642, 3346
Maine, Barry, 692
Mair, David, 3418
Mak, Louisa, 3535
Makau, Josina M., 1465
Malachowski, Ann Marie, 2272
Malamud, Randy, 1598
Malankowsi, James R., 1728
Malatesha, R. N., 801
Malbec, Toby W., 1729
Mallonee, Barbara C., 2926, 3748
Malone, Elizabeth L., 2745, 2825
Maloney, Henry B., 384
Manabe, Takashi, 385
Mandell, Muriel, 2185
Mandell, Stephen, 3305
Mandl, Heinz, 1173
Mandler, Jean, 1174
Mann, Virginia A., 1224
Manna, Anthony, 1636, 2082
Marcus, Harriet, 1730
Marcus, Stephen, 3574, 3575, 3576, 3668
Marcusen, Ann B., 2273
Marder, Daniel, 386
Marechal, Linda S., 1906
Marek, Richard, 1436
Marik, Ray, 2226, 2594
Marino, Jacqueline L., 2185
Marius, Richard, 3277, 3391
Mark, Vera, 992
Markel, Michael H., 3412
Markels, Robin Bell, 387
Markhan, Marsha C., 2595
Markley, Robert P., 1105
Markline, Judy, 1731
Markman, Ellen M., 1110, 1175
Marks, Dorothy, 388
Marling, Cynthia, 3578, 3579, 3580
Marling, William, 3577, 3578, 3579, 3580
Marsh, Herbert W., 3749

Marsh, Robert, 3750
Marshall, Bruce A., 389
Marshall, James D., 10, 11, 2274
Marshall, Kristine E., 1599
Marshall, Melvin Jay, 1466
Marshall, Stewart, 2844
Marsicano, Arthur J., 2877
Marsland, Elizabeth, 693
Martin, Celest A., 2923
Martin, Diane, 3770
Martin, Jerome, 3151
Martin, Kathy, 1732, 1733
Martin, Lee J., 3308
Martin, Marilyn, 993
Martin, Nancy, 1486, 1799
Martinet, Jeanne, 994
Martino, Marta, 2407
Martinson, David, 1504
Marvin, Carolyn, 1467
Masem, Caren, 2765
Mashat, Soraya Hassam, 1337
Mason, George, 3589
Mason, Kenneth M., Jr., 694
Massaro, Dominic A., 807
Masterson, Jacqueline, 808
Masterson, John T., 1380
Matalene, Carolyn, 390
Matalene, H. W., 695
Mateja, John A., 3093
Mather, Patricia L., 1176
Mathes, J. C., 2845
Mathie, Craig, 2275
Mathieson, Kenneth, 696
Matsuhashi, Ann, 237, 391, 2630, 3789
Matteoni, Louise P., 2185
Matthew, Marie-Louise, 3247
Matthews, Dorothy, 2276
Matthews, Frances D., 3751
Matthews, Jacklyn, 2083
Matthews, Kathy, 2046
Matthewson, G. C., 838
Matulich, Loretta, 2846
Mawasha, Abram L., 1853
Maxwell, Donald, 2575
Maxwell, John C., 1907
May, Mary Jo, 2084
Mayer, R. E., 121
Mayher, John S., 392, 995, 1987
Maynard, David, 3591
Mayton, Shirley M., 1367
Mazor, Ayala, 782
McAllister, Carole, 2389, 2440, 3582
McAndrew, Donald A., 393, 394, 395, 1734, 1748

McBaine, Robert, 3152
McBride, Mary, 1177
McCaffery, Larry, 682
McCann, Thomas M., 3583
McCarley, Barbara, 3584
McCarron, William, 396, 2277, 2575, 2596
McCarthy, Bernice, 27
McCarthy, Jan, 778
McCarthy, Lucille, 2085, 2597, 2927
McCarthy, Patricia, 397
McCartney, Kathleen, 996
McCartney, Robert, 398, 2278, 3085
McCauley, Rebecca J., 2804
McClearey, Kevin, 3086
McCleary, Carol Anne, 1178
McCleary, William J., 399, 2598
McClelland, Ben W., 400, 3309
McClelland, J. L., 838
McCloskey, M., 1110
McClosky, Donald N., 1338
McClure, Erica F., 997
McClure, Malcolm McKenzie, 1468
McComb, Karen B., 1469
McConochie, Jean Alice, 998
McCord, Phyllis Frus, 401
McCormick, James R., 3228
McCormick, Mona, 3436
McCoy, Arthuree, 1836
McCoy, Joan, 2847
McCreedy, Lynn A., 999
McCrimmon, James M., 260, 3310
McCroskey, James C., 3850
McCuen, Jo Ray, 3280, 3322
McCulley, George A., 402, 1949
McCullough, C. M., 838
McCully, Belinda, 303
McCully, Michael, 1735
McCurdy, Marla W., 2042
McCutchen, Deborah, 403, 1179
McDermond, Dawn, 1908
McDermott, R. P., 838
McDonald, Agnes, 2279
McDonald, Christie V., 697
McDonald, Irene, 3524
McDonald, Janet L., 1000
McDonald, Joseph P., 2280
McDonald, Joyce, 2086
McDonnell, G., 817
McDonough, Steven, 3087
McDowell, Earl E., 2765, 2854
McFarland, James L., 1287
McGann, Jerome J., 698
McGee, Lea M., 2087

McGinty, Robert L., 2758
McGinty, Susan L., 2758
McGrath, Susan, 1736
McGroarty, Mary, 3032, 3033
McGuiness, Diane, 1180
McGuinnis, Adelaide, 3776
McGuire, John F., 3311
McIlvaine, Robert M., 28, 2405
McKay, James, 1343
McKee, Macey Blackburn, 3034
McKensie, Lee, 2088
McKenzie, Jamieson, 3585
McKenzie, Moira G., 2063
McKenzie, Taylor A., 1470
McKeough, Anne, 404
McKeown, Brian, 2090
McKeown, Margaret, 746, 809, 817, 2089
McKoski, Martin M., 3202
McLane, Joan B., 223
McLaren, Jennifer, 1198
McLaren, Margaret C., 2759
McLaughlin, Barry, 3008
McLaughlin, Daniel, 1339
McLaughlin, Judith Black, 1285
McLean, Deckle, 2928
McLean, James I., 2848, 2929
McLeod, Alan M., 3752
McLeod, Alex, 1799
McMahon, Christine, 2930
McMahon, Marilyn, 3586
McManus, Walter Stewart, 1471
McMillen, Liz, 405
McMorris, Robert F., 3753
McNamara, Leo, 3333
McNamee, Gillian Dowley, 223
McPhail, Irving P., 1836
McPhearson, Bruce, 1285
McPhee, Robert D., 482
McPherson, Elisabeth, 1737, 3125
McPhillips, Shirley P., 406
McQuade, Donald, 407, 3357
McQuade, Thomas F., 2281
McVitty, Walter, 2090
Meacham, John A., 1106, 1114
Mead, C. David, 3276
Mealy, Jim, 38
Meaney, Frank, 2090
Medlin, Douglas L., 1185
Medway, Peter, 1799, 1835
Meek, Margaret, 1799
Meeker, Linda, 2185
Meeker, Michael W., 3587
Meesin, Charoon, 2441

Mehaffy, Robert, 3237, 3238, 3269
Mehlville District Curriculum Office and Teaching
    Staff, 2282
Meichenbaum, D., 1110
Meier, Scott, 397
Meier, Terry Ryan, 3227
Meijs, Willem, 854
Meir, Margaret, 29
Meisenhelder, Susan, 408
Meiser, Mary J., 2442
Melcher, Kate, 2041
Melia, Trevor, 409
Mellon, John C., 191, 916
Melnick, Jane R., 1738
Meloni, Christine, 3013
Meloth, Michael S., 752
Melvin, Mary P., 2283
Memering, W. Dean, 260
Menasche, Lionel, 410
Mendiola, Sandra E., 411
Meriwether, Nell, 1556
Merlin, C., 1256
Merrill, Stephen M., 2760
Merrill, Yvonne, 2284
Metteer, Christine, 2931
Meyer, B. J. F., 121, 1173
Meyer, Bonnie, 412
Meyer, Daisy E., 3814
Meyer, Verne, 3179
Meyers, Alan, 3203
Meyers, G. Douglas, 2599, 2761
Meyers, Miles, 1340
Meyrowitz, Joshua, 413
Meziani, Ahmed, 1001
Miall, David S., 699
Michaels, Kathryn, 3002
Michaels, Sarah, 237, 2063, 2109, 2110, 3499, 3500,
    3754
Michaud, Ruth, 2285
Michener, Darlene M., 2091
Michlin, Michael L., 83
Middleton, Francine K., 1600
Middleton, Stuart, 1835
Midgett, Jeanice, 2101
Mier, Margaret, 1655, 3755, 3756, 3757
Mikelonis, Victoria M., 30
Mikkelsen, Nina, 1601, 1602
Mikulec, Patrick B., 3457
Mikulecky, Larry, 817, 2286, 2953
Miles, C., 1221
Milic, Louis, 407
Miller, Carolyn R., 700
Miller, Doris A., 2277

Miller, Frankie F., 2932
Miller, Gerald R., 414
Miller, J. R., 121
Miller, James E., Jr., 1818
Miller, Jane, 1799
Miller, John C., 2389
Miller, Keith D., 415
Miller, Leann R., 3758
Miller, Margery Staman, 2287
Miller, Mark, 1439, 1440
Miller, Paul M., 222
Miller, S. R., 1002
Miller, Thomas P., 416
Milner, Joseph O., 3589
Milner, Sue, 2542
Milz, Vera, 1596, 2063
Mims, Aquilla A., 2220
Mims, Howard, 3847
Ministry of Education, Jerusalem, 2288
Minor, Dennis E., 417, 418
Mir, Maqsood Hamid, 701
Mischel, Harriet Nerlove, 1106
Mitacek, Barbara, 3709
Mitchell, Catharine C., 3437
Mitchell, Claudia A., 2377
Mitchell, G. A., 1603
Mitchell, Victoria, 3759
Mitre Corporation, 3497
Mittricker, Margaret L., 3476
Mizener, Heather, 702
Mizuno, Jean L., 54
Moberg, Goran, 3257
Mochamer, Randi Ward, 31
Modaff, John, 2092
Moen, Daryl R., 3428
Moffett, James, 260, 318, 419, 1853, 3383
Mohan, Bernard A., 420
Mohr, Marian M., 2600
Moldstad, Mary Frew, 2575
Moll, Luis C., 3055
Monahan, Brian D., 421
Moneyhun, Clyde, 2601
Monroe, Mark Paul, 1472
Monroe, Rick, 2259, 3590
Monson, Dianne L., 32
Moore, George N., 3166
Moore, Mary Candace, 422
Moore, Michael T., 423, 563
Moore, Nick, 3413
Moore, Tony, 2090
Moore, Wayne, Jr., 2602, 3833
Moorhead, Michael, 3760
Moorjani, Angela B., 2702

Moran, Charles, 424, 3476
Moran, Mary Hurley, 33
Moran, Michael G., 33, 425, 2603, 2762, 2849, 3088
Morante, Edward A., 2443, 3761
Morehead, David R., 1739
Moreland, Kim, 2933
Morenberg, Max, 191, 260, 407, 916
Morgan, Ethelyn, 3279, 3373
Morgan, Lyle W., Jr., 1800
Morgan, Margaret, 3762
Morgan, Robert, 3589
Morice, Dave, 1003
Morris, Ann R., 2289
Morris, Barry Alan, 1341
Morris, Bert, 3071
Morris, Chris M., 3768
Morris, Darrell, 318
Morrison, Jerry, 3591
Morrison, Toni, 426
Morrow, Betty R., 3216
Morrow, Daniel Hibbs, 1004
Morrow, John E., 3811
Morrow, Susan R., 1342, 1343
Morse, Donald E., 2604
Morton, Mike, 3089
Moseley, Ann, 1740, 3240
Mosenthal, James H., 810, 1005
Mosenthal, Peter, 2093
Moser, Paul K., 1006
Moses, Carole, 955
Moses, John D., 537
Moss, Andrew, 2444, 3220
Moss, Joy F., 2094
Moss, R. Kay, 2095
Mossip, Judy, 2098
Motley, Michael T., 1181, 1473, 3847
Mott, Tim, 3591
Motto, Anna Lydia, 1842
Mounoud, Pierre, 1182
Mountain, Lee, 3592
Moxley, Joseph M., 427, 2290
Moxley, Roy, 2096
Muehling, Darrel D., 1183
Mulac, Anthony, 1384
Mulderig, Gerald P., 428, 703
Mulesky, Patricia, 1590
Mullen, Thomas P., 1177
Muller, Gilbert H., 3347, 3348
Müller, Kurt E., 1656
Mullican, James S., 778, 2291
Mumford, Michael, 1184
Muncer, Steven J., 811, 1007
Munch, James Michael, 429

Mura, Susan Zachary Swan, 430
Murdock, Phil, 34
Murphey, Sue I., 3103
Murphree, Carolyn T., 3763
Murphy, Bren Adair Ortega, 1474
Murphy, Christine, 2605
Murphy, Gregory L., 1185
Murphy, James J., 431
Murphy, Lackamp, 3163
Murphy, Sandra, 3795
Murray, Donald, 432
Murray, Donald M., 191, 260, 513, 1835, 2606, 2710, 2711, 3438
Murray, Heather, 704
Murray, Patricia Y., 1741, 3183
Murrel, Sharon Lynne, 1475
Muscatine, Charles, 3349
Myers, Alan, 3248, 3249, 3258, 3259
Myers, Doris T., 3384
Myers, Greg, 433
Myers, Miles, 434
Myres, John, 1657, 2292
Myrsiades, Linda S., 2763

Nador, Sue, 1242, 1243
Naff, Beatrice, 2293
Nagahata, Masamichi, 1480
Nageley, John, 3593
Nagy, William E., 812
Nahir, Moshe, 1008
Naitoh, Paul, 1505
Nakamura, Caroline, 2934
Nancarrow, Paula R., 35, 83
Nance, Ellen Harrison, 2294
Nash, Thomas, 1742, 1745
Nash, Walter, 1009
Natalle, Elizabeth Jo, 705
National Science Foundation, 3497
Nattinger, James R., 1010
Nava, John M., 1011
Naylor, Kathleen J., 435
NCTE Commission on Composition, 1909, 1910, 1911, 1912
NCTE Committee on Instructional Terminology, 3851
Neal, Dorothy, 3434
Needham, Lawrence, 656
Neel, Jasper, 33
Neenan, S. A., 3513
Nees-Hatlen, Virginia, 2295, 2935
Nelson, Charles W., 2548
Nelson, David C., 2607
Nelson, Kate, 1476

Nelson, Katharine, 1171
Nelson, Lin, 1186
Nelson, Russ, 3496
Nelson-Le Gall, Sharon A., 1187
Nerem, Tracy, 2404
Nessel, Denise D., 2065
Netsu, Machiko, 1012
Neuleib, Janice, 191, 1743, 3112
Neuner, Jerome L., 436
Neuwirth, Christine M., 3595, 3668
Nevada Joint Council on College Preparation, 2296
Neville, Donald D., 813
Newby, James E., 36
Newell, George E., 1344
Newell, Sara E., 437, 577
Newkirk, Thomas, 83, 400, 438, 439, 440, 814, 1913, 2046, 3764, 3765
Newlin, Peter, 3126
Newman, Judith M., 2097, 2098, 3596
Newton, Frances S., 2297
Newton, Sandra S., 3598
Ng, En Tzu Mary, 441
Nicholas, J. Karl, 3350
Nicholl, James R., 3350, 3589
Nichols, Joe H., 3660
Nichols, Randall G., 2445
Nickell, Samila S., 2608, 2609
Nickens, John, 3682
Nickerson, Jeff, 1188
Nickerson, Raymond S., 2975, 3127
Nickerson, Sheila, 442
Nida, Eugene A., 1013
Niesz, Anthony J., 706
Niles, Alice, 2298
Niles, Lyndrey A., 1345
Nilsen, Alleen Pace, 443
Nilsen, Don L. F., 1014, 2712
Nist, Sherrie L., 3095
Nitsch, K. E., 838
Noble, David F., 3599
Noble, Virginia D., 3599
Nodine, Barbara F., 916, 3346
Nogle, Victoria Louise, 1478
Nold, Ellen, 407
Nomejko, Irene, 2443, 3761
Noppen, Mick, 1744
Nordberg, Beverly, 1914
Nordquist, Richard, 3204
Norman, Barbara Ann, 444
Norman, Rose, 2850
Norment, Nathaniel, Jr., 1015
Norris, Christopher, 707
North, Stephen M., 1288, 1745, 1915

North, Steve, 445
Nothstine, William Lee, 446
Nugent, Harold E., 916, 1604, 2299
Nugent, Susan Monroe, 1604, 2099, 2299
Nunn, Grace G., 447
Nye, Naomi Shihab, 1605
Nystrand, Martin, 2109, 2110, 2610

Oates, William R., 2389
Obenchain, Anne, 916
Ober, Scott, 3769
Oberg, Antoinette, 1431
O'Brien, David P., 1190
O'Brien, Edward Joseph, 448
O'Connell, Barbara, 1051
O'Connell, Daniel, 1218
O'Connor, Finbarr W., 3346
Odell, Lee, 83
O'Dell, Lisa L., 2003
O'Donnell, Angela M., 449
O'Donnell, Holly, 450, 3766, 3767
O'Donnell, Roy C., 1853
O'Donnell, Victoria, 340
O'Donoghue, R., 2851
Oftendahl, Joan L., 1606
Ogbu, John U., 1499
Ogden, Barbara, 2100
Ogilvie, Elisabeth, 2713
Ogle, D., 817
Oglesby, Kent, 1289
Ogren, Roy, 2300
Ogroinsky, Yehudit, 2288
O'Hair, Dan, 1479
O'Hare, Frank, 3176
Ohmann, Richard, 451
Oi, Kyoko M., 1016
Oishi, Noriko, 1480
Oka, Evelyn Reiko, 815
O'Keefe, Barbara J., 1516
O'Keefe, Katherine O'Brien, 2852
Oleksiuk-Velez, Adriana, 3681
Olenn, Valjeane M., 452
Oliu, Walter E., 3414
Oliver, Lawrence J., 453, 454
Ollila, Lloyd O., 1253
Olsen, Leslie A., 3018
Olson, David R., 1431
Olson, Gary A., 1745, 2301, 2302, 2611, 3415
Olson, Gary M., 455
Olson, Judy, 2101
Olson, Lester Clarence, 1481
Olson, Margot A., 3770
Olson, Mary W., 2102

Olson, Miles C., 3771
Olson, Nancy S., 2138
Olson, Sheryl L., 1189
Oluwu, Terry Adekunle, 816
Omanson, Richard C., 746, 2089
O'Neal, Marcia R., 3768
Onghena, Karin, 782
Onore, Cynthia, 2612, 3772
Oplt, Toni, 2613
Oram, Virginia White, 1819, 2614, 2615
Orasanu, Judith, 817
Oravec, Christine, 1482
Orden, J. Hannah, 2303
O'Reilly, Mary Rose, 2936
Oring, Elliott, 456
Orlov, Paul A., 708
Ormrod, Jeanne Ellis, 1483
Orr, Leonard, 709
Orris, JanEdward, 1801
Ort, Daniel, 1820
Orth, Michael, 2853
Ortony, Andrew, 1017
Ory, John C., 3827
Osenlund, Kathryn, 3458
Oster, John E., 2377
Oster, Judith, 3035
Ostereicher, M. H., 2446
Ostrom, Hans, 3601
Ott, Catherine R., 3198
Otto, Paul B., 2937
Overbeck, Lois More, 457
Overton, Willis, 1190
Owen, William Foster, 1018
Owens, William A., 1184
Oxford-Carpenter, Rebecca L., 3015
Ozick, Cynthia, 1484

Pabst, Robert L., 778
Pacanowsky, Michael E., 1526
Packer, Martin J., 458
Pader, K., 3120
Page, Ellis B., 3773
Page, Gina, 459
Page, Ire Adams, 1836
Page, Mirian Dempsey, 2616
Paisner, Marilyn, 1166
Palacas, Arthur L., 191, 916
Palincsar, A. S., 1173
Palmer, James C., 3841
Palmer, William S., 2304
Palmerton, Patricia Ruby, 1485
Palumbo, Roberta M., 2764
Panda Learning Systems, 3602

Panja, Shormishtha, 710
Panwitt, Barbara, 2305
Papagan, Harry G., 1802
Papay, Twila Yates, 1596
Papomchak, Robert Allen, 2714
Paquette, Jerre, 1835
Paramour, Sally, 460
Paris, Pamela, 530
Parish, Charles, 3777
Parker, Frank, 818
Parker, John Reed, 3774
Parker, Robert, 2938
Parker, Robert P., 1486, 1607
Parks, A. Franklin, 3205
Parla, JoAnn, 3036
Parr, Gerald D., 2939
Parris, Peggy, 461, 2617, 2618
Parsons, Jerry M., 2765
Parsons, John W., 1191
Partridge, Harry B., 1019
Patten, Mack, 2306
Patterson, John Willard, 1487
Patton, Vicki, 3037
Paulenich, Fred F., 3128
Paulet, Robert O., 2103
Paulis, Chris, 2104, 2105
Paulson, Jon W., 1413
Paulson, Olaf B., 1245
Paxman, David B., 2619
Paye, Anne, 3224
Payne, Don, 2765
Payne, Steven K., 1092, 1093
Paz, Ruth, 2288
Pea, R. D., 1147
Pea, Roy D., 3603
Pearce, Judy, 2529
Pearce, W. Barnett, 117
Pearl, Karen, 2389
Pearsall, Thomas E., 2854, 3407
Pearse, Steve, 2226
Pearson, P. D., 838
Pearson, P. David, 318, 846, 1633
Pearson, Patricia, 2765
Pearson, Sheryl S., 354
Peck, David, 3192
Pedersen, Elray L., 916, 3775
Pejtersen, Annelise M., 1739
Pellegrini, A. D., 83, 462, 463
Pellegrino, James W., 1192
Pelz, Karen, 2575
Pendergrass, Paula, 2307
Penfield, Elizabeth F., 2620, 2621, 3351, 3776
Peng, Fred C. C., 1020

Penley, Mary Constance, 1488
Penney, M., 817
Penroe, John M., 3604
Perdue, Virginia A., 464
Perelman, Chaim, 465, 466
Peretz, Annette, 2389
Perfetti, Charles A., 1179
Perkins, D. N., 1110
Perkins, David N., 3127
Perkins, Kyle, 3777
Perkins, Leroy, 819
Perkins, Terry M., 467
Perl, Sondra, 260, 407, 468, 1608
Peroni, Patricia, 2622
Perrin, Robert, 1609, 1746, 2106, 2715, 3177, 3752
Perry, Jesse, 1836
Perry-Sheldon, Barbara, 3752
Persouke, Carl, 778
Peters, Douglas, 1644
Peters, Elizabeth, 2716
Peters, R. De V., 1252
Peters, William H., 2308
Petersen, Bruce T., 469, 470, 1193
Peterson, Arlin V., 2939
Peterson, Deborah, 2226
Peterson, Eric, 1103
Peterson, Linda, 471
Petree, Bonny, 3589
Petrosko, Joseph M., 472
Pettegrew, Barbara, 3152
Pettit, John D., Jr., 2755
Pevey, Jo Lundy, 2309
Pfeiffer, William S., 2976
Phelan, James, 3145
Phelps, Louise Wetherbee, 33, 473, 1194
Phelps, Terry O., 1916
Phenix, Jo, 2107
Philips, Leon C., 474
Phillips, Lea, 2623
Phillips, Louis, 1021, 1022, 3090
Piazza, Carolyn L., 475
Piché, Gene L., 83, 829, 839
Pickering, D. M., 820
Pickering, Samuel, Jr., 476
Pickrel, Paul, 477
Pierce, David, 3842
Pierstorff, Don K., 478
Piggins, Carol Ann, 2108
Pilarcik, Marlene A., 1917, 2624
Pinelli, Thomas E., 821
Pinnell, Gay Su, 2063, 2109, 2110
Pipman, Millie H., 2310
Pisano, Arturo, 3535

Pitta, Dennis Anthony, 1195
Pittman, David A., 1610
Pitts, Beverly, 1803, 2311
Pitts, Murray M., 822
Pival, Jean G., 3282
Plake, Barbara S., 87
Plandott, Dinnah, 711
Plante, Patricia R., 1290
Platek, Teri, 3778
Platt, Nancy G., 234, 1291, 2109, 2110
Plattor, Emma, 3129
Plax, Timothy G., 1281
Plomin, Robert, 1141
Podis, JoAnne M., 3312
Podis, Leonard, 260, 3312
Poirier-Bures, Simone, 3752, 3779
Poland, William E., 3842
Polanski, Virginia G., 1918, 2625
Polarin, A. B., 1023
Policastro, M., 1173
Polin, Linda G., 1658, 1953, 1954, 2626, 2627
Pollack, Philip L., 1024
Pollard, Rita, 83, 479, 480, 2312
Pollard-Gott, Lucy, 481
Pollay, Richard W., 1489
Polson, P. G., 1221
Pomerenke, Paula J., 2766
Ponsot, Marie, 3313
Pontius, Anneliese A., 823
Poole, Marshall Scott, 482
Pope, Carol, 2383
Popham, W. James, 3835
Popken, Randall L., 483
Pople, Martha T., 746, 2089
Popp, William, 3586
Popplewell, Scott L., 3780
Porter, James E., 340, 2855
Porterfield, Kay Marie, 2717
Portnoy, Kenneth, 2447
Poscarella, Ernest, 1629
Posey, Della Rose, 2767
Posner, Jeanne, 1025
Posselt, Nancy, 2768
Post, Louis A., 1490
Postlethwait, S. N., 2940
Poston, Lawrence, 3834
Potter, Cheryl L., 37
Potts, Maureen A., 1659
Potts, Richard, 2313
Potvin, Janet H., 2856
Pouncey, Peter R., 1611
Povar, Gail J., 2941
Powell, Joyce E., 2448

Powell, Marcy S., 1026
Powell, Mava Jo, 484
Powell, Philip M., 3130
Powell, Phillip A., 3286
Powell, Tom, 3787
Powers, Donald E., 3781
Powers, Stephen, 1196, 1612
Prabhu, Lalita, 3038
Pradl, Gordon M., 1346, 1553, 2628
Pratee, Doris, 2111
Pratt, Michael W., 1197, 1198
Prelli, Lawrence John, 485
Premack, David, 1199
Presley, John, 3843
Preston, Charlotte, 3363
Preston, Dennis R., 1027, 1028
Preston, James, 2942
Preussner, Alanna, 2449
Preussner, Arnold, 2449
Price, A. Rae, 2857
Price, Gayle B., 260
Price, Glanville, 1029
Price, Julie, 3214
Prigatano, George P., 1491
Pringle, Ian, 1835, 2112
Pritchard, David, 1492
Pritchard, Ruie, 1200, 2314
Prola, Max, 824
Pruchno, R. A., 1201
Pruett, James M., 2906
Pufahl, John P., 486
Puma, Vincent, 38
Pumphrey, Jean, 260
Purves, Alan C., 1747, 3782, 3783
Pytlik, Betty P., 1613, 2629

Qoqandi, Abdulaziz M. Y., 3039
Quarles, Jan, 1440
Queenan, Margaret, 2315
Quellmalz, Edys, 3690, 3784, 3785
Quet, Danielle, 39, 712
Quick, Doris M., 487, 2185
Quinn, Arthur, 713
Quinn, Dennis P., 488
Quinn, Karen B., 391, 2630
Quinn, Mary Ellen, 3024
Quinn, Mary P., 489
Quintilian, 260
Quirk, Randolph, 1030
Quiroz, Sharon, 340

Rabianski-Carriuolo, Nancy, 2450, 2451
Rabin, Joseph, 3612

Rabine, Leslie W., 1493
Rabinowitz, Isaac, 40
Rabinowitz, Nancy Sarkin, 714
Radencich, Marguerite C., 2123, 2452
Radway, Janice, 825
Raffetto, William G., 1919
Rafoth, Bennett A., 490, 491, 3786
Ragno, Nancy N., 3158
Railsback, Celeste Condit, 1494
Raimes, Ann, 492
Raisman, Neal A., 2860
Ramaprasad, Jyotika, 1495
Ramey, Judith A., 2811
Ramos de Perez, J. Maria, 3040
Rampolla, Mary Lynn, 1496
Ramraz, Rachel, 3680
Ramsey, Esther Leota K., 2113, 2114
Ramsey, Paul A., 1836
Ramsey, Shirley, 270, 1324
Rand, Earl, 3535
Randall, Alice F., 2389
Ranieri, Paul, 1614
Rank, Hugh, 1497, 2316, 3476
Rankin, David, 2453
Rankin, Dorothy S., 493
Rankin, Elizabeth D., 494
Ranly, Don, 3428
Rasche, Robert, 3621
Raskin, Victor, 1031
Rasor, Richard A., 3787
Ratman, Nancy, 3091
Ratner, Rochelle, 2977
Ratteray, Oswald M. T., 495
Ravitch, Diane, 1292
Rawski, Evelyn S., 1499
Ray, Richard E., 3415
Raygor, Alton, 3250
Raygor, Robin, 3250
Raymond, James C., 171
Raymond, Richard C., 2861
Reagan, Sally Barr, 2454
Reavley, Katharine R., 2631
Rebhorn, Marlette, 2943
Reddy, Maureen T., 715
Reder, L. M., 1110
Redish, Janice C., 3015
Redlich, Mary Rose, 1972
Redman, Tim, 2423, 3552
Redmond, Claire, 3614
Reed, Linda, 2138
Reed, Michael D., 2317
Reed, Michael W., 1202
Reed, Patricia Ann, 1615

Reed, W. Michael, 496, 2632, 3788
Reegan, Sally B., 2455
Reep, Diana C., 2769
Reese, Paul, 44
Reese, Stephen D., 1410
Reid, Barbara V., 1203
Reid, Joy, 497, 498, 499
Reid-Nash, Naomi Kathleen, 1498
Reif, Frederick, 3567
Reigstad, Thomas J., 1204, 1748, 3789
Reimer, Daniel, 2456
Reimer, Joseph, 1233
Reinhardt, Alan J., 500
Reinke, Barbara J., 1205
Reinking, David, 826
Reiser, Brian J., 1206
Reising, Robert W., 33
Reissman, Rose, 2318, 2319
Reiter, David P., 2633
Reither, James A., 501
Renan, Yael, 716
Renshaw, Betty, 3298
Rentel, Victor M., 1207
Rentz, Kathryn C., 3790
Resch, Kenneth E., 2320
Resch, Paula C., 1920
Resnick, Daniel P., 1499
Resnick, L. B., 1173
Rest, James R., 1208
Reuss, Siegfried, 1155
Rex-Kerish, Lesley, 2634
Reynolds, Mark, 502, 2635
Reynoso, Wendy Demko, 2457
Ribaudo, Michael, 366, 2434
Rice, Donna Steed, 3041
Rice, Eileen M., 503
Rice, Mabel, 1209
Ricento, Thomas, 3005
Rich, Sharon J., 1921
Richard, Jeremy, 2944
Richards, Amy, 3791
Richards, D. Dean, 1451
Richards, Douglas G., 1148
Richards, Thomas, 1546
Richards-Beale, Kaye C., 1616
Richardson, Jacques G., 1500
Richardson, Janette, 717
Richardson, Leonard E., 504
Richgels, Donald J., 2087, 3092, 3093
Richmond, John, 1799
Richmond, Kent C., 3042
Ricketts, Jeffrey Neil, 1293
Ricoeur, Paul, 505

Ridgeway, Doreen, 1032
Rief, Linda, 2046
Riel, Margaret M., 237
Rigg, Pat, 20
Riley, Katherine, 2636
Rinderer, Regina, 397
Ringler, L., 817
Rink, Henry W., 3239
Rissland, E. L., 1110
Rivers, William E., 1821
Roach, Donald A., 827
Roark, Dennis, 3131
Roberts, David D., 1617, 2862
Roberts, David H., 1618
Roberts, Donald F., 828, 1319
Roberts, Elizabeth Ann, 506
Roberts, Jean M., 2115
Roberts, Wayne, 2090
Roberts, William H., 3278
Robertson, Elizabeth, 2509
Robertson, Jean Ellis, 1501
Robertson, S. P., 1173
Robey, Cora, 3279, 3373
Robillard, Douglas, Jr., 2945
Robins, Greg, 2135
Robinson, Ann, 1210
Robinson, E. J., 1211
Robinson, Edward A., 1836
Robinson, James Adolph, 1033
Robinson, Jay L., 507
Robinson, Patricia A., 3416
Robinson, Sam, 1619
Robinson, Susan F., 1294
Rocklin, Thomas, 449
Roddy, Vanessa K., 1502
Roderick, Jessie A., 1620
Roderick, John M., 1922
Rodrigues, Dawn, 1923, 2116, 3617, 3618, 3619, 3668
Rodrigues, Raymond J., 508, 2321, 2322, 3618, 3619, 3668
Rodriguez, William Robert, 2323
Roe, Arnold, 1212
Roe, Kiki V., 1212
Roedel, Harlan, 2847
Roehler, Laura R., 752
Roemer, Kenneth M., 2637
Roen, Duane H., 509, 829, 2638, 2903, 3620
Rogal, Samuel J., 3094
Rogers, Anne, 3752
Rogers, Glenn C., 3221
Rogers, Judy R., 3221
Rogers, Margaret, 1034
Rogers, Robert, 830

Rogers, Zegarra N., 838
Roginski, Jim, 510
Rohatyn, Dennis, 340
Roller, Cathy M., 831
Romano, Tom, 1621
Rompf, Shirley, 3246
Ronald, Katharine J., 2508, 2639
Roodin, Paul A., 1165
Roof, Midge, 2458
Rooney, Pamela S., 15
Root, Robert L., Jr., 511, 512
Roper, Helen D., 2117
Rosa, Alfred F., 3335, 3430
Rose, Janet S., 3835
Rose, Mike, 513, 514, 515, 1660, 1661, 3792
Rosen, Harold, 1853
Rosen, Jay, 516
Rosen, Joan G., 2640
Rosen, Leonard, 3327
Rosen, Lois Matz, 2899
Rosen, Martha, 2046
Rosenbaum, Harvey, 3015
Rosenbaum, Nina Joy, 2324
Rosenberg, Dolly, 2288
Rosenberg, Ruth, 2641, 2642
Rosenblatt, Louise M., 832, 1486
Rosenburg, Ruth, 2118
Rosenhaum, Dolores, 2574
Rosier, James, 3333
Roskelly, Hephzibah, 2639
Rosner, Mary, 1035
Ross, Donald, 35, 83, 2507, 3621, 3668
Ross, William T., 2643
Ross-Larson, Bruce, 3417
Rossman, Mark, 1612
Roth, Audrey J., 3385, 3622
Roth, Froma P., 1036, 1037
Roth, Lorie, 2644
Roth, Richard, 2645
Rothkop, E. Z., 838
Rothwell, William J., 2770, 2771, 2863
Rottenberg, Annette T., 3352
Rottweiler, Gail P., 517
Roubicek, Henry L., 2119
Roueche, James R., 1491
Roueche, John E., 1822, 2459
Roueche, Suanne D., 1822, 2459
Rounds, Jeanine C., 2460, 3793
Rounds, Pat, 870
Roundy, Nancy, 2528, 2864, 2865, 3418
Rouse, John, 1924, 2120
Rouse, Sandra H., 1749
Rouse, William, 1739, 1749

Rousseau, Jean-Jacques, 1038
Rowan, D., 3120
Rowan, Kathleen E., 141
Rowe, H. A. H., 1213
Rowe, Robert D., 237
Rowland, Robert C., 518, 519
Rowley, Gwen, 2529
Rowoth, James D., 2988
Royster, Jacqueline, 1836
Rubano, Gregory, 2325
Rubens, Brenda, 520
Rubin, A., 817
Rubin, Andee, 1039, 3623
Rubin, David C., 1214
Rubin, Donald L., 83, 462, 463, 521, 522, 2138, 3786
Rubin, Dorothy, 3260
Rubin, Lois E., 3794
Rubin, Rebecca B., 3852
Rubin, Yona, 2288
Rubinstein, S. Leonard, 2646
Ruddell, R. B., 838
Ruddell, Robert, 2647
Rude, Carolyn D., 2866
Ruehr, Ruthann, 2867
Ruetten, Mary K., 2621
Ruggiero, Vincent Ryan, 3314, 3392
Rumelhart, D. E., 838
Runco, Mark A., 1215, 1216
Ruscica, Marybeth, 3236
Rushing, Janice Hocker, 1503
Rushing, Joe B., 1925
Ruskiewicz, John J., 3266
Russel, Mark, 1750
Russell, Don, 2090
Russell, James, 1217
Russell, Willis, 1040
Ruth, Leo, 3795
Rutter, Russell, 2868
Ruzich, Constance W., 563
Ryan, Lois Ann, 1922
Ryan, Marie Laure, 718, 719
Ryan, Michael, 1504
Ryder, Eleanor, 2121
Ryder, Randall James, 3589
Ryder, Willet, 2121
Rygiel, Dennis, 523, 524
Ryman, David H., 1505
Ryzewic, Susan R., 366, 2434

Sacksteder, William, 525
Saffran, Murray, 2946
Saidel, Lois F., 2122
Saksena, Anuradha, 1041

Saldiver, Rhoda Gail Hill, 1295
Sale, Don, 3752
Salerno, Douglas, 2648
Salinger, Wendy, 2326
Salmaso, Dario, 755
Salo-Miler, Ilene, 2042
Saloom, B. George, 1347
Salwen, Michael B., 1506
Salzer, Richard T., 833
Samra, Rise Jane, 1507
Samson, George E., 3796
Samuels, J., 838
Samuels, Marilyn Schauer, 526
Samuels, S. Jay, 838, 2109, 2110
Samuels, Shelly, 1751
Sanchez-Escobar, Angel, 527
Sandberg, Alvin, 3195
Sanders, Robert E., 528
Sanders, Scott P., 2798
Santa, C., 817
Santleman, Patricia Kelly, 2869
Santmire, Toni E., 529
Saritsky, Michael, 83
Saunders, Dorothy O., 1992
Sauter, Kevin O'Brien, 1508
Savage, David, 3797
Savale, Zoila A., 3798
Savignon, Sandra J., 3799
Savitz, Fred R., 1296
Sawyer, Thomas M., 2527, 2870
Scallon, Ron, 1431
Scallon, Suzanne B. K., 1431
Scanlon, Leone, 1752, 2575
Scanlon, Patrick M., 720
Scarcella, Robin C., 1042, 1043
Scardamalia, Marlene, 88, 530, 568, 1110, 1173, 1297
Schadler, Margaret, 1218
Schaefer, James Frank, 1044
Schaefer, Lyn, 1299
Schafer, John C., 1567
Schanche, Carol, 1509
Scheffler, Judith, 2461
Schell, John F., 2649
Schieffelin, Bambi B., 1431
Schiff, Jeff, 2650, 2651
Schilb, John, 400
Schlatter, Franklin D., 1298, 1662, 1663, 3836
Schlatterbeck, Rita, 3165
Schleicher, David, 2810
Schmidt, Dan, 2226
Schmidt, Gary D., 2327, 2328, 2557
Schmidt, John L., 3132
Schmidt, Stuart, 1160

Schneider, Annette E., 531
Schneider, Estelle C., 2389
Schneider, Larissa A., 270, 1324, 2718
Schneider, Thomas, 1045
Schnotz, W., 1173
Schnur, Elizabeth Sue, 1046
Schoenberg, Sheila, 2288
Scholastic, 3484
Scholes, Robert, 532, 721, 834, 3315, 3331
Schollmeier, Paul, 533
Schooler, Carmi, 1219
Schooley, Bill Jaye, 1510
Schor, Sandra, 407, 3267
Schorer, Mark, 3353
Schrader, Vincent E., 2329
Schrag, Calvin O., 534
Schreiner, Eleanor Lynn, 1511
Schreiner, Margaret Rizza, 535
Schreiner, Robert, 826
Schuder, R. T., 817
Schuessler, Brian F., 83
Schulte, Ranier, 722
Schultz, Anne, 536
Schultz, Myrna, 1073
Schumacher, Gary M., 537, 1220
Schumaker, Jean B., 761, 1268, 1269
Schumm, Jeanne S., 2123, 2452
Schuster, Charles I., 538, 723, 2719, 2720
Schuster, Edgar H., 1047
Schuster, M. Lincoln, 1436
Schwab, Patricia N., 3043
Schwalm, David E., 2462
Schwartz, Helen J., 45, 1622, 2389, 2772, 3625, 3626,
  3627, 3632, 3668
Schwartz, Jeffrey, 2330
Schwartz, Marc J., 1512
Schwartz, Mimi, 539, 540, 2463, 3438
Schwegler, Robert, 3354
Scibior, Olga, 2098
Scott, Bill, 1048
Scott, James Calvert, 2773
Scott, Jerrie Cobb, 1836
Scott, Kathleen F., 541
Scott, Norval, 2947
Scott, Patrick, 542
Scott, Robert L., 543, 724, 1513, 2948
Scovic, Stephen P., 1926
Scribner, S., 1147
Scruggs, Thomas E., 835
Searls, Evelyn F., 813
Sears, Donald, 3386
Sears, Peter, 2331
Sebranek, Patrick, 3171, 3178, 3179

Secco, T., 1173
Sechrist, Paul W., 3837
Secor, Marie, 340, 725, 3336
Sedgwick, Ellery, 2652
Segal, Erwin M., 1138
Segal, J. W., 1110, 1221
Segedy, Michael, 2332
Segers, May C., 1514
Seibold, David R., 482
Seittelman, Estelle M., 1967
Seldon, Ramsey W., 1804
Self, Warren, 2333
Selfe, Cynthia L., 513, 544, 545, 2507, 3628, 3629,
  3630, 3668
Selman, R. L., 1110
Selzer, Jack, 1927
Semke, Harriet D., 3800
Serebrin, Wayne, 2098
Sereno, Kenneth K., 978
Sevcik, Ann, 1222
Shachak, Miriam, 2288
Shanahan, Joseph B., 546
Shanahan, T., 1223
Shanahan, Timothy, 1049
Shankweiler, Donald, 1224
Shapiro, Nancy S., 547, 1225, 2653
Shaplin, Wanda S., 2172
Sharabany, Ruth, 1134
Sharpe, Pamela J., 3206
Sharplin, Wanda S., 1348, 2654
Shattuck, Roger, 1226
Shaw, Dale G., 3725
Shaw, Henry, 3186
Shaw, Steve, 3591
Shea, George B., Jr., 2334
Sheehan, Daniel S., 3676
Sheen, Sy-Yng, 836
Sheffield, John, 1596
Sheffield, Terry, 2335
Sheilah, Allen, 2336
Shelby, Annette, 2774
Shelden, Michael, 2655
Shell, Kathy L., 3853
Shelly, Lynn B., 548
Shepherd, Gregory J., 1516
Sheppard, Ken, 920
Sher, Lawrence, 2389
Sherman, Dean, 2775
Sherrard, Carol A., 2871
Shields, Ronald Eugene, 1823
Shimkin, David, 3318
Shipley, Joseph T., 1050
Shock, Diane H., 1227

Shoemaker, Pamela J., 1517
Shook, Ronald, 2656
Shore, Cecilia, 1051
Shores, Phyllis, 2337
Shostak, Robert, 3632
Shoval, Peretz, 1755
Shrodes, Caroline, 3355
Shugar, Debora, 549
Shugrue, Michael, 3355
Shultz, Thomas R., 1228
Shuman, R. Baird, 550, 1623, 2338, 3634
Shumway, David R., 551
Shuttleworth, Jack M., 3286
Shuy, Roger W., 817, 2109, 2110, 3028
Sieben, J. Kenneth, 3207
Siefert, Marsha, 1518
Siegel, Alexander W., 1229
Siegel, Gerald, 2978
Siegler, R. S., 1110
Siemers, Curtis Bernard, 552
Sigband, Norman B., 2776, 3419
Sigel, Irving E., 1114
Sigman, Marion, 1230
Sigman, Stuart J., 2949
Sills, Caryl Klein, 2777, 2778
Silva, Dan, 3591
Silverman, Henry, 2575
Silverstein, Anna, 2389
Silverthorn, Lana, 2575
Simard, Rodney, 1745, 1928
Simcox, William A., 2779
Simion, Francesca, 837
Simmonds, Paul, 3801
Simmons, James G., 1130
Simmons, John S., 2339
Simmons, Nancy, 1756
Simmons, W., 1110
Simon, H. A., 1162
Simons, Elizabeth Radin, 2340, 2341
Simons, Herbert W., 124, 553, 554
Simpson, Jeanne H., 1757, 1758, 1759, 2657
Simpson, Michele, 3095
Sinatra, Richard, 2342
Singer, Daniel, 2958
Singer, Hindy, 838, 2343, 2344
Singer, Martha M. L., 2658
Singleton, Barbara, 3128
Sinnott, Jan D., 1105
Sipple, William L., 726
Sirc, Geoffrey, 237
Skeffington, Margaret, 3118
Skelton, John, 3044
Skelton, Terrance, 2872

Skinner, Anna M., 3714
Skinner, B. F., 1664
Skinner, Ellen A., 1106
Skulicz, Matthew, 555, 2464, 2465
Skwire, David, 3316, 3317
Slanger, George, 1929
Slater, Wayne H., 839
SLATE Steering Committee, 1805, 1806, 1807
Slattery, Pat, 2659
Slaughter, Virginia, 2389
Slevin, James F., 556
Sloan, Gary, 557
Sloss, Gail Sam, 558
Slynn, S. M., 121
Small, Robert C., Jr., 1052, 1891, 2255
Small, Sharon, 2660
Smart, William, 3356
Smelstor, Marjorie, 3359
Smeltzer, Larry R., 2780, 2781
Smetana, Judith G., 1231
Smith, Bonnie G., 1519
Smith, Brenda, 3222, 3223
Smith, C. Michael, 1745
Smith, Charles R., 237, 2661, 3668
Smith, Craig R., 1520
Smith, Cyrus F., Jr., 3589
Smith, David M., 1486
Smith, Earl, 1349
Smith, Edward E., 559, 3127
Smith, Elliott L., 3251
Smith, Eugene, 2345, 2662, 2950
Smith, Frank, 318, 1431, 1835
Smith, Franklin E., 3484
Smith, H. Wendell, 3393
Smith, Herb, 1053, 2782
Smith, Hugh T., 560
Smith, J. W., 121
Smith, Jane Bowman, 2302
Smith, John B., 3635
Smith, John H., 561
Smith, Karen, 213, 2127
Smith, Louise Z., 2663
Smith, Lydia A. H., 1232
Smith, Michael, 1054
Smith, Michael Holley, 3439
Smith, Michael W., 2346
Smith, Myrna, 2887
Smith, Nancy J., 2124
Smith, Rochelle, 562
Smith, Roland M., 2125
Smith, Ron F., 1521
Smith, Ronald E., 1624
Smith, Sandy, 1760

Smith, Stephen Austin, 1522
Smith, Suzanne T., 1224
Smith, Terrie, 243
Smith, Terry, 2979
Smith, Tom, 1596
Smith, Vernon H., 2126
Smith, William Flint, 1266
Smith, William L., 191, 563, 1625, 2507
Smith-Burke, M. Trika, 817, 2063
Smitherman, Geneva, 1836, 2347
Smye, Randy, 3636
Smyer, M. A., 1201
Snackey, Jan, 2348
Snarey, John R., 1233
Snodgrass, Sara E., 2951
Snow, Catherine, 759
Snow, Marguerite, 3045
Snow, Susan, 2349
Snyder, Carol, 2664
Snyder, Fritz, 1808
Soares, Eric J., 2783
Software Publishing Corporation, 3637
Sola, Michele, 1350
Sollisch, James, 1761, 1762, 2466
Solomon, Martha, 564
Somay, Bülent, 727
Somers, Margaret L., 2765
Sommerfield, Geoffrey, 407
Sommerfield, Judith Fishman, 407
Sommers, Elizabeth A., 2507, 3638, 3639
Sommers, Jeffrey, 191, 1930, 2665, 3802
Sommers, Nancy, 260, 3310, 3331, 3357
Sonderegger, Theo B., 1234
Sonnenschein, Susan, 1235
Soria, Andrew M., 3046
Soriano, Barbara, 1814
Soskin, Mark D., 2952
Sosnowski, David, 2666
Söter, A., 3783
Southard, Sherry, 2873
Souther, James W., 2811
Southwell, Michael G., 3640, 3668
Soven, Margot, 1626
Sowers, Susan, 223, 2046
Spack, Ruth, 565, 1055, 3047
Spader, Peter H., 3685
Spangler, G. A., 1056
Spann, Sylvia, 187, 766
Sparrow, W. Keats, 1745
Sparshatt, Francis, 566
Speaker, R., 838
Spear, Karen I., 1745
Speck, Bruce W., 728, 2667, 2874, 2875

Speigle, Joan E., 1299
Spekman, Nancy J., 1036, 1037
Spencer, Arlene, 2350
Spencer, Gregory Horton, 1523
Spencer, Margaret, 1835, 1853
Sperling, Melanie, 237
Spicola, Rose, 1552
Spiegel, Dixie Lee, 1273
Spitzer, Michael, 2507
Spooner, Michael, 1939, 1940
Spring, Karen Strom, 3096
Springate, Kay W., 1968
Spurlin, Joni E., 1300
Squire, James R., 318, 1931, 2185
St. Dizier, Byron, 1524
Staab, Claire F., 2127
Stafford, Juliene Lanette, 1236
Stafford, Kim R., 1932
Staiger, R. C., 838
Staitz, Robert L., 3261, 3262
Staley, George, 1933
Staley, R. Eric, 2876
Stalker, Linda, 2128
Stamps, Dory, 1351
Stanback, Marsha Houston, 1057
Standiford, Sally N., 1237
Stanford, Barbara Dodds, 3180
Stanford, Gene, 3180
Stanley, Linda, 3218, 3318
Stanovich, Keith E., 840
Stanton, H. E., 3803
Stanwood, P. G., 567
Staples, Katherine, 1665
Starzcyk, Lawrence J., 3420
Staton, Jana, 2129, 2138
Staudt, Kathleen Henderson, 3083
Stay, Byron L., 2467
Stear, Richard, 2185
Stebbins, Peter J., 1763
Steele, Gary G., 3252
Steele, Louise W., 3644
Steffensen, Margaret S., 997
Steffey, Marda Nicholson, 2784
Stegman, Michael O., 2351
Steiglitz, Francine B., 3261, 3262
Stein, Nancy L., 1173
Stein, Susanna, 1151
Steinbach, Rosanne, 568, 1297
Steinberg, Erwin R., 248
Steinberg, Michael J., 3226
Steinfield, Charles William, 1525
Stephens, Gary, 2668
Stephens, Judith L., 2877

Stern, Barbara B., 2785
Sternberg, R. J., 1110
Sternglass, Marilyn, 569, 570, 1058, 1666
Steuck, Kurt, 1119
Stevens, Edward, 1499
Stevens, Ralph S., III, 237, 2226
Stevens, Vance, 3048
Stevenson, Dwight W., 3838
Stevenson, Harold W., 1301
Stevenson, John W., 571
Steward, Joyce, 3358, 3359
Stewart, Benjamin T., 33
Stewart, Donald C., 33, 120, 171, 572, 573
Stewart, Jon, 1764
Stewart, Judith, 1128
Stewart, Murray, 3804
Stewart, Sharon R., 3110
Sticht, Thomas G., 2953
Stiebel, Arlene, 729
Stiff, Rebecca, 1934
Stiffler, Randall, 3097
Stigler, James, 1301
Stillman, Peter, 2507, 3146, 3208
Stine, Donna, 2735
Stockard, Connie H., 2130, 2352
Stoddard, Eve Walsh, 574
Stoddard, Sara E., 575
Stoddard, Ted D., 2786
Stoddart, Pat, 1765
Stoddart, Susan, 3015
Stoffel, Judy, 2468
Stokes, Shelly J., 1431
Stone, Katherine R., 1117
Stotsky, Sandra, 318, 2131, 2132, 2353, 3263
Stott, Frances M., 223
Stover, Harryette, 3303, 3464
Strage, Amy Alexandra, 1059
Straker, Dolores, 1836
Strandness, Jean, 3226
Stratman, James F., 191
Stratta, Leslie, 1853
Stratton, R. E., 1667
Stratton, Russell E., 2666
Strauss, Gordon D., 1673
Strauss, Harold, 1436
Straw, Stanley B., 916
Street, R. I., 1352
Streff, Craig R., 2354
Strenski, Ellen, 2954
Strickland, Dorothy, 1836
Strickland, James, 576, 1935, 2507, 3647
Strickland, Rennard, 602
Strickland, Robbie W., 2787

Stricklen, Simon A., Jr., 1353
Strine, Mary S., 1526
Stromberg, Linda J., 2076
Strong, William, 191, 400, 916, 2133
Strother, Donna, 3589
Stull, William L., 33, 191, 2355
Stultz, Russell, 3648
Stupple, Donna-Marie, 2356
Stutman, Randall K., 577
Suchan, James, 2788
Sudol, Ronald A., 3649
Suhor, Charles, 46, 1936, 1937, 1938, 1939, 1940, 2138, 3133, 3181
Sulkes, Stan, 1941
Sullivan, Dale, 2878
Sullivan, Frances, 2854
Sullivan, Jenny N., 2357
Sullivan, Kathleen E., 3209
Sullivan, Maureen A., 916
Sullivan, Patricia, 171
Sullivan, Patricia A., 2862
Sullivan, Patricia Ann, 578
Sullivan, Patrick, 1627, 1766, 1767
Sullivan, Phil, 3147
Sullivan, Sally, 3187
Sulzby, Elizabeth, 181, 223
Sumino, Teiko, 1480
Summerlin, Charles Timothy, 2469
Sumners, William, 1060, 1061
Sunnafrank, Michael J., 414
Susi, Geraldine Lee, 1628
Sutton, Jane Susan, 579
Svaldi, David Paul, 580
Svartik, Jan, 1030
Swadener, Marc, 3771
Swaffar, Janet K., 841
Swaino, Jean M., 2879
Swander, Mary, 2358
Swanson, Marti, 2359
Swarts, Heidi, 83
Swarts, Valerie Renee, 1527
Sweedler-Brown, Carol, 2669, 3806
Swenson, Dan H., 2765
Swicord, Barbara, 2134
Swope, John W., 581, 1942, 3752, 3807, 3810

Tabbert, Russell, 1062
Tabor, Kenneth, 2470
Tabor, Patton, 237
Tackach, James, 1768
Taft, Michael, 2377
Takala, Sauli, 3783, 3808
Talal, Marilynn, 730

Talmage, Harriet, 1629
Tanenhaus, M., 1254
Tanner, Deborah, 2360
Tanner, William E., 47, 3213
Tardiff, Kenneth, 1673
Targ, William, 1436
Tarlinskaja, Marina, 1063
Tarpley, J. Douglas, 1528
Tashlik, Phyllis, 2670
Taufen, Phyllis, 582
Taylor, Ann, 3360
Taylor, B. M., 838
Taylor, Barbara M., 842, 1354
Taylor, Carol A., 843
Taylor, David, 3091, 3134
Taylor, Denny, 318
Taylor, Ethel, 1836
Taylor, Karl K., 583, 1943
Taylor, Maravene Elizabeth, 844
Taylor, Michael, 2671
Taylor, Raymond G., 1668, 1669
Taylor, Sharon J., 1630
Teale, William H., 318, 1431
Tebeaux, Elizabeth, 1894, 2789
Teich, Nathaniel, 2135, 2721, 3049
Telotte, J. P., 584
Templeton, Shane, 1064
Terdiman, Rita, 2389
Terpstra, Richard L., 2361
Terrace, H. S., 1238
Terry, Ann, 3165
Tesdell, Lee S., 1065
Testerman, Jean, 2136
Tex, William Winkelman, 1066
Texas Education Agency, Division of Educational
    Assessment, 3809
Thabet, Ahmed A., 3050
Thackeray, William, 2672
Thaiso, Christopher, 2955
Thaiss, Christopher J., 1355, 2137, 2138
Theismeyer, Elaine, 3651
Theismeyer, John, 3651, 3652
Theisz, R. D., 3135
Thierfelder, William R., III, 2880
Thoburn, Tina, 3165
Thoma, Stephen J., 1208
Thomas, Charlene, 1431
Thomas, Dene K., 1769
Thomas, Gordon P., 1067
Thomas, Helen, 3051
Thomas, Jacqueline, 3052
Thomas, Owen, 3477
Thomas, P. G., 3653

Thomas, Patricia, 1064
Thomas, Timothy A., 1944
Thomas, Trudelle, 1945
Thomas-Ruzic, Maria, 585
Thompson, Bruce, 822, 2980
Thompson, C. Lamar, 1631
Thompson, Edgar H., 1632, 2362, 3752, 3810
Thompson, Isabelle, 2790, 2881
Thompson, Loren C., 1946
Thompson, Mary C., 2765
Thompson, Merle O., 2357
Thompson, Nancy S., 3589
Thompson, Neil C., 3151
Thompson, Richard A., 1356
Thompson, W. E., 1221
Thompson-Panos, Karyn, 585
Thomson, John, 2575
Thrush, Jo Ann, 3654
Thrush, Randolph S., 3654
Tibbetts, Arn M., 1068, 2791, 3319
Tibbetts, Charlene, 3319
Tichy, Paul, 1069
Tierney, Robert J., 318, 810, 838, 845, 846, 1005,
    1633
Tiersky, Ethel, 3248, 3249, 3258, 3259
Tietjen, Anne Marie, 1239
Tillinghast, B. S., 3811
Timm, Lenora A., 3053
Timmis, John H., III, 1529
Tinkler, John F., 586
Tipton, Robert M., 1546
Tirrell, Mary Kay, 1634
Tittler, Jonathan, 731
Tolfa, Debra, 835
Tollefson, Nona A., 1973
Tollefson, Stephen K., 3253
Tomkins, Gail E., 2088
Tomlinson, Barbara, 587
Tomlinson, Carl M., 475
Tompkins, Gail E., 2139
Tompkins, Phillip K., 588
Tone, B., 817
Tookey, Mary, 2673
Toole, Joe, 2492
Torbe, Mike, 1835
Tornow, Joan, 3465
Torrison, Beth, 1972
Torsney, Cheryl, 2674
Toth, Marian Davis, 3158
Tough, Joan, 1486
Towns, Sanna Nimtz, 2363
Townsend, Donna, 3165
Towrey, Suzanne, 2364

Trace, Jacqueline, 2792
Trachsel, Mary, 1530
Tracy, Gilman, 2675
Tracz, Richard F., 3379
Trasbasso, Tom, 1173
Travers, D. Molly Murison, 1947
Tregidgo, P. S., 3054
Tremmel, Robert, 2365, 2366, 2471
Trimbur, John, 400, 589, 1670
Trimmer, Joseph F., 1635, 3310, 3361
Tripp, Ellen, 590
Tritt, Michael, 1948
Troyka, Lynn Quitman, 171, 3812, 3813
Trueba, Henry T., 3055
Truscott, Robert Blake, 1770
Tsujimoto, Joseph I., 2367
Tucker, Amy, 3210
Tucker, David L., 1633
Tucker, Robert L., 1809
Tulkoff, Joseph, 1357
Turbill, Jan, 1993, 1994
Turner, Alberta, 591
Turner, Darwin T., 1836
Turner, Judith Axler, 1531
Turner, Susan Douglas, 2083
Turner, Terence J., 838, 1017
Turvey, Joel, 2140
Tutolo, Daniel, 2141
Tversky, Amos, 1132
Tway, Eileen, 2139, 2142, 2143
Tyner, Thomas E., 3211
Tzeng, O. J. L., 838

Uhlig, George E., 3811
Ulatowska, Hanna K., 1125
Ulrich, Clint, 2368
Ulrich, Eugene, 1070, 1071
Ulvund, Stein Erik, 1240
Umland, Marcia, 1596
Underwood, V. L., 1221
Ungerer, Judy A., 1230
Unia, Sumitra, 2098
Updike, Thomas L., 1775
Ur, Penny, 2288
Urkowitz, Stephen, 1596

Vacca, JoAnne, 318, 1636
Vähäpassi, Anneli, 3783, 3808
Vallecorsa, Ada L., 1637
VanAlstyne, Judith, 3421
Vande Kopple, William J., 260, 592, 593
Vanden Bergh, Bruce, 1073
VandenBos, Gary R., 1815

van den Broek, P., 1173
Vanderlaan, Eunice, 3182
Van der Veer, R., 1241
van Didjk, T., 838
van Fiesout, Cornelis F. M., 1251
van Ijzendoorn, M. H., 1241
Vann, Roberta J., 3814
VanOosting, James, 594
Van Ostade, Ingrid Tieken-Boon, 1072
Van Riper, Charles, 1596
Van Sant, Ann Jessie, 3374
Vardell, Sylvia M., 1638
Vargas, Marjorie Fink, 3098
Varner, Iris I., 2765, 2793
Vasos, Helen, 847
Vaughan, John, 2090
Vaughan, Samuel, 1436
Vaughn, Jeannette W., 2754, 2882
Vaught, Susan A., 1998
Vause, Corinne Jordan, 595
Vavra, Edward A., 955
Vavrus, Linda G., 752
Vega, Juan, 2389
Veit, Richard, 1358
Veit, Walter, 596
Velazquez, Clara, 2389
Vernon, Philip A., 1242, 1243
Versluis, Edward B., 3656
Verts, Lita J., 3056
Vick, Richard D., 1771
Viera, Carroll, 2369, 3099
Viglionese, Paschal C., 597
Villani, Frank, 3614
Vipond, Douglas, 848
Vivion, Michael, 1949
Vogeli, Bruce, 2389
Von Blum, Ruth, 3535, 3668
Vondran, Raymond F., 821
von Reyn, Janet, 2046
Vopat, James, 3330
Vorhees, Roy Dale, 2765
Voss, J. F., 121, 1173
Vukovich, Stanyan, 1596
Vukuvich, Diane, 2956
Vulgamore, Melvin L., 598
Vygotsky, L. S., 260

Waddell, Craig, 3658
Wade, James, 1436
Wade, Philip, 2472
Wagner, Betty Jane, 1853
Wagner, Linda W., 732
Wagner, Mary Jo, 1639, 2144

Wahlstrom, Billie J., 3628, 3629, 3630, 3659
Wainer, Howard, 3815
Walden, Ruth, 1532
Waldo, Mark L., 599
Walker, Laurence, 2370
Walker, Lawrence J., 1239, 1244
Walker, Melissa, 3387
Walker, Pat Neff, Jr., 849
Walker, Sue, 600
Wallace, Bill D., 5
Wallace, Jack E., 3394
Wallace, Joan T., 2371
Wallace, M. Elizabeth, 1671, 1672
Wallace, Ray B., 3057
Waller, Gary F., 1950
Wallesch, Claus-W., 1245
Walrath, Norma D., 2372, 2373, 3476
Walsh, Dennis M., 2374
Walshe, R. D., 2090
Walter, Carolyn Calhoun, 2254
Walter, Grace C., 2185
Walter, James A., 2957
Walter, Katya M., 1246
Walter, Otis M., 2676
Walters, Keith, 1533
Waltman, John L., 1534, 2794
Walton, Richard E., 2827
Waltz, Alfred Jacob, 1247
Walvoord, Barbara Fassler, 1951, 2958, 3320
Walzer, Arthur E., 2959
Wander, Philip, 1535
Wang, W. S.-Y., 838
Wangberg, Elaine G., 2980
Want, E. Cleve, 3329
Wapner, Seymour, 1248
Warash, Barbara Gibson, 1969
Warburton, Terrence L., 1536
Ward, Jay A., 2677
Ward, William C., 1124
Ware, Elaine, 2473
Ware, H. W., 1221
Wargetz, Lillian G., 3216
Warner, Michael M., 761
Warnock, John, 33, 1302, 1537, 1745
Warnock, Tilly, 1745
Warren, David J., 1249
Warren, Thomas L., 3422
Warshaw, Mimi, 2248
Warsley, Dale, 2145
Washburn, William, 1835
Washington, Gene, 2678, 2679, 2680
Wason-Ellam, Linda, 601
Wassman, Rose, 3224

Wasson, John M., 3362
Waterman, David C., 778
Waters, Everett, 1032
Waters, Greg, 1642
Waters, Mary Ann, 3438
Watson, Andrea L., 2160
Watson, Arden K., 1538
Watson, Deryn M., 2375
Watson, Dorothy, 2063
Watson, Ken, 1303
Watson, Kittie W., 1374, 2781
Watson, Tom, 2226
Watson, Wendy, 3706
Watson-Gegeo, Karen, 3499, 3500
Watts, John, 1853
Weathers, Winston, 260, 3660
Weatherson, Michael Allen, 1539
Weaver, Barbara, 52, 53, 2681
Weaver, Constance, 850
Weaver, Richard M., 260, 602
Weaver, Robert G., 2646
Webb, Agnes J., 2682
Webb, Judith, 2960
Webb, Suzanne S., 3212, 3213
Webb, Tamsen Banks, 1273
Webber, Richard, 2982
Weber, Barbara, 2883
Weber, Jerry, 3816
Weber, Paul, 1952
Wedell, Richard L., 2765
Weglarz, Mike, 1772
Wegner, Judy A., 2146
Weidenborner, Stephen, 3388
Weiler, Michael, 1540
Weinberg, Henry H., 733
Weinburg, Francine, 3148
Weiner, Bernard, 1250
Weiner, Jack, 1541
Weiner, Linda, 2683
Weiner, Myron F., 2947
Weinman, J., 3817
Weinsheimer, Joel C., 734
Weinstein, C. E., 1221
Weinstein, Eliya, 1134
Weinstein, Gail, 1074
Weis, Monica R., 191
Weisman, Herman, 3423
Weiss, Robert H., 3217
Weissberg, Robert C., 603
Weixelbaum, Elia S., 1075
Welch, Barbara, 1542
Welch, Cyril, 604, 605
Welch, Kathleen Ethel, 340

Welch, Richard Francis, 1543
Wells, Diane, 1228
Wells, Gordon, 1544, 1835, 2109, 2110
Wells, Jan, 2109, 2110
Wendt-Wasco, Nancy J., 1281
Wenzl, Michael, 3301
Werner, Kathleen, 3216
Werner, Randy, 1596
Wertheimer, Molly, 340, 1359
Wertsch, James V., 1114
Wesdorp, Hildo, 3844
Wess, Robert C., 1360, 2684, 2685
West, Edwin G., 1810
West, Janet K., 2226
Westcott, Warren, 3818
Westerfield, Michael W., 2961
Wetherell, Rick, 2376
Wexler, Joyce, 735
Whale, Kathleen B., 2377
Whalen, Tim, 606
Whaley, Charles Philip, 1076
Wheeler, Patricia M., 2378
Whitburn, Merrill D., 171, 1811
White, Edward M., 1953, 1954, 2626, 2627, 3819, 3820, 3821
White, Fred D., 1370, 3321
White, Jack, 2575
White, Kathryn F., 3822
White, Lana J., 607
Whitenton, James B., 1361
Whitin, David J., 2147, 2148
Whitman, R., 1254
Whitson, Caroline, 340
Whittaker, S. J., 1211
Whyte, Douglas A., 2962
Wickens, Garth, 1198
Wicker, Nancy, 3351
Wicking, Jeffrey Bruce, 608
Wiener, Harvey S., 1304, 3231, 3254, 3277
Wiest, Donald, 2379, 3752
Wiethoff, William E., 609, 610
Wiggers, Michiel, 1251
Wilbanks, Charles, 340
Wilcox, Lance, 3547, 3548
Wilcoxson, Barbara Marie, 3058
Wilde, Jack, 2046
Wilder, Jerry R., 1775
Wilkinson, A. M., 2795
Wilkinson, Andrew, 460
Wilkinson, Sarah, 1888
Willert, Jeanette, 2507
Williams, James D., 611, 612
Williams, John A., 3348

Williams, Joseph M., 191, 407, 916, 955, 3440
Williams, Sharon White, 1836
Williams, Stephen Meredith, 1077
Williamson, Larry, 340
Williamson, Michael M., 83, 1362, 2963
Willihnganz, Shirley C., 2003
Willinsky, John, 2149, 2150
Willis, Meredith Sue, 2151, 2380
Wills, Linda Bannister, 1773
Willson, Robert F., Jr., 1774
Wilson, Allison, 2474, 2686
Wilson, Clint C., II, 1545
Wilson, George M., 1078
Wilson, Jay C., 76
Wilson, Nancy, 1608
Wilson, P., 817
Wilson, Robert L., 613, 1955, 2687, 2688, 3823
Wilson, Steven, 2553, 2689
Winchell, Michael W., 2765
Winfield, Evelyn, 243
Winkler, Anthony C., 3280, 3322
Winkler, Victoria M., 54
Winn, Joni, 2722
Winograd, Peter N., 851
Winograd, Terry, 3661
Winter, Henry B., 2765
Winterbauer, Art, 3662
Winterowd, W. Ross, 407, 614, 615, 2381, 3183, 3363
Wirth-Nesher, Hana, 736
Wiseman, Donna, 2152
Witt, Brad, 2723
Witte, Stephen P., 83, 237, 260, 616, 3845
Wittrock, M. C., 318
Wolf, Dennie, 617
Wolf, Morris Philip, 2796
Wolf, Susan J., 2382
Wolfe, Denny, 1305, 2383
Wolfe, Johnny S., 1775
Wolfthal, Maurice, 1306
Wolpow, Edward R., 737, 1079, 1080, 1081
Wolz, James P., 1148
Womack, Deanna F., 340, 519
Womble, Gail, 2384, 2507
Wonderley, Stanley A., 2135
Wong, Samuel G., 618
Wood, Barbara S., 2138
Wood, Karen D., 2153
Wood, Peter H., 1728
Wood, Shaila Penelope, 852
Woodley, Carol, 2154
Woodley, John, 2154
Woodman, Leonora, 3323
Woodmansee, Martha, 738

Woodruff, Earl, 3632
Woodruff, G. Willard, 3166
Woods, William F., 619, 1082, 1307, 2690
Woodson, Nancy P., 620
Woodward, Pauline, 1776
Woodward, Virginia A., 286, 952, 1277
Woolard, Kathryn Ann, 1083
Woolings, Marty, 1956
Woolston, Donald C., 2884
Worley, Lloyd, 3667
Worncik, Barbara, 621
Worthington, Everett L., Jr., 1546
Worthington, Pepper, 1812, 2385, 2691, 3752
Woznick, Robert H., 1091
Wresch, William, 3632, 3668, 3669
Wright, Richard R., 1777
Wright, Sandra, 1084, 2347
Wyatt, David H., 3059, 3672
Wyckham, Robert C., 1085
Wye, Margaret Enright, 3673

Yaden, David B., Jr., 1086
Yager, Joel, 1673
Yancey, Kathleen B., 622
Yap, Johnny N. K., 1252
Yarber, Robert E., 3324
Yarrington, Roger, 2964
Yau, Margaret S. S., 1087
Yearwood, Stephanie, 916
Yeasting, Richard A., 2946
Yee, Nancy, 3846
Yerkes, Barbara H., 2692
Yeshayahu, Shen, 623
Yoos, George E., 171, 624
Yopp, H. K., 838
Yore, Larry D., 1253
Yoshida, Jessie, 2226
Young, Art, 1640, 1674

Young, George M., 625
Young, Marynell, 2850
Young, Richard, 171, 407
Youngblood, Ed, 1957
Youniss, James, 1106

Zakariya, Sally Banks, 853
Zamel, Vivian, 626, 3824
Zander, Sherri, 1778
Zangenberg, Jan, 2389
Zappen, James P., 2885
Zappone, Francis, 2185
Zarnowski, Myra, 2386
Zarobila, Charles, 171
Zarry, Len, 2693
Zasloff, Tela, 1499, 3825
Zbikowski, John, 2387
Zbrodoff, Nadia J., 1308
Zecker, Steven, 1254
Zeider, Martin A., 1547, 2886
Zeiger, William, 627
Zelinski, Elizabeth M., 1255
Zemelman, Steven, 1562
Zenai, Ruth, 1970
Ziegler, Alan, 1958, 2388
Zigmond, Naomi, 1637
Zimmer, JoAnn, 3674
Zimmerman, Jesse, 2475
Zimmerman, Priscilla, 2226
Zin, Nina D., 1672
Zinkhan, George, 1363
Zins, Daniel L., 1364
Zinsser, William, 3441
Ziv, Nina D., 83
Zoran, Gabriel, 739
Zuber, Maarit-Hannele, 26
Zubrick, S. R., 749, 750